ANNOTATED T

SpringBoard®

LEVEL 4

English Textual Power™

THE COLLEGE BOARD
inspiring minds™

About the College Board
The College Board is a mission-driven not-for-profit organization that connects students to college success and opportunity. Founded in 1900, the College Board was created to expand access to higher education. Today, the membership association is made up of more than 5,900 of the nation's leading educational institutions and is dedicated to promoting excellence and equity in education. Each year, the College Board helps more than seven million students prepare for a successful transition to college through programs and services in college readiness and college success — including the SAT® and the Advanced Placement Program®. The organization also serves the education community through research and advocacy on behalf of students, educators and schools.

For further information, visit www.collegeboard.com.

ISBN: 0-87447-922-3
ISBN: 978-0-87447-922-5

3 4 5 6 7 8   11 12 13 14
Printed in the United States of America

Acknowledgments

The College Board gratefully acknowledges the outstanding work of the classroom teachers and writers who have been integral to the development of this revised program. The end product is testimony to their expertise, understanding of student learning needs, and dedication to rigorous but accessible language arts education.

Susie Challancin
English Teacher
Bellevue School District 405
Bellevue, Washington

Paul De Maret
English Teacher
Poudre School District
Fort Collins, Colorado

Suzie Doss
District English/ Language Arts Coordinator
Hobbs Municipal Schools
Hobbs, New Mexico

John Golden
English Teacher
Grant High School
Portland, Oregon

Nancy Gray
English Teacher
West Shore Junior/Senior High School
Melbourne, Florida

Ellen Greig
English Teacher, Consultant
Charlotte, North Carolina

Karen Hanson
Exceptional Student Teacher
Volusia Public Schools
DeLand, Florida

Cheryl Harris
English Teacher Consultant
Bedford, Texas

Susie Lowry
English Teacher
Volusia Public Schools
DeLand, Florida

Julie Manley
Middle School Language Arts Tech-Curriculum Coach and Humanities Teacher
Bellevue School District 405
Bellevue, Washington

Joely Negedly
Secondary Reading and Language Arts Specialists
Volusia Public Schools
DeLand, Florida

JoEllen Victoreen
Instructional Specialist, SpringBoard
San Jose, California

Douglas Waugh
Administrative Coach, SpringBoard
Bellevue, Washington

Nina Wooldridge
Instructional Specialist, SpringBoard
Los Angeles, California

Advisors, Reviewers, Special Feature Writers

The following teachers and writers provided invaluable assistance in creating special features and reviewing manuscript. We gratefully acknowledge their contributions to this revised edition.

Gary Cowan
English/Language Arts Coordinator
Metro Nashville Public Schools
Nashville, Tennessee

Nicki Junkins
Administrative Coach, SpringBoard
DeLand, Florida

Jeanneine Jones
Professor, Departments of Middle, Secondary, and K-12 Education
University of North Carolina
Charlotte, North Carolina

William McBride
Emeritus Professor of English
Colorado State University
Fort Collins, Colorado

Daniel Millet
English Teacher
Weld County School District Re-8
Fort Lupton, Colorado

Melanie Sangalli
English Teacher
Irving Public Schools
Irving, Texas

Special Acknowledgments

The College Board wishes especially to acknowledge the writers of the original *Pacesetter* program. Much of their work continues in use today. The result of their efforts was a program that helped both teachers and students succeed. With its roots in Pacesetter, the current program had an excellent foundation on which to build.

Willie Mae Crews
Educator
Birmingham, Alabama

R. Steven Green, Ed.D.
Educator
Kansas City, Missouri

Ellen Greenblatt
University High School
San Francisco, California

Alice Kawazoe
Educational Consultant, California Academic Partnership Program
San Carlos, California

Jenny Oren Krugman
Vice President, Southern Region
College Board
Miami, Florida

William McBride, Ph.D.
Emeritus Professor of English
Colorado State University
Fort Collins, Colorado

Robert Scholes, Ph.D.
Research Professor, Brown University
Providence, Rhode Island

In addition, we wish to acknowledge the educators and writers whose work on prior editions helped to continue the *Pacesetter* excellence and to establish the high expectations for which the College Board's SpringBoard program is known.

Lance Balla
Bellevue, Washington

Bryant Crisp
Charlotte, North Carolina

Nancy Elrod
Atlanta, Georgia

Ann Foster
Melbourne, Florida

Ana Gandara
Edinburg, Texas

Alex Gordin
Portland, Oregon

Kenyatta Graves
Washington, DC

Don Keagy
Poultney, Vermont

Don Kirk
Poultney, Vermont

Dana Mebane
Baltimore, Maryland

Bob Messinger
Providence, Rhode Island

Debi Miller
Miami, Florida

Melanie Ross Mitchell
Atlanta, Georgia

Lisa Rehm
DeLand, Florida

Penny Riffe
Palm Bay, Florida

Rick Robb
Clarksville, Maryland

Sue Rodriguez
Miami, Florida

Research and Planning Advisors

We also wish to thank the members of our SpringBoard Advisory Council, the SpringBoard Language Arts Trainers, and the many educators who gave generously of their time and their ideas as we conducted research for the program. Their suggestions and reactions to ideas helped immeasurably as we planned the revisions. We gratefully acknowledge the teachers and administrators in the following districts:

Broward County Public Schools
Fort Lauderdale, Florida

Cherry Creek School District
Cherry Creek, Colorado

Chicago Public Schools
Chicago, Illinois

DeKalb County School System
DeKalb County, Georgia

Duval County Public Schools
Jacksonville, Florida

Guilford County Schools
Greensboro, North Carolina

Hillsborough County Public Schools
Tampa, Florida

Hobbs Municipal Schools
Hobbs, New Mexico

Indianapolis Public Schools
Indianapolis, Indiana

Miami-Dade County Public Schools
Miami, Florida

Metropolitan Nashville Public Schools
Nashville, Tennessee

The City School District of New Rochelle
New Rochelle, New York

Orange County Public Schools
Orlando, Florida

School District of Palm Beach County
Palm Beach, Florida

Peninsula School District
Gig Harbor, Washington

Pinellas County Schools
Largo, Florida

San Antonio Independent School District
San Antonio, Texas

Spokane Public Schools
Spokane, Washington

Volusia County Schools
DeLand, Florida

Editorial Leadership

The College Board gratefully acknowledges the expertise, time, and commitment of the language arts editorial manager.

Betty Barnett

Educational Publishing Consultant

Level 4 Contents

Instructional Units

Unit 1 Coming of Age

Unit 2 Defining Style

Unit 3 Exploring Poetic Voices

To the Teacher

Welcome to SpringBoard! In these pages you will find much that is new and much that is familiar. SpringBoard continues to be the highly engaging, student-centered, interactive, and standards-based curriculum it has always been. We continue to offer a variety of assessment opportunities featuring formative assessments that assess growth in skills and knowledge over time and rigorous Embedded Assessments aimed at requiring a synthesis of a complex set of skills and knowledge taught in each unit of instruction. And, as always, we are committed to guiding students toward the goal of being critical thinkers and independent learners by asking them to be metacognitive about their learning and to build a portfolio of work that allows them to self-assess their growth over time.

With this new revision, the SpringBoard program features a more carefully scaffolded and purposeful sequence of instruction, more explicit help for teachers to aid in the successful delivery of instruction, more systematic instruction in vocabulary and grammar, more explicit student instruction in the processes of reading and writing, and a stronger, more deliberate connection to Advanced Placement skills and knowledge.

Our mission remains the same: to inspire, connect and prepare all students for college and post-secondary success. SpringBoard offers a carefully articulated, engaging, and rigorous English Language Arts curriculum of instruction for grades 6-12 that provides students with the skills and knowledge necessary to compete in the 21st century. Students need to be able to collaborate with others to complete a task, to make meaning of any text they encounter, and to communicate effectively in speech and writing. SpringBoard provides students ample opportunity to refine and master strategies that will enhance their ability to understand and analyze any challenging text, to write with clarity and voice, to speak and listen in order to communicate and work effectively with others, and to view media with a critical intelligence.

What Sets SpringBoard Apart from Other English Language Arts Programs?

SpringBoard is the College Board's official Pre-AP program, developed to provide a roadmap for attaining the knowledge and skills students require for success in Advanced Placement courses and in college-level work. Based on the College Board Standards for Success in English Language Arts and current research on best instructional practices, SpringBoard uses a "back-mapping" instructional design that starts with the end in mind, namely, the Embedded Assessments. The skills and knowledge needed for these assessments are scaffolded by the activities leading to each assessment. By using the Embedded Assessments as a starting point for planning instruction, teachers have a clear picture of what students need to know and be able to do as they progress through the units and the course to more easily adjust the learning plan to meet individual needs.

SpringBoard's approach is just the opposite of the "inch deep, mile wide" philosophy that permeates so much of educational instruction today. With SpringBoard, students read deeply and develop the critical-thinking skills needed to emerge as successful readers, writers, and thinkers. Key features of SpringBoard include the following:

- **Educational research** supports the structure of the program, which integrates research findings on best practices for helping students learn, as well as underlying research on how best to present and reinforce new content learning. A key element of the organization of the program is its orientation around the desired results; i.e., determining what students must know to perform well and then scaffolding instruction to deliver that performance.
- **Rigorous standards** provide a pathway to Advanced Placement and support instruction built on the College Board Standards for College Success to meet or exceed state curriculum standards. The CBSCS are the basis of a vertically articulated curriculum, purposefully scaffolded instruction, a recursive instructional design that builds to mastery and successful achievement of complex skills.
- The **instructional framework** is built on "designing with the end in mind." Embedded Assessments are the starting point, with activities scaffolded to teach needed skills and knowledge. **Teaching and learning strategies** are a cornerstone of the instructional design and are embedded in the learning activities to encourage best instructional practices and at the same time develop and sustain independent student learning. "In context" strategic instruction demands a reflective and metacognitive approach to teaching and learning. **Purposeful learning activities** are relevant, rigorous, student-centered, engaging, interactive, and collaborative—developing students' skills in evaluating, analyzing, and communicating effectively.
- **Differentiated instruction** opportunities are built carefully on scaffolded instruction leading toward the Embedded Assessments in the units of instruction.
- **Assessment**, both formative and summative, includes objective end-of-unit tests, performance-based Embedded Assessments, and Portfolio to track growth over time. Along with assessment, recursive calls to reflect on learning all help students work toward successful mastery.
- **Teacher support** and **professional development** honor and value the flexibility and expertise teachers bring to the classroom. A Teacher's Edition offers a wealth of instructional suggestions, while face-to-face training is supported by an online program featuring an interactive professional learning community that invigorates and sustains successful teaching.

How Does Research Inform SpringBoard?

As classroom practitioners, SpringBoard writers understand the role that research plays in curricular design and in creating effective English Language Arts instruction. They also have the hands-on experience of what works in the classroom. Incorporating both research from experts in the field and practical experience, SpringBoard starts with the desired skills and knowledge and scaffolds the instruction students need to achieve learning goals.

SpringBoard Begins with the End in Mind

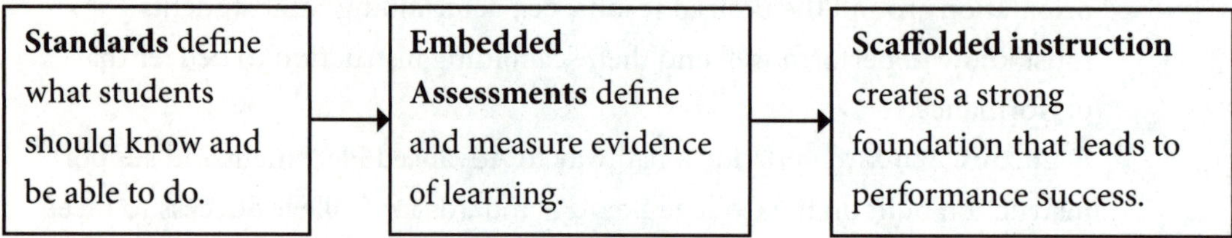

Curricular design begins with the end in mind by "backward mapping" skills and designing carefully scaffolded instruction leading to student understanding that endures beyond the next test.

Instructional Strategies Build Student Success

Research has shown that students learn by doing. To develop a deep understanding of language arts concepts and their applications, the SpringBoard curriculum addresses all learning modalities by including all students in rich discussion and application of concepts. Research also supports the use of specific learning strategies to help students "learn how to learn." Through the use of multiple learning and instructional strategies, students acquire not only the knowledge they need but also the confidence in their own abilities to learn and to communicate effectively in real-world situations.

> Research-based instructional strategies "have a high probability of enhancing student achievement for all students…" (*Classroom Instruction That Works*, Marzano, Pickering, and Pollock, 2001, p. 7)

Assessment Informs Instruction

Research supports assessment to provide the instructor with knowledge about what individual students know and can do. The SpringBoard program provides multiple opportunities for formative assessment, including frequent writing, reading, and analysis tasks that give instructors a snapshot of where individual students are in their learning. The Embedded Assessments, requiring students to synthesize skills and knowledge, provide a broader look at students' abilities on performance-based work.

Research-Based Instruction

Strategic Instruction

- Learning strategies for students.
- Suggested strategies for instruction.

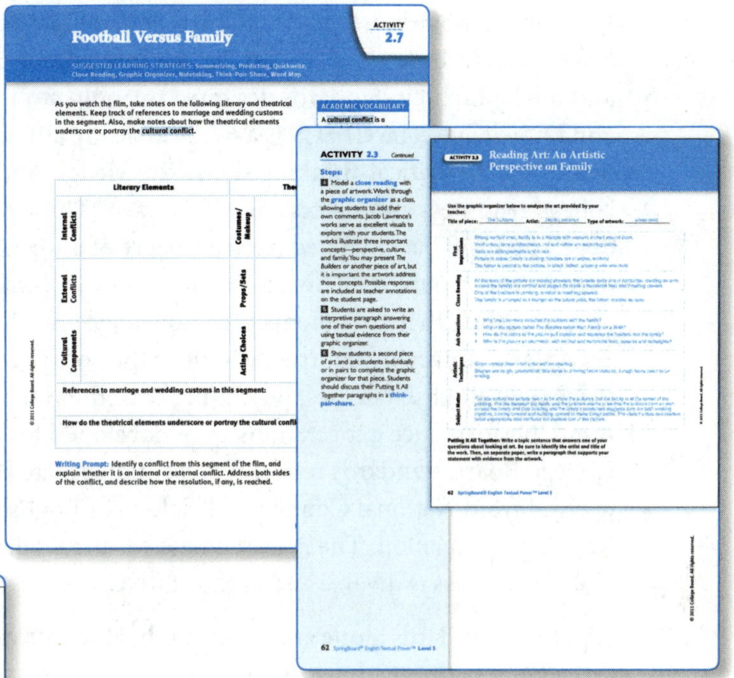

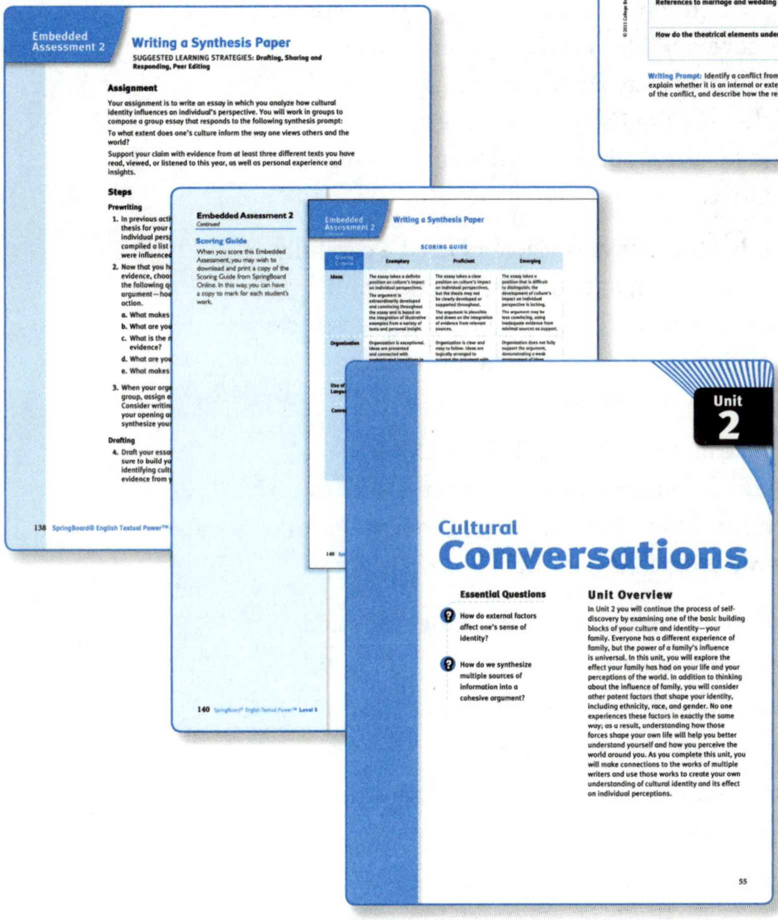

Design That Begins with the End in Mind and Scaffolds Instruction

- Embedded Assessments reflect skills to be learned and provide evidence of learning.
- Scoring Guides define expectations.
- Scaffolding begins with Essential Questions to provide enduring understanding.
- Purposeful activities develop skills and knowledge.

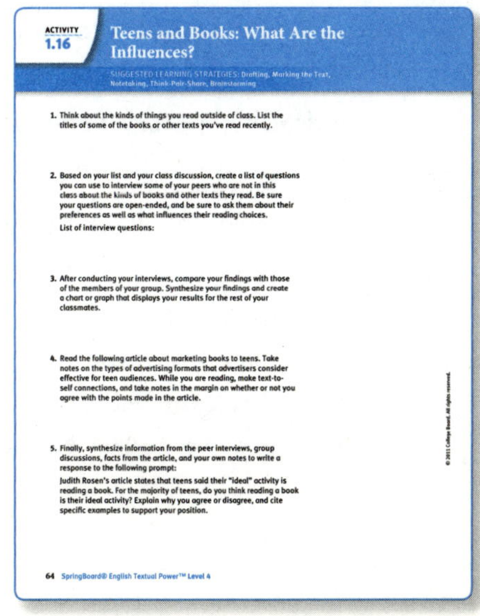

Student-Centered Instruction

- Relevant activities engage student interest.
- Activities address different learning modalities.
- Step-by-step teaching instructions model an effective instructional pathway through the unit.

How Do Rigorous Standards Provide a Pathway to AP?

Rigorous standards are the backbone of curricular development. The College Board Standards for College Success present reading, writing, speaking, listening, and media literacy standards designed to equip students with 21st century skills and knowledge. The CBSCS is a 6-12 vertically aligned set of standards that delineates the critical-thinking skills, knowledge, and behavior essential for college readiness and success in AP courses. These standards have been carefully developed and backmapped from a variety of authoritative sources. Developers used research published by Dr. David Conley in *Understanding University Success* (2003) that documents the knowledge and skills required for success in entry-level university courses, as well as the course requirements of Advanced Placement English courses. Beginning with the final goal of college preparation in mind, performance expectations were developed for each grade level. In addition, College Board standards reflect representative state standards and standards derived from National Council of Teachers of English and the International Reading Association. The research base for the College Board Standards for College Success is diverse and authoritative.

Rigorous standards alone are not enough. Students and teachers need a carefully articulated pathway of instruction that enables them to access, practice, and master the skills these important standards represent. SpringBoard is the vehicle that makes rigorous standards attainable for all students through vertically aligned, carefully scaffolded, strategies-based instruction.

One powerful feature of SpringBoard instruction is the explicit teaching of learning strategies that empower students by equipping them with the skill to know when, why, and how to use them free of teacher support. In this program, teachers will find a systematic development of skills in which:

- Students are consistently exposed to the higher-order thinking skills and behaviors demanded of college-level work.
- Students practice close analysis with pre-AP and AP reading strategies, leading to an ability to independently analyze any new text.
- Students are confronted with increasingly challenging texts, both canonical and contemporary, fiction and nonfiction.
- Students are challenged by complex writing tasks in persuasion, argumentation, literary analysis, and synthesis in order to build capacity to write effectively in these rhetorical modes.

With exposure to AP strategies, prompts, nonfiction texts, and varied writing tasks, students will exit the program equipped with the kind of higher-order thinking **skills**, **knowledge**, and **behaviors** necessary to be successful in AP classes and post-secondary education.

Pathway to AP / College Readiness

Writing Example — Across the Levels

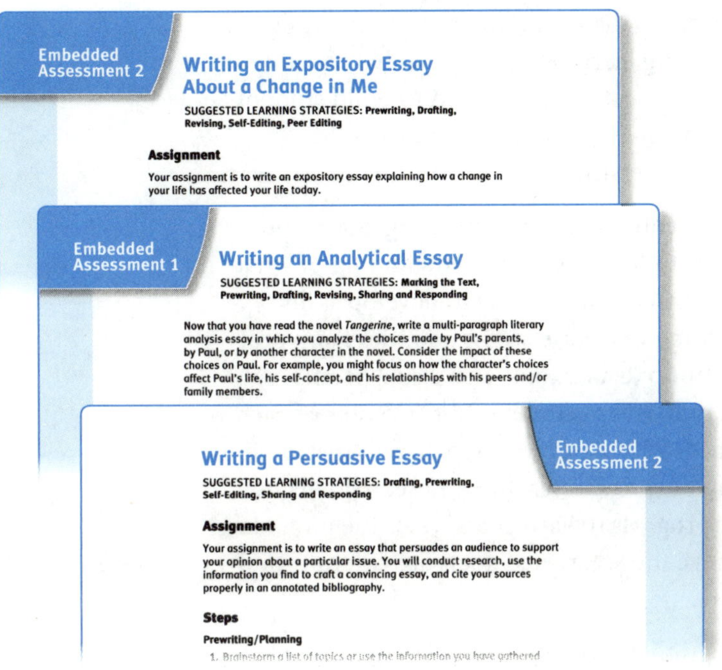

Embedded Assessment 2

Writing an Expository Essay About a Change in Me

SUGGESTED LEARNING STRATEGIES: **Prewriting, Drafting, Revising, Self-Editing, Peer Editing**

Assignment

Your assignment is to write an expository essay explaining how a change in your life has affected your life today.

Embedded Assessment 1

Writing an Analytical Essay

SUGGESTED LEARNING STRATEGIES: **Marking the Text, Prewriting, Drafting, Revising, Sharing and Responding**

Now that you have read the novel *Tangerine*, write a multi-paragraph literary analysis essay in which you analyze the choices made by Paul's parents, by Paul, or by another character in the novel. Consider the impact of these choices on Paul. For example, you might focus on how the character's choices affect Paul's life, his self-concept, and his relationships with his peers and/or family members.

Embedded Assessment 2

Writing a Persuasive Essay

SUGGESTED LEARNING STRATEGIES: **Drafting, Prewriting, Self-Editing, Sharing and Responding**

Assignment

Your assignment is to write an essay that persuades an audience to support your opinion about a particular issue. You will conduct research, use the information you find to craft a convincing essay, and cite your sources properly in an annotated bibliography.

Steps

Prewriting/Planning

1. Brainstorm a list of topics or use the information you have gathered

Middle School

Pre-AP Connections:

- Close reading of a text to determine literary elements.
- Writing with an attention to textual evidence and choosing organizational patterns.
- Identifying and writing rhetorical appeals.

High School

AP Connections:

- Understanding strong relationships among author's purpose, use of literary/stylistic devices, and desired effect.
- Gleaning and synthesizing information from a variety of texts to respond to an AP prompt.
- Writing in response to a synthesis prompt like those used on the AP Language Exam.
- Writing to interpret, evaluate, and negotiate differing critical perspectives in literature.

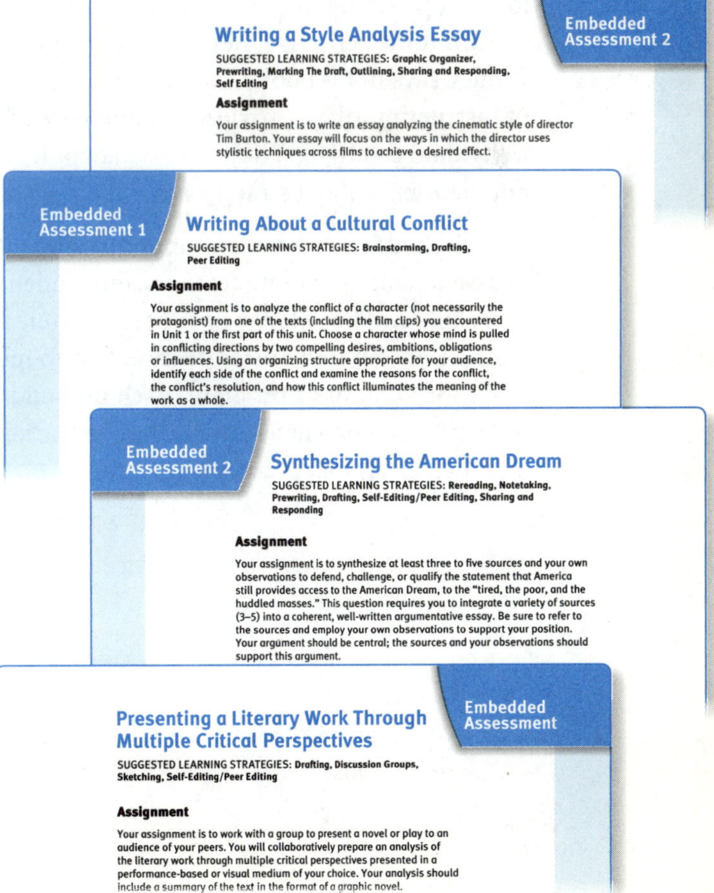

Embedded Assessment 2

Writing a Style Analysis Essay

SUGGESTED LEARNING STRATEGIES: **Graphic Organizer, Prewriting, Marking The Draft, Outlining, Sharing and Responding, Self Editing**

Assignment

Your assignment is to write an essay analyzing the cinematic style of director Tim Burton. Your essay will focus on the ways in which the director uses stylistic techniques across films to achieve a desired effect.

Embedded Assessment 1

Writing About a Cultural Conflict

SUGGESTED LEARNING STRATEGIES: **Brainstorming, Drafting, Peer Editing**

Assignment

Your assignment is to analyze the conflict of a character (not necessarily the protagonist) from one of the texts (including the film clips) you encountered in Unit 1 or the first part of this unit. Choose a character whose mind is pulled in conflicting directions by two compelling desires, ambitions, obligations or influences. Using an organizing structure appropriate for your audience, identify each side of the conflict and examine the reasons for the conflict, the conflict's resolution, and how this conflict illuminates the meaning of the work as a whole.

Embedded Assessment 2

Synthesizing the American Dream

SUGGESTED LEARNING STRATEGIES: **Rereading, Notetaking, Prewriting, Drafting, Self-Editing/Peer Editing, Sharing and Responding**

Assignment

Your assignment is to synthesize at least three to five sources and your own observations to defend, challenge, or qualify the statement that America still provides access to the American Dream, to the "tired, the poor, and the huddled masses." This question requires you to integrate a variety of sources (3–5) into a coherent, well-written argumentative essay. Be sure to refer to the sources and employ your own observations to support your position. Your argument should be central; the sources and your observations should support this argument.

Embedded Assessment

Presenting a Literary Work Through Multiple Critical Perspectives

SUGGESTED LEARNING STRATEGIES: **Drafting, Discussion Groups, Sketching, Self-Editing/Peer Editing**

Assignment

Your assignment is to work with a group to present a novel or play to an audience of your peers. You will collaboratively prepare an analysis of the literary work through multiple critical perspectives presented in a performance-based or visual medium of your choice. Your analysis should include a summary of the text in the format of a graphic novel.

What Is SpringBoard's Instructional Framework?

SpringBoard instruction is organized around five thematically based Model Instructional Units containing scaffolded activities that lead to performance-based Embedded Assessments. SpringBoard's instructional framework, designed with the end in mind, begins by determining learning goals, how that learning will be measured, and what content and instruction are needed to build student knowledge and skills. The purposeful sequence of activities aims to build confidence and skills so students can be successful on the major unit assessments.

Each unit begins with a unit overview, essential questions, learning goals, and academic vocabulary for the unit to give students a clear understanding of what they will be learning. Unit activities are structured not only to develop skills and knowledge, but also to address learning in a variety of modalities from oral interpretations, to written analyses, to group discussions, and visual prompts. Consistent design of content across all units keeps students at the center of each learning experience and provides teachers with a step-by-step plan of instruction that allows for flexibility while ensuring purposeful teaching. Research tells us that students and teachers make better progress toward goals when the target is clear and explicit, and the skills to achieve those targeted goals are carefully and purposefully taught, building to mastery.

More importantly, working from a design that incorporates an "instructional loop" of planning, step-by-step instruction, assessment, and reflection paves the way for more reflective, flexible, and purposeful teaching and learning. As David Conley says in his book *College Knowledge*, SpringBoard is a "complete program of instruction [that] provides a framework in which teachers can express their individual creativity. They can also adapt lessons for the needs of specific student populations without straying from the key standards." (Conley: 55)

Unit Embedded Assessments monitor student progress through various forms of assessment, providing teachers and students with information about how well skills and knowledge have been mastered. Armed with this information, instruction can be adjusted or modified to meet the needs of students as they move forward in the program. Each unit ends with the opportunity for student reflection on content and skills they've learned, strategies they used successfully, and their goals for future learning.

Instructional Framework

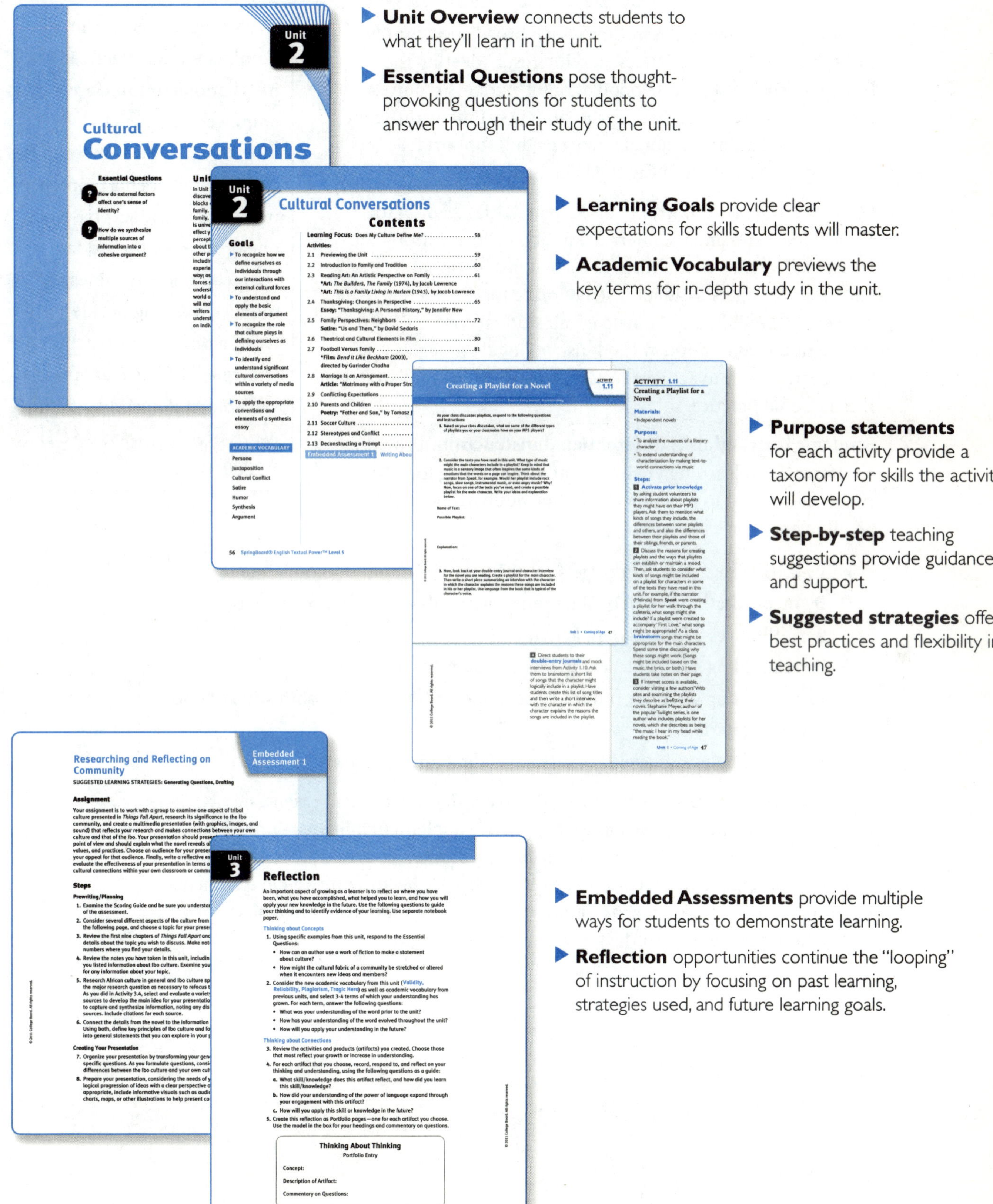

▶ **Unit Overview** connects students to what they'll learn in the unit.

▶ **Essential Questions** pose thought-provoking questions for students to answer through their study of the unit.

▶ **Learning Goals** provide clear expectations for skills students will master.

▶ **Academic Vocabulary** previews the key terms for in-depth study in the unit.

▶ **Purpose statements** for each activity provide a taxonomy for skills the activity will develop.

▶ **Step-by-step** teaching suggestions provide guidance and support.

▶ **Suggested strategies** offer best practices and flexibility in teaching.

▶ **Embedded Assessments** provide multiple ways for students to demonstrate learning.

▶ **Reflection** opportunities continue the "looping" of instruction by focusing on past learning, strategies used, and future learning goals.

How Does SpringBoard Provide Opportunities to Differentiate Instruction?

Students enter today's classrooms with a broad spectrum of skills, knowledge, experiences, and interests. Meeting the learning needs of a diverse population of students requires instructional materials that engage students at many different levels, as well as instructional strategies that support teachers in tailoring instruction to individual needs.

SpringBoard's design, with scaffolded activities leading to Embedded Assessments, offers flexibility for instruction in a variety of learning modalities. Threaded instructional strategies encourage teachers to adapt instruction to their students, while delivering the skills and knowledge all students need. Effective instruction uses multiple, varied instructional strategies that have been proven to achieve results. This is the basis of strategic instructional practice.

Strategic instruction is differentiated instruction. Providing a differentiated learning environment means using tools and practices adapted to learning needs. SpringBoard helps teachers adapt instruction as follows:

According to Carol Ann Tomlinson, "an effective instructional framework empowers teachers to differentiate one or more of the curricular elements (content, process, or product) based on one or more of the student characteristics (readiness, interest, learning profile) using a range of instructional strategies" (*The Differentiated Classroom: Responding to the Needs of All Learners* ASCD, ©2000, p. 11).

- By setting clear learning targets.
- By incorporating a variety of learning materials—such as text, film, oral performances—into student activities.
- By scaffolding student learning through step-by-step activities.
- By integrating learning and teaching strategies throughout both student and teacher materials.
- By providing multiple ways to assess student knowledge and skills.

These elements provide the basis for effective differentiation for extending learning opportunities as well as for supplying supplemental instruction. The flexible design of SpringBoard gives teachers multiple opportunities and resource tools to differentiate instruction in order to support the growth and development of all students. Using a range of strategies, teachers can monitor and adjust instruction, adding more or less scaffolding as needed.

Differentiating Instruction

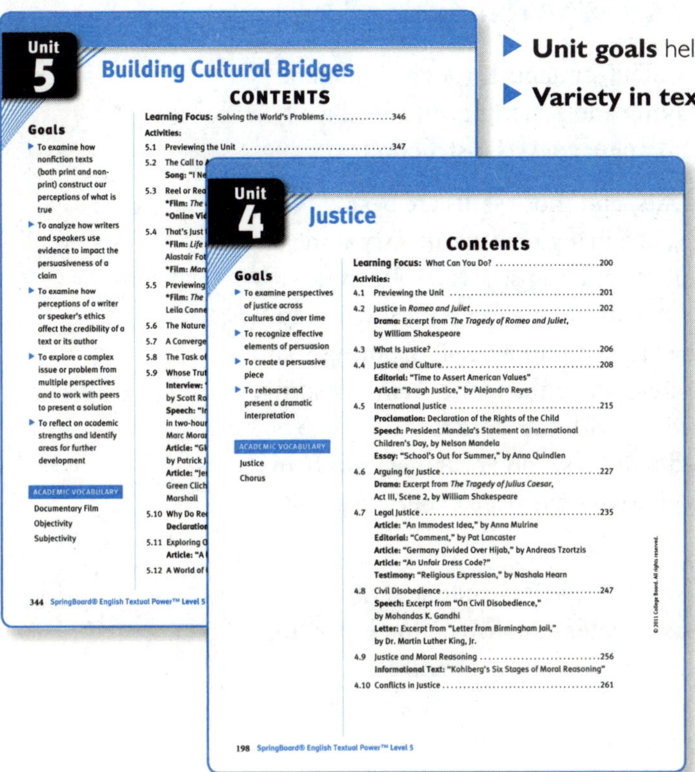

- **Unit goals** help all students understand learning targets.
- **Variety in texts** addresses multiple learning styles.

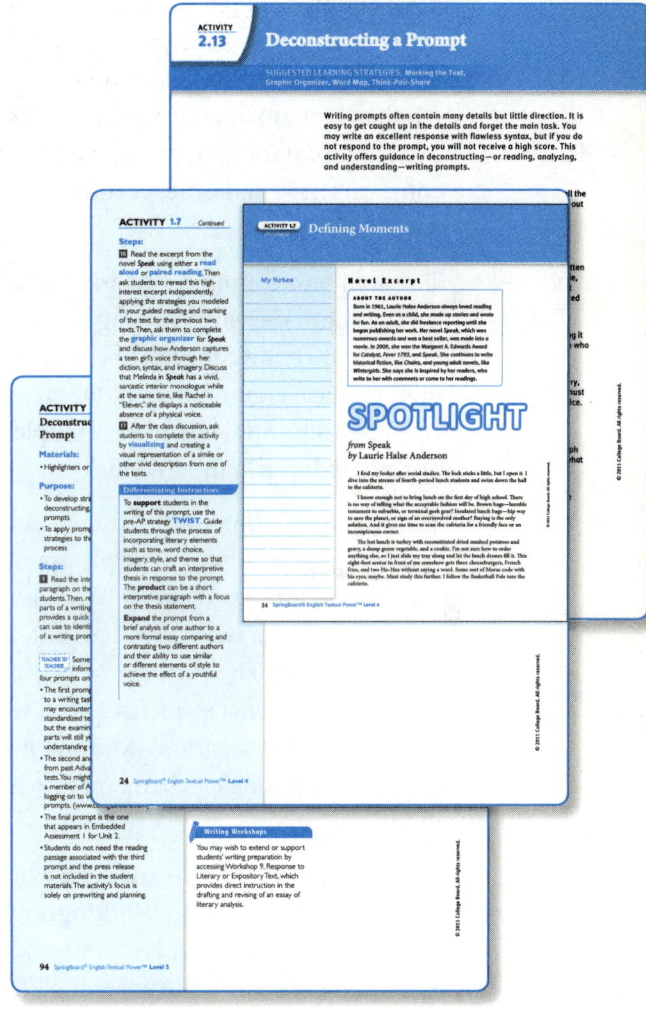

- **Scaffolded activities** allow teachers to adjust pace and content to meet learner's needs.
- **Learning and teaching strategies** in student and teacher materials provide options for all student learning styles.
- **Differentiating Instruction** notes provide suggestions for supporting and extending learning.

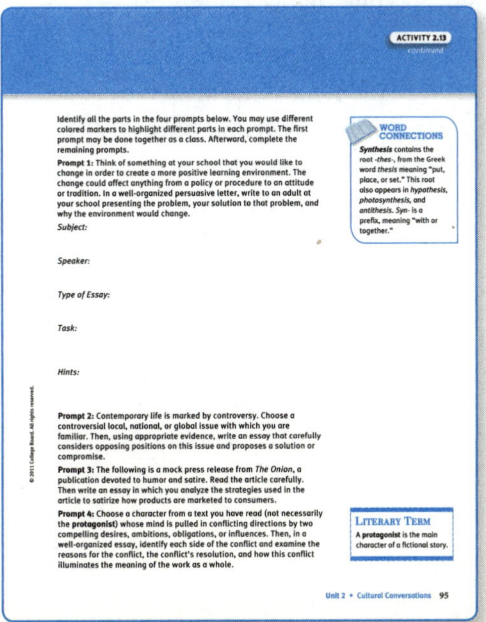

- **Variety in formative assessments** (objective, constructed response in scaffolded activities, and performance-based tasks) provides more flexibility for students to demonstrate learning.

How Does SpringBoard Develop Fluent Communication and Writing Skills Essential for College Readiness?

SpringBoard expands the academic capacity of all students through systematic skill development in Reading, Writing, Speaking and Listening, and Media Literacy—the four main domains of English Language Arts instruction.

Good **reading** skills are essential to all students, and those skills are best developed through reading a variety of texts, acquiring new vocabulary, and determining the writer's meaning using multiple reading strategies. Reading draws upon a student's ability to think inferentially, to analyze critically, and to apply appropriate strategies to enhance and extend comprehension. SpringBoard focuses on vocabulary development and strategies to enhance academic reading, emphasizing interactive reading skills associated with the close reading of texts, such as annotation, marking the text, guided readings, and vocabulary study in context. These and other reading strategies give students deep experiences with reading for purpose.

The ability to communicate in **writing** is a key twenty-first century skill. SpringBoard develops writing skills from basic sentence construction to writing essays and creative pieces. SpringBoard incorporates writing practice in four major areas: argumentation, literary analysis, creative and reflective writing, and research. Students have multiple opportunities to write in all these domains during their SpringBoard work.

Writing instruction in the student activities focuses on all aspects of the writing process. Students have multiple opportunities to practice and master the stages. In addition, online **Writing Workshops** offer a sequence of activities designed to provide direct writing instruction in the writing process and in specific writing genres. The Writing Workshops use the writing process as the core of the instructional sequence. Each workshop guides students through the writing of three separate texts: one that is co-constructed as a class with direct guidance from the teacher, one that is peer constructed, and one that is written independently.

No less important in the modern world of new literacies are the twin skills of **speaking** and **listening**. Working collaboratively and presenting oneself and one's work to others demand ever more skill in these two areas of communication. SpringBoard offers a purposeful pathway of growth in these important areas of personal interactive and presentation skills.

As a complement to and an extension of reading, writing, speaking and listening, **media literacy** is widely recognized as a twenty-first century necessity. From the critical analysis and evaluation of the effect and influence of media in our lives to the ability to manipulate media, students need to be skilled viewers and producers of media in order to compete in modern society.

Developing Communication Skills

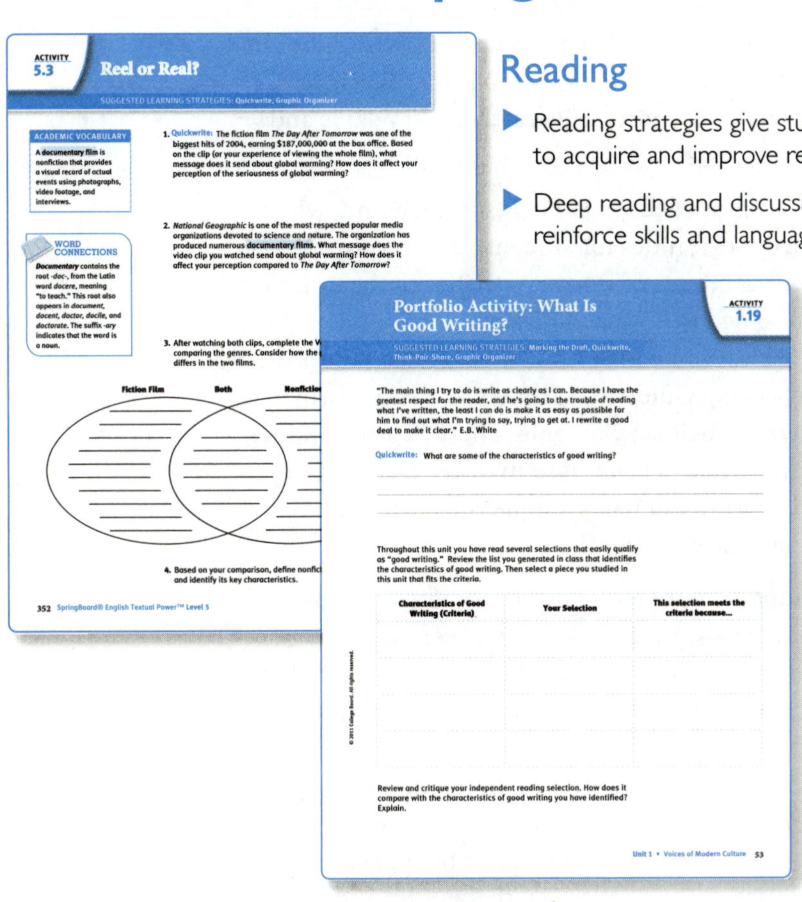

ACTIVITY 5.3

Reel or Real?

SUGGESTED LEARNING STRATEGIES: Quickwrite, Graphic Organizer

ACADEMIC VOCABULARY

A **documentary film** is nonfiction that provides a visual record of actual events using photographs, video footage, and interviews.

WORD CONNECTIONS

Documentary contains the root *-doc-*, from the Latin word *docere*, meaning "to teach." This root also appears in *document, docent, doctor, docile*, and *doctorate*. The suffix *-ary* indicates that the word is a noun.

1. Quickwrite: The fiction film *The Day After Tomorrow* was one of the biggest hits of 2004, earning $187,000,000 at the box office. Based on the clip (or your experience of viewing the whole film), what message does it send about global warming? How does it affect your perception of the seriousness of global warming?

2. *National Geographic* is one of the most respected popular media organizations devoted to science and nature. The organization has produced numerous **documentary films**. What message does the video clip you watched send about global warming? How does it affect your perception compared to *The Day After Tomorrow*?

3. After watching both clips, complete the V[…] comparing the genres. Consider how the […] differs in the two films.

Fiction Film | Both | Nonfictio[…]

4. Based on your comparison, define nonfic[…] and identify its key characteristics.

352 SpringBoard® English Textual Power™ Level 5

Portfolio Activity: What Is Good Writing?

ACTIVITY 1.19

SUGGESTED LEARNING STRATEGIES: Marking the Draft, Quickwrite, Think-Pair-Share, Graphic Organizer

"The main thing I try to do is write as clearly as I can. Because I have the greatest respect for the reader, and he's going to the trouble of reading what I've written, the least I can do is make it as easy as possible for him to find out what I'm trying to say, trying to get at. I rewrite a good deal to make it clear." E.B. White

Quickwrite: What are some of the characteristics of good writing?

Throughout this unit you have read several selections that easily qualify as "good writing." Review the list you generated in class that identifies the characteristics of good writing. Then select a piece you studied in this unit that fits the criteria.

Characteristics of Good Writing (Criteria)	Your Selection	This selection meets the criteria because...

Review and critique your independent reading selection. How does it compare with the characteristics of good writing you have identified? Explain.

© 2011 College Board. All rights reserved.

Unit 1 • Voices of Modern Culture 53

Reading

- Reading strategies give students the tools to acquire and improve reading skills.
- Deep reading and discussion of meaning reinforce skills and language development.

Writing

- The writing process guides writing skills development.
- Extensive and varied writing opportunities reinforce skills.
- Grammar in context supports the writing process.

Speaking and Listening

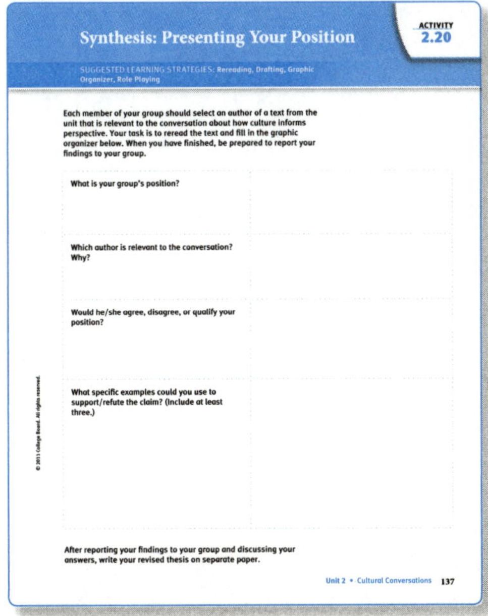

Synthesis: Presenting Your Position

ACTIVITY 2.20

SUGGESTED LEARNING STRATEGIES: Rereading, Drafting, Graphic Organizer, Role Playing

Each member of your group should select an author of a text from the unit that is relevant to the conversation about how culture informs perspective. Your task is to reread the text and fill in the graphic organizer below. When you have finished, be prepared to report your findings to your group.

What is your group's position?	
Which author is relevant to the conversation? Why?	
Would he/she agree, disagree, or qualify your position?	
What specific examples could you use to support/refute the claim? (Include at least three.)	

After reporting your findings to your group and discussing your answers, write your revised thesis on separate paper.

© 2011 College Board. All rights reserved.

Unit 2 • Cultural Conversations 137

- Speaking and listening skills are enhanced through oral presentations, group discussions, and paired student activities.

Media Literacy

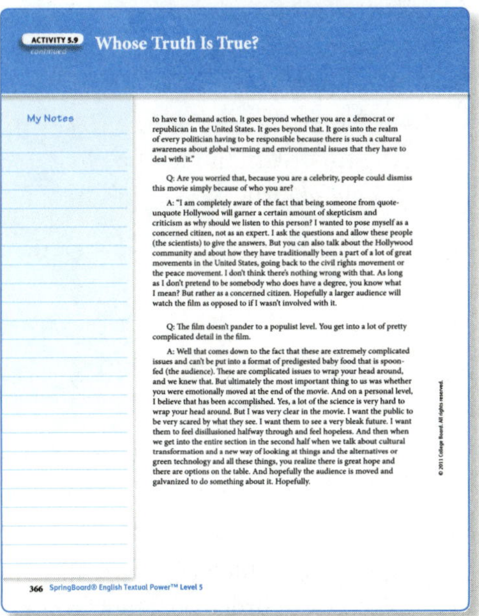

ACTIVITY 5.9 continued

Whose Truth Is True?

My Notes

to have to demand action. It goes beyond whether you are a democrat or republican in the United States. It goes beyond that. It goes into the realm of every politician having to be responsible because there is such a cultural awareness about global warming and environmental issues that they have to deal with it."

Q: Are you worried that, because you are a celebrity, people could dismiss this movie simply because of who you are?

A: "I am completely aware of the fact that being someone from quote-unquote Hollywood will garner a certain amount of skepticism and criticism as why should we listen to this person? I wanted to pose myself as a concerned citizen, not as an expert. I ask the questions and allow these people (the scientists) to give the answers. But you can also talk about the Hollywood community and about how they have traditionally been a part of a lot of great movements in the United States, going back to the civil rights movement or the peace movement. I don't think there's nothing wrong with that. As long as I don't pretend to be somebody who does have a degree, you know what I mean? But rather as a concerned citizen. Hopefully a larger audience will watch the film as opposed to if I wasn't involved with it.

Q: The film doesn't pander to a populist level. You get into a lot of pretty complicated detail in the film.

A: Well that comes down to the fact that these are extremely complicated issues and can't be put into a format of predigested baby food that is spoon-fed (the audience). These are complicated issues to wrap your head around, and we knew that. But ultimately the most important thing to us was whether you were emotionally moved at the end of the movie. And on a personal level, I believe that has been accomplished. Yes, a lot of the science is very hard to wrap your head around. But I was very clear in the movie. I want the public to be very scared by what they see. I want them to see a very bleak future. I want them to feel disillusioned halfway through and feel hopeless. And then when we get into the entire section in the second half when we talk about cultural transformation and a new way of looking at things and the alternatives or green technology and all these things, you realize there is great hope and there are options on the table. And hopefully the audience is moved and galvanized to do something about it. Hopefully.

© 2011 College Board. All rights reserved.

366 SpringBoard® English Textual Power™ Level 5

- Media literacy skills are developed through analysis of media influence and evaluation of media bias.

How Does SpringBoard Integrate Assessment?

Assessment for learning is the philosophical basis of assessment opportunities in SpringBoard. SpringBoard makes assessment and evaluation transparent and explicit so students and teachers can focus more deliberately on key skills and knowledge to be learned.

Central to student learning are the Embedded Assessments in each unit, which were created to provide authentic opportunities for students to demonstrate knowledge and skills learned over the course of study. Activities in the units are purposefully constructed and scaffolded to ensure students will have the skills and knowledge to be successful on the unit Embedded Assessments. Each Embedded Assessment is accompanied by a Scoring Guide that articulates the performance expectations for which students will be held accountable. These Scoring Guides use criteria that are modeled upon writing rubrics used in district, state, and national testing. Each Embedded Assessment has a unique rubric, though the categories assessed are consistent across grade levels.

SpringBoard units also include multiple opportunities for formative "snapshots" of student progress toward learning goals. Every quickwrite, every graphic organizer, every visualization can serve as a check for understanding as students work through unit activities. Each level also includes a Portfolio element that requires students to collect and monitor growth in skills and knowledge over time. End-of-unit objective tests work in tandem with the Embedded Assessments to monitor student proficiency by informing students and teachers about individual progress. Assessment is a fundamental element in the instructional loop of planning, instruction, assessment, and reflection that guides and informs re-teaching and differentiation.

Formative Assessment Opportunities

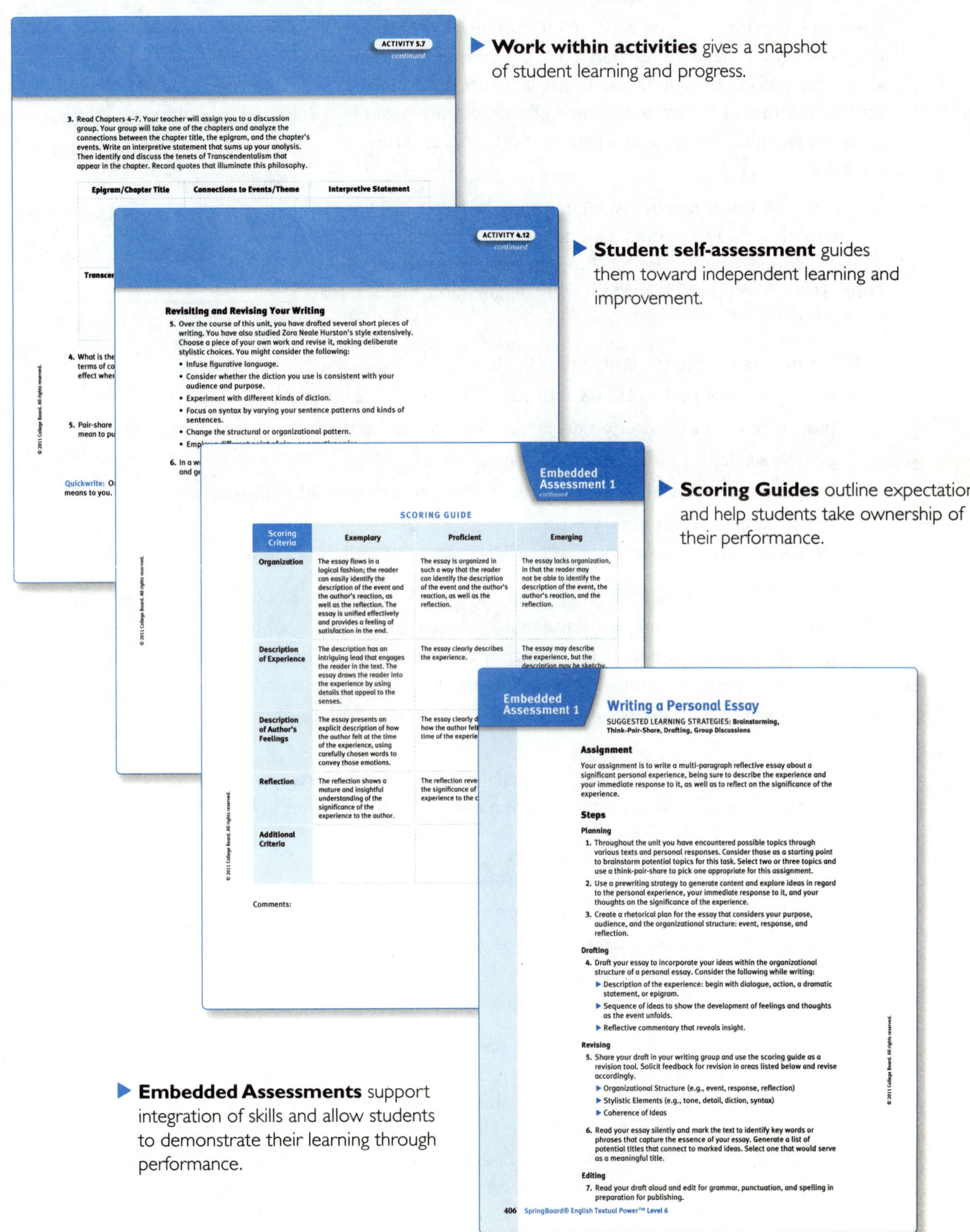

ACTIVITY 5.7 *continued*

3. Read Chapters 4–7. Your teacher will assign you to a discussion group. Your group will take one of the chapters and analyze the connections between the chapter title, the epigram, and the chapter's events. Write an interpretive statement that sums up your analysis. Then identify and discuss the tenets of Transcendentalism that appear in the chapter. Record quotes that illuminate this philosophy.

Epigram/Chapter Title	Connections to Events/Theme	Interpretive Statement

Transcen

4. What is the terms of co effect wher

5. Pair-share mean to pu

Quickwrite: O means to you.

ACTIVITY 4.12 *continued*

Revisiting and Revising Your Writing

5. Over the course of this unit, you have drafted several short pieces of writing. You have also studied Zora Neale Hurston's style extensively. Choose a piece of your own work and revise it, making deliberate stylistic choices. You might consider the following:
   - Infuse figurative language.
   - Consider whether the diction you use is consistent with your audience and purpose.
   - Experiment with different kinds of diction.
   - Focus on syntax by varying your sentence patterns and kinds of sentences.
   - Change the structural or organizational pattern.
   - Empl

6. In a w and ge

Embedded Assessment 1 *continued*

SCORING GUIDE

Scoring Criteria	Exemplary	Proficient	Emerging
Organization	The essay flows in a logical fashion; the reader can easily identify the description of the event and the author's reaction, as well as the reflection. The essay is unified effectively and provides a feeling of satisfaction in the end.	The essay is organized in such a way that the reader can identify the description of the event and the author's reaction, as well as the reflection.	The essay lacks organization, in that the reader may not be able to identify the description of the event, the author's reaction, and the reflection.
Description of Experience	The description has an intriguing lead that engages the reader in the text. The essay draws the reader into the experience by using details that appeal to the senses.	The essay clearly describes the experience.	The essay may describe the experience, but the description may be sketchy.
Description of Author's Feelings	The essay presents an explicit description of how the author felt at the time of the experience, using carefully chosen words to convey those emotions.	The essay clearly d how the author fel time of the experie	
Reflection	The reflection shows a mature and insightful understanding of the significance of the experience to the author.	The reflection reve the significance of experience to the c	
Additional Criteria			

Comments:

Embedded Assessment 1

Writing a Personal Essay

SUGGESTED LEARNING STRATEGIES: **Brainstorming, Think-Pair-Share, Drafting, Group Discussions**

Assignment

Your assignment is to write a multi-paragraph reflective essay about a significant personal experience, being sure to describe the experience and your immediate response to it, as well as to reflect on the significance of the experience.

Steps

Planning

1. Throughout the unit you have encountered possible topics through various texts and personal responses. Consider those as a starting point to brainstorm potential topics for this task. Select two or three topics and use a think-pair-share to pick one appropriate for this assignment.
2. Use a prewriting strategy to generate content and explore ideas in regard to the personal experience, your immediate response to it, and your thoughts on the significance of the experience.
3. Create a rhetorical plan for the essay that considers your purpose, audience, and the organizational structure: event, response, and reflection.

Drafting

4. Draft your essay to incorporate your ideas within the organizational structure of a personal essay. Consider the following while writing:
   - Description of the experience: begin with dialogue, action, a dramatic statement, or epigram.
   - Sequence of ideas to show the development of feelings and thoughts as the event unfolds.
   - Reflective commentary that reveals insight.

Revising

5. Share your draft in your writing group and use the scoring guide as a revision tool. Solicit feedback for revision in areas listed below and revise accordingly.
   - Organizational Structure (e.g., event, response, reflection)
   - Stylistic Elements (e.g., tone, detail, diction, syntax)
   - Coherence of Ideas

6. Read your essay silently and mark the text to identify key words or phrases that capture the essence of your essay. Generate a list of potential titles that connect to marked ideas. Select one that would serve as a meaningful title.

Editing

7. Read your draft aloud and edit for grammar, punctuation, and spelling in preparation for publishing.

406 SpringBoard® English Textual Power™ Level 6

© 2011 College Board. All rights reserved.

▶ **Work within activities** gives a snapshot of student learning and progress.

▶ **Student self-assessment** guides them toward independent learning and improvement.

▶ **Scoring Guides** outline expectations and help students take ownership of their performance.

▶ **Embedded Assessments** support integration of skills and allow students to demonstrate their learning through performance.

How Does SpringBoard Provide Teacher Support?

Since its inception, a cornerstone of SpringBoard has been a deep respect for the work teachers do in the classroom. Research shows that effective teachers are the most significant factor in improving student achievement. SpringBoard offers a host of program elements that provide daily support for classroom teachers.

> "…more can be done to improve education by improving the effectiveness of teachers than by any other single factor."
>
> (from Wright, Horn, & Sanders, 1997, as quoted in *Classroom Instruction That Works*, Marzano, Pickering, and Pollock, 2001, p. 3)

The **Teacher's Edition** provides guidance and suggestions based on the writers' own classroom experiences. Each unit contains an instructional resource for teaching the unit called **About the Unit**. These pages provide the following detailed information for each unit:

- **Context** (situating the unit within the level).
- **Its sequence of instructional activities** (explaining the purpose, progression, and connection of each activity to one another and how each activity scaffolds to the Embedded Assessments).
- **Preparatory materials** (items outside of the SpringBoard materials such as film and the need for library access).
- **Embedded Assessments** (an outline of the essential skills and knowledge required).

In addition, on-page activity purpose statements, suggestions and teaching strategies, plus sample responses for student work, provide a clearly articulated instructional pathway. A complete curriculum online, end-of-unit tests, and correlations to state standards all help teachers plan for and implement instruction.

The SpringBoard program provides unparalleled **professional development** through initial and advanced teacher training institutes that focus on the following:

- Hands-on instruction in best instructional practices.
- Use of strategies to improve instruction and student learning.
- Mapping a standards-based curriculum and vertical articulations of concepts across the grade levels.
- Using assessment to inform instruction.

In addition to training workshops, the program provides train-the-trainer workshops to build district training capacity, support for in-district trainings, online teacher mentors, and access to an online community of SpringBoard teachers and admininstrators for sharing and learning from best practices. Moreover, SpringBoard provides access to English Language Arts Instructional Specialists who can help with implementation questions and online access to a community of SpringBoard teachers eager to share and respond to questions.

How Does SpringBoard Integrate Student Reflection?

The SpringBoard program values reflection as a way to measure student growth, to produce evidence of learning over time, and to promote student self-evaluation as a path to independent learning. SpringBoard students are regularly prompted to stop and think about what they've learned, the strategies they used effectively, and what they still need to learn.

Recursive reflection on the changes in their understanding of key concepts and questions leads to the habit of metacognition, a significant factor in promoting independent and responsible learners. In addition, ongoing Portfolio activities require students to revisit, revise, and reflect on items they have produced and to later select the products that reveal evidence of their growth. Students become reflective thinkers who examine their own learning strategies, the ways they think and express themselves, and the ways they will eventually communicate about themselves to the world. This student-centered interaction produces an enduring understanding of English Language Arts skills as well as confident independent learners ready and able to take on the challenge of lifelong learning.

Students thrive in SpringBoard classrooms because they are empowered to consider what they are learning (content), how they demonstrate learning (product), how they learn best (process and strategies), and who they are as learners. End-of-unit reflection opportunities are built into the program, encouraging both students and teachers to reflect on their learning and teaching experiences.

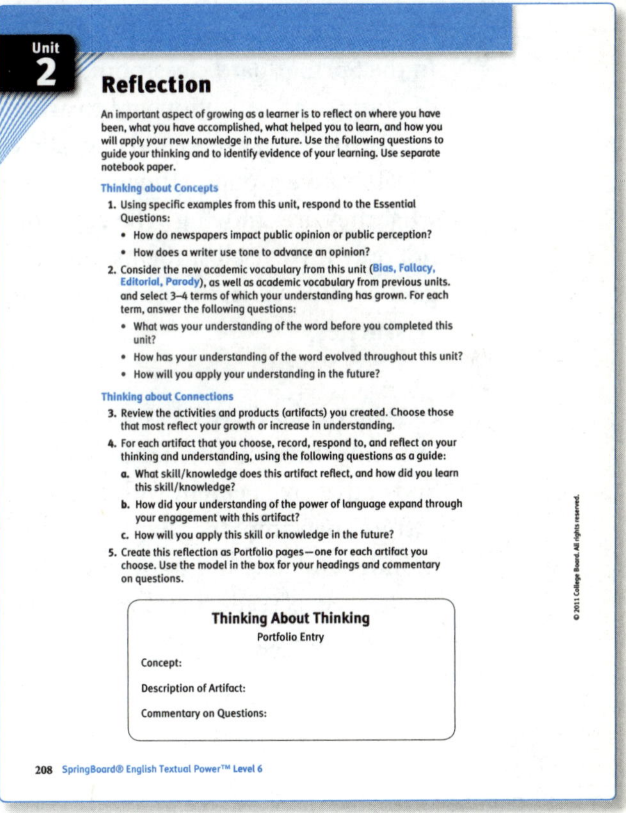
Unit 2

Reflection

An important aspect of growing as a learner is to reflect on where you have been, what you have accomplished, what helped you to learn, and how you will apply your new knowledge in the future. Use the following questions to guide your thinking and to identify evidence of your learning. Use separate notebook paper.

Thinking about Concepts

1. Using specific examples from this unit, respond to the Essential Questions:
   - How do newspapers impact public opinion or public perception?
   - How does a writer use tone to advance an opinion?
2. Consider the new academic vocabulary from this unit (**Bias, Fallacy, Editorial, Parody**), as well as academic vocabulary from previous units, and select 3–4 terms of which your understanding has grown. For each term, answer the following questions:
   - What was your understanding of the word before you completed this unit?
   - How has your understanding of the word evolved throughout this unit?
   - How will you apply your understanding in the future?

Thinking about Connections

3. Review the activities and products (artifacts) you created. Choose those that most reflect your growth or increase in understanding.
4. For each artifact that you choose, record, respond to, and reflect on your thinking and understanding, using the following questions as a guide:
   a. What skill/knowledge does this artifact reflect, and how did you learn this skill/knowledge?
   b. How did your understanding of the power of language expand through your engagement with this artifact?
   c. How will you apply this skill or knowledge in the future?
5. Create this reflection as Portfolio pages—one for each artifact you choose. Use the model in the box for your headings and commentary on questions.

Thinking About Thinking
Portfolio Entry

Concept:

Description of Artifact:

Commentary on Questions:

208 SpringBoard® English Textual Power™ Level 6

© 2011 College Board. All rights reserved.

How Does SpringBoard Make English Language Arts Relevant to Today's Students?

Learning is more effective when the content and the instruction hold students' attention. A multitude of interests vie for students' attention today, and it is important that they see a connection between what they're learning and their own lives. SpringBoard helps students relate to a variety of texts, from fiction and poetry to film and online articles and blogs. Texts included in the SpringBoard program have been selected to meet several criteria: literary merit, skills-based instruction, and interest and relevance to students' lives.

The world is filled with information, but not all of it is sound. SpringBoard gives students the tools to look at multiple sources of information and analyze their purposes, whether to entertain or to inform, and to evaluate their reliability. Reading and analyzing a variety of texts positions students to be more thoughtful and insightful in their own reading and writing.

Interactive Participation

In the SpringBoard classroom, students are encouraged to engage in academic discourse and reflection and to articulate their thoughts and ideas, providing a sense of relevance to and engagement in the learning process. Working in collaborative groups, students also explore their own and others' ideas about what they are studying. The collaborative techniques in SpringBoard classrooms not only involve all students, they also create a setting where students can gain confidence in their own ideas and skills in communicating those ideas to classmates.

Student Ownership of Learning

Students thrive in SpringBoard classrooms as they learn through participation and active engagement with English language arts concepts that stretch and inspire their thinking. Explicitly taught learning strategies enhance students' sense of independence and mastery so that, as they develop confidence in their ability to succeed as readers and writers, they begin to take ownership of their learning in new and exciting ways.

Preview of the Annotated Teacher Edition

English Textual Power, Level 4, focuses on literature that highlights the theme of Coming of Age. Building on their knowledge of literary elements in traditional literary genres, students study the relationship between narrative voice and style, while also analyzing literary and stylistic elements in film and literature. They develop persuasive writing skills by using rhetorical appeals. Performance and oral interpretation of literature build students' speaking and listening skills. Research continues to play an important role as students evaluate social, cultural, and historical influences on texts. Students also continue to evaluate their use of strategies.

About the Unit

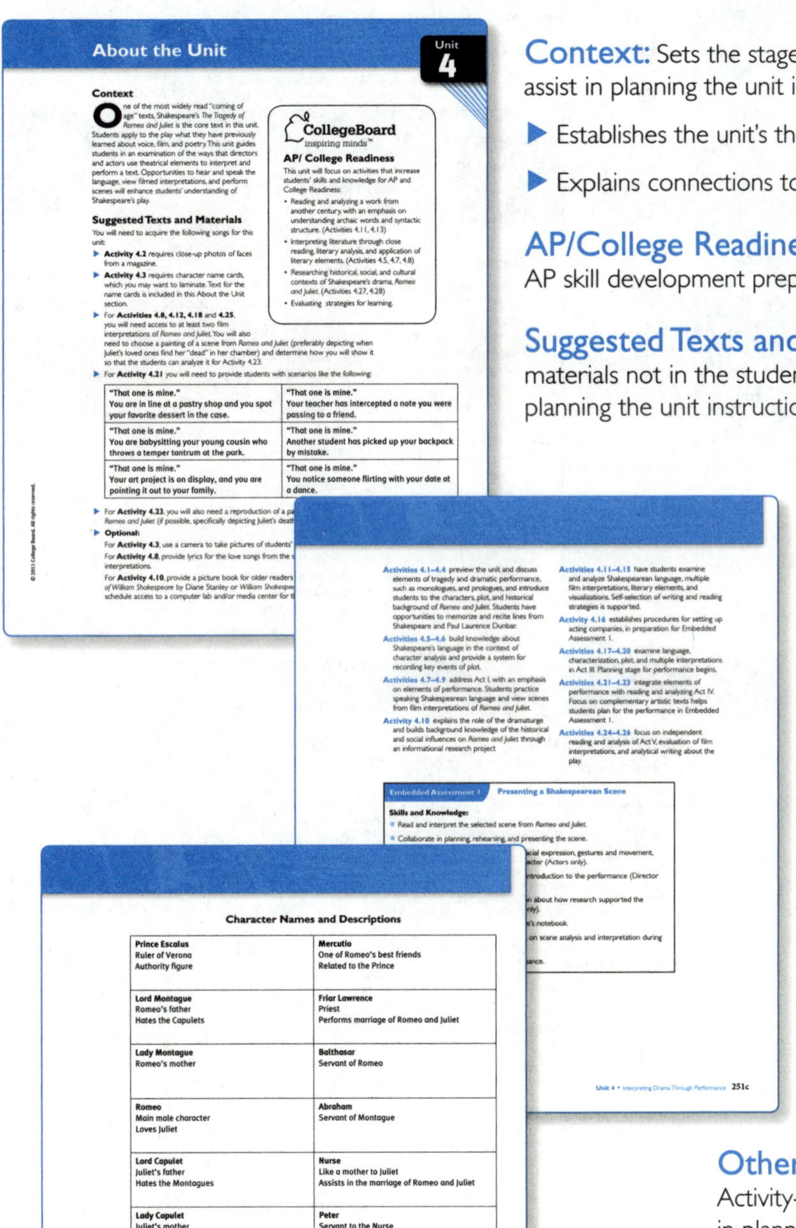

About the Unit

Unit 4

Context

One of the most widely read "coming of age" texts, Shakespeare's *The Tragedy of Romeo and Juliet* is the core text in this unit. Students apply to the play what they have previously learned about voice, film, and poetry. This unit guides students in an examination of the ways that directors and actors use theatrical elements to interpret and perform a text. Opportunities to hear and speak the language, view filmed interpretations, and perform scenes will enhance students' understanding of Shakespeare's play.

CollegeBoard inspiring minds™

AP/ College Readiness

This unit will focus on activities that increase students' skills and knowledge for AP and College Readiness:

- Reading and analyzing a work from another century, with an emphasis on understanding archaic words and syntactic structure. (Activities 4.11, 4.13)
- Interpreting literature through close reading, literary analysis, and application of literary elements. (Activities 4.5, 4.7, 4.8)
- Researching historical, social, and cultural contexts of Shakespeare's drama, *Romeo and Juliet*. (Activities 4.27, 4.28)
- Evaluating strategies for learning.

Suggested Texts and Materials

You will need to acquire the following songs for this unit:

- **Activity 4.2** requires close-up photos of faces from a magazine.
- **Activity 4.3** requires character name cards, which you may want to laminate. Text for the name cards is included in this About the Unit section.
- For **Activities 4.8, 4.12, 4.18** and **4.25**, you will need access to at least two film interpretations of *Romeo and Juliet*. You will also need to choose a painting of a scene from *Romeo and Juliet* (preferably depicting when Juliet's loved ones find her "dead" in her chamber) and determine how you will show it so that the students can analyze it for Activity 4.23.
- For **Activity 4.21** you will need to provide students with scenarios like the following:

"That one is mine." You are in line at a pastry shop and you spot your favorite dessert in the case.	"That one is mine." Your teacher has intercepted a note you were passing to a friend.
"That one is mine." You are babysitting your young cousin who throws a temper tantrum at the park.	"That one is mine." Another student has picked up your backpack by mistake.
"That one is mine." Your art project is on display, and you are pointing it out to your family.	"That one is mine." You notice someone flirting with your date at a dance.

Character Names and Descriptions

Prince Escalus Ruler of Verona Authority figure	**Mercutio** One of Romeo's best friends Related to the Prince
Lord Montague Romeo's father Hates the Capulets	**Friar Lawrence** Priest Performs marriage of Romeo and Juliet
Lady Montague Romeo's mother	**Balthasar** Servant of Romeo
Romeo Main male character Loves Juliet	**Abraham** Servant of Montague
Lord Capulet Juliet's father Hates the Montagues	**Nurse** Like a mother to Juliet Assists in the marriage of Romeo and Juliet
Lady Capulet Juliet's mother	**Peter** Servant to the Nurse
Juliet Main female character Loves Romeo	**Sampson** Servant of Capulet
Tybalt Juliet's cousin Hates the Montagues	**Gregory** Servant of Capulet
Count Paris Wants to marry Juliet Related to the Prince	**Benvolio** One of Romeo's best friends Nephew of Montague

Embedded Assessment 1 Presenting a Shakespearean Scene

Unit 4 • Interpreting Drama Through Performance 251c

Unit 4 • Interpreting Drama Through Performance 251e

Context: Sets the stage and places the unit in context to assist in planning the unit instruction.

- Establishes the unit's thematic and skill elements.
- Explains connections to other units.

AP/College Readiness Connection: Identifies Pre-AP skill development preparing students for AP level work.

Suggested Texts and Materials: Needed texts and materials not in the student books give a heads-up when planning the unit instruction.

Instructional Sequence: Identifies the progression of skills and knowledge in the unit activities.

- Identifies specific scaffolding leading to the Embedded Assessment.
- Shows the scaffolding and recursive paths of instruction.
- Unpacks the skills and knowledge needed for each Embedded Assessment in the unit.
- Allows a view of the "whole picture."

Other Instructional Materials: Activity-specific blackline masters and information to assist in planning and conducting instruction:

- Reading plans to guide the reading of novels.
- Literature circles and how to implement them.
- Film times to guide the selection of film clips.

The Unit at a Glance

Unit Opener sets the stage for the content of the unit.

- **Unit Overview** sets a purpose for the student with a brief introduction to unit concepts and skills.
- **Essential Questions** frame the unit focus in questions whose answers will unfold during the unit and help students make connections to the broader world.

Unit Preview with table of contents gives a quick look at the entire unit.

- **Goal** statements help students focus on what they need to know.
- **Academic Vocabulary** alerts students to the words they'll study in depth as they complete the unit activities.
- **Contents** lists the activities, texts with genre identifications and authors, plus Embedded Assessments in the unit.

Learning Focus pages precede the first activity for each part of the unit. These pages:

- Help students make connections between their lives and what they're learning in the unit.
- Give a context for some of the new vocabulary and literary terms students will learn.
- Focus students' immediate attention on the primary knowledge and skills for the unit.

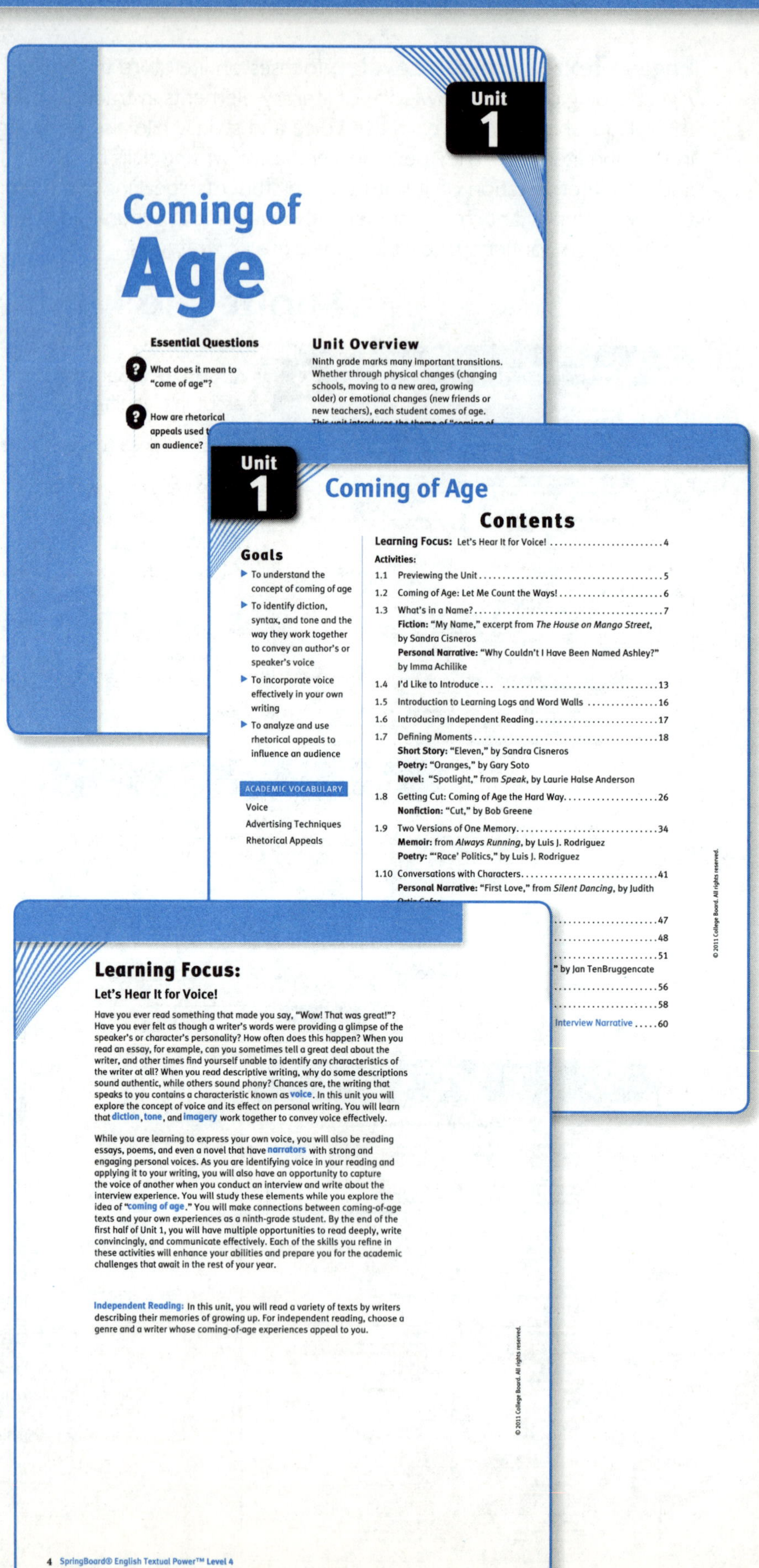

Unit 1

Coming of Age

Essential Questions

What does it mean to "come of age"?

How are rhetorical appeals used t[o] … an audience?

Unit Overview

Ninth grade marks many important transitions. Whether through physical changes (changing schools, moving to a new area, growing older) or emotional changes (new friends or new teachers), each student comes of age.

Unit 1

Coming of Age

Contents

Goals

- To understand the concept of coming of age
- To identify diction, syntax, and tone and the way they work together to convey an author's or speaker's voice
- To incorporate voice effectively in your own writing
- To analyze and use rhetorical appeals to influence an audience

ACADEMIC VOCABULARY

Voice

Advertising Techniques

Rhetorical Appeals

Learning Focus: Let's Hear It for Voice! 4

Activities:

1.1 Previewing the Unit 5

1.2 Coming of Age: Let Me Count the Ways! 6

1.3 What's in a Name? 7

Fiction: "My Name," excerpt from *The House on Mango Street*, by Sandra Cisneros

Personal Narrative: "Why Couldn't I Have Been Named Ashley?" by Imma Achilike

1.4 I'd Like to Introduce ... .13

1.5 Introduction to Learning Logs and Word Walls 16

1.6 Introducing Independent Reading 17

1.7 Defining Moments 18

Short Story: "Eleven," by Sandra Cisneros

Poetry: "Oranges," by Gary Soto

Novel: "Spotlight," from *Speak*, by Laurie Halse Anderson

1.8 Getting Cut: Coming of Age the Hard Way 26

Nonfiction: "Cut," by Bob Greene

1.9 Two Versions of One Memory 34

Memoir: from *Always Running*, by Luis J. Rodriguez

Poetry: "'Race' Politics," by Luis J. Rodriguez

1.10 Conversations with Characters 41

Personal Narrative: "First Love," from *Silent Dancing*, by Judith …

....47

....48

....51

" by Jan TenBruggencate

....56

....58

Interview Narrative 60

© 2011 College Board. All rights reserved.

Learning Focus:

Let's Hear It for Voice!

Have you ever read something that made you say, "Wow! That was great!"? Have you ever felt as though a writer's words were providing a glimpse of the speaker's or character's personality? How often does this happen? When you read an essay, for example, can you sometimes tell a great deal about the writer, and other times find yourself unable to identify any characteristics of the writer at all? When you read descriptive writing, why do some descriptions sound authentic, while others sound phony? Chances are, the writing that speaks to you contains a characteristic known as **voice**. In this unit you will explore the concept of voice and its effect on personal writing. You will learn that **diction**, **tone**, and **imagery** work together to convey voice effectively.

While you are learning to express your own voice, you will also be reading essays, poems, and even a novel that have **narrators** with strong and engaging personal voices. As you are identifying voice in your reading and applying it to your writing, you will also have an opportunity to capture the voice of another when you conduct an interview and write about the interview experience. You will study these elements while you explore the idea of "**coming of age**." You will make connections between coming-of-age texts and your own experiences as a ninth-grade student. By the end of the first half of Unit 1, you will have multiple opportunities to read deeply, write convincingly, and communicate effectively. Each of the skills you refine in these activities will enhance your abilities and prepare you for the academic challenges that await in the rest of your year.

Independent Reading: In this unit, you will read a variety of texts by writers describing their memories of growing up. For independent reading, choose a genre and a writer whose coming-of-age experiences appeal to you.

© 2011 College Board. All rights reserved.

4 SpringBoard® English Textual Power™ Level 4

Unit Activities and Teaching Strategies

Preparing to Teach

Each activity includes point-of-use teaching suggestions.

- **Materials** lists the items you'll need to provide for the activity, such as manipulatives or artwork and other resources to share with students.
- **Purpose** statements identify the skills and knowledge developed in the activity.
- **Steps** provide guidance through suggested teaching strategies (highlighted in blue) and step-by-step ideas for completing the activity.

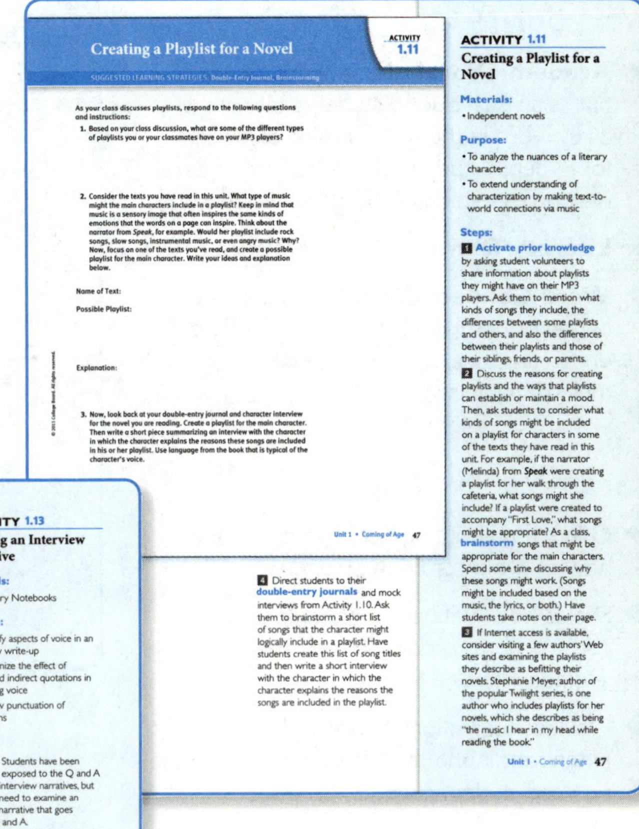

Creating a Playlist for a Novel — ACTIVITY 1.11

SUGGESTED LEARNING STRATEGIES: Double-Entry Journal, Brainstorming

As your class discusses playlists, respond to the following questions and instructions:

1. Based on your class discussion, what are some of the different types of playlists you or your classmates have on your MP3 players?
2. Consider the texts you have read in this unit. What type of music might the main characters include in a playlist? Keep in mind that music is a sensory image that often inspires the same kinds of emotions that the words on a page can inspire. Think about the narrator from *Speak*, for example. Would her playlist include rock songs, slow songs, instrumental music, or even angry music? Why? Now, focus on one of the texts you've read, and create a possible playlist for the main character. Write your ideas and explanation below.

Name of Text:

Possible Playlist:

Explanation:

3. Now, look back at your double-entry journal and character interview for the novel you are reading. Create a playlist for the main character. Then write a short piece summarizing an interview with the character in which the character explains the reasons these songs are included in his or her playlist. Use language from the book that is typical of the character's voice.

© 2011 College Board. All rights reserved.

Unit 1 • Coming of Age 47

ACTIVITY 1.11

Creating a Playlist for a Novel

Materials:
- Independent novels

Purpose:
- To analyze the nuances of a literary character
- To extend understanding of characterization by making text-to-world connections via music

Steps:

1 **Activate prior knowledge** by asking student volunteers to share information about playlists they might have on their MP3 players. Ask them to mention what kinds of songs they include, the differences between some playlists and others, and also the differences between their playlists and those of their siblings, friends, or parents.

2 Discuss the reasons for creating playlists and the ways that playlists can establish or maintain a mood. Then, ask students to consider what kinds of songs might be included on a playlist for characters in some of the texts they have read in this unit. For example, if the narrator (Melinda) from ***Speak*** were creating a playlist for her walk through the cafeteria, what songs might she include? If a playlist were created to accompany "First Love," what songs might be appropriate? As a class, **brainstorm** songs that might be appropriate for the main characters. Spend some time discussing why these songs might work. (Songs might be included based on the music, the lyrics, or both.) Have students take notes on their page.

3 If Internet access is available, consider visiting a few authors' Web sites and examining the playlists they describe as befitting their novels. Stephanie Meyer, author of the popular Twilight series, is one author who includes playlists for her novels, which she describes as being "the music I hear in my head while reading the book."

4 Direct students to their **double-entry journals** and mock interviews from Activity 1.10. Ask them to brainstorm a short list of songs that the character might logically include in a playlist. Have students create this list of song titles and then write a short interview with the character in which the character explains the reasons the songs are included in the playlist.

Unit 1 • Coming of Age 47

Reading an Interview Narrative — ACTIVITY 1.13

SUGGESTED LEARNING STRATEGIES: Quickwrite, Word Map

You have seen interviews written in the Q and A format, but many interview narratives are not presented in this way. As you read "Bethany Only Looking Ahead," consider the ways in which the writer describes Bethany, captures her voice, considers a significant incident in her life, and conveys the significance to the reader.

After reading and discussing the interview narrative with a partner or group, answer the questions below.

Name of Interviewee: Name of Interviewer:

What seems to be the focus of this interview?

Describe the voice of the interviewee.

What does the writer do that makes the voice of the interviewee clear?

Most interview narratives present both **direct** and **indirect quotations**.

- **Direct quotations** are *word-for-word* quotations. Direct quotations

51

ACTIVITY 1.13

Reading an Interview Narrative

Materials:
- Vocabulary Notebooks

Purpose:
- To identify aspects of voice in an interview write-up
- To recognize the effect of direct and indirect quotations in conveying voice
- To review punctuation of quotations

Steps:

TEACHER TO TEACHER Students have been exposed to the Q and A format of interview narratives, but now they need to examine an interview narrative that goes beyond Q and A.

1 As students read the article, "Bethany Only Looking Ahead," remind them to take notes about the focus of the interview, the voice of the interviewee, and the language the writer uses to describe the interviewee.

Unit 1 • Coming of Age 51

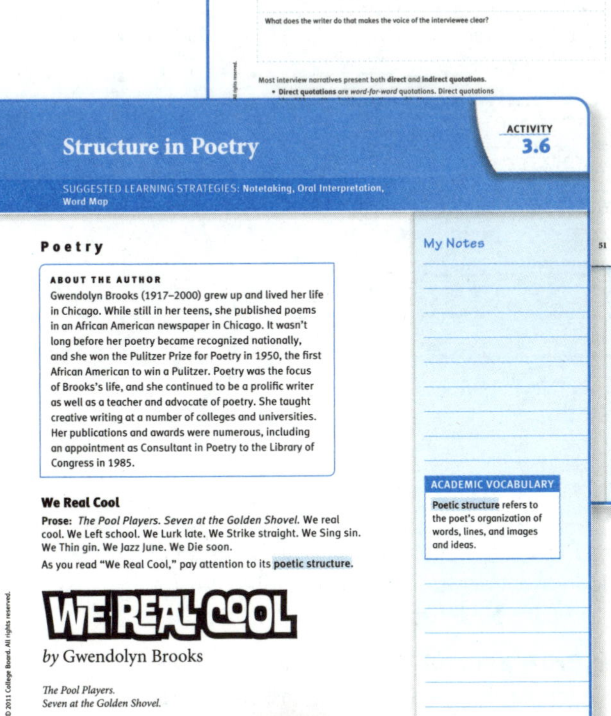

Structure in Poetry — ACTIVITY 3.6

SUGGESTED LEARNING STRATEGIES: Notetaking, Oral Interpretation, Word Map

Poetry

ABOUT THE AUTHOR

Gwendolyn Brooks (1917–2000) grew up and lived her life in Chicago. While still in her teens, she published poems in an African American newspaper in Chicago. It wasn't long before her poetry became recognized nationally, and she won the Pulitzer Prize for Poetry in 1950, the first African American to win a Pulitzer. Poetry was the focus of Brooks's life, and she continued to be a prolific writer as well as a teacher and advocate of poetry. She taught creative writing at a number of colleges and universities. Her publications and awards were numerous, including an appointment as Consultant in Poetry to the Library of Congress in 1985.

We Real Cool

Prose: *The Pool Players. Seven at the Golden Shovel.* We real cool. We Left school. We Lurk late. We Strike straight. We Sing sin. We Thin gin. We Jazz June. We Die soon.

As you read "We Real Cool," pay attention to its **poetic structure**.

WE REAL COOL

by Gwendolyn Brooks

The Pool Players.
Seven at the Golden Shovel.

We real cool. We
Left school. We

Lurk late. We
Strike straight. We

Sing sin. We
Thin gin. We

Jazz June. We
Die soon.

My Notes

ACADEMIC VOCABULARY

Poetic structure refers to the poet's organization of words, lines, and images and ideas.

© 2011 College Board. All rights reserved.

Unit 3 • Exploring Poetic Voices 211

- **Teacher to Teacher** notes point out suggestions based on writers' own classroom experiences and give additional information about the activity or the specific tasks for students.

- **About the Author** features biographical information that helps students understand how authors' experiences influence their writing. This background information helps set the context for the texts students are reading.

Integrated Language Skills

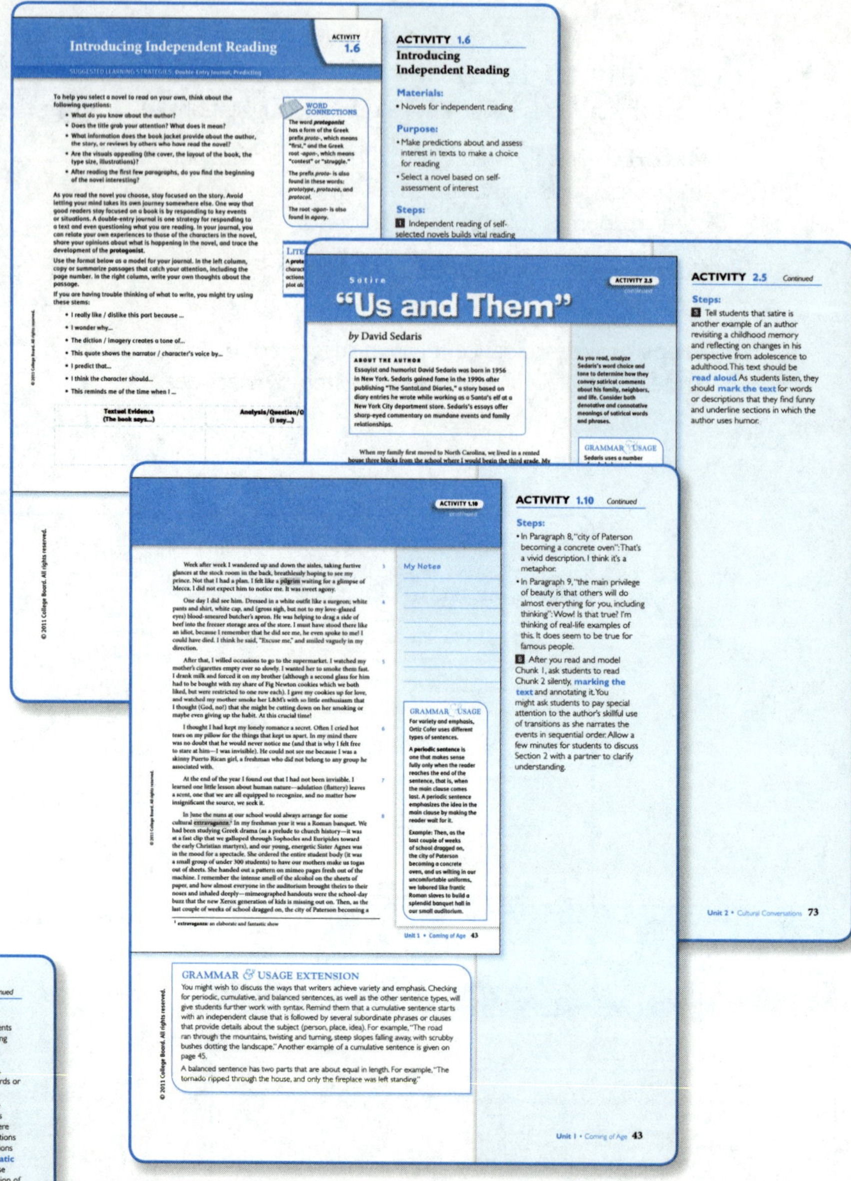

ACTIVITY 1.6
Introducing Independent Reading

Materials:
• Novels for independent reading

Purpose:
• Make predictions about and assess interest in texts to make a choice for reading
• Select a novel based on self-assessment of interest

Steps:
1 Independent reading of self-selected novels builds vital reading

Satire
"Us and Them"
by David Sedaris

ACTIVITY 2.5 *Continued*

Steps:
3 Tell students that satire is another example of an author revisiting a childhood memory and reflecting on changes in his perspective from adolescence to adulthood. This text should be read aloud. As students listen, they should mark the text for words or descriptions that they find funny and underline sections in which the author uses humor.

Unit 2 • Cultural Conversations 73

ACTIVITY 1.10 *Continued*

Steps:
• In Paragraph 8, "city of Paterson becoming a concrete oven": That's a vivid description. I think it's a metaphor.
• In Paragraph 9, "the main privilege of beauty is that others will do almost everything for you, including thinking": Wow! Is that true? I'm thinking of real-life examples of this. It does seem to be true for famous people.
6 After you read and model Chunk 1, ask students to read Chunk 2 silently, marking the text and annotating it. You might ask students to pay special attention to the author's skillful use of transitions as she narrates the events in sequential order. Allow a few minutes for students to discuss Section 2 with a partner to clarify understanding.

GRAMMAR & USAGE EXTENSION
You might wish to discuss the ways that writers achieve variety and emphasis. Checking for periodic, cumulative, and balanced sentences, as well as the other sentence types, will give students further work with syntax. Remind them that a cumulative sentence starts with an independent clause that is followed by several subordinate phrases or clauses that provide details about the subject (person, place, idea). For example, "The road ran through the mountains, twisting and turning, steep slopes falling away, with scrubby bushes dotting the landscape." Another example of a cumulative sentence is given on page 45.
A balanced sentence has two parts that are about equal in length. For example, "The tornado ripped through the house, and only the fireplace was left standing."

Unit 1 • Coming of Age 43

Vocabulary and Word Study

- **Academic Vocabulary** words have a blue tint as a visual clue to students that this is a key word in the unit. Graphic organizers for in-depth study of the words are in the Resources section of the student books.
- **Literary Terms** are defined at point of use.
- **Word Connections** help students use context clues from Latin and other roots, understand analogies, and identify words with multiple meanings.

Grammar & Usage

- Offers tips about points of grammar and how to avoid common errors.
- Shows how writers use grammatical constructions to clarify text, convey meaning, and add interest.
- Provides suggestions for related lesson extensions in the Teacher's Edition under the reduced student page.

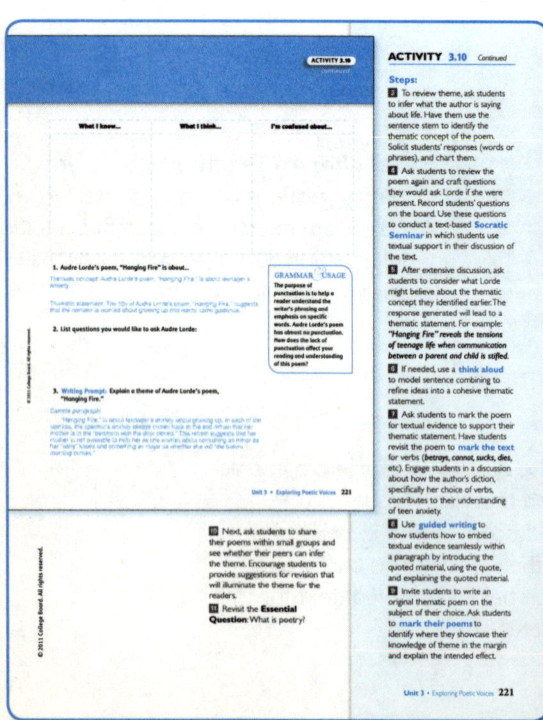

ACTIVITY 3.10 *Continued*

Steps:
3 To review theme, ask students to infer what the author is saying about life. Have them use the sentence stem to identify the thematic concept of the poem. Solicit students' responses (words or phrases), and chart them.
4 Ask students to review the poem again and craft questions they would ask Lorde if she were present. Record students' questions on the board. Use these questions to conduct a text-based Socratic Seminar in which students use textual support in their discussion of the text.
5 After extensive discussion, ask students to consider what Lorde might believe about the thematic concept they identified earlier. The response generated will lead to a thematic statement. For example: *"Hanging Fire" reveals the tensions of teenage life when communication between a parent and child is stifled.*
6 If needed, use a think aloud to model sentence combining to refine ideas into a cohesive thematic statement.
7 Ask students to mark the poem for textual evidence to support their thematic statement. Have students revisit the poem to mark the text for verbs (*betrays, cannot, sucks, dies,* etc.). Engage students in a discussion about how the author's diction, specifically her choice of verbs, contributes to their understanding of teen anxiety.
8 Use guided writing to show students how to embed textual evidence seamlessly within a paragraph by introducing the quoted material, using the quote, and explaining the quoted material.
9 Invite students to write an original thematic poem on the subject of their choice. Ask students to mark their poems to identify where they showcase their knowledge of theme in the margin and explain the intended effect.
10 Next, ask students to share their poems within small groups and see whether their peers can infer the theme. Encourage students to provide suggestions for revision that will illuminate the theme for the readers.
11 Revisit the **Essential Question**: What is poetry?

Unit 3 • Exploring Poetic Voices 221

Writing

- **Writing Process** is integrated into activities and Embedded Assessments; students prewrite, draft, revise, edit, and prepare publishable writing.
- **Writing Prompts and Timed Writings** provide practice in identifying specific writing tasks and writing under timed conditions.
- **Portfolios** are encouraged to showcase students' best work and to demonstrate their growth in skills over the course of study.

Performance-Based Assessment

- **Embedded Assessments** provide opportunities for students to demonstrate their knowledge and skills in a variety of ways—visually, orally, and in writing—to allow all students to perform well.
- **Scoring Guides** provide detailed expectations for what students are to complete for an assessment and how their work will be evaluated.
  - Exemplary, Proficient, and Emerging categories describe the level of work expected for each rating.
  - Previewing the expectations for each sets the standard for students to self-evaluate.
- **College Board Standards** correlations provide a guide to the skills covered in each assessment.

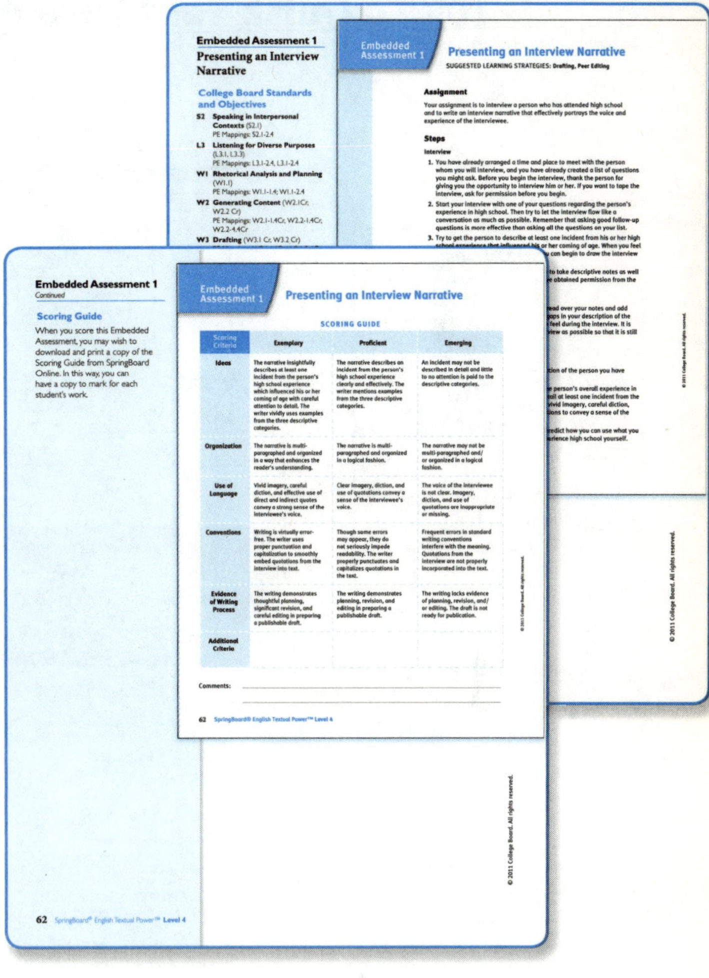

Embedded Assessment 1

Presenting an Interview Narrative

College Board Standards and Objectives

Embedded Assessment 1

Presenting an Interview Narrative

Assignment

Your assignment is to interview a person who has attended high school and to write an interview narrative that effectively portrays the voice and experience of the interviewee.

Embedded Assessment 1 *Continued*

Scoring Guide

When you score this Embedded Assessment, you may wish to download and print a copy of the Scoring Guide from SpringBoard Online. In this way, you can have a copy to mark for each student's work.

Presenting an Interview Narrative

SCORING GUIDE

Scoring Criteria	Exemplary	Proficient	Emerging
Ideas			
Organization			
Use of Language			
Conventions			
Evidence of Writing Process			
Additional Criteria			

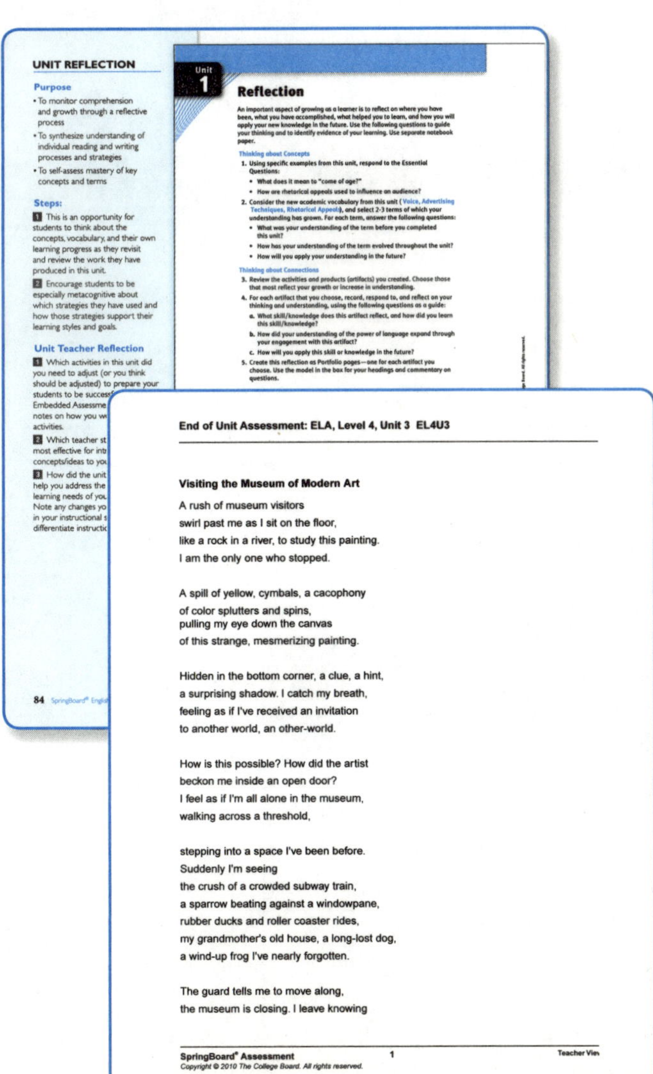

UNIT REFLECTION

Purpose

- To monitor comprehension and growth through a reflective process
- To synthesize understanding of individual reading and writing processes and strategies
- To self-assess mastery of key concepts and terms

Unit 1

Reflection

End of Unit Assessment: ELA, Level 4, Unit 3 EL4U3

Visiting the Museum of Modern Art

A rush of museum visitors
swirl past me as I sit on the floor,
like a rock in a river, to study this painting.
I am the only one who stopped.

A spill of yellow, cymbals, a cacophony
of color splutters and spins,
pulling my eye down the canvas
of this strange, mesmerizing painting.

Hidden in the bottom corner, a clue, a hint,
a surprising shadow. I catch my breath,
feeling as if I've received an invitation
to another world, an other-world.

How is this possible? How did the artist
beckon me inside an open door?
I feel as if I'm all alone in the museum,
walking across a threshold,

stepping into a space I've been before.
Suddenly I'm seeing
the crush of a crowded subway train,
a sparrow beating against a windowpane,
rubber ducks and roller coaster rides,
my grandmother's old house, a long-lost dog,
a wind-up frog I've nearly forgotten.

The guard tells me to move along,
the museum is closing. I leave knowing

SpringBoard® Assessment 1

Unit Reflection

- Promotes student self assessment.
- Provides opportunity for teachers to review instruction and make notes about future instruction.

Unit Assessments

- Available online.
- Cover the skills students learned and practiced in the unit.

Take a Quick Tour Through SpringBoard Online

REPORTS

INSTRUCTIONAL CONTENT

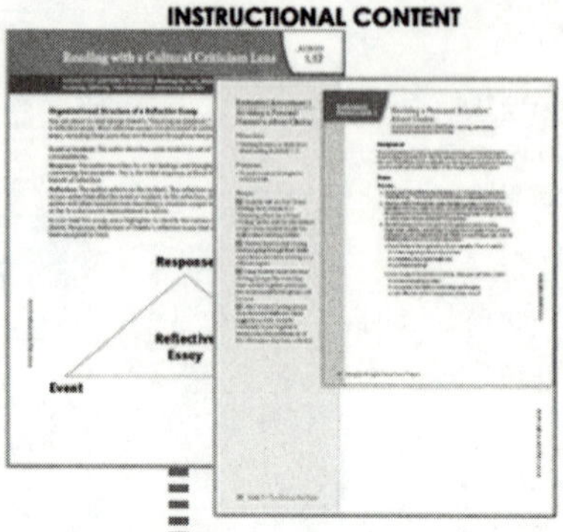

ASSESSMENTS

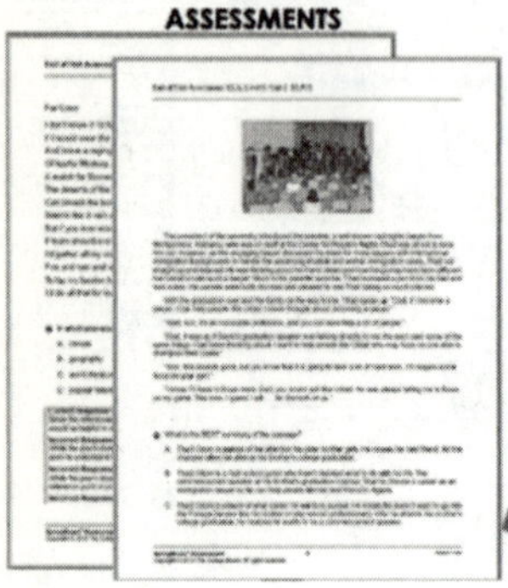

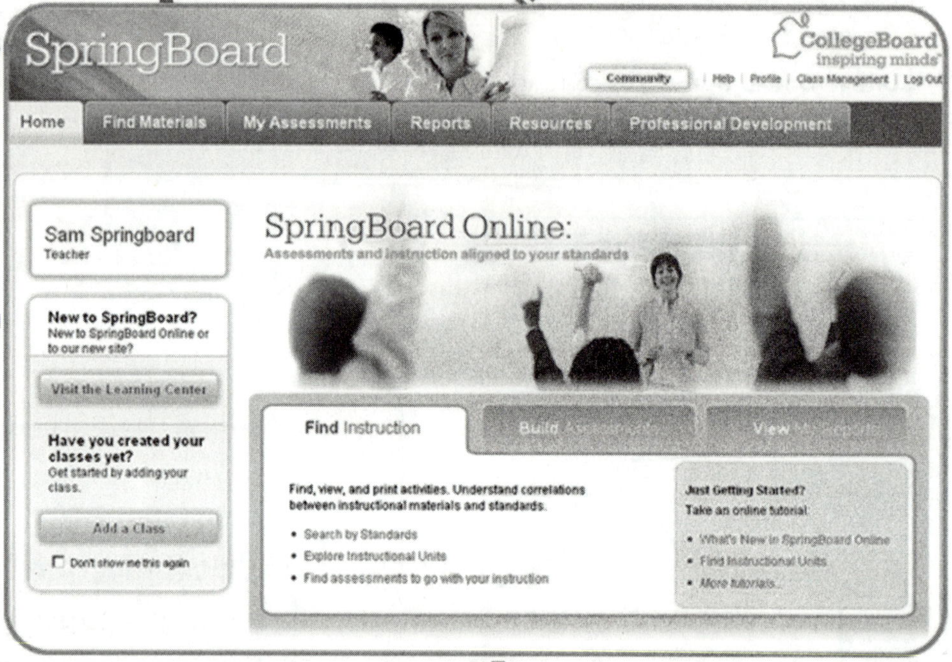

CORRELATED ITEMS

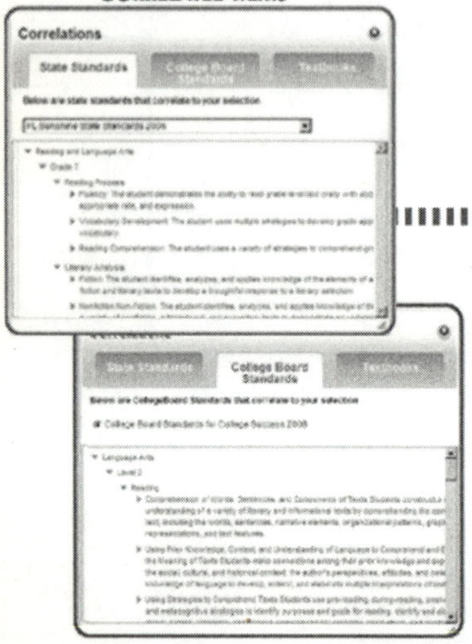

SpringBoard

CollegeBoard
inspiring minds

Community | Help | Profile | Class Management | Log Out

Home | Find Materials | My Assessments | Reports | Resources | Professional Development

Sam Springboard
Teacher

New to SpringBoard?
New to SpringBoard Online or to our new site?

Visit the Learning Center

Have you created your classes yet?
Get started by adding your class.

Add a Class

Don't show me this again

SpringBoard Online:
Assessments and instruction aligned to your standards

Find Instruction

Find, view, and print activities. Understand correlations between instructional materials and standards.

- Search by Standards
- Explore Instructional Units
- Find assessments to go with your instruction

Just Getting Started?
Take an online tutorial

- What's New in SpringBoard Online
- Find Instructional Units
- More tutorials...

COLLABORATIVE SPACE

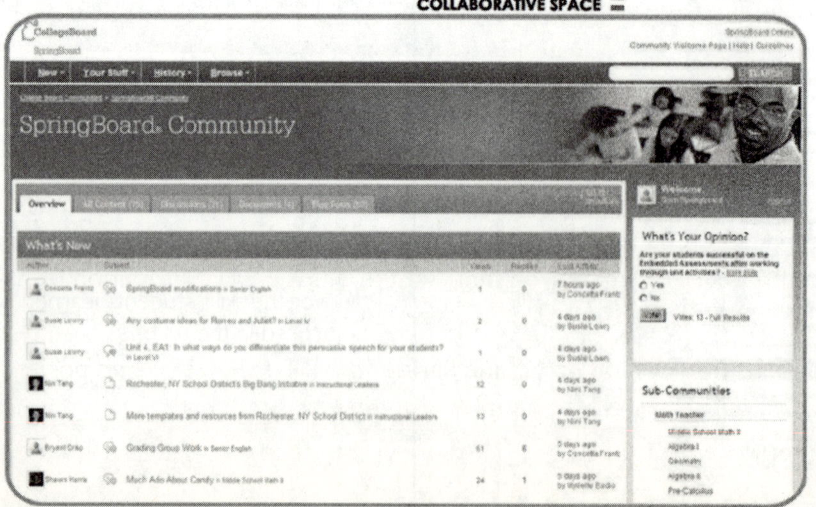

The SpringBoard Classroom

A SpringBoard classroom is an environment that supports high expectations and active participation for all students as they develop and enhance their skills in reading, writing, speaking and listening, and media literacy. Several tools are used to engage students and to ensure participation by all students.

Collaborative Groups

The **student-centered classroom** capitalizes on collaboration. Students are able to engage in purposeful conversation with partners and in small groups. Collaborative groups provide a setting in which students feel confident to explore their own and others' ideas. Group structure follows specific norms of behavior to allow each member to be treated with respect and to allow each person time to share ideas and to listen to others. With collaborative groups, all members are expected to work together to complete a task, while individual students are held accountable for equal participation in the assignment.

Word Wall

The **Word Wall** facilitates vocabulary development for the class. Creating and maintaining a Word Wall is an ongoing activity. It should be an instructional tool, not just a display. Designate a specific space (such as a bulletin board, pocket chart, blank wall space) in the classroom for the Word Wall. Words may be written on index cards, sentence strips, or blank paper.

- As your students encounter new words, add them to the Word Wall.
- Spend time revisiting words on the Wall whenever possible.
- Emphasize the categorization of words to help students see the logic in language. Invite them to generate a list of potential categories to sort words (alphabetical order, theme, parts of speech, genres, ideas, etc.).
- Make the words into manipulatives by writing them on cards so that they can be shifted, added, and/or eliminated.
- Play games using the words. For example, select a word from the Wall and give students clues to guess the word.
- Encourage students to use words from the Wall correctly in their speaking and writing, and specifically on the Embedded Assessments.

Other Visual Displays

You may also want to create displays in your classroom for the skills and knowledge required for each Embedded Assessment. As students complete their preview of an Embedded Assessment and determine the skills and knowledge needed for that assessment, you may want to capture this information on an enlargement of the web graphic organizer and post it in your classroom.

Other visual displays might include SpringBoard learning strategies posters and a writer's checklist, as well as examples of student work.

Vocabulary Notebook

The **Vocabulary Notebook** facilitates vocabulary development for the individual student. It is an intentional tool for students to expand their understanding of academic terms and concepts. The Vocabulary Notebook may be a spiral notebook, a three-ring binder, or a composition notebook. Students can explore terms and concepts directly in the Notebook, or they can use a copy of one of the vocabulary graphic organizers provided and save the completed graphic organizer in their Vocabulary Notebooks.

Portfolio

Portfolios are an important tool for organizing coursework. The work included in the portfolio demonstrates success in meeting course objectives. Portfolio entries also provide the impetus for reflection. Selections for the Portfolio should be culled from the **Working Folder** in which student work for each unit is kept. This Working Folder may be a manila folder or a three-ring binder.

Encourage students to include items in their Portfolios and Working Folders that illustrate a wide range of their work, including examples of reading, writing, oral fluency, and collaborative activities. Strong portfolios will include a variety of work from each unit, including first drafts, final drafts, quickwrites, responses to writing prompts, notes, reading logs, audio and video examples, and graphics that represent a wide variety of genres, forms, and media students create for multiple purposes. The portfolio:

- Gives students a place to feature their work and share it with others.
- Provides an organized way to view growth throughout the year.
- Encourages student reflection on new skills and strategies for learning.
- Encourages ongoing revision to incorporate new learning and skills and to demonstrate growth as writers and communicators.
- Enables you and students to measure growth in reading, writing, speaking, listening, and media skills.

Classroom Arrangement

The activities in this program often call for students to pair up for work or to work in small groups. Students will experience multiple occasions requiring them to be out of their desks for presentation and performance activities such as oral presentations, reader's theater, drama games, and gallery walks. Being able to rearrange the chairs and tables in your classroom facilitates their work.

Suggested Classroom Materials

- Large paper, pens, crayons for creating and presenting
- Highlighters, colored pencils, and Post-it® notes for marking the text
- DVD player/VCR /CD player for visual and audio prompts
- File folders, three-ring binders, composition notebooks for Working Folders and Portfolios
- 3x5 cards for vocabulary development (Word Wall; word sort)

About the Unit

Unit 1

Context

This opening unit introduces "coming of age" as the thematic focus of the year by asking students to explore fictional characters and real individuals who encounter self-defining incidents. As students interact with multiple texts, they refine their understanding of voice, review advertising appeals, and establish a foundational understanding of learning strategies and key concepts they will apply throughout the year.

AP/ College Readiness

This unit focuses on refining three important skill and knowledge areas for AP/College Readiness:

- Understanding and applying the relationship between diction, syntax, and imagery in the creation of an author's voice. (Activities 1.7, 1.9)
- Recognizing the connection between the audience of a writing piece and the rhetorical appeals and advertising techniques used to persuade that audience. (Activities 1.16, 1.17, 1.18)
- Identifying and owning self-selected reading strategies to access a variety of texts. (Activities 1.5, 1.7)

Suggested Texts and Materials

As you prepare for this unit, you will need the following:

- A set of coming-of-age novels for students' independent reading (see Reading Plan on page 1c)
- A video recording of an interview (Activity 1.12)
- A variety of advertisement samples and book jackets (Activity 1.17)

Also, you will need to invite an adult guest for the group interview in Activity 1.14.

Independent Reading

In this unit, students will read a variety of texts by writers describing their memories of growing up. For independent reading, suggest that students choose a genre and a writer whose coming-of-age experiences appeal to them.

Writing Workshops

Writing Workshops that provide a sequence of activities designed for direct writing instruction in the writing process and in specific genres are available for each grade level of the SpringBoard curriculum. Workshops may be accessed at SpringBoard Online and downloaded or printed for student use. Each workshop is accompanied by teaching notes and suggestions. These workshops may be incorporated into unit instruction as follows:

Unit 1: Workshop 1, The Writing Process; Workshop 5, Script Writing

Unit 2: Workshop 9, Response to Literary or Expository Text

Unit 3: Workshop 3, Poetry; Workshop 9, Response to Literary or Expository Text

Unit 4: Workshop 6, Expository Writing

Unit 5: Workshop 10, Research; Workshop 9, Response to Literary or Expository Text

Grammar Handbook

A Grammar Handbook is located in the back of the student books after the last unit. You may want to spend a few minutes having students scan the contents. Encourage students to use this handbook as a reference as they develop their writing skills. Throughout the unit, you may want to incorporate mini-lessons from the Grammar Handbook and the Grammar & Usage features within each unit to reinforce students' grammar and writing skills.

Instructional Sequence

The instruction begins with an introduction to the concepts of coming of age and voice. Students then refine their understanding by reading a variety of short coming-of-age texts and a self-selected novel. Next, students synthesize the concepts by presenting an authentic interview for Embedded Assessment 1. With a rich understanding of these concepts, students then extend their application by reviewing advertising appeals and applying them to independent novels for an advertising campaign for Embedded Assessment 2.

Activities 1.1–1.6 preview the unit and introduce the key concepts of coming of age and voice and establish procedures for ongoing work with strategy Learning Logs and student-selected novels.

Activities 1.7–1.11 use multiple texts, including essays, novel excerpts, and poems, to analyze the components of voice and coming of age.

Activities 1.12–1.15 focus on interviewing skills to capture and convey the voice of another. Students watch a video interview, read a published interview, conduct a group interview, and plan for the independent interview assignment of Embedded Assessment 1.

Embedded Assessment 1 — **Presenting an Interview Narrative**

Skills and Knowledge:

- Understand the concept of coming of age.
- Analyze the components of voice.
- Write with personal voice.
- Conduct an interview, using appropriate speaking and listening skills.
- Organize interview notes into a written narrative.
- Apply understanding of diction, imagery, and tone.
- Incorporate direct and indirect quotations.
- Edit and proofread for correctness.

Activities 1.16–1.19 build to a culminating assignment related to the self-selected novel. Students interview peers to examine the influences on teen reading; they then examine and review advertising techniques and rhetorical appeals in preparation for the advertising campaign in Embedded Assessment 2. In addition, students are introduced to the elements of argumentation.

Embedded Assessment 2 — **Creating an Ad Campaign for a Novel**

Skills and Knowledge:

- Analyze factors that influence readers' selections of books.
- Evaluate key features of a novel.
- Create a variety of advertisements to meet the needs of a target audience.
- Apply an understanding of advertising appeals and rhetorical appeals.

Suggested Pacing

Activity	45 to 50-Minute Class Periods	Class Periods with Homework	Activity	45 to 50-Minute Class Periods	Class Periods with Homework
Learning Focus and 1.1	½		1.13	¾	
1.2	½		1.14	1	
1.3	1 ½	HW	1.15	½	Plan Interview
1.4	1		EA1	1 ½	HW (Interview)
1.5	½		Learning Focus	½	
1.6	¾	HW	1.16	1	
1.7	2		1.17	¾	
1.8	1 ¼		1.18	1	HW
1.9	1	HW	1.19	¼	
1.10	1	HW	EA2	3	
1.11	½		Unit Reflection	½	
1.12	1				
Total Class Periods				22 ¼	

Reading Plan

Unit 1 is a study of voice and coming of age. Thus, selecting novels that contain first-person narration with strong, identifiable voices and that deal with coming-of-age incidents will help students apply the unit concepts. Suggest books from the following list based on your students' interests and reading levels, as well as school policies regarding student texts with mature themes.

The Catcher in the Rye, J. D. Salinger
Monster, Walter Dean Myers
The Secret Life of Bees, Sue Monk Kidd
A Separate Peace, John Knowles
She's So Money, Cherry Cheva
Slam, Walter Dean Myers
Sleeping Freshmen Never Lie, David Lubar
Speak, Laurie Halse Anderson
Stargirl, Jerry Spinelli
Twisted, Laurie Halse Anderson
A Yellow Raft in Blue Water, Michael Dorris
Ellen Foster, Kaye Gibbons
The House on Mango Street, Sandra Cisneros
The Adventures of Huckleberry Finn, Mark Twain

Considerations for Students' Independent Reading

- Depending on the reading levels of your students, you might decide to ask for a minimum number of journal entries.
- You might also consider providing additional checkpoints or opportunities for peer dialogue about the novels as you proceed through the unit.
- Conferencing with students is another widely recognized tool for maintaining student motivation for reading as well as checking for understanding.
- Ask students to look at their journals for specific examples of imagery, diction, syntax, and tone as they identify the features of the narrator's voice. As they read independent novels, students will continue to develop their understanding of these concepts through classroom activities and journal entries.

End-of-Unit Strategies Reflection

You may want to share the graphic organizer on page 1d with students and have them reflect on the learning strategies that work best for them.

Strategic Thinking

Turn to the definitions of learning strategies in the Resources section at the back of your book. Rate your level of understanding of the strategies by placing a checkmark (√) next to the strategies you are familiar with, an asterisk (*) next to the strategies you are unfamiliar with, and a question mark (?) next to the strategies you are familiar with but still find confusing.

Look at the strategies you marked, and select a few strategies that you feel were especially helpful to you as you completed this unit. List those strategies here and explain why and how each strategy was helpful.

Which Strategies Work Best for You?			
Reading	**Writing**	**Oral Literacy**	**Collaborative**
Explanation			

Unit 1

Coming of Age

Essential Questions

- What does it mean to "come of age"?
- How are rhetorical appeals used to influence an audience?

Unit Overview

Ninth grade marks many important transitions. Whether through physical changes (changing schools, moving to a new area, growing older) or emotional changes (new friends or new teachers), each student comes of age. This unit introduces the theme of "coming of age" and explores how each of us shapes our unique voice though our experiences and our exposure to the strong voices around us. You will interview others and produce a narrative of your experiences in this important transition. This unit also explores the ways that we are influenced through advertising techniques and rhetorical appeals in media. By studying an independent novel as well as the likes and dislikes of your classmates, you will begin to understand the complex relationship between an author's purpose, the intended audience, and the ways in which the author appeals to your needs and desires. Your "coming of age" will not only be marked by physical and emotional changes, but also by a heightened understanding of voice, appeals, and persuasive techniques.

UNIT 1

Have students read the Unit Overview. Discuss the ideas in the overview and ask students to relate them to their own lives.

Students will provide responses to the Essential Questions in Activity 1.1. At the end of the unit, they will revisit the Essential Questions to see how their responses have changed after studying the unit.

UNIT 1

Have students read the goals for the unit and **mark** any words that are unfamiliar to them. You may want to create a space in the classroom for these words so students can add information about their meaning as they study the unit.

You may consider posting these goals in a visible place in the classroom for the duration of the unit, allowing you and students to revisit the goals easily and gauge progress toward achieving the goals throughout the unit.

Academic Vocabulary

Point out the academic vocabulary to students, and remind them that they will be studying concepts related to these words throughout the unit. Having students create **graphic organizers** to study these words in depth will greatly enhance their understanding of each word and its relationship to unit concepts. Have students keep their completed graphic organizers in their **Vocabulary Notebooks**.

See the Resources at the back of this book for examples of blackline masters suitable for word study. As students become more acquainted with the use of a **graphic organizer** to explore the meaning of a word, you may want them to create their own graphic organizers.

Unit 1 Coming of Age

Goals

- To understand the concept of coming of age
- To identify diction, syntax, and tone and the way they work together to convey an author's or speaker's voice
- To incorporate voice effectively in your own writing
- To analyze and use rhetorical appeals to influence an audience

ACADEMIC VOCABULARY

Voice
Advertising Techniques
Rhetorical Appeals

Contents

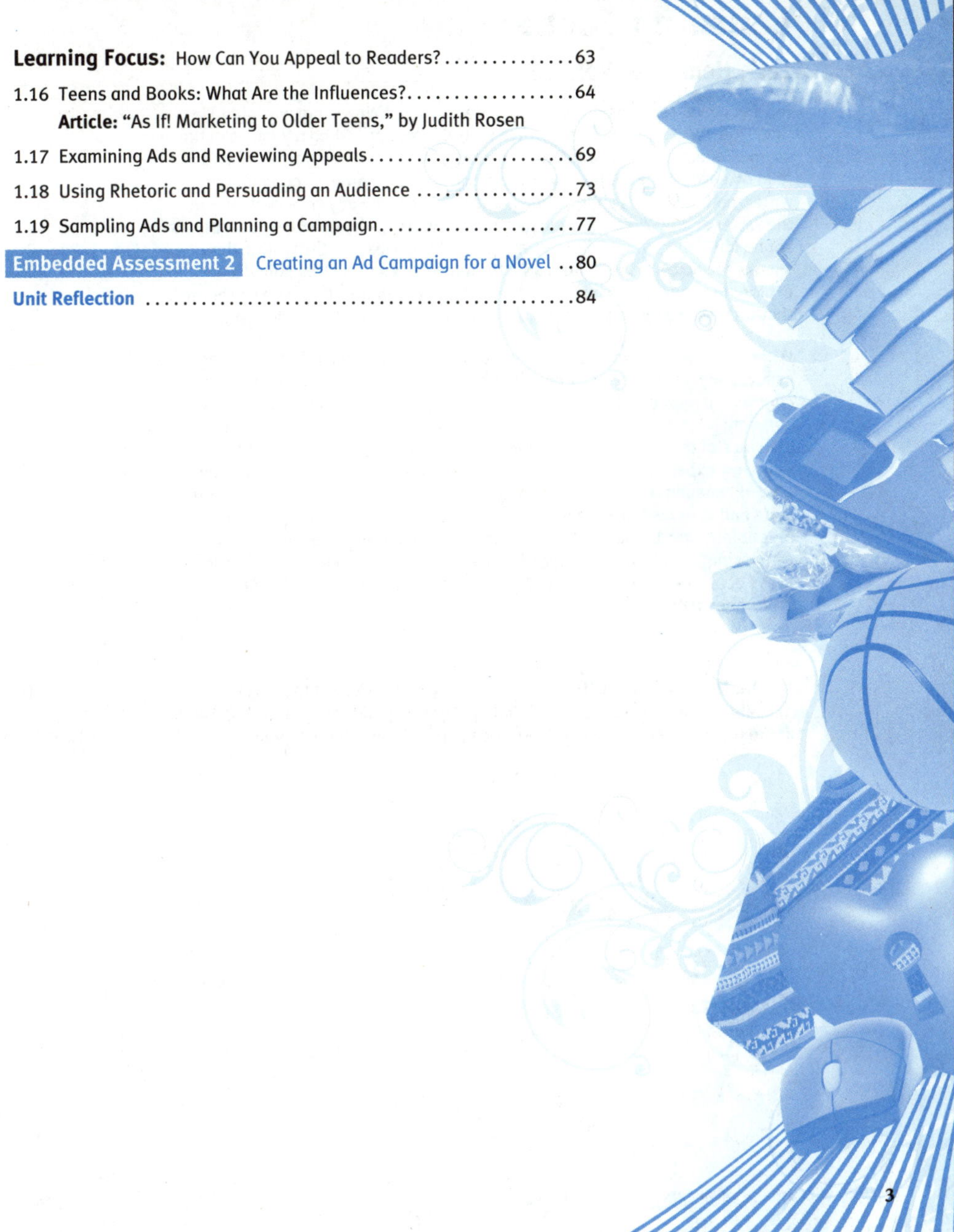

UNIT 1

Teacher Notes

LEARNING FOCUS:
Let's Hear It for Voice!

Read the Learning Focus with students or have them read independently. **Activate prior knowledge** by having students **mark the text** and highlight words or concepts that are familiar (what they know). They might use a question mark to indicate content that is unfamiliar (what they do not know but want to learn).

Students will respond to the information on this page in Activity 1.1.

Teacher Notes

Learning Focus:
Let's Hear It for Voice!

Have you ever read something that made you say, "Wow! That was great!"? Have you ever felt as though a writer's words were providing a glimpse of the speaker's or character's personality? How often does this happen? When you read an essay, for example, can you sometimes tell a great deal about the writer, and other times find yourself unable to identify any characteristics of the writer at all? When you read descriptive writing, why do some descriptions sound authentic, while others sound phony? Chances are, the writing that speaks to you contains a characteristic known as **voice**. In this unit you will explore the concept of voice and its effect on personal writing. You will learn that **diction**, **tone**, and **imagery** work together to convey voice effectively.

While you are learning to express your own voice, you will also be reading essays, poems, and even a novel that have **narrators** with strong and engaging personal voices. As you are identifying voice in your reading and applying it to your writing, you will also have an opportunity to capture the voice of another when you conduct an interview and write about the interview experience. You will study these elements while you explore the idea of "**coming of age**." You will make connections between coming-of-age texts and your own experiences as a ninth-grade student. By the end of the first half of Unit 1, you will have multiple opportunities to read deeply, write convincingly, and communicate effectively. Each of the skills you refine in these activities will enhance your abilities and prepare you for the academic challenges that await in the rest of your year.

Independent Reading: In this unit, you will read a variety of texts by writers describing their memories of growing up. For independent reading, choose a genre and a writer whose coming-of-age experiences appeal to you.

Previewing the Unit

ACTIVITY 1.1

SUGGESTED LEARNING STRATEGIES: **Close Reading, KWL, Marking the Text, Skimming/Scanning, Summarizing/Paraphrasing, Think-Pair-Share**

Essential Questions

1. What does it mean to "come of age"?

2. How are rhetorical appeals used to influence an audience?

Unit Overview and Learning Focus

Predict what you think this unit is about. Use the words or phrases that stood out to you when you read the Unit Overview and the Learning Focus.

Embedded Assessment 1

What knowledge must you have (what do you need to know) to succeed on Embedded Assessment 1? What skills must you have (what must you be able to do)?

ACTIVITY 1.1

Previewing the Unit

Purpose:

- To contextualize prior knowledge about key ideas and concepts
- To analyze the skills and knowledge necessary for success in this unit

Steps:

1 To determine students' existing knowledge about the concepts in this unit, ask them to work in a **think-pair-share** arrangement to respond to the two Essential Questions. Students will revisit these questions throughout the unit to develop a more mature understanding of these ideas.

2 Direct students to **skim and scan** the Unit Overview and Learning Focus pages. **Activate prior knowledge** by asking students to **mark the text**. They may use a check mark to indicate what is familiar to them (know) and a question mark to indicate what is unfamiliar to them (don't know–want to learn). Engage students in a whole class discussion. You may want to record their findings on a **KWL** chart and revisit this chart at the end of the unit to discover what students have learned.

3 Provide students with a clear learning target by asking them to find the Embedded Assessment 1 assignment and Scoring Guide (pages 60-62). Lead students through a **close reading** of the prompt, steps, and Scoring Guide criteria. Instruct students to **mark the text** by underlining or highlighting the places that mention a skill or knowledge necessary to succeed on the Embedded Assessment.

4 Instruct students to **summarize/paraphrase** with a partner or small group the skills/knowledge they have underlined or highlighted. As you conduct a large group discussion, create a web **graphic organizer** that lists the knowledge and skills.

5 Revisit the web graphic organizer throughout the unit. Pointing students back to the web reinforces the purpose of each activity and the skills and knowledge needed for success on the Embedded Assessment. You may want to enlarge the Embedded Assessment web graphic organizer to provide a **visual** in the classroom throughout the course of the unit. Students will preview Embedded Assessment 2 before Activity 1.16.

ACTIVITY 1.2

Coming of Age: Let Me Count the Ways!

Materials:

- Whiteboard, chalkboard, or projector

Purpose:

- To define "coming of age" and identify milestones
- To categorize information

Steps:

1 This activity introduces the thematic concept of both the unit and the level. **Activate prior knowledge** by asking whether students have heard the phrase "coming of age." Ask them to jot down what they think it means. Solicit and discuss responses about the concept, its meaning, and its relevance.

2 Draw or project a number line with the ages twelve through twenty-one marked off. Determine together when the process of "coming of age" starts and when it ends. (Students might not agree on a specific number; the discussion is meant only to inspire them to think about approximate ages.)

3 Ask students to label milestones on the arrow **graphic organizer**: above the line, mark the traditional ages for certain privileges; below the line the approximate ages for certain responsibilities. (For example, privileges might include driving and voting; responsibilities might be working and paying.) Allow students to share with the class.

4 Ask students to work independently to brainstorm words associated with "coming of age." These words might relate to the milestones discussed, feelings, problems, events, fads, traditions, phases, habits, and products.

ACTIVITY 1.2

Coming of Age: Let Me Count the Ways!

SUGGESTED LEARNING STRATEGIES: Graphic Organizer, Think-Pair-Share

"Coming of Age"

What I think this phrase might mean:

Take a few minutes to think about the ages when people traditionally receive certain privileges and responsibilities. Plot the ages on the arrow, and label the privileges and responsibilities. Place the labels for privileges above the line and the labels for responsibilities below the line.

Privileges

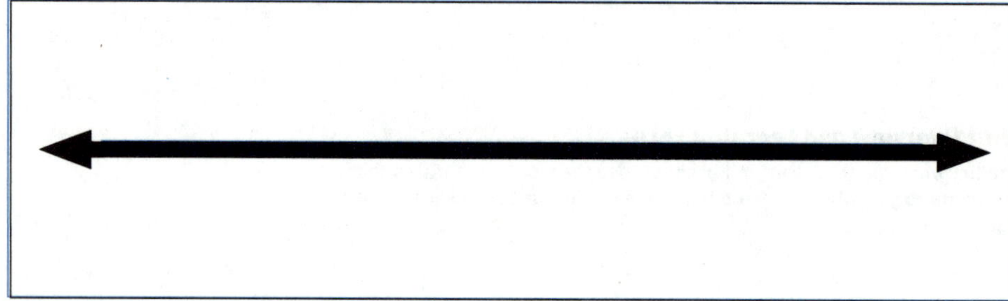

Responsibilities

After your brainstorming and class discussion, reconsider your ideas about the meaning of "coming of age." Write your revised definition below.

Coming of age means:

5 Arrange a **think-pair-share** to allow students to add to their lists. Then, bring the brainstorming session to the whole class and ask the class to identify as many "coming of age" words as possible.

6 Next, ask students to sort the words into categories, such as physical changes, social issues, cultural issues, etc.

7 Create a large chart that shows the categories and the words and phrases that fit under each. Display and discuss the completed charts.

8 End the activity by formulating a class definition of "coming of age." Let students share examples of "coming of age" texts they have read or films they have seen. Then let them know that "coming of age" is the theme for this year's English class. Discuss the **Essential Question**: What does it mean to "come of age"?

What's in a Name?

ACTIVITY 1.3

SUGGESTED LEARNING STRATEGIES: Graphic Organizer, Marking the Text, Quickwrite, Rereading, Word Map, Brainstorming, Drafting

If several different people were asked to describe pizza, you might expect to get a variety of responses. Even though the subject would be the same, the descriptions might be quite different because each used a different voice. In pairs, read the following pizza descriptions and see what you can infer about the speakers. Then, examine each speaker's diction, syntax, and imagery, and identify choices that create four distinctive voices.

- **Diction** – Word choice intended to convey a certain effect
- **Syntax** – The arrangement of words and the order of grammatical elements in a sentence
- **Imagery** – The words or phrases a writer uses to represent persons, objects, actions, feelings, and ideas descriptively by appealing to the senses

Speaker 1: Eating pizza is rather like embarking on a transcontinental excursion. You embark on the journey without being quite certain of what you will encounter. A well-made pizza contains the aromatic essence of fresh basil, oregano, and garlic that beckon invitingly. Once you bite into a perfectly sliced piece of pizza, your taste buds awaken and celebrate. When properly prepared, pizza is an extraordinary culinary creation.

Speaker 2: It's yummy. I like it when the cheese is really gooey. My mom makes it for dinner on the weekends. When it's too hot, I have to wait for it to cool. Mom says if I don't wait I will burn my tongue. I like the way pizza smells. When I smell pizza cooking it always makes me want to eat it right up!

Speaker 3: As long as not one speck of gross disgusting animal flesh comes anywhere near my pizza, I can eat it. I prefer pizza with mushrooms, tomatoes, and spinach. Goat cheese is especially nice too. A thin whole-wheat crust topped with imported cheese and organic vegetables makes a satisfying meal.

Speaker 4: Pizza is, like, one of the basic food groups, right? I mean, dude, who doesn't eat pizza? Me and my friends order it like every day. We usually get pepperoni, and it's great when they are, like, covering the whole top! Dude, hot steamy pizza dripping with cheese and loaded with pepperoni is awesome.

ACADEMIC VOCABULARY

Voice is a writer's (or speaker's) distinctive use of language.

WORD CONNECTIONS

The word ***syntax*** contains the Greek prefix *syn-*, which means "together," and the root *-tax-*, meaning "arrangement" or "order."

The prefix *syn-* is found in words like *synthesis*, *synonym*, and *synchronize*. The root *-tax-* occurs in *taxonomy* and *taxidermy*.

ACTIVITY 1.3
What's in a Name?

Materials:

- Vocabulary Notebooks

Purpose:

- To define diction, imagery, and syntax and identify examples
- To analyze how diction, imagery, and syntax comprise the literary concept of voice
- To infer characteristics of a speaker based on elements of diction, syntax, and imagery
- To address diction, imagery, and syntax in one's own writing

Steps:

1 Begin the discussion of voice with an **Auditory Prompt**: Play a few audio clips of speakers whom students will be likely to recognize. (Select a variety of voices including politicians, musicians, actors, sports stars, your school principal, or even cartoon characters.) As you play the clips, ask students to identify the speakers. Afterwards, **brainstorm** and list others whose voices are immediately recognizable. Then, discuss how voices function like fingerprints to identify their speakers.

2 Move to a discussion of the way a person's written words can also contain a unique "fingerprint" that helps to identify the writer. Explain that, in literary terms, this idea is known as **voice**. Before reading the "Pizza" descriptions, you might ask students to write their own few sentences showing their attitude about pizza in order to experiment with the way their diction, syntax, and imagery establish their voice in writing. Then have students read the descriptions.

Steps:

3 Ask students to complete the **graphic organizer** to analyze the diction, syntax, and imagery in each speaker's pizza description and to make inferences about the speaker.

What's in a Name?

LITERARY TERMS
Tone is a writer's or speaker's attitude toward the subject. Tone is conveyed through the writer's choice of words and detail.

Fill in the organizer with details about diction, syntax, and imagery that you notice about each speaker's description of pizza. Then, make inferences about each speaker and that speaker's **tone** or attitude toward pizza.

Pizza Descriptions

Speaker	Diction (What word choices does the speaker make? Formal or informal?)	Syntax (Are the sentences short, long, simple, complex?)	Imagery (What words and phrases are used to describe sensory details?)	Tone (What can you conclude about the speaker's attitude toward the subject?)	Inferences About the Speaker (What might you infer about the speaker's age, status, preferences?)
1					
2					
3					
4					

"My Name"

from The House on Mango Street

by Sandra Cisneros

ABOUT THE AUTHOR
Sandra Cisneros grew up in Chicago and now lives in San Antonio, Texas. Her novel *The House on Mango Street* reveals the life of a young girl growing up in the Latino section of Chicago. In talking about her writing, Cisneros says she creates stories from things that have touched her deeply: "...in real life a story doesn't have shape, and it's the writer that gives it a beginning, a middle, and an end."

In English my name means hope. In Spanish it means too many letters. It means sadness, it means waiting. It is like the number nine. A muddy color. It is the Mexican records my father plays on Sunday mornings when he is shaving, songs like sobbing. 1

It was my great-grandmother's name and now it is mine. She was a horse woman too, born like me in the Chinese year of the horse — which is supposed to be bad luck if you're born female — but I think this is a Chinese lie because the Chinese, like the Mexicans, don't like their women strong. 2

My great-grandmother. I would've liked to have known her, a wild horse of a woman, so wild she wouldn't marry. Until my great-grandfather threw a sack over her head and carried her off. Just like that, as if she were a fancy chandelier. That's the way he did it. 3

And the story goes she never forgave him. She looked out the window her whole life, the way so many women sit their sadness on an elbow. I wonder if she made the best with what she got or was she sorry because she couldn't be all the things she wanted to be. Esperanza. I have inherited her name, but I don't want to inherit her place by the window. 4

At school they say my name funny as if the syllables were made out of tin and hurt the roof of your mouth. But in Spanish my name is made out of a softer something, like silver, not quite as thick as sister's name — Magdalena — which is uglier than mine. Magdalena who at least can come home and become Nenny. But I am always Esperanza. 5

I would like to baptize myself under a new name, a name more like the real me, the one nobody sees. Esperanza as Lisandra or Maritza or Zeze the X. Yes. Something like Zeze the X will do. 6

My Notes

Note the pattern in the first paragraph of a series of short sentences in the Subject-Verb-Object pattern, followed by a fragment that emphasizes an unusual image.

Paragraph 2 begins with a repeated pattern in sentence 1 followed by a long, compound-complex sentence.

Paragraph 3 begins with a fragment, which creates emphasis.

Additional fragments provide short bursts of information.

In paragraph 4, the juxtaposition of the short and long emphasizes the name.

Steps:

4 As prereading for the two texts, ask students to write their full names at the top of a sheet of paper. Then, ask them to complete a 5–10 minute **quickwrite** in which they write about their names. They might write about the importance of their names, their feelings about their names, whether they would change their names if they could, etc. (If you do this quickwrite along with students, you will have a sample to model in Activity 1.4.)

5 Proceed with a **shared reading** of the texts, pausing to discuss with students the significance of names, and the inferences students can make about the speakers. Then, ask students to **reread** the texts silently and **mark the texts** focusing on imagery, diction, and syntax.

6 You may want to present a specific lesson on sentence types and syntax in these two texts. Direct students' attention to the lengths and types of sentences and ask them to consider the effect of the writer's choices.

© 2011 College Board. All rights reserved.

Steps:

7 As students reread this selection, you might consider having them mark the text in paragraphs 2 and 3 to identify examples of the writer's diction.

What's in a Name?

My Notes

GRAMMAR & USAGE

A compound-complex sentence is one that has two or more independent clauses and one or more subordinate clauses.

Example: I was my parents' first joy, and in their joy, they gave me the name that would haunt me for the rest of my life, Immaculeta Uzoma Achilike.

Personal Narrative

"Why Couldn't I Have Been Named *Ashley?*"

by Imma Achilike

NAAMAN FOREST HIGH SCHOOL

GARLAND, TEXAS

1 "Ashley!" exclaimed Mrs. Renfro, and simultaneously three heads whipped around at attention towards the perturbed[1] teacher. At the same time, all three Ashleys proudly replied, "Yes, ma'am?"

2 When I was a fourth grader, I remember sitting in class that day just before the bell rang for dismissal. I remember thinking of all the names in the world, how I could have possibly been stuck with such an alien one. I thought about all the popular kids in the class. I figured that I wasn't popular because of my weird name. I put some things together in my mind and came up with a plausible[2] equation: COOL NAME = POPULARITY. The dismissal bell rang. As I mechanically walked out to catch my ride, I thought to myself, "Why couldn't I have been named Ashley?"

3 I was born, on July 7th, 1986, at Parkland Hospital of Dallas, Texas. I was the first American-born Nigerian in both of my parents' families. I was my parents' first joy, and in their joy, they gave me the name that would haunt me for the rest of my life, Immaculeta Uzoma Achilike.

4 The first time I actually became aware of my name was on the first day of first grade. I went to school loaded with all my school supplies and excited to see all of my old kindergarten friends. I couldn't wait to see who my new teacher was. As I walked into the classroom, all my friends pushed up to me, cooing my name: "Imma, Imma I missed you so much." The teacher walked in with the attendance sheet. She told everyone to quiet down so she could call roll. Before she started, she said something I thought would have never applied to me. She said, "Before I call roll, I apologize if I mispronounce anyone's name" with a very apologetic look on her face. She looked down at the attendance sheet, paused for a minute, and then looked up with an extremely puzzled look on her face. I remember thinking that there was probably some weird name before mine; although, my name was always the first name to be called in

[1] **perturbed:** troubled or disturbed
[2] **plausible:** credible or believable

GRAMMAR & USAGE EXTENSION

This is an opportunity to review (or introduce) the other types of sentences according to structure (simple, compound, complex) and the four types of sentences according to purpose (declarative, imperative, interrogative, exclamatory).

- You might ask students to identify sentence types in these two texts so that students can explore ways that authors often "break the rules" for effect.
- You might also have students practice the different sentence types in their quickwrites.

kindergarten. Suddenly, my palms started sweating and then she began to hopelessly stutter my name, "Im-Immaculet Arch-liki, I mean, Achei...." Here, I interrupted. My ears burned with embarrassment and droplets of perspiration formed on my nose. "Did I say it right?" she said with the same apologetic look on her face. Before I responded, the laughs that the other kids in class had been holding back suddenly exploded, like a volatile[3] vial of [nitro]glycerin, into peals of laughter. One kid thought it was so funny his chubby face started turning red and I could see a tear gradually making its way down his face. I found myself wishing I could sink into the ground and never come back. I hated being the laughing stock.

5 I never really recovered from the shock of that day. From that day forward, the first day of school was always my most feared day. I didn't know what to do; all I could do was to tell my teachers, "I go by Imma."

6 I felt so alone when all the other girls in my class had sparkly, pink pencils with their names printed on them. You know, the ones they sell in the stores along with name-embossed[4] sharpeners, rulers and pencil pouches. Every year I searched through and rummaged around that rack at the store, but I could never find a pencil with my name on it.

7 The summer of my seventh-grade year, my family and I took a vacation to our "home" in Nigeria, where my parents were born. My cousin and I were playing cards, talking girl talk, and relating our most embarrassing moments. Each tried to see whose story could top whose. I told one story of how I wet the bed at a sleepover, and she told me how she had farted in class during a test. That was a hoot. Then, I told her the story of how I was laughed at because of my weird name. I thought it was pretty funny, but she didn't laugh. She had the most serious look on her face, then she asked me, "Immaculeta Uzoma Achilike, do you know what your name means?" I shook my head at her and that's when she started laughing. I thought she was making fun of me, and as I started to leave she said: "Immaculeta means 'purity', 'Uzoma' means 'the good road' and...." Having heard her words, I stopped walking away and turned around in amazement. What does Achilike mean?" I asked. After a long pause she calmly said, "Achilike means 'to rule without force.'" I was astonished and pleased. I never knew what my name meant.

8 My name is Immaculeta Uzoma Achilike. I am the daughter of first-generation Nigerian immigrants. I am the daughter of hardworking and brave parents. My name means "to rule without force." My grandfather was a wealthy man of generous character. When I say my name in Nigeria, people know me as the granddaughter of a wealthy man of generous character. They know me by my name. There my name is not embossed on any pencil or vanity plate. It is etched in the minds of the people.

My name is Immaculeta Uzoma Achilike.

---

[3] **volatile:** unstable, explosive
[4] **embossed:** raised above the surface

My Notes

ACTIVITY 1.3 *Continued*

Steps:

8 Consider asking students to identify the imagery in paragraph 4.

9 Ask students to examine the juxtaposition of long and short sentences in paragraph 7 and explain the effect.

Steps:

10 Ask students to complete the **graphic organizer**. Provide time for students to work with partners or small groups to share and refine the information they include in their organizers.

11 Ask students to revisit their quickwrites about their names, to brainstorm additional thoughts, and to **draft** a more polished piece of writing from their quickwrites. **Note:** This written piece could be in the form of an essay or a poem. Point out that they will share this writing with a partner in the next activity, so they might not want to write something too personal to share with an audience. You might also develop your own quickwrite to use in Activity 1.4.

12 Instruct students to create an appropriate **word map graphic organizer** in their **Vocabulary Notebooks** to explore the concept of ***voice***. As students work with academic vocabulary in their Vocabulary Notebooks, you may want them to work in pairs or small groups to facilitate discussion and to build confidence and fluency as they internalize new language. Ask students to discuss new academic language as it is introduced, identifying meaning as well as pronunciation and common usage. Students will revisit their Vocabulary Notebooks and add notes during the course of the unit and level.

What's in a Name?

Observations from Published Texts

Text	Diction (What word choices does the speaker make? For example, how does the author describe youth? Formal or informal?)	Syntax (Are the sentences short, long, simple, complex?)	Imagery (What words and phrases are used to describe sensory details?)	Tone (What can you conclude about the speaker's attitude toward the subject?)	Inferences About the Speaker (What might you infer about the speaker's age, status, preferences?)
"My Name"					
"Why Couldn't I Have Been Named Ashley?"					

I'd Like to Introduce...

ACTIVITY 1.4

SUGGESTED LEARNING STRATEGIES: **Marking the Text, Notetaking**

You will interview another student in your class and then introduce that person to the rest of the class.

1. The first information you need is your partner's name:

   ____.

2. Write four questions that you could ask to learn important information about your partner.
   -
   -
   -
   -

3. When you interview someone, it is important to ask open-ended questions. Open-ended questions or statements cannot be answered with a simple "yes" or "no." They give your interviewee an opportunity to provide insight and explanation. In the question pairs below, circle the open-ended question or statement.

   a. Explain some of the best parts of playing soccer.

      Do you like playing soccer?

   b. As the youngest child in your family, do you think you get your own way?

      What are the advantages and disadvantages of being the youngest child in your family?

4. Revise each of the following to be an open-ended question.

   Is it fun to be in the band?

   Revision:

   How many kids are in your family?

   Revision:

5. Look back at the four questions you wrote. Make sure they are open-ended questions or statements. If they are not, revise them as you write them on the next page.

ACTIVITY 1.4
I'd Like to Introduce...

Purpose:

- To create an interview plan
- To conduct an interview and synthesize information
- To compose an introduction of a classmate and present it orally

Steps:

1 To model the interview process, share your "Name" essay from Activity 1.3 and allow students to **generate questions** to ask you based on the information you shared. Working with the questions students ask you, model open-ended questions.

2 Arrange students in pairs. Allow time for partners to read each other's "name" essays from Activity 1.3, and have them formulate a list of possible questions to ask their partners.

Steps:

3 Instruct students to use this page for their interviews. Remind them to be sure that their questions will prompt the interviewee to provide thoughtful information.

I'd Like to Introduce…

6. Write your four interview questions or statements in the Question boxes below. Leave the Answer boxes empty for now.

Question 1:	Question 2:
Answer:	Answer:
Question 3:	Question 4:
Answer:	Answer:

7. Now interview your partner. While your partner is answering, take notes in the Answer boxes on your chart. Try to write down some parts of the answer exactly, using quotation marks to show you are quoting your partner word for word.

Introductions

8. Prepare to introduce your partner to the class. Look back over your interview notes and highlight the parts that seem to be the most important, such as tone of voice, purpose, target audience, circumstances. You will want to include this information in your introduction.

   The hardest part of any presentation can be the beginning. Here are some ways you might begin your introduction (your partner's name goes in the blank):

   - I would like to introduce ____________________.
   - I would like you all to meet ____________________.
   - This is my new friend ____________________.

   Write the opening of your introduction:

9. The other challenging part of any presentation is the closing. Sometimes people do not know how to end the introduction, so they say "That's it." Don't end your introduction that way! You cannot possibly have said all there is to say about your partner in this brief introduction. You want to end your introduction on a strong note that encourages the rest of your class to get to know your partner.

   You might end your introduction like this:

   - I enjoyed getting to talk to ________________ because ________________.
   - ________________ is an interesting person and I'm glad I got the chance to meet my partner because ____________________.

   Write the ending of your introduction:

10. Now write your introduction on a separate sheet of paper. Use the opener you already wrote, include the information from your notes that you highlighted, and then finish with the closing you wrote. Be sure your introduction shows respect for your partner.

    When you introduce your partner, you may use your written introduction, but try not to rely on it the whole time. Avoid hiding behind your paper!

GRAMMAR & USAGE

A **direct quotation** represents a person's exact words. These words are enclosed in quotation marks.

Example: Then she asked me, "Immaculeta Uzoma Achilike, do you know what your name means?"

An **indirect quotation** restates the general meaning of what a person said. Quotation marks are not used with indirect quotations.

Example: She asked whether I knew what my name means.

ACTIVITY 1.4 *Continued*

Steps:

4 Give students a limited amount of time to interview each other. Remind them to **take notes** as they interview. Let them know that they will be presenting their findings in both written and verbal form.

5 Using the framework provided, allow students to use their notes to **draft** a brief written narrative of their partner interview. After the narrative is written, ask students to **mark the text** by highlighting three or four key points that they can share with the class in an oral introduction.

6 Urge students to try to use at least one direct quotation from their interview. They may also include information in the form of indirect quotations; for example, My partner believes that…

7 Review introduction etiquette, and ask the pairs to present brief but engaging introductions of their partners to the rest of the class.

GRAMMAR & USAGE EXTENSION

- Suggest that students practice both direct and indirect quotations in the draft of their partner interviews.
- This is also a timely opportunity to discuss the effectiveness of direct quotations.
- You might also suggest that students try placing direct quotations in different places in a sentence and punctuating them properly in each location. This activity will illustrate (and emphasize) variations in sentence structure as well as proper punctuation of quotations.

ACTIVITY 1.5

Introduction to Learning Logs and Word Walls

Purpose:

- To identify, define, and apply learning strategies
- To evaluate the personal effectiveness of specific learning strategies

Steps:

1 Learning Logs: Direct students to the SpringBoard Learning Strategies in the Resources section at the back of their books and allow them to skim the list, perhaps marking the ones they know. Point out the strategies you used in the preceding activities. After a brief discussion of the four categories, introduce students to the Learning Log format on this page, which will help them identify and reflect on the usefulness of the strategies in their literacy development.

TEACHER TO TEACHER Use of the Learning Log will be suggested periodically throughout Unit 1. Based on students' needs, determine where and how often to use it in the remaining units.

2 Word Walls: Posting significant words in your classroom provides visual cues for students and is highly effective for vocabulary instruction as well as reading and writing support. This would be a good time to create a **Word Wall**. There are a number of ways to generate and categorize words on your Word Wall (e.g., action verbs, words encountered in a specific text or unit of study, tone words, literary terms, etc.). You might start with one of these options:

- List some useful "coming of age" words from completed activities.
- Identify other key vocabulary encountered in class texts.
- Introduce related words students encounter in other courses.

ACTIVITY 1.5

Introduction to Learning Logs and Word Walls

SUGGESTED LEARNING STRATEGIES: Graphic Organizer

In this course, you will use many learning strategies to increase your ability to read, understand, create, and present texts. To help keep track of the strategies that work best for you, you will keep a Learning Log. Use the template below as a model; record information about the new strategies you encounter on a separate sheet of paper.

Strategies Learning Log	
Name of strategy	
Purpose of strategy	
How I used the strategy	
How the strategy helped	
When I might use this strategy again	

3 Consider using a section of your Word Wall for strategies. Students can identify and reflect on the use of these strategies in their Learning Logs and post the names of strategies on the Word Wall. The Learning Logs and Word Wall will enable students to internalize both the strategies and significant vocabulary.

4 Try to use the Word Wall as a flexible tool rather than a static display. Spend time revisiting words whenever you can. Encourage students to use words from the Word Wall in their speaking and writing, and remind them to refer to it for spelling assistance as well. Throughout the year, you might rearrange the Word Wall according to current activities or topics.

Introducing Independent Reading

ACTIVITY 1.6

SUGGESTED LEARNING STRATEGIES: **Double-Entry Journal, Predicting**

To help you select a novel to read on your own, think about the following questions:

- What do you know about the author?
- Does the title grab your attention? What does it mean?
- What information does the book jacket provide about the author, the story, or reviews by others who have read the novel?
- Are the visuals appealing (the cover, the layout of the book, the type size, illustrations)?
- After reading the first few paragraphs, do you find the beginning of the novel interesting?

As you read the novel you choose, stay focused on the story. Avoid letting your mind takes its own journey somewhere else. One way that good readers stay focused on a book is by responding to key events or situations. A double-entry journal is one strategy for responding to a text and even questioning what you are reading. In your journal, you can relate your own experiences to those of the characters in the novel, share your opinions about what is happening in the novel, and trace the development of the **protagonist**.

Use the format below as a model for your journal. In the left column, copy or summarize passages that catch your attention, including the page number. In the right column, write your own thoughts about the passage.

If you are having trouble thinking of what to write, you might try using these stems:

- I really like / dislike this part because ...
- I wonder why...
- The diction / imagery creates a tone of...
- This quote shows the narrator / character's voice by...
- I predict that...
- I think the character should...
- This reminds me of the time when I ...

Textual Evidence (The book says...)	Analysis/Question/Opinion (I say...)

WORD CONNECTIONS

The word ***protagonist*** has a form of the Greek prefix *proto-*, which means "first," and the Greek root *-agon-*, which means "contest" or "struggle."

The prefix *proto-* is also found in these words: ***prototype***, ***protozoa***, and ***protocol***.

The root *-agon-* is also found in *agony*.

LITERARY TERMS

A **protagonist** is the main character who initiates actions that move the plot along.

ACTIVITY 1.6

Introducing Independent Reading

Materials:

- Novels for independent reading

Purpose:

- Make predictions about and assess interest in texts to make a choice for reading
- Select a novel based on self-assessment of interest

Steps:

1 Independent reading of self-selected novels builds vital reading skills. Students will encounter multiple activities that refer to the independent reading prior to Embedded Assessment 2, which asks them to create a marketing campaign for the novel. Ensure that they select appropriate novels and understand them as they read.

2 Conduct brief book talks for the books you recommend for independent reading (see About the Unit for suggested titles). Your summaries and a **shared reading** of an interesting passage can motivate students. Since Embedded Assessment 2 works best as a group project, you will need multiple copies of your selected titles so that several students read the same novel.

3 Have students keep a **double-entry journal** to monitor their understanding while they read. They may use the format on this page. To introduce the journal, you might consider making a transparency or projecting a model of possible entries. Read aloud from one of the novels, and model the kinds of notations and responses students might include. For example, you might suggest the following possibilities for journal entries:

- Identify specific textual features that contribute to the narrator's voice.
- Select quotations that establish a character's voice.
- Comment on the narrator's use of humor.
- React to emotional events that happen in the novel.
- Consider which groups or clubs in school might be likely fits for characters in the novel.
- Identify societal issues presented in the novels and try to infer the author's stance on the issues.
- **Predict** how certain events relate to a character's coming of age.

ACTIVITY 1.7
Defining Moments

Materials:

- Vocabulary Notebooks

Purpose:

- To identify and classify examples of diction, simile, imagery, and syntax in fiction
- To annotate and mark a text to make inferences during a close reading
- To analyze how diction, imagery, and syntax create a distinctive voice

Steps:

1 Explain the purpose of this **graphic organizer**—for recording examples from the texts and making inferences about the speakers.

ACTIVITY 1.7

Defining Moments

SUGGESTED LEARNING STRATEGIES: **Close Reading, Marking the Text, Notetaking, Visualizing, Word Map**

LITERARY TERMS

A **simile** is a comparison of two different things or ideas, using the words *like* or *as*. It is a stated comparison in which the author says one thing is *like* another.

Hyperbole is deliberate, extravagant, and often outrageous exaggeration. It may be used for either serious or comic effect.

"Coming of age" usually occurs over a period of time, but there are often key incidents that individuals can point to as significant milestones in their coming-of-age experience. Follow your teacher's directions for reading the three texts that follow, and use the organizer below to track your observations about how the authors portray youthful voices. After completing the chart, follow your teacher's directions to complete a visual representation based on one of the texts.

In addition to guiding you to trace the elements identified in your graphic organizer, your teacher will also refer to two literary terms: **similes** and **hyperbole**.

Text	Diction	Syntax	Imagery	Tone	Inferences About the Speaker Based on Voice
"Eleven"					
"Oranges"					
Excerpt from *Speak*					

Writing Prompt: Write a brief analysis of one author's use of diction, syntax, and/or imagery to achieve the effect of a youthful voice.

ELEVEN

by Sandra Cisneros

1 What they don't understand about birthdays and what they never tell you is that when you're eleven, you're also ten, and nine, and eight, and seven, and six, and five, and four, and three, and two, and one. And when you wake up on your eleventh birthday you expect to feel eleven, but you don't. You open your eyes and everything's just like yesterday, only it's today. And you don't feel eleven at all. You feel like you're still ten. And you are — underneath the year that makes you eleven.

2 Like some days you might say something stupid, and that's the part of you that's still ten. Or maybe some days you might need to sit on your mama's lap because you're scared, and that's the part of you that's five. And maybe one day when you're all grown up maybe you will need to cry like if you're three, and that's okay. That's what I tell Mama when she's sad and needs to cry. Maybe she's feeling three.

3 Because the way you grow old is kind of like an onion or like the rings inside a tree trunk or like my little wooden dolls that fit one inside the other, each year inside the next one. That's how being eleven years old is.

4 You don't feel eleven. Not right away. It takes a few days, weeks even, sometimes even months before you say Eleven when they ask you. And you don't feel smart eleven, not until you're almost twelve. That's the way it is.

5 Only today I wish I didn't have only eleven years rattling inside me like pennies in a tin Band-Aid box. Today I wish I was one hundred and two instead of eleven because if I was one hundred and two I'd have known what to say when Mrs. Price put the red sweater on my desk. I would've known how to tell her it wasn't mine instead of just sitting there with that look on my face and nothing coming out of my mouth.

6 "Whose is this?" Mrs. Price says, and she holds the red sweater up in the air for all the class to see. "Whose? It's been sitting in the coatroom for a month."

7 "Not mine," says everybody. "Not me."

8 "It has to belong to somebody," Mrs. Price keeps saying, but nobody can remember. It's an ugly sweater with red plastic buttons and a collar and sleeves all stretched out like you could use it for a jump rope. It's maybe a thousand years old and even if it belonged to me I wouldn't say so.

My Notes

ACTIVITY 1.7 *Continued*

Steps:

2 For this **guided reading** of "Eleven," begin with a **shared reading** of the entire text. As you and others read, invite students to examine the text closely and respond in the My Notes area to your guided prompts.

3 Ask students to do a **close reading** and to **mark the text.** Guide them with these prompts:

- In the first two paragraphs, circle the words ***like, you, you're*** and ***they***. Write in the margin to whom you think ***they*** refers and about whom the speaker is talking when she says "you" and "you're."
- Note Cisneros's **syntax**: her use of fragments, run-ons, as well as the repeated use of "And" to begin sentences and clauses.

Discuss with students how these techniques mirror the speaker's **voice** and age.

4 Ask students to find and highlight similes. Start by discussing the three **similes** in Paragraph 3. Have students explain how one of them is like "being eleven years old." Other similes are in paragraphs 5, 8, 13, 14, 18, 19, and 22.

5 In paragraph 5, have students find and highlight the simile and identify the **setting** of the story. Also, have them underline the phrase "nothing coming out of my mouth."

ACTIVITY 1.7 *Continued*

Steps:

6 In Paragraph 9 have students underline the words "when I open my mouth nothing comes out." This is an excellent time to introduce **hyperbole**. Ask students to explain in their notes why nothing comes out of Rachel's mouth. What does that say about her personality? How does the absence of words actually indicate voice?

7 Have students identify other examples of hyperbole in Paragraphs 8, 9, and 18.

8 You might ask students to read in parts the section in which Mrs. Price questions the class about the red sweater (Paragraphs 6–11). Then begin the first-person narration again (Paragraph 12), when the interior monologue begins with "Not mine, not mine, not mine…." Have students put a box around the entire interior monologue, which continues through the end of Paragraph 14. Discuss interior monologue as an element of first-person narration; lead students to see that it reflects internal feelings and creates audience identification. Discuss the following ideas with students:

- Keeping the idea of voice foremost in mind, explain why we use interior monologues every single day in our lives.
- Why does Rachel not voice these feelings?
- What might happen if she did?

Defining Moments

My Notes

9 Maybe because I'm skinny, maybe because she doesn't like me, that stupid Sylvia Saldívar says, "I think it belongs to Rachel." An ugly sweater like that, all raggedy and old, but Mrs. Price believes her. Mrs. Price takes the sweater and puts it right on my desk, but when I open my mouth nothing comes out.

10 "That's not, I don't, you're not . . . Not mine," I finally say in a little voice that was maybe me when I was four.

11 "Of course it's yours," Mrs. Price says. "I remember you wearing it once." Because she's older and the teacher, she's right and I'm not.

12 Not mine, not mine, not mine, but Mrs. Price is already turning to page thirty-two, and math problem number four. I don't know why but all of a sudden I'm feeling sick inside, like the part of me that's three wants to come out of my eyes, only I squeeze them shut tight and bite down on my teeth real hard and try to remember today I am eleven, eleven. Mama is making a cake for me for tonight, and when Papa comes home everybody will sing Happy birthday, happy birthday to you.

13 But when the sick feeling goes away and I open my eyes, the red sweater's still sitting there like a big red mountain. I move the red sweater to the corner of my desk with my ruler. I move my pencil and books and eraser as far from it as possible. I even move my chair a little to the right. Not mine, not mine, not mine.

14 In my head I'm thinking how long till lunchtime, how long till I can take the red sweater and throw it over the schoolyard fence, or leave it hanging on a parking meter, or bunch it up into a little ball and toss it in the alley. Except when math period ends, Mrs. Price says loud and in front of everybody, "Now, Rachel, that's enough," because she sees I've shoved the red sweater to the tippy-tip corner of my desk and it's hanging all over the edge like a waterfall, but I don't care.

15 "Rachel," Mrs. Price says. She says it like she's getting mad. "You put that sweater on right now and no more nonsense."

16 "But it's not —"

17 "Now!" Mrs. Price says.

18 This is when I wish I wasn't eleven, because all the years inside of me — ten, nine, eight, seven, six, five, four, three, two, and one — are pushing at the back of my eyes when I put one arm through one sleeve of the sweater that smells like cottage cheese, and then the other arm through the other and stand there with my arms apart like if the sweater hurts me and it does, all itchy and full of germs that aren't even mine.

GRAMMAR & USAGE

Syntax refers to the arrangement of words and the order of grammatical elements in a sentence—that is, the way the writer puts words together to make meaningful elements, such as phrases and clauses.

Notice the syntax in the last sentence in paragraph 19 (beginning with "My face all hot...").

GRAMMAR & USAGE EXTENSION

Examining the syntax in these texts will help students realize how professional authors manipulate language. Students can experiment with making changes in the original syntax and discuss how sentence type or syntax affects meaning. This experiment will make their analysis more effective and will encourage them to experiment further with their own writing.

© 2011 College Board. All rights reserved.

19 That's when everything I've been holding in since this morning, since when Mrs. Price put the sweater on my desk, finally lets go, and all of a sudden I'm crying in front of everybody. I wish I was invisible but I'm not. I'm eleven and it's my birthday today and I'm crying like I'm three in front of everybody. I put my head down on the desk and bury my face in my stupid clown-sweater arms. My face all hot and spit coming out of my mouth because I can't stop the little animal noises from coming out of me, until there aren't any more tears left in my eyes, and it's just my body shaking like when you have the hiccups, and my whole head hurts like when you drink milk too fast.

20 But the worst part is right before the bell rings for lunch. That stupid Phyllis Lopez, who is even dumber than Sylvia Saldívar, says she remembers the red sweater is hers! I take it off right away and give it to her, only Mrs. Price pretends like everything's okay.

21 Today I'm eleven. There's a cake Mama's making for tonight, and when Papa comes home from work we'll eat it. There'll be candles and presents, and everybody will sing Happy birthday, happy birthday to you, Rachel, only it's too late.

22 I'm eleven today. I'm eleven, ten, nine, eight, seven, six, five, four, three, two, and one, but I wish I was one hundred and two. I wish I was anything but eleven, because I want today to be far away already, far away like a runaway balloon, like a tiny o in the sky, so tiny-tiny you have to close your eyes to see it.

My Notes

ACTIVITY 1.7 *Continued*

Steps:

9 Have students highlight the **images** in Paragraph 19 that describe Rachel crying.

10 In Paragraph 20, have students underline the phrase "only Mrs. Price pretends like everything's okay." Ask: How does that simple statement describe the teacher? What should Mrs. Price have done to handle the situation at this point?

11 In Paragraph 21, have students explain the importance of the phrase "only it's too late." Why is it too late for Rachel? How has the importance of this day been ruined? Lead students to see that one important idea behind the coming-of-age theme is expectation versus reality. What does Rachel perhaps expect her birthday to be versus what really happens?

12 The final paragraph contains two additional similes. Have students highlight those.

13 Discuss the ways "Eleven" fits the concept of coming of age. Ask students to complete the section of their graphic organizer for "Eleven." Then discuss how Cisneros represents the voice of eleven-year-old Rachel through her diction, syntax, and imagery.

Steps:

14 Read the poem "Oranges" in a **shared reading.** Allow students to respond briefly to the poem. Then, using some or all of the following suggestions, invite students to examine it more closely:

- Ask students to **mark the text** by highlighting sensory images. You might want to do this together for the first few lines, highlighting such words and phrases as "cold and weighted down," "Frost cracking beneath my steps," "my breath before me," and so on.
- Ask students to **take notes** in the My Notes area about the speaker and his voice. Ask them to consider such questions as these: Who is the speaker? How old is he? Where does this take place? How does he feel about the girl? What can we determine about his personality based on the incident with the saleslady?
- Ask students to find and highlight the two similes in the poem and explain the comparison.

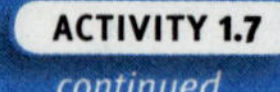

My Notes

Poetry

ABOUT THE AUTHOR

Of Mexican-American heritage, Gary Soto grew up in Fresno, California. In high school, he discovered a love of reading and knew he wanted to be a writer. He started writing while in college. He has written poems, short stories, and novels, which capture the vivid details of everyday life and which have won numerous awards and prizes.

by Gary Soto

The first time I walked
With a girl, I was twelve,
Cold, and weighted down
With two oranges in my jacket.
December. Frost cracking
Beneath my steps, my breath
Before me, then gone,
As I walked toward
Her house, the one whose
Porch light burned yellow
Night and day, in any weather.
A dog barked at me, until
She came out pulling
At her gloves, face bright
With rouge. I smiled,
Touched her shoulder, and led
Her down the street, across
A used car lot and a line
Of newly planted trees,

Until we were breathing
Before a drugstore. We
Entered, the tiny bell
Bringing a saleslady
Down a narrow aisle of goods.
I turned to the candies
Tiered like bleachers,
And asked what she wanted —
Light in her eyes, a smile
Starting at the corners
Of her mouth. I fingered
A nickel in my pocket,
And when she lifted a chocolate
That cost a dime,
I didn't say anything.
I took the nickel from
My pocket, then an orange,
And set them quietly on
The counter. When I looked up,
The lady's eyes met mine,
And held them, knowing
Very well what it was all
About.

Outside,
A few cars hissing past,
Fog hanging like old
Coats between the trees.
I took my girl's hand
In mine for two blocks,
Then released it to let
Her unwrap the chocolate.
I peeled my orange
That was so bright against
The gray of December
That, from some distance,
Someone might have thought
I was making a fire in my hands.

My Notes

Steps:

15 Discuss the ways "Oranges" addresses the concept of coming of age, and ask students to complete the section of their graphic organizer for "Oranges." Discuss how Soto manages to represent an adolescent boy's voice through his diction, syntax, and imagery.

Differentiating Instruction:

After students have identified sensory images in the poem, provide **support** by inviting pairs or small groups to act the scenario in the poem while it is being read aloud by a group member. Have students doing the acting focus on which words help them to create action and feeling.

Extend learning by having students complete a **TP-CASTT** analysis of the poem "Oranges." Encourage students to use this strategy to develop a theme statement that can be supported with examples from the text.

© 2011 College Board. All rights reserved.

ACTIVITY 1.7 *Continued*

Steps:

16 Read the excerpt from the novel *Speak* using either a **read aloud** or **paired reading**. Then ask students to reread this high-interest excerpt independently, applying the strategies you modeled in your guided reading and marking of the text for the previous two texts. Then, ask them to complete the **graphic organizer** for *Speak* and discuss how Anderson captures a teen girl's voice through her diction, syntax, and imagery. Discuss that Melinda in *Speak* has a vivid, sarcastic interior monologue while at the same time, like Rachel in "Eleven," she displays a noticeable absence of a physical voice.

17 After the class discussion, ask students to complete the activity by **visualizing** and creating a visual representation of a simile or other vivid description from one of the texts.

Differentiating Instruction:

To **support** students in the writing of this prompt, use the pre-AP strategy **TWIST**. Guide students through the process of incorporating literary elements such as tone, word choice, imagery, style, and theme so that students can craft an interpretive thesis in response to the prompt. The **product** can be a short interpretive paragraph with a focus on the thesis statement.

Expand the prompt from a brief analysis of one author to a more formal essay comparing and contrasting two different authors and their ability to use similar or different elements of style to achieve the effect of a youthful voice.

Defining Moments

My Notes

Novel Excerpt

ABOUT THE AUTHOR

Born in 1961, Laurie Halse Anderson always loved reading and writing. Even as a child, she made up stories and wrote for fun. As an adult, she did freelance reporting until she began publishing her work. Her novel *Speak*, which won numerous awards and was a best seller, was made into a movie. In 2009, she won the Margaret A. Edwards Award for *Catalyst, Fever 1793*, and *Speak*. She continues to write historical fiction, like *Chains*, and young adult novels, like *Wintergirls*. She says she is inspired by her readers, who write to her with comments or come to her readings.

SPOTLIGHT

from Speak
by Laurie Halse Anderson

I find my locker after social studies. The lock sticks a little, but I open it. I dive into the stream of fourth-period lunch students and swim down the hall to the cafeteria.

I know enough not to bring lunch on the first day of high school. There is no way of telling what the acceptable fashion will be. Brown bags—humble testament to suburbia, or terminal geek gear? Insulated lunch bags—hip way to save the planet, or sign of an overinvolved mother? Buying is the only solution. And it gives me time to scan the cafeteria for a friendly face or an inconspicuous corner.

The hot lunch is turkey with reconstituted dried mashed potatoes and gravy, a damp green vegetable, and a cookie. I'm not sure how to order anything else, so I just slide my tray along and let the lunch drones fill it. This eight-foot senior in front of me somehow gets three cheeseburgers, French fries, and two Ho-Hos without saying a word. Some sort of Morse code with his eyes, maybe. Must study this further. I follow the Basketball Pole into the cafeteria.

My Notes

I see a few friends—people I used to think were my friends—but they look away. Think fast, think fast. There's that new girl, Heather, reading by the window. I could sit across from her. Or I could crawl behind a trash can. Or maybe I could dump my lunch straight into the trash and keep moving right on out the door.

The Basketball Pole waves to a table of friends. Or course. The basketball team. They all swear at him—a bizarre greeting practiced by athletic boys with zits. He smiles and throws a Ho-Ho. I try to scoot around him.

Thwap! A lump of potatoes and gravy hits me square in the center of my chest. All conversation stops as the entire lunchroom gawks, my face burning into their retinas. I will be forever known as "that girl who got nailed by potatoes the first day." The Basketball Pole apologizes and says something else, but four hundred people explode in laughter and I can't read lips. I ditch my tray and bolt for the door.

I motor so fast out of the lunchroom the track coach would draft me for varsity if he were around. But no, Mr. Neck has cafeteria duty. And Mr. Neck has no use for girls who can run the one hundred in under ten seconds, unless they're willing to do it while holding on to a football.

Mr. Neck: "We meet again."

Me:

Would he listen to "I need to go home and change," or "Did you see what that bozo did"? Not a chance. I keep my mouth shut.

Mr. Neck: "Where do you think you're going?"

Me:

It is easier not to say anything. Shut your trap, button your lip, can it. All that crap you hear on TV about communication and expressing feelings is a lie. Nobody really wants to hear what you have to say.

Mr. Neck makes a note in his book. "I knew you were trouble the first time I saw you. I've taught here for twenty-four years and I can tell what's going on in a kid's head just by looking in their eyes. No more warnings. You just earned a demerit for wandering the halls without a pass."

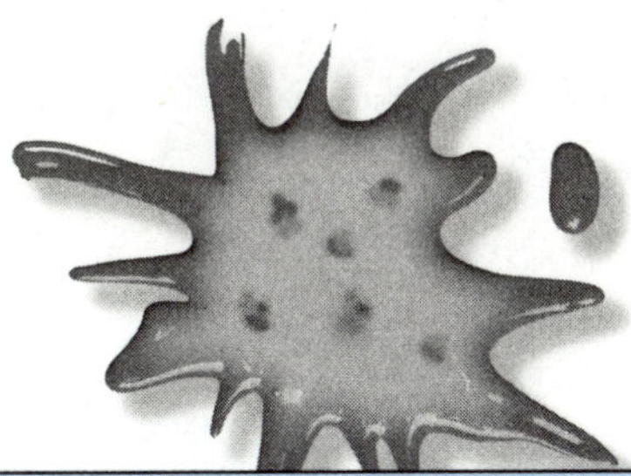

ACTIVITY 1.7 *Continued*

Steps:

18 Ask students to respond to the writing prompt (on page 18) and draft a paragraph or two (or more at your discretion) in which they analyze the way that the diction, imagery, or syntax of one of the authors establishes the narrator's voice. Before assigning the written analysis, conduct a **Guided Writing** on the board in which you model the drafting of an analysis. You might provide sentence starters for students such as the following:

- Cisneros's use of imagery enables the reader to…
- Soto's diction helps define the speaker's voice as one who is….
- Anderson's diction establishes the narrator's tone by….
- Cisneros's syntax helps to establish the speaker's voice by….

19 This might also be a good time to ask students to complete a similar paragraph about how the author establishes a narrator's voice in the novels they are reading independently.

20 Revisit the **Essential Question**: What does it mean to "come of age"?

21 Direct students to revisit their **Vocabulary Notebooks** and elaborate on the concept of ***voice***.

ACTIVITY 1.8

Getting Cut: Coming of Age the Hard Way

Purpose:

- To summarize an incident and identify the effect of the incident
- To explain how a writer's or speaker's voice shapes a reader's response

Steps:

1 Before reading this article, ask students to make a **prediction** about the text based on the title. **Activate prior knowledge** by asking if anyone has ever been cut from something, and allow volunteers to share their experiences.

2 Continue by asking students to **think-pair-share** the ways in which negative experiences can sometimes create positive outcomes. Allow volunteers to share other examples from real life or fictional instances in which a difficult situation resulted in a person's ultimate success.

3 Explain the purpose of this **graphic organizer**—for recording examples from the following texts.

ACTIVITY 1.8

Getting Cut: Coming of Age the Hard Way

SUGGESTED LEARNING STRATEGIES: Diffusing, Graphic Organizer, Predicting, Think-Pair-Share

What does the title "Cut" make you think about? What do you predict this text will be about?

As you read, or read along with, the vignettes in "Cut," take notes on the graphic organizer below.

Vignette	Name	Profession	Describe Incident	How He Felt Then	Effect of Incident in Future
1					
2					
3					
4					
5					

Nonfiction

CUT

by Bob Greene

ABOUT THE AUTHOR

Born in 1947, Bob Greene is best known for the column he wrote for the *Chicago Tribune* for many years. Referring to the breadth of Greene's topics, one writer said, "Water covers two-thirds of the earth, and Bob Greene covers the rest." Greene has written two biographies of basketball player Michael Jordan as well as the novel *All Summer Long*; his columns have also been collected into several books. The following piece tells a lot about Greene and a significant moment in his own "coming of age."

WORD CONNECTIONS

Several words in this text have been glossed to aid understanding. To **gloss** a word is to add an explanation that is not in the original text (see the footnotes on the next pages). The word *gloss* has multiple meanings depending on how it is used; for example, something shiny may have a high gloss, or someone wishing to hide something may gloss over the facts.

My Notes

1

I remember vividly the last time I cried. I was twelve years old, in the seventh grade, and I had tried out for the junior high school basketball team. I walked into the gymnasium; there was a piece of paper tacked to the bulletin board.

It was a cut list. The seventh-grade coach had put it up on the board. The boys whose names were on the list were still on the team; they were welcome to keep coming to practices. The boys whose names were not on the list had been cut; their presence was no longer desired. My name was not on the list.

I had not known the cut was coming that day. I stood and I stared at the list. The coach had not composed it with a great deal of subtlety; the names of the very best athletes were at the top of the sheet of paper, and the other members of the squad were listed in what appeared to be a descending order of talent. I kept looking at the bottom of the list, hoping against hope that my name would miraculously appear there if I looked hard enough.

I held myself together as I walked out of the gym and out of the school, but when I got home I began to sob. I couldn't stop. For the first time in my life, I had been told officially that I wasn't good enough. Athletics meant everything to boys that age; if you were on the team, even as a substitute, it put you in the desirable group. If you weren't on the team, you might as well not be alive.

I had tried desperately in practice, but the coach never seemed to notice. It didn't matter how hard I was willing to work; he didn't want me there. I knew that when I went to school the next morning I would have to face the boys who had not been cut — the boys whose names were on the list, who were still on the team, who had been judged worthy while I had been judged unworthy.

ACTIVITY 1.8 Continued

Steps:

4 Ask for five volunteers, one to **read aloud** each of the five vignettes. Instruct students to complete the graphic organizer as they follow along with the readers.

TEACHER TO TEACHER You might point out that some information is dated, but the speakers' comments are still relevant.

5 Direct students to use the strategy of **diffusing** the text by noting unfamiliar words. Help students discover the meaning of unfamiliar words by using context clues, dictionaries, or footnotes, and replacing selected words with familiar ones.

6 Discuss with students the effect Bob Greene achieves by moving into first-person narration immediately.

Teacher Notes

Getting Cut: Coming of Age the Hard Way

My Notes

As you read, diffuse the text by using the My Notes space to identify the phrases or context clues that help you understand the meanings of glossed words.

GRAMMAR & USAGE

Writers use the subjunctive form of the verb to express a doubt, a wish, a possibility, or a situation contrary to fact. Bob Greene uses the subjunctive in the phrase *as if I were* to express a situation contrary to fact:

"All these years later, I remember it as if I were still standing right there in the gym."

All these years later, I remember it as if I were still standing right there in the gym. And a curious thing has happened: in traveling around the country, I have found that an inordinately[1] large proportion of successful men share the same memory — the memory of being cut from a sports team as a boy.

I don't know how the mind works in matters like this; I don't know what went on in my head following that day when I was cut. But I know that my ambition has been enormous ever since then: I know that for all my life since that day, I have done more work than I had to be doing, taken more assignments than I had to be taking, put in more hours than I had to be spending. I don't know if all of that came from a determination never to allow myself to be cut again — but I know it's there. And apparently it's there in a lot of other men, too.

2

Bob Graham, thirty-six, is a partner with the Jenner & Block law firm in Chicago. "When I was sixteen, baseball was my whole life," he said. "I had gone to a relatively small high school, and I had been on the team. But then my family moved, and I was going to a much bigger high school. All during the winter months I told everyone that I was a ballplayer. When spring came, of course I went out for the team.

"The cut list went up. I did not make the team. Reading that cut list is one of the clearest things I have in my memory. I wanted not to believe it, but there it was.

"I went home and told my father about it. He suggested that maybe I should talk to the coach. So I did. I pleaded to be put back on the team. He said there was nothing he could do; he said he didn't have enough room.

"I know for a fact that it altered[2] my perception of myself. My view of myself was knocked down; my self-esteem was lowered. I felt so embarrassed; my whole life up to that point had revolved around sports, and particularly around playing baseball. That was the group I wanted to be in — the guys on the baseball team. And I was told that I wasn't good enough to be one of them.

"I know now that it changed me. I found out, even though I couldn't articulate[3] it at the time, that there would be times in my life when certain people would be in a position to say 'You're not good enough' to me. I did not want that to happen ever again.

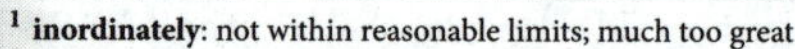

[1] **inordinately**: not within reasonable limits; much too great
[2] **altered**: changed; made different
[3] **articulate**: put into words clearly and easily

GRAMMAR & USAGE EXTENSION

Explore the uses of the subjunctive mood with students. Point out that a verb in the subjunctive mood is often used in a clause beginning with the word *if*. A common error that writers and speakers make is to use the incorrect verb form in such clauses.

Incorrect: If I was rich, I would buy a baseball team.

Correct: If I were rich, I would buy a baseball team.

The subjunctive does not always follow a clause beginning with *if*. For example:

Incorrect: We wish she was able to run the mile faster.

Correct: We wish she were able to run the mile faster.

Teacher Notes

My Notes

"It seems obvious to me now that being cut was what started me in determining that my success would always be based on my own abilities, and not on someone else's perceptions. Since then I've always been something of an overachiever; when I came to the law firm I was very aggressive in trying to run my own cases right away, to be the lead lawyer in the cases with which I was involved. I made partner at thirty-one; I never wanted to be left behind.

"Looking back, maybe it shouldn't have been that important. It was only baseball. You pass that by. Here I am. That coach is probably still there, still a high school baseball coach, still cutting boys off the baseball team every year. I wonder how many hundreds of boys he's cut in his life?"

3

Maurice McGrath is senior vice-president of Genstar Mortgage Corporation, a mortgage banking firm in Glendale, California. "I'm forty-seven years old, and I was fourteen when it happened to me, and I still feel something when I think about it," he said.

"I was in the eighth grade. I went to St. Philip's School of Pasadena. I went out for the baseball team, and one day at practice the coach came over to me. He was an Occidental College student who had been hired as the eighth-grade coach.

"He said, 'You're no good.' Those were his words. I asked him why he was saying that. He said, 'You can't hit the ball. I don't want you here.' I didn't know what to do, so I went over and sat off to the side, watching the others practice. The coach said I should leave the practice field. He said that I wasn't on the team, and that I didn't belong there anymore.

"I was outwardly stoic[4] about it. I didn't want anyone to see how I felt. I didn't want to show that it hurt. But oh, did it hurt. All my friends played baseball after school every day. My best friend was the pitcher of the team. After I got whittled down by the coach, I would hear the other boys talking in class about what they were going to do at practice after school. I knew that I'd just have to go home.

"I guess you make your mind up never to allow yourself to be hurt like that again. In some way I must have been saying to myself, 'I'll play the game better.' Not the sports game, but anything I tried. I must have been saying, 'if I have to, I'll sit on the bench, but I'll be part of the team.'

"I try to make my own kids believe that, too. I try to tell them that they should show that they're a little bit better than the rest. I tell them to think of themselves as better. Who cares what anyone else thinks? You know, I can almost hear that coach saying the words. 'You're no good.'"

[4] **stoic:** indifferent; remaining calm and self-controlled in the face of difficulty

ACTIVITY 1.8 Continued

Steps:

7 Ask students to find the one vignette that contains **imagery** in the form of **similes** and **metaphors**. (Vignette 4)

ACTIVITY 1.8 continued

Getting Cut: Coming of Age the Hard Way

My Notes

4

Author Malcolm MacPherson (*The Blood of His Servants*), forty, lives in New York. "It happened to me in the ninth grade, at the Yalesville School in Yalesville, Connecticut," he said. "Both of my parents had just been killed in a car crash, and as you can imagine, it was a very difficult time in my life. I went out for the baseball team, and I did pretty well in practice.

"But in the first game I clutched. I was playing second base; the batter hit a popup, and I moved back to catch it. I can see it now. I felt dizzy as I looked up at the ball. It was like I was moving in slow motion, but the ball was going at regular speed. I couldn't get out of the way of my own feet. The ball dropped to the ground. I didn't catch it.

"The next day at practice, the coach read off the lineup. I wasn't on it. I was off the squad.

"I remember what I did: I walked. It was a cold spring afternoon, and the ground was wet, and I just walked. I was living with an aunt and uncle, and I didn't want to go home. I just wanted to walk forever.

"It drove my opinion of myself right into a tunnel. Right into a cave. And when I came out of that cave, something inside of me wanted to make sure in one manner or another that I would never again be told I wasn't good enough.

"I will confess that my ambition, to this day, is out of control. It's like a fire. I think the fire would have pretty much stayed in control if I hadn't been cut from the team. But that got it going. You don't slice ambition two ways; it's either there or it isn't. Those of us who went through something like that always know that we have to catch the ball. We'd rather die than have the ball fall at our feet.

"Once that fire is started in us, it never gets extinguished,[5] until we die or have heart attacks or something. Sometimes I wonder about the home-run hitters; the guys who never even had to worry about being cut. They may have gotten the applause and the attention back then, but I wonder if they ever got the fire. I doubt it. I think maybe you have to get kicked in the teeth to get the fire started.

"You can tell the effect of something like that by examining the trail you've left in your life, and tracing it backward. It's almost like being a junkie with a need for success. You get attention and applause and you like it, but you never quite trust it. Because you know that back then you were good enough if only they would have given you a chance. You don't trust what you achieve, because you're afraid that someone will take it away from you. You know that it can happen; it already did.

"So you try to show people how good you are. Maybe you don't go out and become Dan Rather; maybe you just end up owning the Pontiac

[5] **extinguished:** put out; ended

Teacher Notes

dealership in your town. But it's your dealership, and you're the top man, and every day you're showing people that you're good enough."

5

Dan Rather, fifty-two, is anchor of the "CBS Evening News." "When I was thirteen, I had rheumatic fever," he said. "I became extremely skinny and extremely weak, but I still went out for the seventh-grade baseball team at Alexander Hamilton Junior High School in Houston.

"The school was small enough that there was no cut as such; you were supposed to figure out that you weren't good enough, and quit. Game after game I sat at the end of the bench, hoping that maybe this was the time I would get in. The coach never even looked at me; I might as well have been invisible.

"I told my mother about it. Her advice was not to quit. So I went to practice every day, and I tried to do well so that the coach would be impressed. He never even knew I was there. At home in my room I would fantasize that there was a big game, and the three guys in front of me would all get hurt, and the coach would turn to me and put me in, and I would make the winning hit. But then there'd be another game, and the late innings would come, and if we were way ahead I'd keep hoping that this was the game when the coach would put me in. He never did.

"When you're that age, you're looking for someone to tell you you're okay. Your sense of self-esteem is just being formed. And what that experience that baseball season did was make me think that perhaps I wasn't okay.

"In the last game of the season something terrible happened. It was the last of the ninth inning, there were two outs, and there were two strikes on the batter. And the coach turned to me and told me to go out to right field.

"It was a totally humiliating thing for him to do. For him to put me in for one pitch, the last pitch of the season, in front of all the other guys on the team. I stood out there for that one pitch, and I just wanted to sink into the ground and disappear. Looking back on it, it was an extremely unkind thing for him to have done. That was nearly forty years ago, and I don't know why the memory should be so vivid now; I've never known if the coach was purposely making fun of me — and if he was, why a grown man would do that to a thirteen-year-old boy.

"I'm not a psychologist. I don't know if a man can point to one event in his life and say that that's the thing that made him the way he is. But when you're that age, and you're searching for your own identity, and all you want is to be told that you're all right… I wish I understood it better, but I know the feeling is still there."

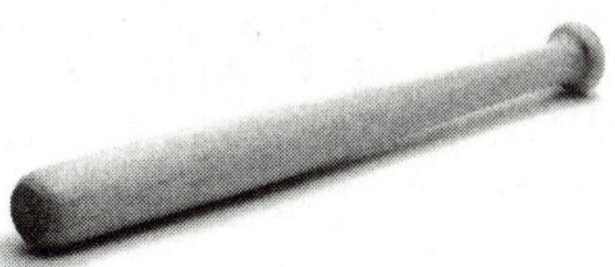

My Notes

WORD CONNECTIONS

An analogy is a comparison of the relationship between two groups of words. One way to analyze an analogy is to look at a relationship that describes a function. For example, eye : see :: ear : hear. Choose an appropriate word to complete the following analogies.

a. architect : building :: coach : team.

b. artist : artwork :: lawyer : case.

ACTIVITY 1.8 *Continued*

Steps:

8 Ask students what they can tell about each man based on the voices represented in the vignettes. After the discussion, prompt students to craft a paragraph explaining how the voice of the speaker helps to shape the reader's response.

9 Finally, as direct scaffolding for Embedded Assessment 1, ask students to consider the types of questions Bob Greene might have asked each of the men in order to obtain the responses he received and included in the vignettes.

Getting Cut: Coming of Age the Hard Way

Writing Prompt: Write a paragraph explaining how the voice of one of the speakers helps to shape the reader's response.

Most of the text included in the vignettes is presented as direct quotations from the men being interviewed. In order to capture the insights of each of the men, Bob Greene, the author, most likely had to ask them a series of questions. What questions might he have asked them? What additional questions or follow-up questions might you want to ask each of these men? Use the subjunctive form to write questions that would elicit responses about each interviewee's doubts, wishes, or possibilities relating the experience of being cut from a team.

- Questions Bob Greene may have asked:

- Follow-up questions you would like to ask:

Strategies Learning Log

Name of strategy:	
Purpose of strategy:	
How strategy was used:	
How strategy helped you make meaning from the text, create a text, or orally present a text:	
When you would use this strategy again:	

Strategies Learning Log

Name of strategy:	
Purpose of strategy:	
How strategy was used:	
How strategy helped you make meaning from the text, create a text, or orally present a text:	
When you would use this strategy again:	

Steps:

10 **Learning Log:** To ensure that students know how to use the Learning Log, you might want to model the reflective process for them. Next, ask students to review the Strategies Appendix to identify the strategies they used to make meaning from the text. Students can use a think-pair-share to reflect on their use of those strategies. Next, ask students to identify two strategies that work well for them and note them on their Learning Logs.

11 Revisit the **Essential Question**: What does it mean to "come of age"?

ACTIVITY 1.9
Two Versions of One Memory

Materials:

- Vocabulary Notebooks

Purpose:

- To compare and contrast the effectiveness of prose and poetry in conveying an experience
- To create open-ended interview questions

Steps:

1 Review with students the difference between prose and poetry. Inform students that while both texts for this activity are by the same author about the same incident, one is a prose version and the other is a poem.

2 Explain that students are to take notes on the **graphic organizer** about the diction, imagery, and syntax in the two texts and to make inferences about the speaker from the information in their notes.

ACTIVITY 1.9

Two Versions of One Memory

SUGGESTED LEARNING STRATEGIES: **Graphic Organizer, Role Playing, Word Map**

LITERARY TERMS

Prose is ordinary written or spoken language, using sentences and paragraphs, without deliberate or regular meter or rhyme; not poetry, drama, or song.

You will read two texts about the same incident by the same author. One version is in **prose** and the other is in poetry. As you listen to both read aloud, visualize the incident and take notes on the graphic organizers below. Think about which version paints the most vivid picture for you.

Prose Version: "Always Running"

Diction	Imagery	Syntax	Inferences About the Speaker Based on Voice

Poetry Version: "'Race' Politics"

Diction	Imagery	Syntax	Inferences About the Speaker Based on Voice

Discussion

Which version do you think is more powerful? Which is easier to visualize and understand? What components of coming of age are present in the two texts?

Memoir

ALWAYS RUNNING

by Luis J. Rodriguez

ABOUT THE AUTHOR
Award-winning author Luis Rodriguez was born near the US-Mexican border. He is a leading Chicano writer and is best known for his memoir of gang life in Los Angeles, *Always Running*. Rodriguez left the gang life in his late teens and has since worked in many jobs, from bus driver to newspaper reporter and community activist. He has developed many outreach programs to assist teens throughout the country. He continues to write both poetry and narrative works and is a co-organizer of the Chicago Poetry Festival.

One day, my mother asked Rano and me to go to the grocery store. We decided to go across the railroad tracks into South Gate. In those days, South Gate was an Anglo neighborhood, filled with the families of workers from the auto plant and other nearby industry. Like Lynnwood or Huntington Park, it was forbidden territory for the people of Watts.

My brother insisted we go. I don't know what possessed him, but then I never did. It was useless to argue; he'd force me anyway. He was nine then, I was six. So without ceremony, we started over the tracks, climbing over discarded[1] market carts and tore-up sofas, across Alameda Street, into South Gate: all-white, all-American.

We entered the first small corner grocery store we found. Everything was cool at first. We bought some bread, milk, soup cans and candy. We each walked out with a bag filled with food. We barely got a few feet, though, when five teenagers on bikes approached. We tried not to pay any attention and proceeded to our side of the tracks. But the youths pulled up in front of us. While two of them stood nearby on their bikes, three of them jumped off theirs and walked over to us.

"What do we got here?" one of the boys said. "Spics to order — maybe with some beans?"

He pushed me to the ground; the groceries splattered onto the asphalt. I felt melted gum and chips of broken beer bottle on my lips and cheek. Then somebody picked me up and held me while the two others seized my brother, tossed his groceries out, and pounded on him. They punched him in the face, in the stomach, then his face again, cutting his lip, causing him to vomit.

[1] **discarded:** thrown away as useless

My Notes

ACTIVITY 1.9 Continued

Steps:

3 Conduct a **shared reading** by either reading the texts yourself or assigning student readers. As students listen and read along, remind them to take notes on the graphic organizer.

Teacher Notes

Two Versions of One Memory

My Notes

I remember the shrill[2], maddening laughter of one of the kids on a bike, this laughing like a raven's wail, a harsh wind's shriek, a laugh that I would hear in countless beatings thereafter. I watched the others take turns on my brother, this terror of a brother, and he doubled over, had blood and spew on his shirt, and tears down his face. I wanted to do something, but they held me and I just looked on, as every strike against Rano opened me up inside.

They finally let my brother go and he slid to the ground, like a rotten banana squeezed out of its peeling. They threw us back over the tracks. In the sunset I could see the Watts Towers, shimmers of 70,000 pieces of broken bottles, sea shells, ceramic and metal on spiraling points puncturing the heavens, which reflected back the rays of a falling sun. My brother and I then picked ourselves up, saw the teenagers take off, still laughing, still talking about those stupid greasers who dared to cross over to South Gate.

Up until then my brother had never shown any emotion to me other than disdain. He had never asked me anything, unless it was a demand, an expectation, an obligation[3] to be his throwaway boy-doll. But for this once he looked at me, tears welled in his eyes, blood streamed from several cuts — lips and cheeks swollen.

"Swear — you got to swear — you'll never tell anybody how I cried," he said.

I suppose I did promise. It was his one last thing to hold onto, his rep as someone who could take a belt whipping, who could take a beating in the neighborhood and still go back risking more — it was this pathetic plea from the pavement I remember. I must have promised.

---

[2] **shrill:** high-pitched and sharp
[3] **obligation:** a duty

Teacher Notes

"Race" Politics

by Luis J. Rodriguez

My brother and I
— shopping for *la jefita* —
decided to get the "good food"
over on the other side
of the tracks.

We dared each other.
Laughed a little.
Thought about it.
Said, what's the big deal.
Thought about that.
Decided we were men,
not boys.
Decided we should go wherever
we damn wanted to.

Oh, my brother — now he was bad.
Tough dude. Afraid of nothing.
I was afraid of him.

So there we go,
climbing over
the iron and wood ties,
over discarded sofas
    and bent-up market carts,
over a weed-and-dirt road,
into a place called South Gate
— all white. All American.

We entered the forbidden
narrow line of hate,
imposed,
transposed,
supposed,
a line of power/powerlessness
full of meaning,
meaning nothing —
those lines that crisscross
the abdomen of this land,
that strangle you
in your days, in your nights.
When you dream.

My Notes

GRAMMAR & USAGE

Rodriguez uses "each other" when he speaks of himself and his brother in line 6.

Each other and *one another* are **reciprocal pronouns.** When you write, use *each other* to refer to two people and *one another* to refer to three or more.

GRAMMAR & USAGE EXTENSION

You might wish to explain that the distinction between *each other* and *one another* is not commonly observed. Nevertheless, in academic or literary usage, students should use the reciprocal pronouns correctly.

Steps:

4 Direct students back to the discussion questions on page 34. Assist students as they answer and discuss the questions. Discuss as a class which version students prefer and why. Ask students to consider which version is easier to read, which version is easier to **visualize**, and why the author might have selected two ways to tell the same story.

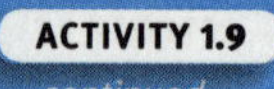

Two Versions of One Memory

My Notes

There we were, two Mexicans,
six and nine — from Watts no less.
Oh, this was plenty reason
to hate us.

Plenty reason to run up behind us.
Five teenagers on bikes.
Plenty reason to knock
the groceries out from our arms —
a splattering heap of soup
cans, bread and candy.

Plenty reason to hold me down
on the hot asphalt; melted gum,
and chips of broken
beer bottle on my lips
and cheek.
Plenty reason to get my brother
by the throat, taking turns
punching him in the face,
cutting his lower lip,
punching, him vomiting.
Punching until swollen and dark blue
he slid from their grasp
like a rotten banana from its peeling.

When they had enough, they threw us back,
dirty and lacerated;
back to Watts, its towers shiny
across the orange-red sky.

My brother then forced me
to promise not to tell anybody
how he cried.
He forced me to swear to God,
to Jesus Christ, to our long-dead
Indian Grandmother —
keepers of our meddling souls.

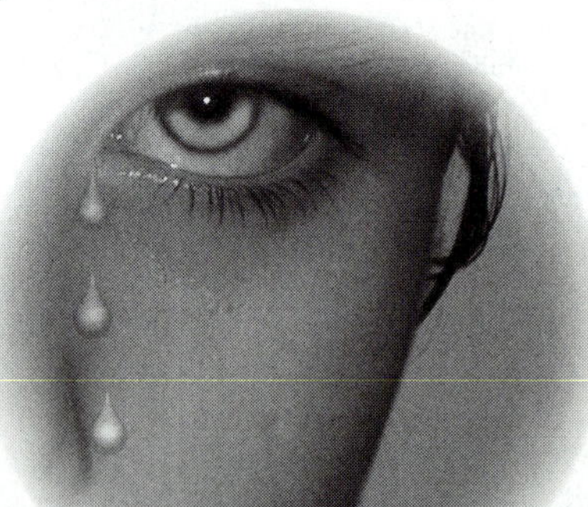

Imagine that the speaker has changed to Rano, the older brother. Write a piece in Rano's voice describing the same incident from his perspective and using sensory images.

How does the speaker influence the telling of the incident?

Steps:

5 Briefly discuss how the story would be different if told through the eyes of Rano, the older brother. Prompt students to write a piece in Rano's voice describing the incident from his perspective and using sensory images.

ACTIVITY 1.9 *Continued*

Steps:

6 Place students into pairs and ask them to **role play** an interview situation in which they answer questions in the voice of one of the characters. Suggest that they refer to their notes in the graphic organizer to help them develop and maintain a character's voice. This interviewing will help students to solidify their understanding of voice as well as to practice asking open-ended interview questions in preparation for Embedded Assessment 1.

7 Direct students to revisit their **Vocabulary Notebook** entries on ***voice*** to further develop their ideas.

ACTIVITY 1.9 *continued*

Two Versions of One Memory

Now choose the voice of one of the characters and practice answering interview questions. With your partner, **role play** how the interview might sound. First, one of you can ask questions while the other answers in the voice of one of the characters. The interviewee should try to maintain the voice of the character by keeping word choice, language, and culture in mind. Once all questions have been asked and answered, switch roles. Now the interviewee will answer in the voice of the other character.

Here are some possible questions to help you get started. Ask additional open-ended follow-up questions. Remember that good interview questions are open-ended — they cannot be answered with a simple "yes" or "no."

Q: Can you tell me what happened today outside the grocery store?

A:

Q: Who would you say is mostly to blame for the incident and why?

A:

Q: Can you think of a way this incident could possibly end up having a positive outcome?

A:

Q: If you could give any advice to the parties involved, what would it be and why?

A:

Q: If you could go back and change the incident, what would you do differently and why?

A:

Q: What did you learn from this incident?

A:

Conversations with Characters

ACTIVITY 1.10

SUGGESTED LEARNING STRATEGIES: Close Reading, Double-Entry Journal, Marking the Text, Sharing and Responding, Think Aloud, Visualization

In class, you have been reading texts that depict an incident that causes the character to grow or mature. "First Love" is another text that addresses the "coming of age" theme. As you read "First Love", notice how the **diction, syntax**, and **imagery** portray the events from the character's **point of view.**

LITERARY TERMS

Point of view refers to the perspective from which a narrative is told.

1. Write a list of the key events in "First Love."

2. Why is this considered a coming-of-age story?

3. What if you had the opportunity to interview the narrator? Write five open-ended questions you would ask as well as possible responses in the voice of the narrator. Complete the organizer to help focus your thoughts.

How would you describe the voice of the character?	What kind of language does the character tend to use?	What kinds of things does the character usually talk about?

Questions to ask the narrator:

4. Now, consider the novel you have been reading independently and review your double-entry journal. On separate paper, write a list of the key events, explain why your novel can be considered a coming-of-age novel, and complete a mock interview of the narrator.

ACTIVITY 1.10

Conversations with Characters

Materials:

- Independent-reading novels

Purpose:

- To apply reading strategies to new reading tasks
- To apply knowledge of diction, syntax, and imagery to understanding a new text
- To plan and generate interview questions

Steps:

1 This activity provides another opportunity for you to model reading strategies, such as **close reading** and **visualization** as well as to **think aloud** as you model **double-entry journal** entries and a character interview.

2 Explain to students that they will return to this page after they have read the text. The "conversation" they have with the narrator of "First Love" will give them guided practice for conducting an imaginary interview with the main character of the novel they are reading independently.

ACTIVITY 1.10 *Continued*

Steps:

3 This text is a little more challenging than the previous texts in this unit. Therefore, you might begin by preteaching some unfamiliar vocabulary and adding the words to the class **Word Wall** as well. Select approximately ten words for instruction based on the needs of your students. Some possibilities are highlighted in the text. You may also consider inviting students to use the diffusing strategy for other unfamiliar words.

4 The narrative has been **chunked** into three sections. Read aloud the first chunk. As you read, **think aloud** about possible **double-entry journal** entries and model some of these for students. To be authentic, you will want to provide some of your own entries and corresponding remarks. Following are some possible locations at which to pause and some possible think-aloud statements you might use:

- In Paragraph 1, "in the great tradition of tragic romance": "I wonder what tragic romance is referring to?" "What other tragic romances do I know about? "
- In Paragraph 1, the boy is described as "not Puerto Rican": "I wonder why it is important that he isn't Puerto Rican…oh… the narrator and her family must be Puerto Rican."
- In Paragraph 3, "sweet agony": Isn't that an interesting expression? That's an oxymoron, right?

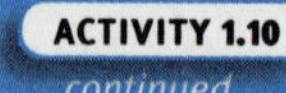

Conversations with Characters

My Notes

Chunk 1

Personal Narrative

ABOUT THE AUTHOR
Judith Ortiz Cofer was born in Puerto Rico, but she grew up in New Jersey. Her family often spent time in Puerto Rico, and she became comfortable with both cultures. Much of her writing addresses the immigrant experience for Puerto Ricans, especially cultural conflicts and the coming-of-age experience for young Puerto Rican Americans.

First Love

from Silent Dancing
by Judith Ortiz Cofer

1 I fell in love, or my hormones awakened from their long slumber in my body, and suddenly the goal of my days was focused on one thing: to catch a glimpse of my secret love. And it had to remain secret, because I had, of course, in the great tradition of tragic romance, chosen to love a boy who was totally out of my reach. He was not Puerto Rican; he was Italian and rich. He was also an older man. He was a senior at the high school when I came in as a freshman. I first saw him in the hall, leaning casually on a wall that was the border line between girlside and boyside for underclassmen. He looked extraordinarily like a young Marlon Brando—down to the ironic little smile. The total of what I knew about the boy who starred in every one of my awkward fantasies was this: that he was the nephew of the man who owned the supermarket on my block; that he often had parties at his parents' beautiful home in the suburbs which I would hear about; that his family had money (which came to our school in many ways)—and this fact made my knees weak: and that he worked at the store near my apartment building on weekends and in the summer.

2 My mother could not understand why I became so eager to be the one sent out on her endless errands. I pounced on every opportunity from Friday to late Saturday afternoon to go after eggs, cigarettes, milk (I tried to drink as much of it as possible, although I hated the stuff)—the staple items that she would order from the "American" store.

continued

Week after week I wandered up and down the aisles, taking furtive glances at the stock room in the back, breathlessly hoping to see my prince. Not that I had a plan. I felt like a pilgrim waiting for a glimpse of Mecca. I did not expect him to notice me. It was sweet agony. 3

One day I did see him. Dressed in a white outfit like a surgeon; white pants and shirt, white cap, and (gross sigh, but not to my love-glazed eyes) blood-smeared butcher's apron. He was helping to drag a side of beef into the freezer storage area of the store. I must have stood there like an idiot, because I remember that he did see me, he even spoke to me! I could have died. I think he said, "Excuse me," and smiled vaguely in my direction. 4

After that, I willed occasions to go to the supermarket. I watched my mother's cigarettes empty ever so slowly. I wanted her to smoke them fast. I drank milk and forced it on my brother (although a second glass for him had to be bought with my share of Fig Newton cookies which we both liked, but were restricted to one row each). I gave my cookies up for love, and watched my mother smoke her L&M's with so little enthusiasm that I thought (God, no!) that she might be cutting down on her smoking or maybe even giving up the habit. At this crucial time! 5

I thought I had kept my lonely romance a secret. Often I cried hot tears on my pillow for the things that kept us apart. In my mind there was no doubt that he would never notice me (and that is why I felt free to stare at him—I was invisible). He could not see me because I was a skinny Puerto Rican girl, a freshman who did not belong to any group he associated with. 6

At the end of the year I found out that I had not been invisible. I learned one little lesson about human nature—adulation (flattery) leaves a scent, one that we are all equipped to recognize, and no matter how insignificant the source, we seek it. 7

In June the nuns at our school would always arrange for some cultural extravaganza.[1] In my freshman year it was a Roman banquet. We had been studying Greek drama (as a prelude to church history—it was at a fast clip that we galloped through Sophocles and Euripides toward the early Christian martyrs), and our young, energetic Sister Agnes was in the mood for a spectacle. She ordered the entire student body (it was a small group of under 300 students) to have our mothers make us togas out of sheets. She handed out a pattern on mimeo pages fresh out of the machine. I remember the intense smell of the alcohol on the sheets of paper, and how almost everyone in the auditorium brought theirs to their noses and inhaled deeply—mimeographed handouts were the school-day buzz that the new Xerox generation of kids is missing out on. Then, as the last couple of weeks of school dragged on, the city of Paterson becoming a 8

[1] **extravaganza**: an elaborate and fantastic show

My Notes

GRAMMAR & USAGE

For variety and emphasis, Ortiz Cofer uses different types of sentences.

A **periodic sentence** is one that makes sense fully only when the reader reaches the end of the sentence, that is, when the main clause comes last. A periodic sentence emphasizes the idea in the main clause by making the reader wait for it.

Example: Then, as the last couple of weeks of school dragged on, the city of Paterson becoming a concrete oven, and us wilting in our uncomfortable uniforms, we labored like frantic Roman slaves to build a splendid banquet hall in our small auditorium.

GRAMMAR & USAGE EXTENSION

You might wish to discuss the ways that writers achieve variety and emphasis. Checking for periodic, cumulative, and balanced sentences, as well as the other sentence types, will give students further work with syntax. Remind them that a cumulative sentence starts with an independent clause that is followed by several subordinate phrases or clauses that provide details about the subject (person, place, idea). For example, "The road ran through the mountains, twisting and turning, steep slopes falling away, with scrubby bushes dotting the landscape." Another example of a cumulative sentence is given on page 45.

A balanced sentence has two parts that are about equal in length. For example, "The tornado ripped through the house, and only the fireplace was left standing."

Steps:

- In Paragraph 8, "city of Paterson becoming a concrete oven": That's a vivid description. I think it's a metaphor.
- In Paragraph 9, "the main privilege of beauty is that others will do almost everything for you, including thinking": Wow! Is that true? I'm thinking of real-life examples of this. It does seem to be true for famous people.

5 After you read and model Chunk 1, ask students to read Chunk 2 silently, **marking the text** and annotating it. You might ask students to pay special attention to the author's skillful use of transitions as she narrates the events in sequential order. Allow a few minutes for students to discuss Section 2 with a partner to clarify understanding.

Teacher Notes

Conversations with Characters

My Notes

concrete oven, and us wilting in our uncomfortable uniforms, we labored like frantic Roman slaves to build a splendid banquet hall in our small auditorium. Sister Agnes wanted a raised dais where the host and hostess would be regally enthroned.

9 She had already chosen our Senator and Lady from among our ranks. The Lady was to be a beautiful new student named Sophia, a recent Polish immigrant, whose English was still practically unintelligible, but whose features, classically perfect without a trace of makeup, enthralled[2] us. Everyone talked about her gold hair cascading past her waist, and her voice which could carry a note right up to heaven in choir. The nuns wanted her for God. They kept saying she had a vocation. We just looked at her in awe, and the boys seemed afraid of her. She just smiled and did as she was told. I don't know what she thought of it all. The main privilege of beauty is that others will do almost everything for you, including thinking.

10 Her partner was to be our best basketball player, a tall, red-haired senior whose family sent its many offspring to our school. Together, Sophia and her senator looked like the best combination of immigrant genes our community could produce. It did not occur to me to ask then whether anything but their physical beauty qualified them for the starring roles in our production. I had the highest average in the church history class, but I was given the part of one of many "Roman Citizens." I was to sit in front of the plastic fruit and recite a greeting in Latin along with the rest of the school when our hosts came into the hall and took their places on the throne.

11 On the night of our banquet, my father escorted me in my toga to the door of our school. I felt foolish in my awkwardly draped sheet (blouse and skirt required underneath). My mother had no great skill as a seamstress. The best she could do was hem a skirt or a pair of pants. That night I would have traded her for a peasant woman with a golden needle. I saw other Roman ladies emerging from their parents' cars looking authentic in sheets of material that folded over their bodies like the garments on a statue by Michelangelo. How did they do it? How was it that I always got it just slightly wrong, and worse, I believed that other people were just too polite to mention it. "The poor little Puerto Rican girl," I could hear them thinking. But in reality, I must have been my worst critic, self-conscious as I was.

Chunk 2

12 Soon, we were all sitting at our circle of tables joined together around the dais. Sophia glittered like a golden statue. Her smile was beatific: a perfect, silent Roman lady. Her "senator" looked uncomfortable, glancing around at his buddies, perhaps waiting for the ridicule that he would surely get in the locker room later. The nuns in their black habits stood in the background watching us. What were they supposed to be, the Fates?

[2] **enthralled**: captivated or fascinated

Nubian slaves? The dancing girls did their modest little dance to tinny music from their finger cymbals, then the speeches were made. Then the grape vine "wine" was raised in a toast to the Roman Empire we all knew would fall within the week—before finals anyway.

13 All during the program I had been in a state of controlled hysteria.[3] My secret love sat across the room from me looking supremely bored. I watched his every move, taking him in gluttonously. I relished the shadow of his eyelashes on his ruddy cheeks, his pouty lips smirking sarcastically at the ridiculous sight of our little play. Once he slumped down on his chair, and our sergeant-at-arms nun came over and tapped him sharply on the shoulder. He drew himself up slowly, with disdain.[4] I loved his rebellious spirit. I believed myself still invisible to him in my "nothing" status as I looked upon my beloved. But towards the end of the evening, as we stood chanting our farewells in Latin, he looked straight across the room and into my eyes! How did I survive the killing power of those dark pupils? I trembled in a new way. I was not cold—I was burning! Yet I shook from the inside out, feeling light-headed, dizzy.

14 The room began to empty and I headed for the girls' lavatory. I wanted to relish the miracle in silence. I did not think for a minute that anything more would follow. I was satisfied with the enormous favor of a look from my beloved. I took my time, knowing that my father would be waiting outside for me, impatient, perhaps glowing in the dark in his phosphorescent white Navy uniform. The others would ride home. I would walk home with my father, both of us in costume. I wanted as few witnesses as possible. When I could no longer hear the crowds in the hallway, I emerged from the bathroom, still under the spell of those mesmerizing[5] eyes.

15 The lights had been turned off in the hallway and all I could see was the lighted stairwell, at the bottom of which a nun would be stationed. My father would be waiting just outside. I nearly screamed when I felt someone grab me by the waist. But my mouth was quickly covered by someone else's mouth. I was being kissed. My first kiss and I could not even tell who it was. I pulled away to see that face not two inches away from mine. It was he. He smiled down at me. Did I have a silly expression on my face? My glasses felt crooked on my nose. I was unable to move or to speak. More gently, he lifted up my chin and touched his lips to mine. This time I did not forget to enjoy it. Then, like the phantom lover that he was, he walked away into the darkened corridor and disappeared.

16 I don't know how long I stood there. My body was changing right there in the hallway of a Catholic school. My cells were tuning up like musicians in an orchestra, and my heart was a chorus. It was an opera I was composing, and I wanted to stand very still and just listen. But, of

[3] **hysteria:** uncontrollable emotion or fear
[4] **disdain:** a feeling of scorn
[5] **mesmerizing:** hypnotizing

GRAMMAR & USAGE

A **cumulative sentence** is one that makes complete sense if brought to close before its actual ending.

Example: Her "senator" looked uncomfortable, glancing around at his buddies, perhaps waiting for the ridicule that he would surely get in the locker room later.

My Notes

Teacher Notes

GRAMMAR & USAGE EXTENSION

Have students locate another cumulative sentence in paragraph 14 (*I took my time, knowing that my father would be waiting outside for me, impatient, perhaps glowing in the dark in his phosphorescent white Navy uniform*).

You may want to give students time to practice writing their own periodic, cumulative, and balanced sentences. Have students write examples, then share with a classmate to discuss the construction that makes their sentences either periodic, cumulative, or balanced.

Steps:

6 Complete a **shared reading** of Chunk 3. Ask students to consider the philosopher's statement in the last paragraph, and invite them to agree or disagree with the statement.

7 Ask students to return to page 43 and respond to the instructions there. Direct them to complete the mock character interview as described. Remind students to think of questions that relate to the coming-of-age concept; that is, students should write about how the character grows or matures. Use **sharing and responding** to allow students to give and receive feedback. Then instruct students to conduct mock interviews based on their novels as an independent assignment, again focusing on the concept of coming of age.

8 **Learning Log:** At the end of these activities, ask students to complete a Learning Log. Then, invite students to form small groups and use their Learning Logs to identify which strategies are listed most often. Ask students to generate a chart listing these strategies on large butcher paper and post it around the room. As students compare lists, invite them to participate in a whole-class discussion about which strategies are most useful to their learning process and how they might use these strategies again in other classes and with other texts.

9 Revisit the **Essential Question**: What does it mean to "come of age"?

Conversations with Characters

My Notes

Chunk 3

course, I heard my father's voice talking to the nun. I was in trouble if he had to ask about me. I hurried down the stairs making up a story on the way about feeling sick. That would explain my flushed face and it would buy me a little privacy when I got home.

17 The next day Father announced at the breakfast table that he was leaving on a six month tour of Europe with the Navy in a few weeks and, that at the end of the school year my mother, my brother, and I would be sent to Puerto Rico to stay for half a year at Mama's (my mother's mother) house. I was devastated. This was the usual routine for us. We had always gone to Mama's to stay when Father was away for long periods. But this year it was different for me. I was in love, and . . . my heart knocked against my bony chest at this thought . . . he loved me too? I broke into sobs and left the table.

18 In the next week I discovered the inexorable[6] truth about parents. They can actually carry on with their plans right through tears, threats, and the awful spectacle of a teenager's broken heart. My father left me to my mother who impassively packed while I explained over and over that I was at a crucial time in my studies and that if I left my entire life would be ruined. All she would say is, "You are an intelligent girl, you'll catch up." Her head was filled with visions of casa and family reunions, long gossip sessions with her mama and sisters. What did she care that I was losing my one chance at true love?

19 In the meantime I tried desperately to see him. I thought he would look for me too. But the few times I saw him in the hallway, he was always rushing away. It would be long weeks of confusion and pain before I realized that the kiss was nothing but a little trophy for his ego. He had no interest in me other than as his adorer. He was flattered by my silent worship of him, and he had bestowed a kiss on me to please himself, and to fan the flames. I learned a lesson about the battle of the sexes then that I have never forgotten: the object is not always to win, but most times simply to keep your opponent (synonymous at times with "the loved one") guessing.

20 But this is too cynical a view to sustain in the face that overwhelming rush of emotion that is first love. And in thinking back about my own experience with it, I can be objective only to the point where I recall how sweet the anguish was, how caught up in the moment I felt, and how every nerve in my body was involved in this salute to life. Later, much later, after what seemed like an eternity of dragging the weight of unrequited love around with me, I learned to make myself visible and to relish the little battles required to win the greatest prize of all. And much later, I read and understood Camus' statement about the subject that concerns both adolescent and philosopher alike: if love were easy, life would be too simple.

GRAMMAR & USAGE

The final sentence is a **balanced sentence.** A sentence is balanced when ideas of similar weight are expressed in similar grammatical structures or lengths.

[6] **inexorable:** unyielding; not to be persuaded

GRAMMAR & USAGE EXTENSION

- Explain that balanced sentences are another effective way to create emphasis. Ortiz Cofer emphasizes her point by balancing the two ideas in the last sentence.
- Then, have students return to some of their earlier writing and practice varying their sentence types with periodic, cumulative, and balanced sentences.

Creating a Playlist for a Novel

ACTIVITY 1.11

SUGGESTED LEARNING STRATEGIES: Double-Entry Journal, Brainstorming

As your class discusses playlists, respond to the following questions and instructions:

1. Based on your class discussion, what are some of the different types of playlists you or your classmates have on your MP3 players?

2. Consider the texts you have read in this unit. What type of music might the main characters include in a playlist? Keep in mind that music is a sensory experience that often inspires the same kinds of emotions that the words on a page can inspire. Think about the narrator from *Speak*, for example. Would her playlist include rock songs, slow songs, instrumental music, or even angry music? Why? Now, focus on one of the texts you've read, and create a possible playlist for the main character. Write your ideas and explanation below.

Name of Text:

Possible Playlist:

Explanation:

3. Now, look back at your double-entry journal and character interview for the novel you are reading. Create a playlist for the main character. Then write a short piece summarizing an interview with the character in which the character explains the reasons these songs are included in his or her playlist. Use language from the book that is typical of the character's voice.

4 Direct students to their **double-entry journals** and mock interviews from Activity 1.10. Ask them to brainstorm a short list of songs that the character might logically include in a playlist. Have students create this list of song titles and then write a short interview with the character in which the character explains the reasons the songs are included in the playlist.

ACTIVITY 1.11

Creating a Playlist for a Novel

Materials:

- Independent novels

Purpose:

- To analyze the nuances of a literary character
- To extend understanding of characterization by making text-to-world connections via music

Steps:

1 **Activate prior knowledge** by asking student volunteers to share information about playlists they might have on their MP3 players. Ask them to mention what kinds of songs they include, the differences between some playlists and others, and also the differences between their playlists and those of their siblings, friends, or parents.

2 Discuss the reasons for creating playlists and the ways that playlists can establish or maintain a mood. Then, ask students to consider what kinds of songs might be included on a playlist for characters in some of the texts they have read in this unit. For example, if the narrator (Melinda) from ***Speak*** were creating a playlist for her walk through the cafeteria, what songs might she include? If a playlist were created to accompany "First Love," what songs might be appropriate? As a class, **brainstorm** songs that might be appropriate for the main characters. Spend some time discussing why these songs might work. (Songs might be included based on the music, the lyrics, or both.) Have students take notes on their page.

3 If Internet access is available, consider visiting a few authors' Web sites and examining the playlists they describe as befitting their novels. Stephanie Meyer, author of the popular Twilight series, is one author who includes playlists for her novels, which she describes as being "the music I hear in my head while reading the book."

ACTIVITY 1.12
Viewing an Interview

Materials:

- Teacher-provided videotaped interview

Purpose:

- To summarize questions and answers from an interview
- To classify interview questions as open-ended and follow-up
- To create open-ended follow-up questions

Steps:

TEACHER TO TEACHER For this activity, you can record something from your local or school news or use a video interview of an author or famous person that you might have in your media center or that you might have online access to. As students watch the video, they will clarify their understanding of follow-up questions. You will probably want to show only a few questions from the entire interview, but be sure to select a segment that includes follow-up questions.

1 First, have students practice writing follow-up questions. Follow a **think-pair-share** process so that students can hear multiple ideas for follow-up questions and can get feedback on their own.

ACTIVITY 1.12 Viewing an Interview

SUGGESTED LEARNING STRATEGIES: Marking the Text, Notetaking, Think-Pair-Share

Pretending to interview a character is easier than interviewing a real person. In a mock interview, you are in complete control. In a real interview, you never know what your interviewee will say. You may have carefully planned questions only to find that the interviewee wants to talk about something different altogether. Although you do want to keep some sense of focus in an interview, sometimes the best thing to do is to follow the lead of your interviewee. That's why it is important to ask good follow-up questions.

Follow-up questions do exactly what the name implies: They follow up on something the interviewee has said. For example:

Q: What was the best thing that happened to you in high school?

A: I guess that would be when my boyfriend broke up with me at the prom.

Follow-up Q: That doesn't sound like a very good thing. Why was it the best thing that happened to you?

You might not have anticipated the answer to that question, but pursuing that topic could lead to some interesting information about your interviewee. That's why you need to be flexible about your planned questions and allow for follow-up questions. Here are a few ways you could follow up on an answer:

- Why do you think that?
- That sounds interesting. Could you tell me more about it?
- What happened next?
- How has that influenced your life?

1. Practice writing follow-up questions to these questions and answers:

   Q: What kind of friends did you hang out with in high school?

   A: Mostly jocks, like me.

   Follow-up Q:

   Q: What is your worst memory from high school?

   A: A kid I knew was badly injured in a car accident.

   Follow-up Q:

2. Make up your own question and answer using the subjunctive form to ask an interviewee about doubts or wishes the person may have had. Include a good follow-up question.

   Q:

   A:

   Follow-up Q:

48 SpringBoard® English Textual Power™ Level 4

© 2011 College Board. All rights reserved.

ACTIVITY 1.12 continued

3. Your teacher will show you a video recording of an interview. As you watch, take notes below, writing down all the questions asked, and summarizing the answers given.

Interviewer:	**Interviewee:**
Questions:	**Answers:**

What seems to be the focus of this interview?

ACTIVITY 1.12 Continued

Steps:

2 As a **visual prompt**, show students the video recording of an interview. Have them **take notes** on the chart on this page. Stop after every answer so students can write down the questions asked and at least a summary of the answers.

ACTIVITY 1.12 *Continued*

Steps:

3 Next, ask students to use three different colors to **mark the text** of their notes. They should identify the new questions and the follow-up questions, and they should write any follow-up questions they wish the interviewer had asked. Ask them to think about why the interviewer might not have asked those particular questions.

4 Finish by asking students to rate the interview and complete a written reflection on the importance of asking good follow-up questions.

ACTIVITY 1.12 *continued*

Viewing an Interview

4. Now that you have watched the interview, go back to your notes and identify the kinds of questions:

- In one color, highlight the first question and any questions that start a new line of questioning.
- In a second color, highlight the follow-up questions.
- In a third color, write any follow-up questions you think the interviewer could have asked but didn't.

5. Choose one of the questions you think the interviewer could have asked but didn't. Why do you think the interviewer didn't ask this (or a similar) question?

6. Circle the number that best describes your evaluation of this interview.

1 = I learned a lot about the person being interviewed.

2 = I learned some things about the person being interviewed, but I wanted to learn more.

3 = I did not learn very much about the person being interviewed.

Why did you choose the rating you did?

7. Write a reflection on the importance of asking follow-up questions.

Reading an Interview Narrative

ACTIVITY **1.13**

SUGGESTED LEARNING STRATEGIES: **Quickwrite, Word Map**

You have seen interviews written in the Q and A format, but many interview narratives are not presented in this way. As you read "Bethany Only Looking Ahead," consider the ways in which the writer describes Bethany, captures her voice, considers a significant incident in her life, and conveys the significance to the reader.

After reading and discussing the interview narrative with a partner or group, answer the questions below.

Name of Interviewee:	**Name of Interviewer:**
What seems to be the focus of this interview?	
Describe the voice of the interviewee.	
What does the writer do that makes the voice of the interviewee clear?	

Most interview narratives present both **direct** and **indirect quotations.**

- **Direct quotations** are *word-for-word* quotations. Direct quotations should be written inside quotation marks. Here are some examples:

  "Have another slice of pie," my mother said.

  "No thank you," I replied. "I can't eat another bite."

- **Indirect quotations** *summarize* and are not written inside quotation marks. For example:

  My mother offered me another slice of pie.

  I told her that I could not eat another bite.

Use one color to highlight the direct quotations in "Bethany Only Looking Ahead." Then use a different color to highlight the indirect quotations.

ACTIVITY 1.13

Reading an Interview Narrative

Materials:

- Vocabulary Notebooks

Purpose:

- To identify aspects of voice in an interview write-up
- To recognize the effect of direct and indirect quotations in conveying voice
- To review punctuation of quotations

Steps:

TEACHER TO TEACHER Students have been exposed to the Q and A format of interview narratives, but now they need to examine an interview narrative that goes beyond Q and A.

1 As students read the article, "Bethany Only Looking Ahead," remind them to take notes about the focus of the interview, the voice of the interviewee, and the language the writer uses to describe the interviewee.

Steps:

2 Suggest that students perform a **shared reading** of the interview narrative with a partner.

3 When the partners have finished reading, ask them to determine the focus of the interview. Allow students to discuss the focus with their partners.

4 Ask students to identify what information is provided in this text that would not be provided in a simple Q and A transcript of an interview. Lead them to identify these three descriptive categories:

- How is the interviewee speaking? "She seems hesitant to go further, but it's just that she's said it all so many times before."
- How is the interviewee acting? "Bethany's right hand is fidgety during the interview, toying with a lacquered chopstick that she uses to arrange her hair."
- How is the interviewee looking? "She looks fine. Surfer's blond hair frames lively eyes and a ready smile. A gold and diamond pendant around her neck is in the shape of a surfboard with a bite taken out of it — looking much like her board did after the attack."

5 Have students reread the text with their partners, annotating examples of each category. As a class, discuss the impact of these descriptions on students' perceptions of Bethany.

Reading an Interview Narrative

My Notes

Article

BETHANY *only looking ahead*

by Jan TenBruggencate

KILAUEA, Kaua'i — Three weeks after a "gray blur" bit off her left arm, Bethany Hamilton is putting her life back together.

The stitches covering the wound caused by the 14-foot tiger shark were to come out yesterday afternoon, and she was eager for her doctor's permission to get back in the water. Bethany is still listed among the top-ranked women surfers, and she insists that she'll be back on the waves soon.

The 13-year-old Princeville girl woke up at 5 a.m. on Halloween morning, eager to surf the reef at Tunnels because the waves had been good nearby the night before. She had cereal for breakfast before her mother drove her to the beach. Her dad was going into the hospital for knee surgery.

Bethany paddled out with her best friend, Alana Blanchard, and Alana's brother, Byron, and father, Holt.

They surfed for about a half-hour and she caught maybe 10 waves before she took a rest, lying on her surfboard parallel to shore, her right hand holding the board, her left dangling in the water.

"We never saw it, or anything, before it bit. It shook me. It lasted about three seconds long. All I saw was, like, a gray blur.

"It let go and I just looked at the red blood in the water."

Holt Blanchard and his son pushed Bethany onto a small wave, then they dragged her in the water, one or the other of them paddling while she held on to their board or their shorts with her remaining hand. When they got into an area shallow enough to stand, the elder Blanchard wrapped his rashguard around her arm. As they reached shore, he used a surfboard leash as a tourniquet.

Until that moment, Bethany had been conscious.

"I was talking. I was praying. I don't know the exact words. I just asked for help," she said.

She passed out as she came ashore, but came to again quickly.

"I woke up and they had a lot of towels on me. I was thinking that the ambulance should hurry up," she said.

She recalls details uncannily, like firefighters asking about the kind of cars her parents drove, like her asking ambulance attendants where they were during the 30-mile ride to the hospital.

And she remembers her mother, trying to keep up with the ambulance to follow her daughter to the hospital and being pulled over by a police officer for speeding. Ambulance attendants radioed the police to explain the situation and her mother was free to go.

At Wilcox Memorial Hospital, Tom Hamilton was hauled out of the operating room to make room for his daughter. He already had been sedated for his scheduled knee operation, and was not able to see Bethany before she underwent surgery.

He got the knee surgery later, and yesterday afternoon, he and Bethany were to have their respective stitches out at the same time.

Within hours of the shark's bite, her story became an international sensation. The family was barraged by media and well-wishers. Friends who saw that they were too fragile to handle the stress stepped up and began trying to manage the situation.

Part-time Kaua'i resident Roy Hofstetter, a Los Angeles entertainment agent, was asked to help handle the media. He is making arrangements for Bethany to be paid for many of her appearances to help secure her future. Although the family has medical insurance, there will be additional uncovered medical costs, including the development of artificial limbs that will have to be replaced as Bethany grows.

Bethany seems to handle the turmoil with aplomb. She credits church and kin for her personal strength and resilience.

"Strong faith and strong family helps me, does it for me," said Bethany, whose family attends North Shore Christian Church.

She seems hesitant to go further, but it's just that she's said it all so many times before. She looks at her dad.

"I wish we had recorded my answers, so we could just play them back," she said.

To some extent, she has been insulated, spending most of her time since the injury with family and a few close girlfriends, including best friend Alana, and that feels normal. Yet, undeniably, life is different.

"Everything's changed. If you just think about it, there's all these people saying, 'How are you feeling?' I just wish I could say, 'I'm fine. You don't have to ask.' But then, I guess I'd ask, too."

GRAMMAR & USAGE

Commas help clarify meaning. When a phrase or a clause is not essential (**nonrestrictive**) to the meaning of a sentence, set it off with commas. However, if it is essential (**restrictive**), do not use commas. Look at these nonrestrictive phrases:

Appositive phrase: Part-time Kaua'i resident Roy Hofstetter, **a Los Angeles entertainment agent**, was asked....

Participial phrase: ...there will be additional uncovered medical costs, **including the development of artificial limbs,**....

The commas indicate that the information in these phrases is additional but not necessary. In your writing, use commas to make clear the distinction between restrictive and nonrestrictive phrases.

ACTIVITY 1.13 Continued

Teacher Notes

GRAMMAR & USAGE EXTENSION

- Explain that *restrictive* elements limit or qualify meaning; they are therefore necessary and are not set off by commas. This concept applies to appositive phrases, participial phrases, and adjective clauses. Students will examine restrictive and nonrestrictive clauses in Activity 5.10.
- To further explore the effect of commas, you might have students explain the difference in meaning in these two examples:

  Bethany surfed with her friend Alana Blanchard.
  Bethany surfed with her friend, Alana Blanchard.

Steps:

6 Have students work individually on a **quickwrite** in which they describe the voice of the interviewee. Allow volunteers to share their descriptions.

7 Then lead the class in a discussion of the methods writers can use to make the voice of the interviewee clear to the readers. Ask students to identify examples of direct and indirect quotations in the text (some are highlighted in the Teacher Version). You might need to review with students how to punctuate direct and indirect quotations and paraphrasing.

Reading an Interview Narrative

My Notes

She looks fine. Surfer's blond hair frames lively eyes and a ready smile. A gold and diamond pendant around her neck is in the shape of a surfboard with a bite taken out of it — looking much like her board did after the attack. It was a gift from a friend who prefers to remain anonymous, she said.

Bethany's right hand is fidgety during the interview, toying with a lacquered chopstick that she uses to arrange her hair. At her left shoulder is a mound of flesh where an arm used to be, a semicircle of scar tissue closing the wound. Bethany appears comfortable with herself, and makes no attempt to shield the injury from view.

This slim, strong teenager doesn't appear to dwell too much on the loss of her arm. It's done, and she said she's ready to move on.

"Consciously or unconsciously, she's doing a lot of stuff on her own," Tom Hamilton said.

"I saw her sitting on the floor, cutting oranges and tangerines, using her feet to hold them."

Bethany is hoping to salvage her semester at school, but it will take hard work. She has been recovering for three weeks, and a couple of weeks of Mainland visits are scheduled in December for national media appearances. The family is talking to her teachers at her online charter school, the Myron B. Thompson Academy, and they're working on bringing her up to speed.

Once she and her dad get their doctor's approval to return to the water, Tom Hamilton said, "we'll probably do some workouts together in the local pool."

When they're ready, it's on to the surf — something they haven't been able to do together for several months because of Tom's bad knee.

"We look forward to surfing together," Tom Hamilton said.

Bethany has a specific goal when she paddles back into the ocean.

"When I first go surfing, I want to make sure I catch the first wave myself. Then, they can help me," she said.

© 2011 College Board. All rights reserved.

54 SpringBoard® English Textual Power™ Level 4

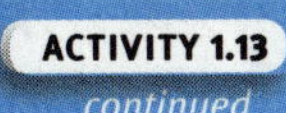

Strategies Learning Log

Name of strategy:	
Purpose of strategy:	
How strategy was used:	
How strategy helped you make meaning from the text, create a text, or orally present a text:	
When you would use this strategy again:	

Strategies Learning Log

Name of strategy:	
Purpose of strategy:	
How strategy was used:	
How strategy helped you make meaning from the text, create a text, or orally present a text:	
When you would use this strategy again:	

Steps:

8 **Learning Log:** Following the format of previous activities, allow time for students to complete another Learning Log and reflect on strategies used throughout the preceding activities.

9 Direct students to revisit their **Vocabulary Notebooks** and elaborate on the concept of ***voice.***

ACTIVITY 1.14
Interviewing Together

Purpose:

- To conduct an interview
- To summarize, paraphrase, and quote
- To synthesize answers and create a report of a Q and A interview

Steps:

1 In this activity, your students will collectively interview a person who has attended high school. You will need to arrange this interview in advance, or you can allow your class to interview you.

2 Provide students with a little background information on the interviewee, which they will include in the K column of their **KWL chart**.

3 Give students time to fill in the W column and write questions they might ask to discover what they want to know. Emphasize that these questions will be used to begin the interview and to move it forward, if needed. Most of the questions they ask should be follow-up questions.

4 Using a **think-pair-share** have students share the three questions they thought of to start the interview. As a class, choose one question to open the interview.

5 When the interviewee is ready, proceed with the interview. Begin with the question the class has chosen, and then have students raise their hands to ask follow-up questions. Remind them that they should only start a new line of questioning if the last one seems finished or if the interviewee seems ready to move on.

ACTIVITY 1.14

Interviewing Together

SUGGESTED LEARNING STRATEGIES: **Drafting, KWL Chart, Marking the Text, Notetaking, Think-Pair-Share**

Your teacher will arrange for your class to interview someone. Your focus for the interview is to find out about an incident that happened while this person was in high school so that you can write about it.

1. Begin by filling in the first two columns of the KWL chart:

Interviewee's name:		
K **What I Know**	**W** **What I Want to Know**	**L** **What I Learned**

2. Based on what you already know, either from your own knowledge of the person or from what your teacher tells you, make a list of questions that you think might get and keep the interview flowing.

-
-
-

Your class will work together to choose the best starting question.

3. During the group interview, take notes on your own paper. Include the questions asked and the interviewee's answers. You will work with a partner. One of you should capture quotes verbatim, while the other summarizes important information from the answers. Remember, the most important information usually comes from follow-up questions, so ask good follow-up questions.

At the end of the interview, be sure to thank the interviewee. Being interviewed by a group of teenagers is not easy.

6 It is very important for students to **take notes** during the interview. You may want to have them work in pairs so that one person can take verbatim notes while the other summarizes what is said. In addition, both students should take note of the three descriptive categories identified in Activity 1.13 (How is the interviewee speaking, behaving, and looking?)

7 At the end of the interview, have students thank the interviewee.

continued

4. Now that the interview is complete, go back to your KWL chart and fill in the L column, explaining what you learned during the interview. You may need to write this on your own paper.
5. Look over the notes that you took during the interview.
   - In one color, highlight the questions that begin a new topic or direction in the questioning.
   - In a second color, highlight the questions that follow up on a previous answer.
   - In a third color, write any follow-up questions that you might have asked, but you either did not have the chance or you did not think of them until later.

   Now look at the L column of your KWL chart. How much of what you learned came from follow-up questions?
6. Circle the number that describes your evaluation of the interview:

   1 = I learned a lot about the person being interviewed.

   2 = I learned some things about the person being interviewed, but I wanted to learn more.

   3 = I did not learn very much about the person being interviewed.

Writing Prompt: Using your notes, write a narrative of the interview on another sheet of paper. Try to capture the voice and personality of the interviewee as you retell his or her coming-of-age experience. Following the model of "Bethany Only Looking Ahead," you can convey the personality of the interviewee by these methods:

- describing how the interviewee is speaking, acting, and looking
- describing the setting of the interview
- conveying the significance of the events discussed
- including both direct and indirect quotations.

ACTIVITY 1.14 *Continued*

Steps:

8 Have students fill in the L column of their KWL charts. Then, direct students to **mark the text** using three different colored pens or pencils to identify the new questions and the follow-up questions, and to indicate any follow-up questions they wish they had asked.

9 Finally, return students to their interview partners and ask them to respond to the Writing Prompt. As they **draft** a narrative of the interview, instruct them to include examples from each of the three descriptive categories, as well as direct and indirect quotations.

Writing Workshops

Before student write Embedded Assessment 1, you may want to review the writing process by using Workshop 1, Writing Process, to guide students through the stages of writing.

ACTIVITY 1.15
Planning an Interview

Purpose:

- To produce a plan for an interview

Steps:

1 To successfully complete the interview process, students will need your guidance in completing each of the four steps outlined in this activity. Step One (brainstorming a list of potential interviewees) can be completed during class or for homework. Step Two (arranging the interview) must be completed for homework. Step Three (writing down the appointment) and Step Four (**brainstorming** a list of questions) may happen in class or for homework.

2 It is essential that you give students a timeline for this process, but allow them a reasonable deadline for conducting the interview.

ACTIVITY 1.15
Planning an Interview

SUGGESTED LEARNING STRATEGIES: Brainstorming

For Embedded Assessment 1, you will conduct an interview and write a narrative in which you present that interview. You have probably noticed that conducting an interview takes a good deal of planning. You need to begin thinking about the interview you will conduct.

The focus of your interview will be to find out about a person's overall experience during high school, and to present at least one important incident during that time that influenced the interviewee's coming of age.

Step One

Make a list of people you might be able to interview. Include only people with whom you could have a face-to-face meeting before the assignment is due.

Name of Person I Might Be Able to Interview	Why I Would Like to Interview This Person About His or Her Experience in High School

Step Two

Contact the people on your list to schedule your interview with one of them. Let them know why you are conducting the interview and that some portions of it may be shared with your classmates.

Step Three

Write the details of your appointment:

- I have arranged to interview:
- Date the interview is scheduled:
- Time:
- Place:

Teacher Notes

Step Four

Brainstorm a list of questions and possible follow-up questions you might ask during the interview. Keep in mind the focus of your interview as you think of potential questions.

1.

2.

3.

4.

5.

6.

Remember, you probably will not ask all of these questions. Once your conversation begins to flow, you will ask follow-up questions. It is important, though, to walk into your interview with a list of questions to start the interview and to keep it going.

Embedded Assessment 1

Presenting an Interview Narrative

College Board Standards and Objectives

S2 Speaking in Interpersonal Contexts (S2.1)
PE Mappings: S2.1-2.4

L3 Listening for Diverse Purposes (L3.1, L3.3)
PE Mappings: L3.1-2.4, L3.1-2.4

W1 Rhetorical Analysis and Planning (W1.1)
PE Mappings: W1.1-1.4; W1.1-2.4

W2 Generating Content (W2.1Cr, W2.2 Cr)
PE Mappings: W2.1-1.4Cr, W2.2-1.4Cr, W2.2-4.4Cr

W3 Drafting (W3.1 Cr, W3.2 Cr)
PE Mappings: W3.1-1.4Cr, W3.1-2.4Cr, W3.1-3.4Cr, W3.2-1.4Cr

W4 Evaluating and Revising Texts (W4.1 Cr, W4.2Cr)
PE Mappings: W4.1-1.4Cr, W4.2-1.4Cr

W5 Editing to Present Technically Sound Texts (W5.1, W5.2, W5.4)
PE Mappings: W5.1-1.4, W5.2-1.4, W5.4-1.4

Steps:

1 Suggest that students review the Scoring Guide criteria to be clear on what they need to achieve in the interview. They might also want to review their interview questions to be sure that the questions will lead to good information.

2 Give students a deadline by which to complete their interviews, or, if you have already done so, remind them of the date.

3 Urge students to follow the format suggested as they draft the interview narrative. To maintain the informal tone of an interview, you may want to encourage students to reproduce contractions in verbatim quotations, pay attention to correct usage of apostrophes in possessives, verb tenses, and pronouns that maintain agreement. Remind students that verbatim quotes may contain incorrect grammar, and they should use the speaker's words as spoken.

Embedded Assessment 1

Presenting an Interview Narrative

SUGGESTED LEARNING STRATEGIES: **Drafting, Peer Editing**

Assignment

Your assignment is to interview a person who has attended high school and to write an interview narrative that effectively portrays the voice and experience of the interviewee.

Steps

Interview

1. You have already arranged a time and place to meet with the person whom you will interview, and you have already created a list of questions you might ask. Before you begin the interview, thank the person for giving you the opportunity to interview him or her. If you want to tape the interview, ask for permission before you begin.
2. Start your interview with one of your questions regarding the person's experience in high school. Then try to let the interview flow like a conversation as much as possible. Remember that asking good follow-up questions is more effective than asking all the questions on your list.
3. Try to get the person to describe at least one incident from his or her high school experience that influenced his or her coming of age. When you feel that you have adequate information, you can begin to draw the interview to a close.
4. As you conduct the interview, remember to take descriptive notes as well as recording the conversation (if you have obtained permission from the interviewee).

Prewriting

5. As soon as possible after the interview, read over your notes and add anything that you can remember. Fill in gaps in your description of the person and the way he or she seemed to feel during the interview. It is important to do this as close to the interview as possible so that it is still fresh in your memory.

Drafting

6. Write a draft of your report.
    - In your introduction, include a description of the person you have interviewed.
    - In your body paragraphs, tell about the person's overall experience in high school. Be sure to describe in detail at least one incident from the person's high school days. Try to use vivid imagery, careful diction, and a mix of direct and indirect quotations to convey a sense of the interviewee's voice in your narrative.
    - In your conclusion, you may want to predict how you can use what you learned from the interview as you experience high school yourself.

Revising and Editing for Publication

7. Share your draft with a partner. Consult the Scoring Guide to revise for the following:
   - Vivid descriptions of the incident and interviewee
   - Clear use of direct and indirect quotes to convey the interviewee's voice
   - Sentence variety that incorporates various sentence structures such as balanced, periodic, and cumulative sentences (Grammar & Usage, pages 43, 45, 46) as well as the subjunctive verb form to express doubt or possibility as appropriate (Grammar & Usage, page 28).
   - Proper punctuation and capitalization of quotations
8. Use your available resources (e.g., spell check, dictionaries, grammar references) to edit for conventions and prepare your narrative for publication. If you are writing your narrative by hand, remember to use legible handwriting.

TECHNOLOGY TIP If you have access to word processing software, use its spell-check and grammar-check features. Be aware, though, that the spell-check program may not recognize proper nouns. The grammar-check feature will often highlight sentences with passive verbs. Look carefully at the suggestions offered, and determine how best to revise your writing to present a document ready for publication.

Embedded Assessment 1

Continued

Steps:

4 As students read each other's drafts, ask them to pay careful attention to the points listed.

5 Instruct students to turn in their interview questions and notes along with their interview narratives.

Embedded Assessment 1
Continued

Scoring Guide

When you score this Embedded Assessment, you may wish to download and print a copy of the Scoring Guide from SpringBoard Online. In this way, you can have a copy to mark for each student's work.

Embedded Assessment 1

Presenting an Interview Narrative

SCORING GUIDE

Scoring Criteria	Exemplary	Proficient	Emerging
Ideas	The narrative insightfully describes at least one incident from the person's high school experience which influenced his or her coming of age with careful attention to detail. The writer vividly uses examples from the three descriptive categories.	The narrative describes an incident from the person's high school experience clearly and effectively. The writer mentions examples from the three descriptive categories.	An incident may not be described in detail and little to no attention is paid to the descriptive categories.
Organization	The narrative is multi-paragraphed and organized in a way that enhances the reader's understanding.	The narrative is multi-paragraphed and organized in a logical fashion.	The narrative may not be multi-paragraphed and/ or organized in a logical fashion.
Use of Language	Vivid imagery, careful diction, and effective use of direct and indirect quotes convey a strong sense of the interviewee's voice.	Clear imagery, diction, and use of quotations convey a sense of the interviewee's voice.	The voice of the interviewee is not clear. Imagery, diction, and use of quotations are inappropriate or missing.
Conventions	Writing is virtually error-free. The writer uses proper punctuation and capitalization to smoothly embed quotations from the interview into text.	Though some errors may appear, they do not seriously impede readability. The writer properly punctuates and capitalizes quotations in the text.	Frequent errors in standard writing conventions interfere with the meaning. Quotations from the interview are not properly incorporated into the text.
Evidence of Writing Process	The writing demonstrates thoughtful planning, significant revision, and careful editing in preparing a publishable draft.	The writing demonstrates planning, revision, and editing in preparing a publishable draft.	The writing lacks evidence of planning, revision, and/ or editing. The draft is not ready for publication.
Additional Criteria			

Comments: ______________________________

Learning Focus:

How Can You Appeal to Readers?

Consider a typical week in your life. How many decisions do you think you make that are affected by advertisers' attempts to persuade you? What areas of your life are most influenced by advertising? Now, think about your reading habits and the reading habits of your peers. Is it possible to use the power of advertising to influence teenagers' reading choices? The next activities give you an opportunity to find out.

You have already studied **voice**, **coming of age**, and interviewing, and you have completed or almost completed reading a coming-of-age novel. Now, you will continue your interviewing skills by interviewing peers about their reading preferences. Then, you'll review **advertising techniques** that you encountered in earlier grades. In addition to advertising techniques, you'll learn about the **rhetorical appeals** of **ethos**, **pathos**, and **logos** and the way they work together with **advertising techniques** to persuade an audience. Finally, you will put all of these pieces together as you work with a group to create an advertising campaign for your novel. Can you use advertising techniques and rhetorical appeals to persuade your peers to read your book? Here's your chance to discover just how persuasive you can be.

LEARNING FOCUS:

How Can You Appeal to Readers?

Previewing Embedded Assessment 2

To preview the skills and knowledge necessary for success on Embedded Assessment 2, instruct students to locate the Assignment and Scoring Guide (pp. 80–83). Guide students through a **close reading** of the prompts, steps, and Scoring Guide criteria.

Steps:

1 Read the Learning Focus with students or have them read independently. **Activate prior knowledge** by having students **mark the text** and highlight words or concepts that are familiar (what they know). They might use a question mark to indicate content that is unfamiliar (what they do not know but want to learn).

2 Engage students in a whole class discussion. You may **revisit** the **KWHL chart** you created at the beginning of the unit to discover what students have learned.

ACTIVITY 1.16

Teens and Books: What Are the Influences?

Purpose:

- To design, conduct, and interpret a peer survey
- To compare and contrast current issues affecting teens' reading choices
- To analyze and create a persuasive text

Steps:

1 Conduct a **think-pair-share** in which students discuss books they have read in the past year that were not assigned. Ask them to discuss what kind of book each was, how they heard about it, and what caused them to read it. If students have not read any unassigned books, allow them to consider what else they might have read (magazines, blogs, etc.).

2 In a shared discussion, focus students' attention on the variety of things they read. Then, ask students to **brainstorm** questions to ask peers outside this class about their reading habits. You might generate a class list of initial questions about the types of reading students do, whether their reading habits have changed over time, and whether or not they discuss books with anyone.

3 Ask students to conduct brief mini-interviews with at least five peers and bring in their notes to share. In the course of the mini-interviews, students can generate their own follow-up questions. Ask them to take notes about the individuals they interview as well as the responses to the questions.

ACTIVITY 1.16

Teens and Books: What Are the Influences?

SUGGESTED LEARNING STRATEGIES: **Drafting, Marking the Text, Notetaking, Think-Pair-Share, Brainstorming**

1. Think about the kinds of things you read outside of class. List the titles of some of the books or other texts you've read recently.

2. Based on your list and your class discussion, create a list of questions you can use to interview some of your peers who are not in this class about the kinds of books and other texts they read. Be sure your questions are open-ended, and be sure to ask them about their preferences as well as what influences their reading choices.

List of interview questions:

3. After conducting your interviews, compare your findings with those of the members of your group. Synthesize your findings and create a chart or graph that displays your results for the rest of your classmates.

4. Read the following article about marketing books to teens. Take notes on the types of advertising formats that advertisers consider effective for teen audiences. While you are reading, make text-to-self connections, and take notes in the margin on whether or not you agree with the points made in the article.

5. Finally, synthesize information from the peer interviews, group discussions, facts from the article, and your own notes to write a response to the following prompt:

Judith Rosen's article states that teens said their "ideal" activity is reading a book. For the majority of teens, do you think reading a book is their ideal activity? Explain why you agree or disagree, and cite specific examples to support your position.

4 Place students in small groups to share their interview findings and synthesize the group's information. Suggest that they share a little about the individuals they interviewed and see if they notice any patterns regarding the reading habits of males, females, athletes, freshmen, upperclassmen, etc. Ask each group to create a bar graph or chart that captures the group's collective findings. Allow groups to post their charts and view other groups' charts.

5 Ask students to synthesize the information from their own and others' interviews and **draft** a response that answers the following questions: What are my peers reading? How are my peers' reading habits similar to or different from my own?

Article

AS IF! Marketing to Older Teens

by Judith Rosen

U.S. teens controlled an estimated $169 billion in disposable income last year—or $91 per week per teen—according to a study by Teenage Research Unlimited. But publishers trying to grab a share of that cash face stiff challenges. "Teens are very savvy and they have a cynical radar. Marketers have to get around that with marketing that doesn't seem like marketing," says Boston College sociology professor Juliet Schor, author of *Born to Buy: The Commercialized Culture and the New Consumerism* (Scribner).

Still, there's reason to think teens could be enticed to buy a lot more books, says Hollywood-based youth culture expert Sharon Lee, co-president and co-founder of market research firm Look-Look Inc. The firm did a recent study in which teens cited writing as one of their main creative outlets. They also said their "ideal" activity is reading a book, followed by exercising and shopping. That's the "ideal." In reality, according to the study, teens are much more likely to spend their free time surfing the Internet, watching TV and listening to music. "I look at as a huge opportunity," Lee says. "The desire to read, the desire to write, the desire to engage with words is there."

Seeking to translate that desire into sales, publishers are using a variety of strategies, ranging from the tech-heavy to traditional-with-a-twist—all tailored to reach those wary but free-spending 14-to-19-year-old consumers.

Cell Phones

Hoping that teens who walk around with cell phones pressed to their ears could be persuaded to sit down with their noses in a book, HarperCollins is running a text-messaging promotion starting next week for Meg Cabot, of Princess Diaries fame. Teen readers can get news on the mobile about the release of her new novel, *Ready or Not: An All-American Girl Novel* (July), and about her monthly online chats. There's also a cell phone screensaver promoting Cabot's books, as well as a ring tone with her voice.

Harper is not the first to try a dial-up campaign. In January Random House used text messaging to promote the paperback edition of the third book in Ann Brashares's Sisterhood of the Traveling Pants series, *Girls in Pants* (Delacorte, Jan.). "The biggest shift in marketing is how important online marketing has become," says Random House Children's Books v-p of marketing Daisy Kline. "We think of driving traffic to our site as hanging onto a reader a little bit longer and having an opportunity of introducing a reader

My Notes

Consider text features (italics, headings, paragraphing) that assist you in understanding and organizing information.

ACTIVITY 1.16 *Continued*

Steps:

6 Ask students to read and **take notes** on "As If! Marketing to Older Teens." Students can **mark the text** and use the My Notes column to note specific ways items are marketed to teens, making connections to their own lives as they read. Then, ask students to compare the information in the article to their peer interview findings. Conduct a class discussion about the role of advertising in the lives of teenagers. Ask them to consider where they view ads, what kinds of ads they view, and how those ads influence their reading habits.

7 Once students have marked the text for understanding, have them respond to the writing prompt on page 64. They will use this response as a draft to revise in the next activity.

Teacher Notes

Teens and Books: What Are the Influences?

My Notes

to another author." Random credits the cell phone promotion, coupled with advance movie trailers for the film, with sending traffic to the Sisterhood Web site soaring 400% higher in the first quarter of the year than during the previous three months.

Playing the Net

After years of experimenting, publishers and authors have become more sophisticated about using the Internet to reach readers. "A few years ago, it was all about developing a presence," says Kira Glass, associate director of Internet marketing for Harcourt. "Now you are budgeting for advertising on the Internet and keyword searches."

For authors, the Web provides a way to connect directly with fans. When asked what prompted her to market her books via her LaurenMyracle.com Web site, the author responded with a question of her own, "Am I marketing? I'd never want to be an Amway salesman for my own books. My job is to tell the best stories I can and to let people know that writers are just people." Myracle plans to IM (instant message) with her teen fans this fall to promote *ttfn* (Ta-ta for Now) (Abrams).

Thirty thousand teens have signed up to receive information on Cabot's books through HarperCollins's Author Tracker e-mail program. In addition, Cabot receives as many as 200 e-mails a day when one of her books is first released, and young people avidly read her blog. "I was very resistant at first to keep a blog," says Cabot. "I thought it would take too much time from my 'real' writing. After I found out how much it increased traffic to my site, I was like 'Um, okay.'" Cabot even started her own online book club—with 8,500 members—and many selections are her own titles.

Phyllis Reynolds Naylor, author of the Alice McKinley series, posts e-mails from young people who look to her as an Ann Landers for teens. "E-mails come to the Web site, and I read them every day," says Naylor, 72, who spends about an hour a day answering teen queries. "They tell me that they feel they can ask me anything. They're terrified of doctors and pelvic exams. They say, 'Even though I love my mother I'm too embarrassed to ask...'"

Giving CDs a Spin

CDs are hardly cutting-edge technology, but publishers are still finding new ways to use them to reach teen consumers. This spring Harper produced 60,000 CD samplers, with 10 authors reading selections from upcoming titles. The CDs, which were tucked inside booklets about the Harper list, were mailed to book and audio buyers and to consumers who ordered from the Alloy catalogue. Harper is also starting to introduce bonus CDs packaged with books. For example, bestselling novelist Louise Rennison's May release, *Then He Ate My Boy Entrancers*, contains a "tell-all" CD on which Rennison answers fan questions.

Teacher Notes

Where the Teens Are

Offline, marketers are following this simple rule: take your message to where the teens are. Tara Lewis, v-p, global marketing for Disney Global Children's Books has seen a jump in sales from viral marketing, such as providing tee-shirts, stickers and posters to Ned Vizzini to promote the hardcover edition of his book *Be More Chill* (Miramax/Hyperion, paperback Sept.) at rock concerts. This fall, she's working on finding a way to ensure that Bat Mitzvah attendees who use the Ladies Room find postcards for Fiona Rosenbloom's *You Are SO Not Invited to My Bat Mitzvah!* (Hyperion, Sept.).

Last spring Abrams staffers distributed copies of two April releases from its year-old Amulet paperback YA line, Lauren Myracle's *ttyl* (Talk to You Later) and William Sleator's *The Boy Who Couldn't Die*, to teens gathered outside MTV's Total Request Live in Times Square. That's not to say that tried-and-true book promotions don't work. Amulet's Jason Wells believes that the 700 book displays for two of Myracle's titles helped push *ttyl* onto bestseller lists.

Scholastic reaches out to young people via marketing partnerships with teen catalogue companies like dELiA*s and Alloy, as well as through clothing and jewelry stores. "If you have the right property you can get into new accounts like Urban Outfitters or Hot Topic," says Scholastic's Jennifer Pasanen, who has placed Jim Benton's *It's Happy Bunny* books in both. Red Wheel/Weiser/Conari has also found a teen audience at those stores for its humorous, edgy books originally conceived for adults. President Michael Kerber attributes 30% of the sales for Voltaire's *What Is Goth?* (Weiser) to Hot Topic and Urban Outfitters, which have taken strong positions on this fall's follow-up, *Paint It Black: A Guide to Gothic Homemaking* (Weiser, Oct.).

Bookstore Events

It's true—teen turnout for bookstore events tends to be so sparse that many retailers don't even bother. But don't count bookstores out as a way to reach teens, who will come out for the right event. Brazos Bookstore in Houston brought Laura Mechling and former Houstonian Laura Moser in for a reading and sold 350 copies of their book, *The Rise and Fall of a 10th-Grade Social Climber* (Houghton/Graphia, May). "I learned early on that when there's a good book by a local author with supportive parents, the usual expectations don't apply," says owner Karl Kilian. In this case Moser's parents, former owners of the now-defunct children's bookstore Stop, Look and Learn, which was located a few blocks from Brazos, supplied their own personal mailing list.

Barring those kinds of connections, group readings show promise. "It's always hard to get an audience," says Barnes & Noble children's buyer Joe Monti, who used to do book readings with three or four authors. This spring he discovered that by increasing the number of writers to 11 he could attract a bigger crowd. "The more the merrier," says Monti. "It gives the reading more the feeling of a party."

My Notes

WORD CONNECTIONS

Some analogies describe the function of one word in relation to the other. For example, clock : time describes the function of the clock to give the time. Complete these analogies using their functions as the basis of the relationship.

a. thermometer : temperature :: hammer : nail

b. eye : see :: tongue : taste

ACTIVITY 1.16 *Continued*

Steps:

8 Introduce students to the elements of an argument. Then ask students to identify each element in the student sample on this page.

9 After a discussion of the elements of argument in the student sample, pair students and ask them to review their responses to the writing prompt on page 68 for evidence of the elements of argument. Have student revise their responses to incorporate the elements of an argument.

10 To further expose students to the elements of argumentation, choose a famous speech and share it with your students. Examples may be found at www.americanrhetoric.com, which includes America's Top 100 Speeches. Ask students to identify the elements of argument in the speech and to evaluate the relevance, quality, and credibility of the evidence given in support of the author's argument for his or her position and audience.

ACTIVITY 1.16 *continued*

Teens and Books: What Are the Influences?

WORD CONNECTIONS

Ad hominem is a term describing an attack on a person's character rather than the argument the person makes. It is an appeal to emotions rather than the logical facts of an argument.

My Notes

Elements of an Argument

Read the elements of an argument. Then read the response below to Judith Rosen's article, and identify the elements of an argument the writer uses.

- The **hook**, which is an opening that grabs the reader's attention and establishes a connection between the reader and the writer.
- The **claim**, which is a clear and straightforward statement of the writer's belief and what is being argued.
- **Concessions** and **refutations**, which are restatements of arguments made by the other side (concessions) and the writer's arguments against those opposing viewpoints (refutations) and why the writer's arguments are more valid.
- **Support**, which is the reasoning behind the argument. Support can include evidence as well as logical and emotional appeals (logos and pathos). It may also anticipate objections and provide reasoning to overcome those objections.
- **Summary/Call to action**, which is a closing statement with a final plea for action.

Student Example

I just read a 600-page book in a day and a half. I couldn't put it down. It had everything a girl could want: romance, friendship, adventure, and fun characters. Unfortunately, it's the only novel I've read all year. Reading just isn't my top priority, and most of my friends would agree.

After reading this article, I asked ten of my friends what their "ideal" activity would be, and not one person answered "reading." Most of my friends would rather go shopping or hang out with friends. My smartest friend, who has a 4.0, said, "I read at least an hour each night for school. Why would I choose to read more than that?" I figure if I spent the entire day as an accountant, I would not want to go home and do math problems! Plus, I have no time. Between soccer, band practice, and my friends, I could watch a movie for two hours or read a book for two weeks! I'm sure the person who says that the book is definitely better than the movie is not a teenager who has no time to read.

I can also hear my Mom telling me that someday I will wish I had read more books. Perhaps she is right, but I don't want that now. What I want now is three extra hours in every day because I have homecoming to help plan and homework to do. So until another "can't miss" book comes out, my to-do list will not include reading a novel.

Revising: Now look at the response you wrote to the writing prompt on page 64. Work with a partner to identify the elements of an argument in your responses. Revise your pieces to incorporate them.

Examining Ads and Reviewing Appeals

ACTIVITY 1.17

SUGGESTED LEARNING STRATEGIES: **Word Map, Brainstorming**

Part 1: Look over the advertisements provided by your teacher, and respond to the following questions:

1. What are some of the first things that you notice? Do you see anything funny, clever, creative?

2. Where is your eye drawn first?

3. Would you buy this product based on this ad? Why or why not?

Part 2: Examine one specific advertisement closely, and answer the following questions:

1. Read the ad's *slogan* carefully. Does it relate to the product at all or is it promoting a lifestyle that can come from this product?

2. Find the *product* itself in the advertisement. Is it there at all? How prominently is it featured? Is the product actually being used?

3. Read the *copy* (the text) of the ad. What is it discussing? Is it relevant to the product? Pay attention to the diction. What do you notice?

ACTIVITY 1.17

Examining Ads and Reviewing Appeals

Materials:

- Samples of print and nonprint advertisements
- Vocabulary Notebooks

Purpose:

- To identify common techniques used in advertising
- To explain why certain advertising techniques appeal to specific audiences

Steps:

1 As a way of **activating prior knowledge**, ask students to **brainstorm** ways that advertisers try to influence consumer choices. Ask them to think about advertising appeals they have learned previously as well as examples from everyday life. During the class discussion, ask students to refer to their survey findings in Activity 1.16, the article they read, and any connections they discovered between advertising and peers' reading habits.

2 Provide groups of students with advertisements from a variety of sources: newspapers, magazines, TV, the Internet, etc. You might ask students to bring in samples of school-appropriate ads so that you include some ads that have captured their attention. Try to include at least a few book jackets as part of your samples.

3 Place students in groups. Have them complete Part 1, listing their initial reactions to each ad.

4 Ask students to complete Part 2, which takes them through a procedure for reading advertisements. Direct students to identify examples of each element and write them in the spaces after each question.

ACTIVITY 1.17 *Continued*

Steps:

5 Next, ask each group to read Part 3, which describes the most common **advertising techniques** and claims that advertisers use to persuade us. As they review each technique, groups can list examples from ads they have seen recently.

ACTIVITY 1.17 *continued*

Examining Ads and Reviewing Appeals

GRAMMAR & USAGE

In examining the ads, note the ways the writers have used language to influence consumer response (**fragments, repetition, rhetorical questions**, for example).

ACADEMIC VOCABULARY

Advertising techniques are the words and images an advertiser uses to hook a reader, viewer, or listener and persuade that person to buy the product or service.

4. Locate the corporate *logo*, slogan, or other designation that lets you know what company sells this product. How prominently is it featured? Why?

5. Try to determine the *plot* of the scene depicted in the ad. Who are the characters, what are they doing, and what is probably going to happen next?

6. Identify the *audience* for this ad. How do you know this?

7. What is the *representation* of males, females, and/or cultural or age groups? What evidence leads you to this conclusion?

8. Look at the ad's *layout* and design. Is the placement of lines, actor's gestures, colors, or other attributes meant to force your eye to look at certain parts of the ad? Why?

9. Are claims made in the ad fact or opinion? Are the claims substantiated or unsubstantiated?

Writing Prompt: Write a paragraph identifying the target audience, the appeals the ad uses to reach this audience, and whether you think the ad was effective in persuading the audience of its message.

GRAMMAR & USAGE EXTENSION

Examining advertisements provides additional opportunities to discuss sentence types and syntax as well as the intended effects. To give students practice in analyzing sentence structure, either bring to class several advertisements or have students collect one or more advertisements. With students working in small groups, have them highlight the sentence fragments, repetitive language, rhetorical questions, and other contructions that are designed to influence the reader.

Teacher Notes

Part 3: Advertisers use many techniques to try to get you to purchase their products. Review the descriptions of various **advertising techniques** below: In the spaces after each technique, name an ad you have seen recently that might use that technique.

Bandwagon: Advertisers make it seem as if everyone is buying this product, so you better buy it too: "*The best car of the year is here.... All your friends and neighbors are driving one....*" This technique makes you feel left out if you are not buying the product.

Avant-garde: This technique is almost the reverse of bandwagon: It makes the product seem so new and so cool that you will be the first on the block to have it. Only super-cool people like you will even know about this product.

Testimonials: Advertisers use celebrities or just regular people to endorse the product. Pay close attention; sometimes the celebrity doesn't even actually say that he or she uses the product.

Facts and Figures: Statistics, percentages, and numbers are used to convince you that this product is better or more effective than another product. Be aware of what the numbers are actually saying. What does "30 percent more effective than the leading brand" really mean?

Transfer: This is a rather complicated technique for persuasion. To recognize it, you really need to pay attention to the background of the ad or to the story of the commercial. This technique gets you to associate the good feelings shown in the ad with the product itself. Then the good feelings transfer to you when you buy the product. A commercial that shows a group of people having a lot of fun while drinking a certain brand of soft drink wants you to believe that you will be a part of fun groups if you buy that brand of soft drink too.

ACTIVITY 1.17 *Continued*

Steps:

6 Next, ask students to work together to create a two or three minute **dramatization** of a commercial that uses two or more advertisting appeals. Their commercials can attempt to sell any common item they have with them in class (a pen, a backpack, a bottle of water, etc.)

7 As each group presents its commercial, have other groups try to identify the appeals that are being used.

8 Finally, ask the class to compose a working definition of ***advertising techniques***, which students can reference throughout the year. Instruct students to create an appropriate **word map graphic organizer** in their **Vocabulary Notebooks** and explore the concept of ***advertising techniques***.

ACTIVITY 1.17 *continued*

Examining Ads and Reviewing Appeals

With your group, create an ad using two or more advertising techniques. Then, as you look at your classmates' advertisements, jot down where you see some of the advertising techniques. Keep in mind that you might not see all of them, and you may see others that were not described on the previous page. List both substantiated and unsubstantiated claims.

Bandwagon	Avant-garde
Testimonials	**Facts and Figures**
Transfer	**Other Techniques**

Based only on your examination of the advertising techniques used, who do you suppose is the audience for one of the ads? How do you know this?

How would you expect the advertising techniques to change if the audience were to change? Explain.

Using Rhetoric and Persuading an Audience

ACTIVITY 1.18

SUGGESTED LEARNING STRATEGIES: Close Reading, Drafting, Graphic Organizer, Word Map

Rhetoric

Rhetoric is the use of words to persuade, either in writing or speech. Aristotle defined rhetoric as "the ability, in each particular case, to see the available means of persuasion." He described three main types of rhetoric: *pathos, ethos,* and *logos*. Authors and speakers use these **rhetorical appeals** in their arguments based on their intended audience as well as on the nature of the argument itself. You might have used these appeals in persuasive writing pieces you created. Advertisers, too, make use of these appeals in their attempts to persuade an audience.

Pathos

Pathos, or emotional appeals, attempt to persuade the reader or listener by appealing to the senses and emotions. Political ads that show politicians kissing babies or shaking hands with the elderly often appeal to the emotions. Also, these appeals usually include statements with vivid sensory details, which awaken the senses and perhaps manipulate the emotions of the audience.

Ethos

Ethos are ethical appeals that attempt to persuade the reader or listener by focusing on the qualifications or the character of the speaker. The speaker's credibility is paramount in an ethical appeal. Ethical appeals focus on the speaker even more than on the situation. Examples of ethical appeals in advertising are expert or celebrity endorsements of products. Other examples of ethical appeals are a teen's argument that he or she should be allowed to do something because he or she has never been in trouble, or because his or her friend is a perfect citizen, and so on.

Logos

Logos, or logical appeals, attempt to persuade readers or listeners by leading them down the road of logic and causing them to come to their own conclusions. Logical appeals state the facts and show how the facts are interrelated. *If/then* statements are examples of logical appeals. Sometimes, the *if/then* can be inferred; for example, if a book jacket indicates the book spent 26 weeks at the top of a bestseller list, a potential reader might infer that since many people read the book it must be a book worth buying. Logical appeals are often used in courtroom situations as well.

ACADEMIC VOCABULARY

Rhetorical appeals are emotional, ethical, and logical appeals used to try to persuade an audience to agree with the writer or speaker.

WORD CONNECTIONS

The word ***pathos*** includes the Greek root *-path-*, which comes from the Greek word meaning "suffering." This root also occurs these English words: *pathetic, sympathy, apathy, empathy, pathology*, and *telepathy*.

LITERARY TERMS

Pathos is a rhetorical appeal to the reader's or listener's senses or emotions.

Ethos is a rhetorical appeal that focuses on the character or qualifications of the speaker.

Logos is a rhetorical appeal to reason or logic.

ACTIVITY 1.18

Using Rhetoric and Persuading an Audience

Materials:

- Vocabulary Notebooks

Purpose:

- To understand the components of rhetoric
- To analyze the use of rhetoric in advertising

Steps:

1 Introduce students to the **rhetorical appeals** of **pathos**, **ethos**, and **logos** by conducting a **close reading** of the information on this page. Consider adding the terms to your Interactive Word Wall. Discuss the rhetorical devices with students, focusing on how they relate to persuasive writing as well as advertising.

ACTIVITY 1.18 *Continued*

Steps:

2 Arrange students in groups to review the ads they examined in Activity 1.17 and look for examples of ethos, pathos, and logos. As in the preceding activity, be sure to include book jackets for some of your examples. Ask students to fill in the chart with examples of rhetorical appeals they can identify in the ads.

ACTIVITY 1.18 *continued*

Using Rhetoric and Persuading an Audience

As you look back at the sample ads, list examples you find of each of the rhetorical appeals listed.

Ethos
Pathos
Logos

One of the most important elements of an advertisement is its need to reach its target audience; if it does not, it has failed. The goal of a media-literate person is to be able to identify that intended audience.

Audience Profile: Look closely at an advertisement. Answer the following questions to determine the audience for the ad.

1. What is the product that is being advertised? ______
2. In general, this product is mainly used by male / female / either.
3. The average age of people who use this product is probably ______
4. The apparent age of the people in the ad (if they are present) is ______
5. The gender of those in the ad (if they are present) is male / female / both.
6. Identify the setting of this ad (outdoors, office, classroom, etc.).

   ______

7. Briefly describe the action in the ad.

   ______

8. Describe people you know who do the actions you identified.

   ______

9. Read the written part of the ad. Rate the diction as easy / medium / difficult / complex.
10. What is the racial or cultural group shown in this ad? ______

Write a statement about the audience for this advertisement. Analyze the relevance, quality, and credibility of the persuasive rhetoric for this audience.

Imagine that this ad was created for a different audience. Describe the new audience. What would be different about this ad? What would remain the same? Why?

ACTIVITY 1.18 *Continued*

Steps:

3 Ask students to select one ad to use for a close reading. Instruct one member of the group to keep track of the group's answers as they read and examine the ad. This page will guide them to analyze the target audience. Ask each group to assign a speaker to share their analysis.

Steps:

4 Now ask students to work individually to **draft** a paragraph that analyzes the ad for the following: target audience, advertising techniques, and rhetorical appeals. Suggest that they begin by analyzing the ad's techniques and appeals. They should take notes in the **graphic organizer** on this page.

5 Guide students to do the following in their drafts:

- Identify the intended audience.
- Comment on the advertising techniques and rhetorical appeals.
- Explain why the appeals and techniques are appropriate for that particular audience.

6 Finally, ask students to think about one of the texts the class has read in this unit and to imagine creating an ad to persuade an audience to read it. Place students into pairs and ask them to do a rough sketch or outline of a print ad for one of the texts. Urge them to be sure their ad includes an example of ethos, pathos, or logos.

7 Direct students to create an appropriate **word map graphic organizer** in their **Vocabulary Notebooks** and explore the concept of ***rhetorical appeals***.

8 Discuss the **Essential Question**: How are rhetorical appeals used to influence an audience?

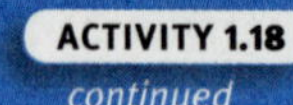

Using Rhetoric and Persuading an Audience

Continue your close examination of a sample ad. Consider how effectively it uses advertising techniques and rhetorical appeals to reach the target audience you identify. Take notes on the organizer. Then write a paragraph in which you analyze the effectiveness of the advertisement. Include a thesis statement that states the product name and the techniques or appeals the advertiser uses to influence the audience. Support your thesis statement with specific examples from the ad. Be sure to mention the target audience and your analysis of the overall effectiveness of the advertisement.

Product: ______________________________

Use of Advertising Appeals	Use of Rhetoric
Target Audience	**Effectiveness**

Sampling Ads and Planning a Campaign

ACTIVITY 1.19

SUGGESTED LEARNING STRATEGIES: Brainstorming

An advertising campaign involves more than a single type of ad. Think about the qualities, strengths, and weaknesses of each the following types of ads. Jot down a few notes about those qualities, and describe the most likely audience for each type of ad.

PRINT ADVERTISEMENTS

- **Magazine ads:**
- **Newspaper ads:**
- **Posters:**
- **Billboards:**
- **Book Displays:**
- **Book Jackets:**

COMMERCIALS

- **Television commercials:**
- **Film or video trailer:**
- **Radio commercials:**

ACTIVITY 1.19

Sampling Ads and Planning a Campaign

Purpose:

- To describe the characteristics of a variety of media channels
- To understand how to select the media channels that are most appropriate for a specific audience

Steps:

1 Ask students to describe the various types of ads listed. For each type, ask them to note which audience might be most receptive to that type of ad. If there are types that students do not know much about, consider bringing in examples or providing time for students to conduct research to obtain examples. Students do not need to list information or have extensive knowledge of every type, but they should have ideas about multiple types. While not all of these types are directly scaffolded in this unit, the basic elements of each are addressed.

Writing Workshops

Students will create an advertising campaign in Embedded Assessment 2. An ad campaign may require a scripted presentation of the campaign narrative. You may want to access Workshop 5, Script Writing, to give students practice or review of the elements of scripts.

Steps:

2 Remind students of the requirements of Embedded Assessment 2. Explain that this is a time to begin **brainstorming** and making plans for their advertising campaigns. Ask them to start thinking about the best media channels to use as well as rhetorical and advertising appeals to include. Urge them to use the brainstorming chart to develop some ideas.

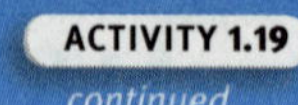

Sampling Ads and Planning a Campaign

INTERVIEWS

- **Television interviews:**
- **Radio interviews:**
- **Podcasts:**

Begin brainstorming how you might persuade your classmates to read the book you read independently. If you want teens to read it, where would you place your ad? On a website? In a podcast? What is it about your book that would appeal to other people and cause them to agree to read it?

Think about what elements of your book you could advertise, who might be interested in reading it, what media channel would be most effective to reach those potential readers, and how you might incorporate advertising techniques and rhetorical appeals. For example, you might market your book to student athletes by creating a poster that would appear in a locker room, and you might also market your book to teachers by creating a book display for the media center or teacher's lounge.

You do not need to make final decisions at this time. Rather, begin jotting down ideas on your own so that you and your group will have a starting point when you begin the Embedded Assessment. Use the Brainstorming chart on the next page.

© 2011 College Board. All rights reserved.

78 SpringBoard® English Textual Power™ Level 4

Teacher Notes

Brainstorming Chart

Features of the book to include in an ad campaign:	
Interests of target audience:	
Effective channels to reach this audience:	
Advertising techniques to incorporate:	
Rhetorical appeals to incorporate:	
Imagery to include:	
Overall diction appropriate for the audience:	

Embedded Assessment 2

Creating an Ad Campaign for a Novel

College Board Standards and Objectives

R2 Using Prior Knowledge, Context, and Understanding of Language to Comprehend and Elaborate the Meaning of Texts (R2.1; R2.3)
PE Mappings: R2.1-1.4, R2.3-2.4

M3 Composing and Producing Media Communication (M3.1; 3.2; 3.3)
PE Mappings: M3.1-1.4, M3.2-4.4, M3.3-1.4

W3 Drafting (W3.1 CR, A, W3.2 CR)
PE Mappings: W3.1-1.4CR, A, W3.1-3.4A, W3.2-3.4CR

W4 Evaluating and Revising Texts (W4.1 CR, A; W4.2 CR, A)
PE Mappings: W4.1-1.4CR, A, W4.2-1.4CR, A

W5 Editing to Present Technically Sound Texts (W5.1; W5.2; W5.4)

S2 Speaking in Interpersonal Contexts (S2.2)
PE Mappings: S2.2-4.4

S3 Preparing and Delivering Presentations (S3.1; S3.2; S3.3; S3.4)
PE Mappings: S3.1-2.4, S3.3-1.4, S3.4-1.4

L3 Listening for Diverse Purposes (L3.1; L3.2)
PE Mappings: L3.1-1.4, L3.2-2.4

Steps:

1 Review the assignment to be sure that students undestand all the requirements. They must create two products as well as a written analysis.

2 Organize students into groups according to the books they read. If a large number has read the same book, you might have two groups on that book.

3 If necessary, direct students back to their work in recent activities to review characteristics of audiences and the various advertising techniques and appeals.

Embedded Assessment 2

Creating an Ad Campaign for a Novel

SUGGESTED LEARNING STRATEGIES: **Drafting, Sharing and Responding, Discussion Groups**

Assignment

Your assignment is to work with a group to create an advertising campaign for your independent reading novel. Your campaign must include two of the three media genres (a dramatized commercial, an interview with an author, a print advertisement) that you have examined in this unit. Your target audience is your classmates. As support for your advertising campaign, write an argument using the five elements of argumentation that you are using to persuade your classmates to read the book. Your project will also include a written analysis of the persuasive techniques and advertising claims that you use and how they appeal to your target audience.

Steps

Prewriting

1. Meet with the group who will be working on the project together. Review the questions in Activity 1.18 to develop a profile of your target audience.
2. Brainstorm a list of features of your book that would appeal to this target audience, such as themes, relevance to their own lives, good dialogue, interesting characters, timely subject matter, etc.
3. Review your work from Activities 1.16–1.19. Decide on two of the three products you have worked on in this unit (dramatization of a commercial, interview with an author, or printed advertisement), which you think would most appeal to your audience.

Drafting

4. Create rough drafts of your advertisements and your persuasive text. Be sure to incorporate a variety of advertising techniques and rhetorical appeals in your ads as well as the five elements of argumentation. Decide how to share the responsibilities of ad creation among the members of your group. One group member might work on the ad design, another member might write the script for the commercial, etc.

Revising

5. With your group, meet with another group in your class and compare your ads. Try to identify the audiences and appeals the other group is using, and provide feedback on how effective their ads are at this point. Consider the following three questions from the peer evaluation form your classmates will use to evaluate your formal presentation:
   - What information have the writers included about the book that appeals to me as a prospective reader?
   - What advertising techniques have they used to motivate me to buy the book?
   - How have they used rhetorical appeals to persuade me to read the book?

© 2011 College Board. All rights reserved.

Embedded Assessment 2
continued

6. Listen as the other group provides similar feedback for your group. Try to incorporate their comments and suggestions as well as any other ideas that come from your group. Examine your ads closely to see how effectively you are incorporating advertising elements to persuade others to read your book. Consult the Scoring Guide to guide your revision.

Editing for Publication

Complete your final versions of your ads. Check to be sure the appearance, design, text, and language conventions are appropriate for your finished product. Make changes as needed. If it is a performance ad, allow rehearsal time.

Presentation

7. Present your finished ads either to small groups or to the whole class, depending on your teacher's directions.

Reflective Analysis

8. Write an essay evaluating your advertising campaign. Include the features of the book you are marketing, the persuasive techniques and rhetorical devices that you use, and quotes from your peer evaluators supporting your assessment of your presentation's effectiveness.

TECHNOLOGY TIP Consider using a graphics program or slide presentation software to create and present your advertising campaign. You may want to incorporate photos of the book you are marketing, as well as interesting graphic elements that support your campaign.

Embedded Assessment 2
Continued

Teacher Notes

© 2011 College Board. All rights reserved.

Steps:

4 Allow time for groups to share with other groups to give and get feedback.

5 Remind students to review their ads carefully as they revise. Point out that mistakes distract an audience. Urge them to check that everything in their ads will appeal to the targeted audience.

6 Depending on time (or on the number of groups), you may have each group present to the class, or you may have the groups present to other groups. As groups present, have the others use the Peer Evaluation Feedback Form to evaluate each group's campaign.

7 Point out that the group's written evaluations of their ad campaign is an important part of this assignment. They may use the information on the Feedback Forms from others as well as their own thoughts about their work in their analyses.

Creating an Ad Campaign for a Novel

Peer Evaluation Feedback Form

Presenters' names:

Book being sold:

What information has the group included about the book that appeals to me as a prospective reader?

What advertising techniques have they used to motivate me to buy the book?

How have they used rhetorical appeals to persuade me to read the book?

Embedded Assessment 2

continued

SCORING GUIDE

Scoring Criteria	Exemplary	Proficient	Emerging
Advertising Campaign	The campaign thoughtfully devises multiple ads that are marked with a clear and consistent purpose to appeal to at least two different audiences.	The campaign ads are crafted with a clear purpose and an attempt to target at least two different audiences.	The purpose and focus of the campaign ads are not always clear. The ads do not capture their intended audience or there is no variety of audience.
Advertising Elements	The campaign shows a skillful use of advertising appeals and rhetorical appeals that work together effectively to entice the audience to read the book.	The campaign shows use of advertising appeals and rhetorical appeals that persuade the audience to read the book.	The campaign does not show the use the advertising appeals and rhetorical appeals. The campaign fails to persuade the audience.
Reflective Text	The reflection insightfully analyzes the features of the book, the persuasive techniques used to reach the intended audiences, and the overall strengths and weaknesses of the campaign.	The reflection analyzes the features of the book, the persuasive techniques used to reach the intended audiences, and some strengths and weaknesses of the campaign.	The reflection includes minimal analysis of the features of the book and persuasive techniques used. It may not identify the intended audiences or address the campaign's strengths or weaknesses.
Conventions	The campaign presents polished ads. Either no errors appear, or they are so slight that they do not interfere with the meaning.	The campaign ads demonstrate control of standard writing conventions. Though some errors may appear, they do not seriously impede readability.	The campaign ads contain frequent errors in standard writing conventions that seriously interfere with the meaning of the texts.
Evidence of Collaboration	The project demonstrates extensive evidence of successful planning and collaboration.	The project shows evidence of adequate planning and collaboration.	Inadequate planning and collaboration are evident.
Additional Criteria			

Scoring Guide

When you score this Embedded Assessment, you may wish to download and print a copy of the Scoring Guide from SpringBoard Online. In this way, you can have a copy to mark for each student's work.

UNIT REFLECTION

Purpose

- To monitor comprehension and growth through a reflective process
- To synthesize understanding of individual reading and writing processes and strategies
- To self-assess mastery of key concepts and terms

Steps:

1 This is an opportunity for students to think about the concepts, vocabulary, and their own learning progress as they revisit and review the work they have produced in this unit.

2 Encourage students to be especially metacognitive about which strategies they have used and how those strategies support their learning styles and goals.

Unit Teacher Reflection

1 Which activities in this unit did you need to adjust (or you think should be adjusted) to prepare your students to be successful on each Embedded Assessment? Add your notes on how you would adjust the activities.

2 Which teacher strategies were most effective for introducing concepts/ideas to your students?

3 How did the unit activities help you address the individual learning needs of your students? Note any changes you would make in your instructional strategies to differentiate instruction.

Unit 1

Reflection

An important aspect of growing as a learner is to reflect on where you have been, what you have accomplished, what helped you to learn, and how you will apply your new knowledge in the future. Use the following questions to guide your thinking and to identify evidence of your learning. Use separate notebook paper.

Thinking about Concepts

1. Using specific examples from this unit, respond to the Essential Questions:
   - What does it mean to "come of age"?
   - How are rhetorical appeals used to influence an audience?
2. Consider the new academic vocabulary from this unit (**Voice, Advertising Techniques, Rhetorical Appeals**), and select 2-3 terms of which your understanding has grown. For each term, answer the following questions:
   - What was your understanding of the term before you completed this unit?
   - How has your understanding of the term evolved throughout the unit?
   - How will you apply your understanding in the future?

Thinking about Connections

3. Review the activities and products (artifacts) you created. Choose those that most reflect your growth or increase in understanding.
4. For each artifact that you choose, record, respond to, and reflect on your thinking and understanding, using the following questions as a guide:
   a. What skill/knowledge does this artifact reflect, and how did you learn this skill/knowledge?
   b. How did your understanding of the power of language expand through your engagement with this artifact?
   c. How will you apply this skill or knowledge in the future?
5. Create this reflection as Portfolio pages—one for each artifact you choose. Use the model in the box for your headings and commentary on questions.

Thinking About Thinking

Portfolio Entry

Concept:

Description of Artifact:

Commentary on Questions:

About the Unit

Unit 2

Context

This unit continues the coming-of-age theme by revealing the unique connection between written texts (short stories) and visual media (film). In this unit, students examine the ways in which authors of short stories and directors of visual media manipulate their audience's reactions through their unique stylistic choices. By studying film alongside short stories, students will come to see film as a separate and unique genre, worthy of serious study along with drama, poetry, fiction, and prose.

Suggested Texts and Materials

You will need to acquire the following films for this unit:

- *Charlie and the Chocolate Factory,* directed by Tim Burton, 2005
- *Edward Scissorhands,* directed by Tim Burton, 1990
- *Big Fish,* directed by Tim Burton, 2004, OR *Corpse Bride,* directed by Tim Burton, 2005

This unit also contains a research activity; therefore, you may want to schedule access to a computer lab for your students.

CollegeBoard
inspiring minds™

AP/ College Readiness

This unit focuses on refining three important skill and knowledge areas for AP / College Readiness:

- Developing a firm understanding of how an author presents themes, ideas, and/or images by means of literary and stylistic elements. (Activities 2.1, 2.7, 2.14)
- Understanding the relationship between an author's purpose, use of literary/stylistic/cinematic devices, and the effect of those choices. (Activities 2.16, 2.19, 2.21)
- Applying the writing process to a literary/style analysis essay. (Activities 2.23, 2.30)

Independent Reading

Although not required for the activities in the unit, independent reading can enhance students' understanding of the unit. Encourage students to read a novel, perhaps one that is related to mystery, fantasy, or magical realism.

Writing Workshops

In this unit, students create write a style analysis essay for Embedded Assessment 2. You may want to access Workshop 9, Response to Literary and Expository Text, as additional or preliminary practice in preparation for the assessment.

Grammar Handbook

Encourage students to use the Grammar Handbook as a reference as they develop their writing skills. You may want to provide mini-lessons from the Grammar Handbook and the Grammar & Usage features to reinforce students' grammar and writing skills.

Instructional Sequence

The instruction begins with several close-reading activities in which students examine stylistic elements (point of view, imagery, etc.) within various short stories. Students will then demonstrate their knowledge of these specific elements by creating a storyboard in Embedded Assessment 1. With a firm understanding of the connection between written text and visual media, students perform a "close reading" of three films by director Tim Burton. These activities introduce students to directorial choices, which they may draw upon for their style analysis essay in Embedded Assessment 2.

Activities 2.1–2.4 preview the unit and establish background information for the short story "The Cask of Amontillado" through personal connections, poetry, and vocabulary.

Activities 2.5–2.8 introduce the short story diagram and other close reading activities as a way to analyze literary elements. In preparation for Embedded Assessment 1, students focus on transferring written imagery to a visual medium.

Activities 2.9–2.13 expand on the connection between setting, characters, and events in a short story and reinforce the understanding of transformation of text. "The Stolen Party" reinforces the Coming of Age theme.

Activity 2.14 moves to independent analysis of "Marigolds" in which students identify key themes, ideas, and images.

Activities 2.15–2.16 introduce film terms, which students apply to a commercial. Students practice storyboarding with "A Poison Tree."

Embedded Assessment 1 | **Creating a Storyboard**

Skills and Knowledge:

- Understand conventions of storyboard format and design.
- Understand cinematic techniques (framing, movement, lighting, sound, editing) and their possible effects.
- Transform written texts into visual texts.
- Create a clear sequence of ideas.
- Consider the connection between shot design and audience appeal.
- Demonstrate presentation skills.

Activities 2.17–2.18 set film in context by asking students to make connections to their personal experiences with film and to research biographical information about Tim Burton.

Activities 2.19–2.21 use both text and film versions of *Charlie and the Chocolate Factory* to draw explicit connections between author's choices of literary techniques and director's choices of cinematic techniques.

Activities 2.22–2.27 guide students through a reading of the film *Edward Scissorhands*. These activities scaffold the process of writing an analytical essay on film.

Activity 2.28 requires students to use strategies independently to analyze a new Tim Burton film.

Activity 2.29 reviews the connections between style in text and film; students develop a thesis for use in Embedded Assessment 2.

Embedded Assessment 2 **Writing a Style Analysis Essay**

Skills and Knowledge:

- Understand cinematic techniques (framing, movement, lighting, sound, editing) and their connection to their stylistic counterparts (diction, imagery, organization, tone, syntax, point of view, etc.).
- Use graphic organizers to identify patterns in a director's style.
- Craft an effective thesis statement.
- Evaluate possible organizational plans for the essay.
- Evaluate the relevance and clarity of stylistic examples as supporting evidence.

Suggested Pacing

Activity	45 to 50-Minute Class Periods	Class Periods with Homework	Activity	45 to 50-Minute Class Periods	Class Periods with Homework
Learning Focus and 2.1	½		Learning Focus	½	
2.2	¾		2.17	½	
2.3	½		2.18	2	
2.4	½		2.19	1	
2.5	1		2.20	¾	
2.6	½		2.21	1	
2.7	½	HW	2.22	½	
2.8	¾	w/presentation	2.23	1	
2.9	¼		2.24	1	
2.10	½		2.25	1	
2.11	½		2.26	1	
2.12	1		2.27	1	
2.13	½		2.28	1 ¾	
2.14	1		2.29	½	
2.15	½		2.30	1 ½	
2.16	1	HW (collage)	EA2	2	HW (writing)
EA1	2	HW	Unit Reflection	½	
Total Class Periods				29 ¾	

Activity 2.6

In this and other activities in this unit, students analyze the elements of a short story. The diagram on page 85d is included in the student book, but you may want to use this page to model part of an analysis or to make extra copies for students to use in their analyses.

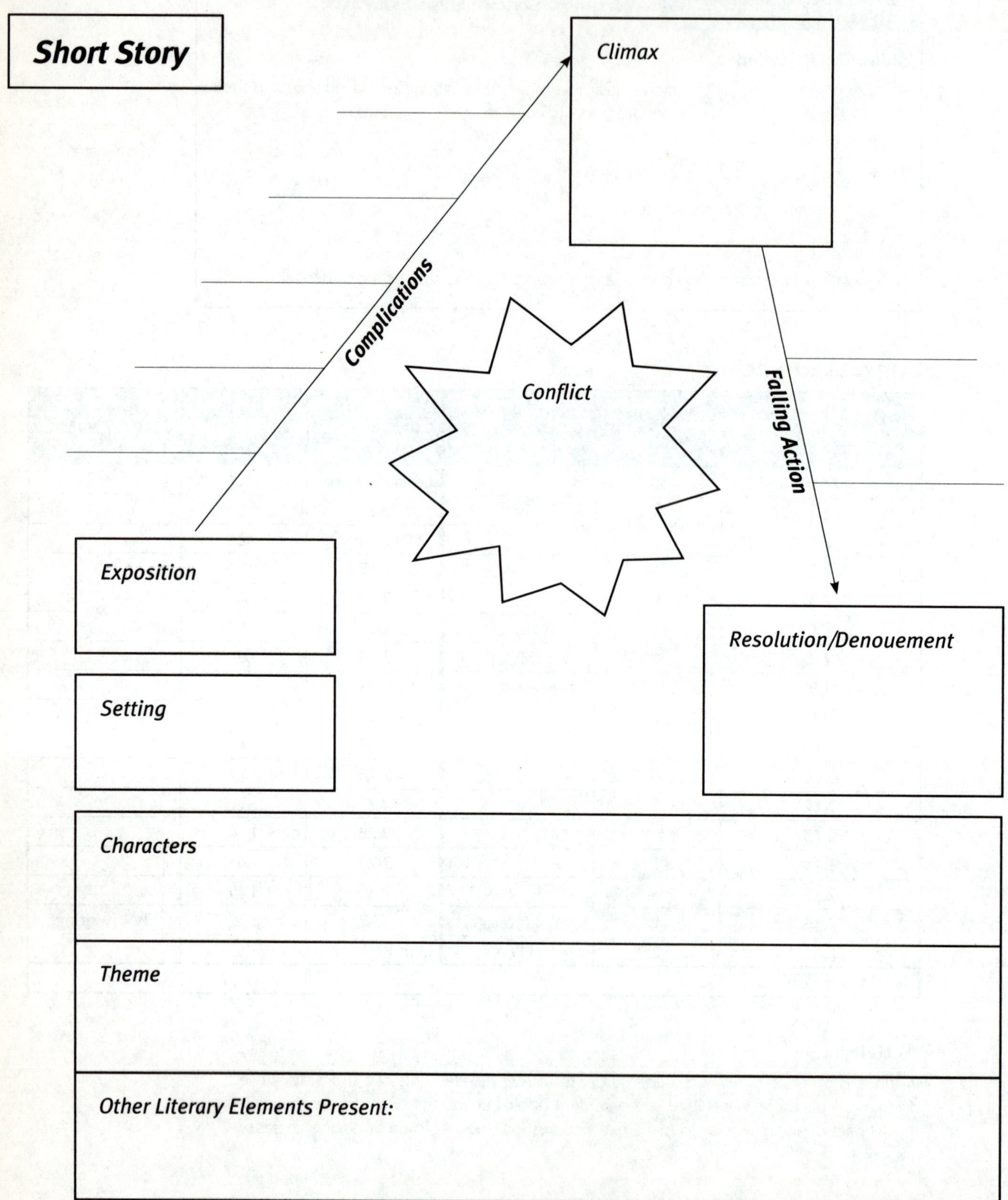
Short Story
Climax
Complications
Conflict
Falling Action
Exposition
Setting
Resolution/Denouement
Characters
Theme
Other Literary Elements Present:

Unit 2

Defining Style

Essential Questions

- How do authors and directors use specific techniques to achieve a desired effect?
- What are the essential features of an effective style analysis?

Unit Overview

Through the ages, stories have been passed from generation to generation. Then, sometime between 1830 and 1835, Edgar Allan Poe began to write structured stories for various magazines. His structure provided a format that characterizes the genre today. Poe felt that a story should be short enough to be read in one sitting and that it should contain a single line of action with a limited number of characters, building to a climactic moment and then quickly reaching resolution. Poe's influence can also be felt in modern cinema through the unique style of film director Tim Burton. This unit will uncover the connection between Poe and Burton along with the commonalities between written texts and visual texts. This unit also introduces the ways that directors of visual media affect or manipulate the audience's reactions. By studying film, you will come to see film as a separate and unique genre, worthy of serious study along with drama, poetry, fiction, and prose.

85

UNIT 2

Have students read the Unit Overview. Discuss the ideas in the overview and ask students to relate them to their own lives.

Students will provide responses to the Essential Questions in Activity 2.1. At the end of the unit, they will revisit the Essential Questions to see how their responses have changed after studying the unit.

UNIT 2

Have students read the goals for the unit and **mark** any words that are unfamiliar to them. You may want to create a space in the classroom for these words so students can add information about their meaning as they study the unit.

You may consider posting these goals in a visible place in the classroom for the duration of the unit, allowing you and students to revisit the goals easily and gauge progress toward achieving the goals throughout the unit.

Academic Vocabulary

Point out the academic vocabulary to students, and remind them that they will be studying concepts related to these words throughout the unit. Having students create **graphic organizers** to study these words in depth will greatly enhance their understanding of each word and its relationship to unit concepts. Have students keep their completed graphic organizers in their **Vocabulary Notebooks**.

See the Resources at the back of this book for examples of blackline masters suitable for word study. As students become more acquainted with the use of a **graphic organizer** to explore the meaning of a word, you may want them to create their own graphic organizers.

Unit 2

Defining Style

Goals

- To identify important cinematic techniques and analyze their effects
- To transform a text into a new genre
- To identify specific elements of an author's style
- To develop an awareness of reading strategies to enhance comprehension
- To analyze the elements of fiction–setting, plot, character, theme–and the steps in plot development–exposition, complications, climax, falling action, resolution (denouement)

ACADEMIC VOCABULARY

Point of View
Commentary
Cinematic Techniques
Style
Effect

Contents

© 2011 College Board. All rights reserved.

UNIT 2

Teacher Notes

**Texts not included in these materials.*

LEARNING FOCUS:

Making the Text Come to Life

Read the Learning Focus with students or have them read independently. **Activate prior knowledge** by having students **mark the text** and highlight words or concepts that are familiar (what they know). They might use a question mark to indicate content that is unfamiliar (what they do not know but want to learn).

Students will respond to the information on this page in Activity 2.1.

Teacher Notes

Learning Focus:

Making the Text Come to Life

Have you ever watched a movie and concluded that it wasn't as good as the book? Conversely, have you ever read a book and assumed the role of a director by creating visual images of the story in your head? This unit is your opportunity to see both sides of the book/movie coin. Now that you have explored the thematic concept "coming of age," it is time to continue your investigation of that theme in two different, but complementary, genres: **short story** and **film**.

You will begin this unit by exploring essential elements of a short story. However, you will do more than just identify important plot points and narrative structure; you will develop your understanding of how authors present themes, ideas, and images through literary and stylistic elements. Some of the elements you will analyze are **point of view, imagery, motif, foreshadowing,** and **irony**.

The exciting part, however, is that you will transform these elements of written text into something visual. Cinematic techniques such as framing, movement, lighting, and sound will be the tools at your disposal to create a storyboard. You will make your directorial debut by creating a storyboard for one of the stories you have read. The goal for your storyboard is to appeal to your intended audience, and to create the effect you want.

Independent Reading: In this unit, you will read short stories and film that are examples of Gothic Literature. For independent reading, look for books or short stories that contain elements of mystery or fantasy.

Previewing the Unit

ACTIVITY 2.1

SUGGESTED LEARNING STRATEGIES: **Close Reading, KWL, Marking the Text, Skimming/Scanning, Summarizing/Paraphrasing, Think-Pair-Share**

Essential Questions

1. How do authors and directors use specific techniques to achieve a desired effect?

2. What are the essential features of an effective style analysis?

Unit Overview and Learning Focus

Predict what you think this unit is about. Use the words or phrases that stood out to you when you read the Unit Overview and the Learning Focus.

Embedded Assessment 1

What knowledge must you have (what do you need to know) to succeed on Embedded Assessment 1? What skills must you have (what must you be able to do)?

ACTIVITY 2.1

Previewing the Unit

Purpose:

- To contextualize prior knowledge about key ideas and concepts
- To analyze the skills and knowledge necessary for success in this unit

Steps:

1 To determine students' existing knowledge about the concepts for the unit, ask them to **think-pair share** responses to the two Essential Questions. Students will revisit these questions throughout the unit to develop a more mature understanding of these ideas.

2 Direct students to **skim and scan** the Unit Overview and Learning Focus pages. **Activate prior knowledge** by asking students to **mark the text**. They may use a check mark to indicate what is familiar to them (know) and a question mark to indicate what is unfamiliar to them (don't know–want to learn). Engage students in a whole class discussion. You may want to record their findings on a **KWL** chart and revisit this chart at the end of the unit to discover what students have learned.

3 Provide students with a clear learning target by asking them to find the Embedded Assessment 1 assignment and Scoring Guide (pages 140-141). Lead students through a **close reading** of the prompt, steps, and Scoring Guide criteria. Instruct students to **mark the text** by underlining or highlighting the places that mention a skill or knowledge necessary to succeed on the Embedded Assessment.

4 Instruct students to **summarize/paraphrase** with a partner or small group the skills/knowledge they have underlined or highlighted. As you conduct a large group discussion, create a web **graphic organizer** that lists the knowledge and skills.

5 Revisit the web graphic organizer throughout the unit. Pointing students back to the web reinforces the purpose of each activity and the skills and knowledge needed for success on the Embedded Assessment. You may want to enlarge the Embedded Assessment web graphic organizer to provide a **visual** in the classroom throughout the course of the unit. Students will preview Embedded Assessment 2 before Activity 2.17.

ACTIVITY 2.2

An Eye for an Eye

Purpose:

- To interpret quotations and synthesize information
- To connect quotations about revenge to personal experience
- To use the writing process to draft a reflective essay

Steps:

1 Revenge and redemption are both underlying ideas in this unit. This theme is explicit in the first short story text, "The Cask of Amontillado" (Activity 2.5).

2 For this activity, divide the class into five groups. Assign each group to interpret one of the quotations. Have them write their interpretations in the appropriate column of the Revenge Quotations **graphic organizer.**

3 Invite groups to share their interpretations with the class. As the groups present their findings, have students complete the Interpretation column in their own charts as well as the remaining columns with their agreement or disagreement and reasons for their responses. Because students are working toward creating a visual, emphasize the imagery in the quotations as well as in the short stories that follow.

ACTIVITY 2.2

An Eye for an Eye

SUGGESTED LEARNING STRATEGIES: **Drafting, Graphic Organizer, Marking the Text, Sharing and Responding**

Read and interpret the following quotations. Do you agree or disagree with them? Fill in the following chart. Then, complete the writing assignment about revenge.

Revenge Quotations

Quotation	Interpretation of Quote	Agree/ Disagree	Reason for Agreement/ or Disagreement
"An eye for an eye only ends up making the whole world blind." — Mahatma Gandhi			
"Don't get mad, get even." — Robert F. Kennedy			
"She got even in a way that was almost cruel. She forgave them." — Ralph McGill (about Eleanor Roosevelt)			
"Success is the sweetest revenge." — Vanessa Williams			
"Revenge is often like biting a dog because the dog bit you." — Austin O'Malley			

Reflect: To which of these quotes might you want to respond? Why? Which quotes have striking *imagery*, and how does that imagery affect your response?

Writing Prompt: Draft a response in which you express your feelings about revenge. Include a personal reflection about a time when you had a choice about taking revenge or when you were the recipient of someone's vengeful attitude or action. Consider using one of the quotations in your essay, crediting the author of the quote.

Steps:

4 **Activate prior knowledge** by having students respond to the Reflection prompt.

5 Then ask them to respond to the Writing Prompt to **draft** an essay about revenge. You might discuss the structure of a reflective essay: an introduction paragraph detailing the event dealing with revenge, body paragraphs that discuss the writer's response to the event, and a conclusion that reflects on the event.

6 After students draft their reflections, ask them to **share and respond** with a partner to get feedback that will help them revise their drafts for clarity of ideas. Encourage them **mark their own text** to note suggestions from their peers and then to revise their drafts accordingly.

7 Have students save this assignment in their Portfolios. They may choose to revisit and further revise this text later.

ACTIVITY 2.3
"A Poison Tree"

Materials:

- Highlighters

Purpose:

- To analyze how an author achieves specific effects of tone and theme
- To apply and reflect on reading strategies that promote comprehension of complex ideas

Steps:

1 Instruct students to read "A Poison Tree" silently. Then call on a volunteer to **read** the poem **aloud** to the class.

2 **Chunk** the poem by assigning two-line increments to student triads. Ask students to **visualize** and sketch each chunk in the margin. Instruct students to specifically create images that reflect important themes or ideas in the text.

3 Allow students to present and explain their sketches to another triad.

4 On the board or overhead, present the following instructions to help students clarify the **tone** and **theme** of the poem. Instruct them to **mark the text** and respond to the following:

- Highlight or underline the different choices the speaker makes about revenge.
- Locate the speaker's shift in attitude and mark it with a star.
- Describe the attitude of the speaker in different places in the poem.
- How does the poem end? Paraphrase the last two lines.
- What causes this to happen?

5 Discuss student responses in order to clarify the poem.

ACTIVITY 2.3 "A Poison Tree"

SUGGESTED LEARNING STRATEGIES: Marking the Text, Visualizing

My Notes

Poetry

ABOUT THE AUTHOR
William Blake (1757–1827) was an artist as well as a poet. Born in London, he was apprenticed to an engraver when he was young. Blake claimed to have mystical visions, which he expressed in his poems and engravings. He engraved both the texts and illustrations for his poems. "A Poison Tree" is from his collection called *Songs of Experience*, which reflect his complex view of a world that includes good and evil, innocence and experience.

A Poison Tree

by William Blake

I was angry with my friend:
I told my wrath, my wrath[1] did end.
I was angry with my foe:
I told it not, my wrath did grow.

And I watered it in fears,
Night and morning with my tears;
And I sunned it with smiles,
And with soft deceitful wiles.[2]

And it grew both day and night,
Till it bore an apple bright.
And my foe beheld it shine.
And he knew that it was mine,

And into my garden stole
When the night had veiled the pole;
In the morning glad I see
My foe outstretched beneath the tree.

[1] **wrath**: Fierce anger; vengeance caused by anger
[2] **wiles**: tricky or clever behavior

92 SpringBoard® English Textual Power™ Level 4

Strategies Learning Log

Name of strategy:	
Purpose of strategy:	
How strategy was used:	
How strategy helped you make meaning from the text, create a text, or orally present a text:	
When you would use this strategy again:	

Strategies Learning Log

Name of strategy:	
Purpose of strategy:	
How strategy was used:	
How strategy helped you make meaning from the text, create a text, or orally present a text:	
When you would use this strategy again:	

Steps:

6 Ask students to select a strategy that contributed to their ability to create/present a text or make meaning from a text and reflect on it in their Learning Logs. Invite students to share the responses in their logs with one another. Add the new strategies to the Word Wall under the appropriate category: reading, writing, collaboration, and oral literacy.

7 Finally, solicit responses to the **Essential Question**: How do authors and directors use specific techniques to achieve a desired effect?

© 2011 College Board. All rights reserved.

ACTIVITY 2.4
Catacombs and Carnival

Materials:

- Pictures of catacombs and Carnival
- Film version of "Cask of Amontillado" (optional)

Purpose:

- To use context clues to clarify the meaning of unknown or ambiguous words
- To develop background knowledge for "The Cask of Amontillado"

Steps:

1 To **activate prior knowledge**, ask students what they know about catacombs and Carnival (in this context, the day before Ash Wednesday). Show pictures of these to give students a frame of reference for the vocabulary.

2 Divide the class into groups of three or four to complete the vocabulary **graphic organizer**. As an **anticipation guide** for the story, explain to students that they should **sort** the **words** on the page into four categories, provide a heading for each category in the top row of each column. Let them know that they may need to guess at placement of some of the words on the chart. Continuing to focus on imagery, urge students to create a drawing of one of the words or its meaning.

3 After students complete their categories, allow groups to share some of their categories and explain how they grouped their words.

ACTIVITY 2.4

Catacombs and Carnival

SUGGESTED LEARNING STRATEGIES: **Diffusing, Graphic Organizer**

The words below are from the story "The Cask of Amontillado." To familiarize yourself with the vocabulary in the story, divide the words below into four categories. Be sure to give each category a heading.

Amontillado	**cask**	**vaults**
connoisseurship	**nitre**	**vintages**
crypt	**pipe**	**palazzo**
parti-striped dress	**De Grave**	**puncheons**
catacombs	**motley**	**roquelaire**
conical cap	**Medoc**	

Word Category Chart			

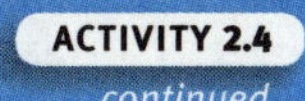

Catacombs and Carnival

Centuries ago, in Italy, the early Christians buried their dead in *catacombs*, which are long, winding underground tunnels. Later, wealthy families built private catacombs beneath their *palazzos*, or palatial homes. These dark and cool chambers, or *vaults*, contained *nitre*, a crystalized salt growth. In order to find their way in their underground tunnels, the owners would light torches or *flambeaux*.

These *crypts* were suitable not only for burial but also for storage of fine *vintage* wines such as *Amontillado, DeGrave*, and *Medoc*. A wine expert, or *connoisseur*, would store wine carefully in these underground vaults. Wine was stored in casks or *puncheons*, which held 72 to 100 gallons, or in *pipes*, which contained 126 gallons (also known as two hogsheads).

Poe's story takes place in the catacombs during Carnival, a celebration that still takes place in many countries. The day before Ash Wednesday is celebrated as a holiday with carnivals, masquerade balls, and parades of costumed merrymakers. During Carnival, people celebrate by disguising themselves as fools, wearing *parti-striped dress* or *motley*, and capes, known as *roquelaires*. Women would celebrate wearing *conical caps*. Carnival is also called Mardi Gras, or Fat Tuesday, because of the feasting that takes place the day before Ash Wednesday. Starting on Ash Wednesday, which is the beginning of Lent, some Christians fast and do penance for their sins.

WORD CONNECTIONS

Mardi Gras is a French term meaning "fat Tuesday." Mardi Gras is celebrated in many countries, including the United States, and it is a day of fun and eating before fasting for Lent.

Word Study: After reading the first paragraph with your teacher, continue using the diffusing strategy by noting unfamiliar words in the space below. Then use context clues, dictionaries, and thesauruses to write definitions.

ACTIVITY 2.4 *Continued*

Steps:

4 Model the **diffusing** strategy while reading at least the first paragraph of "Catacombs and Carnival" aloud, noting unfamiliar words and using context clues, dictionaries, and/or thesauruses. Ask students to continue using this strategy in pairs or small groups as they read the rest of the informational piece.

5 Briefly review the italicized words in the passage and clarify definitions. If students appear to be unclear on what some of the terms are, let them know that the class will revisit many of the terms again. Direct students back to the word sort graphic organizer.

6 As an optional introductory activity, if you have a film version of "The Cask of Amontillado," show it up to the section where the two characters enter the crypt. This will provide essential information on Carnival and the setting. If you cannot locate a copy of this film, assign research topics to student groups to provide essential background information.

ACTIVITY 2.5
Opening the Cask

Purpose:

- To predict outcomes based on clues in text
- To understand and explain nuances of character and the way characterization advances plot

Steps:

1 Lead the class through a **guided reading** of "The Cask of Amontillado." After the first two paragraphs, the text is divided into chunks, and the students will have responsibilities for each chunk.

2 For the first three paragraphs, ask students to **mark the text** as follows: underline anything that is interesting, circle anything confusing, and make notes and drawings in the margins. Allow students to **think-pair-share** responses.

ACTIVITY 2.5

Opening the Cask

SUGGESTED LEARNING STRATEGIES: Graphic Organizer, Predicting, Marking the Text, Think-Pair-Share

My Notes

Short Story

ABOUT THE AUTHOR

Born in Boston, Edgar Allan Poe (1809–1849) was orphaned as a young child and taken in by the Allan family of Richmond Virginia. Poe and the Allans eventually had a falling out because of Poe's irresponsible behavior. This situation was characteristic of Poe's short and tragic life. Despite his personal difficulties and an unstable temperament, Poe was a literary genius, writing short stories, poetry, and literary criticism, for which he became internationally famous. His dark imagination produced stories that are known for their atmosphere of horror.

The Cask of Amontillado

by Edgar Allan Poe

The thousand injuries of Fortunato, I had borne as I best could, but when he ventured upon insult, I vowed revenge. You, who so well know the nature of my soul, will not suppose, however, that I gave utterance to a threat. At *length* I would be avenged; this was a point definitively settled—but the very definitiveness with which it was resolved precluded the idea of risk. I must not only punish, but punish with impunity. A wrong is unredressed when retribution overtakes its redresser. It is equally unredressed when the avenger fails to make himself felt as such to him who has done the wrong.

It must be understood that neither by word nor deed had I given Fortunato cause to doubt my good will. I continued as was my wont, to smile in his face, and he did not perceive that my smile *now* was at the thought of his immolation.

WORD CONNECTIONS

The word ***impunity*** has a Latin root (from *poena*) that means "penalty" or "punishment."

The prefix *in-* (spelled *im-* here) means "not."

To do something *with impunity* is to do it without fear of punishment or consequences.

He had a weak point—this Fortunato—although in other regards he was a man to be respected and even feared. He prided himself on his connoisseurship in wine. Few Italians have the true virtuoso spirit. For the most part their enthusiasm is adopted to suit the time and opportunity to practice imposture upon the British and Austrian millionaires. In painting and gemmary, Fortunato, like his countrymen, was a quack, but in the matter of old wines he was sincere. In this respect I did not differ from him materially; I was skillful in the Italian vintages myself, and bought largely whenever I could.

Chunk 1

It was about dusk, one evening during the supreme madness of the carnival season, that I encountered my friend. He accosted me with excessive warmth, for he had been drinking much. The man wore motley. He had on a tight-fitting parti-striped dress and his head was surmounted by the conical cap and bells. I was so pleased to see him that I thought I should never have done wringing his hand.

I said to him, "My dear Fortunato, you are luckily met. How remarkably well you are looking to-day! But I have received a pipe of what passes for Amontillado, and I have my doubts."

"How?" said he, "Amontillado? A pipe? Impossible!And in the middle of the carnival?"

"I have my doubts," I replied; "and I was silly enough to pay the full Amontillado price without consulting you in the matter. You were not to be found, and I was fearful of losing a bargain."

"Amontillado!"

"I have my doubts."

"Amontillado!"

"And I must satisfy them."

"Amontillado!"

"As you are engaged, I am on my way to Luchesi. If any one has a critical turn, it is he. He will tell me — "

"Luchesi cannot tell Amontillado from sherry."

"And yet some fools will have it that his taste is a match for your own."

"Come, let us go."

"Whither?"

"To your vaults."

My Notes

WORD CONNECTIONS

The word *match* has multiple meanings. Among its meanings are a sports competition, a device to light a fire, and compatibility or similarity. Use context clues to decide its meaning in this sentence: "And yet some fools will have it that his taste is a match for your own."

ACTIVITY 2.5 Continued

Steps:

3 While you read the first three paragraphs aloud, ask students to listen carefully and take notes on the **graphic organizer** on page 104, identifying characteristics about the two characters in the story. When you are finished reading, review student responses and list them on the board or overhead.

© 2011 College Board. All rights reserved.

Teacher Notes

Opening the Cask

My Notes

"My friend, no; I will not impose upon your good nature. I perceive you have an engagement. Luchesi — "

"I have no engagement; come."

"My friend, no. It is not the engagement, but the severe cold with which I perceive you are afflicted. The vaults are insufferably damp. They are encrusted with nitre."

"Let us go, nevertheless. The cold is merely nothing. Amontillado! You have been imposed upon; and as for Luchesi, he cannot distinguish sherry from Amontillado."

Thus speaking, Fortunato possessed himself of my arm. Putting on a mask of black silk and drawing a *roquelaire* closely about my person, I suffered him to hurry me to my palazzo.

Chunk 2

There were no attendants at home; they had absconded to make merry in honour of the time. I had told them that I should not return until the morning and had given them explicit orders not to stir from the house. These orders were sufficient, I well knew, to insure their immediate disappearance, one and all, as soon as my back was turned.

I took from their sconces two flambeaux, and giving one to Fortunato, bowed him through several suites of rooms to the archway that led into the vaults. I passed down a long and winding staircase, requesting him to be cautious as he followed. We came at length to the foot of the descent, and stood together on the damp ground of the catacombs of the Montresors.

The gait of my friend was unsteady, and the bells upon his cap jingled as he strode.

"The pipe," said he.

"It is farther on," said I; "but observe the white webwork which gleams from these cavern walls."

He turned towards me and looked into my eyes with two filmy orbs that distilled the rheum of intoxication.

"Nitre?" he asked, at length.

"Nitre," I replied. "How long have you had that cough?"

"Ugh! ugh! ugh! — ugh! ugh! ugh! — ugh! ugh! ugh! — ugh! ugh! ugh!"

Teacher Notes

My Notes

My poor friend found it impossible to reply for many minutes.

"It is nothing," he said, at last.

"Come," I said, with decision, "we will go back; your health is precious. You are rich, respected, admired, beloved; you are happy as once I was. You are a man to be missed. For me it is no matter. We will go back; you will be ill, and I cannot be responsible. Besides, there is Luchesi — "

"Enough," he said; "the cough is a mere nothing; it will not kill me. I shall not die of a cough."

"True — true," I replied; "and, indeed, I had no intention of alarming you unnecessarily—but you should use all proper caution. A draught of this Medoc will defend us from the damps." Here I knocked off the neck of a bottle which I drew from a long row of its fellows that lay upon the mould.

"Drink," I said, presenting him the wine.

He raised it to his lips with a leer. He paused and nodded to me familiarly, while his bells jingled.

"I drink," he said, "to the buried that repose around us."

"And I to your long life."

Chunk 3

He again took my arm and we proceeded.

"These vaults," he said, "are extensive."

"The Montresors," I replied, "were a great and numerous family."

"I forget your arms."

"A huge human foot d'or, in a field azure; the foot crushes a serpent rampant whose fangs are imbedded in the heel."

"And the motto?"

"Nemo me impune lacessit."[1]

"Good!" he said.

The wine sparkled in his eyes and the bells jingled. My own fancy grew warm with the Medoc. We had passed through walls of piled bones, with casks and puncheons intermingling, into the inmost recesses of the catacombs. I paused again, and this time I made bold tc seize Fortunato by an arm above the elbow.

[1] ***Nemo me impune lacessit:*** No one attacks me with impunity.

ACTIVITY 2.5 Continued

Steps:

4 Continue reading to the end of Chunk 4. Ask students to write their **predictions** regarding Montresor's intentions in the My Notes section and to include support for their predictions from the story. In a **think-pair-share**, allow students to share their predictions with a partner. Encourage volunteers to share their predictions with the whole class.

ACTIVITY 2.5 *continued*

Opening the Cask

My Notes

WORD CONNECTIONS

Crypt derives from a Greek word, ***krypte***, which means "hidden" or "secret." This root is also found in the English words *cryptic* and *cryptogram*.

"The nitre!" I said: "see, it increases. It hangs like moss upon the vaults. We are below the river's bed. The drops of moisture trickle among the bones. Come, we will go back ere it is too late. Your cough—"

"It is nothing," he said; "let us go on. But first, another draught of the Medoc."

I broke and reached him a flagon of De Grave. He emptied it at a breath. His eyes flashed with a fierce light. He laughed and threw the bottle upwards with a gesticulation I did not understand.

I looked at him in surprise. He repeated the movement—a grotesque one.

"You do not comprehend?" he said.

"Not I," I replied.

"Then you are not of the brotherhood."

"How?"

"You are not of the masons."

"Yes, yes," I said, "yes! Yes."

"You? Impossible! A mason?"

"A mason," I replied.

"A sign," he said.

"It is this," I answered, producing from beneath the folds of my *roquelaire* a trowel.

"You jest," he exclaimed, recoiling a few paces. "But let us proceed to the Amontillado."

"Be it so," I said, replacing the tool beneath the cloak, and again offering him my arm. He leaned upon it heavily. We continued our route in search of the Amontillado. We passed through a range of low arches, descended, passed on, and descending again, arrived at a deep crypt, in which the foulness of the air caused our flambeaux rather to glow than flame.

At the most remote end of the crypt there appeared another less spacious. Its walls had been lined with human remains piled to the vault overhead, in the fashion of the great catacombs of Paris. Three sides of this interior crypt were still ornamented in this manner. From the fourth the bones had been thrown down, and lay promiscuously upon the earth, forming at one point a mound of some size. Within the wall thus exposed by the displacing of the bones, we perceived a still interior recess, in depth about four feet, in width three, in height six or seven. It seemed to have been constructed for no special use in itself, but formed merely the interval between two of the colossal supports of the roof of the catacombs, and was backed by one of their circumscribing walls of solid granite. Chunk 4

It was in vain that Fortunato, uplifting his dull torch, endeavoured to pry into the depths of the recess. Its termination the feeble light did not enable us to see.

"Proceed," I said; "herein is the Amontillado. As for Luchesi –"

"He is an ignoramus," interrupted my friend, as he stepped unsteadily forward, while I followed immediately at his heels. In an instant he had reached the extremity of the niche, and finding his progress arrested by the rock, stood stupidly bewildered. A moment more and I had fettered him to the granite. In its surface were two iron staples, distant from each other about two feet, horizontally. From one of these depended a short chain, from the other a padlock. Throwing the links about his waist, it was but the work of a few seconds to secure it. He was too much astounded to resist. Withdrawing the key I stepped back from the recess.

"Pass your hand," I said, "over the wall; you cannot help feeling the nitre. Indeed it is *very* damp. Once more let me *implore* you to return. No? Then I must positively leave you. But I must first render you all the little attentions in my power."

"The Amontillado!" ejaculated my friend, not yet recovered from his astonishment.

"True," I replied; "the Amontillado."

As I said these words I busied myself among the pile of bones of which I have before spoken. Throwing them aside, I soon uncovered a quantity of building stone and mortar. With these materials and with the aid of my trowel, I began vigorously to wall up the entrance of the niche. Chunk 5

I had scarcely laid the first tier of my masonry when I discovered that the intoxication of Fortunato had in a great measure worn off. The earliest indication I had of this was a low moaning cry from the depth of the recess. It was *not* the cry of a drunken man. There was then a long and obstinate silence. I laid the second tier, and the third, and the fourth; and then I heard the furious vibrations of the chain. The noise

After reading the fourth chunk of the story, predict what Montresor intends to do. Support your prediction with clues from the story.

GRAMMAR & USAGE

A **verbal** is a form of a verb that is used as some other part of speech—a noun, an adjective, or an adverb.

A **participle** is a verbal that functions as an adjective.

Example: **Throwing** them aside, I soon uncovered a quantity of stone and mortar. [*throwing* modifies *I*]

A **gerund** is a verbal that ends in *-ing* and functions as a noun.

Example: When at last the **clanking** subsided, I resumed....

An **infinitive** is a verb form that can be used as a noun, an adjective, or an adverb. The word *to* usually appears in front of the verb form.

Example: Unsheathing my rapier, I began **to grope** with it about the recess.

ACTIVITY 2.5 *Continued*

Steps:

5 Instruct students to make new predictions before reading each remaining chunk. Then continue reading aloud. Stop at the end of each chunk and check predictions. Allow students time to confirm or change predictions. Allow student volunteers to share changed predictions and their reasons for the changes.

GRAMMAR & USAGE EXTENSION

- You might point out that both present participles and gerunds end in *-ing*. The way it functions in a sentence determines whether this form of the verb is a participle or a gerund.
- Past participles most often end in *-d* or *-ed*, but irregular verbs have different past participles.
- Have students examine Poe's use of verbals and verbal phrases. Students' recognition that verbs can serve as other parts of speech should contribute significantly to their understanding of a writer's style.

Teacher Notes

Opening the Cask

My Notes

After reading the sixth chunk of the story, I think my prediction was___ (correct or incorrect).

Now I think...

lasted for several minutes, during which, that I might hearken to it with the more satisfaction, I ceased my labours and sat down upon the bones. When at last the clanking subsided, I resumed the trowel, and finished without interruption the fifth, the sixth, and the seventh tier. The wall was now nearly upon a level with my breast. I again paused, and holding the flambeaux over the masonwork, threw a few feeble rays upon the figure within.

A succession of loud and shrill screams, bursting suddenly from the throat of the chained form, seemed to thrust me violently back. For a brief moment I hesitated—I trembled. Unsheathing my rapier, I began to grope with it about the recess; but the thought of an instant reassured me. I placed my hand upon the solid fabric of the catacombs, and felt satisfaction. I reapproached the wall; I replied to the yells of him who clamored. I reechoed—I aided—I surpassed them in volume and in strength. I did this, and the clamorer grew still.

Chunk 6

It was now midnight, and my task was drawing to a close. I had completed the eighth, the ninth, and the tenth tier. I had finished a portion of the last and the eleventh; there remained but a single stone to be fitted and plastered in. I struggled with its weight; I placed it partially in its destined position. But now there came from out the niche a low laugh that erected the hairs upon my head. It was succeeded by a sad voice, which I had difficulty in recognizing as that of the noble Fortunato. The voice said —

"Ha! ha! ha!—he! he!—a very good joke indeed—an excellent jest. We will have many a rich laugh about it at the palazzo— he! he! he!—over our wine—he! he! he!"

"The Amontillado!" I said.

"He! he! he!—he! he! he!— yes, the Amontillado. But is it not getting late? Will not they be awaiting us at the palazzo, the Lady Fortunato and the rest? Let us be gone."

"Yes," I said, "let us be gone."

"For the love of God, Montresor!"

"Yes," I said, "for the love of God!"

But to these words I hearkened in vain for a reply. I grew impatient. I called aloud—

"Fortunato!"

No answer. I called again—

"Fortunato!"

No answer still. I thrust a torch through the remaining aperture and let it fall within. There came forth in return only a jingling of the bells. My heart grew sick—on account of the dampness of the catacombs. I hastened to make an end of my labor. I forced the last stone into its position; I plastered it up. Against the new masonry I reerected the old rampart of bones. For the half of a century no mortal has disturbed them.

In pace requiescat![2]

My Notes

[2] ***In pace requiescat:*** Rest in peace.

ACTIVITY 2.5 *Continued*

Steps:

6 Finish reading the story aloud. Give students the opportunity to respond to the story orally.

ACTIVITY 2.5 *Continued*

Steps:

7 Put students into pairs to complete their notes on Montresor and Fortunato.

ACTIVITY 2.5 *continued*

Opening the Cask

As you read "The Cask of Amontillado," list characteristics you discover or infer about Montresor and Fortunato. Stop after the third chunk of the text to list details you discover about the two characters. As you learn more about the two characters, add your information to the chart.

Montresor	Fortunato
Possible answers: wealthy, vengeful, two-faced, masked, patronizing, in control	Possible answers: wealthy, proud, sick, dressed as a fool, drunk, or dependent

Writing Prompt: "The Cask of Amontillado" begins with this sentence: "The thousand injuries of Fortunato, I had borne as I best could, but when he ventured upon insult, I vowed revenge." Using what you know about the two characters, write a creative story about one of these "injuries." Your story should include a well-developed conflict and resolution as well as dialogue and suspense to enhance the plot.

"The Cask of Amontillado" Story Diagram

ACTIVITY 2.6

SUGGESTED LEARNING STRATEGIES: Graphic Organizer, Marking the Text, Rereading, Skimming/Scanning

With a partner or in your small group, review these elements of the short story. Then, complete the story diagram, filling in the corresponding events from "The Cask of Amontillado."

1. **Setting** — Time and place in which the story happens.
2. **Exposition** — How the stage is set for the story. Characters are introduced, the setting is described, and the conflict begins to unfold.
3. **Complications** — Events that make the plot become more complex. While the characters struggle to find solutions to the conflict, suspense builds (also called rising action).
4. **Climax** — The point of greatest interest or suspense in a story. The climax is the turning point because the action reaches its peak and the outcome of the conflict is decided.
5. **Falling action** — The events between the climax and the resolution.
6. **Resolution/denouement** — The end of the story when loose ends are tied up.
7. **Characters** — People, animals, or imaginary creatures that take part in the action of the story. The short story usually centers on a **Main Character.** Also present are usually one or more **Minor Characters** who are not as complex, but whose thoughts, words, or actions move the story along.
8. **Theme** — The writer's main message about life. Theme is usually not stated directly and is left to the reader to figure out.
9. **Conflict(s)** —The struggle(s) or problem(s) in a story.
10. **Literary Elements Present**
    - **Point of view** — The perspective from which a narrative is told
    - **Verbal Irony** — When a speaker or narrator says one thing while meaning the opposite
    - **Foreshadowing** — The use of hints or clues in a narrative to suggest future action
    - **Motif** — A unifying element in an artistic work, especially any recurrent image, symbol, theme, character type, subject, or narrative detail

WORD CONNECTIONS

Denouement is a French term meaning "an untying" as in untying a plot.

ACTIVITY 2.6

"The Cask of Amontillado" Story Diagram

Materials:

- Highlighters in various colors

Purpose:

- To identify short story elements and analyze their function within a narrative

Steps:

1 After students read "The Cask of Amontillado," **activate prior knowledge** about the elements of the short story by having students work in small groups to review the elements of the short story. Clarify questions student groups may have regarding these elements.

2 Instruct students to **mark the text** of "The Cask of Amontillado" by highlighting the story elements in various colors. For example, as they locate details related to setting, they might highlight them in yellow.

3 Discuss students' findings, and help them summarize the information relating to the various story elements.

© 2011 College Board. All rights reserved.

Unit 2 • Defining Style 105

Steps:

4 Review the Short Story Diagram **graphic organizer**. Instruct students to fill in the appropriate sections of the story diagram. Students may highlight the various sections of the story with colors matching those they used to mark the text.

5 In the final section, Other Literary Elements Present, you may refer students to the definitions of the following literary elements addressed in this unit:

- **Point of view**
- **Irony**
- **Foreshadowing**
- **Motif**

You may specifically wish to include these same terms on your Word Wall.

6 The storyboarding in Embedded Assessment 1 requires that students visualize important elements of a short story. Keeping this requirement in mind, prompt students to **scan** the text, **rereading** passages to identify imagery (visual details) that achieves the following:

- Establishes setting
- Establishes character
- Foreshadows a future event
- Contributes to the resolution.

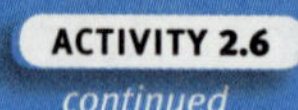

"The Cask of Amontillado" Story Diagram

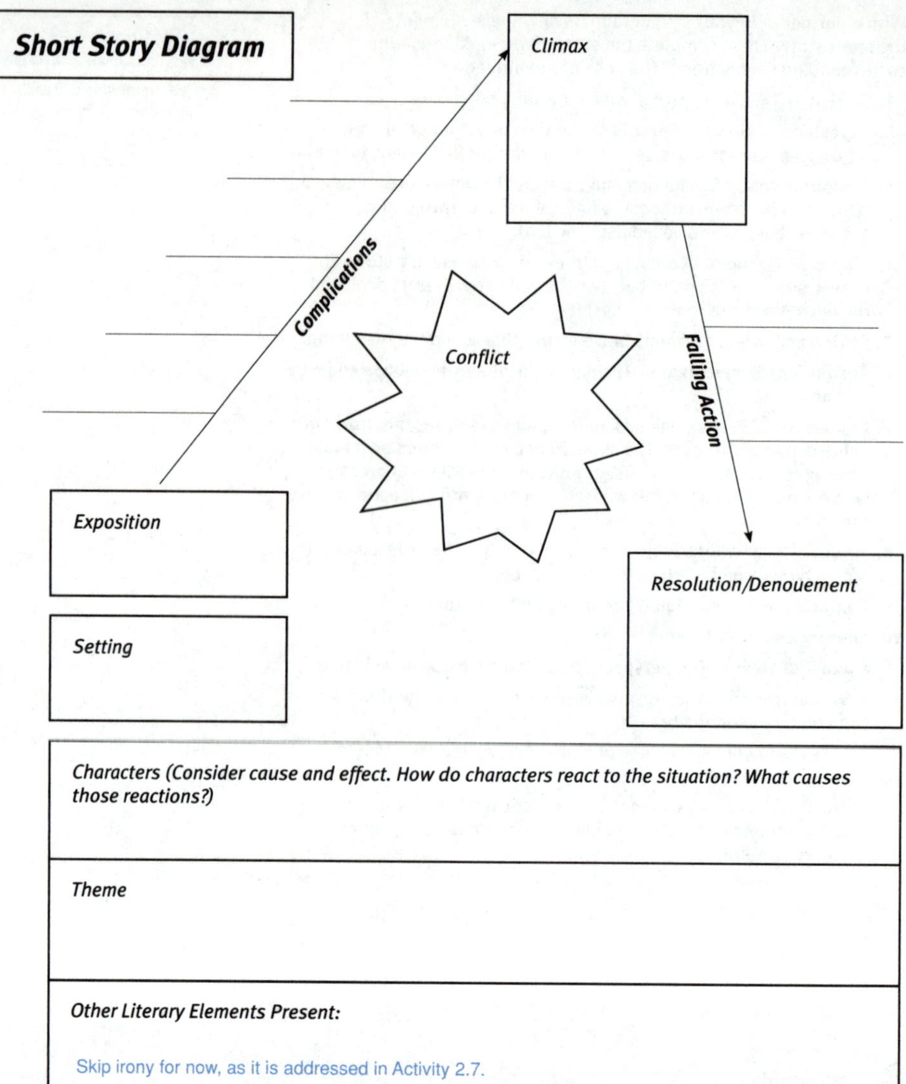

Differentiating Instruction:

To help **support** students' understanding of Edgar Allan Poe, select an additional short story by Poe and lead a guided reading of the text. During the reading, ask students to identify similarities and differences between the content and the style of the two stories. Use a Venn diagram to record answers on the board.

To **expand** students' reading of Poe, select an additional text by the author and have students read it independently. While reading, students should develop level 2 and level 3 questions that can then be used in a structured class discussion or a Socratic seminar.

Irony in "The Cask of Amontillado"

ACTIVITY **2.7**

SUGGESTED LEARNING STRATEGIES: **Close Reading, Rereading**

You reviewed a definition of ***irony*** in the previous activity. One type of irony, *verbal* irony, occurs when a speaker or narrator says one thing while meaning the opposite.

For example, when Fortunato proposes a toast to the dead buried in the crypts around them, Montresor adds, "And I to your long life." Montresor is using verbal irony here, as he intends to end Fortunato's life very soon.

Provide some examples of your own:

Your example:

Your example:

WORD CONNECTIONS

The word ***irony*** has the Greek root *eiron*, referring to someone who, in speaking, conceals true thoughts or feelings.

Verbal Irony in "The Cask of Amontillado"	
What is stated...	**What it means...**

ACTIVITY 2.7

Irony in "The Cask of Amontillado"

Purpose:

- To analyze how the use of irony achieves specific effects

Steps:

1 Review the concept of **irony**, both **verbal** and **situational**. You may notice that the examples below represent primarily situational irony; however, Poe is well-known for his use of verbal irony as well.

2 Explain that "The Cask of Amontillado" contains numerous instances of irony. Instruct students to **reread** the text, **reading closely** to find at least five examples of events or statements that are ironic. Provide one or two examples before students begin the activity. Below are some examples of irony students may locate:

- Fortunato's name suggests he is fortunate or lucky, but in this story he is not lucky at all.
- Montresor acts as though he wants to ask Luchesi about the wine, but really he wants Fortunato to go down in the catacombs with him.
- Montresor gives Fortunato wine to drink supposedly to help his cough but really to get him drunker.
- Montresor pretends to drink to Fortunato's "long life," but really he plans to kill Fortunato.
- The wine vaults are really crypts.
- Fortunato says he will not die of a cough and Montresor says, "True...true," because he knows how Fortunato will die.

3 Allow students to share examples with the class. Create a class list on the board or overhead.

4 Revisit the **Essential Question**: How do authors and directors use specific techniques to achieve a desired effect?

5 As an extension, you might assign the following **writing prompt**:

Write an essay explaining how Edgar Allan Poe's short story "The Cask of Amontillado" uses irony to show Montresor's true intentions. Provide evidence from the text to support your claims. Include a thoughtful introduction, detailed body paragraphs, and an insightful conclusion.

ACTIVITY 2.8

Visualizing the Ending of "The Cask of Amontillado"

Materials:

- Drawing paper
- Markers or colored pencils

Purpose:

- To visualize in order to deepen comprehension of a text
- To identify images from a written text and apply them in a visual rendering

Steps:

1 Students will solidify their understanding of "The Cask of Amontillado" by **visualizing** the ending scene. It might be helpful to review the definition of **imagery**: the use of descriptive words and phrases to represent persons, objects, actions, feelings, and ideas by appealing to the senses.

2 Divide students into triads. Instruct the groups to locate the passage in which Fortunato says, "He is an ignoramus" (chunk 4). They should read from that point to the end of the story and draw a picture that represents how the story ends.

3 Describe these roles for the group members:

- The **Reader** will read the passage orally to the group.
- The **Writer** will take notes on the **graphic organizer**, recording elements from the reading that need to be present in the drawing to accurately represent the text.
- The **Artist** will create the drawing, making sure the elements listed by the writer are present. Emphasize that although the artist actually does the sketching, the drawing should reflect the group's collaborative **visualizing**.

4 Pass out drawing paper (the larger the better) and markers.

ACTIVITY 2.8

Visualizing the Ending of "The Cask of Amontillado"

SUGGESTED LEARNING STRATEGIES: **Graphic Organizer, Visualizing**

With your group, you will create a drawing to represent the ending of "The Cask of Amontillado." Reread the text and make notes on the elements that appeal to the senses in the passage, specifically the visual images.

Consider the following:

- What characters are present in the scene?
- What does this place look like?
- What type of clothing is mentioned in the text?

What visual elements in the text should be in your drawing, for example, a trowel, flambeaux, and so on?

With your group, fill out the following organizer. As your Reader reads the text aloud, the Writer will take notes on things to consider including in your drawing. Your group's Artist will decide how to set up the drawing in the most effective way.

After you complete your drawing, discuss the choices you made for the content of your drawing. Your Reader should record your answers to the reflection questions before you present your drawing to the class.

Writer — What We Could Include from the Text	Artist — How We Could Represent These Items in Our Picture

Reflection

1. Which details from the text did you choose to include in your drawing?
2. Which details from the text did you choose not to include? Why did you make this decision?
3. Why did you choose to set up your drawing the way you did?

5 After students have completed their drawings, have them reflect on the choices they made. Allow each group to make a **presentation** of their drawing to the class along with an explanation of the content of the picture and rationale for drawing it the way they did.

Peer Interviews

ACTIVITY 2.9

SUGGESTED LEARNING STRATEGIES: Think-Pair-Share

Interview

Using the following questions, conduct an informal interview of your assigned partner. First, read through the questions and familiarize yourself with them. Then, create a statement that defines the focus of your interview. Finally, you and your partner will take turns interviewing each other. Take careful notes, and be prepared to share some of your partner's responses with the class.

The name of the person you are interviewing: ______________________

The focus of this interview is ______________________.

1. Describe a time when you were very excited about something but were disappointed about its outcome.

2. Describe an embarrassing event you either experienced or witnessed at a social event.

3. Describe a social event where you felt like an outsider.

Prediction: You will read a story entitled "The Stolen Party." Taking into consideration the prompts for your interview questions, predict what the story might be about.

ACTIVITY 2.9

Peer Interviews

Purpose:

- To draw on prior knowledge and experiences to elaborate on the meaning of events, main ideas, and themes in a text
- To formulate appropriate oral and written responses while interviewing or being interviewed

Steps:

1 This activity revisits and builds on interview skills practiced in Unit 1 and serves as a prereading step for students' close reading of "The Stolen Party." Pair each student with a partner. If you have an uneven number of students, you could either have one group of three students, or you could serve as a partner for one student.

2 Have students refer to the interview questions. Students should take turns asking their partners the questions and responding as their partners ask questions of them. The person asking the questions should take careful notes as the other person gives his or her responses. Encourage students, when responding, to focus on significant images that come to mind when recounting events from their past.

3 When all pairs have completed the interviews, place three or four pairs together to form small groups of students. Conduct a **think-pair-share** within the small groups by having each person share the most interesting response he or she received from his or her partner.

4 Hold a discussion with the whole group about one's expectations and the way that sometimes they mesh with what actually happens and sometimes they do not. Encourage students to keep these thoughts in mind as they read "The Stolen Party" in Activity 2.10.

ACTIVITY 2.10
"The Stolen Party"—Close Reading

Purpose:
- To read and interpret a short story
- To identify and recognize literary elements in a short story
- To identify multiple purposes for reading and select strategies to guide the reading

Steps:

1 To help students make meaning, this text has been divided into **chunks**. Ask students to **mark** and annotate **the text** while reading, following the directives in the My Notes column, in preparation for the discussion following each chunk.

2 Proceed with the reading as follows:

Chunk 1: Read aloud this chunk. Discuss the conflict between mother and daughter.

ACTIVITY 2.10

"The Stolen Party" — Close Reading

SUGGESTED LEARNING STRATEGIES: Marking the Text, Oral Reading

My Notes

Mark and annotate the text so that you can discuss the conflict between mother and daughter.

Short Story

ABOUT THE AUTHOR
Liliana Heker (b. 1943) is an Argentine journalist who also writes fiction. She has received a number of literary prizes in her country. In "The Stolen Party," Heker presents the events of a party through the eyes of a child.

The Stolen Party

by Liliana Heker

translated by Alberto Manguel

Chunk 1

As soon as she arrived she went straight to the kitchen to see if the monkey was there. It was: what a relief! She wouldn't have liked to admit that her mother had been right. Monkeys at a birthday? her mother had sneered. Get away with you, believing any nonsense you're told! She was cross, but not because of the monkey, the girl thought; it's just because of the party.

"I don't like you going," she told her. "It's a rich people's party."

"Rich people go to Heaven too," said the girl, who studied religion at school.

"Get away with Heaven," said the mother.

The girl didn't approve of the way her mother spoke. She was barely nine, and one of the best in her class.

"I'm going because I've been invited," she said. "And I've been invited because Luciana[1] is my friend. So there."

"Ah yes, your friend," her mother grumbled. She paused. "Listen, Rosaura,"[2] she said at last. "That one's not your friend. You know what you are to them? The maid's daughter, that's what."

Rosaura blinked hard: she wasn't going to cry. Then she yelled: "Shut up! You know nothing about being friends!"

---

[1] **Luciana:** (Lū syə´nə)
[2] **Rosaura:** (Rō sah´rə)

© 2011 College Board. All rights reserved.

Every afternoon she used to go to Luciana's house and they would both finish their homework while Rosaura's mother did the cleaning. They had their tea in the kitchen and they told each other secrets. Rosaura loved everything in the big house, and she also loved the people who lived there.

"I'm going because it will be the most lovely party in the whole world, Luciana told me it would. There will be a magician, and he will bring a monkey and everything."

The mother swung around to take a good look at her child, and pompously[3] put her hands on her hips.

Monkeys at a birthday? her mother had sneered. *Get away with you, believing any nonsense you're told!*

Rosaura was deeply offended. She thought it unfair of her mother to accuse other people of being liars simply because they were rich. Rosaura too wanted to be rich, of course. If one day she managed to live in a beautiful palace, would her mother stop loving her? She felt very sad. She wanted to go to that party more than anything else in the world.

"I'll die if I don't go," she whispered, almost without moving her lips.

Chunk 2

And she wasn't sure whether she had been heard, but on the morning of the party she discovered that her mother had starched her Christmas dress. And in the afternoon, after washing her hair, her mother rinsed it in apple vinegar so that it would be all nice and shiny. Before going out, Rosaura admired herself in the mirror, with her white dress and glossy hair, and thought she looked terribly pretty.

Señora Ines[4] also seemed to notice. As soon as she saw her, she said:

"How lovely you look today, Rosaura."

Rosaura gave her starched skirt a light toss with her hands and walked into the party with a firm step. She said hello to Luciana and asked about the monkey. Luciana put on a secretive look and whispered into Rosaura's ear: "He's in the kitchen. But don't tell anyone, because it's a surprise."

Rosaura wanted to make sure. Carefully she entered the kitchen and there she saw it: deep in thought, inside its cage. It looked so funny that the girl stood there for a while, watching it, and later, every so often, she would slip out of the party unseen and go and admire it. Rosaura was the only one allowed into the kitchen. Señora Ines had said: "You yes, but not the others, they're much too boisterous, they might break something." Rosaura had never broken anything. She even managed the jug of orange juice, carrying it from the kitchen into the dining room. She held it carefully and didn't spill a single drop. And Señora Ines had said: "Are you sure you can

[3] **pompously:** (pom′pəs lē), *adv.*: in a self-important way
[4] **Señora Ines:** (se nyōr′ă ē nes′)

GRAMMAR & USAGE

Heker uses the reciprocal pronoun *each other* in this sentence: "They had their tea in the kitchen and they told each other secrets." Writers use *each other* to describe interactions between two people and *one another* for three or more.

My Notes

Mark and annotate the text so that you can discuss Rosaura's attitude.

ACTIVITY 2.10 Continued

Steps:

3 Chunk 2: Select students to **read aloud** this chunk. Discuss Rosaura's attitude.

GRAMMAR & USAGE EXTENSION

Students may find it difficult to remember how to use reciprocal pronouns. Remind them that reciprocal pronouns describe an action that two or more people are doing at the same time; thus, the action is reciprocated. Reciprocal pronouns must describe the same action being done by two or more people. Have students find other examples of reciprocal pronouns in texts and in their own writing. You may want to put *each other* and *one another* on the **Word Wall**, along with descriptions of when to use each as a reminder for students to check their own writing for correct use.

ACTIVITY 2.10 *Continued*

Steps:

4 Chunk 3: Have two students read the dialogue in parts. Discuss the conflict.

5 Chunk 4: Select students to read aloud. Discuss Rosaura's reactions.

ACTIVITY 2.10 *continued*

"The Stolen Party" — Close Reading

My Notes

Mark and annotate the text so that you can discuss the conflicts.

Mark and annotate the text so that you can discuss Rosaura's reactions.

manage a jug as big as that?" Of course she could manage. She wasn't a butterfingers, like the others. Like that blonde girl with the bow in her hair. As soon as she saw Rosaura, the girl with the bow had said:

Chunk 3

"And you? Who are you?"

"I'm a friend of Luciana," said Rosaura.

"No," said the girl with the bow, "you are not a friend of Luciana because I'm her cousin and I know all her friends. And I don't know you."

"So what," said Rosaura. "I come here every afternoon with my mother and we do our homework together."

"You and your mother do your homework together?" asked the girl, laughing.

"I and Luciana do our homework together," said Rosaura, very seriously.

The girl with the bow shrugged her shoulders.

"That's not being friends," she said. "Do you go to school together?"

"No."

"So where do you know her from?" said the girl, getting impatient.

Rosaura remembered her mother's words perfectly. She took a deep breath.

"I'm the daughter of the employee," she said.

Her mother had said very clearly: "If someone asks, you say you're the daughter of the employee; that's all." She also told her to add "And proud of it." But Rosaura thought that never in her life would she dare say something of the sort.

"What employee?" said the girl with the bow. "Employee in a shop?"

"No," said Rosaura angrily. "My mother doesn't sell anything in any shop, so there."

"So how come she's an employee?" said the girl with the bow.

Just then Señora Ines arrived saying shh shh, and asked Rosaura if she wouldn't mind helping serve out the hot dogs, as she knew the house so much better than the others.

"See?" said Rosaura to the girl with the bow, and when no one was looking she kicked her in the shin.

Chunk 4

Apart from the girl with the bow, all the others were delightful. The one she liked best was Luciana, with her golden birthday crown; and then the boys. Rosaura won the sack race, and nobody managed to catch her when they played tag. When they split into two teams to play charades,

Teacher Notes

all the boys wanted her for their side. Rosaura felt she had never been so happy in all her life.

But the best was still to come. The best came after Luciana blew out the candles. First the cake. Señora Ines had asked her to help pass the cake around, and Rosaura had enjoyed the task immensely, because everyone called out to her, shouting "Me, me!" Rosaura remembered a story in which there was a queen who had the power of life or death over her subjects. She had always loved that, having the power of life or death. To Luciana and the boys she gave the largest pieces, and to the girl with the bow she gave a slice so thin one could see through it.

After the cake came the magician, tall and bony, with a fine red cape. A true magician: he could untie handkerchiefs by blowing on them and make a chain with links that had no openings. He could guess what cards were pulled out from a pack, and the monkey was his assistant. He called the monkey "partner."

"Let's see here, partner," he would say, "Turn over a card." And, "Don't run away, partner: time to work now."

The final trick was wonderful. One of the children had to hold the monkey in his arms and the magician said he would make him disappear.

"What, the boy?" they all shouted.

"No, the monkey!" shouted the magician.

Rosaura thought that this was truly the most amusing party in the whole world.

The magician asked a small fat boy to come and help, but the small fat boy got frightened almost at once and dropped the monkey on the floor. The magician picked him up carefully, whispered something in his ear, and the monkey nodded almost as if he understood.

"You mustn't be so unmanly, my friend," the magician said to the fat boy.

"What's unmanly?" said the fat boy.

The magician turned around as if to look for spies.

"A sissy," said the magician. "Go sit down."

Then he stared at all the faces, one by one. Rosaura felt her heart tremble.

"You, with the Spanish eyes," said the magician. And everyone saw that he was pointing at her.

GRAMMAR & USAGE

Independent and **subordinate clauses** can be combined in a variety of ways with coordinating and subordinating conjunctions to form **compound** and **complex** sentences to express relationships among ideas.

Example: Rosaura won the sack race [**independent clause**], and [**coordinating conjunction**] nobody managed to catch her [**independent clause**] when [**subordinating conjunction**] they played tag [**subordinate clause**]. This sentence, with two independent clauses and one dependent clause, is a **compound-complex** sentence.

My Notes

GRAMMAR & USAGE EXTENSION

Examining the independent and subordinate clauses gives students further practice with grammatical and stylistic concepts.

You may wish to discuss the relationship between ***point of view*** (Activity 2.12) and style, as well as the effect of grammar and syntax on writing.

ACTIVITY 2.10 *Continued*

Steps:

6 Chunk 5: Have students read this chunk silently. Discuss Rosaura's feelings.

7 Chunk 6: Select students to read this chunk aloud. Discuss the surprise ending. After students discuss the ending, have them compare the concept of "good versus evil" in "The Cask of Amontillado" and "The Stolen Party."

"The Stolen Party" — Close Reading

My Notes

Mark and annotate the details that convey Rosaura's feelings.

She wasn't afraid. Neither holding the monkey, nor when the magician made him vanish; not even when, at the end the magician flung his red cape over Rosaura's head and uttered a few magic words … and the monkey reappeared, chattering happily, in her arms. The children clapped furiously. And before Rosaura returned to her seat, the magician said:

"Thank you very much, my little countess."

She was so pleased with the compliment that a while later, when her mother came to fetch her, that was the first thing she told her.

Chunk 5

"I helped the magician and he said to me, 'Thank you very much, my little countess.'"

It was strange because up to then Rosaura had thought that she was angry with her mother. All along Rosaura had imagined that she would say to her: "See that the monkey wasn't a lie?" But instead she was so thrilled that she told her mother all about the wonderful magician.

Her mother tapped her on the head and said: "So now we're a countess!"

But one could see that she was beaming.

And now they both stood in the entrance, because a moment ago Señora Ines, smiling, had said: "Please wait here a second."

Her mother suddenly seemed worried.

"What is it?" she asked Rosaura.

"What is what?" said Rosaura. "It's nothing; she just wants to get the presents for those who are leaving, see?"

She pointed at the fat boy and at a girl with pigtails who were also waiting there, next to their mothers. And she explained about the presents. She knew, because she had been watching those who left before her. When one of the girls was about to leave, Señora Ines would give her a bracelet. When a boy left, Señora Ines gave him a yo-yo. Rosaura preferred the yo-yo because it sparkled, but she didn't mention that to her mother. Her mother might have said: "So why don't you ask for one, you blockhead?" That's what her mother was like. Rosaura didn't feel like explaining that she'd be horribly ashamed to be the odd one out. Instead she said:

"I was the best-behaved at the party."

And she said no more because Señora Ines came out into the hall with two bags, one pink and one blue.

Teacher Notes

First she went up to the fat boy, gave him a yo-yo out of the blue bag, and the fat boy left with his mother. Then she went up to the girl and gave her a bracelet out of the pink bag, and the girl with the pigtails left as well.

Finally she came up to Rosaura and her mother. She had a big smile on her face and Rosaura liked that. Señora Ines looked down at her, then looked up at her mother, and then said something that made Rosaura proud:

"What a marvelous daughter you have, Herminia."[5]

Chunk 6

For an instant, Rosaura thought that she'd give her two presents: the bracelet and the yo-yo. Señora Ines bent down as if about to look for something. Rosaura also leaned forward, stretching out her arm. But she never completed the movement.

Señora Ines didn't look in the pink bag. Nor did she look in the blue bag. Instead she rummaged[6] in her purse. In her hand appeared two bills.

"You really and truly earned this," she said handing them over. "Thank you for all your help, my pet."

Rosaura felt her arms stiffen, stick close to her body, and then she noticed her mother's hand on her shoulder. Instinctively she pressed herself against her mother's body. That was all. Except her eyes. Rosaura's eyes had a cold, clear look that fixed itself on Señora Ines's face.

Señora Ines, motionless, stood there with her hand outstretched. As if she didn't dare draw it back. As if the slightest change might shatter an infinitely[7] delicate balance.

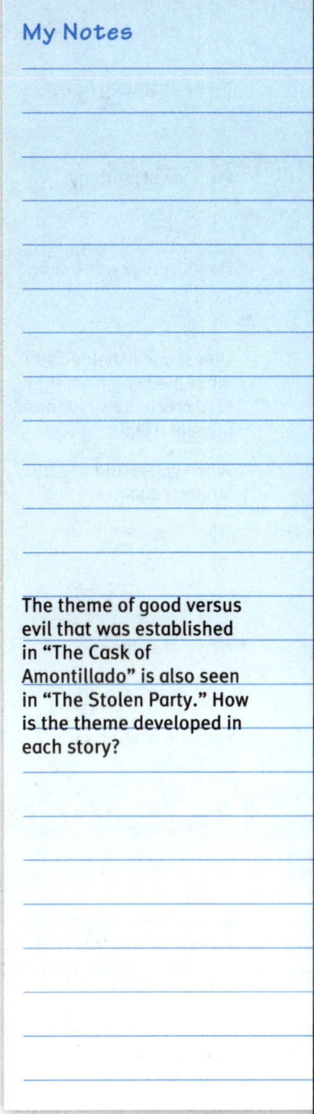

My Notes

The theme of good versus evil that was established in "The Cask of Amontillado" is also seen in "The Stolen Party." How is the theme developed in each story?

[5] **Herminia:** (er mē nyā')
[6] **rummaged:** (rum'ijd), *v.*: searched thoroughly by moving things about
[7] **infinitely:** (in'fə nit lē): endlessly

ACTIVITY 2.10 *Continued*

Steps:

8 Ask students to select a strategy that really contributed to their ability to make meaning from a text or create or present a text. Have them reflect on it in their Learning Log. Invite students to share the responses in their Logs with one another.

9 Finally, add the new strategies to the Word Wall under the appropriate category: reading, writing, collaboration, and oral literacy.

ACTIVITY 2.10 *continued*

"The Stolen Party" — Close Reading

Strategies Learning Log	
Name of strategy:	
Purpose of strategy:	
How strategy was used:	
How strategy helped you make meaning from the text, create a text, or orally present a text:	
When you would use this strategy again:	

Strategies Learning Log	
Name of strategy:	
Purpose of strategy:	
How strategy was used:	
How strategy helped you make meaning from the text, create a text, or orally present a text:	
When you would use this strategy again:	

Visualizing the Ending of "The Stolen Party"

ACTIVITY 2.11

SUGGESTED LEARNING STRATEGIES: Marking the Text, Rereading, Visualizing, Sketching

Reread the final paragraphs of this story, when Señora Ines tries to hand Rosaura money instead of a gift like all the other children received.

"Rosaura felt her arms stiffen, stick close to her body, and then she noticed her mother's hand on her shoulder. Instinctively she pressed herself against her mother's body. That was all. Except her eyes. Rosaura's eyes had a cold, clear look that fixed itself on Señora Ines's face.

Señora Ines, motionless, stood there with her hand outstretched. As if she didn't dare draw it back. As if the slightest change might shatter an infinitely delicate balance."

This is a very powerful moment as all three characters appear to be frozen in time and space. How do you imagine this final scene in the story? Regardless of your artistic abilities, one of the most important reading skills to learn and practice is visualizing what you read. On separate paper, draw what you imagine this final scene looks like. You can focus on whatever you think is most important.

Next, review your drawing and look back at the excerpt from the story. What particular words and phrases helped you create your picture?

Now, imagine what might happen immediately after the scene you have just drawn. If the story were to contain one more scene, what would it look like? Consider what might happen to the money. Who, if anyone, would end up with it? Think through these things; then draw your scene on separate paper.

Writing Prompt: After creating your scene, write a continuation of the narrative to match your vision. Be sure to continue the conflict and perhaps devise an alternative resolution. Use dialogue if possible.

ACTIVITY 2.11

Visualizing the Ending of "The Stolen Party"

Materials:

- Markers or highlighters
- Drawing pencils

Purpose:

- To visualize in order to elaborate and deepen comprehension of increasingly complex texts
- To identify the ways in which an author describes the setting

Steps:

1 Ask students to **reread** the final paragraphs of "The Stolen Party." After students have read the paragraphs once, discuss with them the ways in which the mood of the story shifts when the setting shifts to this final scene by the door.

2 Then, ask them to **visualize** and draw the scene that is represented in the final paragraph. Provide time for students to **sketch** what they are **visualizing**. Encourage students who are reluctant artists to focus on drawing essential features of the description whether or not they are able to draw accurately or to scale.

3 After students have finished their drawings, allow those who are comfortable to share them with the class. Then, give students time to consider their own drawings and the reasons they drew what they did. Instruct them to go back to the paragraphs and **mark the text** that helped them create their drawing.

4 Finally, have students create one more drawing in which they illustrate their prediction of what would most likely occur right after the final scene.

5 Revisit the **Essential Question**: How do authors and directors use specific techniques to achieve a desired effect?

ACTIVITY 2.12
Point of View in "The Stolen Party"

Materials:
- Vocabulary Notebooks

Purpose:
- To identify and distinguish among points of view
- To rewrite a text in another point of view
- To understand that narrative perspective influences the interpretation of events, characters, and themes

Steps:
1 Clarify the three **points of view** and discuss the differences with students.

2 Instruct students to assume the role of a writer and **transform** each excerpt so that it reflects the other two **points of view**. For example, if the passage is written in first person, students will rewrite that passage in third-person limited and third-person omniscient points of view.

ACTIVITY 2.12

Point of View in "The Stolen Party"

SUGGESTED LEARNING STRATEGIES: Graphic Organizer, Think-Pair-Share, Word Map

ACADEMIC VOCABULARY

Point of view is the perspective from which a narrative is told.

Examine and discuss the differences among the three **points of view:**

- **First Person:** The narrator is a character in the story and refers to himself or herself as "I."
- **Third-Person Omniscient:** This type of narrator is not a character, but is all-knowing and is able to recount the background and inside thoughts and feelings of any character.
- **Third-Person Limited:** Like the omniscient narrator, this narrator is not a character in the story, but rather provides the reader the inside thoughts of only one character, and none of the thoughts of any of the other characters.

WORD CONNECTIONS

The word ***omniscient*** has two Latin roots: *omni-*, meaning "all" or "everything," and *-sci-*, meaning "knowing" or "knowledge."

The root *omni-* also occurs in *omnivorous* and *omnipotent*.

The root *sci-* occurs in *science*, *conscious*, *conscience*, and *conscientious*.

Now, use your understanding of point of view to transform each excerpt into the other two points of view.

Excerpt 1

First Person: I ran into my ex-girlfriend Lisa. I did not want to see her again. She always wants to get back with me, and I just want to move on.

Third-Person Limited:

Third-Person Omniscient:

continued

Excerpt 2

First Person:

Third-Person Limited: The city skyline covered the horizon. From the balcony of her high-priced apartment that she shared with Jake, Sarah looked out and wondered if she was happy. Something seemed to be missing. Jake looked over to her and Sarah looked away quickly, hoping that she had not given away her private thoughts.

Third-Person Omniscient:

Excerpt 3

First Person:

Third-Person Limited:

Third-Person Omniscient:

The robber looked over his potential prey for the evening. They all seemed like easy marks to him. *Who would it be*, he wondered.

Feeling someone's eyes on her pocketbook, Jane held it closer to her body. She would not be robbed again, after that last time.

ACTIVITY 2.12 *Continued*

Steps:

3 After students complete the assignment, provide an opportunity for a **think-pair-share** activity, so that students can share their writing. Call on volunteers to read their samples of the transformed points of view. Lead a discussion on the benefits and limitations of each type of narration. Add the names of these three points of view to your Word Wall.

4 Ask students to identify the point of view used in "The Stolen Party." Ask them to return to that story and identify in the margin specific passages of text to provide evidence.

5 Next, pair each student with a partner. Assign one paragraph of the story to each pair. Instruct students to work together to **transform the text** by rewriting the paragraph in a different point of view. Then, ask students to closely examine their new paragraph to ensure that it maintains the new point of view consistently.

6 Guide students to identify the ways in which changing the point of view has altered the effect of the paragraph.

Steps:

7 Ask students, either individually or in pairs, to complete the **graphic organizer** on this page, reflecting on the effects of each point of view.

8 Direct students to select an appropriate **word map graphic organizer** and explore the concept of ***point of view*** in their **Vocabulary Notebooks**.

9 Solicit responses to the **Essential Question**: How do authors and directors use specific techniques to achieve a desired effect?

Point of View in "The Stolen Party"

Reflect: What are the benefits and limitations of each type of narration?

First-Person Point of View	Third-Person Limited	Third-Person Omniscient
Benefits:	Benefits:	Benefits:
Limitations:	Limitations:	Limitations:

© 2011 College Board. All rights reserved.

“The Stolen Party” Story Diagram

ACTIVITY 2.13

SUGGESTED LEARNING STRATEGIES: Graphic Organizer, Marking the Text, Rereading

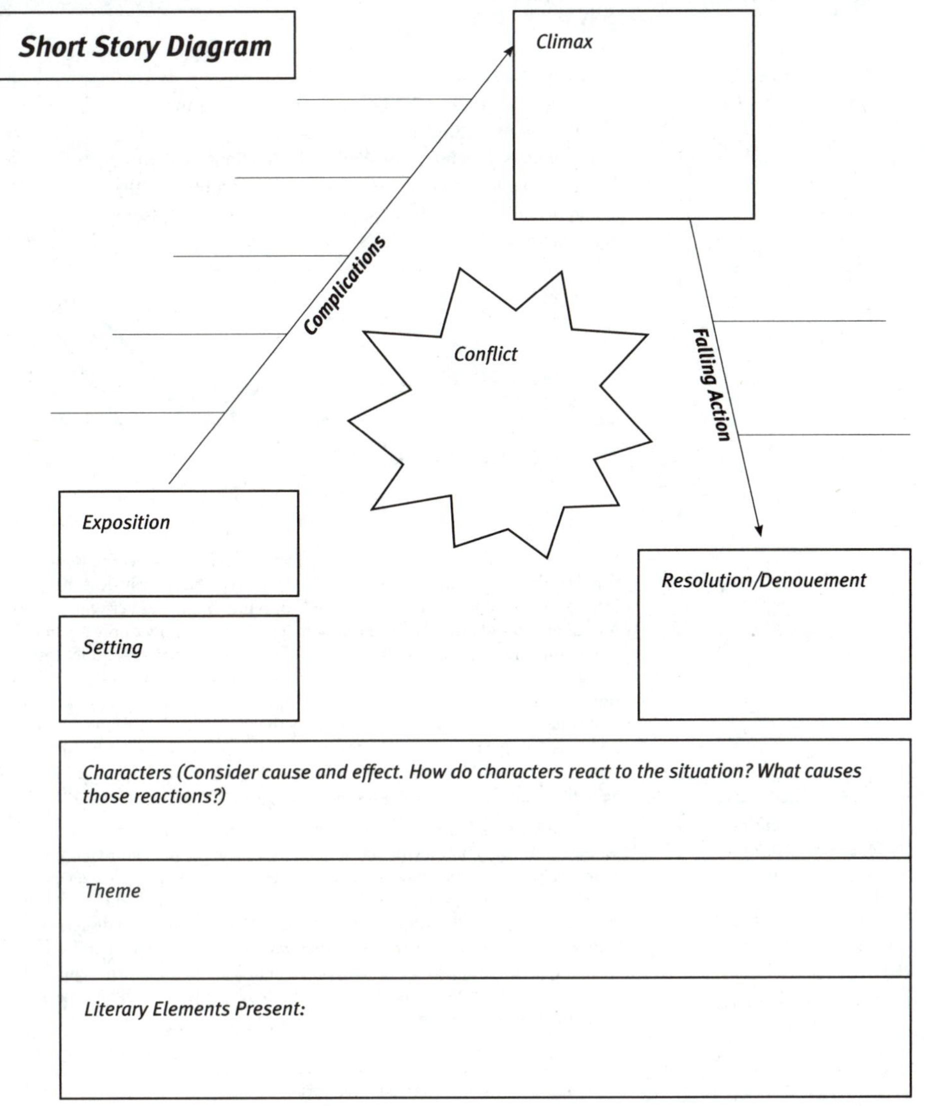

ACTIVITY 2.13

“The Stolen Party” Story Diagram

Materials:

- Highlighters or markers

Purpose:

- To identify short story elements and analyze their function within a narrative
- To diagram major elements of a short story in order to gain a greater understanding of the author’s intended effects

Steps:

1 This activity corresponds to the similar one for “The Cask of Amontillado” in Activity 2.6. Ask students to review the Short Story Diagram. Review each element with students, referring them to the definitions given in Activity 2.6, and answering questions if they arise.

2 Next, ask students to **reread** the story, looking for examples of each element. Suggest that they highlight the examples, using a different color for each major element. In addition, urge them to use the margin to jot down comments or notes regarding the textual examples they locate.

3 After students have reread and **marked the text**, ask them to independently complete the Short Story Diagram. Next, place students in small groups to compare their diagrams, discuss them, and make changes if necessary.

4 Check each group’s diagrams, and discuss the various elements of this story.

5 To directly scaffold Embedded Assessment 1, use this graphic as a way of practicing storyboarding. Divide students into small groups and assign each group an element of the diagram (exposition, conflict, climax, etc.). Instruct them to choose a scene that exemplifies their element and draw it. Remind them that their drawings can be either symbolic or representative.

ACTIVITY 2.14

SIFTing through "Marigolds"

Materials:

- Highlighters in different colors

Purpose:

- To analyze theme, key ideas, main ideas, and supporting ideas within a complex text
- To understand internal and external conflicts

Steps:

1 The **SIFT** (Symbol, Images, Figurative Language, and Tone/Theme) strategy allows students to "sift" through the parts of a text in order to comprehend how a writer uses literary elements and stylistic techniques to convey meaning or theme.

2 Instruct students to read "Marigolds" using appropriate reading strategies for comprehension. Remind students that they are looking for symbols, images, and figurative language that ultimately relate to tone/theme. You might suggest that they **mark the text** by color-coding examples of the elements of SIFT. They can record their findings in the **graphic organizer** on page 132.

3 For more directed instruction, consider the following prompts.

Symbolism: Since the title of a story sometimes includes symbols that hint at theme, ask students what associations they have with marigolds. Then ask them to consider the images of marigolds and dust. Some possible interpretations:

- The marigolds might symbolize hope amidst the surrounding despair.
- The dust might represent a depressing blanket of poverty and sadness that covers the speaker's memory and childhood existence.

ACTIVITY 2.14

SIFTing through "Marigolds"

SUGGESTED LEARNING STRATEGIES: Graphic Organizer, Marking the Text, SIFT, Visualizing

My Notes

Short Story

ABOUT THE AUTHOR

Eugenia Collier (b. 1928) grew up and continues to live in Baltimore. Retired now, she taught English at several universities. She has published two collections of short stories, a play, and many scholarly works. Her noteworthy and award-winning story "Marigolds" powerfully captures the moment of the narrator's coming of age.

by Eugenia W. Collier

When I think of the home town of my youth, all that I seem to remember is dust—the brown, crumbly dust of late summer—arid, sterile dust that gets into the eyes and makes them water, gets into the throat and between the toes of bare brown feet. I don't know why I should remember only the dust. Surely there must have been lush green lawns and paved streets under leafy shade trees somewhere in town; but memory is an abstract painting—it does not present things as they are, but rather as they *feel*. And so, when I think of that time and that place, I remember only the dry September of the dirt roads and grassless yards of the shantytown where I lived. And one other thing I remember, another incongruency[1] of memory—a brilliant splash of sunny yellow against the dust—Miss Lottie's marigolds.

Whenever the memory of those marigolds flashes across my mind, a strange nostalgia comes with it and remains long after the picture has faded. I feel again the chaotic emotions of adolescence, illusive as smoke, yet as real as the potted geranium before me now. Joy and rage and wild animal gladness and shame become tangled together in the multicolored skein of fourteen-going-on-fifteen as I recall that devastating moment when I was suddenly more woman than child, years ago in Miss Lottie's yard. I think of those marigolds at the strangest times; I remember them vividly now as I desperately pass away the time.

WORD CONNECTIONS

The word ***amorphous*** has the Greek root *-morph-*, meaning "shape" or "form." The root comes from Morpheus, the god of sleep—or shaper of dreams.

The Greek prefix *a-* means "not" or "without."

[1] **incongruency**: something that is not appropriate or fitting

© 2011 College Board. All rights reserved.

I suppose that futile waiting was the sorrowful background music of our impoverished little community when I was young. The Depression that gripped the nation was no new thing to us, for the black workers of rural Maryland had always been depressed. I don't know what it was that we were waiting for; certainly not for the prosperity that was "just around the corner," for those were white folks' words, which we never believed. Nor did we wait for hard work and thrift to pay off in shining success, as the American Dream promised, for we knew better than that, too. Perhaps we waited for a miracle, amorphous[2] in concept but necessary if one were to have the grit to rise before dawn each day and labor in the white man's vineyard until after dark, or to wander about in the September dust offering some meager share of bread. But God was chary[3] with miracles in those days, and so we waited—and waited.

We children, of course, were only vaguely aware of the extent of our poverty. Having no radios, few newspapers, and no magazines, we were somewhat unaware of the world outside our community. Nowadays we would be called culturally deprived and people would write books and hold conferences about us. In those days everybody we knew was just as hungry and ill clad as we were. Poverty was the cage in which we all were trapped, and our hatred of it was still the vague, undirected restlessness of the zoo-bred flamingo who knows that nature created him to fly free.

As I think of those days I feel most poignantly the tag end of summer, the bright, dry times when we began to have a sense of shortening days and the imminence of the cold.

By the time I was fourteen, my brother Joey and I were the only children left at our house, the older ones having left home for early marriage or the lure of the city, and the two babies having been sent to relatives who might care for them better than we. Joey was three years younger than I, and a boy, and therefore vastly inferior. Each morning our mother and father trudged wearily down the dirt road and around the bend, she to her domestic job, he to his daily unsuccessful quest for work. After our few chores around the tumbledown shanty, Joey and I were free to run wild in the sun with other children similarly situated.

For the most part, those days are ill-defined in my memory, running together and combining like a fresh watercolor painting left out in the rain. I remember squatting in the road drawing a picture in the dust, a picture which Joey gleefully erased with one sweep of his dirty foot. I remember fishing for minnows in a muddy creek and watching sadly as they eluded my

[2] **amorphous**: without shape or form
[3] **chary**: ungenerous, wary

GRAMMAR & USAGE

Formal diction sometimes requires the use of the **subjunctive** form of the verb to express a doubt, a wish, a possibility, or a situation contrary to fact.

The narrator in "Marigolds" uses the subjunctive to express a wish or possibility in this clause:

... if one **were** to have the grit to rise before dawn each day....

Use this model to write your own sentence expressing a wish or a possibility in either Lizabeth's or Miss Lottie's voice.

My Notes

ACTIVITY 2.14 *Continued*

Imagery: Writers use language to create sensory impressions and evoke specific responses. The author "shows" rather than "tells," thus allowing the reader to participate in the experience more fully. You might encourage students to ask themselves the following:

- What do I see, hear, taste, smell, or feel?
- What effect is the author trying to convey with these images?

Figurative language: Writers often create imagery through figurative language, such as similes, metaphors, and personification. Direct students to consider how figurative language helps to convey an effect. Consider the following questions for discussion:

- What metaphors does the speaker use to describe poverty and the hatred of poverty?
- What do these examples of figurative language have in common and how do they enhance meaning?

GRAMMAR & USAGE EXTENSION

You might explain that the subjunctive mood is no longer commonly used, and most forms have almost disappeared from modern English. However, the subjunctive is usually used in these situations:

- *if* clauses expressing contrary-to-fact conditions
- *that* clauses of recommendation, wish, or command; e.g., "It is important that you be on time." "I wish that she *were* more helpful."
- a few idiomatic phrases, such as "Be that as it may" or "If need be"

The subjunctive is usually the base form of the verb, except for the past of *be*, which is always *were*, not *was*, regardless of the subject.

You might wish to ask students to identify the subjunctive in Juliet's soliloquy in Activity 4.22 (line 8: What if this mixture *do not work* at all?).

Teacher Notes

SIFTing through "Marigolds"

My Notes

cupped hands, while Joey laughed uproariously. And I remember, that year, a strange restlessness of body and of spirit, a feeling that something old and familiar was ending, and something unknown and therefore terrifying was beginning.

One day returns to me with special clarity for some reason, perhaps because it was the beginning of the experience that in some inexplicable[4] way marked the end of innocence. I was loafing under the great oak tree in our yard, deep in some reverie which I have now forgotten, except that it involved some secret, secret thoughts of one of the Harris boys across the yard. Joey and a bunch of kids were bored now with the old tire suspended from an oak limb, which had kept them entertained for a while.

"Hey, Lizabeth," Joey yelled. He never talked when he could yell. "Hey, Lizabeth, let's go somewhere."

I came reluctantly from my private world. "Where you want to go? What you want to do?"

The truth was that we were becoming tired of the formlessness of our summer days. The idleness whose prospect had seemed so beautiful during the busy days of spring now had degenerated to an almost desperate effort to fill up the empty midday hours.

"Let's go see can we find some locusts on the hill," someone suggested.

Joey was scornful. "Ain't no more locusts there. Y'all got 'em all while they was still green."

The argument that followed was brief and not really worth the effort. Hunting locust trees wasn't fun anymore by now.

"Tell you what," said Joey finally, his eyes sparkling. "Let's us go over to Miss Lottie's."

The idea caught on at once, for annoying Miss Lottie was always fun. I was still child enough to scamper along with the group over rickety fences and through bushes that tore our already raggedy clothes, back to where Miss Lottie lived. I think now that we must have made a tragicomic spectacle, five or six kids of different ages, each of us clad in only one garment—the girls in faded dresses that were too long or too short, the boys in patchy pants, their sweaty brown chests gleaming in the hot sun. A little cloud of dust followed our thin legs and bare feet as we tramped over the barren land.

[4] **inexplicable**: unable to be explained or understood

Teacher Notes

When Miss Lottie's house came into view we stopped, ostensibly[5] to plan our strategy, but actually to reinforce our courage. Miss Lottie's house was the most ramshackle of all our ramshackle homes. The sun and rain had long since faded its rickety frame siding from white to a sullen gray. The boards themselves seemed to remain upright not from being nailed together but rather from leaning together, like a house that a child might have constructed from cards. A brisk wind might have blown it down, and the fact that it was still standing implied a kind of enchantment that was stronger than the elements. There it stood and as far as I know is standing yet—a gray, rotting thing with no porch, no shutters, no steps, set on a cramped lot with no grass, not even any weeds—a monument to decay.

In front of the house in a squeaky rocking chair sat Miss Lottie's son, John Burke, completing the impression of decay. John Burke was what was known as queer-headed. Black and ageless, he sat rocking day in and day out in a mindless stupor, lulled by the monotonous squeak-squawk of the chair. A battered hat atop his shaggy head shaded him from the sun. Usually John Burke was totally unaware of everything outside his quiet dream world. But if you disturbed him, if you intruded upon his fantasies, he would become enraged, strike out at you, and curse at you in some strange enchanted language which only he could understand. We children made a game of thinking of ways to disturb John Burke and then to elude his violent retribution.

But our real fun and our real fear lay in Miss Lottie herself. Miss Lottie seemed to be at least a hundred years old. Her big frame still held traces of the tall, powerful woman she must have been in youth, although it was now bent and drawn. Her smooth skin was a dark reddish brown, and her face had Indian-like features and the stern stoicism that one associates with Indian faces. Miss Lottie didn't like intruders either, especially children. She never left her yard, and nobody ever visited her. We never knew how she managed those necessities which depend on human interaction—how she ate, for example, or even whether she ate. When we were tiny children, we thought Miss Lottie was a witch and we made up tales that we half believed ourselves about her exploits. We were far too sophisticated now, of course, to believe the witch nonsense. But old fears have a way of clinging like cobwebs, and so when we sighted the tumbledown shack, we had to stop to reinforce our nerves.

"Look, there she is," I whispered, forgetting that Miss Lottie could not possibly have heard me from that distance. "She's fooling with them crazy flowers."

My Notes

[5] **ostensibly**: for the pretended reason

Teacher Notes

SIFTing through "Marigolds"

My Notes

"Yeh, look at 'er."

Miss Lottie's marigolds were perhaps the strangest part of the picture. Certainly they did not fit in with the crumbling decay of the rest of her yard. Beyond the dusty brown yard, in front of the sorry gray house, rose suddenly and shockingly a dazzling strip of bright blossoms, clumped together in enormous mounds, warm and passionate and sun-golden. The old black witch-woman worked on them all summer, every summer, down on her creaky knees, weeding and cultivating and arranging, while the house crumbled and John Burke rocked. For some perverse reason, we children hated those marigolds. They interfered with the perfect ugliness of the place; they were too beautiful; they said too much that we could not understand; they did not make sense. There was something in the vigor with which the old woman destroyed the weeds that intimidated us. It should have been a comical sight—the old woman with the man's hat on her cropped white head, leaning over the bright mounds, her big backside in the air—but it wasn't comical, it was something we could not name. We had to annoy her by whizzing a pebble into her flowers or by yelling a dirty word, then dancing away from her rage, reveling in our youth and mocking her age. Actually, I think it was the flowers we wanted to destroy, but nobody had the nerve to try it, not even Joey, who was usually fool enough to try anything.

"Y'all git some stones," commanded Joey now and was met with instant giggling obedience as everyone except me began to gather pebbles from the dusty ground. "Come on, Lizabeth."

I just stood there peering through the bushes, torn between wanting to join the fun and feeling that it was all a bit silly.

"You scared, Lizabeth?"

I cursed and spat on the ground—my favorite gesture of phony bravado. "Y'all children get the stones, I'll show you how to use 'em."

I said before that we children were not consciously aware of how thick were the bars of our cage. I wonder now, though, whether we were not more aware of it than I thought. Perhaps we had some dim notion of what we were, and how little chance we had of being anything else. Otherwise, why would we have been so preoccupied with destruction? Anyway, the pebbles were collected quickly, and everybody looked at me to begin the fun.

"Come on, y'all."

Teacher Notes

My Notes

We crept to the edge of the bushes that bordered the narrow road in front of Miss Lottie's place. She was working placidly, kneeling over the flowers, her dark hand plunged into the golden mound. Suddenly *zing*—an expertly aimed stone cut the head off one of the blossoms.

"Who out there?" Miss Lottie's backside came down and her head came up as her sharp eyes searched the bushes. "You better git!"

We had crouched down out of sight in the bushes, where we stifled the giggles that insisted on coming. Miss Lottie gazed warily across the road for a moment, then cautiously returned to her weeding. *Zing*—Joey sent a pebble into the blooms, and another marigold was beheaded.

Miss Lottie was enraged now. She began struggling to her feet, leaning on a rickety cane and shouting. "Y'all git! Go on home!" Then the rest of the kids let loose with their pebbles, storming the flowers and laughing wildly and senselessly at Miss Lottie's impotent rage. She shook her stick at us and started shakily toward the road crying, "Git 'long! John Burke! John Burke, come help!"

Then I lost my head entirely, mad with the power of inciting such rage, and ran out of the bushes in the storm of pebbles, straight toward Miss Lottie, changing madly, "Old witch, fell in a ditch, picked up a penny and thought she was rich!" The children screamed with delight, dropped their pebbles, and joined the crazy dance, swarming around Miss Lottie like bees and changing, "Old lady witch!" while she screamed curses at us. The madness lasted only a moment, for John Burke, startled at last, lurched out of his chair, and we dashed for the bushes just as Miss Lottie's cane went whizzing at my head.

I did not join the merriment when the kids gathered again under the oak in our bare yard. Suddenly I was ashamed, and I did not like being ashamed. The child in me sulked and said it was all in fun, but the woman in me flinched at the thought of the malicious attack that I had led. The mood lasted all afternoon. When we ate the beans and rice that was supper that night, I did not notice my father's silence, for he was always silent these days, nor did I notice my mother's absence, for she always worked until well into evening. Joey and I had a particularly bitter argument after supper; his exuberance[6] got on my nerves. Finally I stretched out upon the pallet in the room we shared and fell into a fitful doze. When I awoke, somewhere in the middle of the night, my mother had returned, and I vaguely listened to the conversation that was audible through the thin walls that separated our

[6] **exuberance**: extreme good cheer or high spirits

Teacher Notes

SIFTing through "Marigolds"

My Notes

rooms. At first I heard no words, only voices. My mother's voice was like a cool, dark room in summer—peaceful, soothing, quiet. I loved to listen to it; it made things seem all right somehow. But my father's voice cut through hers, shattering the peace.

"Twenty-two years, Maybelle, twenty-two years," he was saying, "and I got nothing for you, nothing, nothing."

"It's all right, honey, you'll get something. Everybody out of work now, you know that."

"It ain't right. Ain't no man ought to eat his woman's food year in and year out, and see his children running wild. Ain't nothing right about that."

"Honey, you took good care of us when you had it. Ain't nobody got nothing nowadays."

"I ain't talking about nobody else, I'm talking about *me*. God knows I try." My mother said something I could not hear, and my father cried out louder, "What must a man do, tell me that?"

"Look, we ain't starving. I get paid every week, and Mrs. Ellis is real nice about giving me things. She gonna let me have Mr. Ellis's old coat for you this winter—"

"Damn Mr. Ellis's coat! And damn his money! You think I want white folks' leavings? Damn, Maybelle"—and suddenly he sobbed, loudly and painfully, and cried helplessly and hopelessly in the dark night. I had never heard a man cry before. I did not know men ever cried. I covered my ears with my hand but could not cut off the sound of my father's harsh, painful, despairing sobs. My father was a strong man who could whisk a child upon his shoulders and go singing through the house. My father whittled toys for us, and laughed so loud that the great oak seemed to laugh with him, and taught us how to fish and hunt rabbits. How could it be that my father was crying? But the sobs went on, unstifled, finally quieting until I could hear my mother's voice, deep and rich, humming softly as she used to hum to a frightened child.

The world had lost its boundary lines. My mother, who was small and soft, was now the strength of the family; my father, who was the rock on which the family had been built, was sobbing like the tiniest child. Everything was suddenly out of tune, like a broken accordion. Where did I fit into this crazy picture? I do not now remember my thoughts, only a feeling of great bewilderment and fear.

Teacher Notes

My Notes

Long after the sobbing and humming had stopped, I lay on the pallet, still as stone with my hands over my ears, wishing that I too could cry and be comforted. The night was silent now except for the sound of the crickets and of Joey's soft breathing. But the room was too crowded with fear to allow me to sleep, and finally, feeling the terrible aloneness of 4 A.M., I decided to awaken Joey.

"Ouch! What's the matter with you? What you want?" he demanded disagreeably when I had pinched and slapped him awake.

"Come on, wake up."

"What for? Go 'way."

I was lost for a reasonable reply. I could not say, "I'm scared and I don't want to be alone," so I merely said, "I'm going out. If you want to come, come on."

The promise of adventure awoke him. "Going out now? Where to, Lizabeth? What you going to do?"

I was pulling my dress over my head. Until now I had not thought of going out. "Just come on," I replied tersely

I was out the window and halfway down the road before Joey caught up with me.

"Wait, Lizabeth, where you going?"

I was running as if the Furies[7] were after me, as perhaps they were—running silently and furiously until I came to where I had half known I was headed: to Miss Lottie's yard.

The half-dawn light was more eerie than complete darkness, and in it the old house was like the ruin that my world had become—foul and crumbling, a grotesque caricature. It looked haunted, but I was not afraid, because I was haunted too.

"Lizabeth, you lost your mind?" panted Joey.

I had indeed lost my mind, for all the smoldering emotions of that summer swelled in me and burst—the great need for my mother who was never there, the hopelessness of our poverty and degradation, the bewilderment of being neither child nor woman and yet both at once, the fear

[7] **Furies**: in classical mythology, three spirits of revenge who pursued and punished wrongdoers.

Teacher Notes

SIFTing through "Marigolds"

My Notes

unleashed by my father's tears. And these feelings combined in one great impulse toward destruction.

"Lizabeth!"

I leaped furiously into the mounds of marigolds and pulled madly, trampling and pulling and destroying the perfect yellow blooms. The fresh smell of early morning and of dew-soaked marigolds spurred me on as I went gearing and mangling and sobbing while Joey tugged my dress or my waist crying, "Lizabeth, stop, please stop!"

And then I was sitting in the ruined little garden among the uprooted and ruined flowers, crying and crying, and it was too late to undo what I had done. Joey was sitting beside me, silent and frightened, not knowing what to say. Then, "Lizabeth, look."

I opened my swollen eyes and saw in front of me a pair of large, calloused feet; my gaze lifted to the swollen legs, the age-distorted body clad in a tight cotton nightdress, and then the shadowed Indian face surrounded by stubby white hair. And there was no rage in the face now, now that the garden was destroyed and there was nothing any longer to be protected.

"M-miss Lottie!" I scrambled to my feet and just stood there and stared at here, and that was the moment when childhood faded and womanhood began. That violent, crazy act was the last act of childhood. For as I gazed at the immobile face with the sad, weary eyes, I gazed upon a kind of reality which is hidden to childhood. The witch was no longer a witch but only a broken old woman who had dared to create beauty in the midst of ugliness and sterility. She had been born in squalor and lived in it all her life. Now at the end of that life she had nothing except a falling-down hut, a wrecked body, and John Burke, the mindless son of her passion. Whatever verve there was left in her, whatever was of love and beauty and joy that had not been squeezed out by life, had been there in the marigolds she had so tenderly cared for.

Of course I could not express the things that I knew about Miss Lottie as I stood there awkward and ashamed. The years have put words to the things I knew in that moment, and as I look back upon it, I know that that moment marked the end of innocence. Innocence involves an unseeing acceptance of things at face value, an ignorance of the area below the surface. In that

© 2011 College Board. All rights reserved.

130 SpringBoard® English Textual Power™ Level 4

humiliating moment I had looked beyond myself and into the depths of another person. This was the beginning of compassion, and one cannot have both compassion and innocence.

The years have taken me worlds away from that time and that place, from the dust and squalor of our lives, and from the bright thing that I destroyed in a blind, childish striking out at God knows what. Miss Lottie died long ago and many years have passed since I last saw her hut, completely barren at last, for despite my wild contrition[8] she never planted marigolds again. Yet, there are times when the image of those passionate yellow mounds returns with a painful poignancy. For one does not have to be ignorant and poor to find that his life is as barren as the dusty yards of our town. And I too have planted marigolds.

[8] **contrition**: sorrow or remorse for one's wrongs

My Notes

Tone/Theme: Students should feel comfortable with both of these subjects, but you might wish to offer the following:

- What words or phrases reveal the narrator's attitude, or **tone**, toward her environment, her growth process, and Miss Lottie?
- List the subject or subjects that emerge from the story such as poverty, coming of age, innocence, etc. Then write a thematic statement about each subject based on insights gained from the analysis of the text.

Steps:

4 Allow time for students to complete the SIFT chart.

SIFTing through "Marigolds"

The acronym SIFT stands for Symbol, Images, Figurative Language, and Tone or Theme. You can use this strategy to "sift" through the parts of a story in order to explore how a writer uses literary elements and stylistic techniques to convey meaning or theme.

Record examples from "Marigolds" of each of the SIFT elements in the graphic organizer.

Symbol:	
Imagery:	
Figurative Language:	
Tone/Theme:	

"Marigolds" is a story that examines the coming of age of a young girl, Lizabeth. In order to truly understand the story, as well as Lizabeth's transformation, you must clearly articulate the choices that she makes along the way, both within her own mind and between forces from the outside world. On the following chart, examine the internal and external conflicts Lizabeth faces.

LITERARY TERMS

An **internal conflict** occurs when a character struggles between opposing needs or desires or emotions within his or her own mind.

An **external conflict** occurs when a character struggles against an outside force. This force may be another character, a societal expectation, or something in the physical world.

Internal Conflicts

One side of the conflict	The other side of the conflict

External Conflicts

One side of the conflict	The other side of the conflict

© 2011 College Board. All rights reserved.

Steps:

5 Ask students to consider the internal and external conflicts associated with the main character. Ask them to identify instances of both internal and external conflicts on the chart and make connections to the theme. In addition, ask them to **visualize** these conflicts and represent them visually either through a representative or symbolic drawing.

Differentiating Instruction:

To help **support** students' understanding of "Marigolds," you may want to use the **TWIST** strategy by guiding students through a discussion of the author's **tone**, how the author's **word choice** indicates her feelings, the specific **imagery** or details that evoke specific reactions from readers, how the author's **style** affects the reader's interpretation, and the **theme** the author presents. Focus specifically on how internal and external conflicts help to establish a theme. After the discussion, have students write an interpretive response to the text using the elements of TWIST. This writing will help support their understanding of the text as well as scaffold toward their writing in the end of the unit.

Expand the activity by encouraging students to combine analysis and persuasion and write a persuasive piece on which of the protagonist's choices was the most important in shaping who she was. The product can be a structured paragraph or a complete essay.

ACTIVITY 2.15

Working with Cinematic Techniques: Part I

Materials:

- 8½ x 11 construction paper
- Vocabulary Notebooks

Purpose:

- To analyze and interpret how directors use cinematic techniques to achieve specific effects

Steps:

1 Students will now move from visualizing a moment in a story to creating a plan for filming a chunk of a story. Direct students to the lists of film terms, which they will use to discuss and analyze film.

2 To demonstrate how a film works, have students **manipulate** a paper camera to simulate the effects of a real camera. Instruct them to roll a sheet of construction paper into a tube and hold it up to their eye like a telescope. Ask them to manipulate the paper "camera" to help **visualize** various kinds of shots and angles, as if it were a real camera. You might ask a volunteer to stand in front of the class to be the subject of students' frames.

3 To get a long shot, direct students to unroll the paper to create a large lens in order to get a shot of the student's full body. Ask them what this shot enables the viewer to see.

4 Next, ask students to decrease the size of the lens on the paper camera to get a medium shot (from the waist up). Ask students to consider why a director might use this shot. Further, what does this shot reveal to the viewer?

5 Next, ask students to decrease the size of the lens to get a close up shot (capturing only the face). Ask students to consider why a director might use this shot.

ACTIVITY 2.15

Working with Cinematic Techniques: Part 1

SUGGESTED LEARNING STRATEGIES: Marking the Text, Visualizing, Word Map

ACADEMIC VOCABULARY

Cinematic techniques are the methods a director uses to communicate meaning and to evoke particular emotional responses in viewers.

You have spent a good deal of time visualizing three short stories. In Embedded Assessment 1, you will address film. One of the first steps in filmmaking is visualizing, in the form of storyboarding. To prepare to make a storyboard, examine these cinematic techniques.

Shots and Framing

Shot: a single piece of film uninterrupted by cuts.

Establishing Shot: often a long shot or a series of shots that sets the scene. It is used to establish setting and to show transitions between locations.

Long Shot (LS): a shot from some distance. If filming a person, the full body is shown. It may show the isolation or vulnerability of the character (also called a Full Shot).

Medium Shot (MS): the most common shot. The camera seems to be a medium distance from the object being filmed. A medium shot shows the person from the waist up. The effect is to ground the story.

Close Up (CU): the image takes up at least 80 percent of the frame.

Extreme Close Up: the image being shot is a part of a whole, such as an eye or a hand.

Two Shot: a scene between two people shot exclusively from an angle that includes both characters more or less equally. It is used in love scenes where interaction between the two characters is important.

Camera Angles

Eye Level: a shot taken from a normal height; that is, the character's eye level. Ninety to ninety-five percent of the shots seen are eye level, because it is the most natural angle.

High Angle: the camera is above the subject. This usually has the effect of making the subject look smaller than normal, giving him or her the appearance of being weak, powerless, and trapped.

Low Angle: the camera films subject from below. This usually has the effect of making the subject look larger than normal, and therefore strong, powerful, and threatening.

6 Finally, ask students to roll their paper camera tighter in an effort to zoom into an extreme close up (focusing on one specific aspect, such as an eye or ear). Again, ask students why a director might use this shot.

Camera Movements

Pan: a stationary camera moves from side to side on a horizontal axis.

Tilt: a stationary camera moves up or down along a vertical axis.

Zoom: a stationary camera where the lens moves to make an object seem to move closer to or further away from the camera. With this technique, moving into a character is often a personal or revealing movement, while moving away distances or separates the audience from the character.

Dolly/Tracking: the camera is on a track that allows it to move with the action. The term also refers to any camera mounted on a car, truck, or helicopter.

Boom/Crane: the camera is on a crane over the action. This is used to create overhead shots.

Lighting

High Key: the scene is flooded with light, creating a bright and open-looking scene.

Low Key: the scene is flooded with shadows and darkness, creating suspense or suspicion.

Bottom or Side Lighting: direct lighting from below or the side, which often makes the subject appear dangerous or evil.

Front or Back Lighting: soft lighting on the actor's face or from behind gives the appearance of innocence or goodness, or a halo effect.

Editing Techniques

Cut: most common editing technique. Two pieces of film are spliced together to "cut" to another image.

Fade: can be to or from black or white. A fade can begin in darkness and gradually assume full brightness (fade-in) or the image may gradually get darker (fade-out). A fade often implies that time has passed or may signify the end of a scene.

Dissolve: a kind of fade in which one image is slowly replaced by another. It can create a connection between images.

Wipe: a new image wipes off the previous image. A wipe is more fluid than a cut and quicker than a dissolve.

Flashback: cut or dissolve to action that happened in the past.

Shot-Reverse-Shot: a shot of one subject, then another, then back to the first. It is often used for conversation or reaction shots.

Steps:

7 Students can adjust the paper camera to resemble many different shots, angles, and camera movements. For example, they can simulate a pan by turning their heads from left to right, and they may achieve a low angle may by sitting on the floor and "filming" a clock up on the wall.

8 Allow students to practice other shots and effects in order to develop a conceptual understanding of these film terms. Encourage them to consider the effects of each technique and the kinds of situations in which a director might use them. Engage students in a discussion about the similarities between an author's purpose and a director's choices.

9 After students have practiced various shots and angles, lead them through a summary of the cinematic techniques. Provide a brief explanation of why and how directors use these shots, angles, and camera movements. Allow students to **mark the text** and take notes and make sketches in the margin as you review the film terminology.

10 Instruct students to create an appropriate **word map graphic organizer** in their **Vocabulary Notebooks** to explore the concept of ***cinematic techniques***.

Teacher Notes

Working with Cinematic Techniques: Part 1

Cross Cutting: cut into action that is happening simultaneously. This technique is also called parallel editing. It can create tension or suspense and can form a connection between scenes.

Eye-Line Match: cut to an object, then to a person. This technique shows what a person seems to be looking at and can reveal a character's thoughts.

Sound

Diegetic: sound that could logically be heard by the characters in the film.

Non-Diegetic: sound that cannot be heard by the characters but is designed for audience reaction only. An example might be ominous music for foreshadowing.

Applying Cinematic Techniques

ACTIVITY 2.16

SUGGESTED LEARNING STRATEGIES: Close Reading, Graphic Organizer

Shots and Framing	Camera Angles	Camera Movements	Lighting	Editing	Music/Sound

Analysis: Choose the most significant cinematic technique from your notes above, and write an interpretive statement that explains the effect of this cinematic technique in the commercial.

ACTIVITY 2.16

Applying Cinematic Techniques

Materials:

- Magazines and glue sticks
- A video of a commercial

Purpose:

- To identify cinematic techniques in a commercial
- To revise sketches and transform them into a storyboard
- To explain the effect of the cinematic choices

Steps:

1 Ask students to create a collage of pictures that reflect the various cinematic techniques. Have them search through magazines on a scavenger hunt for examples that demonstrate the various cinematic techniques. They could also take photos themselves to use as some of the examples. To demonstrate their understanding, they should categorize the pictures on their collages (e.g., framing) and label them for viewers (e.g., close up). If students have access to video cameras, they can create a film-terminology video presentation that identifies and displays the film terms in application.

2 Ask students to present their collages in small groups in order to review the film terms.

3 Next, introduce students to the practice of **close reading** a film by showing them a commercial that employs a variety of cinematic techniques (e.g., shots, framing, camera angles, camera movement, lighting, editing, and sound) with sound off. Instruct students to clap to signal a cut from one shot to the next.

4 View the commerical a second time with the sound on and ask students to identify as many cinematic techniques as they can. If this task is too overwhelming, assign students to watch for a single technique; then use a **jigsaw** for sharing. Have students note their observations on the **graphic organizer**. Invite students to revisit the film terminology charts as a resource in their discussion.

5 Ask students to choose the most significant cinematic technique and write an interpretive statement that explains the effect of that technique.

ACTIVITY 2.16 *Continued*

Steps:

6 Discuss the purpose of a storyboard. Be sure to mention that it allows the director to visualize what his or her film will look like, prior to the actual filming. Many DVDs now include the director's storyboards in the bonus materials; consider showing students one or more of these.

7 Ask students to revisit the sketches they created for "A Poison Tree" (Activity 2.3) and to consider how a storyboard of several frames might differ from the single visual representation that they created. Remind students that the poem uses a metaphor to represent an act of revenge; they should brainstorm a plot that presents the poem in a concrete way.

8 Ask students to draw five or six frames of a storyboard adaptation of a section of the poem. Instruct them to make deliberate choices regarding cinematic techniques that would effectively capture the text as a film. This activity might best be done in pairs. You might also consider allowing students to use sticky notes for a first draft so that they can rearrange the frames if they choose.

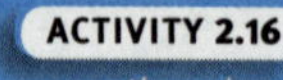

continued

Applying Cinematic Techniques

Storyboarding allows filmmakers to plan the details of the film, shot by shot, in advance, saving time and money. You have visualized a moment in several texts in this unit, beginning with the poem "A Poison Tree" (Activity 2.3). Take a moment to review the sketches you created. Think now about how you might expand that visualization of a single image into a sequence of five or six shots. Describe those shots in the storyboard below.

SHOT #

Describe the Music/Sound:

Dialogue:

Framing: ____________

Lighting:

SHOT #

Describe the Music/Sound:

Dialogue:

Framing: ____________

Lighting:

SHOT #

Describe the Music/Sound:

Dialogue:

Framing: ______________

Lighting:

SHOT #

Describe the Music/Sound:

Dialogue:

Framing: ______________

Lighting:

Reflection: Why did you choose the framing, lighting, and music that you did? What words or phrases from the poem made you picture this? Explain.

Steps:

9 When students are finished, have them answer the reflective questions about their reasons for using particular cinematic elements.

10 If possible, obtain a video showing workplace training. Have students contrast cinematic techniques with fiction and nonfiction topics.

Embedded Assessment 1

Creating a Storyboard

College Board Standards and Objectives

M3 Composing and Producing Media Communication (M3.1, 3.2; 3.3)
PE Mappings: M3.1-1.4, M3.2-4.4, M3.3-1.4

R1 Student Comprehends the Meaning of Words and Sentences (R1.2)
PE Mappings: R1.2-2.4

R4 Using Strategies to Comprehend Texts (R4.3)
PE Mappings: R4.3-3.4

W3 Drafting (W3.1 Cr)
PE Mappings: W3.1-1.4 Cr

S2 Speaking in Interpersonal Contexts (S2.2)
PE Mappings: S2.2-2.4

S3 Preparing and Delivering Presentations (S3.1; S3.2)
PE Mappings: S3.1-1.4, S3.2-2.4

L3 Listening for Diverse Purposes (L3.1)
PE Mappings: L3.1-1.4

Steps:

1 Emphasize to students that this assigment includes an explanation as well as a storyboard. They might want to keep track of reasons for their choices as they make them; they can then later write their explanation from their notes.

2 Arrange students into collaborative groups for this assignment.

3 You may opt to have students use a new short story to extend the concept. If so, consider using a short story with the specific elements discussed in this unit (imagery, foreshadowing, irony, etc.). Also consider the thematic vein: coming of age.

4 Suggest that students use the Short Story Diagram to help them decide the segment to use for their storyboards. You might also assign sequential sections of a single story to different groups so that the entire story is represented.

5 Provide students with copies of the storyboard **graphic organizer** in Activity 2.16.

Embedded Assessment 1

Creating a Storyboard

SUGGESTED LEARNING STRATEGIES: **Graphic Organizer, Sharing And Responding**

Assignment

Your assignment is to work collaboratively to transform a section of a printed text into a storyboard. You will also include a written explanation of the intended effects of your cinematic choices.

Steps

Planning

1. Revisit a short story from this unit that you could imagine as a film. As a group, select a small passage to transform into a storyboard of at least 20 shots. You will not be able to capture the entire story in your storyboard; choose a compelling section that contains many visual elements.
2. As director, decide how you would like to show your version of this text and the effect you want it to have on your audience. Present your ideas to your group, and reach a consensus about your focus.

Drafting

3. Brainstorm a sequence of shots. Consider framing, camera movement, lighting, sound, and editing in each shot. Use sticky notes to sketch out or describe each shot on the Storyboard Graphic Organizer. Be sure to consider the effect you are trying to create with each shot and the words or phrases that communicate your vision. Share this draft within your small group. Even if you plan photographs for your final draft, you should sketch what your photos will look like for this first draft. Decide how to share the responsibilities of producing each element of the storyboard. Create a draft.

Refining

4. As a group, share your ideas with another group. Solicit feedback on
   - Clear sequence of ideas
   - Effective use of cinematic techniques in relation to the story
   - Accurate identification and application of cinematic techniques

   Use the notes generated during the peer group discussion, and revise your storyboard. Add an explanation of the intended effect of your choices. Be specific in terms of your framing, lighting, sound, and other choices, and be sure that your effect is consistent with your cinematic choices. Support your explanation with textual evidence from the short story.

Revising and Editing for Publication

5. Prepare your final draft. Choose a presentation method, such as mounting your frames onto poster board or creating a slide show. Label each frame with all the information required (shot type, angle, lighting, and sound), including intended effect of each shot.

TECHNOLOGY TIP Consider designing and publishing your work using a graphics or presentation software program.

© 2011 College Board. All rights reserved.

Embedded Assessment 1
continued

SCORING GUIDE

Scoring Criteria	Exemplary	Proficient	Emerging
Storyboard **Display of Cinematic Elements**	A compelling section of the selected story is vividly demonstrated through a clear sequence of ideas. The storyboard contains visually appealing frames that skillfully use images to convey a variety of cinematic elements. Each frame is completely and precisely labeled with information about shot type, angle, lighting, and sound.	An appropriate section of the selected story is demonstrated through an organized sequence of ideas. The storyboard contains frames that adequately use images to convey several cinematic elements. Each frame is accurately labeled with information about shot type, angle, lighting, and sound.	The selected section of the story may be inappropriate or may not demonstrate a logical sequence of ideas. The frames of the storyboard are insufficient. Images convey a limited number of cinematic elements. Frames may be labeled inconsistently and/or inaccurately.
Storyboard **Explanatory Text**	The written explanation provides a clear and detailed explanation that uses precise textual evidence to insightfully connect the cinematic choices to short story elements and intended effects.	The written explanation demonstrates a logical understanding of the effect of cinematic elements in relationship to short story elements; cinematic choices are supported by textual evidence.	The written explanation demonstrates a limited understanding of the effect of cinematic choices in relationship to short story elements. Textual support is lacking.
Evidence of Collaboration	The product demonstrates extensive evidence of successful planning and collaboration.	The product shows evidence of adequate planning and collaboration.	Inadequate planning and collaboration are evident.
Additional Criteria			

Comments:

Embedded Assessment 1
Continued

Steps:

6 You might choose to ask students to add a comparison piece in which they select two analogous scenes from different short stories. The scenes might illustrate any of the following:

- Moment of realization
- Foreshadowing
- Character blindness
- Final moment
- Significant dialogue

7 **Sharing** drafts **and responding** to another group's gives students an opportunity to reinforce their understanding of the application of film techniques.

8 As students prepare their final drafts for presentation, you might wish to allow students to enhance this assessment with various technology elements. For example, students can take digital photos or film still shots.

9 Remind students to submit their explanations along with their storyboards.

Scoring Guide

When you score this Embedded Assessment, you may wish to download and print a copy of the Scoring Guide from SpringBoard Online. In this way, you can have a copy to mark for each student's work.

LEARNING FOCUS:
What Is Your Style?

Previewing Embedded Assessment 2

Explain to students that, for Embedded Assessment 2, they will compose a multi-paragraph essay analyzing the cinematic style of director Tim Burton. They will focus on the ways in which the director uses stylistic techniques to achieve a desired effect. Direct students to the Embedded Assessment assignment and the Scoring Guide (pages 181–183). Guide students through a **close reading** of the prompt, steps, and Scoring Guide criteria.

Steps:

1 Read the Learning Focus with students or have them read independently. **Activate prior knowledge** by having students **mark the text** and highlight words or concepts that are familiar (what they know). They might use a question mark to indicate content that is unfamiliar (what they do not know but want to learn).

2 Engage students in a whole class discussion. You may revisit the **KWL chart** you created at the beginning of the unit to discover what students have learned.

Learning Focus:

What Is Your Style?

Whether it is the clothes you wear, how you walk and talk, or the way you decorate your room, you have your own unique **style**. How you choose to present yourself in a variety of situations reflects your individual style. This concept of style is similar in literary works.

Style in a written text can be investigated from a number of vantage points. It may be seen, for instance, in the way in which an author's **diction**, **imagery**, and **rhetorical devices** create a particular effect.

But what about film? In past units, you have viewed film much like a narrative, with plot, characters, conflicts, etc. Now, you will expand your view of film by approaching this visual medium through the lens of the director as author. Thus, you will begin to see the explicit connections between an author's choices of literary techniques and a director's choices of cinematic techniques. You can see some of these comparisons below.

- Tone/Mood may be represented by Lighting and Sound
- Diction may be represented by Dialogue
- Imagery may be represented by Symbolism, Costuming, Setting
- Organization may be represented by Storyboarding
- Syntax may be represented by Editing
- Point of view may be represented by Framing, Shot Type, and Camera Movement

Just as you analyze a short story to understand how its literary elements work together, so too you can analyze a film and how its cinematic elements work together to tell a story. Analyzing style takes this analysis one step further in that it allows you to understand and appreciate the creative craft of the author or director. Authors and directors choose to include certain elements to create certain effects, and these choices in turn reflect the style of the creator. Understanding style in literature is to have a larger understanding of not just the story, but also the craftsmanship of creation.

The imaginative and unusual worlds created by the director Tim Burton in his feature films provide the viewer with clear examples of a unique approach to telling a story. You may already enjoy the films of Tim Burton, and perhaps even appreciate them for their distinctive style of storytelling. Identifying and analyzing the elements of style will give you a vocabulary for explaining your understanding and appreciation of a contemporary, nonprint, literary text.

Film 101

ACTIVITY 2.17

SUGGESTED LEARNING STRATEGIES: **Close Reading, Graphic Organizer**

In the remainder of this unit, you will be viewing film as text. Consider your history of viewing film, and complete the following survey citing specific examples and experiences.

1. Approximately how many movies do you watch a month (on DVD or cable or in a theater)?

WORD CONNECTIONS

The relationship in an analogy may show an object and its description; for example, film : award-winning. Complete the following analogy.

film : award-winning :: novel : best-selling.

2. What are your favorite types of movies? Explain.

3. What are your least favorite types of movies? Explain.

4. List in order the top five best films ever made, in your opinion.

ACTIVITY 2.17
Film 101

Purpose:

- To consider media as a reflection of culture and self
- To draw on relevant prior knowledge and experience to make connections between text and film
- To explore, critique, and evaluate responses in a group discussion

Steps:

1 Give students a few minutes to fill out the film survey. When they have finished, lead them through a whole-class discussion, soliciting their responses.

2 In small groups, prompt students to share their lists of the top five best films ever made and discuss the reasons for their choices. Then ask them to come to consensus and compile one list of the top five films that reflects the group's thinking.

3 As part of an anticipatory set, engage the class in a focused discussion to determine whether they agree or disagree with each group's top-five list. Each group will read its list beginning with number five and ending with number one. If the majority of students agrees with the selections, then you can proceed. If not, ask students to defend their choices orally; allow a discussion to occur.

Steps:

4 To further the discussion, you might consider the following prompts to uncover trends:

- Are your lists a representative cross-section of films? (Consider style, genre, date of production.)
- Are your movies specific to your age group, or are they widely viewed by all ages?
- Would you consider your movies to be part of popular mainstream culture, or are they more obscure?

Film 101

5. What kind of movies do your parents or guardians like to watch? How often do you watch movies with them?

6. What are the differences between watching a movie at home and watching in a theater?

7. What kind of movies do you watch in school?

8. What are you normally asked by the teacher to do while or after watching a film?

© 2011 College Board. All rights reserved.

144 SpringBoard® English Textual Power™ Level 4

Reading a text and viewing a film have similarities and differences. In addition, the author of a text or the director of a film can affect his/her audience through common and/or dissimilar tools, strategies, and methods. Consider the roles of both creator and audience member and fill out the following graphic organizer. You might consider the following prompts to focus your answers:

- What can a director do that an author cannot, and vice versa?
- What tools and strategies do authors and directors share? What tools and strategies are different?
- Are you more entertained by reading books or by watching movies? Why?
- Why might a teacher ask you to read a book rather than watch a movie?
- Is the suggestion that one "should always read the book before watching the movie" valid? Why or why not?

Steps:

5 Direct students to individually fill in the Venn diagram **graphic organizer** to make comparisons between viewing a film and reading a text. Remind students to read through the prompting questions prior to completing the Venn diagram.

6 When students have completed their graphic organizer, elicit responses and record student answers on a class diagram (poster paper, white board, etc.).

ACTIVITY 2.18
Film in Context: An Authorial Study

Materials:
- Internet access

Purpose:
- To recognize that authors both use and deviate from genre norms to achieve specific effects
- To draw appropriate conclusions about research topics
- To develop context for the films to be analyzed
- To identify common themes

Steps:
1 Begin by reviewing the definitions of **subject** and **theme** with your students. It is important for them to differentiate between a theme and a subject as they identify central messages in the text.

2 Point out that students will return to complete this page after they have read the article that begins on the following page.

ACTIVITY 2.18

Film in Context: An Authorial Study

SUGGESTED LEARNING STRATEGIES: Graphic Organizer, Marking the Text, Notetaking, Summarizing

Director Tim Burton's life is as unique as his filming style. With an understanding of what has influenced him, we can begin to understand the directorial choices he has made. However, before we venture into the wild and fantastic world of Tim Burton, we must first review a key term: theme.

LITERARY TERMS
Theme is the central message of a literary work.

Theme is not the same as a **subject**, which can be expressed in a word or two: courage, survival, war, pride, etc. The theme is the idea the author wishes to convey about that subject. It is expressed as a sentence or general statement about life or human nature. A literary work may have more than one theme, and most themes are not directly stated but rather are implied. The reader must think about all the elements of the work and use them to make inferences, or reasonable guesses, about themes in a work. An example of a theme on the subject of pride might be that pride often precedes a fall.

Read carefully the short article entitled "Hollywood Outsider Tim Burton" from CBS News (March 5, 2006). While you read, record two or three possible subjects that might arise in Burton's films that reflect some of his beliefs and experiences.

SUBJECTS:

1.

2.

3.

Once you have created a class list, choose one of the subjects and turn it into a theme statement. Remember that themes must be inferred. You must think about what you have read and make a reasonable guess as to what Burton might believe.

THEME STATEMENT:

Article

Hollywood Outsider

TIM BURTON

from cbsnews.com

The Corpse Bride is a ghoulish animated glee about a shy boy who marries a dead girl by mistake. It's full of crumbling bones, and dead people stealing the show. It all may sound strange, but not to those who know Tim Burton, the director who earned an Oscar nomination for best animated feature.

"Tim's bottled something magical, and I'm drinking it," said Johnny Depp, the voice of Victor, the groom.

"I've always been interested in the juxtaposition of what people say is fantasy versus reality or what's normal versus abnormal," said Burton. "They always seem different to me."

It's a vision that's as dark and oddly appealing as Burton himself is when you sit down with him, as Mika Brzezinski did for a rare interview.

"I did have somebody say their dog liked my work once," he recalled. "I thought it was quite interesting."

"That's weird. I was watching *Corpse Bride* this morning and my dog kept going up to the TV," said Mika.

"That's amazing," Burton replied. "Because somebody's dog says they liked *Nightmare Before Christmas*, too. To me, those are the best compliments because you know they're pure.

Film critic Roger Ebert has been following Burton's career ever since Burton made a very big splash 20 years ago as a very young filmmaker. Burton made such cult favorites as *Edward Scissorhands*, *Beetlejuice*, and *Big Fish*.

"If you go back through all his pictures you find nothing that is conventional," said Ebert. "You find worlds that come completely out of his imagination, as in *Big Fish*, or *Pee Wee's Big Adventure*, one of his early films. His *Batman* pictures have a very distinctive look and feel."

Not to mention successful. *Batman* is well up there on the list of Hollywood's top grossing films.

"Tim is visually astounding, in the way he approaches material," said Danny DeVito, who played the Penguin in *Batman Returns* and also the ringmaster in Burton's 2004 movie *Big Fish*.

"Even when you read the script of *Big Fish*, which is really a terrific script, you don't really get into the world that he's creating until you take that step with him, that first step into a world he's created in his mind," said DeVito.

GRAMMAR & USAGE

In the first paragraph, the writer uses the phrase "but not to those who know Tim Burton." This phrase contrasts with the statement just before it: "It may all sound strange."

A **contrasting expression**, which is set off with commas, gives emphasis to both points.

My Notes

LITERARY TERMS

A **biography** is a description or account of someone else's life or significant events from that person's life. In contrast, an **autobiography** is an account written by a person about his or her own life.

GRAMMAR & USAGE EXTENSION

- Remind students to use commas to set off an element that contrasts with what precedes it.
- The use of a contrasting element can provide rhetorical emphasis. Examining such stylistic devices makes students aware of the effect of syntax. Encourage students to try this stylistic pattern in their writing.

Steps:

3 Have students read this article on Tim Burton. Ask them to **mark the text** for subjects that might arise in Burton's films that reflect some of his beliefs or experiences. After students have read and recorded their individual ideas, have them report out their findings. Generate a whole class list.

4 Using this list, facilitate a class discussion on how to turn theme subjects into theme statements. Remind students that theme statements are usually implied in a text, not stated; students might have to make a reasonable guess about what Burton believes. The following is an example:

- Subject: Being an outsider
- Theme Statement: Being an outsider often allows one to have a unique and important perspective.

Teacher Notes

Film in Context: An Authorial Study

My Notes

DeVito even cast Burton in one of his own movies, *Hoffa*. Burton was, where else, in the coffin.

"His sort of interests, which are more than slightly off center, and a little outside, his interpretation of them does appeal to the masses, which ultimately I think is a very good sign," said Depp.

Burton's creative, quirky, fantastical world, along with his outsider take on life, has won him many fans.

Fans love Burton's creative, quirky, fantastical world, along with his outsider take on life. Among young adults who've grown up with his movies, Burton is a cult hero with a celebrity rare for a director.

In a way, Burton's drawings tell his story. By his own account, he was an odd and solitary kid growing up in Burbank, California, with little use for school or parents. He lived with his grandmother as a teenager, and spent his days drawing and dreaming and watching old monster movies. He even lived near a cemetery.

"I did grow up watching monster movies and I did enjoy playing (in the cemetery), but I thought most kids did. It didn't seem that strange to me."

Are you lashing back from being a tortured child?

"Of course. That's part of what's great about having drawing or writing as an outlet. It's a good way to exorcise those things."

Burton's preoccupation with death and monsters was evident from the start. His drawing talent won him a scholarship to nearby CalArts, founded by Walt and Roy Disney. After that, he landed a job as an animator, working on Disney classics like *The Fox and the Hounds*.

At age 26, he made a short film for Disney called *Frankenweenie*, about a little boy's efforts to revive his dead dog. The Disney folks felt it was too scary too release, but its unique style opened doors.

Next came *Pee Wee's Big Adventure*, which became a cult classic, and that led to *Beetlejuice*, a sleeper hit that received critical raves and earned tons of money for Warner Brothers.

And that led to his first really big budget movie, *Batman*. It was a smash. Suddenly, Tim Burton had Hollywood clout.

The movie he chose to make next was *Edward Scissorhands*, probably Burton's most personal film. It's about a creative misfit in a world that oddly mirrors the one Burton grew up in. But it almost didn't get made.

Teacher Notes

Despite the clout he garnered, movie executive still had trouble giving control to a guy who didn't even comb his hair.

"What they like about you they fear about you," said Burton. "They think you're a somewhat strange person, so they're always a little bit worried."

To play Edward Scissorhands, Burton chose Johnny Depp, who's now shooting Disney's sequel to *Pirates of the Caribbean* in the Bahamas.

"We connected on a number of levels," said Depp. "And it was the beginning of that interesting shorthand that exists between Tim and me."

For Burton, the connection with Depp was immediate and deep.

"He's just somebody who likes to transform," Burton said of his friend. "He's more like an old fashioned Boris Karloff- or Lon Chaney-style actor than he is like a leading man. I enjoy people like that. They're always surprising."

Depp and Burton have gone on to make many movies together, including *Ed Wood*, Burton's loving tribute to the man considered by many Hollywood insiders to be the worst director of all time.

"He deserves to be loved, there's a kind of purity to Ed Wood, which, in terms of intent, is not dissimilar to Tim," said Depp.

"I definitely identified with him," Burton said of Ed Wood. "I grew up seeing his movies and seeing how special they were. Just being in the industry you think there's a real fine line between success and failure, and what makes an artist or not.

Ed Wood may or may not have been an artist, but he was obsessed with movie making. One of his more famous stunts took place in his movie *Plan 9 from Outer Space*, which featured a very old and very ill Bela Lugosi, who died while the movie was being made. Wood got his dentist to fill in for Lugosi.

"The reason (Burton) wanted to make *Ed Wood* is that Ed Wood had so much fun making movies," said Ebert. "And that's where Ed Wood and Tim Burton connect. Tim Burton makes films that are a lot better, but he doesn't make them with any more love."

My Notes

Teacher Notes

Film in Context: An Authorial Study

My Notes

Burton's real life these days seems almost, dare we say it, normal. He lives in England with actress Helena Bonham Carter, and their young son, Billy.

The two often work together. She played a witch in *Big Fish*, Charlie Bucket's mother in *Charlie and the Chocolate Factory*, and she's the voice of the "Corpse Bride."

"It's actually quite nice," said Burton. "She knows what it's all about so there's no ego, no problem whatsoever."

One could argue Burton's life is almost like a fairy tale.

"I'm going to turn into a frog and jump off the stage now," said Burton.

With your classmates, identify and discuss the essential features of a biography that are present in this article.

You will now be assigned one of the following topics:

Johnny Depp
Vincent Price
Edgar Allan Poe
Gothic Literature

For your investigation, you must research your assigned topic, using a minimum of three Internet sources. You will become an expert on your topic and be responsible for teaching your peers what you have learned. Be sure to create a bibliography of your sources. When conducting research, use text features such as captions, illustrations, headings, sidebar information, and footnotes to help you identify information to include in your notes. When you have compiled enough information, respond to the following two questions in preparation for your presentation. You may use the graphic organizer for help.

1. Summarize what you know about the individual/subject you were asked to research
2. Draw connections between your individual/subject and the ideas your class uncovered regarding Tim Burton (hint: this might take some additional research!)

Summary of Topic
Connections to Tim Burton
Bibliography of Sources
Source 1:
Source 2:
Source 3:

Reflection: Evaluate your research process. What did you learn about research, and how will you apply that knowledge to future research tasks? Use the subjunctive stem, "If I had the opportunity to make changes, ..."

© 2011 College Board. All rights reserved.

ACTIVITY 2.18 *Continued*

Steps:

5 Divide the class into groups for a **jigsaw** activity. Assign each group one of the following topics: Johnny Depp, Vincent Price, Gothic Literature, and Edgar Allan Poe.

6 Provide time for students to **research** their topics on the Internet, using at least three sources. To help students create a brief presentation, encourage them to use the **graphic organizer**, which will help them focus their research into a **summary** of the individual or subject and the connections to the ideas the class uncovered regarding Tim Burton.

Steps:

7 Put students in groups of four that include one expert on each topic. While each member of the group reports out his or her findings, encourage the other group members to **take notes** in the area provided.

Film in Context: An Authorial Study

Take notes while you listen to your classmates report on their research.

Subject 1: ____________________

Subject 2: ____________________

Subject 3: ____________________

Writing Prompt: Summarize the influence of these individuals and genres on the contemporary works of Tim Burton.

Setting the Mood: Wonka Two Ways

ACTIVITY 2.19

SUGGESTED LEARNING STRATEGIES: Close Reading, Graphic Organizer, Notetaking, Think-Pair-Share, Word Map

You have uncovered and presented a variety of influences on Tim Burton's unique **style**. You will now have an opportunity to see that style in action through a comparative study between text and film. Both authors and directors thoughtfully consider the **mood** and **tone** they create. Therefore it is important to understand these terms.

By carefully considering the author's choice of words and detail to create a mood, a reader can often uncover the tone of a piece. Similarly, a director can make choices to create a mood and tone. Complete the following steps to compare a written text with a film text.

In passage 1 from *Charlie and the Chocolate Factory*, you will examine the mood. Annotate words and phrases that help to identify the atmosphere or predominant emotion in the text. List those words in the space provided. After you have completed your list of words and phrases, come up with one or two words to describe the mood of the passage.

Literary Terms

Mood is the atmosphere or predominant emotion in a literary work.

Tone is the writer's or speaker's attitude toward a subject, character, or audience. Tone can be serious, humorous, sarcastic, indignant, objective, etc.

Words/Phrases	Mood

ACTIVITY 2.19
Setting the Mood: Wonka Two Ways

Materials:

- Video of *Charlie and the Chocolate Factory*, by Tim Burton (2005)
- TV/DVD player
- Vocabulary Notebooks

Purpose:

- To analyze an author's explicit purpose for writing
- To understand style elements (mood and tone) in two media
- To draw a direct connection between text and film, using textual evidence to support claims

Steps:

1 Before students open to this page, use **think-pair-share** to have them discuss the differences between **mood** and **tone**. These key terms are the cornerstone of this lesson, and students should consider these terms prior to reading the definitions. Then, have students read the introductory material on this page.

2 Introduce the novel *Charlie and the Chocolate Factory* by Roald Dahl. You may consider bibliographic information, other texts by the author, or a simple overview of the story. Like the topics students researched in the previous activity, this novel was a direct influence for Tim Burton's film.

3 Tell students to use the **graphic organizer** to **take notes** from the first passage from *Charlie and the Chocolate Factory*.

Writing Workshops

Students have been viewing and analyzing style as represented by the work of Tim Burton. To prepare them to write a style analysis essay, you might consider using Workshop 9, Response to Literature, to provide direct instruction in writing literary analysis.

ACTIVITY 2.19 *Continued*

Steps:

4 In passage 1, students consider mood. Ask students to do a **close reading** of the text, highlighting words or phrases that help to identify the atmosphere or predominant emotion in the text. Then, prompt them to identify a few words that would describe the mood of this passage. To check for understanding, ask students to identify which specific words contributed to which specific mood.

ACTIVITY 2.19 *continued*

Setting the Mood: Wonka Two Ways

My Notes

Novel Excerpt

From Charlie and the Chocolate Factory

by Roald Dahl

PASSAGE 1

The whole of this family—the six grownups (count them) and little Charlie Bucket—live together in a small wooden house on the edge of a great town.

The house wasn't nearly large enough for so many people, and life was extremely uncomfortable for them all. There were only two rooms in the place altogether, and there was only one bed. The bed was given to the four old grandparents because they were so old and tired. They were so tired, they never got out of it.

Grandpa Joe and Grandma Josephine on this side, Grandpa George and Grandma Georgina on this side.

Mr. and Mrs. Bucket and little Charlie Bucket slept in the other room, upon mattresses on the floor.

In the summertime, this wasn't too bad, but in the winter, freezing cold drafts blew across the floor all night long, and it was awful.

There wasn't any question of them being able to buy a better house—or even one more bed to sleep in. They were far too poor for that.

Mr. Bucket was the only person in the family with a job. He worked in a toothpaste factory, where he sat all day long at a bench and screwed the little caps onto the tops of the tubes of toothpaste after the tubes had been filled. But a toothpaste cap-screwer is never paid very much money, and poor Mr. Bucket, however hard he worked, and however fast he screwed on the caps, was never able to make enough to buy one-half of the things that so large a family needed. There wasn't even enough money to buy proper food for them all. The only meals they could afford were bread and margarine for breakfast, boiled potatoes and cabbage for lunch, and cabbage soup for supper. Sundays were a bit better. They all looked forward to Sundays because then, although they had exactly the same, everyone was allowed a second helping.

The Buckets, of course, didn't starve, but every one of them—the two old grandfathers, the two old grandmothers, Charlie's father, Charlie's mother, and especially little Charlie himself—went about from morning till night with a horrible empty feeling in their tummies.

Charlie felt it worst of all. And although his father and mother often went without their own share of lunch or supper so that they could give it to him, it still wasn't nearly enough for a growing boy. He desperately wanted something more filling and satisfying than cabbage and cabbage soup. The one thing he longed for more than anything else was . . . CHOCOLATE.

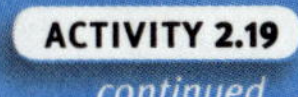

In passage 2, you will consider tone. Highlight words that help to identify the author's attitude toward the children he describes. List those words in the space provided. Then, come up with one or two words that describe the tone of the passage.

Words/Phrases	Tone

ACTIVITY 2.19 *Continued*

Steps:

5 In passage 2, students consider tone. Ask them to highlight words that help to identify the author's attitude toward the children he describes. Then, prompt them to identify a few words that would describe the tone of the passage. Once again, to check for understanding, ask students to identify specific words that correspond to a specific tone.

6 Point out that while ***mood*** and ***tone*** are not interchangeable terms, they often work together. For example, an author may create a dark and depressing mood as a vehicle to express a serious distaste for the restrictive nature of poverty.

Teacher Notes

Setting the Mood: Wonka Two Ways

My Notes

Novel Excerpt

ABOUT THE AUTHOR

Roald Dahl (1916 – 1990) was born in Wales to Norwegian parents. The stories he heard as a child greatly influenced his love of stories and books. Dahl wrote stories for adults and children. Many of his children's stories came about from the bedtime stories he made up for his daughters. *James and the Giant Peach* was his first book, followed by *Charlie and the Chocolate Factory*, both of which enjoyed huge success in the United Kingdom and the United States.

From CHARLIE and the CHOCOLATE FACTORY

by Roald Dahl

PASSAGE 2

The very next day, the first Golden Ticket was found. The finder was a boy called Augustus Gloop, and Mr. Bucket's evening newspaper carried a large picture of him on the front page. The picture showed a nine-year-old boy who was so enormously fat he looked as though he had been blown up with a powerful pump. Great flabby folds of fat bulged out from every part of his body, and his face was like a monstrous ball of dough with two small greedy curranty eyes peering out upon the world. The town in which Augustus Gloop lived, the newspaper said, had gone wild with excitement over their hero. Flags were flying from all the windows, children had been given a holiday from school, and a parade was being organized in honor of the famous youth.

"I just *knew* Augustus would find a Golden Ticket," his mother had told the newspapermen. "He eats so *many* candy bars a day that it was almost *impossible* for him *not* to find one. Eating is his hobby, you know. That's *all* he's interested in. But still, that's better than being a *hooligan* and shooting off *zip guns* and things like that in his spare time, isn't it? And what I always say is, he wouldn't go on eating like he does unless he *needed* nourishment, would he? It's all *vitamins*, anyway. What a *thrill* it will be for him to visit Mr. Wonka's Marvelous factory! We're just as *proud* as can be!"

ADMIT ONE 151744154

Teacher Notes

My Notes

"What a revolting woman," said Grandma Josephine.

"And what a repulsive boy," said Grandma Georgina.

... Suddenly, on the day before Charlie Bucket's birthday, the newspapers announced that the second Golden Ticket had been found. The lucky person was a small girl called Veruca Salt who lived with her rich parents in a great city far away. Once again, Mr. Bucket's evening newspaper carried a big picture of the finder. She was sitting between her beaming father and mother in the living room of their house, waving the Golden Ticket above her head, and grinning from ear to ear.

Veruca's father, Mr. Salt, had eagerly explained to the newspapermen exactly how the ticket was found. "You see, fellers," he had said, "as soon as my little girl told me that she simply *had* to have one of those Golden Tickets, I want out into the town and started buying up all the Wonka candy bars I could lay my hands on. *Thousands* of them, I must have bought. *Hundreds* of thousands! Then I had them loaded onto trucks and sent directly to my *own* factory. I'm in the peanut business, you see, and I've got about a hundred women working for me over at my joint, shelling peanuts for roasting and salting. That's what they do all day long, those women, they sit there shelling peanuts. So I says to them, 'Okay, girls,' I says, 'from now on, you can stop shelling peanuts and start shelling the wrappers off these crazy candy bars instead!' And they did. I had every worker in the place yanking the paper off those bars of chocolate full speed ahead from morning till night.

"But three days went by, and we had no luck. Oh, it was terrible! My little Veruca got more and more upset each day, and every time I went home she would scream at me, "*Where's my Golden Ticket! I want my Golden Ticket!*" And she would lie for hours on the floor, kicking and yelling in the most disturbing way. Well, sir, I just hated to see my little girl feeling unhappy like that, so I vowed I would keep up the search until I'd got her what she wanted. Then suddenly . . . on the evening of the fourth day, one of my women workers yelled, 'I've got it! A Golden Ticket!' And I said, 'Give it to me, quick!' and she did, and I rushed it home and gave it to my darling Veruca, and now she's all smiles, and we have a happy home once again."

"That's even worse than the fat boy," said Grandma Josephine.

"She needs a real good spanking," said Grandma Georgina.

© 2011 College Board. All rights reserved.

Unit 2 • Defining Style 157

ACTIVITY 2.19 *Continued*

Steps:

7 Play the beginning of Tim Burton's ***Charlie and the Chocolate Factory***: Scenes 1-7 (0–0:20:20). Stop the clip after Charlie's parents give him a Wonka bar for his birthday. This segment includes the film sections that correspond to both textual passages that students have examined. During the viewing of the film, ask students to take notes on how the director creates mood and tone in the film.

8 Place students in pairs and have them respond to the two questions on this page.

9 Instruct students to create an appropriate **word map graphic organizer** in their **Vocabulary Notebooks** to explore the concept of ***style***.

10 As an extension, ask students to identify themes or subjects they uncovered that correspond to their research in the previous activity.

ACTIVITY 2.19 *continued*

Setting the Mood: Wonka Two Ways

You will now watch the beginning of Tim Burton's *Charlie and the Chocolate Factory*. While viewing, pay special attention to the ways in which a director's ability to create various moods leads to the shifting tone of the film. Consider these two questions as you watch the film:

1. How does Burton create mood and tone? What does a director have at his disposal that an author does not? (In addition to dialogue/text, a director can use lighting, costuming, sound, color, etc.)
2. In terms of mood and tone, is the film version similar to the written version? What specific instances contribute to the mood/tone?

FILM NOTES:

	MOOD	TONE
LIGHTING		
COSTUMES		
COLOR		
SOUND		

Revisiting "Wonka": Application of Film Terms

ACTIVITY 2.20

SUGGESTED LEARNING STRATEGIES: Close Reading, Drafting, Graphic Organizer, Quickwrite, Role Playing

Your teacher will give your group an index card with cinematic terms on it. In your group, take on the role of director, cameraman, or actors and create a scenario in which you apply the terms.

1. Describe the scene you and your group plan to demonstrate using your assigned cinematic techniques.

2. After you have presented your scene and viewed a clip from *Charlie and the Chocolate Factory*, draft a **quickwrite** in which you respond to the following questions:
   - In your scenario, what effect did you want to have on your audience?
   - What effect do you think Burton wants to have in this scene in the film?
   - What choices did you make in your direction to achieve your desired effect?
   - What choices does Burton make?

3. To elaborate on the concept of cinematic techniques, create a graphic organizer in your Vocabulary Notebook, with one section identifying film technques and another describing the intended and actual effect of that technique.

ACTIVITY 2.20

Revisiting "Wonka": Application of Film Terms

Materials:

- TV/DVD player
- Video of *Charlie and the Chocolate Factory*, directed by Tim Burton, 2005
- Index cards
- Vocabulary Notebooks

Purpose:

- To analyze how media producers use cinematic techniques to achieve specific effects
- To reflect on choices in direction to achieve a desired effect

Steps:

1 Ask students to review the film terms from Activity 2.15 and their collages from Activity 2.16.

2 Next, assign students to groups. Give each group an index card on which you have written three to five film terms, each from a different category. Instruct students to **role play** as director, cameraman, and actors to create a short scenario using the terms on their card. Allow them a specified amount of time to plan and practice using these techniques. Then, have them present their scene demonstrating the terms on their cards.

3 Next, give students an opportunity to **close read** film. Show them the film clip from *Charlie and the Chocolate Factory* that proceeds from Charlie's finding the winning ticket to the first meeting with Willy Wonka: Scenes 10-12 (0:27:36-0:38:00). Ask students to identify the film techniques used in this segment. Consider these suggestions for this activity:

- Turn off the sound, and direct students to identify cuts from one shot to the next by clapping each time a new shot appears.
- Assign specific techniques to individuals and have them trace what they see.

4 Ask students to reflect on both exercises and respond to the **quickwrite**.

5 To elaborate on the concept of *cinematic techniques*, direct students to create another **graphic organizer** in their **Vocabulary Notebooks**, with one section listing film terms and another describing the intended and actual effect of the technique.

ACTIVITY 2.21

Working with Cinematic Techniques: Part 2

Materials:

- TV/DVD player
- Video of *Charlie and the Chocolate Factory*, directed by Tim Burton (2005)

Purpose:

- To analyze how media producers use cinematic techniques to achieve specific effects
- To apply and reflect on effective strategies for reading film

Steps:

1 To move beyond identification of technique and start understanding the connection between film and reader, students will now participate in a more structured **close reading** of a short clip from the film *Charlie and the Chocolate Factory*. Show Scenes 14-16 (0:40:24–0:49:40), when the group is about to enter the room with the chocolate river, and ends when Augustus Gloop is sucked into the pipe.

2 Show this clip once with the sound off and ask students to respond by noting the shots that the director uses. Tell students not to ruin the scene for others if they've already seen this movie. Direct students to use the **graphic organizer** to take notes on the shots and lighting used:

- Long shots to establish the setting
- Medium shots to display the body language of the characters
- Close-up shots to display facial expressions of the characters
- Shot-reverse-shot to show a conversation between characters and the building of tension
- Lighting to establish mood

3 Ask students to generate three questions (**questioning the text**) that they would like to ask the director if he were in the class. Allow students to share their questions in small groups and then predict what the director's response might be.

4 Inform students that when they read film closely, they may find the director's hints about what's to come in this scene (**foreshadowing** the downfall of Augustus Gloop). Have students view this scene again (reread it) with the sound on. Ask them to examine how the director sets up the viewer (reader) for this event. Instruct students not only to notice the specific techniques that the director uses, but also to observe any other details that stand out. After this viewing, ask students to take notes and discuss their findings.

ACTIVITY 2.21

Working with Cinematic Techniques: Part 2

SUGGESTED LEARNING STRATEGIES: Close Reading, Graphic Organizer, Questioning the Text, Think-Pair-Share

Use the graphic organizer to take notes as you view the film clip.

Charlie and the Chocolate Factory	**Observations:** Note what you observe in this scene — camera movement, angles, shots, sound, lighting, setting, characters, etc.	**Interpretation:** What can you infer from your observations?
First viewing — without sound	Example: Shot-reverse-shot between two characters followed by a close up of one character expressing surprise	Example: Maybe they are talking about something that makes one of them uncomfortable
Second viewing — with sound		
Final viewing (Optional)		

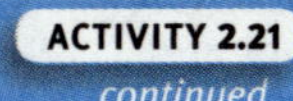

ACTIVITY 2.21
continued

1. How does the director use sound (diegetic and non-diegetic) to enhance this scene?

2. What is the effect of dialogue on the scene?

3. Why does the author use a flashback scene? What does the director accomplish in doing so?

© 2011 College Board. All rights reserved.

ACTIVITY 2.21 *Continued*

Steps:

5 In a **think-pair-share**, ask students to respond to the prompts on this page.

6 Finally, ask students to craft an analytical statement about this scene. Suggest that they use their responses to the questions on this page and any other observations they made to make a statement about the director's use of a cinematic technique and its effect.

7 You may wish to ask students to reflect on the process they used to make meaning of this text (film clip). What strategies did they use while "reading" this clip? Students' lists of reading strategies could include these:

- Making predictions
- Questioning the text
- Responding to the text
- Rereading
- Close Reading
- Making Inferences

This is a great time to point out to students the relationship between reading print text and nonprint texts. Both require particular skills to ascertain meaning.

8 To stress the importance of close reading as a part of literary analysis, solicit responses to the **Essential Question**: What are the essential features of an effective style analysis?

Unit 2 • Defining Style 161

ACTIVITY 2.22

Reading Film: *Edward Scissorhands*

Materials:

- TV/DVD player
- Video of *Edward Scissorhands,* directed by Tim Burton (1990)

Purpose:

- To examine cinematic and literary elements of film (tone, mood, imagery, and motif)
- To clarify how media producers use conventional production elements to achieve specific effects
- To use context clues to make predictions

Steps:

1 Direct students to apply their knowledge of Tim Burton as well as their understanding of film terminology to *Edward Scissorhands*. Instruct them to use the **graphic organizer** on this page to **take notes** on the major visual and literary elements in this film.

2 Point out that viewers often overlook the opening credits and title sequence of a film. Consider guiding students through a **close reading** of the opening of the film in two segments:

- **Segment One:** Show the opening title sequence of the film: Scene 1 (0–0:02:42). As the credits roll, the viewer sees an array of images shot in low-key light of a castle with scientific instruments, cut-out pictures, hands, and faces, all spinning toward the camera. Ask students to **make predictions** about the film based on the imagery in this viewing segment.

ACTIVITY 2.22

Reading Film: *Edward Scissorhands*

SUGGESTED LEARNING STRATEGIES: Close Reading, Graphic Organizer, Making Predictions, Notetaking

Segment of Film	Observations: What is happening in this scene?	Interpretation: What can you infer or predict based on your observations?
The Opening Credits: Images, Shapes, Music		
The Frame Story: Grandmother with Granddaughter		

Segment One: Opening Titles

1. Describe the **tone** in this scene. What type of movie does it remind you of?

2. How does the lighting help create the mood of this opening?

Segment Two: Frame Story — Grandmother with Granddaughter

1. How has the music changed between the opening credits and this scene? Why?

2. What does the camera do when it leaves the room where the story is being told? Why do you think the director does this?

3. What do you think this film will be about? On what do you base your prediction?

ACTIVITY 2.22 *Continued*

Steps:

- **Segment Two**: In the first part of the "frame" of the movie: Scene 2 (0:02:44–0:05:03), an old woman prepares to narrate the story of Edward Scissorhands to her granddaughter. Ask students to read this section closely, being especially observant of the way the camera moves. Then, lead students through a discussion of this opening and again ask them, based on this segment of text, to make predictions about what type of film this is.

ACTIVITY 2.23

Reading Film: Screening Day A

Materials:

- TV/DVD player
- Video of *Edward Scissorhands,* directed by Tim Burton (1990)
- Vocabulary Notebooks

Purpose:

- To analyze how an author or director achieves specific effects and purposes through literary/cinematic devices
- To interpret author's (director's) purpose by analyzing literary/cinematic choices
- To craft an analytical statement and support it with evidence from the text

Steps:

1 This notetaking series in Activities 2.23, 2.24, 2.26, 2.27 is designed to actively engage students with the film. The **text** has been **chunked** into four Screening Days (A-D), giving students the opportunity to view it in four small segments and then re-view (**reread**) key sequences to examine and analyze the effects of these cinematic techniques.

2 Show students the first chunk of the film, Scenes 3-5 (0:05:17–0:26:32), all the way through without interruption.

3 Have students respond to the discussion questions in small **discussion groups**, called "Home Base" groups, ideally with five students, in order to accommodate the jigsaw discussion that follows.

4 Ask the students in each Home Base group to number off from one to five. Then, **jigsaw** students into "Expert" groups: all of the ones together, the twos, and so on.

5 Assign each group a cinematic element on which to become expert for the second reading/viewing of the key sequence: group one—framing/angles; group two—lighting; group three—camera movement; group four—music/sound; group five—editing.

6 Show students the key sequence, Scenes 3–4 (0:11:01–0:16:33), again; have them do a **close reading** and record their observations on the **graphic organizer**. Guide students to notice the changing music and the use of long shots to show that Peg is out of place in the castle. Students should notice, too, the use of long shots of Edward to create fear and suspense, until he is seen in a close-up, at which point viewers know that he is harmless.

7 Ask expert groups to compare their notes, discuss their findings, and come to a consensus about their observations.

ACTIVITY 2.23

Reading Film: Screening Day A

SUGGESTED LEARNING STRATEGIES: Close Reading, Discussion Groups, Graphic Organizer, Rereading, Word Map, Notetaking

Discussion Questions for the Home Base Group

1. What do you know about Peg from this segment?
2. How has the director already established a connection between Edward and Kim?
3. How do you feel about Edward? What do you think will happen to him?
4. How do you feel about the town? Why do you feel this way?

Notes for Jigsaw Discussion of Key Sequence

In the graphic organizer below, note the places where you see particularly interesting or effective examples of your assigned cinematic element. You may need to put your notes on a separate sheet of paper.

Framing/Angles	Lighting	Camera Movement	Music/Sound	Editing

© 2011 College Board. All rights reserved.

164 SpringBoard® English Textual Power™ Level 4

ACTIVITY 2.23
continued

Analytical Statement with Textual Support

As you develop your analytical statement, it is important to understand the following terms:

Author's Purpose: The intended effect or meaning created or suggested by the use of a device (literary, rhetorical, or cinematic)

Effect: The result or influence of using a specific device

Take notes on the graphic organizer about the specific cinematic technique you studied, its effect, and an example from the film.

Purpose of the cinematic element

Example: A purpose of long shots is to make characters look vulnerable

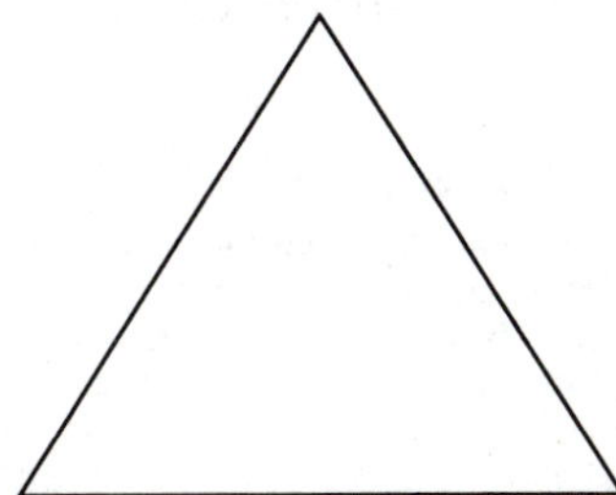

Example(s) of this cinematic element

When Peg is upstairs in the castle

Effect(s) of this cinematic choice

Peg looks very small in that big room. The long shot builds suspense because the viewer is worried about Peg.

One way to pull your observations together for an analytical statement is to follow the model below:

Tim Burton, in *Edward Scissorhands*, uses a long shot *(cinematic element)* in order to show the vulnerablity of characters *(achieve what purpose)*. For example, when Peg is upstairs in the castle, the long shot makes her look small so that the viewer worries about her safety *(evidence from the text to support the topic sentence)*.

ACTIVITY 2.23 *Continued*

Steps:

8 Take time to review and discuss the following Academic Vocabulary words, which are essential to a deep and meaningful discussion: **style** and **effect**. Direct students to create a **word map graphic organizer** in their **Vocabulary Notebooks** to explore the concept of ***effect***. Have them return to their ***style*** word map and further explore this concept.

9 Next, model an analytical statement for students, using the graphic on this page. Ask them to work together to craft one for their assigned cinematic element. Emphasize that they must include an example from the film to support their analysis.

10 Ask students to return to their Home Base groups and share their expertise and analytical statements, along with textual support, from their expert groups. Remind students that they are expected to understand all of the cinematic elements. The Home Base groups should fill out the rest of the graphic organizer during the discussion, so that all students have notes on all the cinematic techniques.

ACTIVITY 2.24

Reading Film: Screening Day B

Materials:

- TV/DVD player
- Video of *Edward Scissorhands*, directed by Tim Burton (1990)

Purpose:

- To analyze how an author or director achieves specific effects and purposes through literary/cinematic devices
- To interpret text by analyzing the author's purpose behind literary/cinematic choices
- To craft an analytical statement, support it with evidence from the text, and include reflective commentary to explain interpretations

Steps:

1 Before students view the second segment of *Edward Scissorhands*, ask them to assemble in their Home Base groups and review the previous day's notes and analyses.

2 Show the second chunk of *Edward Scissorhands*: Scenes 5-13 (0:26:39–0:51:44).

3 After the viewing, have students respond to the questions on this page in their Home Base **discussion groups**.

4 Continue the **jigsaw** by having students return to their expert groups. Assign them a new cinematic element to focus on for the key sequence in this film segment. Show the key sequence: Scenes 7-8 (0:33:13–0:35:24). Have students do a **close reading** of the first flashback to the castle and take notes on the **graphic organizer**. Guide them to think about what triggers this flashback for Edward and how the music, lighting, and tone are different in the flashback. Suggest that students consider the cookie heart as a symbol. Ask students how the bakery's assembly-line structure is similar to the town and its regulated order.

ACTIVITY 2.24

Reading Film: Screening Day B

SUGGESTED LEARNING STRATEGIES: Close Reading, Discussion Groups, Graphic Organizer, Making Predictions, Word Map, Notetaking

Discussion Questions for the Home Base Group

1. Why do the townspeople welcome Edward so quickly into their lives?

2. How does the town seem to change after Edward's arrival?

3. Kim's reaction to Edward is played for humor, but in what way is hers the most natural or realistic response?

4. What hints in this segment indicate that all will not work out well?

Notes for Jigsaw Discussion of Key Sequence

Today, you will become an expert on a different cinematic technique. While re-viewing the key sequence of the text, note the places where you see particularly interesting or effective examples of your assigned cinematic element. Keep in mind that you must have a clear understanding of all of the cinematic techniques, so take good notes during the jigsaw discussion that will follow this viewing.

Framing/Angles	Lighting	Camera Movement	Music/Sound	Editing

5 As with the first segment, have students **take notes** while viewing, and discuss their observations. Ask them to **make** some **predictions** about the story's outcome.

Analytical Statement with Textual Support and Reflective Commentary

In this writing exercise, you will add reflective **commentary** to your analytical statement. Remember that the reflective commentary comes after the example on purpose! The job of the commentary is to show your understanding of the relationship between your example and your original claim. You can make a comment, explain the connection, illustrate the point you made, or perhaps prompt a realization in the mind of the reader. In other words, if your example is the "what," then the reflective commentary is the "so what."

ACADEMIC VOCABULARY

Commentary is your explanation of the importance or relevance of your example and the way your example supports your analysis.

To make your analysis, complete this statement:

Tim Burton, in *Edward Scissorhands*, uses ________________________ in order

(cinematic element)

to ____.

(achieve what purpose)

For example, ____.

(Provide evidence from the text to support the topic sentence.)

____.

____.

(reflective commentary)

© 2011 College Board. All rights reserved.

ACTIVITY 2.24 *Continued*

Steps:

6 Direct students to craft an analytical statement that includes an example to support the statement. Guide students to work on providing **reflective commentary** to explain their interpretation. You might want to **model** commentary to ensure that students are on the right track.

7 Have students return to Home Base groups to share their findings on their cinematic element and their analytical statements with textual examples and commentary.

8 You might want to close this lesson with a whole-group sharing of good student samples.

9 Direct students to select an appropriate **word map graphic organizer** to explore the concept of ***commentary*** in their **Vocabulary Notebooks**.

10 Discuss the **Essential Question**: How do authors and directors use specific techniques to achieve a desired effect?

ACTIVITY 2.25
Director's Chair: Visualizing a Scene

Materials:

- TV/DVD player

Purpose:

- To analyze and make meaning from a printed screenplay
- To predict how the director might capture a particular aspect of a screenplay and craft a reflection that rationalizes the prediction
- To visualize in order to elaborate on comprehension of a text

Steps:

1 Begin by reviewing the purpose of a storyboard. Draw on students' skills and knowledge from Embedded Assessment 1. Remind students that a storyboard allows the director to visualize what his or her film will look like, prior to the actual filming. Many DVDs now include the director's storyboards in the bonus materials; perhaps you might be able to show students one or more of those.

2 Direct students to do a **close reading** of the excerpt from the screenplay of *Edward Scissorhands*. This is a scene that they have not yet viewed in class. Ask students to discuss what this scene shows about the relationships between the characters, as well as any other issues that they discover in the text.

3 Have students **reread** the text, this time **predicting** how Tim Burton would film this scene, based on their growing understanding of Burton's style. Instruct them to mark the text with notes or sketches.

ACTIVITY 2.25 Director's Chair: Visualizing a Scene

SUGGESTED LEARNING STRATEGIES: Close Reading, Making Predictions, Rereading

Dialogue from *Edward Scissorhands*

KIM

You're here. They didn't hurt you, did they? Were you scared? I tried to make Jim go back, but you can't make Jim do anything. Thank you for not telling them about me.

EDWARD

You are welcome.

KIM

It must have been awful when they told you whose house it was.

EDWARD

I knew it was Jim's house.

KIM

You did?

EDWARD

Yes.

KIM

Well, then why did you do it?

EDWARD

Because you asked me to.

(Jim calls out for Kim, who runs outside to see him. Edward watches them together and then stalks off down the hallway, tearing the wallpaper with his hands.)

Imagine how the preceding scene might be filmed by Tim Burton. Predict how he might sequence the shots, and craft a storyboard that will capture the essence of the sequence.

SHOT #

Describe the Music/Sound:

Dialogue:

Framing:

Lighting:

SHOT #

Describe the Music/Sound:

Dialogue:

Framing:

Lighting:

ACTIVITY 2.25 *Continued*

Steps:

4 Direct students to **transform** this screenplay into a storyboard by drawing up to six shots that Burton might film to capture this scene. Tell them to incorporate as many appropriate cinematic elements as possible, to include the dialogue, and to describe the sound and lighting. You might wish to have students do this activity in pairs.

Teacher Notes

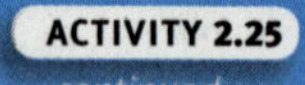

Director's Chair: Visualizing a Scene

SHOT #

Describe the Music/Sound:

Dialogue:

Framing:

Lighting:

SHOT #

Describe the Music/Sound:

Dialogue:

Framing:

Lighting:

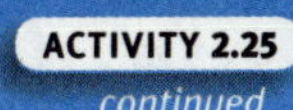
ACTIVITY 2.25 continued

SHOT #

Describe the Music/Sound:

Dialogue:

Framing:

Lighting:

SHOT #

Describe the Music/Sound:

Dialogue:

Framing:

Lighting:

Reflection Questions:

Look back through your shots and, on separate paper, answer these questions.

- Why did you choose the framing, lighting, and music that you did?
- What words or phrases from the screenplay made you picture the scene as you did?
- How did the scenes you have already seen in the movie help you make your choices?
- How does this scene in Burton's film compare to the one that you envisioned? Explain.

ACTIVITY 2.25 *Continued*

Steps:

5 When students have completed their storyboards, have them answer the reflective questions. They will be able to answer the last one only after they have viewed this portion of the film on Screening Day C.

Teacher Notes

ACTIVITY 2.26

Reading Film: Screening Day C

Materials:

- TV/DVD player
- Video of *Edward Scissorhands*, directed by Tim Burton (1990)
- Vocabulary Notebooks

Purpose:

- To analyze how an author or director achieves specific effects and purposes through literary/cinematic devices
- To interpret text by analyzing the author's purpose for making literary/cinematic choices
- To use appropriate closure and summative statements in writing

Steps:

1 Ask students to assemble in their Home Base groups and review their notes and analyses from the previous Screening Days' viewings.

2 Show the third chunk of *Edward Scissorhands*: Scenes 13–19 (0:51:45–1:17:20).

3 After the viewing, have students respond to the questions on this page in their Home Base **discussion groups**.

4 Continue the **jigsaw** by having students return to their expert groups. Assign them a new cinematic element to focus on as they do a **close reading** of the key sequence in this film segment. Instruct them to **take notes** on the **graphic organizer** and discuss their findings afterward.

5 Show the Key Sequence: Scenes 16–17 (1:03:50–1:06:29) of this segment. Have students review, in a close reading, the scene when Edward is locked in Jim's house and the police are outside. Have them listen to the music as he comes out, and examine the low-key lighting and backlighting and the use of the long-shots of Edward from the point of view of the police. Edward is again threatening to those who do not know him.

ACTIVITY 2.26

Reading Film: Screening Day C

SUGGESTED LEARNING STRATEGIES: **Close Reading, Discussion Groups, Graphic Organizer, Notetaking**

GRAMMAR & USAGE

When you write your paragraph of analysis, it is important to use **parallel structure,** that is, to express similar ideas in the same grammatical form. In the following examples, the parallel structures are in boldface type.

The speaker **cajoled, remonstrated,** and **threatened,** but the audience remained unmoved.

Lincoln stressed "...a government **of the people, by the people,** and **for the people** shall not perish from the earth." Gettysburg Address

"I came, I saw, I conquered," wrote Julius Caesar.

Discussion Questions for the Home Base Group

1. Is Edward behaving any differently now than he did before? What is different about the town's treatment of him?

2. What is the effect of the scene with Kim dancing in the ice crystals? How have her feelings about Edward changed? Why?

3. How has Edward tried to fit in? Why has he failed? What does the "ethics lesson" reveal about Edward?

Notes for Jigsaw Discussion of Key Sequence

Note the places where you see particularly interesting or effective uses of your assigned cinematic element. Again, keep in mind that you must have a clear understanding of all of the cinematic techniques, so take good notes during the jigsaw discussion.

Framing/Angles	Lighting	Camera Movement	Music/Sound	Editing

GRAMMAR & USAGE EXTENSION

Stress that elements parallel in thought or meaning must be parallel in grammatical form. Faulty parallelism is sometimes a problem in student writing. Example of faulty parallelism: The athlete enjoyed ***swimming, cycling,*** and ***to row***. You might guide students to identify passages in their writing that they can make parallel.

Analytical Statement with Textual Support, Reflective Commentary and Closure

Tim Burton, in *Edward Scissorhands*, uses ____________________ in order
(*cinematic element*)

to ____.
(*achieve what purpose*)

For example, ____________________________________.
(*Provide evidence from the text to support the topic sentence.*)

____.

____.
(*reflective commentary*)

____.
(*sentence of closure*)

Writing Prompt: With your writing group, create a well-developed paragraph analyzing the element that you focused on for the film segment. Remember to use parallel structure in your writing.

ACTIVITY 2.26 *Continued*

Steps:

6 Direct students to craft an analytical statement with an example to support their statement and reflective commentary. In this statement, they should work on providing a sentence of closure to explain their interpretations. You might want to **model** closing statements to ensure that students are on the right track.

7 Expert groups should now be in a position to collaborate on a paragraph of film analysis. Ask groups to write a well-developed paragraph analyzing the element they focused on in this film segment.

8 Next, ask students to return to their Home Base **discussion groups** to share their findings on their cinematic element as well as their paragraphs.

9 You might want to close this activity by allowing students to share what they liked about each other's paragraphs of film analysis.

ACTIVITY 2.27

Reading Film: Screening Day D

Materials:

- TV/DVD player
- Video of *Edward Scissorhands*, directed by Tim Burton (1990)

Purpose:

- To interpret text by analyzing the author's or director's purpose for literary/cinematic choices
- To craft a paragraph of film analysis

Steps:

1 Students will view the fourth segment of *Edward Scissorhands*. Ask them to assemble in their Home Base groups and review the previous day's notes and analyses.

2 Then, show the last chunk of the film: Scenes 19–24 (1:17:20–1:40:00).

3 After the viewing, have students respond to the questions on this page in their Home Base **discussion groups**.

4 Continue the **jigsaw** by asking students to return to their expert groups. Assign them a new cinematic element to focus on for the close reading of the key sequence. Students should take notes on the **graphic organizer** while viewing and discuss their findings afterward.

5 Show the Key Sequence: Scenes 20–21 (1:23:43–1:26:58). Lead a **close reading** of the flashback when The Inventor dies, including Edward's interaction with Kim before and after the flashback. Ask students to consider, besides the possibility of getting his hands, what Edward lost that day. Make sure students notice the framing and the music during this sequence, especially at the very end. Discuss the implications of Edward's inability to touch people without hurting them.

ACTIVITY 2.27

Reading Film: Screening Day D

SUGGESTED LEARNING STRATEGIES: Close Reading, Discussion Groups, Graphic Organizer, Notetaking, Sharing And Responding

Discussion Questions for the Home Base Group

1. Does Edward's action seem justified?

2. How does Edward appear to feel about Jim's death? How does Kim appear to feel?

3. Why do you think Edward cuts his clothes off?

4. Most fairy tales have a lesson or a moral to teach. What do you think Kim wants her granddaughter to learn from her story?

Notes for Jigsaw Discussion of the Key Sequence

Note the places where you see particularly interesting or effective uses of your assigned cinematic element. Again, keep in mind that you must have a clear understanding of all of the cinematic techniques, so take good notes during the jigsaw discussion.

Framing/Angles	Lighting	Camera Movement	Music/Sound	Editing

Writing Prompt: Write a well-developed paragraph analyzing Burton's use of a cinematic element in *Edward Scissorhands*. Include all the features that you have practiced, including analytical statements with textual support, reflective commentary, and closure.

6 Students should be ready by this time to write a paragraph of analysis independently. Direct them to respond to the Writing Prompt. You might allow time for **sharing and responding** in the expert groups.

7 Ask students to return to Home Base **discussion groups** to share their findings on their cinematic element as well as their analytical paragraphs. You might want to close today's lesson with a whole-group share of random student samples and a discussion of the **Essential Question**: What are the essential features of an effective style analysis?

Independent Viewing

ACTIVITY
2.28

SUGGESTED LEARNING STRATEGIES: Close Reading, Double-Entry Journal, Graphic Organizer, Notetaking

Use the following double-entry journal individually to identify film techniques and their intended effects. You will use these examples in your final writing assessment, so try to identify as many examples as you can.

Film Technique and Example: (Framing/Angles, Lighting, Camera Movement, Music/Sound, and Editing)	**Intended Effect**
1. **Dolly/Tracking:** We see the movement of the fish through its own eyes rather than an omniscient (all-seeing) observer.	1. Establishes a first person point of view and helps the viewer to understand the perspective of the animal as a character rather than an object.

TEACHER TO TEACHER **Summary of *Big Fish*:** This is a beautiful story that revolves around a dying father and his son. In a final reunion, Edward Bloom's son Will tries to learn about his father by piecing together the stories he has gathered over the years. Through this interaction, Will sifts through fact and fantasy, myths and legends, to understand his father's great accomplishments and great failings. It is a story of redemption, family, fantasy, and imagination.

ACTIVITY 2.28
Independent Viewing

Materials:

- TV/DVD
- Video of ***Big Fish*** (2004) and/or ***Corpse Bride*** (2005), directed by Tim Burton
- Vocabulary Notebooks

Purpose:

- To annotate text during and after viewing to identify key concepts, make connections, and question the text
- To identify multiple purposes for reading and apply appropriate strategies during reading
- To understand and identify the connection between technique and effect in film

Steps:

1 Instruct students that they will now participate in a **close reading** of an additional Tim Burton film. For this viewing, they will individually identify and analyze film techniques and theme. You have some flexibility as to which Burton film to use. For accessibility, it's best to show 30-minute clips. You may show two 30-minute clips from the same film or one 30-minute clip from each film. It is important to recognize, however, that students will have to use examples from this exercise in Embedded Assessment 2.

2 Explain to students that they will use the **double-entry** journal **graphic organizer** to **take notes** on the film techniques and effects. Explain that they will use the left column to identify the film technique and example. In the right column, they will record the possible effect on the audience or the directorial reason for using the technique. An example from ***Big Fish*** has been included.

Steps:

3 To help students succeed, stop after the first ten minutes of the film and allow students to discuss their findings in small groups and report out to the class. After this discussion, it is important that students do not share answers; their answers will be used as concrete examples in the final writing assessment.

4 When students have completed their viewing, allow time to clarify examples, record additional thoughts, and respond to the closing question.

5 For conceptual synthesis, direct students to explore the relationship of *style, effect,* and *cinematic techniques* in their **Vocabulary Notebooks**.

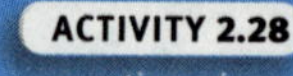

Independent Viewing

Film Technique and Example: (Framing/Angles, Lighting, Camera Movement, Music/Sound, and Editing)	**Intended Effect**

Closing Question: After viewing the film(s), what similarities in style and/or theme did you notice in relation to the other films you watched? Record your ideas on a separate piece of paper for a class discussion.

TEACHER TO TEACHER **Summary of *Corpse Bride*:** This is a stop-motion animated feature that follows a young man (Victor, voiced by Johnny Depp) who is taken to the underworld and married to a mysterious Corpse Bride. In the meantime, his real-life bride waits for him in the Land of the Living. Although the colorful and musical Land of the Dead is a stark contrast to Victor's strict Victorian upbringing, he still yearns to return to his one true love. Set in a nineteenth-century European village, this fantastic film focuses on timeless themes of romance, fantasy, and the power of optimism.

Portfolio Activity: Film Style

ACTIVITY 2.29

SUGGESTED LEARNING STRATEGIES: Graphic Organizer, Prewriting

There are six common literary elements to consider when examining an author's ***style*** in a text: tone, diction, imagery, syntax, organization, and point of view. Some of these terms will be familiar to you from previous years, some were introduced this year, and some might be brand new. Consider what you already know about these elements, and read the definitions provided. Then fill in the right side of the chart with an example from your viewing that is used for the same purpose. Hint: The first one is from a lesson in this unit.

Style Device	Cinematic Technique
Tone: The writer's or speaker's attitude toward a subject, character, or audience; it is conveyed through the author's choice of words and detail. **Mood:** The atmosphere or predominant emotion in a literary work.	
Diction: Word choice intended to convey a certain effect.	
Imagery: The descriptive words or phrases a writer uses to represent persons, objects, actions, feelings, and ideas by appealing to the senses.	
Organization: The narrative structure of a piece—how a text begins and ends, is sequenced, paced, or arranged.	
Syntax: The arrangement of words and the order of grammatical elements in a sentence.	
Point of View: The perspective from which a narrative is told.	

ACTIVITY 2.29

Portfolio Activity: Film Style

Materials:

- Portfolio
- Previous unit notes and activities
- Vocabulary Notebooks

Purpose:

- To create a prewriting document for the assessment style analysis essay
- To draw direct connections between style in film and text
- To demonstrate an understanding of film *as* text

Steps:

1 Explain to students that there are six common elements to consider when examining an author's ***style***. You may wish to review the definitions of these terms. Then, ask them to fill in the right side of the chart with the corresponding cinematic technique a director can use for the same purpose. Ask them also to consider what leads them to make that connection. (After students have worked on this, you may wish to direct them back to the Learning Focus on page 142.)

Steps:

2 Have students use this Venn diagram **graphic organizer** to consider similarities and differences in the films they have viewed. This is an opportunity for students to compile a document that reflects their work and also serves as a prewriting strategy for their assessment. Encourage students to think about similarities and differences in theme, character, and especially cinematic techniques.

3 In preparation for the Embedded Assessment essay, have students formulate a thoughtful thesis that responds to this prompt:

Citing examples from at least two films, explain what cinematic techniques best display the style of Tim Burton. How does he use those techniques to achieve a particular effect?

4 Direct students to revisit their **Vocabulary Notebook** entries on ***cinematic techniques***, ***style***, and ***effect*** to further develop their ideas and to synthesize these concepts.

Portfolio Activity: Film Style

Now consider all of the films you have viewed in class. Fill in the graphic organizer below with similarities and differences in character, theme, and, especially, cinematic techniques. You might want to enlarge the Venn diagram or create your own organizer on a separate page.

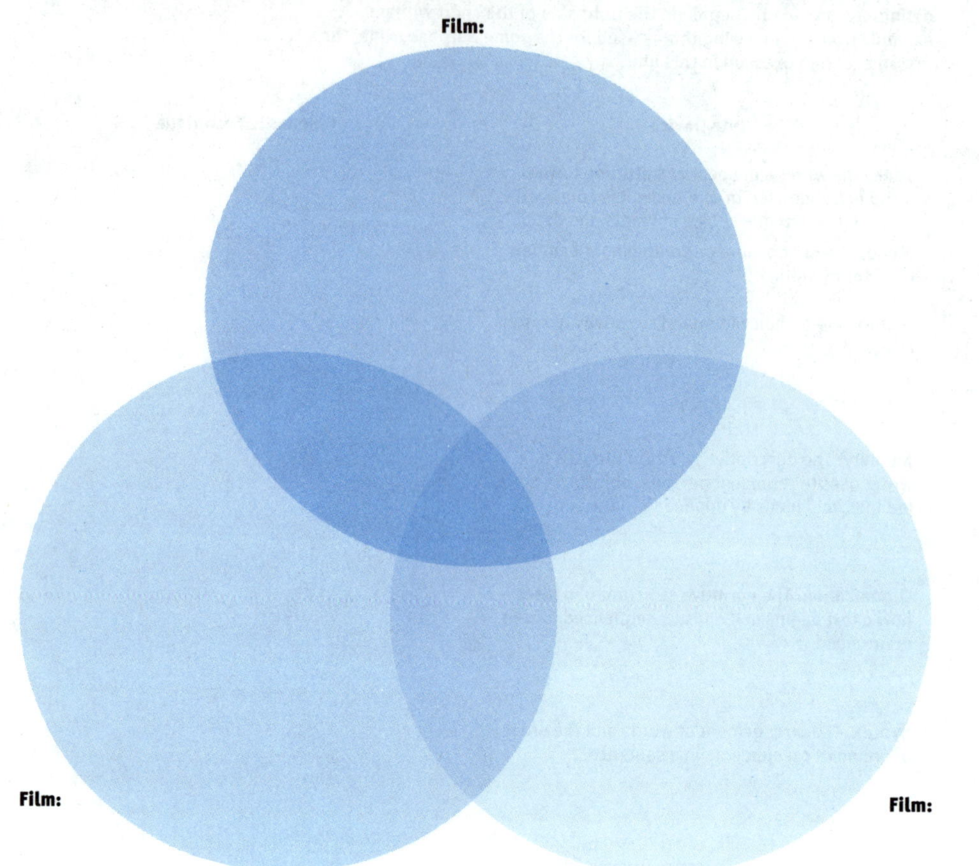

© 2011 College Board. All rights reserved.

Creating a Draft

ACTIVITY 2.30

SUGGESTED LEARNING STRATEGIES: Close Reading, Marking the Draft, Sharing and Responding, Revising

Use the following outline to guide you as you craft your first draft of a multiple-paragraph analytical essay. Use the space in the outline for your notes.

Introduction

Should contain a lead or hook that grabs the reader's attention. Use the subjunctive form to compose a rhetorical question expressing a possibility as a hook.

Should provide a context for the reader (theme) of the movies you will discuss, connecting to two cinematic elements.

Should provide a thesis that interprets Burton's use of your two specified elements.

Should connect to larger themes.

Body Paragraph 1

Focus on one cinematic element and explore its effect in multiple films.

GRAMMAR & USAGE

Consider creating a **compound sentence** by joining independent clauses with a **conjunctive adverb.** A conjunctive adverb joins the clauses and also indicates the relationship between them.

These are some common conjunctive adverbs: *consequently, however, instead, otherwise, therefore, in addition, nevertheless.*

Notice the punctuation and the placement of the conjunctive adverb in the following examples:

> He was an accomplished speaker; **however,** he did not impress the audience.
>
> He was an accomplished speaker; he did not, **however,** impress the audience.

GRAMMAR & USAGE EXTENSION

You might suggest that students use conjunctive adverbs to join independent clauses in their drafts. Draw their attention to the list and examples in the Grammar & Usage feature.

- Explain the punctuation: Usually, a semicolon precedes the conjunctive adverb and a comma follows it.
- Discuss placement: Often the conjunctive adverb may be placed in different locations in a sentence. If it does not fall right after the semicolon, then it is set off with a comma before and after it.

ACTIVITY 2.30
Creating a Draft

Materials:

- Draft of thesis statement
- Rough draft paragraphs

Purpose:

- To draft a text that presents a coherent and smooth progression of ideas and organization
- To evaluate a draft for revision purposes
- To synthesize information from multiple sources

Steps:

1 The purpose of this activity is to help prepare students to write their analysis essays for Embedded Assessment 2. Explain to students that they will be composing a multi-paragraph essay analyzing the cinematic style of director Tim Burton. They will be focusing on the ways in which the director uses stylistic techniques to achieve a desired effect. Instruct students to find the Embedded Assessment assignment and Scoring Guide. Guide students through a **close reading** of the prompt, steps, and Scoring Guide criteria.

2 You may want to begin by reviewing the components of an essay: an introduction, body paragraphs, and a conclusion. Ask students to revisit the structure of a paragraph studied throughout this unit. You may choose to spend time with students to develop coherence as they move from one paragraph to the next (transitions).

3 Ask students to revisit their notes and decide on which two of the five cinematic elements they would like to focus their essay (framing, lighting, camera movement, music/sound, and editing).

4 Direct students to organize their essay using the **outline** template on this page and the next. Each section has important prompts to consider when drafting their essay.

Steps:

5 Provide students time to compose a draft of their text in class. Once students have a draft, allow them to read through their text and **mark the draft** for areas of weakness.

6 As students prepare their drafts, you might work with them on ***unity*** (one single idea per paragraph) and ***coherence*** (moving smoothly from sentence to sentence using repetition of key words, appropriate transitions, etc.).

7 Allow students to share their drafts in small groups and get suggestions for those areas of weakness they identified earlier (**share and respond**). Using the suggestions from the small groups, students should **revise** their text accordingly.

8 You may choose to conduct a mini lesson to meet the varying needs of your students. At some point in your instruction, you might want to ask students to respond to the following reflective sentence starters:

- What I've done really well in this essay is…
- In order to move my draft to a published text, I'll need…
- My priorities for revision on this text are…

9 Prior to the due date, ask students to read through their text, silently and aloud, **editing** any errors they find before they submit their essay to you.

Creating a Draft

Body Paragraph 2

Focus on another cinematic element and explore its effect in multiple films.

Conclusion

Let the following questions shape your concluding thoughts:

- What did you say in regard to Burton's style in this essay?
- Do the cinematic elements you discuss connect to a larger theme?
- What does this interpretive analysis mean?
- Why does it matter?

Writing a Style Analysis Essay

Embedded Assessment 2

SUGGESTED LEARNING STRATEGIES: **Graphic Organizer, Prewriting, Marking The Draft, Outlining, Sharing and Responding, Self Editing**

Assignment

Your assignment is to write an essay analyzing the cinematic style of director Tim Burton. Your essay will focus on the ways in which the director uses stylistic techniques across films to achieve a desired effect.

Steps

Prewriting

1. Review the graphic organizers and double-entry journals you have completed throughout the unit, and consider the multiple examples of Tim Burton's stylistic choices. Make a list of the stylistic elements you can incorporate into your essay. Narrow your list to include only three or four stylistic techniques for which you have clear examples.
2. Create a thesis statement in which you identify the stylistic techniques you will discuss. Then, use a prewriting strategy (e.g., mapping, webbing, or outlining) to develop the details and examples you can include to support each topic. You might consider talking to your Writing Group to refine your thinking about the examples you can include for each stylistic element.

Drafting

3. Draft your essay. Consult your mapping plan and outline. Use ample support for each of your topics. Continue to refer to your graphic organizers and double-entry journal for assistance.

Revising

4. Create manipulative cards on which you write your thesis statement, topics, and supporting details. Consider the relationship between your thesis and topics, and experiment with rearranging the order of your topics or details by shifting the position of the cards.
5. Next, share your draft with your Writing Group. Your peers should consult the Scoring Guide to guide their responses and suggestions with a focus on your essay's ideas, organization, and use of language.
6. Consider the results of your manipulative exercise and writing group discussion, and incorporate desired changes into your new draft.

Editing for Publication

7. Use your available resources (e.g., spell check, dictionaries, Editor's Checklist) to edit for correctness of grammar and conventions and prepare your essay for publication.
8. If you are handwriting your essay, remember to write clearly and legibly.

Embedded Assessment 2

Writing a Style Analysis Essay

College Board Standards and Objectives

M2 Understanding, Interpreting, Analyzing, and Evaluating Media Communication (M2.1)
PE Mappings: M2.1-1.4, M2.1-2.4, M2.1-3.4

W1 Rhetorical Analysis and Planning (W1.1)
PE Mappings: W1.1-1.4, W1.1-2.4

W2 Generating Content (W2.1 L; W2.2 L)
PE Mappings: W2.1-1.4L. W2.1-2.4L, W2.2-1.4L, W2.2-2.4L, W2.2-3.4L, W2.2-4.4L)

W3 Drafting (W3.1 L; W3.2 L)
PE Mappings: W3.1-1.4L, W3.1-2.4L, W3.1-3.4L, W3.2-1.4L, W3.2-2.4L, W3.2-3.4L

W4 Evaluating and Revising Texts (W4.1 L; W4.2 L)
PE Mappings: W4.1-1.4L, W4.2-1.4L

W5 Editing to Present Technically Sound Texts (W5.1; W5.2; W5.4)
PE Mappings: W5.1-1.4, W5.2-1.4, W5.4-1.4

Steps:

1 Be sure students understand the requirements of the assignment. Emphasize that it is important that they use examples from multiple films viewed in this unit to compare how Burton uses stylistic devices to achieve similar effects.

2 Remind students to edit their essays for accuracy in grammar, sentence structure, punctuation, capitalization, subject-verb agreement, appropriate verb tenses, and spelling. If needed, refer students to the Grammar Handbook or provide students with classroom references.

Embedded Assessment 2

Continued

Scoring Guide

When you score this Embedded Assessment, you may wish to download and print a copy of the Scoring Guide from SpringBoard Online. In this way, you can have a copy to mark for each student's work.

Embedded Assessment 2

continued

Writing a Style Analysis Essay

SCORING GUIDE

Scoring Criteria	Exemplary	Proficient	Emerging
Ideas	The writer insightfully identifies and analyzes Burton's stylistic techniques employing textual support from multiple films. The analysis displays an in-depth understanding of how Burton achieves his intended effect on the audience.	The writer clearly identifies and describes Burton's stylistic techniques using support from more than one film. The analysis displays a clear understanding of how Burton achieves his intended effect on the audience.	The writer demonstrates a limited understanding of Burton's stylistic techniques; support is insufficient or inaccurate. The analysis displays a misunderstanding of how Burton achieves the intended effect on the audience and/or may be replaced with plot summary.
Organization	The essay is multi-paragraphed and logically organized to enhance the reader's understanding. It includes an innovative introduction with an insightful lead or hook and strong thesis, coherent body paragraphs, and a perceptive conclusion. Effective transitions exist throughout and add to the essay's coherence.	The essay is multi-paragraphed and organized. It includes an introduction with a lead or hook and clear thesis, detailed body paragraphs, and a conclusion. Transitions create coherence.	Organization is attempted, but key components are lacking. It may include an introduction with an unfocused thesis, undeveloped body paragraphs, and/or inadequate conclusion. Transitions, if attempted, do little to create coherence.
Use of Language	Diction is appropriate for an academic audience. The essay demonstrates a sophisticated use of terminology to knowledgeably discuss film.	Diction is mostly appropriate for an academic essay. The essay demonstrates a basic use of terminology to discuss film.	Diction is informal or inappropriate for an academic essay. The essay may demonstrate limited or inaccurate use of terminology to discuss film.
Conventions	Writing is virtually error-free	Writing is generally error-free.	Writing contains errors that distract from meaning.

SCORING GUIDE

Scoring Criteria	Exemplary	Proficient	Emerging
Evidence of Writing Process	There is extensive evidence that the essay reflects the various stages of the writing process.	There is evidence that the essay reflects stages of the writing process.	There is little or no evidence that the essay has undergone stages of the writing process.
Additional Criteria			

Comments:

Teacher Notes

UNIT REFLECTION

Purpose

- To monitor comprehension and growth through a reflective process
- To synthesize understanding of individual reading and writing processes and strategies
- To self-assess mastery of key concepts and terms

Steps:

1 This is an opportunity for students to think about the concepts, vocabulary, and their own learning progress as they revisit and review the work they have produced in this unit.

2 Encourage students to be especially metacognitive about which strategies they have used and how those strategies support their learning styles and goals.

Unit Teacher Reflection

1 Which activities in this unit did you need to adjust (or you think should be adjusted) to prepare your students to be successful on each Embedded Assessment? Add your notes on how you would adjust the activities.

2 Which teacher strategies were most effective for introducing concepts/ideas to your students?

3 How did the unit activities help you address the individual learning needs of your students? Note any changes you would make in your instructional strategies to differentiate instruction.

Unit 2

Reflection

An important aspect of growing as a learner is to reflect on where you have been, what you have accomplished, what helped you to learn, and how you will apply your new knowledge in the future. Use the following questions to guide your thinking and to identify evidence of your learning. Use separate notebook paper.

Thinking about Concepts

1. Using specific examples from this unit, respond to the Essential Questions:
   - How do authors and directors use specific techniques to achieve a desired effect?
   - What are the essential features of an effective style analysis?
2. Consider the new academic vocabulary from this unit (**Point of View, Style, Cinematic Techniques, Effect, Commentary**) as well as academic vocabulary from previous units, and select 3-4 terms of which your understanding has grown. For each term, answer the following questions:
   - What was your understanding of the term before you completed this unit?
   - How has your understanding of the term evolved throughout the unit?
   - How will you apply your understanding in the future?

Thinking about Connections

3. Review the activities and products (artifacts) you created. Choose those that most reflect your growth or increase in understanding.
4. For each artifact that you choose, record, respond to, and reflect on your thinking and understanding, using the following questions as a guide:
   a. What skill/knowledge does this artifact reflect, and how did you learn this skill/knowledge?
   b. How did your understanding of the power of language expand through your engagement with this artifact?
   c. How will you apply this skill or knowledge in the future?
5. Create this reflection as Portfolio pages—one for each artifact you choose. Use the model in the box for your headings and commentary on questions.

Thinking About Thinking

Portfolio Entry

Concept:

Description of Artifact:

Commentary on Questions:

© 2011 College Board. All rights reserved.

About the Unit

Unit 3

Context

This unit continues the coming-of-age thematic concept by examining diverse perspectives on societal issues, life experiences, community outlook, rites of passage, and character development. Poetry most poignantly conveys the power of words, of feelings, and of images to address issues of importance to writers' unique stylistic choices. A deep understanding of the function and effect of stylistic techniques empowers students to emulate the style of a published author and, in turn, develop a signature style in their own poetry. By studying poetry intensely and writing their own, students will see their voices emerging in the literary community and make their contribution alongside other poets.

Suggested Texts and Materials

You will need to acquire the following songs for this unit:

- "Every Ghetto Every City," by Lauryn Hill
- "Smells Like Teen Spirit," by Nirvana
- "Smells Like Teen Spirit," by Tori Amos

For Activity 3.16, you will need samples from Def Poetry.

CollegeBoard
inspiring minds™

AP/ College Readiness

This unit focuses on refining several important skill and knowledge areas for AP/College Readiness:

- Close reading and analysis of poetry in many forms. (Activities 3.5, 3.6, 3.11)
- Analyzing one poet's style extensively and writing a style analysis essay. (Activities 3.17, EA 2)
- Applying the various stages of the writing process. (Activities 3.18, 3.19, EA 2)
- Writing in a variety of modes. (Activities 3.9, 3.12)
- Oral interpretation and communication. (Activity 3.16)

Independent Reading

To augment your students' experiences with poetry, encourage them to read either a collection of poetry or a story written in poetic form. Students may select their own materials, or you may choose to select poetry and assign it to groups for collaborative study.

Writing Workshops

For Unit 3, you may want to access Workshop 3, Poetry, and Workshop 9, Response to Literary and Expository Text, as additional or preliminary practice in preparation for the Embedded Assessments 1 and 2.

Grammar Handbook

Encourage students to use the Grammar Handbook as a reference as they develop their writing skills. Throughout the unit, you may want to incorporate mini-lessons from the Grammar Handbook and the Grammar & Usage features in this and other units to reinforce students' grammar and writing skills.

Instructional Sequence

The instruction begins with several close-reading activities that ask students to examine the stylistic elements within poems and their impact on the reader. Students will then transfer knowledge of these specific elements (figurative language, poetic form, structure, style, etc.) to the creation of an anthology of their own poetry in Embedded Assessment 1. With a clear understanding of how authors use stylistic features to convey meaning, students are prepared to critically analyze a collection of work from a single poet to identify patterns and trends. These activities provide students with an understanding of an author's choices, which they will use when writing their style analysis essay in Embedded Assessment 2.

Activities 3.1–3.4 preview the unit and introduce the genre of poetry and its distinctive elements (structure, form, figurative language) and its universality.

Activity 3.5 examines how the life and art of an author intersect in a poem to convey theme. Students examine how the life experiences of a poet are reflected in her poetry. This activity provides an example for the brief autobiographical narrative students are asked to write to connect to their own collection of work for Embedded Assessment 1: Creating a Poetry Anthology.

Activities 3.6–3.12 reinforce students' analytical skills by having them examine the function and effect of the stylistic techniques employed by published authors. As students learn poetic elements (e.g., figurative language, structure, and form) from mentor poets, they will emulate these in their own poetry. Students annotate their poetry and critique the effects of their stylistic choices.

Embedded Assessment 1 | **Creating a Poetry Anthology**

Skills and Knowledge:

- Analyze poems for style and craft.
- Analyze poetry for figurative language, structure, form, and theme.
- Understand the function and effect of poetic elements (e.g., figurative language, structure, and form).
- Understand and use suitable diction.
- Create symbolic visuals that connect thematically to students' poetry.
- Annotate a published author's poetry and their own.
- Recognize the essential features of an autobiographical narrative.
- Reflect on and critique stylistic choices.
- Use strategies to interpret poetry (TP-CASTT).
- Generate poetry incorporating a thematic concept (e.g., coming of age).
- Revise poetry.

Activities 3.13–3.15 deepen interpretive skills through the TP-CASTT strategy to analyze poetry for both content and style. Students are guided through the process of analysis and the construction of analytical paragraphs.

Activity 3.16 uses a strategy to analyze poetry for content and style free of teacher support. Students will present an oral interpretation of their poems. This activity directly scaffolds the presentation component for Embedded Assessment 2.

Activity 3.17 guides students through the process of selecting and researching a collection of work by a single poet, and applying their analytical skills to it.

Activities 3.18–3.19 review components of style analysis and guide students through the prewriting and drafting stages for Embedded Assessment 2.

Embedded Assessment 2 **Analyzing and Presenting a Poet**

Skills and Knowledge:

- Use a strategy (TP-CASTT) to analyze poetry.
- Write an analytical paragraph adhering to form (topic sentence, textual support, commentary, sentence of closure).
- Analyze and critique poetry for tone and diction.
- Analyze and critique poetry free of teacher support.
- Interpret poetry orally.
- Identify, interpret, and critique an author's style.
- Write a style analysis essay.
- Generate a thesis and provide textual support.
- Develop and sustain an assertion throughout an essay.
- Revise and edit an essay.
- Conduct research on a poet.

Suggested Pacing

Activity	45 to 50-Minute Class Periods	Class Periods with Homework	Activity	45 to 50-Minute Class Periods	Class Periods with Homework
Learning Focus and 3.1	½		EA1	3	HW
3.2	1		Learning Focus	½	
3.3	¾	HW	3.13	½	HW
3.4	½	HW	3.14	¾	
3.5	1		3.15	¾	HW
3.6	½	HW	3.16	2	HW
3.7	¾	HW	3.17	½	HW (research)
3.8	1	HW	3.18	¾	w/research
3.9	1	HW	3.19	½	
3.10	1	HW	EA2	4	HW
3.11	¾	HW	Unit Reflection	½	
3.12	1	HW			
Total Class Periods				23 ½	

Activity 3.15 Graphic Organizer

In this activity, students will use TP-CASTT to analyze the poem "Young," by Anne Sexton. A blank TP-CASTT diagram is included on page 185d for use in demonstrating the TP-CASTT analysis or for making copies for student use.

TP-CASTT

Poem Title:

Author:

T		
P		
C		
A		
S		
T		
T		

Unit 3

Exploring Poetic Voices

Essential Questions

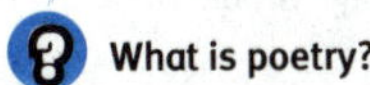
What is poetry?

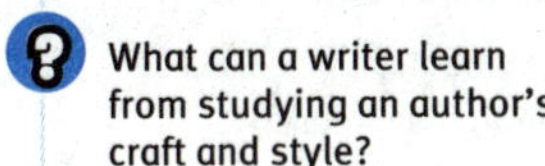
What can a writer learn from studying an author's craft and style?

Unit Overview

Poetry most poignantly conveys the power of words, of feelings, and of images. Since we are surrounded by poetry in its various forms on a daily basis—for example, popular music, billboards, and advertising jingles, it is important to understand the fundamentals of the genre. At the same time, you should appreciate and enjoy poetry independently, free from teacher interpretation. As Walt Whitman noted in his poem, "Song of Myself,"

Stop this day and night with me and you shall possess the origin of all poems,

You shall possess the good of the earth and sun (there are millions of suns left)

You shall no longer take things at second or third hand, nor look through eyes of the dead, nor feed on the spectres in books,

You shall not look through my eyes either, nor take things from me,

You shall listen to all sides and filter them from yourself.

—Walt Whitman, *Leaves of Grass*

UNIT 3

Have students read the Unit Overview. Discuss the ideas in the overview and ask students to relate them to their own lives.

Students will provide responses to the Essential Questions in Activity 3.1. At the end of the unit, they will revisit the Essential Questions to see how their responses have changed after studying the unit.

UNIT 3

Have students read the goals for the unit and **mark** any words that are unfamiliar to them. You may want to create a space in the classroom for these words so students can add information about their meaning as they study the unit.

You may consider posting these goals in a visible place in the classroom for the duration of the unit, allowing you and students to revisit the goals easily and gauge progress toward achieving the goals throughout the unit.

Academic Vocabulary

Point out the academic vocabulary to students, and remind them that they will be studying concepts related to these words throughout the unit. Having students create **graphic organizers** to study these words in depth will greatly enhance their understanding of each word and its relationship to unit concepts. Have students keep their completed graphic organizers in their **Vocabulary Notebooks**.

See the Resources at the back of this book for examples of blackline masters suitable for word study. As students become more acquainted with the use of a **graphic organizer** to explore the meaning of a word, you may want them to create their own graphic organizers.

Unit 3

Exploring Poetic Voices

Goals

- To develop the skills and knowledge to analyze and craft poetry
- To analyze the function and effects of figurative language
- To write original poems that reflect personal voice, style, and an understanding of poetic elements
- To write a style analysis essay
- To present an oral interpretation of a poem

ACADEMIC VOCABULARY

Poetic Structure

Diction

Imagery

Figurative Language

Syntax

Contents

**Texts not included in these materials.*

UNIT 3

Teacher Notes

LEARNING FOCUS:

What Does My Voice Represent?

Read the Learning Focus with students or have them read independently. **Activate prior knowledge** by having students **mark the text** and highlight words or concepts that are familiar (what they know). They might use a question mark to indicate content that is unfamiliar (what they do not know but want to learn).

Students will respond to the information on this page in Activity 3.1.

Teacher Notes

Learning Focus:

What Does My Voice Represent?

We have all had a song, whether we like it or not, get stuck in our heads. It plays over and over and over. Maybe the tune is catchy or maybe the lyrics are contagious; songs are poetry set to music, and lyrics —words— infectiously express an artist's voice. In this unit, you will discover **voice**, a very powerful tool, and you will be exposed to a variety of **poetic voices** that explore coming-of-age issues. Furthermore, you will analyze how poetry frees an artist to express perspectives on personal experiences, community, and societal issues.

As you examine the work of published poets, you will sharpen your ability to read, interpret, and critique poems. You will explore the function and effect of poetic devices (i.e., **poetic structure, figurative language, diction, imagery**). In addition, you will gain a sense of how specific poetic language reinforces ideas and themes, and you will gain a sense of what others' voices can represent.

Careful attention to another's work will help you to explore your own poetic voice, creating original poems that emulate the style and craft of published poets. Once you understand how authors use poetic devices for specific effect, you will be able to use those same devices to create poems that express your feelings about coming of age. As the first half of the unit ends, you will construct an anthology that showcases a collection of your original poems. This task will give you an opportunity to reflect on and critique the stylistic choices you make as a writer, and, as a result, your voice just may contagiously remain in someone else's head!

Independent Reading: Several of the poems in this unit focus on issues of growth, self-realization, and expression. For your own reading, you may want to look for a collection of poems or a story written in poetic form that relates to similar issues that are important to you.

Previewing the Unit

ACTIVITY 3.1

SUGGESTED LEARNING STRATEGIES: Close Reading, KWL Chart, Marking the Text, Skimming/Scanning, Summarizing/Paraphrasing, Think-Pair-Share

Essential Questions

1. What is poetry?

2. What can a writer learn from studying an author's craft and style?

Unit Overview and **Learning Focus**

Predict what you think this unit is about. Use the words or phrases that stood out to you when you read the Unit Overview and the Learning Focus.

Embedded Assessment 1

What knowledge must you have (what do you need to know) to succeed on Embedded Assessment 1? What skills must you have (what must you be able to do)?

ACTIVITY 3.1

Previewing the Unit

Purpose:

- To contextualize prior knowledge about key ideas and concepts
- To analyze the skills and knowledge necessary for success in this unit

Steps:

1 To determine students' existing knowledge about the concepts for the unit, ask them to **think-pair share** responses to the two Essential Questions. Students will revisit these questions throughout the unit to develop a more mature understanding of these ideas.

2 Direct students to **skim and scan** the Unit Overview and Learning Focus pages. **Activate prior knowledge** by asking students to **mark the text**. They may use a check mark to indicate what is familiar to them (know) and a question mark to indicate what is unfamiliar to them (don't know–want to learn). Engage students in a whole class discussion. You may want to record their findings on a **KWL** chart and revisit this chart at the end of the unit to discover what students have learned.

3 Provide students with a clear learning target by asking them to find the Embedded Assessment 1 assignment and Scoring Guide (pages 226–228). Lead students through a **close reading** of the prompt, steps, and Scoring Guide criteria. Instruct students to **mark the text** by underlining or highlighting the places that mention a skill or knowledge necessary to succeed on the Embedded Assessment.

4 Instruct students to **summarize/paraphrase** with a partner or small group the skills/knowledge they have underlined or highlighted. As you conduct a large group discussion, create a web **graphic organizer** that lists the knowledge and skills.

5 Revisit the web graphic organizer throughout the unit. Pointing students back to the web reinforces the purpose of each activity and the skills and knowledge needed for success on the Embedded Assessment. You may want to enlarge the Embedded Assessment web graphic organizer to provide a **visual** in the classroom throughout the course of the unit. Students will preview Embedded Assessment 2 before Activity 3.13.

ACTIVITY 3.2
What Is Poetry?

Materials:

- 3 x 5 index cards

Purpose:

- To activate prior knowledge by exploring beliefs about and experiences with poetry
- To understand the process of making meaning from a poem
- To write a poem expressing perceptions of poetry

Steps:

1 Provide students with an index card and instruct them to label one side "A" and the other side "B." Direct students to review the poetry quotations and select one on which to conduct a **close reading**. Ask students to write their quote on the A side of the card along with a brief interpretation. You might wish to place students in groups to discuss a quotation for deeper understanding.

2 Invite students to participate in a poetry "tea party," moving around the room sharing a selected quotation along with their interpretation with their classmates. Remind students to listen attentively and ask follow-up questions to clarify students' interpretations.

3 Lead students in a **discussion** using the unit's Essential Question, "What is poetry?" Ask students to consider the poems they encounter in life on a regular basis.

Writing Workshops

During the first half of this unit, students will have multiple opportunities to create original poetry. Workshop 3, Poetry, gives students additional practice and direct instruction in writing poetry. You may want to access this workshop early in the unit or wait until students are near Embedded Assessment 1 to provide them with additional opportunities to create poems for their anthologies.

ACTIVITY 3.2

What Is Poetry?

SUGGESTED LEARNING STRATEGIES: Close Reading, Marking the Text, Metacognitive Markers, Quickwrite, Think-Pair-Share

Poets' Perspectives About Poetry

1.	"We don't read and write poetry because it's cute. We read and write poetry because we are members of the human race. And the human race is filled with passion. And medicine, law, business, engineering, these are noble pursuits and necessary to sustain life. But poetry, beauty, romance, love, these are what we stay alive for." *Dead Poets Society*
2.	"Poetry is what gets lost in translation." —Robert Frost
3.	"Poetry is just the evidence of life. If your life is burning well, poetry is just the ash." —Leonard Cohen
4.	"Out of the quarrel with others we make rhetoric; out of the quarrel with ourselves we make poetry." —W.B. Yeats
5.	"Poetry is a packsack of invisible keepsakes." —Carl Sandburg
6.	"Poetry is man's rebellion against being what he is." —James Branch Cabell
7.	"Poetry is the revelation of a feeling that the poet believes to be interior and personal which the reader recognizes as his own." —Salvatore Quasimodo
8.	"Poetry is plucking at the heartstrings, and making music with them." —Dennis Gabor
9.	"Mathematics and poetry are . . . the utterance of the same power of imagination, only that in the one case it is addressed to the head, in the other, to the heart." —Thomas Hill
10.	"Poetry is an orphan of silence. The words never quite equal the experiences behind them." —Charles Simic

Essential Question: What is poetry?

Poetry

Poetry

by Pablo Neruda

ABOUT THE AUTHOR

Chilean author Pablo Neruda (1904–1973) contributed his first poem to a literary journal when he was sixteen and published his first collection of poems the following year. Throughout his life, his poems reflected his world and his work. He wrote political poems, an epic poem about the South American continent, and a series of odes that reflect everyday life—things, events, relationships. In 1971, he was awarded the Nobel Prize in Literature.

And it was at that age . . . poetry arrived
in search of me. I don't know, I don't know where
it came from, from winter or a river.
I don't know how or when,
no they were not voices, they were not
words, nor silence,
but from a street I was summoned,
from the branches of night,
abruptly from the others,
among violent fires
or returning alone,
there I was without a face
and it touched me.

I did not know what to say, my mouth
had no way
with names,
my eyes were blind,
and something started in my soul,
fever or forgotten wings,
and I made my own way,
deciphering[1]
that fire,

My Notes

[1] **deciphering**: figuring out the meaning of something that's not clear

ACTIVITY 3.2 *Continued*

Steps:

4 To explore a published author's perception of poetry, read aloud Neruda's free-verse poem "Poetry" in which he speaks about poetry from the perspective of a writer rather than that of a reader. Ask students to follow along **marking the text** to identify images that capture their attention. Invite students to **pair-share** selected images, and encourage them to think about what these images reveal about Neruda's feelings about poetry.

5 Next, ask students to read the poem silently, using **metacognitive markers**: **?** for a question, ***** for a comment, ___(underline) for verbs, **!** for a connection. Facilitate a text-based discussion, asking students to use their marked text as a point of reference to clarify ideas, make assertions, and interpret the text.

6 Ask for student volunteers to read aloud "Poetry" in sense units. (A sense unit is a complete thought as indicated by punctuation marks. In this poem, there are five complete sentences.) Set a purpose for reading by asking students to consider the essential question from the poet's point of view. Assist students' analysis of Neruda's point of view by directing their attention to the following stylistic techniques:

- Repetition: "I don't know."
- Verb choices: ***know, arrrived, summoned, touched, say, started, deciphering, wrote, saw, wheeled, broke***
- Anaphora: ***and, and, and***
- Form: free verse

Teacher Notes

What Is Poetry?

My Notes

and I wrote the first faint line,
faint, without substance, pure
nonsense,
pure wisdom
of someone who knows nothing,
and suddenly I saw
the heavens
unfastened and open,
planets,
palpitating[2] plantations,
shadow perforated,[3]
riddled
with arrows, fire, and flowers,
the winding night, the universe.

And I, infinitesimal[4] being,
drunk with the great starry
void,
likeness, image of mystery,
felt myself a pure part
of the abyss,
I wheeled with the stars,
my heart broke loose on the wind.

WORD CONNECTIONS

The word ***abyss*** (a bottomless depth) contains the Greek prefix *a-*, which means "without" or "the absence of." This common prefix occurs in other English words like *amoral, apolitical,* and *asocial.*

[2] **palpitating**: pulsating or throbbing rapidly
[3] **perforated**: pierced with holes
[4] **infinitesimal**: so small as to be almost nothing

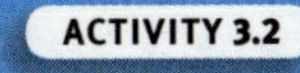

While reading the poem aloud, direct your attention to the following stylistic techniques:

Repetition

Verb Choice

Anaphora

Form

Quickwrite: Revisit the poetry quotations, your classroom discussions, and Neruda's poem and explore the unit's essential question, "What is poetry?"

Literary Terms

Repetition is the use of any element of language—a sound, a word, a phrase, a line, or a stanza—more than once.

Anaphora is a particular kind of repetition in which the same word or group of words is repeated at the beginnings of two or more successive clauses or lines.

Form refers to the particular structure or organization of a work.

Use your ideas about poetry to complete the frame poem below.

A Poem About a Poem

by ____________________

Poetry is ____________________

Poetry is like ____________________

Poetry is about ____________________

Poetry is as important as ____________________

Poetry is as pointless as ____________________

Poetry means ____________________

Poetry is ____________________

ACTIVITY 3.2 Continued

Steps:

7 Ask students to revisit the poetry quotations, classroom discussions, and Neruda's poem to expand their perception of poetry. Have students complete a **quickwrite** responding to the essential question "What is poetry?" to create a personal working definition of poetry.

8 Working collaboratively in small groups, ask students to share their quickwrites. Then ask them to use ideas presented to create a poem about poetry using the frame poem or free verse.

9 Invite each group to share its poetry poems orally via an author's chair, podcast, or another means.

ACTIVITY 3.3

A Writer Speaks About Poetry

Materials:

- Student Poetry Journal

Purpose:

- To discover how authors generate ideas
- To interpret a writer's perspective on poetry
- To analyze the craft and style of professional writers

Steps:

1 Set up a **think-pair-share** in which students share their prior experiences with writing poetry. Ask them to discuss such topics as where ideas come from and what they might be interested in writing about.

2 Remind students that for Embedded Assessment 1, they will create an anthology of their own poetry. Ask students to consider what specific areas they will need more support with in order to be successful.

3 Invite students to examine the writing process of a successful author, Susan Wooldridge. In her collection of essays, ***Poemcrazy,*** she offers an array of suggestions to help emerging poets write poetry.

4 Divide the class into groups of five or six. Assign each group an essay to read. Encourage each group to become experts on their essay by discussing the essay, clarifying ideas, and **marking the text** to highlight specific points to reference.

5 Next, use a **jigsaw** to distribute students into new groups for the purpose of sharing key ideas from the essays. As students listen to the expert, have them mark their texts to perhaps review in depth at a later time.

ACTIVITY 3.3

A Writer Speaks About Poetry

SUGGESTED LEARNING STRATEGIES: **Marking the Text, Think-Pair-Share**

My Notes

Essays

ABOUT THE AUTHOR

Susan Wooldridge is a teacher of creative writing. Her work has been published in numerous journals, though she is best known for her collection of essays, *poemcrazy*. As an observer of nature and the world around her, she is inspired in her writing by everyday events and shares her stories in a distinctive writing style.

From poemcrazy

by Susan Goldsmith Wooldridge

3

collecting words and creating a wordpool

I have a strong gathering instinct. I collect boxes, hats, rusty flattened bottlecaps for collages and creek-worn sticks to color with my hoard of Berol prismacolor pencils. When I was a kid I'd lie in bed imagining I was a squirrel who lived in a hollow tree, foraging for acorns, twigs and whatever it takes to make squirrel furniture.

Most of us have collections. I ask people all the time in workshops, Do you collect anything? Stamps? Shells? '57 Chevys? Raccoons? Money? Leopards? Meteorites? Wisecracks? What a coincidence, I collect them, too. Hats, coins, cougars, old Studebakers. That is, I collect the words. Pith helmet, fragment, Frigidaire, quarrel, love seat, lily. I gather them into my journal.

The great thing about collecting words is they're free; you can borrow them, trade them in or toss them out. I'm trading in (and literally composting) some of my other collections—driftwood, acorns and bits of colored Easter egg shell—for words. Words are lightweight, unbreakable, portable, and they're everywhere. You can even make them up. *Frebrent, bezoncular, zurber*. Someone made up the word *padiddle*.

A word can trigger or inspire a poem, and words in a stack or thin list can make up poems.

Because I always carry my journal with me, I'm likely to jot down words on trains, in the car, at boring meetings (where I appear to be taking notes), on hikes and in bed.

Teacher Notes

My Notes

I take words from everywhere. I might steal *steel*, spelled both ways. *Unscrupulous*. I'll toss in *iron*, *metal* and *magnolias*. Whatever flies into my mind. *Haystack, surge, sidewinder*. A sound, *splash*. A color, *magenta*. Here's a chair. *Velvet. Plush.*

Dylan Thomas loved the words he heard and saw around him in Wales. "When I experience anything," he once said, "I experience it as a thing and a word at the same time, both equally amazing." Writing one ballad, he said, was like carrying around an armload of words to a table upstairs and wondering if he'd get there in time.

Words stand for feelings, ideas, mountains, bees. Listen to the sound of words. I line up words I like to hear, *Nasturtiums buzz blue grass catnip catalpa catalog*.

I borrow words from poems, books and conversations. Politely. Take *polite*. If I'm in a classroom, I just start chalking them onto the board. I don't worry about spelling or meaning. *Curdle. Cantankerous. Linoleum. Limousine.* Listen. *Malevolent. Sukulilli,* the Maidu Indian word for silly. *Magnet cat oven taste tilt titter*.

I call gathering words this way creating a *wordpool*. This process helps free us to follow the words and write poems. In Paradise, California, my students and I looked up insects in a field guide with names like *firebrat, jumping bristletail* and *slantfaced grasshopper*. Then, moving around the room, I asked each person for one word, *any* word.

Everyone started tossing out words. *Tabulate. Magnify. Silence.* We could see the weight and value of each one. Someone said the word *no*. We put yes up there to balance it. Scott said *hate* and then *demolish*. We added *love* and *create* after talking about the importance of opposites. Then we looked for the opposite of *brick, idea, jealousy, tumbleweed* and *cloud*. We piled dozens of words on the board,

toe joust marvel
apparatus dome click
tubed tailstripes
flabbergast horse thought
cumulus cumulo nimbus
nom de plume zodiac zirconium flicker
slip spin serendipity
obsession pyromaniac two-tailed thrips
adobe hypothermia
frost dragon confetti tapioca
observe slither slink snuggle snooze

The rhythm, the music in the words, the circle of voices around the room, the associations, the well of minds casting out words like water in a fountain, words next to words in new ways and the look of them spreading across and down the page takes us to the state of mind poems come from.

Teacher Notes

A Writer Speaks About Poetry

My Notes

I encourage people to toss foreign words into the wordpool. Just the sound can move us into another world very swiftly, like *avra*, breeze in Greek, or *petra*, rock. Add *petrified* and the Maidu word for water that sounds like a spring murmuring, *momoli*. Include place names like the ones I collected in Wales, *Abergavenny, Linthill* and *Skrinklehaven*.

Listed and tossed out this way, words begin to fall into poems by themselves. We put them together in unexpected ways, like *zodiac flicker, tree thought, tumbleweed sadness, magenta jealousy, cloud brick, summer ice, tapioca slithers*.

When I'm playing with words, I don't worry about sounding dumb or crazy. And I don't worry about whether or not I'm writing "a poem." *Word pool. World pool, wild pool, whipoorwill, swing.* Words taken out of the laborious structures (like this sentence) where we normally place them take on a spinning life of their own.

PRACTICE

Write words down. *Flap tip lob. Elope. Scrounge.*

Look around and steal some words. *Lamborghini. Jute. Wombat.*

Go ahead and make up a word. *Losoonie. Flapoon. Noplat.*

Be sloppy. Don't think. You can't make a mistake, there aren't any wrong words. *Phantom strut tumble porch. Dragoon.*

Don't worry too much about meaning for now. Words carry meaning along with them. Put words down and meaning will begin to rush in.

Give each word a color. *Vermilion regret.*

List the senses and give each sense a color. *Peach hearing.*

Toss in words from foreign languages. *Ciao.*

Go for sound: *hum, fizz, fiddle, fandango, zigzag, ziggurat, folderol, armadillo. Tintinabulation.*

Collect field guides. I often bring an insect, rock or butterfly book to workshops and we list words like *window winged moth, globular springtail* or *porphyry*, a purple rock named for the Latin and Greek word for "purple."

My friend Tom's Ford pickup repair manual is chock full of great words: *luminosity probe, diesel throttle control tool, acceleration pump link, swivel, internal vent valve, choke hinge pin. . . .*

Look for a Magnetic Poetry Kit of words that stick to the refrigerator. My friend Arielle got a kit and told me, "Things just come out of you." She wrote about her family's twenty-one-year-old cat, Jumbo,

white puppy petal
you gorgeous milk fluff
sleep all day lick
tiny love from time
and dream

Teacher Notes

My Notes

5

most mad and moonly

Things I love have a way of turning up in my life in unexpected ways. In high school I idolized e. e. cummings because he was irreverent and made me feel free. He played with language and broke all the rules, nourishing my *Catcher in the Rye*, antiestablishment side.

I memorized most of "What of a much of a which of a wind" and several other Cummings poems. My favorite for years was "Somewhere I have never traveled," with the unexpected line that moved me most, "and no one, not even the rain, has such small hands."

During my freshman year of college in New York City I met a Columbia student named Simon Roosevelt, who played Lysander in a production of *A Midsummer Night's Dream*. I painted viney leaves for the set as part of a stage crew that played loud rock music all hours of the night. I helped mend and fit costumes, happiest hanging out behind the scenes. Simon and I went to movies and studied together in the Columbia library. One evening I noticed a worn photo of e. e. cummings in Simon's wallet. "He was my grandfather," Simon told me. e. e. cummings—who died while I was in high school—was turning up again in my world. Life can be like a poem that way, with the unexpected appearing in the room, not just on the page.

cummings plays with words, spacing and capital letters, often putting all the punctuation somewhere unexpected. He experiments with opposites. His poems are both goofy and profound, soft and sharp at the same time, tender and fierce. "What of a much of a which of a wind" opens gently, but soon we're shocked as the wind "bloodies with dizzying leaves the sun / and yanks immortal stars awry."

cummings's words, often like the trail of an acrobat tumbling down the page, invite us to put our *own* words down. Filled with open, white space, his poems leave room for us to enter. We feel we can do this too. cummings's writing inspired a passion in me to create my own world, poke around and explore my boundaries, see how many shades of unnamed color and sound I might find there.

I write this in the car as we zoom home from Berkeley approaching—believe it or not—the "Cummings skyway." Here's Crockett, where the world opens up like a cummings poem into sky, water, sun, ships, and we soar over the Carquinez Strait high in ocean air on a towering erector-set bridge. Back home, my teenage daughter saunters into my room with her hair in a high bun, shoulders low, lips pouting, hips swaying. She's a feminist high-fashion model named Tangerine Valentino. Now she swivels out, ignoring my applause, creating a character sketch for her drama class.

© 2011 College Board. All rights reserved.

Unit 3 • Exploring Poetic Voices 197

Teacher Notes

A Writer Speaks About Poetry

My Notes

cummings reminds me to allow poems to swagger, soar or tiptoe in unexpectedly. I need to be open and ready for them. Poems aren't written from ideas, like essays, and they're not overly controlled. In a poem's "most mad and moonly" spell, out of time, I can break rules and expectations about who I am as well as about writing.

My journal has a memorial page both for e. e. cummings and for his grandson Simon, killed on his red motorcycle the year after we met. At Simon's memorial service someone read a cummings poem that helped us with our shock and sadness,

love is more thicker than forget
more thinner than recall
more seldom than a wave is wet
more frequent than to fail

it is most mad and moonly
and less it shall unbe
than all the sea which only
is deeper than the sea

love is less always than to win
less never than alive
less bigger than the least begin
less littler than forgive

it is most sane and sunly
and more it cannot die
than all the sky which only
is higher than the sky.

The unexpected brings us light and darkness, joy and sorrow, life and death. And it brings discovery. Some of our most important discoveries are made when we're not looking.

PRACTICE

Read some poems by e. e. cummings.

Let a poem write itself as if you were taking dictation from your pen.

Break words up.

Frag

men

t

Let yourself be like a kid. Write your name some way you've never written it before. Draw your name. Use colored pens or pencils.

© 2011 College Board. All rights reserved.

198 SpringBoard® English Textual Power™ Level 4

Teacher Notes

My Notes

Go somewhere outside and turn over a stone.

List in detail what's under the stone that you didn't expect.

Notice three new things in someone's face. Write down what you've seen.

Notice anything that spirals, from the corkscrew to the pasta to the weather patterns on the news.

Write a series of images without stopping. Make some of them absurd. *The snow is black today. It's been raining paint. My dog is singing* La Bohème.

Give colors to ideas and abstractions. *Blue love. Chartreuse agreements. Silver deliberation. Magenta pride.*

Be open to unexpected words and adventures. Spend time being in a state of quiet expectation and see what (or who) comes your way.

Teacher Notes

A Writer Speaks About Poetry

My Notes

6

gas, food, longing

I could glimpse the Hudson River bordering New Jersey when I lived in the Barnard College dorm. This glimpse filled me with longing for I wasn't sure what—maybe a houseboat on the river, a village life I loved or the person I knew I could be.

One weekend I went to a van Gogh exhibit at the Guggenheim Museum. As I rounded a curve in the gallery I saw a painting called *The Sower*. A faceless man, solid as the tree leaning toward him, scatters seeds near a river lit by a huge sun, palpable as a grapefruit in a green sky.

Staring at the painting, I almost stopped breathing. The simple figure in sunset seeding the earth expressed all my feelings of longing, hope and promise. I felt van Gogh had painted the inside of *me*. *I* was the peasant expectantly seeding the field. *I* was the glimpse of river like a blue path. *I* was the low sun about to sink from sight. *I* was the seed in a dark hand waiting to be tossed home. Though it cost more than I could afford, I bought a print of *The Sower* at the show and hung it on a straw mat in my pale green dorm room. The painting made me feel less alone, though I never lost that longing. Even now on the freeway sometimes I'll read the signs as, "Gas, Food, *Longing*."

I still have that print. Tattered and ripped, it's tacked to a wall in my garage, so many years later. I can't throw it out. When I left Barnard and met my future husband, Kent, I was delighted to see a paler version of my *Sower* hanging in his apartment.

For years I've collected paintings on postcards my friend Deborah sends me. I have a large shoebox full. There's Ivan Albright's door, crumbling and bedecked with fading roses like a poem that makes me feel loss and regret.

Albright gave his painting a name that's a poem fragment in itself, *That Which I Should Have Done I Did Not Do*. There's a Magritte room that makes me feel expansive with its clouds for walls, giant comb and shaving brush. Once a student saw this painting and, using the word tickets, wrote, "Suddenly my walls disappear."

In workshops I give each student a postcard to transform into a painting with words. Creating an image with words can express a feeling with color flooding in, as van Gogh's painting does for me.

Image is the root word of imagination. It's from Latin *imago*, "picture," how you see things. Images carry feelings. Saying, "I'm angry," or "I'm sad," has little impact. Creating images, I can make you feel how I feel.

When I read the words of a young student named Cari— "I'm a rose in the shape of a heart / with nineteen days of nothing / but the pouncing of shoes on my dead petals"—I experience desperation through her image.

Teacher Notes

My Notes

Cari doesn't even have to name the feeling—nineteen days, a pale green sky, a pouch of seed held against a sower's heart.

Writing poems using images can create an experience allowing others to feel what we feel. Perhaps more important, poems can put us in touch with our own often buried or unexpected feelings.

Shoua discovered her frustration by using the image of a man shooting pool,

> I hear bang, click, shoosh
> feeling like the white ball
> that does all the work.

Tori used images from a landscape to indicate hopelessness,

> the clouds collapsed,
> they're touching the ground
> trying to come alive,
> but they can't.

Sometime word tickets magically fit with the images in the paintings. One of Tori's words was *jingle*. It helped her convey her developing feeling of hope,

> the glowing water shows shadow
> till we all hear
> the *jingle* of dawn.

Images we create in our poem can not only help us discover our feelings, but can help us begin to transform them.

PRACTICE

Make a wordpool of feeling words, going for opposites: *psychotic stable laughable sober drab vibrant bored blissful frantic calm fragile invincible.*

Find a postcard of a painting, a reproduction in a magazine or book, or a poster on a wall. Any painting will do.

Choose a feeling. Look closely at your painting and find a detail that seems to express your feeling, perhaps one color or the gesture of someone's arm. Perhaps a jug in the corner. Let your words paint the feeling. *I feel as still as a white water jug.*

Say your painting is a landscape. You feel *powerless*. What does that gray cloud look like that expresses your feeling? You might write that the cloud is dissolving, losing its shape. Or you feel *powerful*. Now the cloud is gathering electricity to snap out as lightning.

You might feel *unimportant*, like that tiny leaf on top of the tree, lost in all the others. You might feel like you're *fading* like the last bit of pink light on top of the mountain.

Choose a variety of paintings so you can begin to express the full range of your feelings in one or several poems.

© 2011 College Board. All rights reserved.

Unit 3 • Exploring Poetic Voices 201

Teacher Notes

A Writer Speaks About Poetry

My Notes

7

being here

Once I heard poet Gary Snyder say, "Poetry has an interesting function. It helps people *be* where they are." It's hard to write a poem about a place, an experience or even a state of mind without fully *being* there. When I'm fully present describing a place in a poem it helps bring my reader there too.

I need to breathe in the air, hear the sounds, feel the ground under my feet and join a place to fully describe it. If it's winter, my footprints need to sink in snow or mud beside weblike bird tracks. I need to get wet or muddy, smell, taste and look at things closely. It's important for me to use all my senses in poems: sight, touch smell, taste, hearing and the sixth sense, intuition or "dreamsense" as my friend Mark Rodriguez calls it.

Yesterday morning, on a walk, my writing partner Elizabeth and I got so caught up talking about our kids we barely noticed we were walking along the creek. To write poems I need to be alone. When I avoid being alone I avoid poetry and the messages it brings me.

Alone I open my senses, listen to my surroundings, take in the smells, the light and the way a sycamore curves over the creek like a pale rainbow. "Everything's got to do with listening," the poet W. S. Merwin said of a poem he wrote about the wind. Many of my poems come from what I notice when I'm alone.

Writer Louis Owens says that to most Native Americans, paying this kind of attention is a responsibility. "Our job is to be an awake people . . . utterly conscious, to attend to our world."

This noon I'm on the upper park rim trail on a pockmarked rock. It rained yesterday and there's a veil of mud over the lava cap on the ridge. My dog, Emma, explores as I peer over star thistle at retreating clouds. Thin winter grass is poking up and it's mid-November. Soon I'll find miner's lettuce to feed my kids along with the curly dock I gather for my daughter and me. Everyone else thinks it's too sour.

To experience a place I need to walk in it as often as I can. Abenaki native poet Joseph Bruchac says, "We need to walk to know sacred places, those around us and those within. We need to walk to remember the songs."

Now I've climbed up the hill about fifty feet and I'm sitting against an oak. I'm holding two large acorn caps like small pipe bowls. Here's one of the acorns, long, greenish brown. I rub off the tiny point and polish the acorn with my fingers. Later at home, two acorns will wobble around on the kitchen table shining like bullets.

Bird song. Sweet air. I feel the crumbly oak bark against my back. A darting bird's just above me and I hear thrumming wings. The oak helps me

Teacher Notes

trust and wait and breathe and bend. I feel my body and mind taking in the tree. Soon I'll see what words come.

For now, I'll just be *here*, alone, watching and listening.

PRACTICE

All my poems are suggested by real life and therein have a firm foundation. . . . No one can imitate when you write of the particular, because no others have experienced exactly the same thing. —Goethe

Walk somewhere alone. Listen. Write about what's around you, using all of your senses.

It's important to narrow everything down, make it as specific as you can, down to the tip of a blade of grass, or you'll leave the reader out. For emotion to arise, writing has to be very specific—describing a particular moment or experience in a particular place.

A useful daily practice is to sit (or walk) with a notebook and focus on what's happening right now, in minute detail. "Inside a moment," Emily Dickinson wrote, "centuries of June."

Wherever you are, if it's warm enough, take off your shoes. Breathe deeply. What can you smell?

Look to your right. What's there? Feel your body and mind taking it in.

Look straight down. Notice a color, texture, shape.

Look straight up. Do you see acoustical tiles or blue sky or antique white plaster? Is there a spider up there in a corner webbing herself over? Leave her there, but describe her exactly on paper.

William Blake thought that art and science exist in the organization of "Minute Particulars." Blake saw "a World in a Grain of Sand."

Listen. Do you hear a coffeemaker? Freeway sounds? Tree frogs?

Place your right hand down. What do you feel? A nubby cushion, a chair? Your knee in frayed leggings?

Look closely at something you see all the time. Write as if you've never seen this before.

Keep writing. If you focus on your surroundings, the words may just help you be there. But if they want to take you somewhere else, follow them.

My Notes

Teacher Notes

A Writer Speaks About Poetry

My Notes

8

it looks like

When my son, Daniel, was small he would often compare the way one thing looked to another. Passing a peach cannery I said, "See the smoke coming out of that chimney?" Daniel responded, "Just yike a cigarette." He was always saying, "*It yooks yike, it yooks yike.*" When his sister, Elisabeth, was born, Dan saw her swaddled with only her head visible and remarked, "She yooks yike a hot dog."

When we transplanted a small tree from a pot to a hole in the ground, Daniel said, "The world will be its new pants." As we drove toward the coast one day and saw cows on the hillside, Elisabeth said, "They yook yike popcorn."

I think we naturally see things metaphorically. We're always comparing the way one thing looks to another. Comparison is built into our language. I've noticed that on a highway a hairpin turn, from above, *looks like* a hairpin. Cattails in a swampy area along Lonestar Road *look like* cat's tails. In my garden foxglove looks like a wee "folk's glove," with a pouch for a tiny hand. Georgia O'Keeffe said she painted individual flowers and made them huge so we'd be forced to look closely and notice what flowers really look like. Whether she intended this or not, O'Keeffe's paintings lend themselves to metaphor. Inside her white flower I see

a gown with long white sleeves,
a curled satin slipper with grey on the toe,
a Chinese lantern on low,
a bowl of silver bells, ringing.

Wilfred Funk writes in *Word Origins and Their Romantic Stories* that originally all words were poems, since our language is based, like poems, in metaphor. The names of flowers makes this easier to see. This flower looks like a shooting star. Maybe the next time I see one I'll make the shift from simile to full metaphor and think, This flower *is* a shooting star, or a bird's-eye, a paintbrush, butter and eggs.

In some words we can still see the poem/metaphor, especially flowers and trees like ladyslipper, redbud, spinster blue-eyed Mary. My married name, Wooldridge, must have come from the image of lambs on a ridge.

Metaphor is a bridge bringing things together. The world is a stage. Life is a dream. The navel is a belly button. When she lived in Athens years ago, a friend Sally tells me, some of the delivery bikes had the word METAPHOR printed on their sides—probably a company name. In Greek *metaphor* literally means to bear or carry over.

Sometimes part of writing a poem is as simple as looking carefully and bringing things together through simile and metaphor. This bit of moon looks

© 2011 College Board. All rights reserved.

204 SpringBoard® English Textual Power™ Level 4

like a canoe. The moon *is* a cradle, a wolf's tooth, a fingernail, snow on a curved leaf or milk in the bottom of a tipped glass.

PRACTICE

Take an object and think about what it *looks like*. Describe exactly what you see.

Look around you. Does your lampshade look like a ballerina's illuminated pink pleated skirt? Not exactly, but it's a start. Let yourself go for the farfetched and the ridiculous when you make comparisons.

If you can find a flower, look inside. What does it look like?

Find a painting, abstract or realistic. Choose a detail and stare at it. Focusing on that detail, write,

I see
It looks like
it looks like
I see
It looks like (repeat)

For more practice, list what you see around you and write down what it looks like.

The pine tree looks like a torpedo
That folded piece of paper looks like a flattened sail
The curled telephone cord looks like an earthworm
That man's curly hair looks like. . .
The moth's wing . . .

Keep going.

My Notes

After Reading

What insights about writing does Susan Wooldridge suggest?

ACTIVITY 3.3 Continued

6 Bring closure to this activity by asking students in a whole class discussion to identify Susan Wooldridge's insights that the class can use when writing poetry. Chart these ideas, and encourage students to refer to them throughout the unit if they get writer's block or struggle with a concept.

7 Encourage students to acquire a journal as Wooldridge suggests and begin to log emerging ideas, insights, words, phases, etc.

ACTIVITY 3.4
Literary Devices Scavenger Hunt

Purpose:

- To access prior knowledge about literary devices
- To understand the function and use of literary devices

Steps:

1 Introduce the Personal Poetry Glossary **graphic organizer** and explain that students will use it throughout the unit to define and examine literary devices. They will be expected to use it when analyzing a poem and creating original work.

2 Ask students to review the terms on the graphic organizer and identify each term as follows: **Q** to signal if they have never heard of the device; **H** if they have heard of the device and have a vague understanding of what it is; and **T** if they are very familiar with the device and can teach another student about it.

3 After students have **marked the text,** ask them to share responses with other students to see if they can turn their Qs into Hs and the Hs into Ts.

ACTIVITY 3.4

Literary Devices Scavenger Hunt

SUGGESTED LEARNING STRATEGIES: **Graphic Organizer, Marking the Text, QHT**

Personal Poetry Glossary

Literary Device	Definition	Example from the Text and Explanation of Function and Use	Original Example for My Writer's Toolbox
Refrain			
Tone			
Imagery			
Diction			
Hyperbole			
Allusion			
Connotation			

Extended Metaphor			
Symbol			
Onomatopoeia			
Alliteration			
Rhyme			
Theme			
Anaphora			
Assonance			
Consonance			

Teacher Notes

Steps:

4 Next, ask students to select one of these literary terms to investigate further and find samples of. (You may need to direct them to appropriate resources.) Ask students to create a graphic representation that reinforces their understanding of the term.

5 In this unit, the study of literary devices is designed to develop the students' skill in identifying and analyzing the use of literary devices in poems and then to be able to incorporate them in their original poems. Students can share their growing expertise of the device they selected and become the resident expert when this device is taught explicitly.

6 To bring closure to this activity, invite students as a class to **sort the words** into two categories on the **Word Wall**: literary devices we know and literary devices we are learning.

Literary Devices Scavenger Hunt

WORD CONNECTIONS

Hyperbole contains the Greek prefix *hyper-*, which means "excessive," or "more than normal." This prefix appears in such words as *hyperactive*, *hypersensitive*, *hypertension*, and *hypertext*.

Select a term from the preceding chart that is of particular interest to you, and create a graphic representation that captures the essence of the term.

Literary Device ______________________________

A Catalogue of Coming-of-Age Experiences

ACTIVITY 3.5

SUGGESTED LEARNING STRATEGIES: Freewriting, Marking the Text, Notetaking, Questioning the Text, Think-Pair-Share, Close Reading

Poetry

ABOUT THE AUTHOR

Born in 1943 in Knoxville, Tennessee, Nikki Giovanni is a popular poet and professor of English. Over the years, she has won numerous writing awards. One of her recurring themes, presented through a variety of styles and topics, is love. Once known as "the priestess of Black poetry," she has more recently been called a "national treasure" and named an Oprah Winfrey "Living Legend."

NIKKI ROSA

by Nikki Giovanni

childhood remembrances are always a drag
if you're Black
you always remember things like living in Woodlawn
with no inside toilet
and if you become famous or something
they never talk about how happy you were to have
your mother
all to yourself and
how good the water felt when you got your bath
from one of those
big tubs that folk in Chicago barbecue in
and somehow when you talk about home
it never gets across how much you
understood their feelings

My Notes

LITERARY TERMS

An **autobiography** is written by a person who is telling his or her life's story. What elements in this poem make it autobiographical?

ACTIVITY 3.5

A Catalogue of Coming-of-Age Experiences

Materials:

- Lauryn Hill's "Every Ghetto Every City" (song or lyrics)

Purpose:

- To draft an autobiographical narrative for the introduction of the poetry anthology
- To examine the structure of a free-verse catalogue poem
- To analyze a text for imagery and tone
- To create a free-verse poem in the style of a published author

Steps:

1 In "Nikki Rosa," Nikki Giovanni details a series of moments that create a picture of childhood, highlighting the positive aspect of what her biographers might perceive to be negative experiences. As an **anticipation guide** for the poem, invite students to generate a list of their childhood remembrances that an outsider might perceive to be negative, but are actually positive experiences (e.g., although I had to work and contribute to my family's income, I developed an appreciation for money).

2 Next, invite students to review their lists and **freewrite** in response to this prompt: What do these childhood experiences reveal about who you are as a person?

3 Ask students to silently read "Nikki Rosa." Set a purpose for reading by posing this focus question: What do you learn about the speaker's life from the poem? Students should note their responses in the My Notes area.

4 Read aloud "Nikki Rosa" and ask students to **mark the text** for powerful images. Invite students to **pair-share** their observations. Then ask students to consider questions they would ask the speaker about this poem if she were here in class. Generate a list of students' **levels of questions** on the board (i.e., What is Giovanni's attitude toward her subject and/or readers? Why? Why did she elect to omit punctuation from this poem? What does she capitalize and why?) Use the student-generated questions to conduct a **close reading** of the text.

Steps:

5 In pairs, ask students to **mark the text**, identifying key ideas in the poem that provide insight into the speaker's character. Have the pairs categorize these ideas. Then, to make connections, ask students to reflect on their personal experiences within each identified category. For instance, Giovanni refers to a variety of coming-of-age experiences, such as rituals, holidays, etc.). Isolate one, and point out Giovanni's **diction** and use of **details** that reveal the speaker's character.

6 Present Lauryn Hill's song, "Every Ghetto Every City," or provide the lyrics, to examine how another poet shares insights about coming-of-age experiences and childhood memories.

7 Ask students to emulate either Giovanni's or Hill's style to create an original catalogue poem about their own lives or coming-of-age experiences. The poem should reveal aspects of their character through details. Students should then write a brief autobiography that connects ideas from their poem to an overview of their lives.

8 Revisit the **Essential Question**: What is poetry?

A Catalogue of Coming-of-Age Experiences

LITERARY TERMS
The term ***free verse*** describes poetry without a fixed pattern of meter and rhyme.

My Notes

as the whole family attended meetings about Hollydale
and even though you remember
your biographers never understand
your father's pain as he sells his stock
and another dream goes
and though you're poor it isn't poverty that
concerns you
and though they fight a lot
it isn't your father's drinking that makes any difference
but only that everybody is together and you
and your sister have happy birthdays and very good
Christmases
and I really hope no white person ever has cause
to write about me
because they never understand
Black love is Black wealth and they'll
probably talk about my hard childhood
and never understand that
all the while I was quite happy.

Structure in Poetry

ACTIVITY 3.6

SUGGESTED LEARNING STRATEGIES: **Notetaking, Oral Interpretation, Word Map**

Poetry

ABOUT THE AUTHOR

Gwendolyn Brooks (1917–2000) grew up and lived her life in Chicago. While still in her teens, she published poems in an African American newspaper in Chicago. It wasn't long before her poetry became recognized nationally, and she won the Pulitzer Prize for Poetry in 1950, the first African American to win a Pulitzer. Poetry was the focus of Brooks's life, and she continued to be a prolific writer as well as a teacher and advocate of poetry. She taught creative writing at a number of colleges and universities. Her publications and awards were numerous, including an appointment as Consultant in Poetry to the Library of Congress in 1985.

We Real Cool

Prose: *The Pool Players. Seven at the Golden Shovel.* We real cool. We Left school. We Lurk late. We Strike straight. We Sing sin. We Thin gin. We Jazz June. We Die soon.

As you read "We Real Cool," pay attention to its **poetic structure.**

My Notes

ACADEMIC VOCABULARY

Poetic structure refers to the poet's organization of words, lines, and images and ideas.

WE REAL COOL

by Gwendolyn Brooks

The Pool Players.
Seven at the Golden Shovel.

We real cool. We
Left school. We

Lurk late. We
Strike straight. We

Sing sin. We
Thin gin. We

Jazz June. We
Die soon.

ACTIVITY 3.6
Structure in Poetry

Materials:

- Copies of the prose version of the poem and scissors
- Vocabulary Notebooks

Purpose:

- To interpret a poem, focusing on musical devices
- To analyze a poem's structure (line breaks, stanzas, sense units)
- To present an oral interpretation

Steps:

1 Review with students the **structure of poetry**. Include a **discussion** on line breaks, stanzas, sense units (end punctuation in poetry), etc. Instruct students to take notes in their Personal Poetry Glossary. Ask the class experts to present their findings from the literary devices scavenger hunt (Activity 3.4).

2 In small groups, have students read the prose version of "We Real Cool," and discuss where they would break lines and create stanzas. Give each group a copy of the prose version to cut apart and **manipulate** to create line breaks and stanzas. Ask students to be prepared to explain the reasons for their decisions.

3 Direct students to read Brooks's version and consider why she may have structured the poem (rhythm, rhyme scheme, emphasis on key ideas, etc.) as she did. Ask them to contrast their versions with the author's and discuss how lines and stanzas can affect meaning.

ACTIVITY 3.6 *Continued*

Steps:

4 Instruct students to consider the author's purpose and how the structure (free verse, line breaks, and stanzas), musical devices (consonance, assonance, and alliteration), and rhyme create an effect. Use a **choral reading** to emphasize one of Brooks's choices, and invite students to rationalize what you emphasized in the oral presentation.

5 Ask students to prepare an **oral interpretation** of "We Real Cool" that highlights their understanding of the author's purpose and style.

6 Ask students to **revisit** the catalogue poem they created in Activity 3.5 and revise it to incorporate purposeful line breaks and stanzas. Ask them to explain their authorial choices in the margin.

7 Direct students to choose an appropriate **word map graphic organizer** to explore the concept of ***poetic structure*** in their **Vocabulary Notebooks**.

ACTIVITY 3.6 *continued*

Structure in Poetry

LITERARY TERMS

Rhythm in poetry is the pattern of stressed and unstressed syllables.

Rhyme scheme refers to the consistent pattern of rhyme throughout a poem.

A **stanza** is a group of lines, usually similar in length and pattern, that form a unit within a poem.

Author's purpose: What message about life is Brooks sending to young people with this poem?

How do the structure (free verse, line breaks, stanzas) and musical devices (consonance, assonance, and alliteration) create an effect?

Exploring Diction and Imagery

ACTIVITY 3.7

SUGGESTED LEARNING STRATEGIES: Freewriting, Marking the Text, Think-Pair-Share

Before Reading

Freewrite: Choose a hobby, topic, or interest about which you are passionate, and explain why.

After Reading

Use the Title/Author/Genre (TAG) sentence stem to write an analytical statement examining the author's use of diction or imagery. (For example, Hirsch's poem, "Fast Break" uses the imagery/diction of... to convey...).

ACADEMIC VOCABULARY

Diction refers to a writer's choice of words.

Imagery refers to descriptive or figurative language that appeals to the senses and is used to create word pictures.

LITERARY TERMS

Voice is a writer's distinctive use of language.

ACTIVITY 3.7
Exploring Diction and Imagery

Materials:

- Vocabulary Notebooks

Purpose:

- To analyze a poem for voice, imagery, and diction
- To identify, analyze, and critique the function of voice, imagery, and diction
- To create an original poem emulating the author's style and/or incorporating the literary devices analyzed

Steps:

1 Ask students to generate a list of subjects or topics (i.e., sport, hobby, talent, skill, etc.) about which they are passionate. Then, ask them to choose one and **freewrite** to describe the subject to someone who knows very little about it and share why they enjoy this activity so much. Next, ask them to consider two distinct audiences for their choice and explain how their **voice** (tone, purpose, audience, and context of the message) might change from one audience to the other (e.g., an audience who is familiar with the topic and one who is not). Ask students how the audience may impact one's voice in writing.

ACTIVITY 3.7 *Continued*

Steps:

2 Tell students the next poem presents the knowledge and passion the speaker has for the game of basketball. Invite students to read the poem silently, and identify by highlighting or underlining language or jargon associated with basketball.

3 Next, ask students to read the poem aloud, either in pairs or as a choral reading, circling the verbs chosen by the author. Ask students to discuss the **diction** and the effect of these choices on the reader's appreciation for the action of basketball.

4 Review imagery (language that creates word pictures and appeals to the senses) with students using the Personal Poetry Glossary as a reference tool to take notes. Read the poem aloud again and ask students to **mark the text** for **imagery**. Ask students to **pair-share** their selections and discuss how those details function in the poem to create an effect. Moreover, lead students in a discussion of how the author's use of figurative language conveys the speaker's attitude and passion for basketball.

TEACHER TO TEACHER To reinforce understanding of verb tenses, have students rewrite the verbs in the poem to past tense. Discuss the difference in effect between writing in present tense and past tense.

ACTIVITY 3.7 continued

Exploring Diction and Imagery

My Notes

Poetry

ABOUT THE AUTHOR

Edward Hirsch (b. 1950) is a professor of English and a published author of many poems, essays, and books. His collection of verse, *Wild Gratitude*, was awarded the National Book Critics Circle Award in 1986. Hirsh has also earned a Guggenheim Fellowship and a MacArthur Foundation Fellowship. One of Hirsch's most popular books has been his surprise best-seller, *How to Read a Poem and Fall in Love with Poetry.*

FAST BREAK

In Memory of Dennis Turner, 1946–1984

by Edward Hirsch

A hook shot kisses the rim and
hangs there, helplessly, but doesn't drop,

and for once our gangly starting center
boxes out his man and times his jump

perfectly, gathering the orange leather
from the air like a cherished possession

and spinning around to throw a strike
to the outlet who is already shoveling

an underhand pass toward the other guard
scissoring past a flat-footed defender

who looks stunned and nailed to the floor
in the wrong direction, trying to catch sight

of a high, gliding dribble and a man
letting the play develop in front of him

214 SpringBoard® English Textual Power™ Level 4

in slow motion, almost exactly
like a coach's drawing on the blackboard,

both forwards racing down the court
the way that forwards should, fanning out

and filling the lanes in tandem, moving
together as brothers passing the ball

between them without a dribble, without
a single bounce hitting the hardwood

until the guard finally lunges out
and commits to the wrong man

while the power-forward explodes past them
in a fury, taking the ball into the air

by himself now and laying it gently
against the glass for a lay-up,

but losing his balance in the process,
inexplicably falling, hitting the floor

with a wild, headlong motion
for the game he loved like a country

and swiveling back to see an orange blur
floating perfectly though the net.

My Notes

Steps:

5 After the discussion, direct students to page 213 and ask them to use the Title/Author/Genre (TAG) sentence stem to write an analytical statement examining the author's use of diction or imagery (for example, Hirsch's poem, "Fast Break," uses the diction of … to convey …). Remind students that TAG is an acronym for Title/Author/Genre.

6 Ask students to revisit their freewrite and try to capture in words the essence of the subject for which students are passionate incorporating skillful use of voice, diction, and/or imagery. Students should revise the format of their freewrite into an original poem emulating Hirsch's use of the action-oriented, specialized diction of basketball, or another topic such as skateboarding, hockey, or whatever passion or pastime they want to write about.

7 Encourage students to share their original poems aloud within small groups. Ask students to **mark** their poems to identify where they showcase their knowledge of voice, diction, and/or imagery and in the margin explain their intended effect on the reader.

8 Direct students to explore the concepts of ***diction*** and ***imagery*** in their **Vocabulary Notebooks**.

Differentiating Instruction:

To **support** students in reading the analytical statement in Step 5, place students in groups and have them complete a **TP-CASTT** graphic organizer. Help them focus on a discussion of imagery, diction, and theme.

Expand this activity by having students use the TP-CASTT analysis as the basis for a structured paragraph or essay.

ACTIVITY 3.8
Extended Metaphor and Symbol

Materials:

- Vocabulary Notebooks

Purpose:

- To analyze the function and effect of an extended metaphor
- To create a poem incorporating an extended metaphor
- To make a connection between a poem's content and symbolic visuals

Steps:

1 Have students revisit the poetic devices chart to review symbol and extended metaphor. Remind students that an extended metaphor is a metaphor developed over several lines or throughout an entire poem.

2 Ask students to consider the connotations of the word ***identity***: unique, distinct, original, etc. Then, ask them to **think-pair-share** how these ideas connect with the thematic concept of coming of age.

ACTIVITY 3.8

Extended Metaphor and Symbol

SUGGESTED LEARNING STRATEGIES: **Graphic Organizer, Marking the Text, Skimming/Scanning, Rereading, Think-Pair-Share, Visualizing, Word Map, Brainstorming**

What I know...	What I think...	I'm confused about...

Summary of Identity:

Writing Prompt: After reading the poem "Identity," write an original poem using metaphors, symbols, or repetition to reinforce an idea or concept. You may want to begin with this line: I am like a .... Use figurative language to create an imaginative image of yourself.

© 2011 College Board. All rights reserved.

Poetry

Identity

ACTIVITY 3.8 continued

by Julio Noboa Polanco

ABOUT THE AUTHOR
Julio Noboa Polanco was born in New York and has worked as an educational advocate for Latino communities in several cities. His focus has been on Latino history and heritage, and he writes his poetry in both Spanish and English.

Let them be as flowers
always watered, fed, guarded, admired,
but harnessed to a pot of dirt.

I'd rather be a tall, ugly weed,
clinging on cliffs, like an eagle
wind-wavering above high, jagged rocks.

To have broken through the surface of stone,
to live, to feel exposed to the madness
of the vast, eternal sky.
To be swayed by the breezes of an ancient sea,
carrying my soul, my seed,
beyond the mountains of time or into the abyss of the bizarre.

I'd rather be unseen, and if
then shunned by everyone,
than to be a pleasant-smelling flower,
growing in clusters in the fertile valley,
where they're praised, handled, and plucked
by greedy human hands.

I'd rather smell of musty, green stench
than of sweet, fragrant lilac.
If I could stand alone, strong and free,
I'd rather be a tall, ugly weed.

My Notes

ACADEMIC VOCABULARY
Figurative language is language that uses figures of speech, words, or phrases that describe one thing in terms of another and are not meant to be interpreted literally.

ACTIVITY 3.8 *Continued*

Steps:

3 Ask students to read "Identity" silently. Tell them to record on the **graphic organizer** their response to the ideas as they emerge. Then, have them summarize the poem in a sentence or two. As a class, share and negotiate meaning before moving on.

4 Ask students to **reread** the poem to circle the words ***flowers*** and ***weeds*** (two images central to the poem). Ask them to **brainstorm** the connotations of these two images and infer how they relate to the title, "Identity."

5 Direct students to **mark the text** to identify the author's verbs that elaborate on the two images. Discuss the effect of the author's juxtaposition of images for emphasis; have them note the contrasts in his diction.

6 Lead students in a discussion of what the symbols represent. Invite them to **visualize** the symbols and sketch complementary images in the margin.

7 Ask students to **skim** the poem looking for repeated words or phrases. Ask them why the poet chose to echo these words or phrases. How does the repeated line emphasize the meaning of the poem?

8 Tell students that a poet reaches for a metaphor that makes a comparison between two seemingly unrelated things for the purpose of illuminating them both. Ask students to work in pairs to highlight the metaphors and analyze them in the My Notes area. Direct students to note the repetitive diction that sets up the metaphor: "Let them be" and "I'd rather be."

9 Ask students to interpret the title and discuss how metaphors in the poem reinforce the idea of identity.

10 Encourage students to share their original poems aloud. Ask them to mark their poems to identify their metaphors, symbols, and repetition and explain their intended effect in the margin.

11 Direct students to choose an appropriate **word map graphic organizer** to explore the concept of ***figurative language*** in their **Vocabulary Notebooks**.

ACTIVITY 3.9

Hyperbolic Me with Allusions

Materials:

- Vocabulary Notebooks

Purpose:

- To identify and critique the function of hyperbole and allusion
- To write an analytical statement examining figurative language
- To create an original poem emulating the author's style

Steps:

1 To set a context for "Ego Tripping," write the title on the board and ask students what the title means literally (denotation) and what it suggests (connotation).

2 Direct students to read the poem silently and use **metacognitive markers**: **!** to mark a line that is striking, and **?** for a line that is puzzling. Ask students to **quickwrite** about a striking line.

3 Place students in small groups, and direct them to read the poem aloud together. Then ask them to share their striking lines to engage in a conversation about the poem.

4 Reconvene the class and conduct a dramatic **oral reading** of the poem. Invite students to lead the discussion starting with what they know or notice. Conclude this part of the discussion with an idea wave in which students share questions they still have using this sentence stem: ***I am still wondering about....*** Chart and discuss students' observations.

5 Review ***hyperbole*** (intentional overstatement) and ***allusion*** (references the author thinks the reader should know). Solicit examples from students and invite them to consider how and why they use these devices in their own lives. Next, direct them to work in pairs to identify examples of each within the poem (allusions are highlighted in the Teacher Edition). Follow with a **choral reading** in which students read aloud the hyperbole and allusions as you read. This will help you assess the accuracy of students' understanding.

ACTIVITY 3.9

Hyperbolic Me with Allusions

SUGGESTED LEANING STRATEGIES: Metacognitive Markers, Oral Reading, Quickwrite

My Notes

(there may be a reason why)

by Nikki Giovanni

I was born in the congo
I walked to the fertile crescent and built
    the sphinx
I designed a pyramid so tough that a star
    that only glows every one hundred years falls
    into the center giving divine perfect light.
I am bad

I sat on the throne
    drinking nectar with allah
I got hot and sent an ice age to europe
    to cool my thirst
My oldest daughter is nefertiti
    the tears from my birth pains
    created the nile
I am a beautiful woman

I gazed on the forest and burned
    out the sahara desert
    With a packet of goat's meat
    and a change of clothes
I crossed it in two hours
I am a gazelle so swift
    so swift you can't catch me

    For a birthday present when he was three
I gave my son hannibal an elephant
    He gave me rome for mother's day
My strength flows ever on

My son noah built new/ark and
I stood proudly at the helm
as we sailed on a soft summer day
I turned myself into myself and was
jesus
men intone my loving name
All praises All praises
I am the one who would save

I sowed diamonds in my back yard
My bowels delivered uranium
The filings from my fingernails are
semi-precious jewels
On a trip north
I caught a cold and blew
My nose giving oil to the arab world
I am so hip even my errors are correct
I sailed west to reach east and had to round off
the earth as I went
The hair from my head thinned and gold was laid
across three continents

I am so perfect, so divine so ethereal[1] so surreal
I cannot be comprehended except by my permission

I mean . . . I . . . can fly
like a bird in the sky. . .

[1] **ethereal:** not of the earth; heavenly

GRAMMAR & USAGE

When you incorporate textual evidence to support the assertion in your analytical statement, put quotation marks around words and phrases you take directly from the poem to show that you are quoting verbatim.

My Notes

GRAMMAR & USAGE EXTENSION

Share these guidelines with students for inserting quotations in sentences:

- Write the quoted material exactly as it is in the poem.
- If the quotation finishes the sentence, end the sentence with the same puncutation as the quotation.
- If the sentence continues, then use a comma after the quotation, close the quotes, and finish the sentence.

ACTIVITY 3.9 *Continued*

Steps:

6 **Chunk** the poem by numbering each stanza. Discuss the function and effect of hyperbole and allusion in the first stanza. For the second stanza, allow students to assist you in identifying the function of the literary devices. For the third stanza, allow students to work in pairs and note their findings in the margin. Ask students to analyze the remaining stanzas independently.

7 Ask students to write an analytical statement including the title, author, and genre (TAG) in which they discuss the function and use of hyperbole and allusion in the poem. Next, ask students to mark the text to identify evidence that supports the assertion made in the analytical statement and incorporate that evidence into their interpretation. You might need to review the format and punctuation for embedded quotations.

8 Invite students to write an original poem on a subject of their choice emulating the style in "Ego Tripping." Ask them to use hyperbole and allusion and to mark these devices in the poem and explain in the margin their intended effect.

9 Encourage students to share their original poems aloud and solicit feedback for revision to enhance their use of figurative language.

10 Direct students to revisit their **Vocabulary Notebooks** to elaborate on the concept of ***figurative language***.

ACTIVITY 3.10
Exploring Theme

Purpose:

- To analyze a poem to identify a thematic concept
- To write a response to literature making an assertion about theme
- To identify and critique the function of a literary device
- To create an original poem emulating the author's style and/or incorporating the use of the literary devices analyzed

Steps:

1 Invite students to read Lorde's free-verse poem, "Hanging Fire." Have them use the **graphic organizer** on the next page to jot down what they know, think, and are confused about as they read. Allow students to **pair-share** responses.

2 Ask students to consider what the phrase, "momma's in the bedroom with the door closed" could mean. Review the purpose of a refrain—a repeated line or group of lines—and ask students to infer why this line is repeated. Invite students to note the details leading up to the refrain and discuss how these details contribute to their analysis of the repeated line.

Differentiating Instruction:

To **support** students in examining theme, use **TP-CASTT** as a prewriting strategy and develop a group theme statement. Then have students use the writing organizer from Activity 2.26 (page 173) to add textual support, reflective commentary, and closure to their individual paragraphs.

Extend the product by asking students to synthesize two different poems they have read that share a similar theme. Ask students to support claims with textual elements from each poem and to contrast the authors' approaches to theme.

ACTIVITY 3.10

Exploring Theme

SUGGESTED LEARNING STRATEGIES: **Graphic Organizer, Marking the Text, Think Aloud, Think-Pair-Share**

ABOUT THE AUTHOR
Born in Harlem in New York, Audre Lorde (1934–1992) was a poet and essayist. Her first poem was published in *Seventeen* magazine while she was in high school. Lorde's writing, especially her poetry, explores personal, political, and social issues, focusing on the emotions of relationships, especially in urban life. She had been the New York State poet laureate when she died.

My Notes

Poetry

Hanging Fire

by Audre Lorde

I am fourteen
and my skin has betrayed me
the boy I cannot live without
still sucks his thumb
in secret
how come my knees are
always so ashy
what if I die
before the morning comes
and momma's in the bedroom
with the door closed.

I have to learn how to dance
in time for the next party
my room is too small for me
suppose I die before graduation
they will sing sad melodies
but finally
tell the truth about me
There is nothing I want to do
and too much
that has to be done
and momma's in the bedroom
with the door closed.

Nobody even stops to think
about my side of it
I should have been on Math Team
my marks were better than his
why do I have to be
the one
wearing braces
I have nothing to wear tomorrow
will I live long enough
to grow up
and momma's in the bedroom
with the door closed.

GRAMMAR & USAGE EXTENSION

- You might wish to explore with students the primary purpose of punctuation—how it aids both in reading and understanding written text. You might also explore the effectiveness of the poet's avoidance of traditional punctuation.
- This poem also provides an opportunity to illustrate the use of the rhetorical question.

What I know...	What I think...	I'm confused about...

1. Audre Lorde's poem, "Hanging Fire" is about...

Thematic concept: Audre Lorde's poem, "Hanging Fire," is about teenager's anxiety.

Thematic statement: The title of Audre Lorde's poem, "Hanging Fire," suggests that the narrator is worried about growing up and wants some guidance.

2. List questions you would like to ask Audre Lorde:

GRAMMAR & USAGE

The purpose of punctuation is to help a reader understand the writer's phrasing and emphasis on specific words. Audre Lorde's poem has almost no punctuation. How does the lack of punctuation affect your reading and understanding of this poem?

3. **Writing Prompt:** Explain a theme of Audre Lorde's poem, "Hanging Fire."

Sample paragraph:

"Hanging Fire," is about teenager's anxiety about growing up. In each of the stanzas, the speaker's anxiety always comes back to the sad refrain that her mother is in the "bedroom with the door closed." This refrain suggests that her mother is not available to help her as she worries about something as minor as her "ashy" knees and something as major as whether she will "die before morning comes."

ACTIVITY 3.10 *Continued*

Steps:

3 To review theme, ask students to infer what the author is saying about life. Have them use the sentence stem to identify the thematic concept of the poem. Solicit students' responses (words or phrases), and chart them.

4 Ask students to review the poem again and craft questions they would ask Lorde if she were present. Record students' questions on the board. Use these questions to conduct a text-based **Socratic Seminar** in which students use textual support in their discussion of the text.

5 After extensive discussion, ask students to consider what Lorde might believe about the thematic concept they identified earlier. The response generated will lead to a thematic statement. For example: ***"Hanging Fire" reveals the tensions of teenage life when communication between a parent and child is stifled.***

6 If needed, use a **think aloud** to model sentence combining to refine ideas into a cohesive thematic statement. Also remind students that thematic statements about literary works are always written in present tense. Have students share their statements and edit them for the correct tense.

7 Ask students to mark the poem for textual evidence to support their thematic statements. Have students revisit the poem to **mark the text** for verbs (***betrays, cannot, sucks, dies,*** etc). Engage students in a discussion about how the author's diction, specifically her choice of verbs, contributes to their understanding of teen anxiety.

8 Use **guided writing** to show students how to embed textual evidence seamlessly within a paragraph by introducing the quoted material, using the quote, and explaining the quoted material.

9 Invite students to write an original thematic poem on the subject of their choice. Ask students to **mark their poems** to identify where they showcase their knowledge of theme, and explain the intended effect in the margin.

10 Next, ask students to share their poems within small groups and see whether their peers can infer the theme. Encourage students to provide suggestions for revision that will illuminate the theme for the readers.

11 Revisit the **Essential Question**: What is poetry?

ACTIVITY 3.11

Odes to Someone Special

Materials:

- Vocabulary Notebooks

Purpose:

- To analyze odes for figurative language
- To create an original ode emulating the authors' style

Steps:

1 Introduce the qualities of an ode, a lyric poem expressing feelings or thoughts of a speaker, often celebrating a person, event, or a thing. Ask students to identify persons or things to which they might pay homage, honor, praise, or respect. Students should generate a list individually and provide a brief note explaining why.

2 Invite students to share ideas with the class. Students may add to their lists when they hear a shared interest. They will revisit these lists later.

3 Read aloud "Ode to My Socks." Have students **mark the text** to identify the figurative language (similes, extended metaphor). Invite students to speculate why Neruda might have paid homage to his socks. Ask students to identify the function of the figurative language and discuss its effect.

4 Direct students to revisit their **Vocabulary Notebooks** to elaborate on the concept of ***figurative language***.

ACTIVITY 3.11

Odes to Someone Special

SUGGESTED LEARNING STRATEGIES: Marking the Text, Sharing and Responding

My Notes

WORD CONNECTIONS

The origin of ***ode*** is the Greek word *oide*, for a song.

A related spelling, *-ody*, is found in *melody, parody, rhapsody*.

Poetry

ABOUT THE AUTHOR

Pablo Neruda (1904–1973) was born in Chile. He began writing at an early age and published his first literary work as a teenager. Neruda spent much of his life living in different countries, and his writing reflects the political and social matters of his time.

ODE TO MY SOCKS

by Pablo Neruda
translated by Robert Bly

Mara Mori brought me
a pair of socks
which she knitted herself
with her sheepherder's hands,
two socks as soft as rabbits.
I slipped my feet into them
as if they were two cases
knitted with threads of twilight and goatskin,
Violent socks,
my feet were two fish made of wool,
two long sharks
sea blue, shot through
by one golden thread,
two immense blackbirds,
two cannons,
my feet were honored in this way
by these heavenly socks.

My Notes

They were so handsome for the first time
my feet seemed to me unacceptable
like two decrepit firemen,
firemen unworthy of that woven fire,
of those glowing socks.

Nevertheless, I resisted the sharp temptation
to save them somewhere as schoolboys
keep fireflies,
as learned men collect
sacred texts,
I resisted the mad impulse to put them
in a golden cage and each day give them
birdseed and pieces of pink melon.
Like explorers in the jungle
who hand over the very rare green deer
to the spit and eat it with remorse,
I stretched out my feet and pulled on
the magnificent socks and then my shoes.

The moral of my ode is this:
beauty is twice beauty
and what is good is doubly good
when it is a matter of two socks
made of wool in winter.

Teacher Notes

ACTIVITY 3.11 *Continued*

Steps:

5 Introduce "Abuelito Who," which describes the relationship between a child and her aging grandfather. The poem pays homage to the grandfather by honoring what he says and does, and by referring to objects that invoke memories. Ask students to consider how the refrain, images, and metaphors work together to honor the speaker's grandfather in her memory.

6 Invite students to refer to their list of possible topics for homage. Ask them to choose one and draft an original ode that uses figurative language.

7 Ask students to **share and respond** to those of others in small groups. Ask them to work collaboratively to revise the poems as follows:

- Refine line breaks, stanzas, refrains.
- Add, delete, or reorder lines.
- Add in or refine figurative language.

8 Propose several publication opportunities for these poems, such as the school newspaper, a poetry journal, a podcast, a blank card on which to write the ode to give to the subject of the ode.

Odes to Someone Special

My Notes

Poetry

ABOUT THE AUTHOR

Sandra Cisneros (b. 1954) grew up in Chicago and now lives in San Antonio, Texas. Cisneros has written extensively about the experiences of growing up as a Latina. In talking about her writing, Cisneros says she creates stories from things that have touched her deeply; "...in real life a story doesn't have shape, and it's the writer that gives it a beginning, a middle, and an end."

Abuelito Who

by Sandra Cisneros

Abuelito[1] who throws coins like rain
and asks who loves him
who is dough and feathers
who is a watch and glass of water
whose hair is made of fur
is too sad to come downstairs today
who tells me in Spanish you are my diamond
who tells me in English you are my sky
whose little eyes are string
can't come out to play
sleeps in his little room all night and day
who used to laugh like the letter k
is sick
is a doorknob tied to a sour stick
is tired shut the door
doesn't live here anymore
is hiding underneath the bed
who talks to me inside my head
is blankets and spoons and big brown shoes
who snores up and down up and down up and down again
is the rain on the roof that falls like coins
asking who loves him
who loves him who?

[1] **Abuelito:** Spanish term for "grandfather"

Coming of Age in Sonnets

ACTIVITY 3.12

SUGGESTED LEARNING STRATEGIES: Diffusing the Text, Paraphrasing

Sonnet

ABOUT THE AUTHOR

Little is known about the early life of William Shakespeare (1564–1616) except that he was born and grew up in Stratford-on-Avon in England. He is considered one of the greatest playwrights who ever lived. In addition to thirty-seven plays (comedies, tragedies, and histories), he also wrote a series of 154 sonnets in a style that has become known as the Shakespearean sonnet, which includes three quatrains and a couplet.

Sonnet 18

by William Shakespeare

Shall I compare thee to a summer's day?
Thou[1] art more lovely and more temperate.
Rough winds do shake the darling buds of May,
And summer's lease hath all too short a date.
Sometime too hot the eye of heaven shines,
And often is his gold complexion dimmed;
And every fair from fair sometime declines,
By chance, or nature's changing course untrimmed.[2]
But thy eternal summer shall not fade
Nor lose possession of that fair thou ow'st;[3]
Nor shall death brag thou wand'rest in his shade,
When in eternal lines to time thou grow'st,
So long as men can breathe or eyes can see,
So long lives this, and this gives life to thee.

1. What is the purpose of each quatrain?
2. How does the couplet bring closure to ideas presented in the poem?
3. How does the poem address the thematic concept of coming of age?

[1] **thee, thou:** you
[2] **untrimmed:** stripped of beauty
[3] **fair thou ow'st;** beauty you possess

My Notes

LITERARY TERMS

A **quatrain** is a four-line stanza in a poem.

A **couplet** is two consecutive lines of verse with end rhyme. A couplet usually expresses a complete unit of thought.

Iambic pentameter describes a rhythmic pattern: five feet (or units) of one unstressed syllable followed by a stressed syllable.

ACTIVITY 3.12

Coming of Age in Sonnets

Materials:

- Vocabulary Notebooks

Purpose:

- To examine the structure of a sonnet
- To create an original sonnet

Steps:

1 Read aloud Sonnet 18, and ask students to **diffuse** the text. Invite students to jot down their initial interpretation of the poem.

2 Have students **chunk the text** as follows to highlight the structure of this Shakespearean sonnet:

- Chunk 1: Put a blue box around the first quatrain (first four lines) of the sonnet.
- Chunk 2: Put a red box around the second quatrain.
- Chunk 3: Put a green box around the third quatrain.
- Chunk 4: Put a circle around the rhyming couplet (last two lines).

3 Read aloud chunk 1, asking students to listen to the rhyme scheme. Direct them to label the rhyme scheme as ABAB. Ask them to label the CDCD rhyme in the second chunk and the EFEF pattern in the third chunk.

4 Instruct students to label the final couplet GG. Ask them to consider the function of these lines in the sonnet.

5 Next, ask students to count the syllables in each line as they read aloud and tap the beat of each syllable. They should identify ten syllables per line. Introduce the term ***pentameter*** (five similar units per line). Have them count the ten syllables in the next four lines.

6 Next, introduce ***iambic pentameter***, a line of poetry that contains five iambs: a metrical foot with an unstressed syllable followed by a stressed syllable. Invite students to read the poem aloud in pairs, stressing one syllable in each iamb.

7 Direct students to **paraphrase** each chunk, and invite pairs to collaborate to make meaning. Ask students in small groups to create a title and provide a rationale for their title. List titles on the board and have students agree on one. Encourage students to revisit their original poems to ensure that they have appropriate titles.

8 Invite students to choose a topic and write a sonnet. Ask them to annotate their sonnets to identify the structure. Encourage students to consider using multimedia outlets (i.e., podcast, cinepoems, etc.) to present their sonnets.

9 Direct students to revisit their **Vocabulary Notebooks** and elaborate on the concept of ***poetic structure***.

Embedded Assessment 1

Creating a Poetry Anthology

College Board Standards and Objectives

W1 Rhetorical Analysis and Planning (W1.1)
PE Mappings: W1.1-1.4, W1.1-2.4

W2 Generating Content (W2.1 Cr; W2.2 Cr)
PE Mappings: W2.1-1.4CR, W2.2-1.4Cr, W2.2-3.4Cr, W2.2-4.4Cr

W3 Drafting (W3.1 Cr; W3.2 Cr)
PE Mappings: W3.1-1.4Cr, W3.1-3.4Cr, W3.2-1.4Cr, W3.2-3.4Cr, W3.2-4.4Cr

W4 Evaluating and Revising Texts (W4.1 Cr; W4.2 Cr)
PE Mappings: W4.1-1.4Cr, W4.2-1.4Cr

W5 Editing to Present Technically Sound Texts (W5.1; W5.2; W5.4)
PE Mappings: W5.1-1.4, W5.2-1.4, W5.4-1.4

Steps:

1 Review the assignment with students to ensure that they understand the requirements.

2 Point out to students that they may need to create additional poems if they do not have enough. You may wish to guide them to create additional types—for example, lyric or narrative.

3 You may wish to set up writing groups for **sharing and responding**.

4 Encourage students to illustrate their poems to enhance the figurative language and imagery.

5 As students prepare their autobiographical introduction, point out that they need not include a full autobiography. Emphasize that they should include significant events that relate to the topics of their poems.

6 Stress the importance of their reflection in which they explain their purpose and desired effects.

7 As students prepare their final copy for publication, remind them of the importance of visual appeal.

Embedded Assessment 1

Creating a Poetry Anthology

SUGGESTED LEARNING STRATEGIES: **Marking the Draft, Sharing and Responding, Self-Editing/Peer Editing**

Assignment

Your assignment is to create a thematic poetry anthology with an introduction to the collection, seven or eight original poems with complementary visuals, and a reflection explaining the style and content of the work.

Steps

Planning and Drafting the Collection

1. Revisit the poems you generated throughout this unit. Select ones you think will work well for this assignment. If necessary, draft additional poems using the various structures (sonnet, free verse, catalogue, ode).
2. Revise your poems for purposeful use of figurative language and literary devices to capture your theme.
3. Share your poems with your peers and solicit feedback for revision on:
   - Refining line breaks, stanza, refrains.
   - Adding, deleting, or reordering lines.
   - Adding in or refining figurative language and poetic devices.
4. Annotate each poem by marking the text and creating marginal notes identifying the literary devices and explaining their effect.
5. Think about the imagery and symbolism in your poems. Find pictures or make sketches to represent the thematic concepts.
6. Reread, revise, and edit your poems to prepare final drafts for publication. Be sure each poem contains an appropriate title.

Planning and Drafting the Introduction and Reflection

7. Write a brief autobiography to introduce your poetry anthology. Focus on what the reader needs to know about you to better understand your poems.
8. Write a reflection to explain your favorite selections, and discuss the style and form used to capture the ideas in your poems. What was your intended effect on the reader? How did you design your poems to accomplish this? Discuss your creative process and what inspires you as a poet.

Refining the Anthology for Publication

9. Consult the Scoring Guide, and review your poetry anthology in its entirety to revise and edit each section, preparing for publication.
10. Create a cover with a unique title and thematic visual.
11. Organize your anthology and bind it in this order: cover page, table of contents, introduction, annotated original poems with visuals, and reflection.

TECHNOLOGY TIP You may want to use a software program to create your anthology. Many word processing programs have attractive templates for creating booklets, or you can design your own.

Embedded Assessment 1

Continued

Scoring Guide

When you score this Embedded Assessment, you may wish to download and print a copy of the Scoring Guide from SpringBoard Online. In this way, you can have a copy to mark for each student's work.

Embedded Assessment 1

continued

SCORING GUIDE

Scoring Criteria	Exemplary	Proficient	Emerging
Original Poems	The collection of poems displays skillful use of format and structure to capture key ideas within the poetic form (i.e., line breaks, stanzas, refrain, title, etc.). The poetry contains knowledgeable use of word choice, figurative language, and literary devices to reinforce the thematic concept and have an impact on the reader. Each poem contains an insightful connection to the thematic concept of the unit appealing to the universal level.	The collection of poems contains a clear format or structure appropriate to the poetic form (i.e., line breaks, stanzas, refrain, etc.). The poetry contains appropriate word choice, figurative language, and literary devices that reinforce the thematic concept of the collection. Each poem contains an appropriate connection to the thematic concept of the unit.	The poems presented do not contain a clear format or structure. If devices are present, the poems in this collection contain a limited understanding of these literary devices and how they are used to add meaning to the text. The poems do not show a connection to the thematic concepts addressed within the unit.
Annotated Poems	The poet marks the poems, identifies literary devices used, and provides insightful analysis of the function and purpose of the device and its impact on the reader.	The poet is able to identify, appropriately label some of the literary devices used, and analyze the literary devices' function and purpose in marginal notes.	The poet is unable to identify the literary devices used and/ or does not provide appropriate analysis of the function and purpose of the devices.
Introduction	The engaging introduction highlights significant and influential moments of the poet's life that thoroughly provide the reader an insight about the poet's collection of work.	The introduction is clear and contains relevant information about the poet's life that helps the reader better understand the collection of work.	The introduction is unfocused and vaguely discusses the life and work of the poet. The reader is unable to draw connections between the life events shared and the collection of poems.

Embedded Assessment 1
Continued

Teacher Notes

Embedded Assessment 1
continued

Creating a Poetry Anthology

SCORING GUIDE

Scoring Criteria	Exemplary	Proficient	Emerging
Reflection	The reflection insightfully explains and provides examples of the poet's purpose, creative process, challenges encountered, and use of symbolic visuals. It clarifies learning within the unit on poetic form, style, and content.	The reflection insightfully explains and provides examples of the poet's purpose, creative process, challenges encountered, and use of symbolic visuals. It reveals learning in some or all aspects of poetic form, style, and content.	The reflection is unclear and/or incomplete. It does not adequately explain the process, product, or learning of poetic form, style, and content.
Organization and Presentation	The poetry anthology is a polished collection of work that contains: • a creative cover page with an insightful title • an accurate table of contents • a well written introduction • insightful annotated original poems with symbolic visuals to support the ideas in the poem • a thoughtful reflection.	The poetry anthology is an organized collection of work that contains: • a cover page and title • a table of contents • a clear introduction • annotated original poems with complementary visuals • a clear reflection.	The poetry anthology is not well organized or may contain some or all of the following: • a missing or vague cover page, no title • a missing or inaccurate table of contents • a missing or limited introduction • a limited number of poems that are not annotated or are missing complementary visuals • a missing or limited reflection.
Additional Criteria			

Comments:

© 2011 College Board. All rights reserved.

Learning Focus:

A Signature Style

What is a signature style in writing? Is a signature style one that reveals a clear understanding of self? Is a signature style one that is emulated by others? During the second half of this unit, you will choose a published author whose signature style speaks to you. In your analysis of this writer's work, you will distinguish between a thematic concept, a subject of a text, and a theme—the author's underlying message about life inferred by the reader. Independently, you will know when, why, and how to use strategies to interpret and critique a poet's work. To deepen your understanding of the poet's work, you will conduct research to learn about the poet's life.

You will demonstrate your analysis at the end of the unit by creating a literary analysis essay. You will use the writing process to explain your poet's thematic ideas and style. As you develop your essay, you will create complex thesis and topic sentences, and you will seamlessly embed quotations. In addition to writing your analysis, you will present a poem of your choice to your peers. This presentation will allow you to show what you have learned about your author, about theme, and about the significance of the poet's style. This in turn will help you to understand the power of style in your own writing as you continue to encounter and create new texts.

LEARNING FOCUS:

A Signature Style

Previewing Embedded Assessment 2

To preview the skills and knowledge necessary for success on Embedded Assessment 2, instruct students to locate the Assignment and Scoring Guide (pp. 246–249). Guide students through a **close reading** of the prompts, steps, and Scoring Guide criteria.

Steps:

1 Read the Learning Focus with students or have them read independently. **Activate prior knowledge** by having students **mark the text** and highlight words or concepts that are familiar (what they know). They might use a question mark to indicate content that is unfamiliar (what they do not know but want to learn).

2 Engage students in a whole class discussion. You may revisit the **KWL chart** you created at the beginning of the unit to discover what students have learned.

ACTIVITY 3.13

More Work with Connotation

Purpose:

- To analyze a poem for connotation
- To reinforce poetry analysis
- To write a style-analysis paragraph

Steps:

1 Prepare to read this poem by writing the complete title on the board. Ask students to consider it carefully and make a **prediction**. **Activate prior knowledge** by asking students to consider what they know about Executive Order 9066. You might want to provide a brief historical context.

2 Ask students to read the poem and identify the key ideas in each stanza. Then, direct students to review these ideas and create a synthesis statement for each stanza. You might model this process with the first stanza. Allow students to work in pairs on the remaining stanzas. Ask students to discuss their statements to identify the poem's theme.

3 Next, invite students to select a line that may be confusing or challenging and work with a partner to **paraphrase** it to clarify meaning.

4 Revisit the title and have students confirm or negate initial predictions. Ask students how their knowledge of the poem illuminates the title. Further, ask students to consider the format of the poem—a letter—and its intended audience.

5 Move students to a deeper, more metaphorical interpretation of the text. Review the difference between denotation and connotation. Model a close reading for connotation in the first stanza. Next, direct students in small groups to do a **close reading** of the remaining stanzas to identify connotations of words and infer meaning.

ACTIVITY 3.13

More Work with Connotation

SUGGESTED LEARNING STRATEGIES: **Close Reading, Paraphrasing, Predicting**

ABOUT THE AUTHOR

Dwight Okita (b. 1958) was born and continues to live in Chicago. His first book of poems, *Crossing with the Light*, was published in 1992. He continues to be an active writer, working on poetry, stage plays, a screenplay, and fiction—both stories and novels.

My Notes

Poetry

In Response to Executive Order 9066: All Americans of Japanese Descent Must Report to Relocation Centers

by Dwight Okita

Dear Sirs:
Of course I'll come. I've packed my galoshes
and three packets of tomato seeds. Denise calls them
love apples. My father says where we're going
they won't grow.

I am a fourteen-year-old girl with bad spelling
and a messy room. If it helps any, I will tell you
I have always felt funny using chopsticks
and my favorite food is hot dogs.
My best friend is a white girl named Denise—
we look at boys together. She sat in front of me
all through grade school because of our names:
O'Connor, Ozawa. I know the back of Denise's head very well.

I tell her she's going bald. She tells me I copy on tests.
We're best friends.

I saw Denise today in Geography class.
She was sitting on the other side of the room.
"You're trying to start a war," she said, "giving secrets
away to the Enemy.[1] Why can't you keep your big
mouth shut?"

I didn't know what to say.
I gave her a packet of tomato seeds
and asked her to plant them for me, told her
when the first tomato ripened
she'd miss me.

Writing Prompt: Follow your teacher's instructions to construct a paragraph analyzing the function of connotation in "In Response to Executive Order 9066."

[1] **Enemy:** the Japanese, who were at war against the United States in World War II.

6 Revisit the title again, and ask students to consider the connotation of the title in relationship to what they now understand about the text. Invite students to refine earlier predictions and critique the effectiveness of the title.

7 Use **guided writing** to model the construction of a paragraph analyzing the function of connotation in "In Response to Executive Order 9066."

Tone Deaf—Exercises on Tone in Poetry

ACTIVITY 3.14

SUGGESTED LEARNING STRATEGIES: Close Reading

"Smells Like Teen Spirit" is a song originally written by and recorded by Nirvana. Later, Tori Amos recorded it with her own signature style. Listen to both artists' versions of the song, and use the graphic organizer below to note words or phrases that may describe the tone that the artist conveys in the song.

Nirvana's Version: "Smells Like Teen Spirit"	Tori Amos's Version: "Smells Like Teen Spirit"
Comments About Tone:	Comments About Tone:

1. What are the differences between these two versions of one song?

2. What tone (attitude) does each artist create? Incorporate phrases and images from the song to support your opinion.

3. Where do you see or hear a shift? Explain.

Writing Prompt: Follow your teacher's directions to write a style analysis paragraph identifying the tone and explain how it shifts between the two songs.

ACTIVITY 3.14

Tone Deaf—Exercises on Tone in Poetry

Materials:

- "Smells Like Teen Spirit" by Nirvana and by Tori Amos

Purpose:

- To understand tone
- To write an analytical paragraph on the effect of tone

Steps:

1 Review the concept of tone, the speaker's attitude toward the subject, and ask students to generate a list of tone words (e.g., ***joyful, apologetic, pitiful***). List these words on the board, and ask students to sort them into categories. Place these words on the Word Wall.

2 Play "Smells Like Teen Spirit" as performed by two different artists: Nirvana's version from the CD ***Nevermind*** and Tori Amos's version from the CD ***Crucify***. Ask students to do a **close reading** as they listen to the two versions, and note adjectives that describe the feeling or attitude revealed in the lyrics. After each song, invite students to share their observations to gain insights into each song.

3 Lead students through a discussion noting the differences between the two versions of the song. Invite them to make connections about tone from their initial reading, from Amos's version, and from Nirvana's version.

4 Next, explain the concept of a **poetic shift**, in tone, syntax, ideas, etc. Ask students to consider the shift in tone from the lyrics as well as within Nirvana's song. Ask students how that shift reinforces their understanding of the text.

5 Ask students to consider how the tone of each song advances the thematic message of "Smells Like Teen Spirit."

6 Bring closure to this discussion by asking students to respond to the Writing Prompt with a paragraph identifying the tone and analyzing how it shifts between the two versions of the song. Ask students to discuss how the shift is created and its intended effect on the reader. Use **guided reading** to assist students' analysis of the text.

ACTIVITY 3.15

Poetry Analysis of "Young"

Purpose:

- To analyze poetry

Steps:

1 Review the **TP-CASTT** strategy with students. TP-CASTT is a fluid process; however, for students' first encounter, it might be best to model the process with a **guided reading** of "Young." Students should take notes in the My Notes area as you chart their responses on the board.

2 Begin by asking students to make predictions based on the title.

3 Read "Young" aloud to students and ask them to paraphrase confusing lines in the My Notes space. Use **think-pair-share** to review responses and negotiate meaning.

4 Ask students to read the poem silently and mark all the words or phrases with strong connotations. Use a **choral reading** to check for understanding: Read the poem aloud again, asking students to chime in with the words or phrases they marked. Discuss what feelings or images these words evoke and what they contribute to students' understanding of the text.

5 Ask students to **skim** the poem to identify the tone, write it in the margin, and **mark the text** to support their assertion. Invite students to discuss their observations on tone and the textual support.

6 Ask students to use **shared reading** to identify where a shift occurs, what kind of shift it is, and how it contributes to their understanding of the poem.

ACTIVITY 3.15

Poetry Analysis of "Young"

SUGGESTED LEARNING STRATEGIES: Marking the Text, Skimming, Think-Pair-Share, TP-CASTT

My Notes

Poetry

ABOUT THE AUTHOR

Anne Sexton (1928–1974) discovered her poetic voice as an adult when she joined writing groups and met other poets who encouraged her work. She published several successful collections of poetry and was awarded a Pulitzer Prize for Poetry in 1967. Much of her work explores personal issues or issues specific to women.

YOUNG

by Anne Sexton

A thousand doors ago
when I was a lonely kid
in a big house with four
garages and it was summer
as long as I could remember,
I lay on the lawn at night,
clover wrinkling under me,
the wise stars bedding over me,
my mother's window a funnel
of yellow heat running out,
my father's window, half shut,
an eye where sleepers pass,
and the boards of the house
were smooth and white as wax
and probably a million leaves
sailed on their strange stalks
as the crickets ticked together
and I, in my brand new body,
which was not a woman's yet,
told the stars my questions
and thought God could really see
the heat and the painted light,
elbows, knees, dreams, goodnight.

Writing Workshops

If you have not already used Workshop 9, Response to Literature, you may want to access it at this point to provide extended practice with literary analysis. This workshop is focused more specifically on style analysis, but practice in the elements and structure of analysis will still be helpful for students.

© 2011 College Board. All rights reserved.

TP-CASTT Analysis

Title of Poem:

Author:

Title: Make a prediction. What do you think the title means before you read the poem?

Paraphrase: Restate the main ideas of the poem in your own words.

Connotation: What words or phrases suggest something beyond their literal meanings? What do you think the poet is saying in this poem? Go beyond the literal meanings (denotation) or the plot of the poem.

Attitude: Describe the speaker's attitude. Use specific adjectives to describe your ideas.

Shifts: Describe where the poem appears to shift, either in subject, speaker, or tone.

Title: Re-examine the title. What do you think it means now in the context of the poem?

Theme: What do you think is the underlying message about life expressed in this poem?

Reflection: How does the TP-CASTT strategy assist you to make meaning of a complex poem?

WORD CONNECTIONS

In analyzing analogies, look at the parts of speech in the word pairs. Parts of speech are consistent within an analogy; for example, if an adjective is used in one pair, the second pair also will use an adjective. Look at this analogy:

carpenter : hammer :: musician : piano. Complete the following analogy.

youth: child :: adult : woman or man

ACTIVITY 3.15 *Continued*

Steps:

7 Revisit students' earlier predictions to confirm or negate them. Ask students to apply their understanding of the poem to explain the significance of the title.

8 Ask students to review their notes and complete the TP-CASTT analysis on this page including a thematic statement conveying the underlying message about life presented in "Young."

9 Invite students to reflect on how the process of TP-CASTT assisted in making meaning from a complex poem.

© 2011 College Board. All rights reserved.

ACTIVITY 3.16

Poetry Café

Materials:

- Samples from Def Poetry Jam

Purpose:

- To independently apply a poetry analysis strategy
- To plan and present an oral interpretation of a poem

Steps:

1 Tell students that they will analyze a poem in small groups and present an oral interpretation of that poem to the class. Review the process of **TP-CASTT** as needed.

2 Divide the class into groups of four and assign each group one poem to analyze using TP-CASTT. Students should work together to make meaning from their assigned poem and note observations on this page.

3 Use a search engine to find a clip from Def Poetry Jam. Play this for students to model an oral interpretation of a poem and to set expectations for their own oral deliveries. Ask students how the poets convey meaning (i.e., inflection, movement, gestures, facial expressions, sound effects, props etc.).

4 Ask students to reconvene in their small groups and create an **oral interpretation** of their poem. Their interpretation should demonstrate their understanding of the poem through movement, inflection, gestures, facial expressions, sound effects, props, and so on. Consider these options for publication: live presentation, cinepoem, podcast, slide show.

5 After sufficient planning and rehearsal time, have students present their oral interpretations to the class using the following format:

- Introduce the author and title of the poem.
- Present the group's oral interpretation.
- Conclude with a brief analysis of the poem connecting the group's analysis to the oral interpretation.

ACTIVITY 3.16

Poetry Café

SUGGESTED LEARNING STRATEGIES: **TP-CASTT, Oral Interpretation**

TP-CASTT Analysis

Title of Poem:

Author:

Title: Make a prediction. What do you think the title means before you read the poem?

Paraphrase: Restate the main ideas of the poem in your own words.

Connotation: What words or phrases suggest something beyond their literal meanings? What do you think the poet is saying in this poem? Go beyond the literal meaning or the plot of the poem.

Attitude: Describe the speaker's attitude toward the subject. Use specific adjectives to describe your ideas.

Shifts: Describe where the poem appears to shift, either in subject, speaker, or tone.

Title: Re-examine the title. What do you think it means now in the context of the poem?

Theme: What do you think is the underlying message about life the author is expressing in this poem?

Poetry

Combing

by Gladys Cardiff

ABOUT THE AUTHOR
Gladys Cardiff (b. 1942) is an American poet and writer of Irish, Welsh, and Cherokee descent. Her poetry tends to reflect her heritage. She has published two books of poems, *To Frighten a Storm* and *A Bare Unpainted Table*. She is an associate professor of poetry, American literature, and Native American literature at Oakland University.

Bending, I bow my head
And lay my hand upon
Her hair, combing, and think
How women do this for
Each other. My daughter's hair
Curls against the comb.
Wet and fragrant— orange
Parings. Her face, downcast,
Is quiet for one so young.

I take her place. Beneath
My mother's hands I feel
The braids drawn up tight
As a piano wire and singing,
Vinegar-rinsed. Sitting
before the oven I hear
The orange coils tick
The early hour before school.

She combed her grandmother
Mathilda's hair using
A comb made out of bone.
Mathilda rocked her oak-wood
Chair, her face downcast,
intent on tearing rags
In strips to braid a cotton
Rug from bits of orange
And brown. A simple act,

Preparing hair. Something
Women do for each other,
Plaiting the generations.

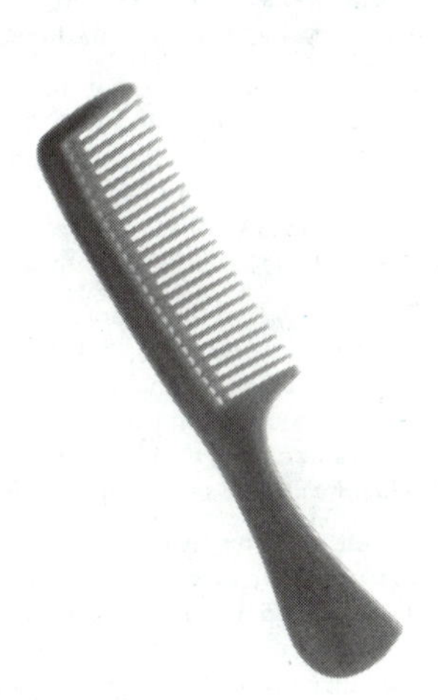

My Notes

Teacher Notes

Teacher Notes

My Notes

Poetry

ABOUT THE AUTHOR

William Wordsworth (1770–1850) was a British poet who lived in the Lake District in Northern England. He was an innovator in that he wrote lyric poetry in the language of ordinary people rather than in the "poetic" diction that was common at the time. He wrote about his love of nature in a way that later came to be known as Romanticism.

I Wandered Lonely as a Cloud

by William Wordsworth

I wandered lonely as a cloud
That floats on high o'er vales and hills,
When all at once I saw a crowd,
A host, of golden daffodils;
Beside the lake, beneath the trees,
Fluttering and dancing in the breeze.

Continuous as the stars that shine
And twinkle on the milky way,
They stretched in never-ending line
Along the margin of a bay:
Ten thousand saw I at a glance,
Tossing their heads in sprightly dance.

The waves beside them danced; but they
Outdid the sparkling waves in glee:
A poet could not but be gay,
In such a jocund company:
I gazed—and gazed—but little thought
What wealth the show to me had brought:

For oft, when on my couch I lie
In vacant or in pensive mood,
They flash upon that inward eye
Which is the bliss of solitude;
And then my heart with pleasure fills,
And dances with the daffodils.

© 2011 College Board. All rights reserved.

Teacher Notes

Poetry

My Notes

ABOUT THE AUTHOR

Langston Hughes (1902–1967) was born in the Midwest but came to New York to attend Columbia University. He became a prominent figure in the period of American literature known as the Harlem Renaissance. Much of his work—poetry, prose, and plays—evoked life in the Harlem section of New York. In fact, he was known as the "poet laureate of Harlem." In his work, he focused on the struggles and feelings of ordinary individuals.

HARLEM

by Langston Hughes

What happens to a dream deferred?

Does it dry up
like a raisin in the sun?
Or fester like a sore—
And then run?
Does it stink like rotten meat?
Or crust and sugar over—
like a syrupy sweet?

Maybe it just sags
like a heavy load.

Or does it explode?

Teacher Notes

Poetry Café

My Notes

Poetry

ABOUT THE AUTHOR

Emily Dickinson (1830–1886) lived her entire life in her father's house in Amherst, Massachusetts. She was somewhat reclusive, yet her imagination was extremely active. Using her own peculiar style of punctuation and capitalization, she wrote more than 1,700 short poems, of which only a few were published (anonymously) in her lifetime. The others were found after her death. She is regarded as one of America's greatest poets.

"HOPE" IS THE THING WITH FEATHERS

by Emily Dickinson

"Hope" is the thing with feathers—
That perches in the soul—
And sings the tune without the words—
And never stops—at all—

And sweetest—in the Gale—is heard—
And sore must be the storm—
That could abash the little Bird
That kept so many warm—

I've heard it in the chillest land—
And on the strangest Sea—
Yet, never, in Extremity,
It asked a crumb— of Me.

238 SpringBoard® English Textual Power™ Level 4

Teacher Notes

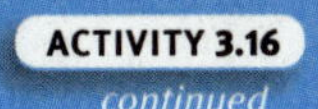

Poetry

ABOUT THE AUTHOR

Daniel Halpern (b. 1945) is a literary editor, translator, and writer. He has published eight collections of his own poetry. He has also edited two collections of international short stories and several collections of writings on a variety of topics, such as nature and artists.

by Daniel Halpern

They are the short stories of the flesh,
can evoke the entire event
in a moment–the action, the scent
and sound–place you there a second time.

It's as if the flesh decides to hold
onto what threatens its well-being,
They become part of the map marking
the pain we've had to endure.

If only the heart were so ruthless,
willing to document what it lived
by branding even those sensitive
tissues so information might flow back.

It's easy to recall what doesn't heal,
more difficult to call back what leaves
no mark, what depends on memory
to bring forward what's been gone so long,

The heart's too gentle. It won't hold
before us what we may still need to see.

My Notes

© 2011 College Board. All rights reserved.

Unit 3 • Exploring Poetic Voices 239

Teacher Notes

My Notes

Poetry

ABOUT THE AUTHOR

Essex Hemphill (1957–1995) was a poet, essayist, and editor. He began writing when he was fourteen, and, over time, he published three volumes of poetry. His poetry also appeared in a variety of magazines and in several films and documentaries. Some of his poems, like "American Hero," reflect on self-acceptance and social acceptance or denial.

AMERICAN HERO

by Essex Hemphill

I have nothing to lose tonight.
All my men surround me, panting,
as I spin the ball above our heads
on my middle finger.
It's a shimmering club light
and I'm dancing, slick in my sweat.
Squinting, I aim at the hole
fifty feet away. I let the tension go.
Shoot for the net. Choke it.
I never hear the ball
slap the backboard. I slam it
through the net. The crowd goes wild
for our win. I scored
thirty-two points this game
and they love me for it.
Everyone hollering
is a friend tonight.
But there are towns,
certain neighborhoods
where I'd be hard pressed
to hear them cheer
if I move on the block.

© 2011 College Board. All rights reserved.

240 SpringBoard® English Textual Power™ Level 4

Getting Kidnapped by a Poet

ACTIVITY 3.17

SUGGESTED LEARNING STRATEGIES: **Graphic Organizer, Quickwrite**

Poetry

"Poetry, to me, is the association of disassociated ideas. I like clear simple images, clear simple metaphors, making clear simple statements about not-so-clear, not-so-simple human beings." – Nikki Giovanni

The BEEP BEEP Poem

by Nikki Giovanni

i should write a poem
but there's almost nothing
that hasn't been said,
and said and said
beautifully, ugly, blandly
excitingly
    stay in school
    make love not war
    death to all tyrants
    where have all the flowers gone
and don't they understand at kent state[1]
the troopers will shoot . . . again

i could write a poem
because i love walking
 in the rain
and the solace[2] of my naked
body in a tub of warm water
cleanliness may not be next
to godliness but it sure feels
 good

i wrote a poem
for my father but it was so constant[3]
i burned it up
he hates change
and i'm baffled by sameness

i composed a ditty
about encore american and worldwide news

[1] **kent state:** on May 4, 1970, National Guard troops fired at student protestors at Kent State University in Ohio, killing four students and wounding nine others.
[2] **solace:** comfort in times of disappointment
[3] **constant:** unchanging, faithful, dependable

My Notes

ACTIVITY 3.17
Getting Kidnapped by a Poet

Purpose:

- To examine stylistic elements in an author's work

Steps:

1 In preparation for Embedded Assessment 2, "Analyzing and Presenting a Poet," ask students to conduct a **quickwrite** on the unit's second **Essential Question:** What can a writer learn from studying an author's craft and style?

2 Next, give students a few minutes to review the poems in this unit. In small groups, invite students to discuss their favorite ones and share why.

3 Direct students to read Nikki Giovanni's quotation on writing poetry and discuss her commentary. Next, direct students to read and interpret "The Beep-Beep Poem." Then, ask them to make connections between her commentary and this poem. Use **guided reading** to examine each of the stanzas. Discuss the use of **onomatopoeia** (the use of words that mimic the sounds they describe: e.g., "hiss," hum, and "bang") to emphasize an image in the title and final line.

Steps:

4 Place students in small groups to read and make meaning from "kidnap poem." Ask students to identify the author based on the style. Students should be able to recognize Nikki Giovanni as the author after studying "Ego-Tripping" and "Nikki-Rosa." Explain to students that they were most likely able to recognize her work by her signature style. Ask students what aspects of her style are easily recognizable. Chart students' observations on the board. Direct students to transfer their observations to the Style Chart **graphic organizer** on the next page, and complete the chart by adding textual examples and analysis.

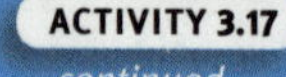

Getting Kidnapped by a Poet

My Notes

but the editorial board
said no one would understand it
as if people have to be tricked
into sensitivity
though of course they do

i love to drive my car
hours on end
along back country roads
i love to stop for cider and apples and acorn squash
three for a dollar
i love my CB when the truckers talk
and the hum of the diesel in my ear
i love the aloneness of the road
when I ascend[4] the descending curves
the power within my toe delights me
and i fling my spirit down the highway
i love the way i feel
when i pass the moon and i holler to the stars
i'm coming through

Beep Beep

kidnap poem

ever been kidnapped
by a poet
if i were a poet
i'd kidnap you
put you in my phrases and meter
you to jones beach
or maybe coney island
or maybe just to my house
lyric you in lilacs
dash you in the rain
blend into the beach
to complement my see
play the lyre for you
ode you with my love song
anything to win you
wrap you in the red Black green
show you off to mama
yeah if i were a poet i'd kid
nap you

GRAMMAR & USAGE

The subjunctive verb describes a wish or something contrary to fact. Giovanni uses the subjunctive in the third line of "Kidnap Poem" when she says "if I were a poet."

[4] **ascend:** move upward; rise to a higher level

GRAMMAR & USAGE EXTENSION

You may want to review the main verb moods at this point: the indicative mood, the imperative mood, and the subjunctive mood. Provide these descriptions and examples for students.

Indicative mood: Use this mood to express facts and opinions.

Examples: Marilinda debates well.

Imperative: Use this mood to give orders or make requests.

Example: Please come to class on time.

Subjunctive: Use this mood to express hypothetical statements or something wished for or contrary to fact.

Example: If I were 16, I could drive myself to work.

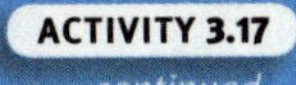

Writing Prompt: Write a short poem expressing a wish for yourself. Model Giovanni's phrasing "If I were a ..."

Style Chart

Poet or Lyricist: Nikki Giovanni

Author's Style	Example from the Poems/ Song Lyrics	Analysis

ACTIVITY 3.17 *Continued*

Steps:

5 Ask students what poets or poems have the potential to kidnap them. Brainstorm a list of potential authors and lyricists to study for Embedded Assessment 2.

6 Have students select an author whose work they would like to analyze.

© 2011 College Board. All rights reserved.

Unit 3 • Exploring Poetic Voices 243

ACTIVITY 3.18
Syntax Surgery

Materials:
- Overhead transparency
- Vocabulary Notebooks

Purpose:
- To apply poetry analysis strategies
- To generate a strong thesis
- To analyze and revise draft statements for syntax
- To apply revision techniques

Steps:
1 Use the work of Nikki Giovanni to model a style analysis for Embedded Assessment 2. Revisit the Style Chart students completed (Activity 3.17). Use **guided writing** to model construction of a working thesis that identifies a stylistic technique.

2 Ask students to reflect on the strategies they used to analyze Giovanni's style and to use similar strategies to make meaning from their selected author's work. Students should complete the **graphic organizer** on their author's style.

3 Next, ask students to review their author's work and to identify a stylistic technique particular to his or her style. Have students use the given criteria to craft a working thesis and revise it.

4 Place students in small groups to read one another's thesis statements and select the best one. Provide students with an overhead pen and a transparency on which to write this statement. Encourage each group to work collaboratively to revise or refine this statement.

5 Write *Syntax Surgery* on the board, and invite students to infer meaning. Tell students they will **role play** a doctor, diagnose the working thesis statements (major or minor surgery=revision; no surgery/revision required), and prescribe a treatment—revising the sentence to create a strong thesis. The entire class should work to revise the sentences. Your role is to provide mini-lessons as needed.

6 Bring closure to *Syntax Surgery* by having students revise their own thesis statements. Students whose statements were treated by the class can assist others in need during this time.

7 Direct students to choose an appropriate **word map graphic organizer** to explore the concept of ***syntax*** in their **Vocabulary Notebooks**.

ACTIVITY
3.18
Syntax Surgery

SUGGESTED LEARNING STRATEGIES: Graphic Organizer, Marking the Text, Word Map

Poet or Lyricist: ____________________

Author's Style	Example from the Poems/ Song Lyrics	Analysis

ACADEMIC VOCABULARY

Syntax refers to the arrangement of words and the order of grammatical elements in a sentence; the way in which words are put together to make meaningful elements, such as phrases and clauses.

Criteria for thesis statement:
- Include title, author, genre
- Identify the stylistic technique and its effect

Example:

In "The Beep Beep Poem," Giovanni's artful use of diction causes the reader to ponder considerably before gaining clarity.

Generate a working thesis on your poet or lyricist. Mark the text to identify where you have met the criteria of a strong thesis.

GRAMMAR & USAGE

A verb form must **agree** in number (singular or plural) with its subject. Notice that in the sample thesis statement the singular verb *causes* agrees with the singular subject *use*:

In "The Beep Beep Poem," Giovanni's artful **use** of diction **causes** the reader to ponder considerably before gaining clarity.

If needed, use the space below to revise your thesis statement to incorporate missing criteria or strengthen your thesis.

ACTIVITY 3.19

Generating a Rhetorical Plan

SUGGESTED LEARNING STRATEGIES: **Marking the Text, Think-Pair-Share**

Model outline of analysis of Giovanni's style:

Thesis: *In "The Beep Beep Poem," Giovanni' s artful use of diction causes the reader to ponder considerably before gaining clarity.*

- Topic Sentence 1: Giovanni's connotations are elusive because they comprise various shades of suggestion making a simple object a complex idea.

  Possible examples for support:

- Topic Sentence 2: Giovanni weaves formal and informal diction together seamlessly to assert an informed, yet humble opinion.

  Possible examples for support:

As you work on your rhetorical plan, consider—and use—the grammatical knowledge and skills you have studied and practiced throughout this unit.

Your Outline:

I. Thesis

II. Topic Sentence 1:
Possible examples:

III. Topic Sentence 2:
Possible examples:

ACTIVITY 3.19

Generating a Rhetorical Plan

Purpose:

- To extract ideas from the thesis to explore in topic sentences
- To create a rhetorical plan for the essay
- To generate a first draft

Steps:

1 Now that students have a thesis, they can design a rhetorical plan for their essays. **Activate prior knowledge** by asking students to review the organizational structure for literary analysis—what goes in each section of the essay and why?

2 Review the model thesis statement on Giovanni's style. Use a think aloud to show students how to unpack the thesis, the driving force of the essay, to generate supporting topic sentences. Begin by having students **mark the text** to identify key ideas that warrant further support in the body paragraphs.

TEACHER TO TEACHER It's possible to have a thesis statement that does not mention the title. This would allow for body paragraphs that draw support from more than one text. Your ELL students may need assistance in crafting a thesis statement that clearly communicates the topic and includes correct grammar, especially agreement between subject and verb and appropriate use of verb tenses.

3 Show students how you arrived at this outline, moving from a broad thesis statement to more specific topic sentences. Then, invite them to brainstorm examples from Giovanni's texts to support the topic sentences.

4 Ask students to create a rhetorical plan for their essay and note all of the possible examples. Students should **pair-share** their outlines, discussing and explaining ideas before generating a first draft.

Embedded Assessment 2

Analyzing and Presenting a Poet

College Board Standards and Objectives

R1 Comprehension of Words, Sentences, and Components of Texts (R1.2)
PE Mappings: R1.2-6.4

R3 Author's Purpose, Audience, and Craft (R3.2)
PE Mappings: R3.2-1.4, R3.2-2.4

R4 Using Strategies to Comprehend Texts (R4.1; R4.2; R4.4)
PE Mappings: R4.1-1.4, R4.2-2.4, R4.4-2.4

W1 Rhetorical Analysis and Planning (W1.1)
PE Mappings: W1.1-1.4

W2 Generating Content (W2.1 L; W2.2 L)
PE Mappings: W2.1-1.4L, W2.1-2.4L, W2.2-1.4L, W2.2-2.4L W2.2-3.4L, W2.2-4.4L

W3 Drafting (W3.1 L, W3.2 L)
PE Mappings: W3.1-1.4L, W3.1-2.4L, W3.1-3.4L, W3.2-1.4L

W4 Evaluating and Revising Texts (W4.1 L, W4.2 L)
PE Mappings: W4.1-1.4L, W4.2-1.4L

W5 Editing to Present Technically Sound Texts (W5.1, W5.2, W5.3, W5.4)
PE Mappings: W5.1-1.4, W5.2-1.4, W5.3-1.4, W5.4-1.4

S3 Preparing and Delivering Presentations (S3.1, S3.3; S3.4)
PE Mappings: S3.1-1.4, S3.2-1.4, S3.3-1.4, S3.4-1.4

Steps:

1 Students may already have selected a poet and drafted a thesis and outline in the previous two activities. If so, refer them to the work they have done. If not, you may need to guide students in selecting a poet.

2 Allow time for students to research the poet's work and select specific poems to analyze.

3 Urge students to review the criteria for organization on the Scoring Guide as they begin to revise their drafts. As students edit their essays for publication, remind them to read for correct punctuation and grammar, especially in the use of verb tenses and subject-verb agreement. You may want to have students review pages 430 and 432-434 of the Grammar Handbook for information on subject-verb agreement and verb tenses.

4 Allow students to **share and respond** in writing groups, focusing specifically on analysis of style and clarity of ideas.

Embedded Assessment 2

Analyzing and Presenting a Poet

SUGGESTED LEARNING STRATEGIES: **Drafting, TP-CASTT, Marking the Text, Self-Editing, Oral Interpretation, Sharing and Responding**

Assignment

Your assignment is to analyze a collection of work from a poet, and write a style-analysis essay. You will then select one of the poems you analyzed and present an oral interpretation of the poem to the class.

Steps

Planning

1. Review the list of poets provided by your teacher and briefly research potential poets for this assignment. Select a poet that is of interest to you.
2. Read through a collection of the poet's work and choose three to five poems to analyze for this task. Mark and annotate the texts using TP-CASTT or another strategy.

Drafting

3. Review the analyzed poems and look for recurring patterns within the text. Generate a working thesis that identifies the author's stylistic technique and its effect.
4. Create an outline to organize and structure ideas for the essay.
5. Generate a first draft to develop the ideas from the outline.

Revising

6. Review and evaluate your draft by color-coding the text to identify elements of organization listed in the Scoring Guide. Revise your draft and add any missing elements into it to ensure that ideas flow coherently.
7. Share your draft with your peers and get feedback to revise for the following:
   - Analysis of style.
   - Clarity of ideas.

   Review the suggestions from your peers and consult the Scoring Guide to revise accordingly.

Editing for Publication

8. Reread and edit your draft for seamless integration of quotations and for correct grammar, punctuation, and spelling. If you are handwriting your essay, write legibly.
9. Create an appropriate title, and prepare a final draft for publication.

TECHNOLOGY TIP If you are using word processing software to create your essay, use its spell-check features to help you create a publishable final product. Also, consult a style manual such as that published by the Modern Language Association or *The Chicago Manual of Style* to find general guidelines for formatting your essay.

Embedded Assessment 2 *continued*

Planning and Rehearsing for Presentation

10. Select the poem that most intrigues you and prepare an oral interpretation of the poem. Mark and annotate this poem for purposeful use of movement, gestures, inflection, props, sound effects, etc.
11. Rehearse your oral interpretation in a mirror, and practice within a group of your peers. Ask for suggestions to refine your oral interpretation.
12. Use the format below to organize your performance:
    - Brief introduction of the poet and his or her style.
    - Oral interpretation of the poem.
    - Brief rationale for your oral interpretation.
13. Check that your presentation has a logical progression of ideas and a clearly stated point of view.
14. Consult the Scoring Guide criteria, and use peer feedback to refine your presentation.

Embedded Assessment 2

Continued

Steps:

5 Emphasize the importance of including textual evidence. You might wish to have students revisit Activity 3.9 to review how to incorporate quotations in the drafts.

6 Allow students time to rehearse their oral presentations. Depending on time, you may have students present their poems in small groups or to the whole class.

7 As students practice and rehearse in groups, encourage them to listen and respond to each other's presentations, so they can provide assistance to their peers. Encourage all students and especially ELL students to use strategies such as asking questions, using nonverbal cues, and making inferences in order to clarify meaning.

Embedded Assessment 2

Continued

Scoring Guide

When you score this Embedded Assessment, you may wish to download and print a copy of the Scoring Guide from SpringBoard Online. In this way, you can have a copy to mark for each student's work.

Embedded Assessment 2

continued

Analyzing and Presenting a Poet

SCORING GUIDE

Scoring Criteria	Exemplary	Proficient	Emerging
Ideas	The essay demonstrates an insightful analysis of the poet/lyricist's style. It makes relevant connections within the text at a sophisticated level.	The presentation and essay demonstrate an accurate analysis of the poet/lyricist's style.	The presentation and essay demonstrate a sustained misinterpretation of the text and/or a lack of appropriate analysis, relying primarily on summary.
Organization	The essay's structure contains: • a well-written introduction with an engaging lead, TAG, and a sophisticated thesis • coherent and concise body paragraphs with complex topic sentences, strong textual support, and insightful commentary • effective transitions that show relationship between ideas • a reflective conclusion that extends the key ideas of the essay.	The essay's structure contains: • an introduction with a clear lead, TAG, and thesis • coherent body paragraphs with topic sentences, adequate textual support, and relevant commentary • transitions that show a relationship between ideas • a logical conclusion that extends the key ideas of the essay.	The essay's structure may or may not contain: • a limited introduction with an unfocused lead, inaccurate TAG, and/or an unclear thesis • incoherent body paragraphs with topic sentences that do not support the thesis, inadequate textual support, and irrelevant commentary • inappropriate transitions • a limited conclusion that is repetitive and/or does not extend the ideas presented in the essay.
Use of Language	The writing contains a clear, consistent academic voice and seamless integration of quotations woven in with commentary.	The writing contains an academic voice and integration of quotations with commentary.	Writing may contain inconsistent/inappropriate voice, ineffective sentence structure (run-ons, fragments), and/or freestanding quotations not connected with commentary.
Evidence of Writing Process	The writing demonstrates thoughtful planning, significant revision, and careful editing in preparing a publishable draft.	The writing demonstrates planning, revision, and editing in preparing a publishable draft.	The writing lacks evidence of planning, revision, and/or editing. The draft is not ready for publication.

Embedded Assessment 2
continued

SCORING GUIDE

Scoring Criteria	Exemplary	Proficient	Emerging
Presentation	The oral interpretation of the poem is convincingly performed with skillful use of movement, gestures, inflection, props, and/or sound effects. The brief introduction and rationale enlighten the audience, communicating a deep understanding of the poem. Focused rehearsal is evident.	The oral interpretation of the poem is performed with purposeful use of movement, gestures, inflection, props, and/or sound effects. The brief introduction and rationale inform the audience, communicating a clear understanding of the poem. Adequate rehearsal is evident.	The oral interpretation lacks movement, gestures, inflection, props, and/or sound effects, or the performance elements may be distracting. The brief introduction and rationale do little to communicate a clear understanding of the poem or may be missing. There is little or no evidence of rehearsal.
Additional Criteria			

Comments:

Embedded Assessment 2
Continued

Teacher Notes

UNIT REFLECTION

Purpose

- To monitor comprehension and growth through a reflective process
- To synthesize understanding of individual reading and writing processes and strategies
- To self-assess mastery of key concepts and terms

Steps:

1 This is an opportunity for students to think about the concepts, vocabulary, and their own learning progress as they revisit and review the work they have produced in this unit.

2 Encourage students to be especially metacognitive about which strategies they have used and how those strategies support their learning styles and goals.

Unit Teacher Reflection

1 Which activities in this unit did you need to adjust (or you think should be adjusted) to prepare your students to be successful on each Embedded Assessment? Add your notes on how you would adjust the activities.

2 Which teacher strategies were most effective for introducing concepts/ideas to your students?

3 How did the unit activities help you address the individual learning needs of your students? Note any changes you would make in your instructional strategies to differentiate instruction.

Unit 3

Reflection

An important aspect of growing as a learner is to reflect on where you have been, what you have accomplished, what helped you to learn, and how you will apply your new knowledge in the future. Use the following questions to guide your thinking and to identify evidence of your learning. Use separate notebook paper.

Thinking about Concepts

1. Using specific examples from this unit, respond to the Essential Questions:
   - What is poetry?
   - What can a writer learn from studying an author's craft and style?
2. Consider the new academic vocabulary from this unit (**Diction, Imagery, Poetic Structure, Figurative Language, Syntax**) as well as academic vocabulary from previous units and select 3-4 terms of which your understanding has grown. For each term, answer the following questions:
   - What was your understanding of the word before you completed this unit?
   - How has your understanding of the term evolved throughout the unit?
   - How will you apply your understanding in the future?

Thinking about Connections

3. Review the activities and products (artifacts) you created. Choose those that most reflect your growth or increase in understanding.
4. For each artifact that you choose, record, respond to, and reflect on your thinking and understanding, using the following questions as a guide:
   a. What skill/knowledge does this artifact reflect, and how did you learn this skill/knowledge?
   b. How did your understanding of the power of language expand through your engagement with this artifact?
   c. How will you apply this skill or knowledge in the future?
5. Create this reflection as Portfolio pages—one for each artifact you choose. Use the model in the box for your headings and commentary on questions.

Thinking About Thinking

Portfolio Entry

Concept:

Description of Artifact:

Commentary on Questions:

About the Unit

Unit 4

Context

One of the most widely read "coming of age" texts, Shakespeare's *The Tragedy of Romeo and Juliet* is the core text in this unit. Students apply to the play what they have previously learned about voice, film, and poetry. This unit guides students in an examination of the ways that directors and actors use theatrical elements to interpret and perform a text. Opportunities to hear and speak the language, view filmed interpretations, and perform scenes will enhance students' understanding of Shakespeare's play.

CollegeBoard
inspiring minds™

AP/ College Readiness

This unit will focus on activities that increase students' skills and knowledge for AP and College Readiness:

- Reading and analyzing a work from another century, with an emphasis on understanding archaic words and syntactic structure. (Activities 4.11, 4.13)
- Interpreting literature through close reading, literary analysis, and application of literary elements. (Activities 4.5, 4.7, 4.8)
- Researching historical, social, and cultural contexts of Shakespeare's drama, *Romeo and Juliet*. (Activities 4.27, 4.28)
- Evaluating strategies for learning.

Suggested Texts and Materials

You will need to acquire the following materials for this unit:

- **Activity 4.2** requires close-up photos of faces from a magazine.
- **Activity 4.3** requires character name cards, which you may want to laminate. Text for the name cards is included in this About the Unit section.
- For **Activities 4.8, 4.12, 4.18** and **4.25**, you will need access to at least two film interpretations of *Romeo and Juliet*. You will also need to choose a painting of a scene from *Romeo and Juliet* (preferably depicting when Juliet's loved ones find her "dead" in her chamber) and determine how you will show it so that the students can analyze it for Activity 4.23.
- For **Activity 4.21** you will need to provide students with scenarios like the following:

"That one is mine." You are in line at a pastry shop and you spot your favorite dessert in the case.	**"That one is mine." Your teacher has intercepted a note you were passing to a friend.**
"That one is mine." You are babysitting your young cousin who throws a temper tantrum at the park.	**"That one is mine." Another student has picked up your backpack by mistake.**
"That one is mine." Your art project is on display, and you are pointing it out to your family.	**"That one is mine." You notice someone flirting with your date at a dance.**

- For **Activity 4.23**, you will also need a reproduction of a painting of a scene from *Romeo and Juliet* (if possible, specifically depicting Juliet's death scene).
- **Optional:**

  For **Activity 4.3**, use a camera to take pictures of students' tableaux.

  For **Activity 4.8**, provide lyrics for the love songs from the soundtracks of the film interpretations.

  For **Activity 4.10**, provide a picture book for older readers (such as *Bard of Avon: The Story of William Shakespeare* by Diane Stanley or *William Shakespeare & the Globe* by Aliki) and schedule access to a computer lab and/or media center for the research part of the activity.

Independent Reading

Encourage outside reading as a part of this unit of instruction. You may want to suggest that students explore an additional play, a collection of short stories, or a nonfiction book that connects to Shakespeare or to Shakespearean themes.

Writing Workshops

For Unit 4, you may want to access Workshop 6, Expository Writing, as additional practice in preparation for Embedded Assessment 2, Writing a Metacognitive Reflection.

Grammar Handbook

Remind students to refer to the Grammar Handbook in the back of their books. Encourage them to use this handbook and the Grammar & Usage features throughout this and other units as reference for helping them develop their writing skills. You may want to incorporate mini-lessons from the Grammar Handbook and the Grammar & Usage features to reinforce students' grammar and writing skills.

Instructional Sequence

This unit, while challenging, offers great rewards and requires careful planning for instruction. Students (and therefore teachers) will be multi-tasking: reading and grappling with Shakespeare's text, conducting research, and planning and rehearsing a presentation of a scene from *Romeo and Juliet*. Many of these tasks will need to happen simultaneously, and students will need help juggling these activities. Notice that scaffolding for the second Embedded Assessment, Writing a Metacognitive Reflection, is woven through the entire unit.

The sequence of instruction begins with several activities that help students gain confidence speaking in front of an audience and build background knowledge about *Romeo and Juliet*. Then students are guided through the play. They interpret and analyze Shakespeare's language, characters, and plot and make connections to their own lives. They also view film interpretations of key scenes, identify directors' choices, and discuss the effects of those choices. Students reflect on strategies for reading and writing, and evaluate how specific strategies are working for them. An informal research project allows students to refine their research skills as they learn about the historical and social context of the play.

After reading Act II, students form acting companies. In their companies, they read and interpret Acts III through V, moving from identification of theatrical elements to planning their own performances. By the time students finish reading the play, they have extensive practice reading and interpreting. They perform a scene from the play for Embedded Assessment 1. The final activities ask students to use their portfolios as a guide to self-reflection on their growth as speakers, listeners, readers, and writers. Embedded Assessment 2, Writing a Metacognitive Reflection, benefits students as they evaluate and write about the strategies that help them take charge of their own learning.

Activities 4.1–4.4 preview the unit and discuss elements of tragedy and dramatic performance, such as monologues, and prologues, and introduce students to the characters, plot, and historical background of *Romeo and Juliet*. Students have opportunities to memorize and recite lines from Shakespeare and Paul Laurence Dunbar.

Activities 4.5–4.6 build knowledge about Shakespeare's language in the context of character analysis and provide a system for recording key events of plot.

Activities 4.7–4.9 address Act I, with an emphasis on elements of performance. Students practice speaking Shakespearean language and view scenes from film interpretations of *Romeo and Juliet*.

Activity 4.10 explains the role of the dramaturge and builds background knowledge of the historical and social influences on *Romeo and Juliet* through an informational research project

Activities 4.11–4.15 have students examine and analyze Shakespearean language, multiple film interpretations, literary elements, and visualizations. Self-selection of writing and reading strategies is supported.

Activity 4.16 establishes procedures for setting up acting companies, in preparation for Embedded Assessment 1.

Activities 4.17–4.20 examine language, characterization, plot, and multiple interpretations in Act III. Planning stage for performance begins.

Activities 4.21–4.23 integrate elements of performance with reading and analyzing Act IV. Focus on complementary artistic texts helps students plan for the performance in Embedded Assessment 1.

Activities 4.24–4.26 focus on independent reading and analysis of Act V, evaluation of film interpretations, and analytical writing about the play.

Embedded Assessment 1 **Presenting a Shakespearean Scene**

Skills and Knowledge:

- Read and interpret the selected scene from *Romeo and Juliet*.
- Collaborate in planning, rehearsing, and presenting the scene.
- Perform with appropriate vocal delivery, facial expression, gestures and movement, using props and costumes to convey character (Actors only).
- Write, memorize, and recite an engaging introduction to the performance (Director only).
- Write, memorize, and recite an explanation about how research supported the performance of the scene (Dramaturge only).
- Create an actor's, director's, or dramaturge's notebook.
- Reflect on the acting company's collaboration on scene analysis and interpretation during rehearsals.
- Evaluate dress rehearsal and final performance.

Activities 4.27–4.28 guide self-assessment and reflection on speaking and listening, reading, and writing.

Embedded Assessment 2 **Writing a Metacognitive Reflection**

Skills and Knowledge:

- Self-assess growth in use of reading, writing, oral literacy, and collaborative strategies.
- Organize and write a reflective essay.
- Describe texts and purpose of assignments for audience.

Suggested Pacing

Activity	45 to 50-Minute Class Periods	Class Periods with Homework	Activity	45 to 50-Minute Class Periods	Class Periods with Homework
Learning Focus and 4.1	½		4.17	1	HW
4.2	1		4.18	2	HW
4.3	1		4.19	1	
4.4	1	HW	4.20	1	
4.5	1		4.21	1	
4.6	¼		4.22	1	HW
4.7	1 ½	HW	4.23	¾	
4.8	1 ½	HW	4.24	½	
4.9	¾	HW	4.25	1 ½	HW
4.10	2 ½	HW	4.26	2	HW
4.11	½		EA1	7	
4.12	1	HW	Learning Focus	½	
4.13	½		4.27	¼	
4.14	1		4.28	1	
4.15	1	HW	EA2	2	
4.16	1		Unit Reflection	½	
Total Class Periods				39	

Character Names and Descriptions

Prince Escalus Ruler of Verona Authority figure	**Mercutio** One of Romeo's best friends Related to the Prince
Lord Montague Romeo's father Hates the Capulets	**Friar Lawrence** Priest Performs marriage of Romeo and Juliet
Lady Montague Romeo's mother	**Balthasar** Servant of Romeo
Romeo Main male character Loves Juliet	**Abraham** Servant of Montague
Lord Capulet Juliet's father Hates the Montagues	**Nurse** Like a mother to Juliet Assists in the marriage of Romeo and Juliet
Lady Capulet Juliet's mother	**Peter** Servant to the Nurse
Juliet Main female character Loves Romeo	**Sampson** Servant of Capulet
Tybalt Juliet's cousin Hates the Montagues	**Gregory** Servant of Capulet
Count Paris Wants to marry Juliet Related to the Prince	**Benvolio** One of Romeo's best friends Nephew of Montague

Reading Plan

By speaking the lines and playing the parts, students can make a drama and its language their own. In order to provide ample time for rehearsing and presenting scenes from the play, you must plan your pacing carefully.

Ideas to Consider

- Try to move students through the play quickly, using a variety of methods to read the text. Listening to audiotapes, reading aloud in parts, viewing scenes, and even summarizing some sections will allow students to be exposed to the entire play.
- One purpose of research is to set a historical and social context for the drama. Activity 4.10 provides students with an opportunity to learn about Shakespeare and his world, which may enhance their understanding of the play. As students conduct their research, help them assess the validity of online sources.
- Have students form acting companies and review Embedded Assessment 1 requirements before they read Act III of *Romeo and Juliet*. The suggested scenes for performance appear in Acts III through V. Consider asking the companies to rehearse by reading selected scenes on their feet.
- Provide time for students to plan and rehearse their scenes. Intersperse this planning and rehearsal time with the reading of the drama. Think about places on your campus where groups may rehearse, keeping in mind how you might orchestrate a dress rehearsal for the acting companies.
- Maximize student engagement by varying the methods you use for reading the scenes. Let the students "perform" as much as possible, in order to prepare them for Embedded Assessment 1.

Suggested Reading Methods

Act, Scene	Suggested Reading Methods	Act, Scene	Suggested Reading Methods
Prologue	Teacher reads aloud. Listen to audio.	III, 1	Have seated readers read aloud while class directs actors.
I, 1	Listen to audio.	III, 2	Analyze the portrayal of Juliet on an audio.
I, 2	Listen to audio.	III, 3	Watch films, if possible; use an audio version if not. Friar has long speeches.
I, 3	Listen to audio.	IV, 2	Read in parts.
I, 4	Listen to audio.	IV, 3	Juliet's soliloquy: Multiple readings. Teacher reads first, and then volunteers read same passage.
I, 5	Compare film interpretations; party scenes.	IV, 4	Use an audio version so students can hear the humor.
II, 1	Read in parts aloud.	IV, 5	Might stop at the comic relief.
II, 2	Compare film interpretations' balcony scene.	V, 1	Read in parts, up to Balthasar's exit. Finish the scene reading independently.
II, 3	Listen to audio.	V, 2	Read in parts or watch a film version.
II, 4	Watch video.	V, 3	Read in parts or watch a film version.
II, 5	Listen to audio.		
II, 6	Listen to audio.		

Resources

Film Interpretations of *Romeo and Juliet*

Campbell, N. (Director). (1993). *Romeo & Juliet.* Filmed stage production.

Castellani, R. (Director). (1954). *Romeo and Juliet.*

Cukor, G. (Director). (1936). *Romeo and Juliet.* Stars Leslie Howard and Norma Shearer. Available through Vintage Classics.

Horrox, A. (Director). (1994). *Romeo and Juliet.* A television version starring Geraldine Sommerville and Jonathan Firth.

Kemp-Welch, J. (Director). (1976). *Romeo and Juliet.* Made for television. Shakespeare Collection

Luhrmann, B. (Director). (1996). *William Shakespeare's Romeo and Juliet.* Contemporary setting.

Rakoff, A. (Director). (1978). *Romeo and Juliet.* Made for television. BBC and TIME-LIFE films.

Robbins, J. and Wise, R. (Directors). (1961). *West Side Story.* With music by Leonard Bernstein. A musical adaptation set in New York City.

Zeffirelli, F. (Director). (1968). *Romeo and Juliet.* Renaissance setting.

(1966) *The Royal Ballet performing* Romeo and Juliet. Starring Rudolf Nureyev and Margot Fonteyn. Prokofiev's adaptation of the story. No dialogue.

(1999) *Standard Deviants: Shakespeare Tragedies — Titus Andronicus, Romeo and Juliet, and Hamlet.* A comic approach to Shakespeare's tragedies especially designed for high school and college students, which presents complicated material in engaging ways.

Written Texts

Berry, C. (1991). *Voice and the Actor.* New York: Wiley. Foreword by Peter Brook. Gielgud, J. (2000). *Acting Shakespeare.* New York: Applause Books.

O'Brien, P. (ed). (1993). *Shakespeare Set Free: Teaching Romeo and Juliet.* New York: The Folger Shakespeare Library. Essential text for the teaching of Shakespeare through performance.

Unit 4

Interpreting Drama Through Performance

Essential Questions

- What are the essential features of an effective drama and/or dramatic performance?
- How have the strategies I have learned this year helped me to be a better reader, writer, speaker, and listener?

Unit Overview

"All the world's a stage and all the men and women merely players..."

—*William Shakespeare (1564–1616)*

In this line from *As You Like It*, William Shakespeare reminds us of the connection between drama and our lives. One of his most famous plays is *The Tragedy of Romeo and Juliet*, a "coming of age" drama widely read by students. The play has everything an Elizabethan or a modern audience could ask for—romance, combat, comedy, and death. Over the centuries, the play has inspired artists, musicians, choreographers, and filmmakers. It has even been the basis for different texts such as the musical *West Side Story* and the action film *Romeo Must Die*. Shakespeare's language, his insight into human nature, and his creative sense of theater are the qualities that make his plays memorable. By speaking lines, performing scenes, hearing the language, and viewing various directors' interpretations, your experience with *Romeo and Juliet* will bring the play to life.

UNIT 4

Have students read the Unit Overview. Discuss the ideas in the overview and ask students to relate them to their own lives.

Students will provide responses to the Essential Questions in Activity 4.1. At the end of the unit, they will revisit the Essential Questions to see how their responses have changed after studying the unit.

UNIT 4

Have students read the goals for the unit and **mark** any words that are unfamiliar to them. You may want to create a space in the classroom for these words so students can add information about their meaning as they study the unit.

You may consider posting these goals in a visible place in the classroom for the duration of the unit, allowing you and students to revisit the goals easily and gauge progress toward achieving the goals throughout the unit.

Academic Vocabulary

Point out the academic vocabulary to students, and remind them that they will be studying concepts related to these words throughout the unit. Having students create **graphic organizers** to study these words in depth will greatly enhance their understanding of each word and its relationship to unit concepts. Have students keep their completed graphic organizers in their **Vocabulary Notebooks**.

See the Resources at the back of this book for examples of blackline masters suitable for word study. As students become more acquainted with the use of a **graphic organizer** to explore the meaning of a word, you may want them to create their own graphic organizers.

Unit 4

Interpreting Drama Through Performance

Goals

- To engage in authentic research related to performing *Romeo and Juliet*
- To explore multiple interpretations of *Romeo and Juliet* through performance and film
- To examine the "coming of age" concept in context of the play
- To be intentional in the use of strategies and to evaluate how well they work
- To reflect on one's growth as a learner

ACADEMIC VOCABULARY

Drama
Tragedy
Theatrical Elements
Interpretation
Metacognition

Contents

*Texts not included in these materials.

UNIT 4

Teacher Notes

LEARNING FOCUS:

Expressing Your Vision of Shakespeare

Read the Learning Focus with students or have them read independently. **Activate prior knowledge** by having students **mark the text** and highlight words or concepts that are familiar (what they know). They might use a question mark to indicate content that is unfamiliar (what they do not know but want to learn).

Students will respond to the information on this page in Activity 4.1.

Teacher Notes

Learning Focus:

Expressing Your Vision of Shakespeare

Just as reading another writer's poetry and writing your own poetry are entirely different experiences, reading a play and performing someone else's play are demanding and rewarding in different ways. Performers have many tools by which they convey **dramatic interpretations**. Perhaps you found it challenging and satisfying to express your personal and unique voice through poetry. Performance is another opportunity to express your interpretation of words and ideas.

Actually performing a drama allows you to understand more deeply the multiple layers of dramatic interaction—from dealing with physical movement as you wield props to memorizing lines and communicating the emotions of the characters. Your involvement with the reality of a play allows you to make a text come alive for yourself and for viewers.

Shakespeare's understanding of human nature is timeless. In the course of this unit, you will strive to get inside the minds of the characters in *Romeo and Juliet*. You have already learned how to use different voices in different situations. Shakespearean text is often difficult for modern readers, but the words coupled with clear voices and actions guide an audience's understanding. The characters find themselves in situations where they are not always able to express their true voices. As a reader and performer, you will look for the **subtext** beneath the words the characters say.

Interpretation of a work of literature comes from a desire to convey an understanding of the work itself through close readings and a thoughtful appreciation of the author's purpose. Film interpretations allow you to see how different directors and actors bring their own interpretations to Shakespeare's words and ideas.

Directors use theatrical elements such as set design, props, costumes, music and other sounds, lighting, and editing to express a vision or interpretation of Shakespeare's words and ideas. As you deliver Shakespeare's dramatic language, you will practice a deliberate vocal delivery and careful blocking of movement to match the words to the actions. Understanding Shakespeare's sense of **inverted syntax** and the comedy of **puns**, as well as all the figurative language of the poetry, will help you perform the text.

Independent Reading: In this unit, you will study one of Shakespeare's most famous tragedies. For independent reading, look for another play, perhaps one by Shakespeare. You might also consider a collection of short stories or informational text about Shakespeare's life and influence on literature.

© 2011 College Board. All rights reserved.

Previewing the Unit

ACTIVITY 4.1

SUGGESTED LEARNING STRATEGIES: Think-Pair-Share, Close Reading, Summarizing/Paraphrasing, Graphic Organizer

Essential Questions

1. What are the essential features of an effective drama and/or dramatic performance?

2. How have the strategies I have learned this year helped me to be a better reader, writer, speaker, and listener?

Unit Overview and Learning Focus

Predict what you think this unit is about. Use the words or phrases that stood out to you when you read the Unit Overview and the Learning Focus.

Embedded Assessment

What knowledge must you have (what do you need to know)? What skills must you have (what will you need to do to complete the Embedded Assessment successfully)? Write your responses below.

ACTIVITY 4.1

Previewing the Unit

Purpose:

- To contextualize prior knowledge about key ideas and concepts
- To analyze the skills and knowledge necessary for success in the unit

Steps:

1 To reveal existing knowledge about the concepts for the unit, ask students to **pair-share** responses to the two Essential Questions. Students will revisit these questions throughout the unit to develop a more mature understanding of these ideas.

2 Provide students with a clear learning target by asking them to find the Embedded Assessment 1 assignment and Scoring Guide (pp. 319–325). Lead students through a **close reading** of the prompt, steps, and scoring guide criteria. Instruct students to **mark the text** by underlining or highlighting the places the text that mentions a skill or knowledge necessary to succeed on the Embedded Assessment.

3 Instruct students to **summarize/paraphrase** with a partner or small group the skills/knowledge they have underlined or highlighted. As you conduct a large group discussion, create a web graphic organizer that lists the knowledge and skills.

4 Revisit the web **graphic organizer** throughout the unit to reinforce the skills and knowledge developed in the unit activities. You may want to enlarge the web graphic organizer to provide a **visual** in the classroom. Repeat the process for the second part of the unit in preparation for Embedded Assessment 2.

ACTIVITY 4.2
Mask Monologues

Materials:

- Photographs from magazines

Purpose:

- To build fluency, confidence and poise when speaking in front of an audience
- To use simple props effectively
- To demonstrate appropriate volume in vocal delivery

Steps:

1 Provide or instruct students to bring in photographs of faces from magazines and newspapers to use as visual prompts the day before this activity. Collect the photos and redistribute them, one picture per student, if possible.

2 Remind students that a monologue is a speech delivered by a single character. Tell students to **draft** a short monologue in the voice of the person in their photograph.

3 Tell students to hold the picture in front of their faces as they role-play their characters, delivering their monologues to a partner, a small group, or the class. Listening students should provide feedback.

4 Have listening students ask questions of the character. The "masked" student should answer in the voice of the character.

ACTIVITY 4.2

Mask Monologues

SUGGESTED LEARNING STRATEGIES: **SIFT, Marking the Text, Discussion Groups**

LITERARY TERMS

A **monologue** is a dramatic speech delivered by a character.

Look closely at the pictures provided by your teacher and consider the following:

- The person's gender, age, and ethnicity
- His or her facial expression
- The kind of person you think he or she is; what he or she might sound like; what he or she might talk about; what body movements or gestures he or she would use

Write a short **monologue** in the voice of the person to deliver to others. Cover topics that you think the person would discuss as you try to "speak for" him or her.

What I look like:

What I might say or talk about:

How I might move:

Then, hold up your mask in front of your face as you deliver the *monologue* to others. Speak at an appropriate volume. Allow your audience to pose questions that you answer in the voice of your "masked" character. You will have a chance to pose questions to other students' characters.

Next, read the poem "We Wear the Mask" by Paul Laurence Dunbar and use the SIFT strategy to guide your marking of the text. Discuss the poem, including its relevance to the monologue activity you completed earlier. Consider the following questions: How do we wear masks in our daily lives? What do people really know about us if we wear a mask to hide our true feelings? How do you think this poem may relate to the play *Romeo and Juliet*?

© 2011 College Board. All rights reserved.

Poetry

WE WEAR THE MASK

by Paul Laurence Dunbar

ABOUT THE AUTHOR

The son of former slaves, Paul Laurence Dunbar (1872–1906) was the first African American writer to earn his living solely by writing poetry and fiction. He was also the first to gain a national audience of mostly white readers.

We wear the mask that grins and lies,
It hides our cheeks and shades our eyes—
This debt we pay to human guile[1];
With torn and bleeding hearts we smile,
And mouth with myriad[2] subtleties.

Why should the world be over-wise,
In counting all our tears and sighs?
Nay, let them only see us, while
We wear the mask.

We smile, but, O great Christ, our cries
To thee from tortured souls arise.
We sing, but oh the clay is vile[3]
Beneath our feet, and long the mile;
But let the world dream other-wise,
We wear the mask.

[1] **guile**: deception
[2] **myriad**: countless
[3] **vile**: repulsive or wretched

My Notes

Symbols:

Images:

Figures of Speech:

Tone and Theme:

Steps:

5 Read aloud the poem "We Wear the Mask" by Paul Laurence Dunbar. Have students use the **SIFT** strategy to help them analyze the symbols, images, figures of speech, tone, and theme of poem, **marking the text** with their notes. Lead a **group discussion** of the poem. Challenge students to draw on their prior knowledge and predict how the poem might relate to the play ***Romeo and Juliet***.

ACTIVITY 4.3

Who's Who in Verona

Materials:

- Vocabulary Notebook
- Character name cards (see Unit 4 About the Unit)
- Cast of characters from *Romeo and Juliet*
- Materials for bookmarks
- Digital camera (optional)

Purpose:

- To explore the concept of drama
- To analyze relationships between characters in a play
- To demonstrate understanding of visual delivery
- To evaluate group work

Steps:

1 Use a **graphic organizer** such as a word map to help students brainstorm words and phrases associated with the word ***drama***. Record students' responses on the board. Add ***drama*** to the Word Wall and ask students to save the word map in their **Vocabulary Notebooks**. Follow large-group discussion with small groups or partners in which students discuss and share their new understanding to build on the concept and to gain fluency with new language.

2 Have students read and form an initial response to the **Essential Question**, "What are the essential features of an effective drama and/or dramatic performance?"

3 To **preview** the drama, create 4 x 6 cards of the character names and descriptions to use as nameplates for students. It would be a good idea to laminate these cards for future use. You might use different colors to the separate households (for example, red for Capulet and blue for Montague). Show students the cast of characters page in the edition of the play they will be using.

4 Assign students to groups. Have each group choose a director. This person must be able to judge the effect of the group's tableau and may have to explain the tableau to the class. Hand out a character card to every student except the director. Students should attach the cards to themselves, so others will know whom they are portraying.

ACTIVITY 4.3

Who's Who in Verona

SUGGESTED LEARNING STRATEGIES: **Graphic Organizer, Previewing**

ACADEMIC VOCABULARY

A **drama** is a play written for stage, radio, film, or television, usually about a serious topic or situation.

1. Create a graphic organizer, such as a word map, on separate paper and then brainstorm all of the words and phrases you can think of that are associated with **drama**. As your class discusses this academic vocabulary term, take notes and be sure to save your work in your vocabulary notebook for later use.
2. Next, consider the essential question "What are the essential features of an effective drama and/or dramatic performance?"
3. To preview *The Tragedy of Romeo and Juliet*, your teacher will give you a card with a character's name and description on it. You will then "become" the character and work in a group to create a tableau. A *tableau* is a purposeful arrangement of characters frozen as if in a painting or a photograph. In your tableau, convey as much information as you can about the characters and their relationships.
4. Read your card aloud to the others in the group, along with any additional information from the cast of characters in your copy of *Romeo and Juliet*.
5. Practice arranging yourselves according to your descriptions. Assign one student the role of director so he or she can give the group feedback to help you create the effect you want. Think about the following as you prepare your tableau:
   - Body positions (who you stand next to, distance, and how you pose)
   - Postures
   - Facial expressions
   - Gestures
   - Simple props to convey your character
6. After you have rehearsed, pose your tableau. Create a freeze-frame image for your classmates. Then either step out of the tableau one at a time and tell why you chose to place yourself as you did, or have your director explain your group's choices.

WORD CONNECTIONS

An analogy may help understanding with a second word that describes the first. For example, a tableau may present a striking scene of a group of people. Complete the following analogy.

tableau : group :: flock : birds, sheep

Write a sentence describing the relationship of the two sets of words.

A tableau is a group of people, while a flock is a group of birds or sheep.

continued

7. Using what you learned from the tableau and the *Dramatis Personae* (Cast of Characters) in your edition of *Romeo and Juliet*, write each of the characters listed below under the correct family heading. Highlight or draw asterisks next to the names of the two **protagonists**.

Prince Escalus	Romeo	Juliet
Benvolio	Mercutio	Tybalt
Count Paris	Nurse	Friar Lawrence
Lord Capulet	Lady Capulet	Apothecary (druggist)
Lord Montague	Lady Montague	Peter
Sampson	Balthasar	Abraham

LITERARY TERMS

Protagonists are the main, or most important, characters in a play.

Capulet	Montague	Unaffiliated

8. To help you keep track of the characters, create a bookmark to use while you are reading *Romeo and Juliet*. Fold a sheet of paper in half lengthwise, and write the Capulets on one side, the Montagues on the other side, and unaffiliated characters inside. Write what you know about each character.

9. On separate paper, reflect on how well your group worked together. Describe the effective speaking and listening skills that members of your group practiced, and explain why they were effective.

Steps:

5 After students have some understanding of the characters, instruct them to **rehearse** by placing themselves in a tableau as if in a freeze-frame photograph. Students should position themselves in a way that conveys the characters' relationships, using elements such as body positioning, posture, facial expression, frozen gestures, and perhaps simple props to convey information. Remind the groups that the audience will need to be able to see all of the characters.

6 Have the groups present their tableaux for the class. If possible, take a photograph of each tableau and save it for use later in the unit. At the end of each presentation, have each student step out of the tableau and present his or her character and positioning/visual delivery. The director might be asked to explain each character and relationship instead.

7 Tell students to **take notes** on the **graphic organizer** on the student page to categorize the characters as Capulets, Montagues, or Unaffiliated. You might have them begin by sorting the name cards in a kinesthetic exercise. Be sure that students can identify Romeo and Juliet as the protagonists of the play.

8 Have students use the completed graphic organizer as the basis for a bookmark they can refer to when reading the play. They could fold a sheet of paper in half and write Capulets on one side, Montagues on the other side, and unaffiliated characters inside the fold.

9 Finally, ask students to evaluate independently how their group worked together. You might ask each student to create a pie chart, showing a representation of each person's contribution, and then rate the overall success of the group on a scale of 1 to 5.

ACTIVITY 4.4

The Prologue: So Much from One Sonnet

Materials:

- Prologue
- Dictionaries
- Vocabulary Notebook

Purpose:

- To understand tragedy
- To recognize the function of the chorus
- To reinforce understanding of the Shakespearean sonnet
- To memorize, paraphrase, and deliver verse

Steps:

1 Remind students of the work they did with sonnets in Unit 3 and have them **mark the text** by writing the rhyme scheme of the Prologue on the student page.

2 Explain the function of the chorus in the play—a single actor who performs the Prologue, an overview of the play.

3 To introduce students to the sounds of Shakespeare's language, lead a **shared reading** of the Prologue. Or show film adaptations so students can see different versions of the Prologue.

4 Pose the following questions to gauge students' comprehension:

How many families (households) are involved in this fight? (two) How long has it been going on? (years; the grudge is ancient) How do the lovers stop the fighting? (with their "end")

ACTIVITY 4.4

The Prologue: So Much from One Sonnet

SUGGESTED LEARNING STRATEGIES: Marking the Text, Diffusing, Think-Pair-Share, Predicting, Oral Interpretation

ACADEMIC VOCABULARY

A **tragedy** is a dramatic play that tells the story of a main character, usually of a noble class, who meets an untimely and unhappy death or downfall, often because of a specific character flaw or twist of fate.

The story of ***Romeo and Juliet*** was well known to those who attended the play in Shakespeare's day. The audience knew the end result would be a **tragedy**. The Prologue served as an introductory speech where an actor, in this case probably just one man called the "Chorus," provided the audience with a brief outline for the plot.

In this case, the Prologue is a 14-line poem with a defined structure that is called a Shakespearean **sonnet**. Using what you learned about sonnets in Unit 3, label the lines of the Prologue to show its **rhyme scheme**.

Listen to the Prologue as it is read aloud. Close your eyes and envision an actor speaking the words. In the space below, describe how the Prologue aids your understanding of the play.

GRAMMAR & USAGE

The general sentence pattern in modern English is subject-verb-complement. Shakespeare frequently uses **inverted order**, in which the verb precedes the subject.

Example: LADY MONTAGUE: "*O where* ***is*** (verb) *Romeo?* (subject). ***Saw*** (verb) ***you*** (subject) *him today?*"

GRAMMAR & USAGE EXTENSION

- You might wish to explain that, although Shakespeare's kind of inversion is no longer in use, we still use an inverted sentence pattern in questions and in sentences beginning with *Here* and *There*. Additionally, inverting normal word order is a way to achieve emphasis or build suspense, as in this sentence: Into the dark cave strode the intrepid explorer.
- Remind students that a verb must agree with its subject, even when the subject follows the verb.

Sonnet PROLOGUE

from *The Tragedy of Romeo and Juliet* by William Shakespeare

ABOUT THE AUTHOR
William Shakespeare (1564–1616) is considered one of the most gifted and perceptive writers in the English language. He left his home in Stratford-upon-Avon for London, where he pursued a career as an actor. He was more successful as a playwright and poet, however, producing more than three dozen plays, which are still performed centuries after his death.

Enter Chorus

Two households, both alike in dignity, A
In fair Verona, where we lay our scene, B
From ancient grudge break to new mutiny, A
Where civil blood makes civil hands unclean. B
From forth the fatal loins of these two foes C
A pair of star-crossed lovers take their life, D
Whose misadventured piteous overthrows C
Doth with their death bury their parents' strife. D
The fearful passage of their death-marked love, E
And the continuance of their parents' rage, F
Which, but their children's end, naught could remove, E
Is now the two hours' traffic of our stage; F
The which if you with patient ears attend, G
What here shall miss, our toil shall strive to mend. G

My Notes

WORD CONNECTIONS
Prologue **contains the root *-log-*, from the Greek word *logos*, meaning *word*. This root also appears in *dialogue*, *catalogue*, and *eulogy*. The prefix *pro-* means "before."**

Steps:

5 Some students have likely picked up the gist of the Prologue, but it would be helpful to use a **think aloud** and paraphrase the Prologue. Invite students to make notes in the margins as you share.

6 Have students work in pairs or small groups to **diffuse** the text of the Prologue. Working with partners, students should identify unfamiliar words and replace them with synonyms they know.

Steps:

7 Ask students to review the **word map graphic organizer** for *drama* in their **Vocabulary Notebooks**. Then read aloud the definition of the word ***tragedy***. Ask students to draw in their notebooks a graphic representation of the masks of comedy and tragedy. (You may need to show students an example.) Have students label the masks. Based on their understanding of the Prologue, ask students to **predict** which kind of play they will read.

8 Underneath the tragedy mask, ask students to generate a list of words they associate with ***tragedy***. Allow students to **think-pair-share** their ideas. Then discuss how tragedy is different from comedy. Have students save their notes in their **Vocabulary Notebooks**.

9 Once students have an understanding of the Prologue, use **choral reading** to boost students' confidence in speaking Shakespeare's words. Divide the class in half and direct the sides to take turns reading in unison, alternating lines of the Prologue. Let the class read this way a couple of times to build fluency. You may also want students to read in pairs to help build their confidence.

10 Continue guiding a whole-class choral reading as you assign a smaller number of students to read certain lines in unison. Have students number off from 1 through 7 (or assign letters A through G), but don't have them change seats. Using the markings students made when they labeled the rhyme scheme of the sonnet, assign the 1's to read in unison the lines labeled A, the 2's to read in unison the lines labeled B, and so on, with the 7's reading the lines labeled G. Again, repetition of this choral reading allows all students to build fluency with Shakespeare's language.

The Prologue: So Much from One Sonnet

Shakespeare's plays and poems are written in Modern English, although the language sounds quite different from the English we speak today. It is possible to understand Shakespeare's language if you know a few strategies.

Go back and read through the Prologue and underline words that you do not know. Try to guess at the meanings, if using context clues help. Then, use a dictionary to determine the meaning of the unfamiliar words. Write a synonym for each unknown word. For example, the word *mutiny* appears in line 3. One dictionary defines it as a noun that means "an open rebellion against authorities, especially by soldiers or sailors against their officers." A mutiny is a rebellion, so you may write *rebellion* above *mutiny*.

1. Review your word map for *drama*. You have probably seen the graphic representation of drama—the comedy and tragedy masks. Sketch those masks beside each other on the same sheet of paper. Underneath **Tragedy**, write a bulleted list of words that come to mind. You might find some of these words in the Prologue.

Based on what you have learned from the Prologue, why do you think *Romeo and Juliet* is called a tragedy?

Later in this unit, you will be acting scenes from the play. Practicing reading aloud in unison with your classmates can help you get used to speaking Shakespeare's words. After you participate in several choral readings of the Prologue, rate your comfort level with saying Shakespeare's words, with 1 being "I do not feel comfortable at all" and 10 being "I'm ready for Broadway!"

1 2 3 4 5 6 7 8 9 10

2. Explain your self-rating:

11 Tell students that when they read Shakespeare's verse, they should not pause at the ends of the lines, but rather at the punctuation marks. Create small groups and direct the first group to read only to a punctuation mark, at which point the second group reads.

12 This would be a good time to review iambic pentameter, practicing the rhythm with the Prologue.

ACTIVITY 4.4 continued

An important skill in drama is the ability to memorize lines. This is another method that can help you get used to Shakespeare's language. To practice this skill, you will memorize the Prologue.

Memorizing is easier than it seems; you have memorized hundreds of lines from TV shows, movies, jokes, and songs. This is no harder; it just takes a little patience and practice.

Start slowly and work on a line or two at a time and visualize what is happening in each line. Practice by saying the lines into a tape recorder or writing them down. Say them aloud to yourself until you can finally write or say the entire Prologue without help.

Below you will find the Prologue, but some of the words are left out. Once you think you know the Prologue, fill in the blanks. Keep trying until you know the Prologue and can fill in all the blanks.

Two ______________, both alike in ______________,

In fair ______________, where we ______________ our scene,

From ancient ______________ break to new ______________,

Where civil ______________ makes civil ______________ unclean.

From forth the fatal ______________ of these two ______________

A ______________ of ______________ lovers take their life;

Whose ______________ piteous overthrows

Doth with their death ______________ their parents' ______________.

The fearful ______________ of their death-marked ______________,

And the continuance of their parents' ______________,

Which, but their ______________ end, naught could ______________,

Is now the two hours' ______________ of our ______________;

The which if you with ______________ ears attend,

What here shall ______________, our toil shall strive to ______________.

Essential Question 2: How have the strategies I have learned this year helped me to be a better reader, writer, speaker, and listener? What is your initial response to this question?

ACTIVITY 4.4 *continued*

Steps:

13 Explain that for Embedded Assessment 1, students will perform a scene from ***The Tragedy of Romeo and Juliet.*** The skills of memorizing words, phrases, and lines will be important to acquire. Allow students time to use the exercise on the student page to memorize the Prologue. Then ask volunteers to either write the Prologue from memory or perform an **oral interpretation** for the class.

14 If you want to extend students' oral interpretations, ask volunteers to audition for the part of the Chorus. Hold a mock open-mike competition to see who performs the best Chorus.

15 Guide students to respond to the **Essential Question**, "How have the strategies I have learned this year helped me to be a better reader, writer, speaker, listener, critical thinker?" Encourage students to take note of the strategies they used during this activity as well as those they used independently or in small groups.

ACTIVITY 4.5

A Sorrowful Son, a Dutiful Daughter

Materials:

- Copy of ***Romeo and Juliet*** (Act I, Scenes I-4)

Purpose:

- To recognize evolution in the English language
- To understand and analyze syntax
- To analyze author's use of figurative language

Steps:

1 The first part of this activity examines Romeo's state of mind at the beginning of the play. Students should know that the play begins with Romeo pining over a young woman, Rosaline, who does not return his love. Have students **paraphrase** Montague's description of Romeo's behavior. Discuss what Romeo's behavior suggests about his state of mind.

2 Students may be confused by Shakespeare's use of inverted syntax (sentence structure). You may need to review the grammatical concepts of subject and verb. Guide students through the process of comparing the syntax of Shakespearean and modern speech, using the examples on the student page. Demonstrate the inversion of Lady Capulet's words by writing the words on index cards and using them as **manipulatives**.

3 Students may also feel intimidated by Shakespeare's use of archaic words. Creating a glossary of commonly used words can lessen their confusion. Add a section to your **Word Wall** for the archaic words covered in this activity. Suggest that students also use the glossary to **diffuse** archaic words like ***thou*** with contemporary replacements.

ACTIVITY 4.5

A Sorrowful Son, a Dutiful Daughter

SUGGESTED LEARNING STRATEGIES: **Diffusing, Think-Pair-Share, Paraphrasing**

In Act 1, Romeo's parents are concerned about their son because he has been behaving strangely. After the street brawl in Act I, Scene 1, Lady Capulet asks Romeo's friend Benvolio:

> "O, where is Romeo? Saw you him today?
>
> Right glad I am he was not at this fray."

Notice the way Lady Capulet reverses the order of the subject and the verb in her second question. We would probably say, "I am glad" not "glad I am." We would also say, "Did you see him today?" instead of "Saw you him today?" Putting the verb before the subject is called *inversion*.

1. Try rewriting these inverted sentences the way we would say them today.
   - Pining over unreturned love is our hero Romeo.
   - A promise to stay pure has his love made.

Romeo's friend Benvolio tries to cheer up his love-sick friend, but Romeo is not interested in his solutions. He says to Benvolio:

> "Farewell. Thou canst not teach me to forget."

Thou and *canst* are archaic, or old, forms of words. *Thou* means *you*; *canst* means "can." Romeo is saying, "Goodbye. You cannot teach me to forget."

2. Using *can* as a model, try to determine the meanings of these words used in Shakespeare's day.

canst	can
didst	
hadst	
wouldst	
dost	

In Act 1, Scene 1, Benvolio proposes that Romeo compare Rosaline with the other lovely girls at the feast. Don't let Benvolio's words *thee* and *thy* confuse you; these are archaic forms of *you* and *your*. Benvolio is saying, "I will make you think your swan is a crow."

> "Compare her face with some that I shall show,
>
> And I will make thee think thy swan a crow."

3. Use this glossary to update the lines from the play that follow by writing the more modern word above the older one in the sentences below.

thee: you	*art:* are
thy: your	*thou:* you
hath: has	*mine:* my

Dost thou not laugh?

This love that *thou hast* shown/*Doth* add more grief to too much of *mine* own.

Why, Romeo, *art thou* mad?

Ay, *mine* own fortune in my misery.

4. When we first meet Juliet (Act I, Scene 4), she is an obedient and courteous daughter. When her mother tells her that Paris is interested in her, Juliet answers that she will honor her mother's wishes and consider him. In this conversation, Shakespeare uses figurative language (metaphor, simile, personification) to paint word pictures of characters. Look for three comparisons that the Nurse and Lady Capulet use to describe Paris vividly. What does each say about Paris?

To what is Paris compared?	What does this comparison tell you about Paris?

5. Work in pairs to discuss what Lady Capulet and the Nurse value about Paris. Does this match what you would look for?

Steps:

4 The next part of the activity introduces the character of Juliet, who is presented as an obedient daughter. Discuss Juliet's relationships with her mother and the Nurse.

5 Next, examine Shakespeare's use of vivid language to describe Paris. Point out how the character is compared to a wax figure, a flower, and a beautifully bound book. Have students **think-pair-share** what the Nurse and Juliet's mother suggest about Paris through these comparisons.

ACTIVITY 4.6
A Timeline of Events

Materials:

- Copy of *Romeo and Juliet*

Purpose:

- To identify plot events
- To analyze how plot is advanced

Steps:

1 Point out the **graphic organizer** to students at the beginning of the play and explain that the action in the play unfolds quickly and over a short period of time. At the end of every act or major plot event, have students revisit the graphic organizer to identify the act, scene, and event. Creating a timeline to display in your classroom during the reading of the play can be a teaching tool as well.

2 At the end of the play, ask students to talk about the timeline of events in **discussion groups**. If time allows, have them discuss or write about the following questions:

- Why do you think Shakespeare compresses the action into so few days?
- What does the time compression say about real love or love at first sight?
- What do the words ***rash*** and ***impetuous*** mean and how do they apply to Romeo and Juliet?

ACTIVITY 4.6

A Timeline of Events

SUGGESTED LEARNING STRATEGIES: Graphic Organizer, Discussion Groups

Scholars have indicated that the action of this play occurs in a short period of time. At the end of each act or major plot event, take notes in the following chart to help you review and summarize the play.

Day	Act(s)/Scene(s)	Setting(s)	Plot Events
Sunday a.m. **p.m.**			
Monday a.m. **p.m.**			
Tuesday a.m. **p.m.**			
Wednesday a.m. **p.m.**			
Thursday a.m. **p.m.**			
Early Friday a.m.			

You Are Cordially Invited

ACTIVITY 4.7

SUGGESTED LEARNING STRATEGIES: Role Playing

Below are famous lines from *Romeo and Juliet*. Choose one that appeals to you and practice saying it quietly. When the line feels familiar, rehearse it again, using movement, gestures, inflection, and intonation to convey the feelings behind it.

- How does this rehearsal help you make sense of the line?
- Which character do you think said the line, and what do you think it means in the play?

WORD CONNECTIONS

Intonation contains the root *-ton-*, from the Greek word *tonos*, meaning "a stretching tone or pitch." The root also appears in the words *tonic* and *astonish*. The suffix *-ation* indicates that the word is a noun.

"O Romeo, Romeo! Wherefore art thou Romeo?"	Spoken by:
"Oh, I am fortune's fool!"	
"Good night, good night! Parting is such sweet sorrow."	
"But, soft! What light through yonder window breaks? It is the East, and Juliet is the sun!"	
"What's in a name? That which we call a rose By any other name would smell as sweet."	
"A plague o' both your houses!"	
"O happy dagger! This is thy sheath; there rest, and let me die."	
"My only love sprung from my only hate! Too early seen unknown and known too late!"	
"O true apothecary! Thy drugs are quick. Thus with a kiss I die."	
"For never was a story of more woe Than this of Juliet and her Romeo."	

In *Romeo and Juliet*, the nobles speak in poetry, using **formal diction**, while the servants speak in prose, using **informal diction**. Keep the level of language in mind as you create an invitation from Lord Capulet to the feast (Act I, Scene 2).

LITERARY TERMS

Diction is a writer or speaker's choice of words.

ACTIVITY 4.7

You Are Cordially Invited

Materials:

- Copy of ***Romeo and Juliet*** (Act I, Scene 2)
- Materials for making masks (construction paper, markers, glue, scissors)

Purpose:

- To demonstrate appropriate oral delivery
- To use simple props
- To analyze author's use of language structure, distinguishing between verse and prose
- To apply understanding of elements of visual delivery

Steps:

1 Help students prepare for the performances they will give in Embedded Assessment 1 by asking them to **rehearse** a famous line from the play until they can say it without reading it. You may assign lines to students or allow them to choose from the list on the student page.

2 Invite students to create masks for the character whose lines they speak. Provide construction paper and other materials, such as beads, sequins, feathers, ribbon, buttons, stickers, glitter, tissue paper, and crayons. The masks should be colorful, creative, and fun. Refer to the poem in Activity 4.2, "We Wear the Mask." Ask students how the wearing of masks might affect a celebration.

3 Explain that in ***Romeo and Juliet***, the nobles speak in poetry while the servants speak in prose. Discuss how diction signals this distinction between social classes.

4 After they read Act I, Scene 2, instruct students to create an attractive invitation from Lord Capulet to the feast, keeping their audience in mind. If possible, display students' work in the room.

5 The final activity before students read the scene would be a type of **drama game**, a cast party. Invite students to bring their invitations, wear their masks, and **role play** their famous lines to each other. From time to time, give a signal for all the students to halt and try to determine to whom they are speaking. At your signal, they should begin mingling again until they have spoken to everyone.

ACTIVITY 4.8

Comparing Film Interpretations: An Old Accustomed Feast

Materials:

- Two or more film interpretations of *Romeo and Juliet*
- Vocabulary Notebook
- Lyrics to songs in film interpretations (optional)

Purpose:

- To understand interpretation and theatrical elements
- To compare and evaluate filmed productions
- To compare and contrast media versions with written text

Steps:

TEACHER TO TEACHER Try to obtain at least two different film interpretations of ***Romeo and Juliet*** to use as **visual prompts** for discussion. The most accessible films may be the Franco Zeffirelli version and the Baz Luhrmann version. See Unit 4 About the Unit for a complete list of film versions.

1 In Zeffirelli's interpretation, show Clip 1, Scenes 5–6 (0:22:49–0:38:47). Begin when guests are being welcomed to the party and end after Juliet realizes who Romeo is. In Luhrmann's interpretation, show Clip 2, scenes 8–12 (0:25:30–0: 33:12). Begin after Romeo submerges his face in the water and end after the Nurse tells Juliet who Romeo is.

2 Have students use the **graphic organizer** on the student page for **note taking** and to engage in a **close reading** of the theatrical elements of each film. Have them focus primarily on costumes and music. You may assign a row of students certain elements on which to concentrate and they can then share in a **jigsaw**.

ACTIVITY 4.8

Comparing Film Interpretations: An Old Accustomed Feast

SUGGESTED LEARNING STRATEGIES: **Graphic Organizer, Close Reading, Revisiting Prior Work, Notetaking, Drafting**

ACADEMIC VOCABULARY

An **interpretation** is the act of making meaning from something, such as a text. **Theatrical elements** are physical, visual, and oral means the director uses to convey meaning.

Your teacher will show you the same scene from at least two different film **interpretations** of *Romeo and Juliet*. An interpretation is based on the reader, actor, or director's own experiences as well as on the actual words of the text. As you watch, write notes in the chart below, paying attention to the **theatrical elements** of costumes and music in each version. Ask yourself, "Why would the director choose those costumes and music for the first meeting between Romeo and Juliet?"

Act I, Scene 5: The Capulets' party — first meeting between Romeo and Juliet

Version: Director's Name	Costumes: Colors, Style	Music: Vocals, Instruments, Lyrics	What is the effect of the director's choices?

3 If you choose, print out the lyrics to theme songs from both films ("What Is Youth?" and "Kissing You," available through an online search) to compare the similarities. A search using the key terms "Romeo and Juliet + lyrics" should offer useful results.

4 When students have compiled their notes, lead a class discussion in which students compare the two film versions and discuss the effectiveness of both directors' craft.

In Unit 2, you considered the similarities and differences between reading a text and viewing a film. Now consider the similarities and differences between viewing a film and watching a live performance. Fill out the following graphic organizer. Consider the following prompts to help focus your answers:

- What can a film do that live performance cannot and vice versa?
- What tools and strategies do directors of plays and directors of films share? What tools and strategies are different?
- Are you more entertained by watching movies or watching live performances? Why?

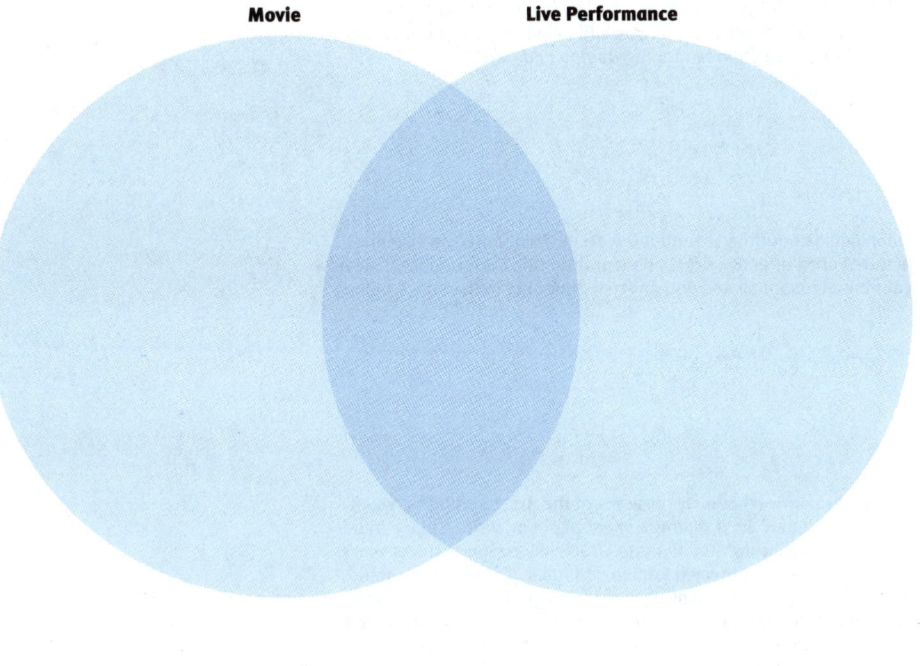

© 2011 College Board. All rights reserved.

Steps:

5 Students should now consider the tools that film directors use to convey meaning. Have students use the Venn diagram to identify how a stage director's tools are similar to and different from the tools of a film director. This conversation will be most effective if students have seen a live or a filmed stage production.

ACTIVITY 4.8 *continued*

Steps:

6 ***Interpretation*** and ***theatrical elements*** are academic vocabulary terms for this unit. Now that students have been introduced to these concepts, have them reinforce their understanding. Begin with ***interpretation***, asking students to work with a partner to come up with a definition and an original sentence that uses the word. After students have come to an agreement, they should join with another pair and compare their work. Allow pairs to then revise their definitions or sentences, based on their conversations with another pair.

7 Ask students to create a **graphic organizer** such as a bubble cluster or an outline, with Theatrical Elements as the main topic and Costumes and Music as secondary topics. Have them add additional theatrical elements as they come up. They should save their work in **Vocabulary Notebooks**.

8 At this point, have students **revisit** their answers to the **Essential Question**, "What are the essential features of an effective drama and/or dramatic performance?"

9 Have students respond to the writing prompt at the bottom of their page. Make your expectations clear, as the topic could be addressed in a paragraph or in an essay. You might consider allowing students to **draft** in other genres, such as poetry, as they express their thoughts.

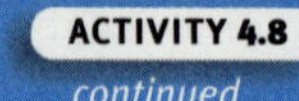

Comparing Film Interpretations: An Old Accustomed Feast

You have seen two interpretations of the same scene from *Romeo and Juliet*. **Interpretation** is an academic vocabulary word for this unit. Work with a partner to come up with your own definition and an original sentence that uses this word.

Theatrical elements include sets, props, costumes, lighting, and sound effects—anything that helps bring a story to life on the stage. On separate paper, create a graphic organizer to help you remember these elements. Use theatrical elements as the main topic, with costumes and music as the secondary topics. You will be adding additional theatrical elements as you continue reading *Romeo and Juliet*.

Think again about the Essential Question, "What are the essential features of an effective drama and/or dramatic performance?" Review your initial response and add any new thoughts in the space below.

Writing Prompt: What is the essence of the first meeting between Romeo and Juliet? On a separate sheet of paper, write a piece that explains which interpretation more effectively captures the essence of the first meeting between Romeo and Juliet. Your writing should include a thesis or analytical statement along with textual support from your notes and reflective commentary. Be sure to make specific references to theatrical elements from the film, such as costumes, music, props, and actions.

Persuasive Prompt

ACTIVITY 4.9

SUGGESTED LEARNING STRATEGIES: **Brainstorming, Graphic Organizer, Drafting, Sketching**

Below is a writing prompt based on ideas from Act I of *Romeo and Juliet*. Read the prompt and think about the writing strategies you can use. Think carefully about how best to proceed.

Before you begin writing, look over the writing strategies and identify the ones that you plan to use for prewriting, drafting, revising, and editing. Then respond to the writing prompt.

Name of Strategy	Why I Plan to Use This Strategy

Writing Situation

Your best friend has met a boy or girl at a party and has fallen in love. You know that your friend's family will be set against the relationship because the boy or girl is from a family with a different set of values. Your best friend is unhappy about the situation; he or she does not want to give up the relationship, but how can it continue if the family is against it? Think about reasons your friend might use to convince his or her family to accept the relationship.

Writing Prompt: Write a letter to your best friend with suggestions that may convince family members to allow her or him to date the boy or girl. Keep your audience's concerns in mind as you think through your writing plan. Also consider the persuasive appeals you learned in Unit I.

ACTIVITY 4.9

Persuasive Prompt

Materials:

- Vocabulary Notebook

Purpose:

- To compose a persuasive text in response to a prompt
- To reflect on the use of strategies

Steps:

1 This activity will help students prepare for the metacognitive writing assignment in Embedded Assessment 2.

2 Read aloud or have students read the writing prompt on the student page. After they have read and understood the situation and the prompt, they may want to **brainstorm** what "different values" means to them.

3 Then ask students use the **graphic organizer** on the student page to record the writing strategies they will use to address the prompt. Elicit discussion from students about strategies they have used in the past. You might also want to refer them to the SpringBoard Learning Strategies charts in the Resources section of their books.

4 After **drafting**, and during the revision stage of the writing process, have students exchange letters with a partner. Suggest that partners read the letters from the viewpoint of the friend's parents and evaluate the effectiveness of the support.

Differentiating Instruction:

To help scaffold the writing process, remind students of the elements of argumentation presented in Unit 1. Encourage students to use these elements (hook, claim, concessions/refutations, support, and summary/call to action) as an outline for their drafts. As students evaluate each other's drafts, have them identify each of these elements in the partner's paper.

Extend the activity by allowing students to consider the prompt overnight. Then present the persuasive prompt as an in-class timed writing. Students will need to manage their time and use prewriting strategies that are quick and help them to successfully organize their essays for completion within the time limit.

© 2011 College Board. All rights reserved.

Steps:

5 Explain that ***metacognition*** is one of the academic vocabulary words in Unit 4. Guide students to use roots and affixes to make sense of this word. Write ***metacognition*** on the board and demonstrate a **think-aloud**. ***Meta-*** means "higher"; ***cognition*** means "thinking, understanding;" ***–ition*** indicates that the word is a noun.

6 Ask students to **sketch** an illustration or symbolic representation of the word ***metacognition***. They should write a caption that explains the visual. These should be saved for later use in their **Vocabulary Notebooks**.

7 After students revise and edit their letters, ask them to reflect on their use of strategies, using the rating system provided. Remind them that their reflection is an example of metacognition.

Persuasive Prompt

ACADEMIC VOCABULARY

Metacognition is the ability to know and be aware of one's own thought processes. It is a tool that helps students identify and evaluate their learning goals.

In your vocabulary notebook, use roots and affixes to determine the meaning of the academic vocabulary word **metacognition**. Create a visual representation of metacognition and write a caption below your sketch. Save the sketch in your vocabulary notebook for later use.

After you write your letter, decide how effective the strategies that you selected were and note if you used strategies that you had not originally planned to use. You may use these ratings and descriptions:

1 The strategy worked well for the assignment; I would use it again for a similar writing task.
2 The strategy worked pretty well, but I found that I needed other strategies to complete the task.
3 The strategy did not work well for this writing task; it might work better for a different writing task.
4 The strategy did not work well for me; in fact, I may never use this strategy again.
5 Although I thought I might, I did not use this strategy after all.

Strategy	Rating/Description	Notes/Explanation

Developing Dramaturges

ACTIVITY 4.10

SUGGESTED LEARNING STRATEGIES: **Brainstorming, KWHL Chart, Notetaking**

Review everything you have heard, read, or learned about Shakespeare, Elizabethan England, and the play *Romeo and Juliet*. There are many interesting topics to research, such as male actors playing the parts of girls or girls marrying at age 14. From your recent exposure to the play and other background information, generate a list of topics that you find interesting.

List topics that you are interested in:

Choose the topic that most interests you at this point:

Is it about Shakespeare, Elizabethan England, or the play itself?

On a separate sheet of paper, create a KWHL chart for the topic that most interests you, filling in the first three columns.

1. Your teacher will have you share your topic and one of the questions with the class. Then give your questions to somebody who is interested in that topic and have them answer the questions as best they can. They may not know all the answers, since you have not yet researched most topics related to the author and the play. The idea here is to find topics that are interesting that you will want to research. You will, in turn, answer someone else's questions.
2. In addition, try to offer ideas for how the other student can find out more information about his or her topic, and he or she will try to give you additional ideas.

ACTIVITY 4.10
Developing Dramaturges

Materials:

- Copy of ***Romeo and Juliet***
- Background information on social and historical influences on ***Romeo and Juliet***
- Vocabulary Notebook

Purpose:

- To formulate research topics grounded in a text
- To use print and electronic resources to research information

Steps:

TEACHER TO TEACHER An important role in an acting company is that of the dramaturge. The dramaturge helps the director make informed decisions by providing context and information for the play. The role of dramaturge is one that students will take on when they form their acting companies, but in this activity all students will conduct research on the role of the dramaturge.

1 Now that students have read Act I, they are ready to research historical and social influences on ***Romeo and Juliet***. Begin with a student-friendly overview, based on picture books, such Diane Stanley's biography ***Bard of Avon: The Story of William Shakespeare***, or ***William Shakespeare & the Globe*** by Aliki. Or offer students information you have researched that can be presented visually. Students should **take notes** on topics that interest them.

2 Have the students individually list topics about the background of ***Romeo and Juliet***, its author, or its text. Lead the class in a **brainstorming** session, listing their suggestions on the board. Once the students' ideas are exhausted, guide them to additional topics, including:

- Shakespeare's biography
- Queen Elizabeth I's influence on the arts and on Shakespeare specifically
- life in Elizabethan England, including the economy, prominent beliefs, courtship and marriage customs, and popular forms of entertainment
- Elizabethan theater, including gender roles; costuming, props, and scenery; traveling troupes; patrons; acting companies; theaters such as the Swan, the Rose, and the Globe
- Topics that will help students understand ***Romeo and Juliet*** in particular include Petrarch's sonnets, Verona, falconry terms, and fencing.

3 You may also choose to allow students to research films based on ***Romeo and Juliet***, including information such as the year it was filmed, the ages of the actors, the style and body of work of the director, the reception of the film when it was released, awards the film won, and so on. This presentation will be most meaningful if made the next time you show clips from the films.

ACTIVITY 4.10 *continued*

Steps:

4 Now have students formulate a **KWHL chart** on separate paper from their chosen topics. They should include what they know, what they want to know and how they might find out; later they will fill in what they have learned.

5 Students should then share their topics with the class so that everyone can hear the types of topics and questions that have been generated.

6 Then ask students to exchange their KWHL charts with partners whose topics also interest them. In discussion, students should ask "Want to know" questions. They should also try to offer each other suggestions about where to look for information.

7 In pairs, groups, or independently, students should conduct research into their selected topics. The research activity is meant to be informal and require a minimal amount of time—one class period at most. Ask students to share their research results in a brief oral presentation, with visuals. Or allow them to share their findings in a **jigsaw** format or a gallery walk. Make sure students provide bibliographies for their sources.

8 Point out to students that this activity is designed to build background knowledge that will enhance their reading of ***Romeo and Juliet*** and their performances. Now that they have been introduced to the role of the dramaturge, they should add the word to their word maps for drama that they saved in their **Vocabulary Notebooks**.

ACTIVITY 4.10 *continued*

Developing Dramaturges

Share one of your questions and its possible answer with the whole class. Take notes below while others are presenting topics.

Interesting topics I heard from others:

You will now take on the role of *dramaturge*, an important member of an acting company. The dramaturge helps the director make informed decisions by providing pertinent information related to the play. Add *dramaturge* to your word map for *drama*, and write an explanation of the role.

1. Using the appropriate style as directed by your teacher, research your topic of interest and prepare to share your findings with your classmates. Keep in mind that the information you and your classmates learn from each other will help you better understand the play and will enhance your performance of a scene from the play.
2. Keep track of your sources so you can create a bibliography or works cited page later. In addition, make notes about your research process and focus questions for a later reflection. As you continue your research, consider the quantity and quality of information you are finding. Do not be afraid to modify your process or change your focus questions to achieve better results.

I Pray You, Speak Plainly, Please

ACTIVITY 4.11

SUGGESTED LEARNING STRATEGIES: Oral Interpretation

Below are some chunks of text from Act II, Scene 2 of *Romeo and Juliet*. With a friend, translate the lines into the other forms below or forms suggested by your teacher. After you read the examples, think of at least one other format for translation, such as a foreign language or a secret code.

Translation Formats

Standard English: The widely accepted way of speaking.

Computer messaging: Instant Messenger and e-mail chat.

Examples:

Original Text:	O Romeo, Romeo! Wherefore art thou Romeo? Deny thy father and refuse thy name! Or, if thou wilt not, be but sworn my love, And I'll no longer be a Capulet.
Standard English:	O Romeo, Romeo. Why does your name have to be Romeo? Give up your father and your name; or if you can't, then tell me you love me and I will marry you and no longer be a Capulet.
Computer messaging:	O R. R.! Why r u a R.? Deny ur father and refuse ur name. Or, tell me u luv me 2 n I will no longer b a C.
Other:	

ACTIVITY 4.11

I Pray You, Speak Plainly, Please

Materials:

- Copy of ***Romeo and Juliet*** (Act II, Scene 2)

Purpose:

- To translate Shakespearean language into current English
- To demonstrate appropriate vocal delivery

Steps:

1 Have students work together to decipher and "translate" Shakespeare's lines from Act II, Scene 2, on the student pages, to current English. Ask them to translate the lines several ways, including into Standard English — the language we expect in their essays — and computer lingo — instant messenging or e-mail slang. Encourage students to think of other dialects or ways of speaking,

Teacher Notes

I Pray You, Speak Plainly, Please

1. JULIET: "What's in a name? That which we call a rose
By any other name would smell as sweet."

Standard English:

Other translation of your choice:

2. ROMEO: "With love's light wings did I o'er-perch these walls;
For stony limits cannot hold love out"

Standard English:

Other translation of your choice:

3. JULIET: "Or if thou think'st I am too quickly won,
I'll frown, and be perverse, and say thee nay,
So thou wilt woo; but else, not for the world.
In truth, fair Montague, I am too fond,
And therefore thou mayst think my 'havior light;"

Standard English:

Other translation of your choice:

4. ROMEO: "O blessed, blessed night! I am afeard,
Being in night, all this is but a dream,
Too flattering-sweet to be substantial."

Standard English:

Other translation of your choice:

Choose one of these sets of lines and rehearse saying it in a translation of your choice. Get feedback on your pitch (how high or low your voice is) and the rate or speed at which you speak.

Steps:

2 Give students time to **rehearse** speaking Shakespeare's lines in the new formats. They should focus on elements of vocal variety such as pitch and rate. Allow students to share with the class or with a wider audience, if possible.

ACTIVITY 4.12

Comparing Film Interpretations: The Balcony Scene

Materials:

- Two different film interpretations of *Romeo and Juliet*
- Vocabulary Notebook

Purpose:

- To compare and evaluate media productions
- To compare and contrast media versions with written text
- To analyze blocking in a scene
- To develop a plan for blocking in performances
- To plan and reflect on use of strategies

Steps:

1 Explain that the scene students are about to view as a **visual prompt** is the famous "balcony scene," one that many students may already know. If any students conducted research about the film for Activity 4.11, this would be a good time to ask them to share their findings.

2 In Zeffirelli's interpretation, show Clip 1, Scene 7 (0:40:18–0:51:39). The scene begins when Romeo says, "He jests at scars that never felt a wound" and ends when Romeo leaves Juliet's home. Show the same scene in Luhrmann's interpretation, Clip 2, Scene 14 (0:35:38–0:45:05).

3 The **graphic organizer** on the student page has three rows if you want to add a third film. Have students watch the film versions of the scene closely and **take notes** on staging. You may want to assign specific columns to certain students and then have them **share** with the large group.

4 Lead a class discussion in which students share the information they recorded on their charts. Explain that just as an author chooses words carefully, a director chooses the set and the actors' movements carefully.

ACTIVITY 4.12

Comparing Film Interpretations: The Balcony Scene

SUGGESTED LEARNING STRATEGIES: Graphic Organizer, Drafting, Brainstorming, Notetaking, Discussion Groups

You will view at least two different film versions of the same famous scene from *Romeo and Juliet*. This scene is the balcony scene in which Romeo and Juliet first declare their love for each other. Watch closely and take notes on the chart provided below.

1. **The focus of this chart is staging. In other words, look closely at where the actors stand on the stage or set and how they move in relation to one another and to the props and objects around them. Look closely at the *mise en scène*, or "everything in the scene." As you view the scene, write your responses to the questions below.**

Version: Director's Name and Year	**Set Design: What does it look like?** What does the set look and feel like? How does its design affect the way the actors move?	**Movements of Actors on Stage or Set** Why did the director place the actors where he did? (blocking)	**Effect of the Director's Choices**

Have students discuss the directors' effectiveness and technique.

5 Now that students have analyzed set design and movement, they should add these terms to the graphic organizer about theatrical elements in Activity 4.8 and save it in their **Vocabulary Notebooks**.

6 Since students will be performing a scene from ***Romeo and Juliet***, they should view the film interpretations with their own performances in mind. Ask students to examine, in small **discussion groups**, the effect that is created by the set design and the blocking. They should **brainstorm** how they might achieve a similar effect in their own performances, using the resources they have at hand.

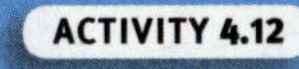

The importance of this scene is that it is the first time the young couple declare their love for each other, after knowing each other for a very short period of time.

2. Discuss with a small group how the staging of this scene adds to its emotional impact. How does the way the director staged the scene help you to understand it better? Which version seems more effective and why? How could you achieve a similar effect with the resources available to you?

3. You can see that the two film clips have similarities and differences. Write a short essay in which you compare the two films, considering the set design, actors' movements, and other theatrical elements. Begin by thinking about how you want to organize your writing. There are two ways you could organize the points of comparison:

    Subject-by-subject: Discuss all the elements (set design, actor movement, music, props, etc.) of one film version first and then discuss the elements of the other.

    Feature-by-feature: Go back and forth in your discussion of the two film interpretations, comparing and contrasting each element.

Remember to use transition words to help your reader follow your ideas.

GRAMMAR & USAGE

The reciprocal pronoun *one another* describes interactions among three or more people. Use *each other* to describe interactions between two people.

Transition Words and Phrases for Comparison:

also | in the same way | likewise | similarly | in addition | moreover | another

Transition Words and Phrases for Contrast:

but | however | in contrast | instead | yet | although | nevertheless | on the other hand

Strategies Reflection: As you have been doing throughout the unit, plan which strategies you will use and then reflect on how well they worked for you.

ACTIVITY 4.12 *continued*

Steps:

7 At the top of this student page is a brief writing assignment. Students are asked to write an essay comparing the two films. Have students read the writing prompt and organizational strategies. Remind them to use transitions effectively in their writing. Again, students should select strategies to use in their writing and then reflect on those strategies after **drafting**. Ask them to save these reflections in preparation for Embedded Assessment 2.

8 The strategy reflection is another opportunity for students to enhance their self-awareness as learners.

GRAMMAR & USAGE EXTENSION

You may want to provide a mini-lesson on pronouns. Give examples for the following types of pronouns, and have students explain how each is used in writing.

Personal pronouns: I, me, you, he, him, she, etc.

Demonstrative pronouns: this, that, these, those, etc.

Possessive pronouns: mine, hers, his, ours, etc.

Reflexive pronouns: myself, herself, himself, yourself, etc.

Interrogative pronouns: who, whom, what, which, etc.

Reciprocal pronouns: each other, one another

Indefinite pronouns: anyone, nobody, another, etc.

Relative pronouns: who, whom, which, where, when, etc.

ACTIVITY 4.13

Poetry, Paraphrased

Materials:

- Copy of *Romeo and Juliet* (Act II, Scene 3)

Purpose:

- To build fluency with Shakespeare's language
- To identify literary devices and their effects
- To reflect on use of paraphrasing as a strategy

Steps:

1 Explain that **paraphrasing** is a strategy students may use to make meaning of Shakespeare's words. After students have read or listened to Act II, Scene 3, have them practice paraphrasing Shakespeare's words.

2 To begin, divide students into six **discussion groups** and assign each group to revisit prior work from Unit 3, specifically their Personal Poetry Glossary, so they can define one of the literary devices listed on the student page. This practice will help students dig deeper into the language of the scene, moving them to analysis.

3 Each group should then reread Act II, Scene 3, identifying at least one example of its assigned literary device. As a group, students should discuss the effect of the literary device on the scene. **Jigsaw** the groups for an analysis of Shakespeare's use of literary devices.

4 From these groups, have students break out into pairs. All pairs will work on the same dialogue, beginning with Romeo's line, "Thou chid'st me oft for loving Rosaline," and going to the end of Scene 3. Pairs will collaborate on **paraphrasing** this dialogue.

5 After paraphrasing, have students choose parts and **rehearse** saying the paraphrased lines. They should face each other and make eye contact. Encourage them to use the elements of vocal delivery (volume, pitch, rate, pauses, pronunciation, and articulation) to show feeling.

6 Next, have students change partners and say the paraphrased dialogue again. Students may need to modify their lines to make sense with their new partner. Have students **think-pair-share**.

7 Finally, ask students to reflect independently on the strategies they used and their effectiveness in helping to learn and understand this dialogue. Allow students to discuss any new insights they may have about the **Essential Question**, "How have the strategies I have learned this year helped me to be a better reader, writer, speaker, and listener?"

ACTIVITY 4.13

Poetry, Paraphrased

SUGGESTED LEARNING STRATEGIES: **Paraphrasing, Discussion Groups, Think-Pair-Share**

LITERARY TERMS

Imagery is language that appeals to the senses, particularly the sense of sight.

A **metaphor** is a figure of speech that compares two or more unlike things. Metaphors do not use the words *like* or *as* to make the comparison.

Hyperbole is a figure of speech that uses exaggeration to express a strong feeling.

An **allusion** refers to a literary, historical, or cultural moment, figure, or event.

Personification is a figure of speech that describes an object as if it were a living creature.

One reason Shakespeare's plays are so well loved is the poetic language that he uses. Every scene of *Romeo and Juliet* is enriched by the use of poetic devices you learned in Unit 3. Choose one of the following literary devices and find an example and comment on its effect: **imagery, metaphor, hyperbole, allusion,** and **personification.**

Literary device:

Example in Act II, Scene 3:

Effect of the literary device on the scene:

Paraphrasing, or restating in your own words, is a strategy that can help you gain understanding of the play. A paraphrased text will be about as long as the original text. Work with a partner to paraphrase the dialogue in Act II, Scene 3, between Romeo and the Friar that begins with Romeo's line, "Thou chid'st me oft for loving Rosaline" and ends at the close of Scene 3.

Both partners should write the entire dialogue on separate paper. Then with your partner, rehearse saying the dialogue in different ways.

Finally, reflect on how the strategies you used helped you understand the scene.

Writing Prompt: Choose at least ten lines of dialogue, and transform the interaction into an email or an instant message conversation. Your content will be similar, but your syntax and voice will change. Be sure to use the proper structure for your format.

Foiled Again

ACTIVITY 4.14

SUGGESTED LEARNING STRATEGIES: **Graphic Organizer, Think-Pair-Share**

You may have noticed Shakespeare's use of wordplay in *Romeo and Juliet*. For example, Shakespeare makes liberal use of **puns**, or plays on words that have two meanings. In Act II, Scene 4, Mercutio and Romeo engage in an exchange in which Mercutio scolds Romeo for giving his friends "the counterfeit" the night before. Romeo, still on top of the world after spending the evening with his new love Juliet, goes along with Mercutio's joke. The next several lines capitalize on the dual meanings of *counterfeit* and *slip*.

WORD CONNECTIONS

Many writers, including Shakespeare, are known for their wordplay. The word *repartee* is a French word that describes a type of wordplay with witty replies or retorts.

1. Why do you think puns are known as "thinking man's humor?"

2. In this scene, the wordplay between Romeo and Mercutio helps characterize their friendship and reveals contrasts between them. Compare the characters in the chart below.

Mercutio	Romeo

When a character in a text is seemingly the opposite of another character, yet complements that character, we say he or she is a **character foil**. Use your comparison chart to show how Mercutio serves as a *character foil* for Romeo.

LITERARY TERMS

A **character foil** is a person who, in contrast to the main character—the protagonist—accentuates the main character's distinctive qualities or characteristics.

ACTIVITY 4.14
Foiled Again

Materials:

- Copy of ***Romeo and Juliet***, Act II, Scene 4

Purpose:

- To recognize how puns affect and inform characterization
- To understand how a character foil enhances the understanding of the main character

Steps:

1 Explain to students that Act II, Scene 4 showcases clever wordplay between Mercutio and Romeo and reinforces Mercutio as a foil to Romeo. Point out the exchange in which Mercutio and Romeo play on the words ***counterfeit*** and ***slip***. To help students appreciate Shakespeare's use of puns, ask them to tell appropriate jokes that are funny because of the dual meanings of words.

2 Guide students as they fill in the T-chart **graphic organizer** on the student page, by directing them to think about each character's view of love, women and beauty, and dreams.

3 Introduce the concept of ***character foil***. Point out how Mercutio serves as Romeo's foil. Use **think-pair-share** to check for students' understanding.

ACTIVITY 4.15
Short Shrift: A Quick Wedding

Materials:
- *Romeo and Juliet*, Act II, Scene 6
- Art materials

Purpose:
- To visualize a scene and plan a performance
- To build fluency with Shakespeare's language
- To apply the concept of coming of age to ***Romeo and Juliet***

Steps:

1 Have students read or listen to Act II, Scene 6, which ends before the wedding of Romeo and Juliet. You may want students to return to the chart in Activity 4.6, to chart the passage of time and course of events in the play.

2 Ask students to think about why the wedding, an important occasion, takes place off-stage. Ask them why Shakespeare may have decided to leave this scene out. How would its inclusion have affected the pace of the play or its course of events?

3 Ask students to **visualize** the costumes, music, and staging that they would use to stage the wedding scene, if it had been included in the play. First have students imagine the scene in Shakespeare's day. Then have them imagine it in a modern production.

4 Students should **take notes** on the theatrical elements of costumes, music, and staging in the **graphic organizer** on the student page and share their work with others. Ask students to discuss how theatrical elements in the past might be different from those of today.

ACTIVITY 4.15

Short Shrift: A Quick Wedding

SUGGESTED LEARNING STRATEGIES: **Visualizing, Graphic Organizer, Rereading**

The art of visualizing is the ability to picture what something looks like. Consider the following questions and then fill in the chart below with your ideas.

Shakespeare does not write a scene for the wedding of Romeo and Juliet. Why does the wedding take place off-stage?

If the wedding were added to the action of the play, how would you show it in two different time periods—Shakespeare's and now? Describe in detail your choices below and justify them in the space provided.

Time Period: Shakespeare's Time		
Costumes: Colors and styles for all three characters (Draw, describe, or cut out pictures.)	Music: Instruments, vocals, artists, specific songs, etc.	Staging: What would the set look like?
Intended effect?	Intended effect?	Intended effect?

© 2011 College Board. All rights reserved.

Teacher Notes

Time Period: Now		
Costumes: Colors and styles for all three characters (Draw, describe, or cut out pictures.)	Music: Instruments, vocals, artists, specific songs, etc.	Staging: What would the set look like?
Intended effect?	Intended effect?	Intended effect?

Steps:

5 Discuss the romanticized language that Romeo and Juliet use to describe each other and their love. Have students **reread** the lines where Romeo and Juliet speak about their love. With these lines as inspiration, have students **draft** wedding vows for Romeo and Juliet.

6 Finally, have students answer causes and consequences questions that will help prepare them for the writing they will do in Activity 4.26.

Short Shrift: A Quick Wedding

Wedding Vows

Writing Prompt: Shakespeare did not stage Romeo and Juliet's vows, but you can imagine what the characters said. Reread lines in Act II that help you get a sense of the protagonists' voices. Take notes about the way they talk to and about each other. Then, on a separate sheet of paper, write a script with wedding vows for the star-crossed lovers. In your script, include descriptions of gestures, movement, and staging that evoke a definite tone or mood.

Causes and Consequences

1. How does the concept of coming of age relate so far to Romeo? What about Juliet?

2. Does the emotional behavior of Romeo and Juliet have more to do with their age or with love at first sight? Why do you say that?

3. Why do the Friar and the Nurse, adults who care deeply about the young lovers, allow Romeo and Juliet to act so quickly?

Acting Companies

ACTIVITY 4.16

SUGGESTED LEARNING STRATEGIES: Drafting, Brainstorming, Discussion Groups

Performance Scenes

Your acting company will perform a scene from *Romeo and Juliet*. See the list of possible scenes below. Your teacher may add to or delete from this list. Some of the scenes include long speeches from which lines may be cut with your teacher's direction and approval. In addition, a few research topics are provided for your group's dramaturge.

Act and Scene	Description	Characters	Research Topics for the Dramaturge
Act III, Scene 1 Begin — TYBALT: Follow me close, for I will speak to them. End — ROMEO: O, I am fortune's fool!	Mercutio, Tybalt, and Romeo engage in a fight in the street. **104 lines**	Mercutio Tybalt Romeo Benvolio	Fencing, banishment laws
Act III, Scene 5 Begin — LADY CAPULET: Marry, my child, early next Thursday morn ... End — LADY CAPULET: Talk not to me, for I'll not speak a word.	Juliet, her parents, and the Nurse argue about her proposed marriage to Paris. **98 lines**	Lady Capulet Juliet Capulet Nurse	Courtship customs, females' rights
Act IV, Scene 3 Begin — JULIET: Farewell! — God knows when we shall meet again. End — JULIET: Romeo, I come! this do I drink to thee.	Juliet drinks the Friar's potion. **45 lines**	Juliet	Burial vaults, herbal potions

ACTIVITY 4.16
Acting Companies

Materials:

- Art supplies for making invitations
- Sticky notes (optional)

Purpose:

- To collaborate on planning for a performance
- To draft a text for a specific audience

Steps:

1 To begin preparations for Embedded Assessment 1, students should form acting companies before they begin reading Act III. They should be thinking about their performances as they read the rest of the play.

2 Student acting companies should choose a name for their group and a scene they would like to perform. Also have each group choose a director and a dramaturge. A list of scenes with descriptions is provided on the student page. You may add other scenes if you choose. Note that some scenes identified here have been examined closely in the preceding unit activities. Use your own discretion about offering those scenes as options for students. Many of the scenes are long and should be shortened so that students can perform them effectively.

3 In addition to specific scenes, the student pages also identify possible topics for the dramaturge to research. Some topics suggested may already have been addressed in your class in a previous activity. You may want to meet with the dramaturges and guide them to research topics and sources that will enhance their scenes.

Steps:

4 Decide whether more than one group may choose the same scene. Viewing multiple presentations of the same scene does allow students to recognize the potential for interpretation in a drama.

Acting Companies

Act and Scene	Description	Characters	Research Topics for the Dramaturge
Act IV, Scene 5 Begin — NURSE: I must needs wake her. End — FRIAR: Move them no more by crossing their high will.	The Nurse thinks Juliet is dead, and she informs the household. **91 lines**	Nurse Capulet Lady Capulet Friar Paris	Funeral customs, astrology
Act V, Scene 3 Begin — ROMEO: For here lies Juliet, and her beauty makes / This vault a feasting presence full of light. End — JULIET: This is thy sheath; there rest, and let me die.	Romeo and Juliet commit suicide. Note: The exchange between Friar Lawrence and Balthasar may be deleted from this scene **90 lines**	Romeo Juliet Friar Lawrence Balthasar	Burial customs
Act V, Scene 3 Begin — PRINCE: What misadventure is so early up, ... End — PRINCE: For never was a story of more woe / Than this of Juliet and her Romeo.	All is revealed and resolved. Note: Friar Lawrence has a long speech that could be cut or edited. **126 lines**	Prince Capulet Lady Capulet First Watch Montague Friar Lawrence Balthasar Page	Statues as memorials, famous feuds and truces

© 2011 College Board. All rights reserved.

286 SpringBoard® English Textual Power™ Level 4

In Shakespeare's day, acting companies named themselves just as bands do today. Sometimes the acting companies honored their patron (the person who provided financial support) in their name. Shakespeare belonged first to the Lord Chamberlain's Men and later to the King's Men.

1. Your acting company should think of a name that reflects the characteristics of your group. Try to incorporate something you have learned about Shakespeare, the Renaissance, Elizabethan theater, or *Romeo and Juliet* into your company's name.

   Once you reach an agreement, write, sign, and turn in a contract like the one below to your teacher.

   We, the _________________ (name of acting company), pledge to

   plan, rehearse, and perform _________________ (act and scene)

   from William Shakespeare's *The Tragedy of Romeo and Juliet*.

Cast:

(Name of student) as (name of character)

Director:

Dramaturge:

Date of performance:

2. Once you know the role you will play, read the rest of the play, paying attention to what your character says and does. Take notes as you read. You may also need to do research in preparation for the performance.
3. With your acting company, brainstorm people whom you could invite to your performance and then prepare invitations. Keep your audience's interests in mind as you create the invitation.

ACTIVITY 4.16 continued

Steps:

5 Have each acting company complete a contract. Post the date for your Shakespeare festival and a schedule of the performances.

6 Have the acting companies brainstorm people to invite to their performance, such as family members, school faculty, younger students, senior citizens, and other community members. Ask acting companies to craft invitations that appeal to their audience.

7 After the acting companies have been formed and scenes selected, take time to review the products students will need to prepare for Embedded Assessment 1.

8 Once the actors know their roles, they should pay particular attention to their character as they read the play. Give students sticky notes or have them create a **graphic organizer** for taking notes about their character and to jot down ideas about how they will perform the part.

9 Directors should identify passages in the play that connect to the scene they will direct. Dramaturges will conduct research on the topics that will inform their company's performance. Allow dramaturges to meet periodically to share resources, if applicable.

10 During class reading of the play, as you encounter scenes students will be performing, allow the acting companies to read their scenes while standing. This will give them some initial practice with their scenes.

ACTIVITY 4.17

"A Plague o' Both Your Houses!"

Materials:

- Copy of *Romeo and Juliet*, Act III, Scene 1
- Vocabulary Notebook

Purpose:

- To orally interpret a literary text
- To draft a persuasive text

Steps:

1 Before they read Act III, Scene 1, have students do a **quickwrite** about the way angry feelings can escalate. Ask volunteers to share their ideas.

2 As they read the fight scene, ask students to **visualize** the scene and to record their thoughts about the characters' behavior and motivations. If one of the acting companies in your class has chosen the fight scene from Act III, Scene 1 for Embedded Assessment 1, have that group read the scene in parts. Read until Mercutio says, "Go, villain, fetch a surgeon."

3 Have students fill in the **graphic organizer** on the student page and then **think-pair-share** their thoughts about the characters' behavior and motivations.

4 In a **role-playing** activity, have the acting company or volunteers act out the scene in front of the class as they read. Allow the class to provide feedback on the blocking of Tybalt stabbing Mercutio under Romeo's arm. Ask them to read on their feet until Romeo says, "O, I am fortune's fool!"

ACTIVITY 4.17

"A Plague o' Both Your Houses!"

SUGGESTED LEARNING STRATEGIES: **Quickwrite, Graphic Organizer, Think-Pair-Share, Role Playing, Marking the Text, RAFT, Drafting , Visualizing, Oral Interpretation**

Quickwrite: Before you read Act III, Scene 1, think about action scenes that you have seen on TV or in video games or movies. On a separate sheet of paper, quickwrite about action scenes that involve fighting. Use the following questions to guide your thinking, but do not limit yourself to answering just these questions:

- Why do people fight?
- Who usually wins in a fight? Why?
- Under what circumstances would you fight?
- What are the consequences of fighting?

While you are reading Act III, Scene 1, try to imagine the action in your head and think about why the characters are doing what they are doing.

Character	How is he behaving?	Why is he behaving in this way? What is his motivation?
Romeo		
Mercutio		
Tybalt		
Benvolio		

Reread the Prince's decision at the end of the scene. How does the Prince feel? What thoughts may be going through his mind? Pretend you are a director and make notes on the script below to indicate how you want the actor playing the Prince to deliver the lines. Begin by identifying where you would have the Prince pause for effect. Using pauses and silence is part of vocal variety, just as pitch, rate and intonation are. Include in your planning all the elements of visual delivery (gestures, posture, movement, eye contact, facial expression and props) and vocal delivery (volume, pitch, rate, pauses, vocal variety, and pronunciation/articulation). You will use these notations later to mark your text for the performance of your scene from the play.

Act III, Scene 1

PRINCE: And for that offence

Immediately we do exile him hence.

I have an interest in your hate's proceeding,

My blood for your rude brawls doth lie a-bleeding;

But I'll amerce you with so strong a fine

That you shall all repent the loss of mine.

I will be deaf to pleading and excuses;

Nor tears nor prayers shall purchase out abuses.

Therefore use none. Let Romeo hence in haste,

Else, when he's found, that hour is his last.

Bear hence this body and attend our will.

Mercy but murders, pardoning those that kill.

2. After you have heard some oral interpretations of this speech, note how they differ. What does the speaker do and to what effect? Which interpretation best expresses your ideas of how the Prince must be feeling at this moment? Why?

Steps:

5 Have students read the rest of the scene aloud, paying particular attention to the Prince's speech, which appears on the student page. Have the students work in their acting companies or with a partner to **mark the text**. Remind students that, as actors, they will be expected to prepare a script marked for performance. Ask volunteers to perform, and, as a class, discuss the different **oral interpretations**. Take time to refine the definitions of ***interpretation*** that students wrote earlier and saved in their **Vocabulary Notebooks**.

Steps:

6 Finally, have acting companies meet and use the questions and the **graphic organizer** on the student page to help them decide whether the Prince's sentence is fair. Acting companies should use the **RAFT** strategy to generate a response to the writing prompt, supporting or opposing his decree. Remind them to keep their audience in mind.

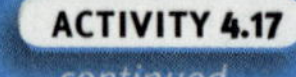

"A Plague o' Both Your Houses!"

3. After you have read Act III, Scene 1, analyze the arguments made by each side. The Prince must sentence Romeo to some kind of punishment for killing Tybalt.
   - What punishment for Romeo does Lady Capulet demand?
   - What punishment does Lord Montague suggest?
   - What is the Prince's decree or decision?

Characters' Responses to Romeo's Sentence

Romeo	Juliet
The Montagues	**The Capulets**

Writing Prompt: Do you think this is a fair punishment for the crime? Choose one of the characters above and, on a separate sheet of paper, work with your acting company to write his or her response to the Prince's decree. Use RAFT to help you form your response.

© 2011 College Board. All rights reserved.

Comparing Film Interpretations: "And Fire-eyed Fury Be My Conduct Now"

ACTIVITY 4.18

SUGGESTED LEARNING STRATEGIES: Graphic Organizer, Discussion Groups, Drafting

From the opening of the play, the conflict between the Capulets and the Montagues has inspired "fire-eyed fury," or anger that has erupted into violence and murder. As you watch at least two interpretations of Act III, Scene 1, pay attention to the portrayals of the major characters. Take notes on any shifts in the emotions of the characters and consider how the director presents the shift.

Director:

	Romeo	Mercutio	Tybalt
How does the character behave? (Consider visual and vocal delivery to show emotion.)			
Why does the character behave this way?			
What causes the shift in behavior?			
How does the character's behavior change?			
Why does the character behave in this new way?			

How does the director signal change in the mood of the scene? Consider any changes in set, props, costumes, music and other sounds, lighting, and editing.

ACTIVITY 4.18

Comparing Film Interpretations: "And Fire-eyed Fury Be My Conduct Now"

Materials:

- Copy of ***Romeo and Juliet***, Act III, Scene 1
- Multiple film interpretations of ***Romeo and Juliet***
- Vocabulary Notebook

Purpose:

- To compare and evaluate film productions
- To plan for performances
- To draft a response to a writing prompt

Steps:

1 Now that students have worked with Act III, Scene 1, show them at least two film interpretations as **visual prompts** for this scene.

- In Zeffirelli's film, show Clip 1, Scene 11 (1:12:08–1:27:00). Begin with Benvolio's line, "By my head, here come the Capulets" and end with Romeo's "I am Fortune's fool!"
- In Luhrmann's interpretation, show Clip 2, Scenes 20–21 (0:58:30–1:10:06). Begin and end with the same dialogue as in the Zeffirelli film.

2 Have students complete the **graphic organizers** on the student pages for each version of the scene. Tell them to pay particular attention to shifts in the behaviors of the characters. They should also watch how mood is suggested by the set, props, costumes, music and sound effects, and lighting.

Steps:

3 You may want to use a **jigsaw** approach, with some students taking notes on Romeo, others on Tybalt, and the rest on Mercutio. Form groups of students who studied the same character and have them share ideas. Then rearrange the groups so that each one contains an expert on a different character.

4 Students can now flesh out their notes on theatrical elements (set, props, costumes, music and other sounds, lighting and editing) in their **Vocabulary Notebooks**.

5 Have students work with their acting companies (**discussion groups**) to discuss the mood they want to create in their own scenes and how they might use the resources they have to create it.

6 Ask students to read the writing prompt on the student page and **draft** a response. Students' writing should explain the reasons for their choice and use textual support and reflective commentary.

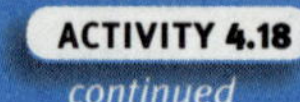

Comparing Film Interpretations: "And Fire-eyed Fury Be My Conduct Now"

Director:

	Romeo	Mercutio	Tybalt
How does the character behave? (Consider visual and vocal delivery to show emotion.)			
Why does the character behave this way?			
What causes the shift in behavior?			
How does the character's behavior change?			
Why does the character behave in this new way?			
How does the director signal a change in the mood of the scene? Consider any changes in set, props, costumes, music and other sounds, lighting, and editing.			

In your acting company, discuss the mood created in these film interpretations, then brainstorm ways that your company could create a similar mood with the resources you have available.

Writing Prompt: On separate paper, write an essay that explains which film version more powerfully conveys the seriousness of "fire-eyed fury." Be sure to provide textual support and reflective commentary. Be mindful of the strategies you use in the writing process.

Emotional Roller Coaster

ACTIVITY 4.19

SUGGESTED LEARNING STRATEGIES: Graphic Organizer

Coming of age stories involve young characters who are just learning how to deal with the intense emotions and experiences of young adulthood. At times the characters seem to be on an emotional roller coaster. In Act III, Romeo and Juliet both experience a broad range of emotions. For example, one minute Juliet is anxiously awaiting a message from her love, and the next she is grieving the death of her cousin.

Create a list of significant events in each character's story so far (you might update your timeline chart from Activity 4.6). Number them in a key below the graph. Next, plot the numbers of the events on the emotional graph below. When you have finished reading Act III, connect the points you have plotted for each character's emotions.

Juliet's Emotions

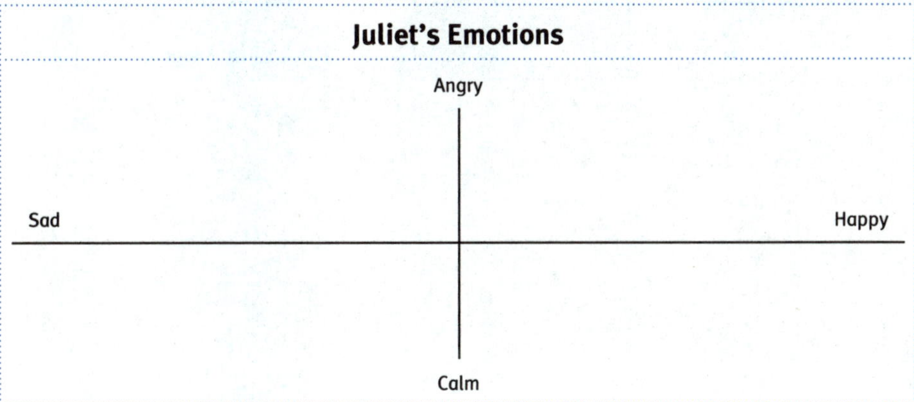

Key: Incidents in the story that reveal Juliet's emotions

1.

2.

3.

4.

5.

ACTIVITY 4.19

Emotional Roller Coaster

Materials:

- Copy of ***Romeo and Juliet***, Act III
- Vocabulary Notebook

Purpose:

- To recognize conflicts in a drama
- To analyze an author's use of figurative language

Steps:

1 After they have read Act III, scene 1, lead students in a review of the most important moments in the play so far. Then have students use the **graphic organizers** on the student pages to plot the emotions of the characters during those moments.

2 You may want to use a **jigsaw** approach; ask half the class to work individually to plot Juliet's emotions and the other half to plot Romeo's and then form groups for sharing notes. Next, rearrange the groups so that Juliet experts can meet with Romeo experts. Have students continue to plot the characters' emotions as they read the rest of Act III.

Steps:

3 The language Juliet uses to describe Romeo in Act III, Scene 2 shows her turbulent feelings. Have students visualize and illustrate the oxymorons Juliet uses to describe Romeo (in her speech beginning with "O serpent heart hid with a flow'ring face!"). Lead a discussion of the effect of the comparisons.

Emotional Roller Coaster

When Juliet first receives the news about Tybalt's fate, she reacts with a wide range of feelings. The figurative language she uses to describe Romeo in Act III, Scene 2, shows her confusion. Identify the oxymorons that Juliet uses to describe Romeo (see the speech beginning with "O serpent heart . . . "). An ***oxymoron*** is an expression that combines contradictory ideas into a single, unusual expression; for example, "cold fire" or "sweet sorrow."

In the space below, illustrate or create a symbolic representation of the descriptions she uses.

Romeo's Emotions

Key: Incidents in the story that reveal Romeo's emotions

1.

2.

3.

4.

5.

Look back at the graphs you have drawn. What do the characters' ranges of emotion reveal about them and their situations?

Steps:

4 After they have read all of Act III, ask students to meet in small groups to discuss the emotions of Romeo and Juliet thus far in the play. What do their emotional roller coasters say about the characters? Students may begin to see that external circumstances, combined with the inexperience of the characters, contribute to their great emotional turmoil.

5 Have students revisit their notes about tragedy, which they saved in their **Vocabulary Notebooks**, and compare them to what they are learning about the characters of Romeo and Juliet. They may have new ideas to add, or they may want to edit some ideas.

ACTIVITY 4.20

"But Now I'll Tell Thee Joyful Tidings, Girl"

Materials:

- Copy of *Romeo and Juliet*, Act III, Scene 5
- Timeline

Purpose:

- To analyze characterization and conflict
- To explore and evaluate a character's options
- To draft a persuasive text

Steps:

1 Before students read Act III, Scene 5, ask them to do a **quickwrite** about a time when the adult(s) in their lives made a decision for them that was contrary to their own wishes.

2 Next, **activate prior knowledge** by asking students what they know about arranged marriages. Let them discuss with a partner or small group what kind of person they think their parents would choose for them.

3 Ask students to complete the **graphic organizer** on the student page, identifying what each adult wants Juliet to do. (Have students **reread** the conversation between Lord Capulet and Paris in Act I, Scene 2, and compare Capulet's statements there to those in Act III, Scene 5.)

4 Students will create a graphic organizer such as a bubble cluster where they will **brainstorm** all of Juliet's options and the consequences of each. You may need to model the brainstorming process.

5 Once students have thought about Juliet's options, have them **draft** a letter of advice to her.

6 Finally, students should continue to update the Timeline of Events from Activity 4.6.

ACTIVITY 4.20

"But Now I'll Tell Thee Joyful Tidings, Girl"

SUGGESTED LEARNING STRATEGIES: Quickwrite, Graphic Organizer, Rereading, Brainstorming, Drafting

Quickwrite: Think of a time when the adult(s) in your life made a decision for you that was contrary to your wishes. What happened? How did you feel?

Act III, Scene 5

Part of the process of coming of age is learning and accepting that sometimes parents and other trusted adults make mistakes. Juliet's father has good intentions when he decides that Juliet should marry Paris. Juliet's mother thinks the news will dry Juliet's tears. The Nurse sides with the Capulets. No wonder Juliet is confused! Take notes on what the adults want Juliet to do.

Lord Capulet tells Juliet to . . .		because
Lady Capulet tells Juliet to . . .		because
The Nurse tells Juliet to . . .		because
The Friar tells Juliet to . . .		because

What are Juliet's options? On separate paper, create a graphic organizer that identifies what Juliet might do and what the consequences of each decision might be.

Below the organizer, write your advice to Juliet.

© 2011 College Board. All rights reserved.

"And, If Thou Darest, I'll Give Thee Remedy"

ACTIVITY 4.21

SUGGESTED LEARNING STRATEGIES: Oral Interpretation, Marking the Text, Graphic Organizer

1. Write your own explanation of **subtext** and give an example.

2. Why is it important to keep the subtext in mind when you are performing a scene?

3. In Act IV, Scene 1, Juliet has a conversation with Paris during which she must hide her true feelings. Using sticky notes, mark the text by writing the subtext—Juliet's true thoughts—which you find "between the lines."

4. Your teacher will ask your acting company to pantomime either the things Juliet would rather do than marry Paris or the Friar's plan for Juliet. Remember that in a pantomime, you act out something without using words. Your audience must guess the action from your movements and expressions.

What Juliet Would Rather Do Than Marry Paris	Pantomime Plan (Movements, expressions, gestures)

Steps in the Friar's Plan for Juliet	Pantomime Plan (Movements, expressions, gestures)

ACTIVITY 4.21

"And, If Thou Darest, I'll Give Thee Remedy"

Materials:

- Copy of ***Romeo and Juliet***, Act IV, Scene 1
- Sticky notes

Purpose:

- To interpret a subtext
- To analyze conflict in drama
- To rehearse oral interpretation and movement
- To evaluate characters' choices

Steps:

1 To introduce the concept of *subtext*, put students into small groups and give each a card with a scenario on it (see page 251a for scenarios). Be sure that no two students in a group have them same scenario.

2 Explain that each student has the same line, "That one is mine" but will be saying it differently, depending on the scenario. Have each student read his or her scenario silently and consider how to deliver the line.

3 In each group, students should take turns saying the line with the appropriate expression to convey the scenario (**oral interpretation**). The rest of the group should determine the emotion the speaker is feeling.

4 Bring the class together and explain that subtext is what goes on "between the lines" or "in the background." Have students read Act IV, Scene 1, until Paris kisses Juliet and exits. Discuss how the subtext—Juliet is secretly married to Romeo—affects the meaning of the scene. Have students use sticky notes to **mark the text**, writing Juliet's true thoughts and feelings next to the words she says to Paris.

ACTIVITY 4.21 *continued*

Steps:

5 Remind students of the mask monologues they performed in Activity 4.2. Guide them to make a connection to the false face Juliet has put on for Paris.

6 After they have read Act IV, Scene 1, have the acting companies meet. Tell half the acting companies to pantomime things Juliet is willing to do rather than marry Paris. Ask the other half to pantomime the Friar's plan. Allow for rehearsal time.

7 Have at least one of the acting companies from each of the two groups to present. After the companies present, lead the class in a discussion of the choices the company made in its pantomime.

8 As students evaluate the Friar's plan for Juliet, ask them to consider the subtext of the Friar's decision. Do they think it is wise? Why or why not?

9 Finally, students should update their timelines from Activity 4.6.

"And, If Thou Darest, I'll Give Thee Remedy"

Quickwrite: Evaluate the Friar's plan for Juliet. Be sure to explain the subtext of his plan. Does it seem wise? Why or why not?

"... I Needs Must Act Alone"

ACTIVITY 4.22

SUGGESTED LEARNING STRATEGIES: **Role Playing, Discussion Groups, Graphic Organizer, Close Reading, Marking the Text, Quickwrite, Summarizing**

In Act IV, Scenes 2–3, Juliet must conceal her emotions once again. Role-play parts of the scenes, having one of the actors say Juliet's lines while another actor stands nearby and pantomimes Juliet's true feelings. Discuss what the scenes suggest about Juliet and her family.

WORD CONNECTIONS

Soliloquy contains the root *-sol-* from the Latin word *soli*, meaning "one, alone, or lonely." This root also appears in *solo, solitary,* and *solitude*.

Work with your acting company to create a graphic organizer that shows all the characters with whom Juliet has interacted. Show on your organizer those with whom she speaks in her true voice and those with whom she "wears a mask." For each, explain why. Describe the most important event in Act IV, Scene 3.

A close reading reveals that Juliet has much to fear if she follows the Friar's plan. Read carefully Juliet's soliloquy from Act IV, Scene 3, which appears on the next page. Underline all the potential outcomes that frighten Juliet. In the margin, summarize Juliet's fears.

Highlight the words and phrases that you associate with death. In the margin, write which sense each word appeals to (sight, hearing, taste, touch, smell). What is the effect of all this death imagery?

Quickwrite: Do you think Juliet made a good decision in drinking the potion? Why or why not?

Differentiating Instruction:

To provide additional **support**, use the **diffusing** strategy and have students identify unfamiliar words or phrases. Ask them to use context clues, dictionaries, and thesauruses to help clarify their understanding of unfamiliar words.

Extend the activity by having students work independently to analyze the text using the pre-AP strategy **SOAPSTone**.

ACTIVITY 4.22
"... I Needs Must Act Alone"

Materials:

- Copy of ***Romeo and Juliet***, Act IV, Scenes 2-3

Purpose:

- To analyze a character's voice
- To develop a plan for a performance

Steps:

1 Ask one of the acting companies to read on their feet Act IV, Scene 2, beginning when Capulet says, "What, is my daughter gone to Friar Lawrence?" One of the actors should recite Juliet's lines while another actor **role-plays** or pantomimes Juliet's hidden feelings.

2 Move students into their acting groups, which will serve as **discussion groups** as they update their timelines (Activity 4.6) to reflect events in the scene.

3 Then, in groups, each student should create a **graphic organizer** to use during discussion of Juliet's ability to express her voice.

4 Remind students that their **close reading** and **marking the text** of Juliet's soliloquy is practice for the work they will do in preparation for their performance. Tell them to practice marking and **summarizing** and reading aloud to deepen their understanding. As students **quickwrite** about Juliet's decision to drink the potion, ask them to infer the scene's subtext, or hidden meanings.

Teacher Notes

"... I Needs Must Act Alone"

My Notes

Drama

From ROMEO AND JULIET

by William Shakespeare

Juliet

Farewell! — God knows when we shall meet again.
I have a faint cold fear thrills through my veins
That almost freezes up the heat of life.
I'll call them back again to comfort me.
Nurse! — What should she do here?
My dismal scene I needs must act alone.
Come, vial.
What if this mixture do not work at all?
Shall I be married then to-morrow morning?
No, no! This shall forbid it. Lie thou there.
[Laying down her dagger.]

What if it be a poison, which the friar
Subtly hath minister'd to have me dead,
Lest in this marriage he should be dishonoured,
Because he married me before to Romeo?
I fear it is; and yet, methinks, it should not,
I will not entertain so bad a thought.
For he hath still been tried a holy man.
How if, when I am laid into the tomb,
I wake before the time that Romeo
Come to redeem me? There's a fearful point!

© 2011 College Board. All rights reserved.

300 SpringBoard® English Textual Power™ Level 4

Teacher Notes

Shall I not, then, be stifled in the vault,
To whose foul mouth no healthsome air breathes in,
And there die strangled ere my Romeo comes?
Or, if I live, is it not very like,
The horrible conceit of death and night,
Together with the terror of the place,
As in a vault, an ancient receptacle
Where, for this many hundred years, the bones
Of all my buried ancestors are packed;
Where bloody Tybalt, yet but green in earth,
Lies fest'ering in his shroud; where, as they say,
At some hours in the night spirits resort—
Alack, alack, is it not like that I,
So early waking—what with loathsome smells,
And shrieks like mandrakes torn out of the earth,
That living mortals, hearing them, run mad—
O, if I wake, shall I not be distraught,
Environed with all these hideous fears,
And madly play with my forefathers' joints,
And pluck the mangled Tybalt from his shroud,
And, in this rage, with some great kinsman's bone
As with a club dash out my desp'rate brains?
O, look! Methinks I see my cousin's ghost
Seeking out Romeo, that did spit his body
Upon a rapier's point. Stay, Tybalt, stay!
Romeo, I come! This do I drink to thee.
[Throws herself on the bed.]

Writing Prompt: Choose an example of a subjunctive possibility from Juliet's speech, and rewrite it in modern English.

My Notes

© 2011 College Board. All rights reserved.

Unit 4 • Interpreting Drama Through Performance 301

Steps:

5 Next, students should copy an excerpt from Juliet's speech (from the previous student pages) and **mark** it as a director would, indicating elements of visual and vocal delivery. You might have students revisit their understanding of the **Essential Question**, "What are the essential features of an effective drama and/or dramatic performance?"

6 Have students pair up with another member of their acting companies to practice directing and being directed. They should trade director's notes and take turns following the directions in a rehearsal. If confusion or misunderstanding occurs, the director can verbally re-direct.

7 Have students draft a reflection on directing and being directed.

"... I Needs Must Act Alone"

After your group has read the previous scene, individually choose one part that you feel is important. Imagine that you are directing an actor. What would you tell her to do in order to create an effective performance?

Rewrite part of the speech here. Then review the essential features of an effective dramatic performance. Mark the speech, indicating how the actor should use vocal delivery and visual delivery to convey the essence of the speech.

Trade papers with a classmate and follow each other's directions in a rehearsal. Practice a few times until you each feel that your partner is delivering the lines the way you want.

Writing Prompt: Reflect on your experiences both as a director and an actor. Which did you prefer? Why? Write your response on a separate sheet of paper.

Shakespeare in Art

ACTIVITY 4.23

SUGGESTED LEARNING STRATEGIES: Close Reading, Graphic Organizers, Discussion Groups

Shakespeare's works have inspired artists for over four hundred years. As you examine a piece of art inspired by the tragedy of *Romeo and Juliet*, think about the connections between the drama and the artwork and how the artist achieves them.

Name of painting:

Artist:

Part of *Romeo and Juliet* depicted:

Which Characters Appear?	What Are the Characters Doing?	How Do the Characters Appear to Feel?

How Would You Describe the Grouping of the Characters?	Why Do You Think the Artist Chose to Group the Characters in This Way?

ACTIVITY 4.23
Shakespeare in Art

Materials:

- Copy of ***Romeo and Juliet***, Act IV, Scene 4
- Photos from tableaux, Activity 4.3 (optional)
- Reproduction of artwork inspired by a scene from ***Romeo and Juliet***

Purpose:

- To interpret a visual text
- To plan for performances

Steps:

1 Many artists have been inspired by Shakespeare's works, and artistic renderings of Juliet on her deathbed (as well as many other scenes from the drama) are readily available online. These include James Stephanoff's "Juliet's Chamber, Act IV, Scene 5;" Frederick Leighton's "The Discovery of Juliet Apparently Lifeless," and "Count Paris….;" and Jean Pierre Simon's engraving based on John Opie's "Act IV, Scene 5: Juliet's Supposed Death."

2 Use the artworks mentioned above or others as **visual prompts** and have students do a **close reading** of the artwork, using the **graphic organizers** on pages 303–305. Students should focus on character, setting, and use of color and indicate what feelings the painting evokes in them and how it evokes those feelings.

Teacher Notes

Shakespeare in Art

How Would You Describe the Setting?	What Effect Is Created by This Setting?

What Colors are Used in the Painting?	What Effect Do You Think the Artist was Trying to Achieve by Using These Colors?

What Feelings Does the Painting Evoke in You?	What About the Painting Evokes These Feelings?

Meet with your acting company to discuss how you can apply your thoughts about the artwork you analyzed to your own performance. Discuss what visual and emotional effects you want to achieve and how you might use elements such as the placement of the actors (blocking), simple sets and props, and color to create them. Be sure to take notes during this discussion.

Steps:

3 If you were able to photograph the students' tableaux in Activity 4.3, revisit them now. Ask students to **close read** their tableaux in the same way that they have considered the artworks.

4 Acting companies (**discussion groups**) should meet to discuss how they may apply their close readings and interpretations of the art to their own performances. They should discuss what effects they will strive for and how they might use elements such as the placement of the actors (blocking), simple sets and props, and color to achieve them.

© 2011 College Board. All rights reserved.

ACTIVITY 4.24

"Then I Defy You, Stars!"

Materials:

- Copy of ***Romeo and Juliet***, Act V, Scene I

Purpose:

- To apply reading strategies in order to read a challenging text independently
- To plan and reflect on use of strategies
- To appraise a character's options

Steps:

1 You have introduced a variety of methods to help students read the play so far. With this foundation, students should be able to read Act V, Scene I independently. Have them first identify which reading strategies they intend to use. After reading, they should be able to explain Romeo's plan.

2 After they have read, give students an opportunity to assess the effectiveness of the reading strategies that they selected.

3 Have students do a **think-pair-share** for the steps in Romeo's plan.

4 Discuss with students what Romeo means by "Then I defy you, stars!"

5 Individually, with partners, or acting companies, students should **brainstorm** Romeo's options and their possible outcomes. Challenge students to predict which option Romeo will choose.

ACTIVITY 4.24

"Then I Defy You, Stars!"

SUGGESTED LEARNING STRATEGIES: **Think-Pair-Share, Brainstorming**

1. You have read most of *Romeo and Juliet* with your class, so you should be ready to read Act V on your own. First, think about the reading strategies you have used in the past and identify which you intend to use. After reading Act V, reflect on the effectiveness of those strategies in the space provided below.

2. Rather than marry Paris, Juliet decides to drink the Friar's potion so she will appear dead and then be interred in her family's vault. When Romeo hears news of Juliet's death, he, too, makes a difficult decision. As you read Act V, Scene 1, look for evidence that tells you what Romeo intends to do.

3. Based on the details you identified, what is Romeo's plan?

4. What does Romeo mean when he says, "Then I defy you, stars!"?

5. What are Romeo's options? On separate paper, create a graphic organizer such as a bubble cluster, and brainstorm every option you can see for Romeo and the possible outcomes of each option.

Comparing Film Interpretations: "Thus with a Kiss I Die"

ACTIVITY 4.25

SUGGESTED LEARNING STRATEGIES: Quickwrite, Close Reading, Graphic Organizer, Drafting

In Shakespeare's time, the stage would have looked similar to the drawing below. The theater in London where many of Shakespeare's productions were staged is the Globe Theatre. Modern-day stages are not so different, though seating for the audience is arranged differently.

Stage directions written into a play are usually given from the point of view of an actor facing the audience.

ACTIVITY 4.25

Comparing Film Interpretations: "Thus with a Kiss I Die"

Materials:

- Copy of ***Romeo and Juliet*** (Act V)
- Multiple film interpretations of the death scene from ***Romeo and Juliet***

Purpose:

- To compare and evaluate film interpretations
- To draft a response

Steps:

1 If students have not already researched theaters as part of their earlier work, you may want to have them research the Globe Theatre, both the one existing in Shakespeare's time and the modern-day version in London. Have students share their findings in class, drawing conclusions about the size of the theatre and how the closeness of the audience would affect the actors' use of gestures and expressions.

Steps:

2 Using the diagram on the student page, ask students to label the parts of the stage.

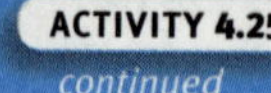

Comparing Film Interpretations: "Thus with a Kiss I Die"

Look at the stage directions below and imagine you are an actor facing the audience.

Using the information already provided for you, label areas of the stage:

Upstage

Stage Right

Stage Left

Center Stage

Downstage

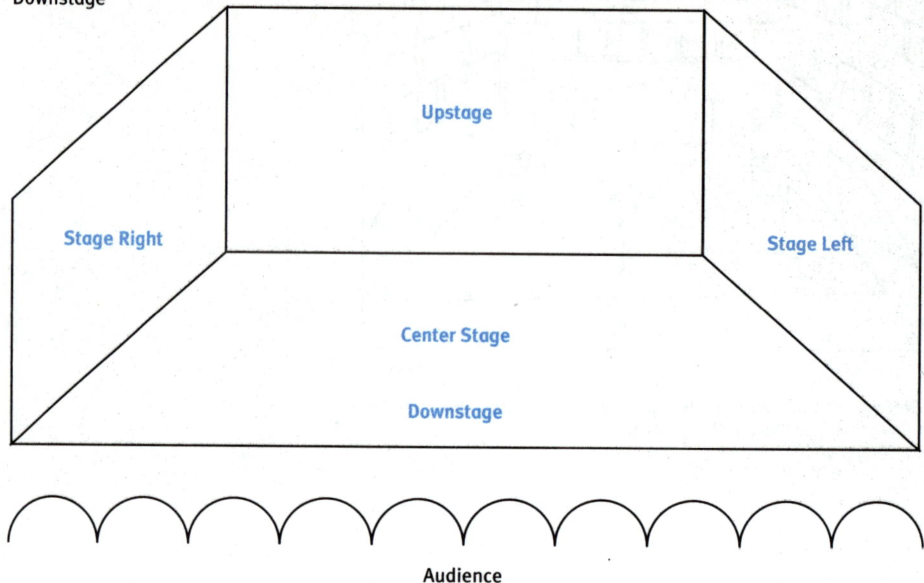

Audience

Find an area in your classroom and pretend it is your stage. See if you can identify the different areas of the stage.

308 SpringBoard® English Textual Power™ Level 4

The Tragedy of Romeo and Juliet has been performed countless times since Shakespeare's company first staged the drama, in part because audiences around the world respond emotionally to the young lovers who cannot be together.

1. What emotions does Act V of *Romeo and Juliet* create in you?

2. List the props you would need to create your vision of this scene.

3. The scene when Romeo and Juliet die is obviously one of the most important scenes in the play. Think about how you might stage this scene. Draw a diagram of your set and mark where your actors and props would be.

© 2011 College Board. All rights reserved.

Steps:

3 After reading Act V, have students do a **quickwrite** about the emotions created by this act.

4 Then have students visualize how they would stage Act V, Scene 3, and do the following:

- Draw a diagram of their set.
- Plan the lighting and music.
- Make a list of props.

Have students create their staging on pages 309–310 of their books.

Teacher Notes

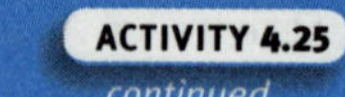

Comparing Film Interpretations: "Thus with a Kiss I Die"

What Kind of Lighting Would You Use to Create the Effect You Want?	What Kind of Music Would You Use to Create the Effect You Want?

TECHNOLOGY TIP If appropriate resources are available, work with peers to capture your ideas for staging a scene by filming short enactments or your discussions of props and staging.

As you watch film interpretations of the deaths of Romeo and Juliet, take notes on what each film does to create an emotional response. Think about all the theatrical elements directors use to create their intended effect:

- Actors' visual delivery (gestures, posture, movement, eye contact, facial expression)
- Actors' vocal delivery (volume, pitch, rate, pauses, vocal variety, pronunciation/articulation)
- Costumes/Props
- Setting
- Music/Sounds
- Lighting
- Editing

Title / Director	Intended Effect	How Director Creates Effect

Steps:

5 Next, ask students to do a **close reading** of at least two film interpretations of the deaths of Romeo and Juliet. Give them time to complete the **graphic organizer** on the student page after each viewing.

6 Begin with Romeo's entrance to the crypt and end with the deaths of both Romeo and Juliet.

- Zeffirelli: Clip 1, Scene 16 (2:00:53–2:12:36)
- Luhrmann:Clip 2, Scene 27 (1:41:55–1:51:22)

Steps:

7 The death scene provides an excellent opportunity to visualize the concept of dramatic irony. (If necessary, review this term.) Ask volunteers to share their responses. Make sure that they give evidence from the film to support their ideas.

8 Close by having students **draft** an essay that explains which version of *Romeo and Juliet* they enjoyed most and thought was more effective.

Comparing Film Interpretations: "Thus with a Kiss I Die"

Title / Director	Intended Effect	How Director Creates Effect

Literary Terms
Dramatic irony occurs when the audience knows something that a character does not.

Some directors emphasize **dramatic irony** in this scene. Explain any example of dramatic iron that you noticed. What knowledge did you have that the characters did not? How did your knowledge affect the way you felt during the scene?

Writing Prompt: Write a piece that explains which interpretations of *Romeo and Juliet* you found effective. Be sure to make specific references to theatrical elements, such as costumes, props, gestures, music, and other details to support your response.

"Some Shall Be Pardoned, and Some Punished"

ACTIVITY **4.26**

SUGGESTED LEARNING STRATEGIES: **Discussion Groups, Drafting, Graphic Organizer, Paraphrasing**

Review what you know about tragedy. Revisit any notes you have taken about tragedy and add to and refine them, showing how your understanding has grown after reading *Romeo and Juliet*.

LITERARY TERMS

A **theme** is a central idea or message of a literary work. Unlike a topic (for example, love, revenge, or death), a statement of theme is a complete thought; for example, not every love story is meant to have a happy ending.

Now that you have read *Romeo and Juliet*, consider the important themes that Shakespeare's play suggests. A literary work can have more than one theme, and the author does not generally directly state a theme but rather implies it. List several thematic statements about the subjects that Shakespeare treats in the play.

Which of these themes is most relevant to teenagers today? Explain.

ACTIVITY 4.26

"Some Shall Be Pardoned, and Some Punished"

Materials:

- Copy of ***Romeo and Juliet***

Purpose:

- To plan for an essay of argumentation
- To write a response to literature under time constraints

Steps:

TEACHER TO TEACHER This assignment is designed to give students practice in responding to a timed-writing prompt. The preparation for the writing can be done a day or two ahead. On the day of the timed writing, students should bring their notes. The actual writing of the essay should take place in a class period of about 45 to 50 minutes. This writing could provide a diagnostic instrument to help students improve future timed writings.

1 Have students revisit the notes they took during the unit about tragedy. They should add to and refine those notes in a **discussion group**.

2 Have the discussion groups identify major themes in the tragedy and share those with others in a **jigsaw**.

ACTIVITY 4.26 *continued*

Steps:

3 The discussion groups should next consider the various causes of the deaths of Romeo and Juliet. They should use the **graphic organizer** on pages 314–315 to record evidence for each of the causes and find quotations from the text to support their ideas.

"Some Shall Be Pardoned, and Some Punished"

During your reading of *Romeo and Juliet* you have considered the causes of Romeo's and Juliet's deaths. The major causes leading to their untimely demise are as follows:

- Romeo's and Juliet's youth and inexperience,
- The interference of the adults in the play,
- The influence of fate and/or chance on the lives of the characters.

Now look back through the play to locate actions and lines that support each of these causes. Use the chart below to organize your findings.

Youth and Inexperience	Adults' Interference	Fate/Chance
Act I	Act I	Act I
Act II	Act II	Act II
Act III	Act III	Act III

© 2011 College Board. All rights reserved.

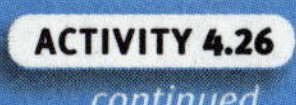

Youth and Inexperience	Adults' Interference	Fate/Chance
Act IV	Act IV	Act IV
Act V	Act V	Act V

Thesis Statement: After compiling your evidence and thinking about the causes of the deaths of Romeo and Juliet, write a thesis statement that addresses the question: Who or what is responsible for the deaths of Romeo and Juliet?

ACTIVITY 4.26 *continued*

Steps:

4 Have students craft a thesis statement and think about how they will organize and support their thesis.

Steps:

5 To help students begin the process of organizing, ask them to complete the outline provided on the student page.

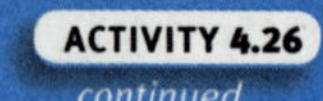

"Some Shall Be Pardoned, and Some Punished"

Now write topic sentences that address three possible causes of Romeo's and Juliet's deaths. Put the causes in order from least to most important.

Cause 1 (least important)

Cause 2 (important)

Cause 3 (most important)

Use the following outline to draft your essay:

Introduction

Lead or hook to grab the reader's attention

TAG (Title, Author, Genre) and minimal plot summary

Thesis—your opinion on the subject that you are trying to prove

Body Paragraphs

Topic sentences in each body paragraph that express ideas in support of your thesis.

Evidence from the text that supports your topic sentence

Commentary or explanations of the significance of your evidence

Conclusion

Summary of your main points

Expression of your own thoughts

Brief considerations of related questions, such as:

- How does a major theme of the play relate to the causes of the characters' deaths?
- What lesson can be learned from the characters' fates?
- What was Shakespeare trying to tell us about life through this story?

© 2011 College Board. All rights reserved.

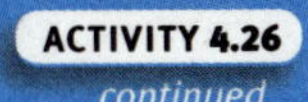

Timed Writing

At the end of *Romeo and Juliet*, the Prince states that some characters will be pardoned and others punished. You have considered the actions of Romeo and Juliet themselves, the adults in their lives, and fate or chance. Which do you think is primarily to blame for the deaths of Romeo and Juliet? Write your thesis here.

Compose a persuasive essay in which you argue that one of the three causes is the most important. Discuss each of the causes. Show which is the most important by organizing your essay from least to most important. Use transitions to reflect your organization. Also, consider the five elements of argumentation (hook, claim, concessions/refutations, support, and summary/call to action). Look at the Scoring Criteria on the next page to help guide your writing.

Writing Prompt: For Embedded Assessment 1, you will be presenting a Shakespearean scene. Work with your classmates to write two class advertisements for your performance. Use language and images to attract your audience. If possible, add sound to your advertisements, and film them for presentation to the class.

Steps:

6 Students should respond to the timed-writing prompt on this page by **drafting** a persuasive essay with ideas supported by the quotations they located earlier and by using **paraphrased** information.

7 Have students read the Scoring Criteria for their timed writings on page 318 to ensure that they incorporate these expectations into their pieces.

Teacher Notes

"Some Shall Be Pardoned, and Some Punished"

Scoring Criteria	Exemplary	Proficient	Emerging
Ideas and Organization	Essay opens with a clearly stated purpose that grabs readers' attention. Author provides opinions and supports them with evidence from the play. Author concludes with a thought-provoking ending.	Essay contains an opening with a clear purpose. Author states clear opinions and supports them with evidence from the play and concludes by giving the reader a sense of closure.	The essay lacks a clear purpose and opinions, as well as relevant evidence from the play. The conclusion does not address ideas expressed in essay.
Use of Language (Persuasive Techniques)	The author's skillful use of persuasive techniques works effectively to sway the reader. The author has a clear sense of effective tone for that audience.	The author uses persuasive techniques in an attempt to sway the reader. The author is aware of and uses an appropriate tone for that audience.	The author lacks appropriate techniques of persuasion and appropriate tone for the audience.
Conventions	The writer demonstrates strong control and mastery of standard conventions. Either no errors appear, or they are so slight that they do not interfere with meaning.	The writer demonstrates control of standard writing conventions. Though some errors may appear, they do not seriously impede readability.	There are frequent errors in standard conventions that seriously interfere with meaning.
Additional Criteria			

Comments:

© 2011 College Board. All rights reserved.

318 SpringBoard® English Textual Power™ Level 4

Presenting a Shakespearean Scene

Embedded Assessment 1

SUGGESTED LEARNING STRATEGIES: **Discussion Groups, Oral Interpretation**

Assignment

Your assignment is to work with your acting company to interpret, rehearse, and perform a scene from *The Tragedy of Romeo and Juliet*. In addition to the performance, actors, the director, and the dramaturge will prepare notebooks to accompany the scene.

Steps

Planning

1. When you formed your acting companies, you selected roles and a scene from the play to perform for the class. As you prepare for the performance, each member of the company must prepare a staging notebook specific to his or her role. (The content will be determined by the role of director, actor, or dramaturge.)
2. Review the essential features of an effective dramatic performance. Discuss how your acting company will integrate those features into your performance.
3. Begin the process by rereading your selected scene, getting comfortable saying the lines, and understanding the action in the scene. Plan appropriate visual and vocal delivery.
4. Remember, the goal is to interpret a scene. The acting company's success depends on how well members work together to create a polished and interesting performance.
5. The director will guide the acting company, making lists of props, costume pieces, and background music that will enhance the performance. The dramaturge will provide needed background information to enhance your performance.

Rehearsing

6. Rehearse your scene several times, using the strategies you have learned in this unit. The director's feedback and the dramaturge's research should enhance the acting company's performance.
7. If possible, videotape one of your rehearsals to help you improve the quality of the performance. Pay attention to your positions on stage, the pacing of your speeches, and the volume at which you speak. If videotaping is not practical, ask another group to watch and provide feedback on how you might improve your performance. Consult the Scoring Guide to help facilitate your rehearsals.

2 As students rehearse, remind them to ask for suggestions about ways to improve their performances. Especially encourage ELL students to solicit help from their peers by using strategies such as asking questions, using nonverbal cues, and asking for clarification to gain understanding.

© 2011 College Board. All rights reserved.

Embedded Assessment 1

Presenting a Shakespearean Scene

College Board Standards and Objectives

R1 Student Comprehends the Meaning of Words and Sentences (R1.1, R1.2)
PE Mappings: R1.1-2.4, R1.1-3.4, R1.2-2.4 , R1.2-3.4

R2 Using Prior Knowledge, Context, and Understanding of Language to Comprehend and Elaborate the Meaning of Texts (R2.1; R2.3)
PE Mappings: R2.1-1.4, R2.1-2.4, R2.3-1.4

R3 Author's Purpose, Audience, and Craft (R3.2)
PE Mappings: R3.2-2.4

R4 Using Strategies to Comprehend Text (R4.2, R4.3, R4.4)
PE Mappings: R4.2-1.4, R4.2-2.4, R4.2-3.4, R4.3-1.4, R4.4-1.4

S3 Preparing and Delivering Presentations (S3.3, S3.4)
PE Mappings: S3.3-1.4, S3.4-1.4

L3 Listening for Diverse Purposes (L3.1)
PE Mappings: L3.1-1.4

W2 Generating Content (W2.1 Cr; W2.2 Cr)
PE Mappings: W2.2-1.4 Cr, W2.2-2.4 Cr, W2.2-3.4 Cr

W3 Drafting (W3.1cr; 3.2cr)
PE Mappings: W2.1-1.4 Cr, W3.1-1.4 Cr, W3.2-1.4 Cr

W4 Evaluating and Revising Texts (W4.1 Cr; W4.2 Cr)
PE Mappings: W4.1-1.4 Cr, W4.2-1.4 Cr

W5 Editing to Present Technically Sound Texts (W5.1; W5.2; W5.4)
PE Mappings: W5.1-1.4, W5.2-1.4, W5.4-1.4

Steps:

1 By now, students should be familiar with their assignment for this assessment. Remind them to review the Scoring Criteria to ensure they know the expectations for their work.

Teacher Notes

Presenting a Shakespearean Scene

Performing

8. Perform your scene on the agreed-upon day. The director will introduce the scene, and, after the performance, the dramaturge will explain how the performance reflects his or her research.

Reflecting

9. After your performance, write a metacognitive reflection of the entire process including the scene analysis, rehearsals, and performance itself. Include your commentary on the challenges you faced, how you worked to overcome them, and your evaluation of the final performance. You may want to revisit the Scoring Guide to ensure your understanding of the criteria for this piece.

TECHNOLOGY TIP If appropriate resources are available, film your rehearsals for use in critiquing and improving your performance. Pay particular attention to speaking skills and delivery of your lines.

Embedded Assessment 1

continued

Director's Notebook

In preparation for your acting company's performance of a scene from *Romeo and Juliet*, you will create a staging notebook. Completing each item listed below will help you understand the scene and your responsibilities in the scene.

Text

Type or paste a copy of your scene on white paper. Leave plenty of room in the margins to take notes about the visual and vocal delivery by each character. Actors will take notes about their own characters, based on your direction, but you should have notes about all the characters. Plan to sit near your acting company during the performance and be prepared to feed lines to the actors if they forget.

Diagram of the Set

You will need to draw the set, so be sure to ask your teacher where you will be performing your scene. Include a sketch of the set from the audience's perspective as well as an aerial view (a view from above).

Lighting and Sound

Create a plan for lighting that will enhance your acting company's performance. Also list any sound effects or music that your group will use. For both lighting and sound, include an explanation as to why you think your choices are appropriate for your scene.

Props

Make a list of the props for your scene and where you will get them.

Introduction

Write an introduction for the scene and memorize it. You will present this introduction before your acting company performs.

Meeting Log

After every meeting, you will be responsible for writing a dated log that records how the meeting went. Some questions you might answer in your log include the following:

- What did the group accomplish?
- What obstacles were identified?
- Which problems have been resolved? How?
- What needs to be done before and at the next meeting?

Embedded Assessment 1

Continued

Teacher Notes

Teacher Notes

Presenting a Shakespearean Scene

Actor's Notebook

To help you prepare for your performance of a scene from *Romeo and Juliet*, you will create a staging notebook. Completing each of the items listed below should help you understand your scene and your part in the scene.

Text

Type or paste a copy of your scene on white paper. Highlight your own lines, and paraphrase them to help you understand them. There should be plenty of room in the margins for you to take notes about vocal and visual delivery. Write down everything that you and your director decide you should do to convey your interpretation of your character.

Costume

You will need to decide on an appropriate costume for your character. This page of your staging notebook will have two parts: the first part will show your ideal costume, and the second part will show your real costume.

- Your **ideal costume** is the one you would wear if you had all the resources you could wish for. You can draw, trace, or cut a picture out of a magazine for your ideal costume.
- Your **real costume** might be very simple, but it should reflect the character in some recognizable way. You may draw, trace, or attach a picture of yourself wearing your real costume.

Explain why the costume is appropriate for your character.

Character Analysis

Write a character analysis or explain your interpretation of your character.

- If you write a character analysis, choose a genre that will allow you to convey your character's thoughts, desires, actions, and obstacles.
- If you explain your artistic interpretation, think of a way to express these concerns visually. For example, you might draw an outline of a body and write your analysis on the corresponding body parts:

  Head: thoughts of your character

  Heart: desires of your character

  Arms: actions of your character

  Legs: obstacles for your character

Teacher Notes

Dramaturge's Notebook

Research Questions

As soon as your acting company has selected its scene, you will need to generate research questions related to the scene. These questions might address the context of the play, or they might focus on the history of its performance. You might need to research references made in the play or the meanings of unfamiliar words or phrases. In short, your assignment is to answer questions so that your company's performance is as authentic as possible.

Notes

Conduct research to answer questions and take careful notes.

Bibliography

Create a bibliography of the works you consulted in your research.

Suggestions

Based on your research findings, prepare a list of suggestions for the director and the actors. Present them to the group and be prepared to explain your reasons for the suggestions.

Explanation

Write an explanation of how your research helped the acting company interpret its scene. Memorize this explanation and present it after your group's performance.

Reflection

Write a reflection considering the research for your role as dramaturge. Did the process work effectively? Did you modify your major research question during research? How would you change the process for future research?

Scoring Guide

When you score this Embedded Assessment, you may wish to download and print a copy of the Scoring Guide from SpringBoard Online. In this way, you can have a copy to mark for each student's work.

Presenting a Shakespearean Scene

SCORING GUIDE

Scoring Criteria	Exemplary	Proficient	Emerging
Staging Notebook	The staging notebook demonstrates an insightful understanding of the scene and of the student's responsibilities. Each required entry is complete and detailed. The format of the notebook is exceptionally neat, organized, and well presented.	The staging notebook demonstrates a clear understanding of the scene and of the student's responsibilities. Required entries are complete. The format of the notebook is organized.	The staging notebook inadequately demonstrates an understanding of the scene and of the student's responsibilities. Required entries may be incomplete or missing. The format of the notebook is disorganized and difficult to follow.
Performance	The groups' interpretation of the scene is insightful, and the intended effect is clearly communicated to the audience. Participants demonstrate a polished performance by: • skillfully using various theatrical elements; • strategically using all elements of vocal delivery to effectively fulfill their role within the acting company; • effectively using elements of visual delivery to create focus and maintain energy for the scene.	The groups' interpretation of the scene is plausible, and the intended effect is communicated to the audience. Participants demonstrate an organized performance by: • adequately using various theatrical elements; • knowledgeably using elements of vocal delivery to appropriately portray their character(s) or to communicate information related to their role within the acting company; • using elements of visual delivery to create coherence for the scene.	The groups' interpretation of the scene may be unclear, and/or the intended effect is not successfully communicated to the audience. Participants demonstrate a disorganized performance and may: • not utilize various theatrical elements; • not use elements of vocal delivery to portray their character(s) or to communicate information related to their role within the acting company; • use elements of visual delivery that are unclear or detract from the quality of the scene.
Evidence of Collaboration	Throughout the entire process of planning and presenting, the group cooperates and works successfully to maintain purpose and to achieve goals. The equal sharing of responsibility is evident.	Throughout the process of planning and presenting, the group works together adequately to maintain purpose and achieve goals. The sharing of responsibility is mostly balanced.	Throughout the process of planning and presenting, the group members' cooperation is lacking, which impedes their ability to maintain a purpose or achieve goals. Responsibilities may not be equally divided.

SCORING GUIDE

Scoring Criteria	Exemplary	Proficient	Emerging
Reflective Text	The writer's metacognition demonstrates a thorough and detailed analysis of the entire process including analyzing, rehearsing, and performing the scene. It includes insightful commentary on challenges faced, how they were overcome, and an evaluation of the final performance.	The writer's metacognition demonstrates adequate analysis of the process of analyzing, rehearsing, and performing the scene. It includes commentary on challenges faced, how they were overcome, and an evaluation of the final performance.	The writer's metacognition demonstrates inadequate analysis of the process of analyzing, rehearsing, and performing the scene. Commentary on the challenges faced, how they were overcome, and an evaluation of the final performance may be weak or missing. Analysis and evaluation may be replaced by summary.
Additional Criteria:			

Comments:

Teacher Notes

LEARNING FOCUS: Measuring My Growth

Previewing Embedded Assessment 2

To preview the skills and knowledge necessary for success on Embedded Assessment 2, instruct students to locate the Assignment and Scoring Guide (pp. 333–335). Guide students through a **close reading** of the prompts, steps, and Scoring Guide criteria.

Steps:

1 Read the Learning Focus with students or have them read independently. **Activate prior knowledge** by having students **mark the text** and highlight words or concepts that are familiar (what they know). They might use a question mark to indicate content that is unfamiliar (what they do not know but want to learn).

2 Engage students in a whole class discussion.

Learning Focus:

Measuring My Growth

You and your group have presented your interpretation of a scene from a Shakespearean play, which is quite an accomplishment. Some parts of the assignment may not have gone as you had planned, while other parts may have gone better than you expected. One thing is certain—you learned along the way. You probably learned about the play itself as well as the playwright and the different contexts of his work, but more importantly, you may have learned about yourself.

You have used reading, writing, speaking, and listening skills to help you learn about and perform Shakespeare's drama. Now is your opportunity to take a close look at your growth as a learner, a reader, a writer, and a communicator. The second part of the unit focuses on **metacognition**. Metacognition is the ability to evaluate your growth and recognize the strategies that contributed to it so that you can continue to meet new learning goals.

You will have several opportunities to reflect on the learning strategies that are effective for you. Metacognition is an important skill to master because while your teachers and others may guide your education, ultimately you need to know and understand your strengths and challenges as a learner.

© 2011 College Board. All rights reserved.

Reflecting on Growth: Speaking and Listening

ACTIVITY 4.27

SUGGESTED LEARNING STRATEGIES: Revisiting Prior Work, Graphic Organizer

Think about your acting company's presentation of a scene from *Romeo and Juliet*. Now take some time to reflect on the presentation and your part in it.

What did you do well?	
Next time, what would you do differently?	
What did you learn about yourself?	
What did you learn about working with others?	
How did you grow or change as a result of the experience?	

ACTIVITY 4.27
Reflecting on Growth: Speaking and Listening

Materials:

- Staging notebook
- Portfolio of year's work

Purpose:

- To reflect on processes for creating and presenting a performance
- To reflect on growth in speaking and listening

Steps:

1 Revisit the Essential Question, "How have the strategies I have learned this year helped me to be a better reader, writer, speaker, and listener?" Explain to students that Embedded Assessment 2 will ask them to write a metacognitive, or self-reflective, essay. In order to manage the reflection process, this activity focuses on speaking and listening, and Activity 4.28 focuses on reading and writing. Both activities require that students have access to their work from this and previous units.

2 Have students complete the reflection questions in the **graphic organizers** on this page and the next. The questions focus on their acting company's presentation of a scene from ***Romeo and Juliet***.

Writing Workshops

You may want to have students complete Workshop 6, Expository Writing, prior to Embedded Assessment 2. This workshop provides direct instruction on organizing and developing an expository essay. While the workshop specifically focuses on cause and effect, students will benefit from the practice in organizing, drafting, and revising an essay as support for writing the Embedded Assessment essay.

Steps:

3 Next, ask students to think back on the opportunities they had throughout the year to perform or speak in front of others. They should **revisit prior work** by looking through their portfolios, their strategy learning logs, and their portfolio reflections, to refresh their memory and reflect on their growth as a performer or speaker.

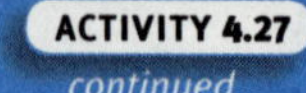

Reflecting on Growth: Speaking and Listening

You have had many opportunities for speaking and performing in front of an audience this year. Review your portfolio for activities in which you spoke to or performed for others. In this unit, you engaged in role playing, participated in a dress rehearsal, and performed a scene from a play.

Complete the graphic organizer about yourself as a speaker and/or performer.

In the past, as a speaker or performer I was...	
When I had to speak or perform before an audience, I felt...	
While I spoke or performed, I used to...	
Now, as a speaker or performer, I am...	
Now when I have to speak or perform before an audience, I feel...	
In the future, when I speak or perform, I will...	

© 2011 College Board. All rights reserved.

Part of the experience of performing scenes is serving as audience for your classmates' performances. Give yourself a rating, with 10 being the best score, as a listener/audience member.

1 2 3 4 5 6 7 8 9 10

Why did you give yourself this rating?

Working collaboratively also requires listening. Rate yourself as a listener in your acting company.

1 2 3 4 5 6 7 8 9 10

Why did you give yourself this rating?

How would you rate yourself as a listener in other activities you have completed?

1 2 3 4 5 6 7 8 9 10

Why did you give yourself this rating?

What can you do to be a better listener?

Which speaking and listening strategies have helped you most? Explain.

Steps:

4 Students should also rate themselves as listeners, both as audience members and as small group members, and set goals toward being a better listener.

5 Finally, ask students to review the speaking and listening strategies they have used and to choose those that helped them most. Ask students to explain their choices.

© 2011 College Board. All rights reserved.

Unit 4 • Interpreting Drama Through Performance 329

ACTIVITY 4.28

Reflecting on Growth: Reading and Writing

Materials:

- Students' portfolios of year's work

Purpose:

- To recognize elements that connect readers to texts
- To reflect on growth in reading and writing through use of strategies

Steps:

1 Ask students to **revisit their prior work** over the year and to identify pieces that demonstrate their growth and development as readers and writers. Ask students to focus on their use of the four types of strategies (Reading, Writing, Oral Literacy, and Collaborative). Make sure that students add the strongest pieces from this year to their portfolios.

2 Students should review Unit 4 for activities that challenged them in the use of reading and writing strategies. They should identify activities that required them to stretch their abilities.

3 Ask students to trace their thoughts about these activities and related texts in the **graphic organizer** on the student page. As students complete the organizer, remind them to note the use of strategies in those activities and to include that information as well.

ACTIVITY 4.28

Reflecting on Growth: Reading and Writing

SUGGESTED LEARNING STRATEGIES: Graphic Organizer, Drafting, Revising, Revisiting Prior Work

Identify activities from the unit that fit the descriptors listed at the bottom of the page. Write the activity in the Title(s) column. Then choose a descriptor that describes your response(s) to the activities. You can use the same activity more than once.

Type of Activity	Title(s)	Descriptor Words*	Strategies Used
Activities Where Your Feelings Changed as You Worked			
Activities Where Your Feelings Changed After You Finished Working			
Activities That the Class and/or Teacher Seemed to Enjoy But You Did Not			
Activities That Were Very Challenging			

***Descriptor Words**

curiosity	doubt	humor	surprise	fear
unwillingness	boredom	confidence	realization	confusion
amazement	empathy	joy	intimidation	awakening
anger	serenity	anticipation	engagement	compassion
disdain	dread	frustration	questioning	encouragement
delight	nostalgia	comfort	reminding	connection
disengagement	agitation	beauty	regret	admiration

On separate paper, write a response to an activity and text that you completed in this unit. Try to trace your connection (or lack of it) to this activity throughout the whole process of completing the task. In your response, discuss the strategies you used and their effect on the activity. You are not writing a review of the activity (saying whether or not it was good) but focusing on your response to that activity and text.

After writing your response, answer the following reflection questions.

1. As you review the challenging activities you listed on the previous page, what did strategies add to the activity, if anything? Explain.

2. You may have used some strategies more than others in this unit. Which strategies did you use most often? Why?

ACTIVITY 4.28 *continued*

Steps:

4 Next, students should **draft** a piece that describes their response to one activity that particularly affected them in some way (positively or negatively). They should include specific details about the strategies they used. The piece should be written as a narrative that traces their developing feelings about a text.

5 Ask students to answer the reflection questions that appear on the student pages.

Teacher Notes

Reflecting on Growth: Reading and Writing

3. What pieces of work, if any, do you plan to include in your portfolio as measurements of growth during this unit? Why did you select those pieces? How do they reflect your growth? Fill in the organizer below.

Name of Activity or Activities	Reason for Including This Activity in the Portfolio as an Example of Growth

4. In which strategies do you feel you have improved the most in this unit?

5. Which strategies, if any, are not comfortable for you at this point? Why?

Writing a Metacognitive Reflection

Embedded Assessment 2

SUGGESTED LEARNING STRATEGIES: **Drafting, Revising**

Assignment

Your assignment is to write a reflective essay about your growth as a reader, writer, speaker, and listener. Your essay should include examples of reading, writing, speaking, listening, and collaborative strategies you have used this year. You should also explain how those strategies helped you to improve your ability to read and comprehend challenging texts as well as write and present original texts.

Steps

Planning

1. Review the activities you completed this year. Also, refer to your list of strategies you have used this year. Be sure to consider strategy learning logs and end-of-unit reflections, as well as the pieces you have saved in your portfolio throughout the year.
2. Identify two or three strategies from each category (Reading, Writing, Speaking and Listening, Collaborative) that you used often and found to be most helpful in your tasks.
3. Using a prewriting strategy of your choice, develop a plan for a reflective essay in which you describe yourself as a reader, a writer, a speaker and a listener.

Drafting

4. Draft your essay. Include examples of your strengths, the challenges and obstacles you have encountered, and the strategies you have used to overcome them. Be sure to identify the strategies you have used, their effectiveness, and reasons you think they worked well for you. Use your portfolio as a resource and provide specific examples of texts you have read and created. Conclude by describing how you will meet new challenges and opportunities as a speaker, listener, and writer. Consult the Scoring Guide to review criteria.

Revising and Publishing

5. When you revise and edit your essay, make sure that your references to specific texts and assignments are accurate.
6. Share your metacognitive reflection with an audience of your choice.

Embedded Assessment 2

Writing a Metacognitive Reflection

College Board Standards and Objectives

W2 Generating Content (W2.1 Cr; W2.2 Cr)
PE Mappings: W2.1-1.4 Cr, W2.2-1.4 Cr, W2.2-2.4 Cr, W2.2-3.4 Cr, W2.2-4.4 Cr

W3 Drafting (W3.1 Cr; W3.2 Cr)
PE Mappings: W3.1-1,4 Cr, W3.1-3.4 Cr, W3.2-1.4 Cr, W3.2-2.4 Cr, W3.2-3.4 Cr

W4 Evaluating and Revising Texts (W4.1 Cr; W4.2 Cr)
PE Mappings: W4.1-1.4 Cr, W4.2-1.4 Cr

W5 Editing to Present Technically Sound Texts (W5.1; W5.2; W5.4)
PE Mappings: W5.1-1.4, W5.2-1.4, W5.4-1.4

Steps:

1 Review the assignment and Scoring Guide criteria with students to ensure they understand expectations for this Embedded Assessment.

2 In Step 6, Revising and Publishing, you may want students to ask their audiences for written feedback on their accomplishments.

3 As students edit their papers for publication, remind them to pay special attention to accuracy of grammar, punctuation, and spelling. Since this reflection is to be written in first person, students should also pay attention to their pronoun use and subject-verb agreement.

Embedded Assessment 2
Continued

Scoring Guide

When you score this Embedded Assessment, you may wish to download and print a copy of the Scoring Guide from SpringBoard Online. In this way, you can have a copy to mark for each student's work.

Embedded Assessment 2
continued

Writing a Metacognitive Reflection

SCORING GUIDE

Scoring Criteria	Exemplary	Proficient	Emerging
Evidence of Metacognition	The text insightfully and descriptively discusses the writer's strengths and the obstacles/challenges encountered in reading, writing, speaking, and listening. It provides reflective commentary on the effectiveness of strategies used as a reader, speaker, listener, and writer and demonstrates a perceptive analysis of strategies the student will apply in the future.	The text discusses the writer's strengths and the obstacles/challenges encountered in reading, writing, speaking, and listening. The text evaluates the effectiveness of particular strategies as a reader, speaker, listener, and writer. Commentary also shows an adequate evaluation of the strategies the student will apply in the future.	The text attempts to discuss the writer's strengths and the obstacles/challenges encountered in reading, writing, speaking, and listening. Commentary does little to explain the strategies to support experiences with challenging texts and opportunities as a speaker, listener, and writer. Parts of the reflective evaluation and evidence of personalized strategies to apply in the future may be missing.
Examples of Strategy Application	Specific and varied examples of texts the writer read and created and examples of speaking and listening opportunites support the identified strategies. They directly connect to the writer's analysis.	Clear examples of texts the writer read and created and examples of speaking and listening opportunities support the identified strategies. They relate to the writer's analysis.	Examples are difficult to identify from the description the student provides.
Organization	The text is multi-paragraphed and logically organized to enhance reader's understanding.	The essay is multi-paragraphed and organized in a coherent manner.	Organization is attempted, but key components are lacking in coherence.

Embedded Assessment 2

continued

SCORING GUIDE

Scoring Criteria	Exemplary	Proficient	Emerging
Additional Criteria			

Comments:

Embedded Assessment 2

Continued

Teacher Notes

© 2011 College Board. All rights reserved.

UNIT REFLECTION

Purpose:

- To monitor comprehension and growth through a reflective process
- To synthesize understanding of individual reading and writing processes and strategies
- To self-assess mastery of key concepts and terms

Steps:

1 This is an opportunity for students to think about the concepts, vocabulary, and their own learning progress as they revisit and review the work they have produced in this unit.

2 Encourage students to be especially metacognitive about which strategies they have used and how those strategies support their learning styles and goals.

Unit Teacher Reflection

1 Which activities in this unit did you need to adjust (or you think should be adjusted) to prepare your students to be successful on each Embedded Assessment? Add your notes on how you would adjust the activities.

2 Which teacher strategies were most effective for introducing concepts/ideas to your students?

3 How did the unit activities help you address the individual learning needs of your students? Note any changes you would make in your instructional strategies to differentiate instruction.

Unit 4

Reflection

An important aspect of growing as a learner is to reflect on where you have been, what you have accomplished, what helped you to learn, and how you will apply your new knowledge in the future. Use the following questions to guide your thinking and to identify evidence of your learning. Use separate notebook paper.

Thinking about Concepts

1. Using specific examples from this unit, respond to the Essential Questions:
   - What are the essential features of an effective drama and/or dramatic performance?
   - How have the strategies I have learned this year helped me to be a better reader, writer, speaker, and listener?
2. Consider the new academic vocabulary from this unit (**Drama, Tragedy, Theatrical Elements, Interpretation, Metacognition**) as well as academic vocabulary from previous units, and select 3–4 terms of which your understanding has grown. For each term, answer the following questions:
   - What was your understanding of the term before you completed this unit?
   - How has your understanding of the term evolved throughout the unit?
   - How will you apply your understanding in the future?

Thinking about Connections

3. Review the activities and products (artifacts) you created. Choose those that most reflect your growth or increase in understanding.
4. For each artifact that you choose, record, respond to, and reflect on your thinking and understanding, using the following questions as a guide:
   a. What skill/knowledge does this artifact reflect, and how did you learn this skill/knowledge?
   b. How did your understanding of the power of language expand through your engagement with this artifact?
   c. How will you apply this skill or knowledge in the future?
5. Create this reflection as Portfolio pages—one for each artifact you choose. Use the model in the box for your headings and commentary on questions.

Thinking About Thinking
Portfolio Entry

Concept:

Description of Artifact:

Commentary on Questions:

About the Unit

Unit 5

Context

Novels are a product and reflection of the life and times of their authors, even though they often present experiences that transcend those defining influences. In this unit, as students read *To Kill a Mockingbird*, they examine how an understanding of a novel's social, cultural, historical, and geographical context enhances their experience of the text. This unit also challenges them to become increasingly aware of how authors use literary elements—such as character, setting, and conflict—to represent and evaluate various points of view within those contexts. Thematically, the exploration of *To Kill a Mockingbird* engages students in an examination of the diverse meanings of coming of age.

AP/ College Readiness

Students develop the following important skills and knowledge areas for AP/College Readiness in this unit:

- Researching the cultural, historical, social, and geographical context of a novel and applying the research to an understanding and appreciation of the work. (Activities 5.5, 5.6, 5.7)
- Reading and analyzing a novel of literary merit. (Activities 5.11, 5.12)
- Applying close textual analysis for use of language and the complex relationships between literary elements and thematic development. (Activities 5.15, 5.17, 5.18)

Suggested Texts and Materials

You will need to acquire the following texts for this unit:

- Photos of images of the segregated South from the 1930s through the 1960s for the opening gallery walk
- Copies of the novel *To Kill a Mockingbird* by Harper Lee, for each student
- A DVD of the film *To Kill a Mockingbird*, directed by Robert Mulligan, 1962

The first part of this unit involves a group research project and presentation. If possible, schedule adequate computer lab time for research, and plan to have an LCD projector available for presentations.

Independent Reading

Students will participate in an in-depth study of a complex text in Unit 5. To extend this unit's focus on the theme of coming of age, encourage students to read an outside text that relates to a theme from the novel (prejudice, community, or tolerance) that resonates with them. Students might also consider a piece of historical fiction to help them explore the connection between historical context and construction of text.

Writing Workshops

The embedded assessments for this unit require students to complete a historical investigation and presentation and analyze a passage from *To Kill a Mockingbird*. For Unit 5, you may want to access Workshop 10, Research, and Workshop 9, Response to Literary and Expository Text, as additional or preliminary practice for the Embedded Assessments in this unit.

Grammar Handbook

As students continue to develop their writing skills, encourage them to refer to the Grammar Handbook and to the Grammar & Usage features in this and previous units to help them improve the mechanics of their writing. You may want to incorporate mini-lessons from the Grammar Handbook and the Grammar & Usage features to reinforce students' grammar and writing skills.

Instructional Sequence

The instruction begins with investigations of the novel's background, or context. Working in groups, students select topics, research and develop content, and craft a presentation (Embedded Assessment 1) designed to engage their classmates and inform them of relevant contextual information. When students are prepared with this background, you will lead them through a close examination of Part One of the novel, modeling active reading and thinking skills. In Part Two, the instructional emphasis shifts to close textual analysis of language and literary elements. To prepare students for Embedded Assessment 2, the literary analysis of a passage, students practice crafting interpretive statements about the text and identifying and evaluating textual passages as supporting evidence for those claims.

Activities 5.1–5.3 preview the unit and introduce students to issues and images that will be explored in the text.

Activities 5.4–5.6 establish the meaning of context, and engage students in an examination of a model topic (Jim Crow laws) to prepare them for their own investigations.

Activities 5.7–5.9 walk students through the research and presentation process, helping them to collect and organize information, shape the content to appeal to their target audiences, and evaluate their success as presenters.

Embedded Assessment 1 | **Historical Investigation and Presentation**

Skills and Knowledge:

- Understand literary context.
- Understand and practice effective public speaking.
- Craft an effective thesis statement.
- Develop key questions to guide organization of content.
- Use effective transitions to connect ideas.
- Evaluate audio-visual resources as tools for engaging audiences.
- Organize presentation responsibilities.
- Design an organizational notetaking tool for audience members.
- Understand and apply the conventions of an annotated bibliography.

Activities 5.10–5.14 model active reading skills (making predictions and connections, drawing inferences) and scaffold these skills for independent reading of the text.

Activities 5.15–5.18 guide students through the process of generating interpretive claims about the text and identifying quotations as supporting evidence for those claims.

Activities 5.19–5.27 examine the connection between the portrayal of setting, character, and conflict in key passages and the themes of the novel as a whole, scaffolding the process students will use in Embedded Assessment 2.

Embedded Assessment 2 **Analyzing a Passage from *To Kill A Mockingbird***

Skills and Knowledge:

- Understand the connection between literary elements (setting, conflict, character) and the meaning of a work as a whole.
- Identify a significant passage that pertains to coming of age.
- Interpret a textual passage.
- Connect the larger themes of the novel to the content and literary elements in a short passage from the novel.
- Craft a clear and effective thematic statement.
- Evaluate quotes as textual evidence in support of an interpretive claim.
- Develop a topic outline.
- Use peer feedback to guide revision.
- Seamlessly integrate quotes from the novel.
- Edit and revise for publication.

Activity 5.28 asks students to consider the impact of the novel and how it continues to be received.

Suggested Pacing

Activity	45 to 50-Minute Class Periods	Class Periods with Homework	Activity	45 to 50-Minute Class Periods	Class Periods with Homework
Learning Focus and 5.1	½		5.15	½	
5.2	¾		5.16	1 ½	HW
5.3	1		5.17	¼	
5.4	¼		5.18	1	HW
5.5	1		5.19	1	HW
5.6	2	HW	5.20	1	
5.7	2	HW	5.21	1	HW
5.8	1		5.22	2	HW
EA1	3	HW	5.23	1	HW (reading)
Learning Focus	½		5.24	1	HW (reading)
5.9	½		5.25	¾	HW (reading)
5.10	1	HW (reading)	5.26	1	HW (reading)
5.11	1 ½	HW	5.27	½	
5.12	1	HW (reading)	EA2	3	
5.13	1	HW (reading)	5.28	½	
5.14	1	HW (reading)	Unit Reflection	½	
Total Class Periods				34 ½	

Reading Plan: *To Kill a Mockingbird*

To Kill a Mockingbird is one of the most studied books in the American canon, but it has also been, at times, one of the most controversial. The narrative core—the coming of age of Scout, Jem, and Dill—still resonates today. In addition, the novel's exploration of racism, justice, gender roles, and the nature of heroism remains relevant, even after more than 50 years of social change. Atticus Finch, both on the page and in Gregory Peck's beloved film portrayal of him, ranks in the pantheon of literary creations, while the tragic fate of Tom Robinson reminds us that injustice all too often triumphs—a harsh and disillusioning reality, which Scout, and Jem, and Dill must come to terms with on their journey to maturity and adulthood.

This unit is designed to teach students to be close readers and interpreters of extended texts through a variety of active reading strategies. Activities explore the significance of setting, character, and conflict as they relate to the development of the novel's themes. Students examine these elements as the means by which the author articulates the social and cultural tensions that swirl within the setting of the novel, as well as at the time of its publication in 1960. Both contexts are thus central to the students' experience of the novel.

Prereading

Embedded Assessment 1 requires students to generate a body of contextual knowledge to understand the very different world of 1930s, and to a lesser extent, 1960s Alabama. In order to activate prior knowledge and prepare students for the novel, the first part of the unit gives students an opportunity to explore relevant background, and establish norms for active reading, listening, and participating.

While Reading the Novel

Part One of the novel, closely taught, is designed to help students "come of age" as academic readers as you model various active-reading strategies, strategies that are second nature to experienced readers. It also sets up the close analysis of the central experience of Part One—the children's relationship with Boo Radley. This relationship prepares the main characters with a lesson about how to combat the poison of rumors, gossip, and stereotyping that is encapsulated by Atticus' advice that "You never really understand a person until you consider things from his point of view—until you climb into his skin and walk around in it." This relationship and this lesson are keys to understanding how the children avoid "Maycomb's usual disease"—racism.

Students read Part Two of the novel more independently. Throughout both Parts, students engage in close readings of passages. This focus prepares them to choose and interpret a passage about the "coming of age" of Jem and Scout and then relate this passage to central themes of the novel about stereotyping, about being a gentleman or a lady, about courage, about walking in another's skin, about injustice and intolerance (thematic subjects of the novel)—the task of Embedded Assessment 2.

Chapters	Activities	
1	5.10 A Scouting Party 5.11 Visualizing Setting	Students closely read several passages, begin a character-based (Boo [Arthur] Radley) double-entry journal, and use visualization as they read.
2-3	5.12 Making Connections	Students make links to prior knowledge, personal experience, and other texts.
4-5	5.13 Making Predictions	Students make predictions and apply strategies for comprehending new vocabulary.
6-7	5.14 Drawing Inferences	Students analyze textual details to draw inferences.
8	5.15 Lessons from the Neighborhood	Students focus on lessons learned from Jem and Scout's interactions with Boo Radley.
9-10	5.16 Questioning the Text 5.17 Examining the Title	Students generate levels of questions in preparation for more independent and small group work in Part Two. Students also read a passage closely to draw conclusions about the significance of the novel's title.
11	5.18 Pin the Quote on Atticus 5.19 Exploring the Issues in *To Kill a Mockingbird*	Students write topic sentences and paragraphs focused on Atticus as a heroic figure. Jem's experience with Mrs. Dubose and the lesson he learns about courage ends Part One of the novel.
After Chapter 11, students stop to identify key thematic elements of the novel in preparation for reading Part Two more independently. Students synthesize the facts about the children's relationship to Boo Radley and articulate what they are learning that will be important in Part Two.		
12-13	5.20 Changing the Scene	Students consider the significance of a change in setting (to Calpurnia's church where they "walk around" in another person's skin) and the introduction of a new, key character (Aunt Alexandra).
14-15	5.21 Comparing Print and Film Text	Students contrast their reading of the jail porch scene with the film version.
16-20	5.22 Analyzing Atticus's Closing Argument	Students again contrast the text with the film version, this time focusing on how Atticus's speech is modified to suggest a change in the intended audience (from readers to viewers).
21-23	5.23 Reflection on the Verdict	Students hold a Socratic Seminar responding to issues of justice in the novel (reinforcing a key thematic element).

24	5.24 The World of Fragrant Ladies	Students examine the changing relationship between Scout and Aunt Alexandra, who is trying to teach Scout how to be a proper Southern lady (linking to the theme of gender norms in the book).
25-28	5.25 Exploring Insights 5.26 Standing in Borrowed Shoes	Students create a character collage and discuss how characters function as symbolic representations of points of view and experiences central to the South.
After Chapter 25, students interpret several quotations that link to key themes in the novel.		
29-31	5.27 Scout and Boo	Students consider how Scout's perception of Boo has changed and how this change is emblematic of her changing view of the world

Throughout Part Two, you might supplement activities with additional small group or large group discussions, but the goal of discussing only some of these chapters in depth is to push students to take responsibility for critical, independent, engagement with the text.

Post-Reading

After students finish the novel and the final essay, the unit ends with a discussion of how texts function within and beyond the context in which they are created, examining the novel's reception by various readers since its publication.

The year concludes with a final Reader's Theater activity revisiting texts from throughout the year and inviting students to reflect on how their encounters with the various texts and activities this year have affected them.

Unit 5

Coming of Age Amidst Controversy

Essential Questions

- What are the essential elements of an effective informative presentation?
- What impact does historical, cultural, geographical, and social context have on a novel and on the reaction of readers to it?

Unit Overview

In this unit, you will encounter a longer, more complex text that deals with the concept of coming of age. Like Romeo and Juliet, who are confronted with prejudice in their world, Jem and Scout in Harper Lee's novel *To Kill a Mockingbird* confront prejudice in their community. Jem and Scout are more fortunate than Romeo and Juliet because their father is a model of tolerance, rationality, and compassion. The two children learn from their father and from their experiences how best to live in a less-than-perfect world. In your reading, you will trace a sustained development of character, setting, conflict, and you will examine how these relate to theme. Also, you will consider how social, cultural, geographical, and historical context can affect both the writer's construction of a text and the readers' responses to it.

UNIT 5

Have students read the Unit Overview. Discuss the ideas in the overview and ask students to relate them to their own lives.

Students will provide responses to the Essential Questions in Activity 5.1. At the end of the unit, they will revisit the Essential Questions to see how their responses have changed after studying the unit.

UNIT 5

Have students read the goals for the unit and **mark** any words that are unfamiliar to them. You may want to create a space in the classroom for these words so students can add information about their meaning as they study the unit.

You may consider posting these goals in a visible place in the classroom for the duration of the unit, allowing you and students to revisit the goals easily and gauge progress toward achieving the goals throughout the unit.

Academic Vocabulary

Point out the academic vocabulary to students, and remind them that they will be studying concepts related to these words throughout the unit. Having students create **graphic organizers** to study these words in depth will greatly enhance their understanding of each word and its relationship to unit concepts. Have students keep their completed graphic organizers in their **Vocabulary Notebooks**.

See the Resources at the back of this book for examples of blackline masters suitable for word study. As students become more acquainted with the use of a **graphic organizer** to explore the meaning of a word, you may want them to create their own graphic organizers.

Unit 5 Coming of Age Amidst Controversy

Goals

- To gather and synthesize information for an oral presentation on the social, cultural, historical, and geographical context of the novel
- To explore the signficance of setting, conflict, and the growth of characters in relation to the theme of coming of age
- To extrapolate from a short passage the larger themes and literary elements of the novel

ACADEMIC VOCABULARY

Context
Annotated Bibliography
Thematic Statement
Characterization
Audience Analysis

Contents

UNIT 5

Teacher Notes

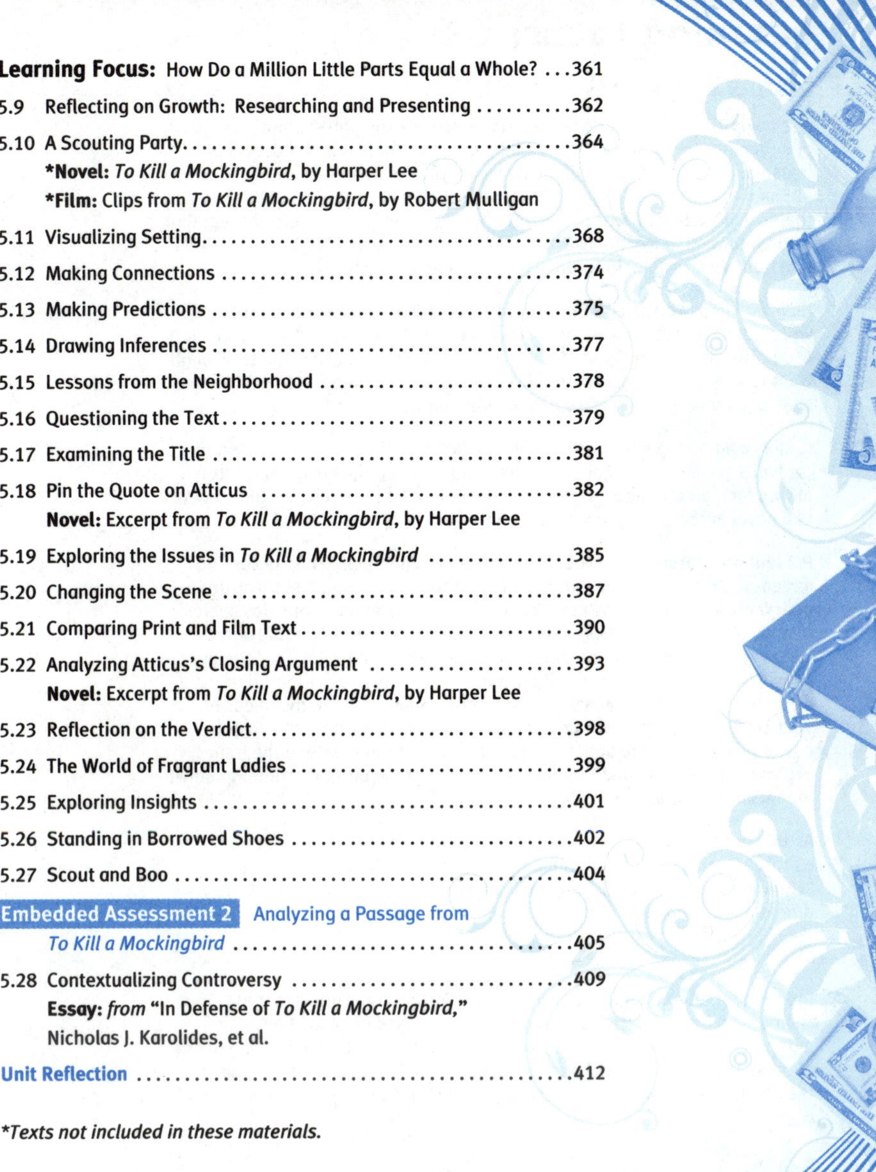

**Texts not included in these materials.*

339

LEARNING FOCUS:
Setting the Context

Read the Learning Focus with students or have them read independently. **Activate prior knowledge** by having students **mark the text** and highlight words or concepts that are familiar (what they know). They might use a question mark to indicate content that is unfamiliar (what they do not know but want to learn).

Students will respond to the information on this page in Activity 5.1.

Teacher Notes

Learning Focus:
Setting the Context

The novel *To Kill a Mockingbird*, by Harper Lee, is the perfect combination of engaging story-telling and hard-edged social commentary. Recognizing injustices through the eyes of an innocent narrator makes those injustices all the more memorable. The novel is very much about the "**coming of age**" theme you have studied all year, but it's also about a controversial event that creates turmoil in a fictional community—an event that reflects the tensions that defined a certain time and place in real American history.

Have you ever wondered where authors get inspiration for the things they write? Or how "real" a work of fiction might be? Or why a novelist sets a story in a particular time and place? Have you ever questioned why someone might want to ban a book that others think everyone should read? Research is the way to get answers to these kinds of questions.

Understanding the social, cultural, historical, and geographical **context** of a novel's setting, as well as the time period in which the novel was written, allows for a greater understanding of the immediate and long-lasting impact of a novel in the society in which it is published.

Presenting information to your classmates is a challenging and rewarding endeavor. As you present your research on social, cultural, historical, and geographical issues of the novel's context, you will enable your classmates to make connections between the novel and the real world it represents. One way to enhance your presentation is to understand what your audience knows and wants to know about the subject. As with any presentation, an **audience analysis** helps you to tailor the presentation to the needs of your classmates. After your presentation, it is also important to evaluate how effective you were at helping your audience to understand the issues explored in the novel and their relevance both to the author's contemporary readers and to readers of today.

As this level ends, you will also have an opportunity to think about how cultural, historical, and contemporary contexts reflect themes such as "coming of age." Theme is present in all genres, from poetry and film to drama and the novel.

Independent Reading: Reading in this unit focuses on a novel that explores issues such as prejudice, community, tolerance, and coming of age. For independent reading, look for a text that expands your understanding of one of these themes. You could also select historical fiction that helps illuminate the connection between historical context and the construction of a fictional work.

Previewing the Unit

ACTIVITY 5.1

SUGGESTED LEARNING STRATEGIES: Close Reading, KWL Chart, Marking the Text, Skimming/Scanning, Summarizing/Paraphrasing, Think-Pair-Share

Essential Questions

1. What are the essential elements of an effective informative presentation?

2. What impact does historical, cultural, geographical, and social context have on a novel and on the reaction of readers to it?

Unit Overview and **Learning Focus**

Predict what you think this unit is about. Use the words or phrases that stood out to you when you read the Unit Overview and the Learning Focus.

Embedded Assessment 1

What knowledge must you have (what do you need to know) to succeed on Embedded Assessment 1? What skills must you have (what must you be able to do)?

ACTIVITY 5.1 Previewing the Unit

Purpose:

- To contextualize prior knowledge about key ideas and concepts
- To analyze the skills and knowledge necessary for success in the unit

Steps:

1 To determine students' existing knowledge about the concepts for the unit, ask them to **think-pair share** responses to the two Essential Questions. Students will revisit these questions throughout the unit to develop a more mature understanding of these ideas.

2 Direct students to **skim and scan** the Unit Overview and Learning Focus pages. **Activate prior knowledge** by asking students to **mark the text**. They may use a check mark to indicate what is familiar to them (know) and a question mark to indicate what is unfamiliar to them (don't know–want to learn). Engage students in a whole class discussion. You may want to record their findings on a **KWL** chart and revisit this chart at the end of the unit to discover what students have learned.

3 Provide students with a clear learning target by asking them to find the Embedded Assessment 1 assignment and Scoring Guide (pages 358–360). Lead students through a **close reading** of the prompt, steps, and Scoring Guide criteria. Instruct students to **mark the text** by underlining or highlighting the places that mention a skill or knowledge necessary to succeed on the Embedded Assessment.

4 Instruct students to **summarize/paraphrase** with a partner or small group the skills/knowledge they have underlined or highlighted. As you conduct a large group discussion, create a web **graphic organizer** that lists the knowledge and skills.

5 Revisit the web graphic organizer throughout the unit. Pointing students back to the web reinforces the purpose of each activity and the skills and knowledge needed for success on the Embedded Assessment. You may want to enlarge the Embedded Assessment web graphic organizer to provide a **visual** in the classroom throughout the course of the unit. Students will preview Embedded Assessment 2 before Activity 5.9.

ACTIVITY 5.2
Exploring My Opinions

Materials:

- Posted signs—Agree, Disagree

Purpose:

- To set a context for study of thematic ideas
- To defend and discuss opinions and evidence
- To apply listening and speaking strategies to large group discussions

Steps:

1 Note that the "opinionnaire" serves as an **Anticipation Guide** in that the statements relate to concepts and issues in the novel: equality, gender, heroism, vigilante action, and prejudice.

2 Make two large signs—one that reads "Agree" and one that reads "Disagree." Post them conspicuously on two opposite sides of the room. After students have responded to the statements, read the statements aloud and have students move to the signs that reflect their opinion. You may want to have students do this in response to only a few selected statements rather than all of them.

3 When students are situated, solicit reasons for their opinions. In this way, students participate in a structured discussion about their opinions. They must listen and respond to one another politely. Post the following stems, and ask students to use them as they present their responses to others' opinions:

- I agree with you _____; however ....
- I hear what you're saying _____, but have you considered...?
- I really disagree with you _______, because...
- I disagree because.... Have you considered....?

ACTIVITY 5.2

Exploring My Opinions

SUGGESTED LEARNING STRATEGIES: Quickwrite

WORD CONNECTIONS

The word ***prejudice*** means a preconceived idea or judgment. The Latin prefix *pre-* means "before." The Latin root *-judic-* means to "judge" or "decide." Other words using this root include *judge* and *judicial*.

Opinionnaire

Respond to the following statements by placing either **A** (Agree) or **D** (Disagree) next to each one to indicate your feelings. Your response should simply be your first impression in response to each statement. You can also jot down comments about a statement, examples to support your point of view, or mixed feelings you have about the statement. Be prepared to present your perspectives to your classmates.

A = Agree D = Disagree

Beginning of Unit		Statement	Conclusion of Unit
_____	1.	All men and women are treated equally in society.	_____
_____	2.	Girls should act like girls, and boys should act like boys.	_____
_____	3.	In society, it's okay to be different from what others consider normal.	_____
_____	4.	People are either all good or all evil; there is no in-between.	_____
_____	5.	Some words are so offensive that they should never be stated or written.	_____
_____	6.	Under our justice system, all citizens are treated fairly in our courts of law.	_____
_____	7.	This old saying still applies in society today: "Sticks and stones may break my bones, but words will never hurt me."	_____
_____	8.	Speaking standard English proves that a person is smart.	_____
_____	9.	A hero is born, not made.	_____
_____	10.	We should follow only the laws in society that make sense to us.	_____
_____	11.	Education gives everyone an equal opportunity to succeed.	_____
_____	12.	When the law does not succeed in punishing a criminal, citizens should be able to punish the criminal themselves.	_____
_____	13.	If someone is on trial for murder, that person is probably guilty.	_____
_____	14.	Killing under any circumstance is wrong.	_____
_____	15.	Good parents set limits for their children.	_____
_____	16.	Every individual in society is prejudiced about something.	_____

After you have responded to the questionnaire and discussed your responses, work in pairs or small groups to sort the sixteen questions into general topic areas, such as justice or education.

4 As students hear a peer's points, encourage them to move toward a posted sign to indicate the degree to which they are persuaded by a point.

5 This activity is designed to teach students to thoughtfully articulate views on a subject while considering the perspectives of others, an important concept as they read the novel in this unit. You may conclude by having students respond to this **quickwrite** prompt:

Choose one statement with which you disagree strongly. Write about why you feel so strongly.

6 To set up later research work, ask students to categorize the questions, which fall generally into these groups: gender, justice, labeling/stereotyping, heroes, prejudices.

A Time and a Place

ACTIVITY 5.3

SUGGESTED LEARNING STRATEGIES: Graphic Organizer, Word Map

To develop some understanding of the context for the novel *To Kill a Mockingbird*, view the photographs your teacher has provided. Note your observations and questions on the graphic organizer.

ACADEMIC VOCABULARY

Context refers to the circumstances or conditions in which something takes place.

Photo #	Observation: Note the details of the image in the photograph.	Reflection: What is your response to the images in the photograph?	Questions: What questions come to mind that might lead to further exploration or research?

ACTIVITY 5.3
A Time and a Place

Materials:

- Photographs from the 1930s to set a context for *To Kill a Mockingbird*

Purpose:

- To demonstrate inquiry-based research
- To identify and assess aspects of the social, historical, cultural, and geographical context of the novel
- To illustrate aspects of the novel's setting

Steps:

1 Gather six or seven dramatic photographs that capture the essence of Southern life during the 1930s. Include photos that illustrate the times of the Great Depression, the poverty of whites and blacks, small-town rural living, and Jim Crow laws. You can find many Web sites with images of the 1930s. Number each photograph, and post them equidistant from one another around the room in preparation for a gallery walk.

2 While students are seated, ask them to select one photograph that particularly interests them, and then direct them to move to that picture. This procedure will break the class into smaller groups to facilitate the gallery walk. Next, direct students to move clockwise around the room as though they were at an art gallery. Have them record their responses to the photographs on the **graphic organizer**. Students may engage in light conversation in response to images, but they should focus on taking notes. You might want to ring a bell, or say "switch" every two or three minutes to keep the traffic moving.

3 Encourage students to respond to, reflect upon, and question the photographs. Urge them especially to ask questions about the images as a way to create inquiry or focus questions for the upcoming research project.

4 Put students in small groups to share and to develop more questions about the historical, geographical, social and/or cultural context of the novel.

5 Inform students that *To Kill a Mockingbird* is set in the 1930s in Alabama. Then, lead a large group discussion of students' comments and questions about the social, cultural, historical, geographical aspects depicted in the photos.

6 To prepare for the visual portion of Embedded Assessment 1, use their responses to create a list of criteria for choosing visuals that engage an audience. Connect the criteria to a discussion of the **Essential Question**: What are the essential elements of an effective informative presentation?

ACTIVITY 5.4
What Is Context?

Materials:

- Vocabulary Notebooks

Purpose:

- To analyze the meaning of social, historical, cultural, and geographical context
- To review the skills and knowledge necessary to investigate and present information on a topic

Steps:

1 Have students work with a partner to create a web **word map** for *context*. You might wish to point out that *context* comes from the Latin word *contexere*, which means "to weave together." Context weaves together the circumstances or conditions under which something exists or occurs. When students have explored the word, have them add the words ***historical, social, cultural, geographic*** to the web. Then, link what they've learned about these terms to the photos they have seen. Instruct students to add this word and its graphic organizer to their **Vocabulary Notebooks**.

2 Remind students of the research and presentation skills they'll need for Embedded Assessment 1. They will apply these skills to learn about the context for *To Kill a Mockingbird*.

3 You may want students to think about context from a different perspective by posing this prompt for discussion or writing:

- How would the context of the time when the novel was written (1960) affect its creation?

You might use this prompt as an effective differentiation by introducing another context for the novel.

ACTIVITY 5.4

What Is Context?

SUGGESTED LEARNING STRATEGIES: Graphic Organizer, Word Map

You have viewed photographs to give you a context for the novel *To Kill A Mockingbird*, which you are about to read. But what exactly is context? With a partner, brainstorm what you already know about the idea of context. Then, find out its meaning and derivation in a dictionary. Create a web graphic organizer below, exploring the relationships of historical, cultural, social, and geographical settings to context.

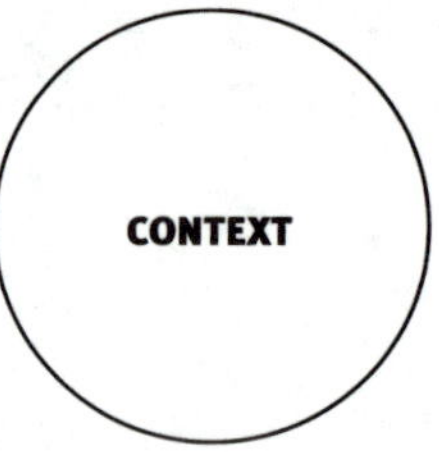

Once you have investigated the idea of context, add branches for historical, cultural, social, and geographical aspects. What does each term incorporate?

Putting the Text in Context

ACTIVITY 5.5

SUGGESTED LEARNING STRATEGIES: Close Reading, KWHL Chart, Marking the Text, Skimming/Scanning

Reflecting on the images from the gallery walk and other information from your class discussion, fill out the first two columns of the chart below.

K: What do I know about life in the South during the 1930s?	**W:** What do I want to know about life in the South during the 1930s?	**H:** How will I find information? (Which resources, web pages, texts, methods, etc.)	**L:** What have I learned about life in the South during the 1930s?

ACTIVITY 5.5

Putting the Text in Context

Materials:

- Highlighters
- Chart paper
- Vocabulary Notebooks

Purpose:

- To define and identify significant terms that illuminate the novel's context
- To categorize and analyze elements of the social, legal, and cultural context of the novel
- To develop questions for possible research

Steps:

1 Direct students to the **KWHL chart**, and have them fill in the K column (what they know about the South in 1930s). You might also want to use this chart to expand the discussion by asking students about the 1960s (when the book was published).

Steps:

2 Read the short excerpt from the article "Shorthand for Separation" aloud, and ask students to **mark the text** by highlighting the statements that define the term "Jim Crow." Work with students to create a working definition of Jim Crow laws.

Putting the Text in Context

My Notes

What were Jim Crow laws? As you read the following article, mark the text to identify the words and phrases that help you to define the meaning of the term *Jim Crow* and understand its importance in American history.

Informational Text

JIM CROW: SHORTHAND FOR SEPARATION

by Rick Edmonds

"Jim Crow" the term, like Jim Crow the practice, settled in over a long period of time. By the 1950s, *Jim Crow* was the colloquialism whites and blacks routinely used for the complex system of laws and customs separating the races in the South. Hardly anyone felt a particular need to define it or explore its origins.

The term appears to date back at least to the eighteenth century, though there is no evidence that it refers to an individual. Rather it was a mildly derogatory slang for a black everyman (Crow, as in black like a crow.) A popular American minstrel song of the 1820s made sport of a stereotypic Jim Crow. "Jump Jim Crow" was a sort of jig. By the mid-1800s, a segregated rail car might be called the "Jim Crow." As segregation laws were put into place—first in Tennessee, then throughout the South—after Reconstruction, such diverse things as separate public facilities and laws restricting voting rights became known collectively as Jim Crow.

A bit like "political correctness" in recent years, the term was particularly popular with opponents of the practice. It was a staple of NAACP conversations of the '30s and '40s. Ralph Bunche once said he would turn down an appointment as ambassador of Liberia because he "wouldn't take a Jim Crow job." A skit at Morehouse College during Martin Luther King's student days portrayed a dramatic "burial" of Jim Crow. And . . . at the eventful Republican National Convention of 1964 in San Francisco, picketers outside the hall chanted, "Jim Crow (clap, clap) must go." . . .

From material in *American Heritage Dictionary, Safire's Political Dictionary,* and *From Slavery to Freedom.*

GRAMMAR & USAGE

The second sentence in this essay begins with a prepositional phrase, "By the 1950s." A prepositional phrase consists of a preposition, its object, and any modifiers of the object.

Common prepositions include *about, across, in, by, after, onto, until,* and *up*. A preposition shows the relationship or connection between its object and some other word. In the sentence identified above, for example, *by* shows the relationship between "1950s" and the term "Jim Crow."

GRAMMAR & USAGE EXTENSION

While students are looking at prepositional phrases, you could introduce the use of the comma after initial prepositional phrases.

- **Behind the house at the far end of the lot**, the dog buried its bone. (after two or more introductory prepositional phrases)
- **In front of the roses, snapdragons, and mums**, she planted some onions. (after a long introductory prepositional phrase)
- **At my desk** I keep a cup of pens and pencils. (after a short introductory prepositional phrase only if the comma is necessary to make the meaning clear)

You might have students find other examples of introductory prepositional phrases in this essay and discuss the punctuation.

Use text features such as boldface type or italics to aid your comprehension of the text. Work with other members of your group to scan the following laws. Use the bold type as a guide to create a list of possible categories into which you might sort the laws.

Once you have arrived at four or five categories, read the entire text of each law, and put the law into one of the categories you have created. You might need to create more or change or delete categories. Also, note in the margin any questions you may have. Discuss your responses as you read and categorize. Be prepared to share your categories and your reactions and questions with the whole class.

My Notes

Sample Jim Crow Laws

Created by the Interpretive Staff of the Martin Luther King, Jr., National Historic Site

1. **Nurses** No person or corporation shall require any white female nurse to nurse in wards or rooms in hospitals, either public or private, in which negro men are placed. *Alabama*
2. **Buses** All passenger stations in this state operated by any motor transportation company shall have separate waiting rooms or space and separate ticket windows for the white and colored races. *Alabama*
3. **Restaurants** It shall be unlawful to conduct a restaurant or other place for the serving of food in the city, at which white and colored people are served in the same room, unless such white and colored persons are effectually separated by a solid partition extending from the floor upward to a distance of seven feet or higher, and unless a separate entrance from the street is provided for each compartment. *Alabama*
4. **Pool and Billiard Rooms** It shall be unlawful for a negro and white person to play together or in company with each other at any game of pool or billiards. *Alabama*
5. **Intermarriage** The marriage of a person of Caucasian blood with a Negro, Mongolian, Malay, or Hindu shall be null and void. *Arizona*
6. **Intermarriage** All marriages between a white person and a negro, or between a white person and a person of negro descent to the fourth generation inclusive, are hereby forever prohibited. *Florida*
7. **Education** The schools for white children and the schools for negro children shall be conducted separately. *Florida*
8. **Mental Hospitals** The Board of Control shall see that proper and distinct apartments are arranged for said patients, so that in no case shall Negroes and white persons be together. *Georgia*

WORD CONNECTIONS

Legal documents use many foreign words and phrases, including *quid pro quo* and *ipso facto*. *Quid pro quo* is Latin and describes giving something of value to get something else of value in return. *Ipso facto* means "by the fact itself." It may be used to describe factual evidence.

Steps:

3 Form students into small groups of three or four. Ask each group to appoint a recorder, and give each group a large piece of butcher paper. Direct groups to **scan** the sample Jim Crow laws, using the boldface descriptors to create categories. Possibilities include these: Marriage, Education, Transportation, Entertainment, Work, Public Buildings, Personal Behavior.

4 After a short time, you may want to have a brief large group discussion about the categories. Then ask groups to undertake a **close reading** to sort the laws into categories. Explain that the categories are flexible; some may be added, some changed, some deleted.

Steps:

5 As students read and categorize these laws, ask them to record questions they have about the laws.

TEACHER TO TEACHER Leave time for a whole group discussion after this small group activity in order to acknowledge the blatant racism of these laws. Point out that these laws reached into every facet of daily life. Solicit from students laws they found especially shocking, irrational, or ridiculous. Note the geographic extent of these laws. As an extension, you might ask students to research information about the context in which these laws were enacted and abolished.

6 Connect this activity to the discussion about social, historical, cultural, geographical context in Activity 5.4. Solicit responses to the **Essential Question**: What impact does historical, cultural, geographical, and social context have on a novel and on the reaction of readers to it?

Putting the Text in Context

My Notes

9. **Barbers** No colored barber shall serve as a barber [to] white women or girls. *Georgia*

10. **Burial** The officer in charge shall not bury, or allow to be buried, any colored persons upon ground set apart or used for the burial of white persons. *Georgia*

11 **Restaurants** All persons licensed to conduct a restaurant shall serve either white people exclusively or colored people exclusively and shall not sell to the two races within the same room or serve the two races anywhere under the same license. *Georgia*

12. **Amateur Baseball** It shall be unlawful for any amateur white baseball team to play baseball on any vacant lot or baseball diamond within two blocks of a playground devoted to the Negro race, and it shall be unlawful for any amateur colored baseball team to play baseball in any vacant lot or baseball diamond within two blocks of any playground devoted to the white race. *Georgia*

13. **Parks** It shall be unlawful for colored people to frequent any park owned or maintained by the city for the benefit, use and enjoyment of white persons. . .and unlawful for any white person to frequent any park owned or maintained by the city for the use and benefit of colored persons. *Georgia*

14. **Reform Schools** The children of white and colored races committed to the houses of reform shall be kept entirely separate from each other. *Kentucky*

15. **Circus Tickets** All circuses, shows, and tent exhibitions, to which the attendance of. . .more than one race is invited or expected to attend shall provide for the convenience of its patrons not less than two ticket offices with individual ticket sellers, and not less than two entrances to the said performance, with individual ticket takers and receivers, and in the case of outside or tent performances, the said ticket offices shall not be less than twenty-five (25) feet apart. *Louisiana*

16. **The Blind** The board of trustees shall. . .maintain a separate building. . . on separate ground for the admission, care, instruction, and support of all blind persons of the colored or black race. *Louisiana*

17. **Railroads** All railroad companies and corporations, and all persons running or operating cars or coaches by steam on any railroad line or track in the State of Maryland, for the transportation of passengers, are hereby required to provide separate cars or coaches for the travel and transportation of the white and colored passengers. *Maryland*

18. **Promotion of Equality** Any person. . .who shall be guilty of printing, publishing or circulating printed, typewritten or written matter urging or presenting for public acceptance or general information, arguments or suggestions in favor of social equality or of intermarriage between whites

© 2011 College Board. All rights reserved.

348 SpringBoard® English Textual Power™ Level 4

and negroes, shall be guilty of a misdemeanor and subject to fine not exceeding five hundred (500.00) dollars or imprisonment not exceeding six (6) months or both. *Mississippi*

19. **Intermarriage** The marriage of a white person with a negro or mulatto or person who shall have one-eighth or more of negro blood, shall be unlawful and void. *Mississippi*

20. **Hospital Entrances** There shall be maintained by the governing authorities of every hospital maintained by the state for treatment of white and colored patients separate entrances for white and colored patients and visitors, and such entrances shall be used by the race only for which they are prepared. *Mississippi*

21. **Prisons** The warden shall see that the white convicts shall have separate apartments for both eating and sleeping from the negro convicts. *Mississippi*

22. **Education** Separate free schools shall be established for the education of children of African descent; and it shall be unlawful for any colored child to attend any white school, or any white child to attend a colored school. *Missouri*

23. **Intermarriage** All marriages between. . .white persons and negroes or white persons and Mongolians. . .are prohibited and declared absolutely void. . . . No person having one-eighth part or more of negro blood shall be permitted to marry any white person, nor shall any white person be permitted to marry any negro or person having one-eighth part or more of negro blood. *Missouri*

24. **Education** Separate rooms [shall] be provided for the teaching of pupils of African descent, and [when] said rooms are so provided, such pupils may not be admitted to the school rooms occupied and used by pupils of Caucasian or other descent. *New Mexico*

25. **Textbooks** Books shall not be interchangeable between the white and colored schools, but shall continue to be used by the race first using them. *North Carolina*

26. **Libraries** The state librarian is directed to fit up and maintain a separate place for the use of the colored people who may come to the library for the purpose of reading books or periodicals. *North Carolina*

27. **Transportation** The. . . Utilities Commission. . . is empowered and directed to require the establishment of separate waiting rooms at all stations for the white and colored races. *North Carolina*

28. **Teaching** Any instructor who shall teach in any school, college or institution where members of the white and colored race are received and enrolled as pupils for instruction shall be deemed guilty of a misdemeanor, and upon conviction thereof, shall be fined in any sum not

My Notes

WORD CONNECTIONS

The word ***transportation*** means "a method of moving passengers or goods from one place to another." The Latin prefix *trans-* means "across" or "beyond." The Latin root *-port-* means "to carry" or "to bear."

The root *-port-* is found in many other English words, such as *portable, portfolio, import, export, report,* and *support.*

Some of the words in which the prefix *trans-* appears are *transfer, transform, transition, translate,* and *transparent.*

ACTIVITY 5.5 continued

Steps:

7 Direct students back to the **KWHL chart** to add to the K column. Then, in the W column, have them write key questions they have about life in the South in the 1930s. Urge students to also include questions they created based on the photos they viewed. These questions are to set the stage for an inquiry-based research investigation and presentation. End by asking students to fill in the H column with possible resources they might use to find answers to their questions.

8 Direct students to revisit the *context* **graphic organizer** in their **Vocabulary Notebooks** to expand on the concept.

Teacher Notes

Putting the Text in Context

My Notes

less than ten dollars ($10.00) nor more than fifty dollars ($50.00) for each offense. *Oklahoma*

29. **Fishing, Boating, and Bathing** The [Conservation] Commission shall have the right to make segregation of the white and colored races as to the exercise of rights of fishing, boating and bathing. *Oklahoma*
30. **Telephone Booths** The Corporation Commission is hereby vested with power and authority to require telephone companies. . . to maintain separate booths for white and colored patrons when there is a demand for such separate booths. That the Corporation Commission shall determine the necessity for said separate booths only upon complaint of the people in the town and vicinity to be served after due hearing as now provided by law in other complaints filed with the Corporation Commission. *Oklahoma*
31. **Lunch Counters** No persons, firms, or corporations, who or which furnish meals to passengers at station restaurants or station eating houses, in times limited by common carriers of said passengers, shall furnish said meals to white and colored passengers in the same room, or at the same table, or at the same counter. *South Carolina*
32. **Libraries** Any white person of such county may use the county free library under the rules and regulations prescribed by the commissioners court and may be entitled to all the privileges thereof. Said court shall make proper provision for the negroes of said county to be served through a separate branch or branches of the county free library, which shall be administered by [a] custodian of the negro race under the supervision of the county librarian. *Texas*
33. **Education** [The County Board of Education] shall provide schools of two kinds; those for white children and those for colored children. *Texas*
34. **Railroads** The conductors or managers on all such railroads shall have power, and are hereby required, to assign to each white or colored passenger his or her respective car, coach or compartment. If the passenger fails to disclose his race, the conductor and managers, acting in good faith, shall be the sole judges of his race. *Virginia*
35. **Theaters** Every person. . .operating. . .any public hall, theatre, opera house, motion picture show or any place of public entertainment or public assemblage which is attended by both white and colored persons, shall separate the white race and the colored race and shall set apart and designate. . .certain seats therein to be occupied by white persons and a portion thereof, or certain seats therein, to be occupied by colored persons. *Virginia*
36. **Intermarriage** All marriages of white persons with Negroes, Mulattos, Mongolians, or Malayans hereafter contracted in the State of Wyoming are and shall be illegal and void. *Wyoming*

WORD CONNECTIONS

The word ***provision*** begins with the Latin prefix *pro-*, meaning "before" or "for." The root *-vis-* means "see."

The Latin word *provisio* means "a foreseeing." The word *provision* means "something provided or supplied for the future."

Some of the words in which the root *-vis-* (and its alternate spelling *-vid-*) appear include *vision, visible, visualize, video,* and *evident.*

Writing Workshops

In the next activity, students will begin the process of creating a group research project. Prior to that work, you may want to access Workshop 10, Research. This workshop will give you an opportunity to guide students through the process of creating a research project by having them create a research plan, find and evaluate sources, and incorporate research into a presentation.

Preparing for Research

ACTIVITY 5.6

SUGGESTED LEARNING STRATEGIES: Think-Pair-Share

1. Form groups of three to plan, organize, and prepare a research project, which you will present in Embedded Assessment 1. Your group will investigate the historical, cultural, social, or geographical *context* of the novel *To Kill a Mockingbird*. Using the information from your viewing of 1930s photographs, your reading of Jim Crow laws, and your thinking on the KWHL chart, choose a research topic.

2. List possible topics to investigate and present with a Guiding Question for research:

   Jim Crow Laws – Why were Jim Crow Laws created?

3. List possible focus questions for your investigation of the Guiding Question:

   What was the basis of the Jim Crow laws?
   When and where did they start?
   How were the laws enforced?
   What was the effect of these laws on the lives of African Americans?
   What was the effect of these laws on the lives of white Americans?

4. Prepare a group proposal sheet with the following information:
   - Group members' names (no more than three members)
   - Topic expressed as a universal question or Guiding Question. Focus areas: related questions that fall within the overall topic area (Example: What kinds of jobs did women hold in the 1930s?)
   - Possible resources you might use to find answers to your questions
   - Individual responsibilities at this point (who will look for what, including visuals)

5. Find and collect resources about your topic. Your group must find five sources of information. You must use at least three different types of sources (e.g., magazine, reference source, Internet) in the presentation.

WORD CONNECTIONS

An analogy may use both words and phrases. For example, Jim Crow laws : segregation as negligence : accident. This analogy shows a cause-effect relationship. Write two additional cause-effect analogies, either on your own or as part of a class activity. Use both phrases and words.

ACTIVITY 5.6

Preparing for Research

Materials:

- Internet access for research

Purpose:

- To formulate a guiding question and additional focus questions for research on a topic
- To devise a group plan for research

Steps:

1 Have students form groups of three for the research project that they will present as Embedded Assessment 1. Review with the entire class what they know about life in the South in the 1930s and the questions they have developed. Direct them to decide in their small groups on a topic area for their investigation. Guide them to balance their interests with information that will enrich their understanding of ***To Kill a Mockingbird***. You might lead them toward one of these areas:

- Status of Women/Women's Roles
- Education and Schools
- Economic Concerns
- Status of African Americans
- The Great Depression
- Class Divisions in the South
- Franklin Delano Roosevelt's presidency
- Supreme Court Case: Plessy v. Ferguson

2 Additionally, you may want to expand their research to include topics connected to the context of the novel's publication in 1960:

- Harper Lee
- Supreme Court Case: Brown v. Board of Education of Topeka
- Civil Rights Movement

3 Using the topic of Jim Crow as a model, guide students through the process of creating a guiding question, using the resources they have previously read. Then, work with students to come up with additional focus questions that could help direct research on the Jim Crow laws. You may choose to allow students to use this topic if they come up with a different guiding question.

4 Now, instruct groups to develop a guiding question and formulate additional questions for research. Have students submit a group proposal.

5 Direct students to do the research, either as homework or as an assignment day in your media center. Instruct them to find five sources of information and at least three different types of sources (e.g., magazine article, reference source, Internet). You may wish to review the difference between previously published articles found in an online database and information found on Web sites. Encourage students to print hard copies or make photocopies of sources, if possible.

ACTIVITY 5.7
Collecting Resources

Materials:

- Internet access
- Hard copies of sources
- Vocabulary Notebooks

Purpose:

- To evaluate and choose sources appropriate to the guiding question
- To identify relevance of information from secondary sources to research questions
- To summarize and synthesize information from a secondary source
- To produce an annotated bibliography

Steps:

1 Guide students to evaluate the relevance of the sources they have collected to their guiding questions and focus questions. Then instruct each member of the research group to select at least one source for which to complete an ***annotated bibliography*** entry.

2 Review the terms ***annotate*** and ***bibliography*** with students. Then ask them to create a **word map** for ***annotated bibliography*** in their **Vocabulary Notebooks**.

3 Analyze the model annotated bibliography entry, having students identify the required parts of the annotation. Model the annotation process with **guided writing** as you complete the second entry (or provide an additional article). You might also provide examples for an encyclopedia entry, a book, and other common types of sources, or provide students with a Web site where complete MLA formatting guidelines are posted.

ACTIVITY 5.7

Collecting Resources

SUGGESTED LEARNING STRATEGIES: **Drafting, Marking the Text, Word Map**

You and your group have collected sources to research your topic in preparation for a presentation to your classmates.

First, evaluate the relevance of the sources you have collected. Then select five sources, keeping in mind that you must reference at least three different types (e.g., magazine article, reference source, Internet) in your presentation.

For each source you use, you will create an **annotated bibliography** entry in the MLA format. Annotated bibliographies are tools for tracking and processing your research work. Entries typically consist of two parts: a *bibliographic citation* for the source and an *annotation* (a brief summary of or commentary about the source).

ACADEMIC VOCABULARY

A **bibliography** is a list of the sources used for research. This list may also be called a Works Cited list. An **annotated bibliography** includes comments or summaries about each of the sources and the information found there.

For this task, the annotation will consist of three elements:

- A summary of the information you found in the source
- An assessment of the degree to which the source was helpful in your research
- A reflection on how the information might be used in your presentation.

Below are sample formats and entries. Your teacher may provide resources that have more examples.

For an Article:

Author(s). "Title of Article." *Magazine Title*. Publication date or issue: page number.

Sample Entry with Annotation:

Edmonds, Rick. "Jim Crow: Shorthand for Separation." *FORUM Magazine*. Summer 1999: 7.

Edmonds reviews the origins of the term "Jim Crow" and the significance of Jim Crow laws and customs as a social factor in the South. He also traces how awareness of the term's meaning has changed over time as our society has become more politically correct. This source was helpful for understanding how racial attitudes led to the creation of separate-but-equal laws. We might use it to show how political the term became in the 1930s through 1960s.

For a Web site:

Author(s). "Name of Page." Date of Posting/Revision. Name of Institution/Organization Affiliated with the Site. Date of access. <electronic address>.

Sample Entry:

Martin Luther King, Jr., *National Historic Site*. "Jim Crow Laws." 15 Nov. 2004. National Parks Service. 5 January 2008. <http://www.nps.gov/malu/documents/jim_crow_laws.htm>.

Annotation: This site gave a shocking list of laws that existed across the South—but also in other states (such as Arizona and Wyoming). It shows how Jim Crow regulated things ranging from the use of public facilities and transportation to marriage and schools. We might use it to engage our audience with some shocking examples—or to challenge their belief that this only happened in the South.

Once you have completed your annotated entries, compile a complete annotated bibliography as a group, placing the entries in alphabetical order. Use the next page to write your annotated bibliography.

Use the MLA format to create a complete bibliographic citation for each source. Include an annotation of each source based on your research group's understanding and discussion.

Steps:

4 Direct students to reread their sources as resources, **marking the text** to identify key information related to their focus questions. Suggest that this might be a time to add focus questions or delete those that don't seem relevant.

Steps:

5 Have each group member complete annotated bibliography entries on their own articles. Then ask the group to compile the entries in alphabetical order into one document.

6 Instruct group members to share and examine their source information, focusing their discussion on possible answers to their related questions and deciding which information is relevant.

7 Direct students respond to the Writing Prompt individually, **drafting** a one-page expository text that answers the questions guiding the group's research and uses the information the group has gathered. This task holds all students responsible for processing the information they will present to their peers.

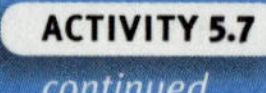

Collecting Resources

Annotated Bibliography

Source 1: Citation:

Annotation:

Source 2: Citation:

Annotation:

Source 3: Citation:

Annotation:

Source 4: Citation:

Annotation:

Source 5: Citation:

Annotation:

Writing Prompt: Individually, craft a one-page paper that uses information you have gained from your research to answer the question guiding your group's research. You may also address some or all of your group's focus questions. Be sure to cite information from your sources appropriately.

© 2011 College Board. All rights reserved.

354 SpringBoard® English Textual Power™ Level 4

Audience Analysis

ACTIVITY 5.8

SUGGESTED LEARNING STRATEGIES: **Graphic Organizer, Questioning the Text, Word Map**

Whether you are writing a paper or preparing a presentation, knowing who your audience will be is one of the most important steps toward planning your final product. For your presentation, complete an **audience analysis** by answering these questions.

1. What do you want your classmates—your audience—to get from your presentation?

2. What background knowledge or assumptions does your audience have about your subject?

   How will this background affect the types of information and vocabulary you use as you present?

3. How might your audience's values, opinions, and beliefs affect their perspective towards your subject?

4. What audio/visual components can you include in your presentation to engage your audience and convey your information effectively?

5. What connections can you make between your subject and your target audience to make your topic relevant to them?

6. What additional materials will you need to present your subject successfully?

ACADEMIC VOCABULARY

An **audience analysis** is an evaluation of the characteristics and knowledge of the people who will read a work or hear a speech. Examples of information that might be useful would be average age, prior experience with your topic, or formal education about the topic.

ACTIVITY 5.8
Audience Analysis

Materials:
- Research articles and visuals
- Vocabulary Notebooks

Purpose:
- To analyze how presenters can encourage active engagement by listeners and overcome barriers to listening
- To construct an oral presentation plan, organizing information around key concepts
- To use levels of questioning to generate and evaluate questions for listening

Steps:
1 Introduce the academic vocabulary term ***audience analysis***; ask students to create a **word map** in their **Vocabulary Notebooks**. Then, as a class, discuss the purpose of analyzing an audience. As students add to their Vocabulary Notebooks, remind them to use their partners or small groups to practice meaningful oral use of new academic language.

2 Ask the research groups to complete the ***audience analysis*** on this page to determine how best to make their presentation accessible, engaging, and informative for their target audience.

Steps:

3 Tell groups that they will create **levels of questions** that will both guide the organization of their presentation and help the audience take notes. Guide students through the sample questions, and help them evaluate the purpose of each level of question and the effectiveness of the questions at guiding listeners to identify key information.

4 Direct groups to complete the graphic organizer, generating questions for their own topic. Urge them to consider questions that will help their listeners identify key information from their presentation, as well as questions that will lead to full class discussions and personal connections to their content. They may revisit and use the original questions they generated with their group members, but they should move beyond these to develop questions that fully account for new information they have discovered through research.

5 When the group has identified its best questions, have them put each focus question on a note card. They can then rearrange the note cards as **manipulatives** to find the order that flows most logically and would most appeal to audience members.

6 To help students further organize and develop their presentation, you may want to teach a mini-lesson on three-fold transitions. These transitional sentences help students make logical connections among their points. Explain that a three-fold transition sentence does the following:

- Refers subtly to the idea discussed in the previous paragraph
- Refers briefly to the overall thesis idea
- Refers more specifically to new ideas to be discussed in the next paragraph.

You might share the examples provided at the bottom of this page.

Audience Analysis

Levels of Questioning

1. Work collaboratively to write questions about your topic. Your presentation will be the "text," so the questions will guide both the structure and organization of your speech and the audience's notetaking on your presentation.
   - Level 1 questions reveal key factual information in your presentation.
   - Level 2 questions should push listeners to consider how prevailing attitudes (towards race, class, gender, etc.) affect social practices.
   - Level 3 questions should prompt the audience to consider connections beyond the presentation, such as to their personal experience, current social issues, or other texts they have encountered.

You might use questions you previously generated if you think they will work to organize your information for your audience. However, you still need a balance of Level 1, 2, and 3 questions in your presentation.

Level of Questions	Questions on Your Topic
Level 1 **Questions of Fact:** **What does the text say?** For example: Which states had laws restricting interracial marriage?	1.
	2.
In what three major ways did Jim Crow laws affect schools?	3.
Level 2 **Questions of Interpretation:** **The how or why of the text** For example: How were the laws enforceable?	1.
	2.
What do people mean today when they refer to something as being "Jim Crow"?	3.

Sample thesis with three-fold transitions:

Thesis: Jim Crow Laws were enacted specifically to ensure that certain services, pleasures, and basic human rights would be denied to a people.

Transition sentence (topic sentence): Jim Crow laws denied access to the most basic services.

Transition sentence (topic sentence): Not only was access to basic services denied, but it was also denied to the pleasures of daily life.

Transition sentence (topic sentence): But most important, states created laws against basic human rights.

continued

Level 3 **Questions That Go Beyond the Text: Why does it matter?** For example: How could the United States have ever allowed Jim Crow laws to exist? Are racist laws still a major factor in the United States today?	1.
	2.
	3.

2. Once you have generated questions for your presentation, review your *audience analysis* on the previous page. Then answer the following questions.
   - What is the purpose of an audience analysis?
   - How can it help you evaluate what information to include in your presentation?
   - How can it help you choose which questions to use to organize and structure your presentation?
   - How can it help you to create an engaging presentation?

3. Based on your audience analysis and your answers to the questions above, design a notetaking handout, in the form of a graphic organizer, for your classmates to use while you present your topic. Design your handout so that classmates will have ample room to record answers to a limited number of questions that will best help them to understand the topic of your group's presentation of the 1930s South.

On the back of your organizer, be sure to leave ample space for the audience to take notes on connections they make while reading *To Kill a Mockingbird*.

ACTIVITY 5.8 *continued*

Steps:

7 Instruct the groups to **draft** both an outline of questions and a draft of the notetaking handout they will give to classmates. Their handout should use their questions to prompt listener **notetaking**.

8 Remind students to leave space at the bottom of the handout graphic organizer for audience questions provoked by the presentation. The presentations should be interactive, not passive!

9 Solicit responses to the **Essential Question**: What are the essential elements of an effective informative presentation?

Embedded Assessment 1

Historical Investigation and Presentation

College Board Standards and Objectives

R2 Using Prior Knowledge, Context, and Understanding of Language to Comprehend and Elaborate the Meaning of Texts (R2.1; R2.2)
PE Mappings: R2.1-1.4, R2.2-1.4

S3 Preparing and Delivering Presentations (S3.1; S3.2; 3.3; 3.4)
PE Mappings: S3.1-1.4, S3.2-3.4, S3.2-4.4, S3.3-1.4, S3.4-1.4

W1 Rhetorical Analysis and Planning (W1.1)
PE Mappings: W1.1-1.4, W1.1-3.4

W2 Generating Content (W2.1R; W2.2R)
PE Mappings: W2.1-1.4R, W2.1-2.4R, W2.2-1.4R, W2.2-2.4R, W2.2-3.4R, W2.2-4.4R, W2.2-2.4Cr, W2.2-3.4Cr, W2.2-4.4Cr

W3 Drafting (W3.1R; W3.2R)
PE Mappings: W3.1-1.4R, W3.1-2.4R, W3.1-3.4R, W3.2-4.4R

W4 Evaluating and Revising Texts (W4.1R)
PE Mappings: W4.1-1.4R

W5 Editing to Present Technically Sound Texts (W5.1; W5.2; W5.3; W5.4)
PE Mappings: W5.1-1.4, W5.2-1.4, W5.3-1.4, W5.4-1.4

L3 Listening for Diverse Purposes (L3.1)
PE Mappings: L3.1-1.4

M2 Understanding, Interpreting, Analyzing, and Evaluating Media Communication (M2.1)

M3 Composing and Producing Media Communication (M3.1; M3.2; M3.3)
PE Mappings: M3.1-1.4

Steps:

1 Students have already done some research and planning for this presentation. Explain that now they will actually prepare and deliver the presentation. Have them review and evaluate their research, their proposal, and their levels of questions. If they need to do additional research or make changes, have them address those concerns now.

2 Be sure they have a plan for dividing the responsibilities fairly.

Embedded Assessment 1

Historical Investigation and Presentation

SUGGESTED LEARNING STRATEGIES: **Drafting, Notetaking, Rehearsal**

Assignment

Your assignment is to work collaboratively to investigate the historical, cultural, social, or geographical *context* of the novel *To Kill a Mockingbird*. You will make an oral presentation of your findings, with audio or visual support, and you will prepare a notetaking handout for your audience to use.

Planning

1. Review your work on the skills and knowledge required of the investigation and presentation in order to identify key expectations for your presentation. Review your group proposal and, if necesssry, revise how you will share the responsibilities of the investigation and presentation.

Drafting and Creating

2. Draft your presentation outline or script covering the following:
   - Thesis regarding the significance of your topic and its importance in the historical, social, cultural, or geographical context of the 1930s or the 1960s.
   - Key questions that will guide the structure of your presentation
   - Transitions to link your points together.

   Place your information on 3 x 5 note cards. Include the following with your outline:
   - Audio-visual resources you will use and their placement in the presentation
   - A speaking plan for who will cover what during the presentation

3. Decide on an interactive way to present your research to the class (e.g., digital slides, a Web page, online blog, tri-fold presentation board). Update your group proposal to include a plan of what you will do in your presentation and the materials you need to be successful. If you create PowerPoint slides, consult a style manual such as that published by The Modern Language Association to help you format your presentation.
4. Finalize a one-page graphic organizer handout of questions for your classmates to use to take notes on your presentation. The title of your organizer may be your guiding question. Choose a few other questions designed to help listeners identify information relevant to that question.

358 SpringBoard® English Textual Power™ Level 4

© 2011 College Board. All rights reserved.

Rehearsal and Performance

5. Review the guidelines for effective public speaking that you generated in Unit 1 and your self-evaluation as a speaker from Unit 4. Using these, determine your goals for improvement. Refine each group member's roles and responsibilities.
6. Plan the oral components of your presentation, and rehearse. Consult the Scoring Guide for specific criteria, and use peer feedback to refine your presentation.
7. Deliver your presentation to your class.

Presentation Follow-up

As you read and study *To Kill A Mockingbird*, take notes on how your topic (or another that interests you more) surfaces in the novel. Record both textual evidence and personal commentary. After you have finished the novel, you will connect the information you have presented to your understanding of the novel.

TECHNOLOGY TIP If you have the appropriate resources, consider recording your rehearsals for use in reviewing your performance. You may also want to record your notes and commentary for later use.

Steps:

3 Point out to students that they need to include audio or visual media in their presentations. As they are making selections, revisit the criteria you identified in Activity 5.7 to remind students how to evaluate potential resources.

4 Remind students to keep their audience analysis in mind as they make choices and decisions. What will appeal to the audience? What will inform them? What is the best way to communicate the group's information to them?

5 Set a date for the presentations. Remind students to **rehearse** to prepare for their presentations. As students rehearse, remind them to help each other by asking questions, clarifying meaning, and using nonverbal cues to solicit suggestions for improvement. Encourage ELL students to use their group's suggestions to help them gain confidence and fluency in speaking. You may wish to set a minumum and maximum time for presentations. Have presenters distribute their notetaking guides; tell the listeners to **take notes** during the presentations.

6 After each group has presented, you may want to revisit both Essential Questions to deepen students' understanding and allow for self-reflection on the act of oral presentation and the concept of historical, cultural, geographical, and social context.

Embedded Assessment 1

Continued

Scoring Guide

When you score this Embedded Assessment, you may wish to download and print a copy of the Scoring Guide from SpringBoard Online. In this way, you can have a copy to mark for each student's work.

Embedded Assessment 1

continued

Historical Investigation and Presentation

SCORING GUIDE

Scoring Criteria	Exemplary	Proficient	Emerging
Presentation: Analysis of the Subject	The presentation is thoughtfully and effectively organized. It demonstrates a comprehensive understanding of significant aspects of the topic and its relevance to the novel.	The presentation is organized and displays a solid understanding of the topic. The connection between the topic and the novel as a whole is clear to the audience.	The presentation is somewhat organized. The information presented demonstrates a limited understanding of the topic and fails to make any connection to the novel as a whole.
Presentation: Use of Media	The presentation skillfully uses a variety of audio/visual resources to keep the audience engaged. The audio/visual selections are thoughtfully chosen and demonstrate critical thinking.	The presentation uses some audio/visual components to engage the audience. The selections are relevant and creative and serve the purpose of the presentation.	The presentation may or may not contain audio/visual components to supplement the information. The materials chosen are not relevant or are distracting and fail to serve the group's purpose.
Presentation: Oral Delivery	The presenters demonstrate effective oral communication skills. Each group member participates equally. The presentation actively engages audience members. It is is well-planned and successfully coordinated.	The presenters display adequate oral communication skills. All members participate, but the balance may be unequal. The presentation is engaging. Adequate collaboration is evident.	The presenters lack adequate oral communication skills. Some group members participate little or not at all. The presentation lacks energy and enthusiasm and is unengaging.
Audience Guide	The graphic organizer is clearly organized with thoughtful questions to focus the information for viewers. The layout skillfully provides space for recording information and reflecting on its importance. It contains no errors.	The graphic organizer is adequately organized with questions to help focus information for viewers. The layout provides space for recording information and reflecting on its importance. It contains no errors.	The graphic organizer lacks clear organization or may confuse viewers. The layout is inadequate for following and recording information, or it provides no space for reflection. It may contain errors.
Additional Criteria			

Comments:

Learning Focus:

How Do a Million Little Parts Equal a Whole?

In earlier units, you've studied the ways in which authors and directors use **stylistic choices** to suggest meaning in their texts. But how do choices work with a text as complicated as a novel? Does every word really matter when there are 60,000 of them? Is everything really a symbol of something more? As you begin the second part of this unit, you'll immerse yourself in the world of Scout Finch, the narrator of *To Kill a Mockingbird*. As you do so, though, you'll go beyond the story of what happens to Scout and the folks of Maycomb, Alabama, to focus as well on *how* Harper Lee tells the story. In particular, you'll explore how the **setting**, **conflict**, and **characters** develop **themes** within the text.

As you read Part One of the novel, you'll apply various strategies for active reading:

- Visualizing the Text
- Marking/Annotating the Text
- Making Connections
- Making Predictions
- Drawing Inferences
- Questioning the Text
- Diffusing Vocabulary

As you move into Part Two of the novel, you'll become more independent in your reading, while class activities will focus more on analyzing the language used to tell the story. Like a detective, you'll interpret quotations and passages as clues to the novel's thematic meaning. You'll develop a **thematic statement** and write a **literary analysis** explaining how the meaning of a passage contributes to the meaning of the novel as a whole. It's a way to end the year by applying all the skills you've developed as a reader and writer—and by grappling with the ways texts challenge us to question the world around us.

LEARNING FOCUS:

How Do a Million Little Parts Equal a Whole?

Previewing Embedded Assessment 2

To preview the skills and knowledge necessary for success on Embedded Assessment 2, instruct students to locate the Assignment and Scoring Guide (pp. 405–408). Guide students through a **close reading** of the prompts, steps, and Scoring Guide criteria. Urge them to keep this assignment in mind as they proceed to read and analyze ***To Kill a Mockingbird***.

Steps:

1 Read the Learning Focus with students or have them read independently. **Activate prior knowledge** by having students **mark the text** and highlight words or concepts that are familiar (what they know). They might use a question mark to indicate content that is unfamiliar (what they do not know but want to learn).

2 Engage students in a whole class discussion. You may **revisit** the **KWL chart** you created at the beginning of the unit to discover what students have learned.

ACTIVITY 5.9

Reflecting on Growth: Researching and Presenting

Materials:

- Presentation materials
- Portfolio

Purpose:

- To reflect on and evaluate processes of research and delivering a presentation
- To reflect on and self-assess growth in speaking and listening

Steps:

1 Have students complete the reflection questions about their research skills, citing examples from the unit and throughout the year to support their self-evaluations.

ACTIVITY 5.9

Reflecting on Growth: Researching and Presenting

SUGGESTED LEARNING STRATEGIES: Graphic Organizer

You have engaged in a number of activities as a researcher. Being an effective researcher requires several key skills. These skills are listed below. For each of these skills, review your work from this unit and from the year as a whole to find evidence of your practice of the skill. Then discuss your current level of mastery of the skill, citing examples to support your evaluation.

- **Assessing your current knowledge of your subject and identifying areas to address through research:**
- **Defining and revising research questions to guide research:**
- **Identifying and evaluating potential sources of information:**
- **Using strategies to monitor comprehension while engaging with complex texts:**
- **Using strategies to organize, restructure, and synthesize text content from research sources:**
- **Effectively incorporating and citing information from outside sources in your own texts:**

Think about your group's presentation of your research topic. Take some time to reflect on the presentation and your part in it.

What did you do well?	
Given another opportunity to present, what would you do differently?	
What did you learn about organizing information?	
What did you learn about how to effectively engage an audience?	
How have you most improved as a researcher this year?	
What goals do you have for improving as a researcher?	

Steps:

2 Have students answer the questions on this page, reflecting on their presentation skills, including their ability to use research effectively.

ACTIVITY 5.10

A Scouting Party

Materials:

- *To Kill a Mockingbird*, by Harper Lee
- *To Kill a Mockingbird* DVD

Purpose:

- To predict, infer, and interpret, based on close reading of print and nonprint materials
- To identify the novel's point of view
- To apply strategies for understanding new vocabulary

Steps:

1 Remind students of ways to **preview** a text (title, pictures, synopsis, reviews, knowledge of the author). Lead them through a **guided reading** of the novel's covers. If any of these elements are missing from students' copies, skip them.

- Ask students to examine the cover art and note their observations. Ask them to describe the art and predict what the images might represent.
- Have students predict, based on the title, what this novel might be about.
- Ask students whether they've heard of the author, Harper Lee. Have they read anything by her?
- Next, ask students to examine the synopsis on the back of the book and make meaning from the commentary. Ask: What insight about this novel does this information provide?
- Share the reviews of the novel in the opening pages of the book. As an extended activity, you might direct students to locate and read additional reviews of this novel. Based on the reviews, ask students to consider what they believe the author might have wanted to make readers think about.

ACTIVITY 5.10

A Scouting Party

SUGGESTED LEARNING STRATEGIES: Diffusing the Text, Graphic Organizer, Previewing, Quickwrite, Think Aloud, Think-Pair-Share, Visualizing, Notetaking, Marking the Text

View the opening clip of *To Kill a Mockingbird*, and note your observations on this graphic organizer. After watching the opening credits, share your findings in groups of three. Add your groups' findings to your graphic.

First Viewing of the Opening Credits of *To Kill a Mockingbird*

What did you observe? What images did you see on screen?	What did you notice about the lighting?	What did you notice about the sound?	Based on your observations, what predictions can you make?

View the opening credits again. This time each member of your small group should take notes on one element in one column. After the second viewing, share and note your observations.

From the sound and the images, what can you infer about the *point of view* from which this story will be told?

Child's voice humming; children's playthings; children's writing
The story will be a child's story told from a child's point of view.

2 Next, introduce students to the film *To Kill a Mockingbird* by showing only the opening credits in Scene 1 (0–0:02:57). Show this clip twice. On the first viewing, direct students to note their general observations. For the second viewing, direct each student (within a group of three) to view the clip for a specific element: lighting, sound, and images and **take notes** on the **graphic organizer**. After each viewing, allow students to **think-pair-share** and note their observations, first within their group and then with the class.

3 Then, have students synthesize their observations by answering the questions after the graphic organizer.

ACTIVITY 5.10
continued

Something to Ponder: When this film was made, color film technology was available. The director made a conscious decision to shoot this film in black and white. Why do you think the director might have made this choice?

Literary Terms
A **flashback** is an interruption in the sequence of events to relate events that occurred in the past.

As your teacher reads the opening of *To Kill a Mockingbird*, highlight the part that indicates the story is a **flashback**. In addition, note what you are learning about the narrator and her perspective, both from what she talks about and from the language she uses to do so. Finally, make a list below of the characters who are introduced in Chapter 1.

Facts about the narrator	Character names

Quickwrite: What *perspective* is established in the opening credits of the film that contrasts with the perspective that opens the novel?

ACTIVITY 5.10 *continued*

Steps:

4 Because the opening of the novel may be a challenge even to proficient readers, conduct a **shared reading** of the beginning of Chapter 1. As you read aloud, model active reading strategies. The goal is to guide students through Part One of the novel modeling effective habits of good readers. Students will apply the strategies and reflect on their effectiveness. In Part Two students read this text more independently using the strategies practiced in Part one.

5 As they read along, direct students to **mark the text** to note characters' names, either with sticky notes, or highlighting or annotation. Use this oral reading as an opportunity to conduct a **think aloud** of difficult portions of the passage, actively **diffusing** unfamiliar vocabulary by substituting easier synonyms for challenging vocabulary, and by wondering aloud about the narrator's age, gender, and purpose in telling the story.

6 Stop after the first four paragraphs. As a whole class, create a list of names mentioned. Discuss and clarify the characters and their stories. The time you spend clarifying the beginning will help students as they go forward. Establishing the narrative perspective, or ***point of view***, is especially significant in the beginning of the novel—in this case, the perspective is that of an adult looking back and creating a context for childhood. Remind students of the idea of a ***flashback***, and ask how old the narrator seems to be. Ask students to predict the effect of the narrator's age on the telling of the story.

7 Ask students to complete the **Quickwrite**. Then lead them in a discussion of how the perspective in each text engages the reader or viewer.

8 Read the next four paragraphs, and ask students to add to the list of characters. Also, clarify with them what is happening.

9 After Scout has given some of the history of her family, she begins to set the scene for the flashback, which becomes the plot of the novel. Continue to read up until "That was the summer Dill came to us." Ask students to note words they don't know. **Diffuse** the text by directing students to collaboratively come up with synonyms for the unfamiliar words. Have them place the synonyms in the margin near the unfamiliar words and create a vocabulary bookmark for the definitions. Reread this passage aloud, replacing the unfamiliar words with the synonyms students have identified.

Steps:

10 Direct students to the line in the novel, "That was the summer Dill came to us." Have students create a script for this dialogue by writing the character names in their books before each section of dialogue. Ask students to read the dialogue in parts with you taking the narration. Then, ask students to **visualize** these major characters and what they're doing by drawing them together in relation to one another.

11 Assign the rest of Chapter 1 to be read silently or for homework.

A Scouting Party

My Notes

Visualizing the Characters

As you read, highlight all the images and details that describe what the children look like and are doing.

Novel

ABOUT THE AUTHOR

American writer Nelle Harper Lee (b. 1926) was born and grew up in Alabama. As an adult, she moved to New York City, where she wrote and published several short stories. She then took a year off from work to write *To Kill a Mockingbird*, using her father as a model for Atticus Finch. *To Kill a Mockingbird* won much acclaim when it was published and a Pulitzer Prize in 1961. Harper Lee has never written another novel.

from To Kill a MOCKINGBIRD

by Harper Lee

Early one morning as we were beginning our day's play in the back yard, Jem and I heard something next door in Miss Rachel Haverford's collard patch. We went to the wire fence to see if there was a puppy—Miss Rachel's rat terrier was expecting—instead we found someone sitting looking at us. Sitting down, he wasn't much higher than the collards. We stared at him until he spoke:

"Hey."

"Hey yourself," said Jem pleasantly.

"I'm Charles Baker Harris," he said, "I can read."

"So what?" I said.

"I just thought you'd like to know I can read. You got anything needs readin' I can do it. . . ."

"How old are you," asked Jem, "four-and-a-half?"

"Goin' on seven."

"Shoot no wonder, then," said Jem, jerking his thumb at me. "Scout yonder's been readin' ever since she was born, and she ain't even started to school yet. You look right puny for goin' on seven."

"I'm little but I'm old," he said.

Jem brushed his hair back to get a better look. "Why don't you come over, Charles Baker Harris?" he said. "Lord, what a name."

"'s not any funnier'n yours. Aunt Rachel says your name's Jeremy Atticus Finch."

Jem scowled. "I'm big enough to fit mine," he said. "Your name's longer'n you are. Bet it's a foot longer."

"Folks call me Dill," said Dill, struggling under the fence.

"Do better if you go over it instead of under it," I said. "Where'd you come from?"

Dill was from Meridian, Mississippi, was spending the summer with his aunt, Miss Rachel, and would be spending every summer in Maycomb from now on. His family was from Maycomb County originally, his mother worked for a photographer in Meridian, had entered his picture in a Beautiful Child contest and won five dollars. She gave the money to Dill, who went to the picture show twenty times on it.

"Don't have any picture shows here, except Jesus ones in the courthouse sometimes," said Jem. "Ever see anything good?"

Dill had seen *Dracula*, a revelation that moved Jem to eye him with the beginning of respect. "Tell it to us," he said.

Dill was a curiosity. He wore blue linen shorts that buttoned to his shirt, his hair was snow white and stuck to his head like duck-fluff; he was a year my senior but I towered over him. As he told us the old tale his blue eyes would lighten and darken; his laugh was sudden and happy; he habitually pulled at a cowlick in the center of his forehead.

When Dill reduced *Dracula* to dust, and Jem said the show sounded better than the book, I asked Dill where his father was: "You ain't said anything about him."

"I haven't got one."

"Is he dead?"

"No . . ."

"Then if he's not dead you've got one, haven't you?"

GRAMMAR & USAGE

Relative clauses can be **restrictive** (essential) or **nonrestrictive** (nonessential). Notice the use and punctuation of the adjective clauses in the following examples:

Nonrestrictive: She gave the money to Dill, **who went to the picture show twenty times on it.**

Restrictive: He wore blue linen shorts **that buttoned to his shirt....**

In your writing, use commas to set off nonrestrictive adjective clauses in complex sentences.

My Notes

After Reading

After you have read the conversation, visualize and sketch the scene and the characters on another sheet of paper. How would they be standing in relation to each other? What features would you emphasize? Where are they?

Teacher Notes

GRAMMAR & USAGE EXTENSION

- As students read Chapter 1, you may wish to point out the use and punctuation of restrictive (essential) and nonrestrictive (nonessential) clauses. The following sentence contains a noun clause and an adjective clause, both beginning with relative pronouns:

  "I maintain **that the Ewells started it all** (*restrictive*), but Jem, **who was four years my senior** (*nonrestrictive*), said it started long before that."
- Encourage students to use these structures before they are given the terms. Students will be far more effective writers when they can skillfully manipulate the language.

ACTIVITY 5.11
Visualizing Setting

Materials:

- *To Kill a Mockingbird*, Chapter 1
- Vocabulary Notebooks

Purpose:

- To analyze a passage for diction and imagery
- To apply close reading as a strategy for making meaning from a text
- To develop an interpretive statement about the effect of setting
- To identify a subplot and trace the relationships among main and secondary characters

Steps:

1 This lesson is intended to model a close reading to analyze diction and imagery in creating setting.

2 Guide students through a **close reading** of the description of Maycomb. Work with them to identify diction and imagery that that enable them to **visualize** the setting. Have students **annotate** the text. Guide them to develop an interpretive statement about the effect of the diction and imagery.

3 As you discuss the interpretive or ***thematic statements*** the students create, have them create a **word map** and add this concept to their **Vocabulary Notebooks**. It is important that they understand connections that tie together ***theme, thematic subject, interpretation, thematic statement, topic sentence,*** and ***thesis statement***.

ACTIVITY 5.11

Visualizing Setting

SUGGESTED LEARNING STRATEGIES: Close Reading, Double-Entry Journal, Word Map, Visualizing, Marking the Text, Notetaking

GRAMMAR & USAGE
In the second sentence of the second paragraph, notice that the author uses a series without a conjunction before the last item. This effect is called **asyndeton**.

My Notes

As your teacher reads aloud this passage, underline or highlight images and words—adjectives and verbs in particular—that create a vivid picture of the town where the novel takes place. Consider what effect the author wants to create in this description, then answer the questions on the next page.

from ***To Kill a Mockingbird***, Chapter 1

Maycomb was an old town, but it was a tired old town when I first knew it. In rainy weather the streets turned to red slop; grass grew on the sidewalks, the courthouse sagged in the square. Somehow, it was hotter then: a black dog suffered on a summer's day; bony mules hitched to Hoover carts flicked flies in the sweltering shade of the live oaks on the square. Men's stiff collars wilted by nine in the morning. Ladies bathed before noon, after their three-o'clock naps, and by nightfall were like soft teacakes with frostings of sweat and sweet talcum.

People moved slowly then. They ambled across the square, shuffled in and out of the stores around it, took their time about everything. A day was twenty-four hours long but seemed longer. There was no hurry, for there was nowhere to go, nothing to buy and no money to buy it with, nothing to see outside the boundaries of Maycomb County. But it was a time of vague optimism for some of the people: Maycomb County had recently been told that it had nothing to fear but fear itself.

GRAMMAR & USAGE EXTENSION

- You might draw students' attention to the use of asyndeton as a rhetorical device. Explain that general usage calls for a conjunction before the final item in a series. Ask: What is the effect of not using that conjunction?
- You might wish to point out another example of asyndeton, in Activity 1.9, p. 36: "He had never asked me anything, unless it was a demand, an expectation, an obligation to be his throwaway doll."

Teacher Notes

1. Which **images** help you to visualize life in Maycomb? Write several of the images that enable you to "see" the town.
   "streets turned to red slop," "bony mules...flicked flies," "stiff collars wilted," "Ladies ...were like soft teacakes," "People... shuffled in and out of stores."

2. Write down specific words or **diction** that create a picture. What effect is created by these words? What does this effect suggest is Scout's attitude toward the town she grew up in?
   "old," "tired," "rainy," "sagged," "suffered," "sweltering," "wilted," "ambled," "shuffled," "nowhere," "nothing," "no money"

3. Write an interpretive statement about the specific effect the **diction** and **imagery** create in this passage about the setting. An interpretive statement can be used as a topic sentence because it presents an assertion about a specific topic.
   Maycomb is a town characterized by slowness and inactivity with little hope of more action or interest.

Steps:

4 Ask students to work in pairs to conduct a close reading of the short description of the Radley place. Then, open the discussion to the whole group.

Visualizing Setting

My Notes

Reread this passage that introduces the Radley place. Underline or highlight sensory images and words—adjectives and verbs in particular—that create a vivid picture of the house. Consider what effect the author wants to create in this description.

from ***To Kill a Mockingbird***, Chapter 1

The Radley Place jutted into a sharp curve beyond our house. Walking south, one faced its porch; the sidewalk turned and ran beside the lot. The house was low, was once white with a deep front porch and green shutters, but had long ago darkened to the color of the slate-gray yard around it. Rain-rotted shingles drooped over the eaves of the veranda; oak trees kept the sun away. The remains of a picket drunkenly guarded the front yard—a "swept" yard that was never swept—where johnson grass and rabbit-tobacco grew in abundance.

GRAMMAR & USAGE

Notice the punctuation in the final sentence of the excerpt: the **quotation marks** around *swept* indicate irony, and the **dashes** emphasize the parenthetical nature of the information.

1. Which images help you to visualize the Radley place? In the My Notes space, write several of the images that help you to "see" the house.

2. Write down specific words or diction that create a picture. What effect is created by these words? What does this effect suggest is Scout's attitude towards the Radley place?

3. Write an *interpretive sentence* about the specific effect the *diction* and *imagery* create in this passage about the setting.

GRAMMAR & USAGE EXTENSION

Call students' attention to the use of quotation marks around words used in special senses, such as to express irony or sarcasm or to indicate an invented word. You might solicit from students other special senses that require the use of quotation marks.

Brief Review of the Elements of a Paragraph

- Topic sentence (an *interpretive sentence* about effect)
- Evidence from the text to support *claims made*
- Reflective commentary on the *evidence*
- Sentence of closure

Writing Prompt: Write a paragraph explaining how the diction and imagery in the description of either the town of Maycomb or the Radley place creates a certain effect. Your *topic sentence* (an interpretive statement) must state the effect created by the words and images in the passage.

Steps:

5 To begin scaffolding for Embedded Assessment 2, have students complete the Writing Prompt. You might have students do a peer review of these paragraphs.

© 2011 College Board. All rights reserved.

Unit 5 • Coming of Age Amidst Controversy 371

Steps:

6 The ***interpretive statement*** can set the stage for students' long-term task of keeping a double-entry journal of the children's contacts with the Radleys. Based on their reading of Chapter 1, work with students to begin **notetaking** in a **double-entry journal** on Boo (Arthur) Radley throughout Part One of the novel. Taking notes will help students to recognize how Harper Lee creates and sustains the character of Boo Radley, a secondary character, as an extended metaphor for how to combat the poisonous effects of prejudice. Ask students to record all information about Boo that they encounter throughout the text. Have them note points in Jem and Scout's interactions with Boo that enable them to change their perspectives on him.

Note: page references may vary depending on the edition you are using.

Visualizing Setting

Main Idea and Detail Notes

As you read the novel, take notes on Boo Radley whenever he is mentioned. Include page numbers for your notes. Look for any changes in the way that Jem and Scout react to Boo, and make note of these changes.

Incidents Involving Boo Radley	Details from the Text
CHAPTER 1:	FACT:
Radley place and family story described – pgs 8–13	Boo's father locked him in the house after his misbehavior; he was suspected of stabbing his father in the leg at age 33; he was locked in the courthouse basement for a time; the family isolated themselves; when Mr. Radley died, Boo's brother Nathan took charge of the house.
Children are afraid of Boo because they only know about him from listening to gossip and rumor about the Radleys.— pgs 8–13	RUMORS: Boo is a "phantom;" "peeped in windows"; azaleas froze because he "breathed on them"; "Radley pecans would kill you." Boo was "chained to the bed"; "dined on raw squirrels"; hands were "bloodstained"; "teeth yellow and rotten"; he "drooled most of the time."
Summer begins. Dill wants to make Boo Radley come out. Pgs 8 and 13 Dill dares Jem, and Jem touches the house.– pg 15	Kids thought they saw an inside shutter move.
CHAPTERS 2 AND 3	
Jem and Scout run past the Radley house on the way to school.	Jem runs by the Radley place only when alone.
CHAPTER 4	
In a knothole in the tree on the Radley property, Scout finds two pieces of chewing gum.— pg 33	When Scout tells Jem, he makes her spit it out because it might be poison.
In the knothole, Jem and Scout find a box with two pennies in it.— pg 34	The box is covered with tinfoil from chewing gum wrappers and the pennies are Indian heads – very valuable and shined up. Jem thinks they are important to someone and saves them.
Scout ends up on the Radley front porch after tire hits the house and Jem retrieves the tire.— pg 38	
Jem thinks up a new game – Boo Radley.— pg 38	
CHAPTERS 5–8	
Jem tries to give a letter, to look in window, Jem's pants, ball of twine in knothole, soap figures, pocket watch, knife, Mr. Radley plugs the hole with cement, Boo covers Scout's shoulders with a blanket during the fire.	Scout heard someone laughing when she got out of the tire.—pg 41 The kids reenact the Radley story. Scout wants to stop.

Strategies Reflection

You have used several reading strategies as you have begun reading *To Kill a Mockingbird*:

- Read-Aloud/Think-Aloud
- Marking the Text
- Annotating the Text
- Diffusing Vocabulary
- Close Reading
- Double Entry Journaling

Writing Prompt: Write a short paragraph starting with a *topic sentence* on how effective these strategies are for you in making meaning of the text. Which is most effective, which will you need more practice with, and which do you feel confident about?

Steps:

7 Finally, ask students to reflect on the strategies they used to make meaning from the text. Have them respond to the Writing Prompt in which they evaluate the effectiveness of these strategies Make this a regular practice to bring closure to each lesson in this unit.

© 2011 College Board. All rights reserved.

ACTIVITY 5.12 Making Connections

Materials:

- *To Kill a Mockingbird*, Chapters 2 and 3

Purpose:

- To identify and discuss textual connections as a strategy for making meaning
- To analyze character through an oral interpretation

Steps:

1 Begin reading Chapter 2 aloud. **Think aloud**, making connections and identifying the type of connections so that students can see the habits of a good reader:

- As Scout attends school for the first time, you could make text-to-self connections by recalling your first day of school, how you learned to read, or an unfavorable encounter you had in school with a teacher.
- You could make a text-to-text connection referencing a text using first-person point of view that students are familiar with.
- You could introduce a text-to-world connection based on Scout and Miss Caroline's struggle with each other. You could refer to the difficulty teachers and students often have in their view of education because of their lack of agreement about cultural norms.

2 You might open Chapter 3 by emphasizing the importance of **oral interpretation** via a Reader's Theater. Cast five students in the roles of Jem, Scout, Calpurnia, Walter Cunningham, and Atticus. You might read the narration. Begin the Reader's Theater with the opening sentence of Chapter 3 and conclude with the paragraph beginning "I returned to school and hated Calpurnia steadily...."

ACTIVITY 5.12

Making Connections

SUGGESTED LEARNING STRATEGIES: Oral Interpretation, Think-Pair-Share

Reading Strategies

Good readers are strategic, and being strategic requires that readers use an array of strategies to make meaning from text. Making connections while reading is a strategy that keeps you engaged in the text and enables you to understand the text more deeply. These are some types of connections you can make while reading:

- Text-to-self: when the text makes you think of your own life.
- Text-to-text: when the text makes you think of another text.
- Text-to-world: when the text makes you think of world events.

As you read Chapters 2 and 3, fill in the circles with your own connections.

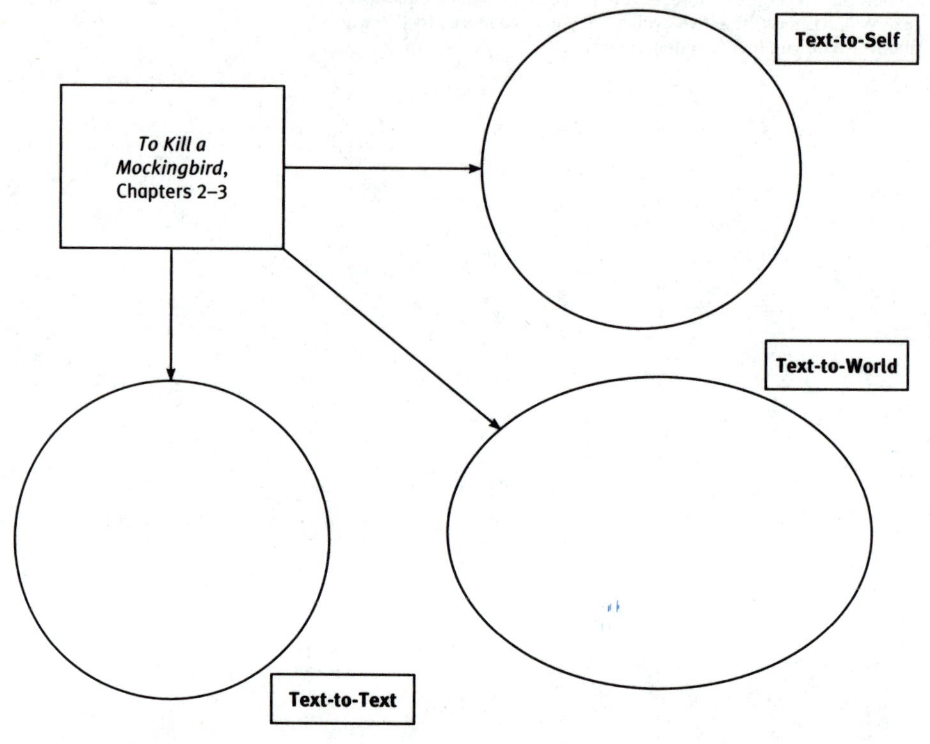

3 Direct students to finish reading Chapter 3. Then, have them engage in a **think-pair-share** to practice making connections: text-to-self, text-to-text, and text-to-world. Direct them to take notes as they and their partner verbalize their connections. The goal is for students to practice using an effective strategy so that it becomes a habit.

4 Close the lesson by asking students to describe the strategies they used to help them make meaning from the text. Ask then to evaluate the effectiveness of these strategies.

© 2011 College Board. All rights reserved.

374 SpringBoard® English Textual Power™ Level 4

Making Predictions

ACTIVITY 5.13

SUGGESTED LEARNING STRATEGIES: Double-Entry Journals, Drafting, Notetaking, Predicting, Word Map

Good readers **make predictions** while they read, and then they confirm or negate these predictions based on the information in the text. The focus of this read-aloud/think-aloud will be to model the practice of predicting and then confirming or negating predictions as the chapter unfolds. As you read Chapters 4 and 5, record details about the growing relationship between Boo and the children, and predict what you think is likely to happen. Then, check these predictions as you go.

Incidents Involving Boo Radley	Predictions
CHAPTER 4	
In a knothole in the tree on the Radley property, Scout finds two pieces of chewing gum. — pg 33	Scout will tell Atticus about what she has found.
In the knothole, Jem and Scout find a box with two pennies in it.— pg 34	Boo Radley is putting the objects in the knothole for the children.
Scout ends up on Radley front porch after tire hits the house and Jem retrieves the tire.—pg 38	It is Boo Radley that Scout hears laughing.
Jem thinks up a new game – Boo Radley. pg 38	Boo Radley will come out and play with kids.
CHAPTER 5	
Scout talks to Miss Maudie about Boo and asks her about all the stories and rumors.—pg 44-46	The kids will obey Atticus, or they will not give up their efforts to make contact with Boo.
Jem tries to give a letter, to look in window, but is caught in the act by Atticus.—pg 48-49	
Atticus tells Jem and Scout and Dill to "stop tormenting that man."— pg 49	
Atticus told the kids to stop "putting his [Boo's] life's history on display for the edification of the neighborhood."	
Jem's pants, ball of twine in knothole, soap figures, pocket watch, knife, Mr. Radley plugs the hole with cement.	

ACTIVITY 5.13
Making Predictions

Materials:

- *To Kill a Mockingbird*, Chapters 4 and 5
- Vocabulary Notebooks

Purpose:

- To infer and to predict based on textual evidence
- To synthesize information about a character in order to write from the character's point of view

Steps:

1 Read aloud the first half of Chapter 4 (to the end of page 35). During your reading, make inferences about the events and some predictions about what will happen between the children and Boo. Direct students to their **double-entry journals** to update **notes** on the relationship between Boo and the children

2 Ask students to use their double-entry journals to make predictions and to provide textual evidence for the predictions. Have students finish Chapter 4 silently; then, discuss the predictions you and they made. Instruct students to **take notes** in their double-entry journals about Boo and the children after you finish the class discussion.

3 Ask students to read Chapter 5 aloud in small groups or pairs. Have them use the predictions chart to identify and verify their predictions. Bring the class together and ask students to share their predictions. You might write the predictions on the board so that they can confirm or negate them as the novel unfolds.

4 Have students also add further information about Boo's attempts to reach out to the children to their double-entry journals.

ACTIVITY 5.13 *continued*

Steps:

5 Guide students to think about the concept of *characterization*, especially how characters are created. Have them also think about terms related to fictional characters. They are creating a vocabulary with which to discuss their reading. Direct students to explore the concept of ***characterization*** on a **word map** in their **Vocabulary Notebooks**.

6 Ask students to respond to the Writing Prompt, **drafting** a diary entry in Boo's voice commenting on the children's latest pranks. Ask students to consider, based on evidence from the story, how Boo might view their antics.

7 Finally, ask students to reflect upon the strategies they used to make meaning from the text and evaluate the effectiveness of these strategies.

ACTIVITY 5.13 *continued*

Making Predictions

ACADEMIC VOCABULARY

Characterization is the way a writer portrays a character.

In your Vocabulary Notebook, write all you know about the word characterization. What do you know about terms associated with characterization, with how characters are developed and how they function?

Four methods of character development: what characters do, what they say, what they look like; what others say about them.

Other terms: primary and secondary characters, foil, protatgonist, main character, major and minor characters, round and flat characters

Writing Prompt: **Write a diary entry in Boo's voice (use first-person point of view) commenting on the children's latest pranks. Be sure to communicate Boo's attitude toward the children through the diction and imagery you use to write about them. Think about how you could use the subjunctive mood to begin your diary entry; for example, "If I could talk to Jem and Scout, I would ..."**

The strategies I used to make meaning from this text are...

© 2011 College Board. All rights reserved.

Drawing Inferences

ACTIVITY 5.14

SUGGESTED LEARNING STRATEGIES: **Close Reading, Double-Entry Journal, Think-Pair-Share**

Active readers *infer* much, or "read between the lines." You infer to discover character motivation and to consider the symbolic and thematic implications of textual details. As you read Chapters 6 and 7, identify textual details that suggest something more to you, and interpret what these suggestions are.

Incidents Involving Boo Radley	Making Inferences and Drawing Conclusions from Inferences
CHAPTERS 6 AND 7 1. Jem wants to peep in the window.— pg 51 2. Kids run aways as a great shadow appears and a shotgun blast frightens them.— pg 53	
3. Jem loses his pants, and decides to go back to the Radley yard to fetch them and says, "We shouldn'a done that tonight. Scout…" Scout realls, "It was then, I suppose, that Jem and I first began to part company. Sometimes I did not understand him, but my periods of bewilderment were short-lived. This was beyond me." — Pg 56	3. Jem recognizes that what he did was wrong and does not want to disappoint his father. Conclusion: Jem is maturing. He is beginning to take responsibility for his actions, but Scout does not understand Jem's maturation and is mystified by his secrecy.
4. ball of twine in knothole — pg 58 5. soap figures — pg 59 6. pocket watch, knife — pg 60	4. – 6. Jem and Scout begin to expect the things they find in the knothole and know they are gifts specifically intended for them. Conclusion: Jem understands more about who is putting the gifts in the knothole. Scout doesn't put the evidence together the way he does.
7. Mr. Radley plugs the hole with cement, and says the tree is dying. Jem cries about this. — pg 62-63	7. Jem questions Mr. Radley and his father about cementing up the knothole, and he comes to his own conclusion. Conclusion: Jem cries not because he won't get any more presents, but because he realizes Mr. Radley is stopping Boo's attempts to reach out to the children with gifts.

ACTIVITY 5.14
Drawing Inferences

Materials:

- *To Kill a Mockingbird*, Chapters 6 and 7

Purpose:

- To make inferences and draw appropriate conclusions
- To identify evidence from the text to support inferences
- To read interpretively as well as literally

Steps:

1 Students will practice a **close reading** of the text to infer meaning and draw conclusions, which is the basis of literary interpretation. Begin by asking students to infer meaning from the statement "Go to your room." Moreover, what conclusions can they draw from this statement?

2 Begin Chapter 6 with a **read aloud/think aloud** in which you model developing inferences from the text. Use the inferences you make to draw significant conclusions. For example, you could model a close reading of a short passage beginning with "I pulled him down beside me on the cot" and going to the end of the chapter. Next, based upon Jem's comment, "Maybe so, but — I just wanta keep it that way, Scout. We shouldn'a done that tonight, Scout." Model the inference that Jem recognizes that what he did was wrong and he does not want to disappoint his father. One conclusion that readers can draw from this inference is that Jem is maturing and beginning to take responsibility for his actions.

3 After you've modeled this strategy thoroughly, instruct students to read Chapter 7 and engage in a **think-pair-share** using the **double-entry journal** to practice close reading, inferring, and drawing conclusions.

4 Close this lesson by asking students to reflect on the strategies they used to make meaning from text and to evaluate the effectiveness of these strategies.

5 Assign Chapter 8 as homework, or give students silent reading time in class.

ACTIVITY 5.15

Lessons from the Neighborhood

Materials:

- *To Kill a Mockingbird*, Chapter 8

Purpose:

- To synthesize evidence from the text to create an interpretation
- To evaluate how a minor character has affected the major characters
- To infer and predict the significance of a character's role
- To discuss the function of motif in understanding theme

Steps:

1 Chapter 8 is the last chapter in Part One that deals with the growing relationship between the children and Arthur Radley. Ask students to add the last bit of information about Boo and the children to their **double-entry journals**. It is time for them to synthesize all they know and have been noting about Boo's and the children's attempts to "climb into [another's] skin and walk around in it" (Chapter 3). Boo's act of concern for the children's welfare during the fire foreshadows his final act of self-sacrifice for them.

2 After discussing the blanket scene, ask students to **discuss** the questions on this page in small groups. Instruct them to use textual evidence noted in their **double-entry journals**. Next ask students, first individually, then in pairs, then as a large group, to craft an interpretive sentence that synthesizes their new understanding of the relationship between the children and Arthur Radley.

3 From now on the children will become increasingly affected by the concerns of the wider community, specifically the trial of Tom Robinson and their father's involvement. But point out the insightful way the children will continue to refer to Boo as they encounter the injustices, intolerance, and prejudice of their community.

4 As students continue to read the novel, encourage them think how the motif (a recurring subject, theme, idea) of Boo Radley prepares the children to encounter the problems of the wider world of Maycomb County prejudices and stereotyping.

5 Ask students to reflect on the strategies they used to make meaning from text and to evaluate the effectiveness of these strategies.

ACTIVITY 5.15

Lessons from the Neighborhood

SUGGESTED LEARNING STRATEGIES: **Discussion Groups, Double-Entry Journal**

LITERARY TERMS

A **motif** is a unifying element in an artistic work, especially any recurrent image, symbol, theme, character type, subject, or narrative detail.

Lessons from the Neighborhood — Who Is Arthur Radley?

1. In small groups, using the notes you have collected, answer the following questions to discuss the character of Boo Radley as a **motif**. Take notes in your double-entry journal about your conclusions.
   - Who is most affected by the contacts the children have had with Boo (Arthur Radley)? How do you know, and what has been the effect?
   - Review the rumors and gossip the children hear about Boo. What is the effect of all that stereotyping? What is the truth of the rumors, gossip, and stereotyping?
   - What has been Atticus's role in the children's relationship to Boo?
   - Discuss Harper Lee's purpose in including this story of the children and Boo Radley. What are the children learning from this experience as they come of age in Maycomb, Alabama?

2. Once you have discussed the questions above, synthesize all the incidents by writing an interpretive sentence that shows your understanding of how the relationship has changed from the beginning of the novel to now.

Sample statements:

- The children first stereotype Boo as an evil freak, capable of horrible acts of violence, but as he reaches out to them with kindness and concern, and as they try to contact him, the children discover he deserves their kindness and sympathy, not their fear and hatred.
- The children, especially Jem, have begun to leave behind the fear and stereotyping of their early thinking about Boo Radley because these ideas are being replaced by real contacts that create a connection of kindness and curiosity between Boo and them.
- Because of the efforts of the children to know Boo, and Boo's kindness and concern for the children. Scout and, especially, Jem have learned to empathize and sympathize with him.

WORD CONNECTIONS

The word ***synthesize***, which means "to combine parts or elements into a whole," has a Greek prefix, *syn-*, meaning "together" or "united," and the Greek root *thesis*, which is "something laid down, like a statement."

Questioning the Text

ACTIVITY 5.16

SUGGESTED LEARNING STRATEGIES: Questioning the Text, Close Reading

Levels of Questioning

Write three questions about Chapter 10 for each level of questioning.

Level of Questions	Your Questions
Level 1 **Questions of Fact:** **What did the text say?** For example: When did Atticus scold Scout for fighting?	**1.**
	2.
	3.
Level 2 **Questions of Interpretation:** **What does the text mean?** For example: Why does Jem encourage Scout to ask Atticus about Cecil Jacobs's comments instead of just explaining them to her?	**1.**
	2.
	3.

ACTIVITY 5.16

Questioning the Text

Materials:

- *To Kill a Mockingbird*, Chapters 9 and 10

Purpose:

- To compose levels of questions to interpret text

Steps:

1 Review **Levels of Questions** with students (Activity 5.8). Next, **read aloud/think aloud** Chapter 9, and model questions on different levels. For example, during the first two paragraphs you could ask these questions:

Factual: When did Atticus scold Scout for fighting?

Interpretive: Why does Jem encourage Scout to ask Atticus about Cecil Jacobs's comments instead of just explaining them to her?

Universal: How do you explain racism to a child?

2 Now, guide students through the process of developing levels of questions. Involve students in a **close reading** of Chapter 9; then, select a passage for them to read independently:

- Ask for two Level-1 questions for that section. Solicit from students some of the literal-level questions. Further, discuss the importance and limitations of these questions.
- Have students work in pairs to develop Level-2 questions for the same passage. These questions usually begin with ***how*** or ***why***. Discuss the value of this deeper level of thinking.
- Ask students to develop Level-3 questions and share them aloud with the class. These questions go beyond the text and require the reader to explore the larger implications of the text.

Steps:

3 Complete Chapter 9 with a read aloud/think aloud in which you continue to make your thinking public as you model answering these questions on different levels:

- What is "Maycomb's usual disease"?
- According to Scout, how is Uncle Jack's treatment of her unfair?
- Why doesn't Scout want Atticus to know why she was fighting with Francis?
- Why does Scout fight with Cecil Jacobs and with her cousin Francis?
- Why does the author present news about the trial of Tom Robinson through the children?
- Why does Atticus want Scout to overhear his discussion with Uncle Jack?
- Why doesn't Atticus tell the children about the trial before they hear about it in an ugly way?

You may use these questions and the ones your students develop as the basis of a class discussion.

4 Direct students to read Chapter 10 silently or in small groups (or as homework). Ask students to work collaboratively to write three questions at each level based on this chapter. Then, have them write responses to each question on a separate sheet of paper.

5 Assign groups to exchange questions with another group and answer the other group's questions. When groups have finished answering questions, have them return the questions to the originators. Have students assess the answers to their questions provided by the other group. Discuss how the other group's answers are similar to or different from the originator's.

6 Finally, ask students to reflect on the effectiveness of the strategies they used to make meaning from this text.

Questioning the Text

Level 3 **Questions That Go Beyond the Text: Why does it matter?** For example: How do you explain racism to a child?	**1.**
	2.
	3.

The strategies I used to make meaning from this text are...

Examining the Title

ACTIVITY 5.17

SUGGESTED LEARNING STRATEGIES: Close Reading, Discussion Groups, Marking the Text, Quickwrite, Rereading

Conduct a close reading of the passage below from Chapter 10. As you read, highlight references to the title and think about why Harper Lee chose this the title for her novel. Keep track of your ideas by noting your thoughts in the margin.

from ***To Kill a Mockingbird,*** Chapter 10

When he gave us our air rifles Atticus wouldn't teach us to shoot. Uncle Jack instructed us in the rudiments thereof; he said Atticus wasn't interested in guns. Atticus said to Jem one day, "I'd rather you shot at tin cans in the back yard, but I know you'll go after birds. Shoot all the bluejays you want, if you can hit 'em, but remember it's a sin to kill a mockingbird."

That was the only time I ever heard Atticus say it was a sin to do something, and I asked Miss Maudie about it.

"Your father's right," she said. "Mockingbirds don't do one thing but make music for us to enjoy. They don't eat up people's gardens, don't nest in corncribs, they don't do one thing but sing their hearts out for us. That's why it's a sin to kill a mockingbird."

1. How does Miss Maudie's information about mockingbirds add to Atticus's comment that "it's a sin to kill a mockingbird"?

2. Based on the passage above, predict what you think may happen in the novel.

3. A *motif* is a repeated image; expect to encounter more mentions of the mockingbird. As you do, note them in your double-entry journal, and think about how the image helps you understand Harper Lee's thinking when she named her novel.

GRAMMAR & USAGE

Most novels and short stories contain dialogue, as do some nonfiction forms, such as memoirs and biographies. In dialogue, the speaker's exact words are always enclosed in quotation marks. The rules for other punctuation marks with quotations include the following:

- **A direct quotation can be set off from the rest of a sentence by a comma, a question mark, or an exclamation mark.**
- **Commas and periods are placed inside quotation marks.**
- **Colons and semicolons are placed outside closing quotation marks.**
- **Question marks and exclamation marks are placed inside if the quotation itself is a question or exclamation.**

GRAMMAR & USAGE EXTENSION

You might extend this lesson on dialogue with the following information:

- An interrupting expression should not be inside the quotation marks. Example: "Let's go into shore," Carlos shouted, "before the seas get too rough."
- With two or more sentences by the same speaker, only one set of quotation marks is needed. Example: She answered, "No, I don't want to go to the party. I'm in the mood for a movie tonight."
- Generally, a direct quotation begins with a capital letter. When an interrupting expression divides the quoted sentence, the second part should not be capitalized. (See the first example above.)

ACTIVITY 5.17
Examining the Title

Materials:

- *To Kill a Mockingbird*, Chapter 10

Purpose:

- To consider the meaning of the title
- To practice close reading and inferring meaning

Steps:

1 You might need to review ***motif***: a recurring image used to symbolize an idea. The motif of Boo Radley represents how stereotyping, gossip, and rumor can so mischaracterize someone that it leads to prejudicial feelings of fear and hatred. The motif of the mockingbird, along with the Boo Radley motif and the idea of walking in another's skin, contributes to the metaphorical meaning of the novel.

2 In Chapter 10, the novel's title surfaces in the text; in this activity students participate in a **close reading** to consider the meaning of the title *To Kill a Mockingbird*. Ask students to **reread** this passage from Chapter 10 silently. Direct them to express their interpretation of the passage in a **quickwrite**, and **mark the text**, circling details that support their interpretive statements. Next, ask students, in **small discussion groups**, to share their interpretations, discuss them, and respond to the questions on this page.

3 It is too early to ask students to discuss why the text is titled *To Kill a Mockingbird*, but from this point forward ask students to use their double-entry journals about Boo to record this reference (with page numbers) and all future additional references to mockingbirds. At the end of the novel, have students come back to their notetaking to see the link between Boo and Tom and mockingbirds.

ACTIVITY 5.18

Pin the Quote on Atticus

Materials:

- *To Kill a Mockingbird*, Chapter 11
- Life-sized paper cutout of Atticus

Purpose:

- To connect a chapter to a larger understanding of the novel
- To evaluate evidence in support of an interpretive claim
- To analyze a character based on textual evidence
- To independently apply reading strategies to new text

Steps:

1 Chapter 11, the last chapter in Part One, is an important turning point. Starting in Part Two, the setting moves from the secure confines of Scout and Jem's neighborhood into the wider community of Maycomb, including Calpurnia's church, the jail, and the courthouse. The last encounter of Part One, with Mrs. Dubose, foreshadows the prejudice the children will encounter and the bravery of their father.

2 You may want to divide the class into seven groups and divide the chapter up into seven segments for students to practice close analysis. Ask students in groups to apply all the reading strategies they have practiced (**rereading, questioning the text, inferring, predicting, marking the text**) to understand this portion of the text.

3 Before students begin, model a close reading or analysis with the opening passage, reproduced on this page.

4 As groups of students read their passages, ask them to **mark the text**, highlighting or underlining parts they think are particularly significant. Discuss Mrs. Dubose's wrathfulness and sharp tongue.

ACTIVITY 5.18

Pin the Quote on Atticus

SUGGESTED LEARNING STRATEGIES: **Marking the Text, Questioning the Text, Rereading, Predicting, Scanning**

WORD CONNECTIONS

The word ***conceal*** is formed from the Latin prefix *con-*, meaning "together," and the Latin verb *celare*, meaning "to hide."

Many English words have the prefix *con-*, including *conceited, conceive, concentrate*, and *concentric*.

GRAMMAR & USAGE

An independent clause is a group of words that contains a subject and a verb and can stand alone as a sentence. A sentence having more than one independent clause is a **compound sentence**. One way to combine two such clauses is to use a coordinating conjunction: *and, or, but*. Unless the clauses are both short and simple, you need to place a comma before the coordinating conjunction between the two independent clauses.

Example: I did not remember our mother, but Jem did....

Analysis begins with a close reading of the novel. Read the passage below from the beginning of Chapter 11. Apply all the strategies you have practiced—rereading, diffusing vocabulary, questioning the text, inferring, predicting, and marking the text—to show your understanding as you read.

from ***To Kill a Mockingbird***, Chapter 11

When we were small, Jem and I confined our activities to the southern neighborhood, but when I was well into the second grade at school and tormenting Boo Radley became passé, the business section of Maycomb drew us frequently up the street past the real property of Mrs. Henry Lafayette Dubose. It was impossible to go to town without passing her house unless we wished to walk a mile out of the way. Previous minor encounters with her left me with no desire for more, but Jem said I had to grow up some time.

Mrs. Dubose lived alone except for a Negro girl in constant attendance, two doors up the street from us in a house with steep front steps and a dog-trot hall. She was very old; she spent most of each day in bed and the rest of it in a wheelchair. It was rumored that she kept a CSA pistol concealed among her numerous shawls and wraps.

Jem and I hated her. If she was on the porch when we passed, we would be raked by her wrathful gaze, subjected to ruthless interrogations regarding our behavior, and given a melancholy prediction on what we would amount to when we grew up, which was always nothing. We had long ago given up the idea of walking past her house on the opposite side of the street; that only made her raise her voice and let the whole neighborhood in on it.

We could do nothing to please her. If I said as sunnily as I could, "Hey, Mrs. Dubose," I would receive for an answer, "Don't you say hey to me, you ugly girl! You say good afternoon, Mrs. Dubose!"

She was vicious. Once she heard Jem refer to our father as "Atticus" and her reaction was apoplectic. Besides being the sassiest, most disrespectful mutts who ever passed her way, we were told that it was quite a pity our father had not remarried after our mother's death. A lovelier lady than our mother never lived, she said, and it was heartbreaking the way Atticus Finch let her children run wild. I did not remember our mother, but Jem did—he would tell me about her sometimes—and he went livid when Mrs. Dubose shot us this message.

GRAMMAR & USAGE EXTENSION

You might extend this lesson by showing students others ways to join independent clauses:

- ***With a semicolon:*** She left the house to go to the movie; he slammed the door behind her forcefully.
- ***With a conjunctive adverb***: She said goodbye with a sarcastic voice; however, she also managed a small smile and a wave of her hand.

Ask students to look through the excerpt for other compound sentences and identify how the clauses are joined.

1. On index cards, write quotations of important things Atticus says that teach Jem and Scout about people and life. Share a quote with the class, and discuss why you selected it before you place it on the Atticus outline. A sample index card has been prepared for you.

> "You just hold your head high and be a gentleman. Whatever she says to you, it's your job not to let her make you mad." (page 100)

2. What does this quotation reveal about Atticus?

3. Create a web of adjectives that describe Atticus's character:

wise
courageous
considerate
kind
respectful

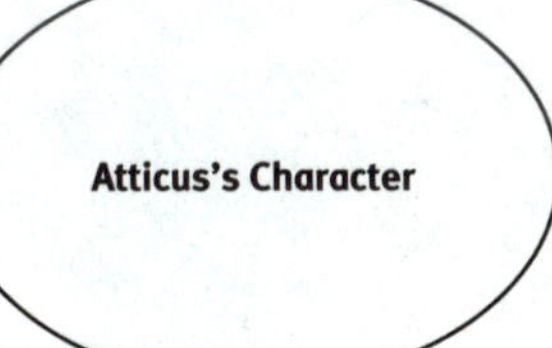

intuitive
loving
ethical
fair
independent

humble
thoughtful
friendly
polite

© 2011 College Board. All rights reserved.

Steps:

5 After a discussion about Mrs. Dubose, focus the passage analysis on evaluating Atticus's character in this novel. Solicit from students any words of wisdom or advice or concerns spoken by Atticus. On three different occasions Atticus makes a point he knows will be important in the future. Have students write Atticus's words of wisdom on 3x5 index cards. Use this opportunity to discuss his role as father, gentleman, and lawyer and as a heroic figure to his family and the community.

6 Create a full-scale outline of a person, and tell students that this figure represents Atticus Finch. Post students' collected quotes from Atticus on the outline.

7 Then, assign a chapter (from Chapters 1–10) to each group. Ask groups to **scan** the chapters and find quotations in which Atticus gives advice or makes significant comments, or comments by others about Atticus, that show his character. Have students write each quotation on an index card, with a statement that clarifies what is being taught to the children.

8 Place these quotes on "Atticus"; have students share the significance of the quote as well what it teaches Jem and Scout.

9 Next, ask students to create a web of adjectives that describe Atticus's character. Add these adjectives to the outline of Atticus.

Unit 5 • Coming of Age Amidst Controversy 383

ACTIVITY 5.18 *continued*

Steps:

10 Direct students to write topic sentences using two of these adjectives that are complementary yet not the same. Have students share their topic sentences aloud so all can hear samples of good writing.

11 You may want to have students draft a complete paragraph characterizing Atticus.

12 Direct students to revisit their **Vocabulary Notebooks** and elaborate on the concept of *characterization.*

ACTIVITY 5.18 *continued*

Pin the Quote on Atticus

4. Select two adjectives from your web that are complementary yet not the same, and organize them into a coherent topic sentence with a subject (Atticus) and an opinion (character trait).

Write your topic sentences here:

Sample topic sentences:

- Atticus is respectful and strict with his children.
- Atticus, a man of integrity, is a model of great patience.
- As a father, Atticus is fair and thoughtful; as a lawyer he is brave and determined.

Share your topic sentences with your neighbor.

5. Work collaboratively in small groups to find evidence from all the quotations you've gathered to support your claims.

Exploring the Issues in *To Kill a Mockingbird*

ACTIVITY 5.19

SUGGESTED LEARNING STRATEGIES: Predicting, Previewing, Questioning the Text, Brainstorming

Review Embedded Assessment 2. What will you need to do to successfully complete this assessment?

Embedded Assessment 2 asks you to discuss the connection between a passage in the book and a central subject of the text. Create a web of the many thematic subjects Harper Lee explores in Part One of *To Kill a Mockingbird*. In addition to the central journey of Coming of Age, list the various subjects Scout, Jem, and Dill must come to terms with as they discover what coming of age means. You will add to this web as you read Part Two.

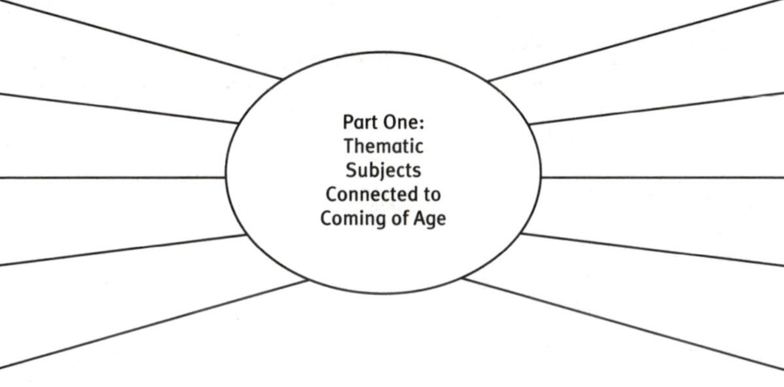

ACTIVITY 5.19
Exploring the Issues in *To Kill a Mockingbird*

Materials:

- *To Kill a Mockingbird*, Chapters 1–11

Purpose:

- To identify the skills and knowledge necessary to analyze a passage
- To brainstorm topics relevant for an essay about "coming of age"
- To identify foreshadowing and make predictions

Steps:

1 You may want to review the requirements of Embedded Assessment 2, and review some of the major themes or ideas related to "coming of age" in ***To Kill a Mockingbird.***

2 Return to the excerpted passages from ***To Kill a Mockingbird*** that the class has studied closely, and reflect on how these passages function in the novel in terms of character and setting and conflict.

3 Ask students to **brainstorm** issues Jem and Scout have encountered as they grow up and come of age in Maycomb, Alabama, in the 1930s. You might start this discussion by asking what "coming of age" might mean for Scout and Jem. (This discussion may include prejudice, courage, integrity, gender roles, family relationships, and tolerance.) Create a web or a list of these on chart paper, and post the list so students can add to it as they continue through the novel.

Writing Workshops

This might be a good time to revisit Workshop 9, Response to Literature. Since students have already been introduced to the direct instruction in this workshop, you could modify the third activity in the workshop to ask students to analyze a passage rather than an entire short story as they practice writing a literary analysis.

ACTIVITY 5.19 *continued*

Steps:

4 **Preview** the beginning of Part Two. The incidents with Cecil Jacobs, Francis Hancock, and Mrs. Dubose **foreshadow** what is to come. Ask students to summarize these incidents, and predict what might happen. Ask students to respond to the Writing Prompt, explaining why the author might have used these three characters and incidents to foreshadow the action of Part Two.

5 Remind students of the statement Atticus makes early in the novel (Chapter 3), "You never really understand a person until you consider things from his point of view—until you climb into his skin and walk around in it." You might already have this statement on the "Pin the Quote" figure. This motif becomes increasingly significant in Part Two, starting with the children's visit to Calpurnia's church.

6 Chapter 12 takes the children out of the familiarity of their neighborhood to the Quarters for the first time, where they have a chance to see things from another point of view, while Chapter 13 reintroduces Aunt Alexandra, who represents a very different point of view. Begin reading Chapters 12 and 13 with students, and assign the rest as homework. You may want to ask students to use **levels of questioning** to create six questions (two literal, two interpretive, and two universal) based on their reading. These questions can be used as a reading quiz or as a preview of the questions asked in the next activity.

Exploring the Issues in *To Kill a Mockingbird*

LITERARY TERMS

Foreshadowing is the use of hints or clues in a narrative to suggest future action.

Briefly summarize the incidents involving Cecil Jacobs, Francis Hancock, and Mrs. Dubose. How are these three incidents related? What might these characters and these incidents **foreshadow**?

- Scout and Cecil Jacobs:

- Scout and Francis Hancock:

- Jem and Scout and Mrs. Dubose:

Writing Prompt: Write a piece explaining why Harper Lee used these three characters and three incidents to foreshadow the action of Part Two. Include in your text the lessons Atticus wants his children to learn and why.

Changing the Scene

ACTIVITY 5.20

SUGGESTED LEARNING STRATEGIES: **Discussion Groups**

Part Two of *To Kill A Mockingbird* begins with two dramatic developments in Jem and Scout's life: the visit to First Purchase African M.E. Church and Aunt Alexandra's arrival for a prolonged stay.

The following questions will help you to consider how these developments contribute to the text's overall meaning. They will help you examine how setting, conflict, and character development within specific scenes function in connection with the rest of the text.

Question Set 1:

1. What details does Scout provide when describing Calpurnia's church? The events of the service? What do these reveal about the nature of the Quarters as a community, especially in contrast to life in Scout and Jem's own neighborhood?

2. This scene shows that Calpurnia is a **dynamic** rather than a **static** character. What is revealed about Calpurnia through the conflict with Lula? Through Scout's conversation with her following the service (e.g., linin', her "double life," her "command of two languages")?

3. Based on the events of this chapter, what values does Calpurnia seem to represent in the book? Find quotes that support your conclusion.

4. How do Calpurnia and the trip to her church influence Scout's perspective? Find quotes that support your conclusions regarding the impact of the church scene and the conversation on Scout's view of the world.

WORD CONNECTIONS

The word ***dynamic*** comes from the Greek word meaning "powerful." The root *dyna-* appears in *dynamo, dynamite,* and *dynasty.*

Static also comes from a Greek word, *statikos*, referring to a stand or a pause or something firm or fixed. Other words in English with the root *-stat-* include *status, station, statistics,* and *statue.*

ACTIVITY 5.20
Changing the Scene

Materials:

- *To Kill a Mockingbird*, Chapters 12 and 13
- Vocabulary Notebooks

Purpose:

- To analyze the significance of a new setting and a new character in the novel
- To discuss major ideas in small groups
- To independently analyze how textual elements support thematic interpretations

Steps:

1 This activity requires students to analyze how setting, characters, and conflict develop the major theme of the novel. Split the class into small **discussion groups** (three students per group), and assign each group one of the two question sets. Explain that each group is responsible for answering the questions and then sharing its responses with a group who answered the other set of questions.

2 Combine the groups into larger groups (of six) to share their responses.

Steps:

3 Lead a whole class discussion in response to the following questions: What is the effect of starting Part Two with the material in Chapter 12? Of placing the scene in Chapter 13 immediately after Chapter 12? What is emphasized by the shift from Calpurnia to Alexandra as the focal point in Scout's narrative?

Changing the Scene

Question Set 2:

1. Describe the shift regarding Calpurnia that occurs in the first sentence of Chapter 13. How else is Calpurnia referred to during this chapter?
2. Why does Scout say "Aunt Alexandra fitted into the world of Maycomb like a hand into a glove"? How is this connected to the extended description of Maycomb's history in this chapter?
3. What is revealed about Aunt Alexandra through Scout's conversation with her about Cousin Lily and Cousin Joshua? Through Atticus's conversation with Scout and Jem on her behalf?
4. Based on the events of this chapter, what values does Aunt Alexandra represent? Find quotations that support your conclusion.

Now that you have examined the significance of setting and of characters in more detail, it's time to write thematic statements. A **thematic statement** articulates your interpretation of the text's central meaning or message. Earlier, you identified thematic subjects *To Kill a Mockingbird* explores, such as prejudice and courage. You may want to add more subjects to your classroom web. Your thematic statement would clarify what Harper Lee seems to be saying about these subjects.

For Embedded Assessment 2, you will analyze a passage and explain how it contributes to the meaning of the novel as a whole. You can focus on a character, conflict, or setting within the passage to develop your analysis. Based on your discussions in this activity, write a thematic statement for each of these three elements. You may use the following stems, but feel free to write your own.

1. Character: Aunt Alexandra's fascination with family history symbolizes _______________.
2. Conflict: The confrontation between Calpurnia and Lula shows that _______________.
3. Setting: The trip to Calpurnia's church reveals that _______________.

Exchange your thematic statements with a partner, and evaluate the statements using the following criteria:

- A thematic statement should not be stated as an order. (Example: "People should not be racist.")
- It should not be a cliché. (Example: "Blood is thicker than water.")
- It should not be restricted to the characters themselves. (Example: "Calpurnia looks beyond skin color.")
- It should not be stated as an absolute. (Example: "All white Southerners are racist.")

Revise your thematic statements based on your peer's feedback.

ACADEMIC VOCABULARY

A **thematic statement** is an idea a writer wishes to convey about a subject.

Steps:

4 Review the term ***thematic statement***, and link it to Embedded Assessment 2. Remind students of their exploration of this term in their **Vocabulary Notebooks**. This would be a good time to add more thematic subjects to the class web you created in Activity 5.19. Then, direct students to complete this page.

5 Call on students to share some thematic statements. Write them on the board, and discuss the effectiveness of each, revising as necessary. You might ask students to explain why each of the criteria is an important one to keep in mind.

6 You might want to have students **visualize** and draw a map of the Finch children's neighborhood now as they move from the security of their close neighborhood and out into the larger arena of Maycomb.

ACTIVITY 5.21

Comparing Print and Film Text

Materials:

- *To Kill a Mockingbird*, Chapter 15
- *To Kill a Mockingbird* DVD

Purpose:

- To analyze a passage closely and explain it within the context of the entire novel
- To compare and contrast aspects of character and conflict as presented in print and film text
- To observe and analyze the effects of a director's choices in film and an author's choices in text

Steps:

1 Note that the confrontation/discussion between Atticus and members of the town in front of his house ***foreshadows*** the central ***conflict*** of this chapter.

2 Ask students to do a **close reading** of the latter half of Chapter 15, starting with "As we walked up the sidewalk…" (This scene involves Atticus protecting Tom Robinson at the jail.) Assign each student a character to track as they read. Have them **mark the text** and **take notes** on the **graphic organizer** on their assigned character, noting the character's appearance, words, actions, and what others say to the character.

TEACHER TO TEACHER This scene has seven identified characters: Scout, Atticus, Jem, Mr. Walter Cunningham, Tom Robinson, Dill, and Mr. Underwood. Five unidentified men from the mob speak—Walter Cunningham is identified when he first speaks; the others are not. You may want to assign all unidentified men to one student.

ACTIVITY 5.21

Comparing Print and Film Text

SUGGESTED LEARNING STRATEGIES: **Close Reading, Graphic Organizer, Marking the Text, Rereading, Notetaking**

Reread Chapter 15. Your teacher will give you a particular character to observe. As you reread the chapter, complete the following chart for that character.

Then, your class will perform a Reader's Theater interpretation of the scene. Finally, your teacher will show you the film version of the scene. In each version, note how your character is portrayed and how this portrayal influences your perspective on the character. You will then compare the versions.

Name of Character ______	**Notes from Novel**	**Notes from Reader's Theater**	**Notes from Film Clip**
What your character says, and how			
What your character does			
Your character's appearance			
What others say **about** your character (you may look outside Chapter 15 for this information)			
What others say **to** your character, and how			

3 After students read the passage, ask for one volunteer from each of the character groups to perform in a **Reader's Theater**, as well as one to read the part of the narrator. Explain that a Reader's Theater is an oral interpretation of a scene in which students stand in front of the classroom and, using their texts, perform the roles of the characters. As this group performs the scene, have the rest of the class add to their notes.

Reflect on your notes, focusing on differences and similarities between how the novel and the movie portray the scene.

1. How did the Reader's Theater interpretation affect your impressions of the chracters? Why?

2. In the film, how are framing, lighting, sound, and other **cinematic elements** used to communicate meaning in this scene? Describe how each element is used and its effect. See Activity 2.15 to review film terms.
   - **Angles and Framing** (high and low angles, long shot, medium shot, close-ups):
   - **Lighting** (high key and low key):
   - **Sound** (diegetic and non-diegetic):
   - **Other elements** (camera movement):

ACTIVITY 5.21 continued

Steps:

4 You may want to review cinematic elements from Activity 2.15. Show students the film version of Scene 21 (01:01:58–01:07:10). Ask them to take notes on the same things in the film version that they noted in the print version. They will then analyze the similarities and differences between the two texts. You may want to show the clip a second time to enable students to focus on the use of cinematic techniques in the clip.

© 2011 College Board. All rights reserved.

Unit 5 • Coming of Age Amidst Controversy 391

Steps:

5 Lead students in a discussion of the scene's significance in the book as a whole. How do the central conflict, the setting, and the characters function in the scene? Why is it one of the most dramatic moments in the book? How does this scene link to the central theme(s) of the text? Ask students to write a statement explaining the significance of this scene to the novel as a whole. Then, have them share these statements with the class.

6 Direct students to complete the Writing Prompt.

Differentiating Instruction:

To provide **support** for writing, create a more structured writing experience by having students use a drafting/brainstorming strategy (such as **TWIST**) to create a thesis. In their thesis, students should examine the importance of a character to the scene. Have students follow this basic outline:

- Topic sentence: importance of the character
- Example: how the character deals with conflict
- Commentary: what the character's actions reveal about the character
- Example: how setting helps illuminate a character
- Summary: connection to the novel as a whole

Extend the activity by changing the prompt to a more complex analysis between film and text. Ask students to argue which medium does a better job of describing a character and the character's connection to a broader theme.

Comparing Print and Film Text

3. What changes in dialogue were made? Why? What is the effect of these changes?

4. Cite specific changes made in the transformation from print to film. Why might those changes have been made?

Writing Prompt: Explain the significance of conflict and setting in this scene. Then, choose a character and discuss the significance of his or her role in the outcome of the scene. How does this scene contribute to the meaning of the novel as a whole?

Analyzing Atticus's Closing Argument

ACTIVITY 5.22

SUGGESTED LEARNING STRATEGIES: Close Reading, Marking the Text, SMELL

from ***To Kill a Mockingbird***, Chapter 20

"Gentlemen," he was saying, "I shall be brief, but I would like to use my remaining time with you to remind you that this case is not a difficult one, it requires no minute sifting of complicated facts, but it does require you to be sure beyond all reasonable doubt as to the guilt of the defendant. To begin with, this case should never have come to trial. This case is as simple as black and white.

"The state has not produced one iota of medical evidence to the effect that the crime Tom Robinson is charged with ever took place. It has relied instead upon the testimony of two witnesses whose evidence has not only been called into serious question on cross-examination, but has been flatly contradicted by the defendant. The defendant is not guilty, but somebody in this courtroom is.

"I have nothing but pity in my heart for the chief witness for the state, but my pity does not extend so far as to her putting a man's life at stake, which she has done in an effort to get rid of her own guilt.

"I say guilt, gentlemen, because it was guilt that motivated her. She has committed no crime, she has merely broken a rigid and time-honored code of our society, a code so severe that whoever breaks it is hounded from our midst as unfit to live with. She is the victim of cruel poverty and ignorance, but I cannot pity her: she is white. She knew full well the enormity of her offense, but because her desires were stronger than the code she was breaking, she persisted in breaking it. She persisted, and her subsequent reaction is something that all of us have known at one time or another. She did something every child has done—she tried to put the evidence of her offense away from her. But in this case she was no child hiding stolen contraband: she struck out at her victim—of necessity she must put him away from her—he must be removed from her presence, from this world. She must destroy the evidence of her offense.

"What was the evidence of her offense? Tom Robinson, a human being. She must put Tom Robinson away from her. Tom Robinson was her daily reminder of what she did. What did she do? She tempted a Negro.

"She was white, and she tempted a Negro. She did something that in our society is unspeakable: she kissed a black man. Not an old Uncle, but a strong young Negro man. No code mattered to her before she broke it, but it came crashing down on her afterwards.

"Her father saw it, and the defendant has testified as to his remarks. What did her father do? We don't know, but there is circumstantial evidence to indicate that Mayella Ewell was beaten savagely by someone who led almost exclusively with his left. We do know in part what Mr. Ewell did: he did what any God-fearing, persevering, respectable white man would do under the

My Notes

WORD CONNECTIONS

Circumstantial is an adjective meaning "having to do with certain facts or conditions." The prefix *circum-* derives from the Latin word *circum*, meaning "around." English has many words beginning with *circum-*. They include *circumference*, *circumnavigate*, and *circumvent*.

ACTIVITY 5.22

Analyzing Atticus's Closing Argument

Materials:

- *To Kill a Mockingbird*, Chapters 16–20
- *To Kill a Mockingbird* DVD

Purpose:

- To analyze a speaker's rhetorical appeals
- To identify the connection between audience, context, and a speaker's appeals
- To evaluate how effectively a print text was transformed into a film text

Steps:

1 Chapters 16–20 deal with the trial of Tom Robinson, which occurs over the course of one day. You can have students read these chapters independently, or you could ask students to read in parts, especially Atticus's examination of Mayella and Tom Robinson. Be sure students note where Jem, Scout, and Dill are during the trial and the differences in their reactions to the events of the trial.

(Dill reacts emotionally to the cross-examination of Tom; Jem, being logical, thinks Atticus has convinced the jurors; and Scout has little outward reaction.)

2 Have students turn to page 396, and explain the acronym **SMELL** to students. Lead the class in a discussion of the S element of the acronym to establish the difficulties Atticus faces as he presents his final appeals for Tom Robinson's innocence.

3 Returning to this page, direct students to do a **close reading** of Atticus's closing argument. Instruct them to **mark the text** when they find appeals of emotion, logic, or language.

Teacher Notes

Analyzing Atticus's Closing Argument

My Notes

circumstances—he swore out a warrant, no doubt signing it with his left hand, and Tom Robinson now sits before you, having taken the oath with the only good hand he possesses—his right hand.

"And so a quiet, respectable, humble Negro who had the unmitigated temerity to 'feel sorry' for a white woman has had to put his word against two white people's. I need not remind you of their appearance and conduct on the stand—you saw them for yourselves. The witnesses for the state, with the exception of the sheriff of Maycomb County, have presented themselves to you gentlemen, to this court, in the cynical confidence that their testimony would not be doubted, confident that you gentlemen would go along with them on the assumption—the evil assumption—that *all* Negroes lie, that *all* Negroes are basically immoral beings, that *all* Negro men are not to be trusted around our women, an assumption one associates with minds of their caliber.

"Which, gentlemen, we know is in itself a lie as black as Tom Robinson's skin, a lie I do not have to point out to you. You know the truth, and the truth is this: some Negroes lie, some Negroes are immoral, some Negro men are not to be trusted around women—black or white. But this is a truth that applies to the human race and to no particular race of men. There is not a person in this courtroom who has never told a lie, who has never done an immoral thing, and there is no man living who has never looked upon a woman without desire."

Atticus paused and took out his handkerchief. Then he took off his glasses and wiped them, and we saw another "first": we had never seen him sweat—he was one of those men whose faces never perspired, but now it was shining tan.

"One more thing, gentlemen, before I quit. Thomas Jefferson once said that all men are created equal, a phrase that the Yankees and the distaff side of the Executive branch in Washington are fond of hurling at us. There is a tendency in this year of grace, 1935, for certain people to use this phrase out of context, to satisfy all conditions. The most ridiculous example I can think of is that the people who run public education promote the stupid and idle along with the industrious—because all men are created equal, educators will gravely tell you, the children left behind suffer terrible feelings of inferiority. We know all men are not created equal in the sense some people would have us believe—some people are smarter than others, some people have more opportunity because they're born with it, some men make more money than others, some ladies make better cakes than others—some people are born gifted beyond the normal scope of most men.

GRAMMAR & USAGE

Parallel structure is the use of the same grammatical structures—words, phrases, or clauses—to balance related ideas. Writers perform this balancing act because it makes their writing more effective. Readers can see the commonalities and relationships clearly when the structures are parallel.

Example: . . . the assumption . . . *that all Negroes lie, that all Negroes are basically immoral beings, that all Negro men are not to be trusted around our women.* . . . (parallel adjective clauses)

GRAMMAR & USAGE EXTENSION

You can extend this lesson by pointing out other examples of parallel structure in this excerpt from ***To Kill a Mockingbird***. For example, point out the parallel uses of "some Negroes" in the paragraph beginning "Which, gentlemen...." This example and the one in the feature box are actually good examples of repetition as well as parallel structure. You might also point out the last sentence in the paragraph beginning with "One more thing. . . ." It contains a series of clauses beginning with "some."

Teacher Notes

"But there is one way in this country in which all men are created equal—there is one human institution that makes a pauper the equal of a Rockefeller, the stupid man the equal of an Einstein, and the ignorant man the equal of any college president. That institution, gentlemen, is a court. It can be the Supreme Court of the United States or the humblest J.P. court in the land, or this honorable court which you serve. Our courts have their faults, as does any human institution, but in this country our courts are the great levelers, and in our courts all men are created equal.

"I'm no idealist to believe firmly in the integrity of our courts and in the jury system—that is no ideal to me, it is a living, working reality. Gentlemen, a court is no better than each man of you sitting before me on this jury. A court is only as sound as its jury, and a jury is only as sound as the men who make it up. I am confident that you gentlemen will review without passion the evidence you have heard, come to a decision, and restore this defendant to his family. In the name of God, do your duty."

Atticus's voice had dropped, and as he turned away from the jury he said something I did not catch. He said it more to himself than to the court. I punched Jem. "What'd he say?"

"'In the name of God, believe him,' I think that's what he said."

When you have read this passage, analyze Atticus's speech for the rhetorical structures and devices he uses to convince the reader. Highlight the five elements of an argument (hook, claim, concessions/refutations, support, and summary/call to action).

My Notes

WORD CONNECTIONS

Legal arguments often use a persuasive technique of *ad hominem*, which is Latin for "argument against the person." An *ad hominem* appeal points out that a person may be disposed to take a particular position. Find an example of *ad hominem* in the excerpt from Chapter 20 of *To Kill a Mockingbird*.

Steps:

4 Have students complete the SMELL chart, providing detailed evidence. You might give them an example of each to help focus their reading:

Emotion: "I have nothing but pity in my heart for the chief witness of the state."

Logic: "There is circumstantial evidence to indicate that Mayella Ewell was beaten savagely by someone who led almost exclusively with his left."

Language: ". . . the assumption—that evil assumption—that all Negroes lie . . ."

5 Ask students to share their responses in small groups or with the whole class.

Analyzing Atticus's Closing Argument

Perform a close reading of Atticus's famous closing statement. Use the SMELL strategy to analyze the quality and credibility of his evidence for this particular audience.

S = Sender-Receiver relationship. Atticus is the sender. The jury and the audience are the receivers. What is the relationship among Atticus, the jury, and the audience? Whom does Atticus mean to influence with his statement? What attitudes and assumptions does his target audience hold towards his subject? Towards Atticus himself?

Most of the men of the jury are from the surrounding countryside, rather than city men. Atticus knows they have already made up their minds about Tom Robinson's guilt. The jury knows that Atticus has tried to break down their prejudices by confronting them with factual evidence that proves Tom incapable of the crime he is accused of. They cannot waver from their prejudices. Atticus speaks to his community as much as to the jury, hoping to create a chink in the armor of prejudice.

M = Message. What is Atticus's message? Summarize the statements made in his closing argument.

Tom Robinson is on trial because Mayella and Tom Ewell need a scapegoat for their own code-breaking behavior – she for desiring a black man's attention, he to justify his savage beating of his daughter. There is no evidence of the crime, and much evidence suggesting the crime of rape was impossible. The case is "as simple as black and white." He asks the jury to rise above prejudice in their deliberations.

E = Emotional strategies. Does Atticus use any statements that are meant to get an emotional reaction from his audience? Explain. If so, what is the desired effect?

"...nothing but pity in my heart for the chief witness"; "She is the victim of cruel poverty and ignorance"; "...unspeakable: she kissed a black man"; "...a quiet, respectable, humble Negro who had the unmitigated temerity to 'feel sorry' for a white woman." Atticus tries to create empathy and sympathy for both the victim and the accused. He cannot make a martyr of the victim but must try to get them to understand her motives.

L = Logical strategies. Does Atticus use any statements or appeals that are logical? Explain. How does the logic (or its absence) affect the message?

All the statements he makes about evidence appeal to logic: left- and right-handedness, physical evidence of a crime.

The psychological logic of scapegoating is also presented.

L = Language. Look for specific words and phrases chosen by Atticus, and consider how the language affects his message.

...a quiet, respectable, humble Negro who had the unmitigated temerity to 'feel sorry' for a white woman": Here Atticus reminds the jury of Tom's place in society.

"...but in this country our courts are the great levelers, and in our courts all men are created equal." Here Atticus uses the language of historical ideals of the country to make an ethical appeal.

As you watch the film version of the courtroom scene, fill out the chart below, looking for specific elements from the scene.

What images does the director present to the audience in this scene?	What images does the director consciously choose NOT to present to the audience?	What did you notice about the relationship between the speech and the images?	What changes or deletions did you notice in the text of Atticus's speech?

Discussion Questions:

1. How do the director's choices affect the way we respond to the scene?
2. How do the changes in the text of the speech affect the message of the speech (if they do)?
3. Why do you think the director changed the speech in this way (other than to shorten it)?

Writing Prompt: Write a paragraph analyzing the use of appeals in Atticus's closing argument. In your paragraph, relate your analysis to the ideas of justice and equality.

ACTIVITY 5.22 *continued*

Steps:

6 Show the class the film clip of Atticus's closing argument to the jury, Scene 28 (1:31:39–1:38:57). Have students complete the viewing guide as they watch the scene. Discuss their answers to the questions. You might encourage students to revisit their notes from the classroom presentations to consider how the changes from text to film might be related to the social and cultural climate of the day.

7 Finally, ask students to respond to the Writing Prompt.

8 Add the ideas of justice and equality to the thematic web the class created in Activity 5.19 (if they are not already there).

ACTIVITY 5.23
Reflection on the Verdict

Materials:

- *To Kill a Mockingbird*, Chapters 21–23

Purpose:

- To participate in an oral evaluation of an event through a Socratic Seminar
- To discuss how prejudice influences justice in the novel
- To understand the influence of context on the construction of a text

Steps:

1 Divide students into small groups. Have students reread the last pages of Chapter 22 and the beginning of Chapter 23, and write thoughtful **interpretive and evaluative questions** about issues. They may write their personal responses to the verdict.

2 Conduct a **Socratic Seminar**. Pose an open-ended question, such as the ones students have just created or the samples provided. Direct the question to the group. Keep the discussion focused on the text as participants express ideas.

3 Place a twenty-minute time limit on the discussion. Suggest the following guidelines:

- Discuss ideas, not opinions. This is not a debate!
- Refer to the text continually throughout the discussion.
- Don't raise hands. Take turns speaking, and speak one at a time.
- Converse with each other. Do not direct comments to the teacher.

4 Encourage students to respond to each other by agreeing or disagreeing and by providing evidence from the text. Students should ask for clarification when needed. If necessary, provide follow-up questions to keep the discussion going. This may be an opportunity to return to the **Essential Question**:

What impact does historical, cultural, geographical, and social context have on a novel and on the reaction of readers to it?

5 When students have finished the discussion, have them complete a **RAFT** response to the Writing Prompt. You might first define some additional options in each category, or you might further restrict their choices, depending on your objectives.

6 Assign Chapter 24 in preparation for the next activity.

ACTIVITY 5.23

Reflection on the Verdict

SUGGESTED LEARNING STRATEGIES: Questioning the Text, RAFT

Socratic Seminar: Your teacher will place you in a group. Your group will be given a question regarding the verdict to begin the discussion. Write the question below, and write your initial response. Reread or scan the last pages of Chapter 22 and the first six pages of Chapter 23, as you think about your answer and as you begin to talk in your Socratic circles.

- Why is Atticus so impressed by Jem's questions and responses?
- Why is Jem so hopeful about the eventual verdict?
- Why did the judge give this case to Atticus?
- What was fair and unfair (just and unjust) about this trial?
- Why do we have juries in our system of justice?
- Why does Atticus continue to believe in the justice system?

Writing Prompt: Use **RAFT** to write a piece that expresses your reaction (as a character) to the verdict convicting Tom.

ROLE	AUDIENCE	FORMAT	TOPIC
Scout	Readers of the *Maycomb Tribune*	Letter to the editor	The Tom Robinson verdict
Jem	A friend in some other part of the country	Personal letter	
Atticus	A paper in some other part of the country	Other:	
Tom Robinson	Other:		
Judge Taylor			
Other:			

The World of Fragrant Ladies

ACTIVITY 5.24

SUGGESTED LEARNING STRATEGIES: **Discussion Groups, Graphic Organizer**

As you discuss these questions, consider the significance of Chapter 24 to the meaning of the novel as a whole. Consider, also, the different perspectives on racial equality represented by each of the characters who appear in the scene.

1. **What values does Mrs. Grace Merriweather seem to represent in the novel? Is there anything ironic about her name? Find textual evidence to support your answer.**

2. **What is the effect of revealing Tom Robinson's death during this scene? Why do you think the author chose to do so here instead of elsewhere?**

3. **Does your impression of Aunt Alexandra change in this chapter from the impressions you had of her earlier the book? Is she a *static character* or a *dynamic character*? Explain your answer.**

4. **How does Scout's perspective on what it means to be a lady evolve during this scene? Find textual evidence to support your answer.**

ACTIVITY 5.24

The World of Fragrant Ladies

Materials:

- *To Kill a Mockingbird*, Chapter 24
- Chart paper and markers
- Vocabulary Notebooks

Purpose:

- To explore the relationship between conflict and theme
- To analyze how characters represent competing points of view in a text
- To read a passage closely for textual evidence

Steps:

1 This chapter contrasts Miss Maudie's and Mrs. Merriweather's perspectives on racism and contrasts Mrs. Merriweather's moral hypocrisy with Aunt Alexandra's respect for decorum and propriety. It also expands on the gender-role aspect of the coming-of-age theme, as Scout comments several times on what it means to become a lady.

You might begin with a definition and discussion of the word ***hypocrisy***. Clarify how the kind of hypocrisy and dishonesty Maycomb residents live with because of racism is evident in the life of Dolphus Raymond; it also foreshadows incidents at the tea party and Scout's classroom.

2 Place the students into small **discussion groups** to respond to the questions on this page. You might want to assign each group a question and then have them report back to the whole class; encourage other students to respond to the comments of each presenter.

Steps:

3 After the class discussion, ask students to write a thematic statement using one of the discussion topic areas as a starting point. Have them share these in their groups; then have each group share one back to the class. Write each on the board and evaluate it with the class. Direct students to revisit their **Vocabulary Notebooks** and elaborate on the concept of ***thematic statement.***

4 Have groups follow the instructions to create a **graphic organizer** showing the levels of racism each represents. Remind them to find a quotation that represents each character's attitude toward race and racial equality.

5 If you think your students are mature enough, end with a discussion of Miss Maudie's final statement to Aunt Alexandra: "The handful of people in this town who say that fair play is not marked White Only; the handful of people who say a fair trial is for everybody, not just us; the handful of people with enough humility to think, when they look at a Negro, there but for the Lord's kindness am I . . . The handful of people in this town with background, that's who they are." As students respond to this quote, ask: To what extent are we encouraged to accept Miss Maudie's perspective as enlightened? To what extent do students accept it as actually being enlightened? To what extent does the novel seem to actively challenge all aspects of racism?

6 Assign Chapters 25 and 26. Ask students to look especially for references to the title, to Boo Radley, and to another good example of hypocrisy.

The World of Fragrant Ladies

After you have completed your discussions, choose the question you most strongly responded to, and use it as a starting point for a thematic statement. Incorporate the idea of coming of age into your statement. Be prepared to share this with your discussion group.

Sample Thematic Statements

As Scout comes of age in Maycomb, she confronts the blatant hypocrisy of people like Mrs. Merriweather who express Christian concern about the far away Mrunas tribe but contempt and racism toward members of her own community.

Scout learns that to grow up in Maycomb is to ignore the hypocrisy of her neighbors and, like her Aunt and Miss Maudie, "be a lady."

Scout is literally shaken by the news of Tom's death, but learns from Miss Maudie and Aunt Alexandra that a lady must not let her emotions show and must be "together" in front of others.

With your group members, make a list of all the characters who appear in this chapter. Next, rank them in terms of the level of racism they seem to portray. Create a graphic organizer to represent your conclusions using whatever visual layout seems most insightful. For each character, include a quotation (possibly from another chapter, if necessary) that represents his or her attitude towards race and racial equality. Be prepared to explain your organizer to your classmates. Make notes below; then use separate paper to create your graphic organizer.

Character names:

Rank:

Potential Quotes:

Exploring Insights

ACTIVITY 5.25

SUGGESTED LEARNING STRATEGIES: **Close Reading, Questioning the Text**

Each of the following quotations links to the novel's exploration of what it means to come of age. After each quote, explain which thematic subject(s) (from the class list) you think it best links to, and explain why.

"He jerked his head at Dill: 'Things haven't caught up with that one's instinct yet. Let him get a little older and he won't get sick and cry. Maybe things'll strike him as being—not quite right, say, but he won't cry, not when he gets a few years on him.'"
—Dolphus Raymond to Jem, Dill, and Scout, Chapter 20

"'This is their home, sister,' said Atticus. 'We've made it this way for them, they might as well learn to cope with it.'"
—Atticus to Alexandra, Chapter 22

"The older you grow the more of it you'll see. The one place where a man ought to get a square deal is in a courtroom, be he any color of the rainbow, but people have a way of carrying their resentments right into a jury box."
—Atticus to Jem, Chapter 23

"As you grow older, you'll see white men cheat black men every day of your life, but let me tell you something and don't you forget it—whenever a white man does that to a black man, no matter who he is, how rich he is, or how fine a family he comes from, that white man is trash."
—Atticus to Jem, Chapter 23

"There was no doubt about it, I must soon enter this world, where on its surface fragile ladies rocked slowly, fanned gently, and drank cool water."
—Scout, Chapter 24

Writing Prompt: Choose a quotation and write about what it means, how it relates to coming of age, and how it connects to one of the thematic subjects presented in the novel.

ACTIVITY 5.25

Exploring Insights

Materials:

- *To Kill a Mockingbird*, Chapters 25 and 26

Purpose:

- To evaluate quotations as evidence for an interpretive claim
- To articulate key thematic subjects of the novel

Steps:

1 As a check for understanding, review the references to the title in Chapter 25 ("the slaughter of songbirds") and the reference to Boo Radley in Chapter 26, as well as earlier references in Chapter 14 and the end of Chapter 23. Ask students to infer the thematic significance of these references and explain how they relate to the conflict of the novel.

2 Instruct students to think about a passage—of no more than two pages—that they consider a key scene or a significant point in which the children learn something as they come of age in Maycomb. You may want students in groups to scan the chapters and locate possible passages for a **close reading** in preparation for an analytic essay.

3 Have students analyze the quotations on this page. You may want to use the first one to model how to interpret the implications in regard to becoming an adult. Ask: What toll does it take on the idealism of youth? What realities about human nature and/or society must we accept as we mature?

4 Have students choose the quotation they think best captures a thematic subject in the novel and that they relate to most strongly. Have them discuss it in small groups, and then share out to the class as a whole.

5 As students read Chapters 27–28 independently, you might have them generate **levels of questions** related to specific scenes or passages in the book.

ACTIVITY 5.26

Standing in Borrowed Shoes

Materials:

- *To Kill a Mockingbird*
- Poster paper, pens, markers, etc.
- Vocabulary Notebooks

Purpose:

- To evaluate quotations as evidence for interpretive claims
- To analyze the function of characters as representations of competing values in the novel
- To examine and categorize the relationships between primary, dynamic characters and secondary, or flat, static characters

Steps:

1 Students will create character posters to understand how each character represents different values and perspectives in the novel. It is important that students understand that characterization has the function of developing thematic subjects. For example, Dolphus Raymond, Mrs. Merriwether, and Mrs. Dubose all function to develop the thematic connection between hypocrisy and racism.

2 Lead students in a discussion of the difference between a primary (major) character and a secondary (minor) character. A primary character carries the weight of the narrative and may be described as round or dynamic. A secondary character generally remains flat or static and appears to serve a function connected to the growth of the primary character(s).

3 Have students **think-pair-share** to brainstorm a list of characters they feel are significant enough to be considered primary and secondary (as opposed to background) characters. You may ask students to continue to build on the concept of ***characterization*** in their Vocabulary Notebooks.

ACTIVITY 5.26

Standing in Borrowed Shoes

SUGGESTED LEARNING STRATEGIES: **Graphic Organizer, Think-Pair-Share**

"Atticus was right. One time he said you never really know a man until you stand in his shoes and walk around in them."

In the chart below, define each of the terms. Then work in a small group to list all the primary (major) and secondary (minor) characters you can identify from the novel. When you have finished, compare your list with that of other groups to determine which characters should be added or deleted based on their importance in the story. Then, make notes on how the secondary, or minor, characters represent certain thematic subjects in the novel.

Primary Characters:	Secondary Characters:
Atticus Scout Jem Dill Miss Maudie Calpurnia Arthur (Boo) Radley	Miss Stephanie – gossip and stereotyping Mrs. Merriweather – hypocrisy and racism Mayella Ewell – ignorance and racism Tom Ewell – violence and racism Tom Robinson } kindness, the black community Helen Robinson Reverend Sykes Link Deas, Mr. Underwood, Heck Tate, Judge Taylor } enlightened citizens Mr. Walter Cunningham – } individual in a mob

© 2011 College Board. All rights reserved.

Working with a partner, create a character profile poster. Your poster should include the following elements:

- A picture or graphic representation
- A physical description from the novel
- A list of several adjectives describing his or her personality, values, and/or motives
- An explanation of the function he or she serves in advancing the novel's plot
- A quotation about him or her from another character
- A quotation by him or her that reveals the character's values

These profiles will go up on the wall in a class collage, so make your poster visually appealing! Be prepared to present your poster to your classmates, explaining the information you have included.

Steps:

4 Have students select partners and create a character-profile poster. You want to have posters for as many different characters as possible to facilitate a discussion of how each functions in the novel's exploration of thematic subjects.

5 Display the completed posters in a collage on the wall, and have each pair present its poster to the class. Lead a discussion of how the characters function relative to each other. You might begin with the ranking exercise students completed in Activity 5.24, but move the discussion beyond the issue of race to include other thematic concerns.

© 2011 College Board. All rights reserved.

Unit 5 • Coming of Age Amidst Controversy 403

ACTIVITY 5.27
Scout and Boo

Materials:

- *To Kill a Mockingbird*, Chapters 29–30

Purpose:

- To explain the connection between two major motifs and themes
- To interpret the significance of the title and its relationship to character
- To articulate a character's function in the expression of the novel's theme

Steps:

1 Direct students to review the double-entry journal of quotations they've collected, including new entries from chapters 26-30. Tell them to complete the **graphic organizer** as follows:

- Cite evidence that demonstrates Scout's thoughts about Boo prior to meeting him.
- Use quotations to describe what Boo was really like.
- Discuss your reactions to Scout's views of Boo after actually meeting him. Note how this encounter with Boo changes Scout's view of the world.

2 Ask students to consider the accuracy of Jem's assessment of Boo in the quotation at the top of this page. What are the implications of thinking of Boo's reclusiveness as a dramatic device that reveals the only option if we choose not to accept the harsh realities of the world?

3 Have students respond to the **quickwrite**, reflecting on their notes.

ACTIVITY 5.27

Scout and Boo

SUGGESTED LEARNING STRATEGIES: Graphic Organizer, Quickwrite

"If there's just one kind of folks, why can't they get along with each other? If they're alike, why do they go out of their way to despise each other? Scout, I think I'm beginning to understand something. I think I'm beginning to understand why Boo Radley's stayed shut up in the house all this time . . . it's because he wants to stay inside."

—Jem to Scout, Chapter 23

Using notes from your double-entry journal on Boo and from the text of *To Kill a Mockingbird*, fill out the following grid:

Scout's mental picture of Boo before Chapter 29	
The reality of Boo	
Scout's vision of Boo after she meets him	

Quickwrite: After her encounter with Boo, how does Scout's changed perception of him connect to your broader understanding of what it means to come of age? How does this understanding link to Atticus's closing words, "Most people are [real nice], Scout, when you finally see them"?

4 Lead students in a discussion of Scout's changed understanding of Boo as a symbol of the narrator's changing understanding of realities of life. How do the contrasting images of Bob Ewell's racism, ignorance, and hatred and Boo Radley's innocence and protectiveness reinforce the theme that coming of age means letting go of illusions about human nature?

Embedded Assessment 2

Analyzing a Passage from *To Kill a Mockingbird*

SUGGESTED LEARNING STRATEGIES: **Close Reading, Drafting, Marking the Text, Revising**

Assignment

Your assignment is to write a literary essay that analyzes a short passage that depicts a key scene from *To Kill a Mockingbird*. Your analysis must discuss the passage in terms of the literary elements of the novel – setting, conflict, or character—and explain how that passage relates to the thematic development of the work as a whole.

Steps

Prewriting

1. Select a passage from the novel that illustrates a defining moment in a setting, conflict, or development of character as it pertains to the overall thematic concept: coming of age.
2. Make a photocopy of the passage, and do a close reading on your copy. Mark and annotate the text to make sure you understand it and its significance in terms of the themes of the novel. You will attach this copy of the passage to your essay.
3. Review your annotations and explore the significance of this passage. Generate a working thematic statement that identifies the significance of the passage as it relates to the theme.
4. In pairs, share a summary of your analyzed text and your thematic statement, using the criteria established in Activity 5.20 to evaluate the statement's effectiveness. Use the feedback of your peers to revise accordingly.

Drafting and Revision

5. Create a topic outline for your essay that contains the thematic statement, supporting topic sentences, and textual support in the form of direct and indirect quotations and paraphrasing. Share your outline with your writing partner.
6. Write your first draft and incorporate your writing partner's suggestions.
7. Gather in writing groups to share your passages and your first draft. Analyze drafts for the following:
   - Organizational structure of a literary analysis: look for effective three-fold transition sentences.
   - Interpretation of the text: claim, evidence, commentary, and closure in each paragraph; clarity of ideas.

   As you share and respond in your writing groups, you may want to consult the Scoring Guide criteria.

3 Remind students to review their work in this unit on analyzing passages, making thematic statements, and supporting interpretative statements with textual evidence.

Embedded Assessment 2

Analyzing a Passage from *To Kill a Mockingbird*

College Board Standards and Objectives

R1 Student Comprehends the Meaning of Words and Sentences (R1.1; R1.2)
PE Mappings: R1.1-2.4, R1.1-3.4, R1.2-1.4, R1.2-2.4, R1.2-3.4, R1.2-4.4

R2 Using Prior Knowledge, Context, and Understanding of Language to Comprehend and Elaborate the Meaning of Texts (R2.1; R2.2; R2.3)
PE Mappings: R2.1-1.4, R2.1-2.4, R2.2-1.4, R2.2-2.4, R2.3-1.4, R2.3-2.4

R3 Author's Purpose, Audience, and Craft (R3.2)
PE Mappings: R 3.2-1.4, R3.2-2.4

R4 Using Strategies to Comprehend Texts (R4.2; R4.3; R4.5)
PE Mappings: R4.2-1.4, R4.2-2.4, R4.2-3.4, R4.2-4.4, R4.3-1.4, R4.3-3.4, R4.3-4.4

W2 Generating Content (W2.1L; W2.2L)
PE Mappings: W2.1-1.4L, W2.1-2.4L, W2.2-1.4L, W2.2-2.4L, W2.2-3.4L, W2.2-4.4L

W3 Drafting (W3.1L; W3.2L)
PE Mappings: W3.1-1.4L, W3.1-2.4L, W3.1-3.4, W3.2-1.4L, W3.2-2.4L, W3.2-3.4L, W3.2-4.4L

W4 Evaluating and Revising Texts (W4.1L; W4.2L)
PE Mappings: W4.1-1.4L, W4.2-1.4L

W5 Editing to Present Technically Sound Texts (W5.1; W5.2; W5.4)
PE Mappings: W5.1-1.4, W5.2-1.4, W5.4-1.4

S2 Speaking in Interpersonal Contexts (S2.2)
PE Mappings: S2.2-2.4

L3 Listening for Diverse Purposes (L3.1; L3.2)
PE Mappings:L3.1-1.4, L3.2-2.4

Steps:

1 Review the assignment and Scoring Guide criteria to be sure students understand the requirements.

2 Students may have a tendency to choose an over-long passage. Guide them to select a passage of approximately one page.

Embedded Assessment 2

Continued

Steps:

4 You might suggest that students organize their essays by ideas:

- Link to coming of age
- Link to element—conflict, character, or setting
- Link to a thematic subject (prejudice, gender roles, justice, racism, family relationships, etc.)

5 As students work in writing groups, have them color-code their drafts to identify claim, evidence, commentary, and closure for purposes of revision.

6 You may need to review with students proper in-text citation of textual evidence.

7 Urge students to use all available resources to correct spelling and grammar as they prepare their final drafts.

8 Remind students to turn in their marked copy of the passage along with their essay.

Analyzing a Passage from *To Kill a Mockingbird*

8. Revise your draft for seamless integration of quotations using this strategy: introduce the quote, use the quote, and explain the quote. Share your draft in your writing group to ensure that quotes flow within the context of the essay and are properly cited. Mark the text as you read to make sure each source is adequately introduced, correctly cited, and effectively extended with commentary.
9. Read through your draft, and generate a list of possible titles for your essay that capture key ideas, words, or phrases. Select a memorable title that captures the essence of your essay.

Editing for Publication

10. Proofread your essay, and mark the text making final edits in grammar, punctuation, and spelling. Prepare for submission by using publication software to type and edit your draft for spelling and grammar. Consult an appropriate style manual to find general guidelines for formatting your essay.

SCORING GUIDE

Scoring Criteria	Exemplary	Proficient	Emerging
Ideas	The writer insightfully links the chosen passage to a thematic interpretation of coming of age as well as elements of literature. Supporting details from *To Kill a Mockingbird* richly enhance the understanding of the writer's position. All commentary relates directly back to the thesis.	The writer adequately links the chosen passage to a thematic interpretation of coming of age as well as elements of literature. Supporting details from *To Kill a Mockingbird* are relevant to understanding the writer's position. Most commentary relates directly back to the thesis, but some commentary may lack development.	The writer attempts to link the chosen passage to a thematic interpretation of coming of age and/or elements of literature. Supporting details from *To Kill a Mockingbird* may be present but may lack development or may not be concrete enough to give a full understanding of the writer's position. Commentary may not relate directly to the thesis. The writer may replace commentary with plot summary.
Organization	The essay is multi-paragraphed and logically organized to enhance the reader's understanding. Transitions establish fluent connections between the ideas. It includes an innovative introduction with an insightful lead and a strong thesis, coherent body paragraphs, and a perceptive conclusion.	The essay is multi-paragraphed and organized. Transitions establish connections between ideas. It includes an introduction with a lead and a clear thesis, detailed body paragraphs, and a conclusion.	Organization is attempted, but key components are lacking. Transitions are absent or ineffective. It may include an introduction with an unfocused thesis, undeveloped body paragraphs, and/or an inadequate conclusion.
Use of Language	The writer shows command of language and employs purposeful, appropriate diction for an academic audience.	The writer's language is adequate, using diction that is appropriate for an academic essay, but may use some unsophisticated or incorrect words.	The writer's language is coherent yet simplistic, and may be inappropriate for an academic audience, using slang or informal word choice.

Embedded Assessment 2
Continued

Scoring Guide

When you score this Embedded Assessment, you may wish to download and print a copy of the Scoring Guide from SpringBoard Online. In this way, you can have a copy to mark for each student's work.

Teacher Notes

Analyzing a Passage from *To Kill a Mockingbird*

SCORING GUIDE

Scoring Criteria	Exemplary	Proficient	Emerging
Conventions	Writing is virtually error-free. The writer uses proper punctuation and capitalization to smoothly embed quotations into text.	Writing is generally error-free. The writer uses proper punctuation and capitalization to embed quotations into text.	Writing contains errors that at times distract from meaning. At times, the writer attempts proper punctuation and capitalization to incorporate quotations into text.
Evidence of Writing Process	The writing demonstrates thoughtful planning, significant revision, and careful editing in preparing a publishable draft.	The writing demonstrates planning, revision, and editing in preparing a publishable draft.	The writing lacks evidence of planning, revision, and/or editing. The draft is not ready for publication.
Additional Criteria			

Comments:

Contextualizing Controversy

ACTIVITY 5.28

SUGGESTED LEARNING STRATEGIES: RAFT

Essay

ABOUT THE AUTHOR
Nicholas Karolides is an author and editor of books for young adults. He has often written about the topics of the politics of suppression and censorship of literary works.

From

IN DEFENSE OF *To Kill a Mockingbird*

by Nicholas J. Karolides, et al.

The critical career of *To Kill a Mockingbird* is a late twentieth-century case study of censorship. When Harper Lee's novel about a small southern town and its prejudices was published in 1960, the book received favorable reviews in professional journals and the popular press. Typical of that opinion, Booklist's reviewer called the book "melodramatic" and noted "traces of sermonizing," but the book was recommended for library purchase, commending its "rare blend of wit and compassion." Reviewers did not suggest that the book was young-adult literature, or that it belonged in adolescent collections; perhaps that is why no one mentioned the book's language or violence. In any event, reviewers seemed inclined to agree that *To Kill a Mockingbird* was a worthwhile interpretation of the South's existing social structures during the 1930s. In 1961 the book won the Pulitzer Prize Award, the Alabama Library Association Book Award, and the Brotherhood Award of the National Conference of Christians and Jews. It seemed that Harper Lee's blend of family history, local custom, and restrained sermonizing was important reading, and with a young girl between the ages of six and nine as the main character, *To Kill a Mockingbird* moved rapidly into junior and senior high school libraries and curriculum. The book was not destined to be studied by college students. Southern literature's critics rarely mentioned it; few university professors found it noteworthy enough to "teach" as an exemplary southern novel.

My Notes

Differentiating Instruction:

To provide **support** for understanding the text, have students use the pre-AP strategy of **SOAPSTone** to analyze the author's craft.

Extend the activity by asking students to research additional critical commentary on ***To Kill a Mockingbird***. Have students summarize the additional position and write their own position statement.

ACTIVITY 5.28
Contextualizing Controversy

Materials:

- *To Kill a Mockingbird*

Purpose:

- To discuss how context influences a reader's response to a text
- To explore the nature of censorship

Steps:

1 Have students number each paragraph of the essay in the margins. **Chunk the text** by paragraph. Divide students into five groups, and instruct them to read their assigned paragraph for explanations of why the book has sometimes been controversial and even banned.

2 **Jigsaw** students from each group to report on the insights offered in their chunk of the text. Have each group compile a list of the major arguments that have been used against ***To Kill a Mockingbird***.

3 After each group has shared, conduct a whole class discussion of four topics.

- Which of the arguments presented have the most credibility? How would students answer the argument?
- Is the novel still controversial today? Why or why not?
- Is censorship still an issue today? In what contexts and why?
- How do our personal values and experiences influence our reactions to the contents of a literary or media text?

Teacher Notes

Contextualizing Controversy

GRAMMAR & USAGE

Verbs have **active** and **passive voice** in all six tenses. A passive-voice verb always contains a form of *be* with the past participle of the verb.

Examples:

- Active voice (past perfect): Things **had changed** in the South...
- Passive voice (past perfect): Things **had been changed**...

Note the following examples of passive-voice verbs on this page:

- Two national leaders... were assassinated....
- John F. Kennedy was killed...

These examples demonstrate one reason to use passive voice: when you want to emphasize the receiver of the action.

WORD CONNECTIONS

The word ***psychological*** is an adjective meaning "mental" or "of the mind." The prefix *psycho-* comes from the Greek word *psychē*, meaning "soul" or "spirit." Other words with the prefix *psycho-* include *psychoanalysis*, *psychobabble*, and *psychodrama*.

By the mid-sixties *To Kill a Mockingbird* had a solid place in junior and senior high American literature studies. Once discovered by southern parents, the book's solid place became shaky indeed. Sporadic lawsuits arose. In most cases the complaint against the book was by conservatives who disliked the portrayal of whites. Typically, the Hanover County School Board in Virginia first ruled the book "immoral," then withdrew their criticism and declared the ruckus "was all a mistake" (*Newsletter* [*on Intellectual Freedom*] 1966). By 1968 the National Education Association listed the book among those which drew the most criticism from private groups. Ironically it was rated directly behind *Little Black Sambo* (*Newsletter* 1968). And the seventies arrived.

Things had changed in the South during the sixties. Two national leaders who had supported integration and had espoused the ideals of racial equality were assassinated in southern regions. When John F. Kennedy was killed in Texas on November 27, 1963, many southerners were shocked. Populist attitudes of racism were declining, and in the aftermath of the tragedy southern politics began to change. Lyndon Johnson gained the presidency: blacks began to seek and win political offices. Black leader Martin Luther King had stressed the importance of racial equality, always using Mahatma Gandhi's strategy of nonviolent action and civil disobedience. A brilliant orator, King grew up in the South; the leader of the [Southern Christian Leadership Conference], he lived in Atlanta, Georgia. In 1968, while working on a garbage strike in Memphis, King was killed. The death of the 1965 Nobel Peace Prize winner was further embarrassment for white southerners. Whites began to look at public values anew, and gradually southern blacks found experiences in the South more tolerable. In 1971 one Atlanta businessman observed [in *Ebony*], "The liberation thinking is here. Blacks are more together. With the doors opening wider, this area is the mecca...." Southern arguments against *To Kill a Mockingbird* subsided. *The Newsletter* on *Intellectual Freedom* contained no record of southern court cases during the seventies or eighties. The book had sustained itself during the first period of sharp criticism; it had survived regional protests from the area it depicted.

The second onslaught of attack came from new groups of censors, and it came during the late seventies and early eighties. Private sectors in the Midwest and suburban East began to demand the book's removal from school libraries. Groups, such as the Eden Valley School Committee in Minnesota, claimed that the book was too laden with profanity (*Newsletter* 1978). In Vermont, New York, Reverend Carl Hadley threatened to establish a private Christian school because public school libraries contained such "filthy, trashy sex novels" as *A Separate Peace* and *To Kill a Mockingbird* (*Newsletter* 1980). And finally, blacks began to censor the book. In Warren, Indiana, three blacks resigned from the township Human Relations Advisory Council when the Warren County school administration refused to remove the book from Warren junior high school classes. They contended that the book "does psychological damage to the positive integration process and represents institutionalized racism" (*Newsletter* 1982). Thus, censorship of *To Kill a*

GRAMMAR & USAGE EXTENSION

Remind students of the importance of using active voice in most cases: it is more direct, more forceful, and more concise. Nevertheless, there are important reasons to use passive voice. In addition to the reason given on the student page, there are two other reasons: (1) when you do not know the performer of the action and (2) when you do not want readers to know the performer of the action.

- The plants were stripped bare of their tomatoes overnight. (do not know who/what performed the action)
- Someone was discovered eating the snacks we were saving for tomorrow. (do not want to say who performed the action)

Mockingbird swung from the conservative right to the liberal left. Factions representing racists, religious sects, concerned parents, and minority groups vocally demanded the book's removal from public schools....

The censors' reactions to *To Kill a Mockingbird* were reactions to issues of race and justice. Their moves to ban the book derive from their own perspectives of the book's theme. Their "reader response" criticism, usually based on one reading of the book, was personal and political. They needed to ban the book because it told them something about American society that they did not want to hear. That is precisely the problem facing any author of realistic fiction. Once the story becomes real, it can become grim. An author will use first-person flashback in a story in order to let the reader lie in another time, another place. Usually the storyteller is returning for a second view of the scene. The teller has experienced the events before and the story is being retold because the scene has left the storyteller uneasy. As the storyteller recalls the past, both the listener and the teller see events in a new light. Both are working through troubled times in search of meaning. In the case of *To Kill a Mockingbird* the first-person retelling is not pleasant, but the underlying significance is with the narrative. The youthful personalities who are recalled are hopeful. Scout tells us of a time past when white people would lynch or convict a man because of the color of his skin. She also shows us three children who refuse to believe that the system is right, and she leaves us with the thought that most people will be nice if seen for what they are: humans with frailties. When discussing literary criticism, Theo D'Haen suggested [in *Text to Reader*] that the good literary work should have a life within the world and be "part of the ongoing activities of that world." *To Kill a Mockingbird* continues to have life within the world; its ongoing activities in the realm of censorship show that it is a book which deals with regional moralism. The children in the story seem very human; they worry about their own identification, they defy parental rules, and they cry over injustices. They mature in Harper Lee's novel, and they lose their innocence. So does the reader. If the readers are young, they may believe Scout when she says, "nothin's real scary except in books." If the readers are older they will have learned that life is scary, and they will be prepared to meet some of its realities.

My Notes

ACTIVITY 5.28 *continued*

Steps:

4 You might end this activity with a **RAFT**, asking students to write a letter to a parent, teacher, censor, or administrator defending or challenging the book's place in their ninth-grade curriculum.

5 You may want to have students go back to the research they did as part of their presentation for Embedded Assessment 1. Ask them to write one page connecting their reseach to their understandings of the novel.

UNIT REFLECTION

Purpose:

- To monitor comprehension and growth through a reflective process
- To synthesize understanding of individual reading and writing processes and strategies
- To self-assess mastery of key concepts and terms

Steps:

1 This is an opportunity for students to think about the concepts, vocabulary, and their own learning progress as they revisit and review the work they have produced in this unit.

2 Encourage students to be especially metacognitive about which strategies they have used and how those strategies support their learning styles and goals.

Unit Teacher Reflection

1 Which activities in this unit did you need to adjust (or you think should be adjusted) to prepare your students to be successful on each Embedded Assessment? Add your notes on how you would adjust the activities.

2 Which teacher strategies were most effective for introducing concepts/ideas to your students?

3 How did the unit activities help you address the individual learning needs of your students? Note any changes you would make in your instructional strategies to differentiate instruction.

Unit 5

Reflection

An important aspect of growing as a learner is to take the time to reflect. It is important to take into account where you have been, what you have accomplished, what helped you to learn, and how you will apply your new knowledge in the future. Use the following process to record your thinking and to identify evidence of your learning.

Thinking about Concepts

1. Using specific examples from this unit, respond to the following Essential Questions
   - What are the essential elements of an effective informative presentation?
   - What impact does historical, cultural, geographical, and social context have on a novel and on the reaction of readers to it?
2. Consider the new academic vocabulary from this unit (**Context, Annotated Bibliography, Audience Analysis, Characterization, Thematic Statement**) as well as academic vocabulary from previous units, and select 3 - 4 terms of which your understanding has grown. For each term, answer the following questions:
   - What was your understanding of the term before this unit?
   - How has your understanding of the word evolved throughout this unit?
   - How will you apply your understanding in the future?

Thinking about Connections

3. Reflecting on key concepts (Essential Questions, Academic Vocabulary, and Important Themes), select one or two concepts that reflect your most growth or greatest understanding. Then, find an example (or "artifact") from your work that can serve as evidence of your understanding of your selected concepts
4. For each artifact that you choose, record, respond to, and reflect on your thinking and understanding, using the following questions as a guide:
   a. What skill/knowledge does this artifact reflect, and how did you learn this skill/knowledge?
   b. How did your understanding of the power of language expand through your engagement with this artifact?
   c. How will you apply this skill or knowledge in the future?
5. Create this reflection as Portfolio pages—one for each artifact you choose. Use the model in the box for your headings and commentary on questions.

Thinking About Thinking

Portfolio Entry

Concept:

Description of Artifact:

Commentary on Questions:

Teacher Notes

The material in this Handbook is from The Writing Lab & The OWL at Purdue and is used by permission of Purdue University[1].

Grammar Handbook

Part 1: Using Pronouns Clearly

Because a pronoun REFERS BACK to a noun or TAKES THE PLACE OF that noun, you have to use the correct pronoun so that your reader clearly understands which noun your pronoun is referring to. Therefore, pronouns should:

1. Agree in number

If the pronoun takes the place of a singular noun, you have to use a singular pronoun.

> If a student parks a car on campus, he or she has to buy a parking sticker.
> (**NOT:** If a student parks a car on campus, they have to buy a parking sticker.)

Remember: the words **everybody**, **anybody**, **anyone**, **each**, **neither**, **nobody**, **someone**, **a person**, etc. are singular and take singular pronouns.

> Everybody ought to do his or her best. (NOT: their best)
> Neither of the girls brought her umbrella. (NOT: their umbrellas)

NOTE: Many people find the construction "his or her" wordy, so if it is possible to use a plural noun as your antecedent so that you can use "they" as your pronoun, it may be wise to do so. If you do use a singular noun and the context makes the gender clear, then it is permissible to use just "his" or "her" rather than "his or her."

2. Agree in person

If you are writing in the "first person" (I), don't confuse your reader by switching to the "second person" (you) or "third person" (he, she, they, it, etc.). Similarly, if you are using the "second person," don't switch to "first" or "third."

> When a person comes to class, he or she should have his or her homework ready.
> (**NOT:** When a person comes to class, you should have your homework ready.)

3. Refer clearly to a specific noun.

Don't be vague or ambiguous.

> **NOT:** Although the motorcycle hit the tree, it was not damaged. (Is "it" the motorcycle or the tree?)
> **NOT:** I don't think they should show violence on TV. (Who are "they"?)
> **NOT:** Vacation is coming soon, which is nice. (What is nice, the vacation or the fact that it is coming soon?)
> **NOT:** George worked in a national forest last summer. This may be his life's work. (What word does "this" refer to?)
> **NOT:** If you put this sheet in your notebook, you can refer to it. (What does "it" refer to, the sheet or your notebook?)

[1] Copyright © 1995-2009 by The Writing Lab & The OWL at Purdue and Purdue University. All rights reserved. This material may not be published, reproduced, broadcast, rewritten, or redistributed without permission.

Teacher Notes

Pronoun Case

Pronoun case is really a very simple matter. There are three cases.

- Subjective case: pronouns used as subject.
- Objective case: pronouns used as objects of verbs or prepositions.
- Possessive case: pronouns which express ownership.

Pronouns as Subjects	Pronouns as Objects	Pronouns that show Possession
I	me	my (mine)
you	you	your (yours)
he, she, it	him, her, it	his, her (hers), it (its)
we	us	our (ours)
they	them	their (theirs)
who	whom	whose

The pronouns **this, that, these, those,** and **which** do not change form.

Some problems of case:

1. **In compound structures, where there are two pronouns or a noun and a pronoun, drop the other noun for a moment. Then you can see which case you want.**

   Not: Bob and me travel a good deal.
   (Would you say, "me travel"?)
   Not: He gave the flowers to Jane and I.
   (Would you say, "he gave the flowers to I"?)
   Not: Us men like the coach.
   (Would you say, "us like the coach"?)

2. **In comparisons. Comparisons usually follow than or as:**

   He is taller than I (am tall).
   This helps you as much as (it helps) me.
   She is as noisy as I (am).

Comparisons are really shorthand sentences which usually omit words, such as those in the parentheses in the sentences above. If you complete the comparison in your head, you can choose the correct case for the pronoun.

   Not: He is taller than me.
   (Would you say, "than me am tall"?)

3. **In formal and semiformal writing:**

Use the subjective form after a form of the verb to be.

   Formal: It is I.
   Informal: It is me.

Use whom in the objective case.

   Formal: To whom am I talking?
   Informal: Who am I talking to?

Teacher Notes

Part 2: Appositives

An appositive is a noun or pronoun — often with modifiers — set beside another noun or pronoun to explain or identify it. Here are some examples of appositives (the noun or pronoun will be in blue, the **appositive will be in boldface**).

Your friend **Bill** is in trouble.
My brother's car, **a sporty red convertible with bucket seats**, is the envy of my friends.
The chief surgeon, **an expert in organ-transplant procedures**, took her nephew on a hospital tour.

An appositive phrase usually follows the word it explains or identifies, but it may also precede it.

A bold innovator, Wassily Kadinsky is known for his colorful abstract paintings.
The first state to ratify the U. S. Constitution, Delaware is rich in history.
A beautiful collie, Skip was my favorite dog.

Punctuation of Appositives

In some cases, the noun being explained is too general without the appositive; the information is essential to the meaning of the sentence. When this is the case, do not place commas around the appositive; just leave it alone. If the sentence would be clear and complete without the appositive, then commas are necessary; place one before and one after the appositive. Here are some examples.

The popular US president **John Kennedy** was known for his eloquent and inspirational speeches.

Here we do not put commas around the appositive, because it is essential information. Without the appositive, the sentence would be, "The popular US president was known for his eloquent and inspirational speeches." We wouldn't know which president was being referred to.

John Kennedy, **the popular US president**, was known for his eloquent and inspirational speeches.

Here we put commas around the appositive because it is not essential information. Without the appositive, the sentence would be, "John Kennedy was known for his eloquent and inspirational speeches." We still know who the subject of the sentence is without the appositive.

Part 3: What is the Difference Between Adjectives and Adverbs?

The Basic Rules: Adjectives

Adjectives modify nouns. To modify means to change in some way. For example:

- "I ate a meal." *Meal* is a noun. We don't know what kind of meal; all we know is that someone ate a meal.
- "I ate an enormous lunch." *Lunch* is a noun, and *enormous* is an adjective that modifies it. It tells us what kind of meal the person ate.

Adjectives usually answer one of a few different questions: "What kind?" or "Which?" or "How many?" For example:

- "The *tall* girl is riding a *new* bike." *Tall* tells us which girl we're talking about. *New* tells us what kind of bike we're talking about.
- "The *tough* professor gave us the *final* exam." *Tough* tells us what kind of professor we're talking about. *Final* tells us which exam we're talking about.
- "*Fifteen* students passed the midterm exam; *twelve* students passed the final exam." *Fifteen* and *twelve* both tell us how many students; *midterm* and *final* both tell us which exam.

So, generally speaking, adjectives answer the following questions: Which? What kind of? How many?

Teacher Notes

The Basic Rules: Adverbs

Adverbs modify verbs, adjectives, and other adverbs. (You can recognize adverbs easily because many of them are formed by adding *-ly* to an adjective, though that is not always the case.) The most common question that adverbs answer is **how.**

Let's look at verbs first.

- "She sang *beautifully.*" *Beautifully* is an adverb that modifies *sang.* It tells us **how** she sang.
- "The cellist played *carelessly.*" *Carelessly* is an adverb that modifies *played.* It tells us **how** the cellist played.

Adverbs also modify adjectives and other adverbs.

- "That woman is *extremely* nice." *Nice* is an adjective that modifies the noun *woman. Extremely* is an adverb that modifies *nice*; it tells us **how** nice she is. **How** nice is she? She's extremely nice.
- "It was a *terribly* hot afternoon." *Hot* is an adjective that modifies the noun *afternoon. Terribly* is an adverb that modifies the adjective *hot.* **How** hot is it? Terribly hot.

So, generally speaking, adverbs answer the question **how.** (They can also answer the questions **when**, **where**, and **why**.)

Part 4: Verbals

Gerunds

A gerund is a verbal that ends in *-ing* and functions as a noun. The term *verbal* indicates that a gerund, like the other two kinds of verbals, is based on a verb and therefore expresses action or a state of being. However, since a gerund functions as a noun, it occupies some positions in a sentence that a noun ordinarily would, for example: subject, direct object, subject complement, and object of preposition.

Gerund as subject:

- Traveling might satisfy your desire for new experiences. (**Traveling** is the gerund.)
- The study abroad program might satisfy your desire for new experiences. (The gerund has been removed.)

Gerund as direct object:

- They do not appreciate my singing. (The gerund is **singing**.)
- They do not appreciate my assistance. (The gerund has been removed)

Gerund as subject complement:

- My cat's favorite activity is sleeping. (The gerund is **sleeping**.)
- My cat's favorite food is salmon. (The gerund has been removed.)

Gerund as object of preposition:

- The police arrested him for speeding. (The gerund is **speeding**.)
- The police arrested him for criminal activity. (The gerund has been removed.)

A Gerund Phrase is a group of words consisting of a gerund and the modifier(s) and/or (pro)noun(s) or noun phrase(s) that function as the direct object(s), indirect object(s), or complement(s) of the action or state expressed in the gerund, such as:

The gerund phrase functions as the subject of the sentence.

Finding **a needle** **<u>in a haystack</u>** would be easier than what we're trying to do.

Finding (gerund) **a needle** (direct object of action expressed in gerund) **<u>in a haystack</u>** (prepositional phrase as adverb)

Teacher Notes

The gerund phrase functions as the direct object of the verb *appreciate*.

I hope that you appreciate **my** offering **you *this opportunity***.

my (possessive pronoun adjective form, modifying the gerund)
offering (gerund)
you (indirect object of action expressed in gerund)
this opportunity (direct object of action expressed in gerund)

The gerund phrase functions as the subject complement.

Ned's favorite tactic has been **lying to** his constituents.

lying to (gerund)
his constituents (direct object of action expressed in gerund)

The gerund phrase functions as the object of the preposition *for*.

You might get in trouble for **faking** an illness ***to avoid work***.

faking (gerund)
an illness (direct object of action expressed in gerund)
to avoid work (infinitive phrase as adverb)

The gerund phrase functions as the subject of the sentence.

Being the boss made Jeff feel uneasy.

Being (gerund)
the boss (subject complement for Jeff, via state of being expressed in gerund)

Punctuation

A gerund virtually never requires any punctuation with it.

Points to remember:

1. A gerund is a verbal ending in -ing that is used as a noun.
2. A gerund phrase consists of a gerund plus modifier(s), object(s), and/or complement(s).
3. Gerunds and gerund phrases virtually never require punctuation.

Participles

A participle is a verbal that is used as an adjective and most often ends in *-ing* or *-ed*. The term *verbal* indicates that a participle, like the other two kinds of verbals, is based on a verb and therefore expresses action or a state of being. However, since they function as adjectives, participles modify nouns or pronouns. There are two types of participles: present participles and past participles. Present participles end in *-ing*. Past participles end in *-ed*, *-en*, *-d*, *-t*, or *-n*, as in the words *asked*, *eaten*, *saved*, *dealt*, and *seen*.

- The *crying* baby had a wet diaper.
- *Shaken*, he walked away from the *wrecked* car.
- The *burning* log fell off the fire.
- *Smiling*, she hugged the *panting* dog.

A participial phrase is a group of words consisting of a participle and the modifier(s) and/or (pro)noun(s) or noun phrase(s) that function as the direct object(s), indirect object(s), or complement(s) of the action or state expressed in the participle, such as:

Example: Removing his coat, Jack rushed to the river.

The participial phrase functions as an adjective modifying *Jack*.

Teacher Notes

Removing (participle)
his coat (direct object of action expressed in participle)

Example: Delores noticed her cousin **walking along the shoreline.**

The participial phrase functions as an adjective modifying *cousin*.
walking (participle)
along the shoreline (prepositional phrase as adverb)

Example: Children **introduced to music** early develop strong intellectual skills.

The participial phrase functions as an adjective modifying *children*.
introduced (to) (participle)
music (direct object of action expressed in participle)
early (adverb)

Example: Having been a gymnast, Lynn knew the importance of exercise.

The participial phrase functions as an adjective modifying *Lynn*.
Having been (participle)
a gymnast (subject complement for Lynn, via state of being expressed in participle)

Placement: In order to prevent confusion, a participial phrase must be placed as close to the noun it modifies as possible, and the noun must be clearly stated.

- *Carrying a heavy pile of books,* his foot caught on a step.
- *Carrying a heavy pile of books,* he caught his foot on a step.

In the first sentence there is no clear indication of who or what is performing the action expressed in the participle carrying. Certainly foot can't be logically understood to function in this way. This situation is an example of a **dangling modifier** error since the modifier (the participial phrase) is not modifying any specific noun in the sentence and is thus left "dangling." Since a person must be doing the carrying for the sentence to make sense, a noun or pronoun that refers to a person must be in the place immediately after the participial phrase, as in the second sentence.

Punctuation: When a participial phrase begins a sentence, a comma should be placed after the phrase.

- *Arriving at the store,* I found that it was closed.
- *Washing and polishing the car,* Frank developed sore muscles.

If the participle or participial phrase comes in the middle of a sentence, it should be set off with commas only if the information is not essential to the meaning of the sentence.

- Sid, *watching an old movie,* drifted in and out of sleep.
- The church, *destroyed by a fire,* was never rebuilt.

Note that if the participial phrase is essential to the meaning of the sentence, no commas should be used:

- The student *earning the highest grade point average* will receive a special award.
- The guy *wearing the chicken costume* is my cousin.

If a participial phrase comes at the end of a sentence, a comma usually precedes the phrase if it modifies an earlier word in the sentence but not if the phrase directly follows the word it modifies.

- The local residents often saw Ken wandering through the streets.
  (The phrase modifies *Ken*, not *residents*.)
- Tom nervously watched the woman, alarmed by her silence.
  (The phrase modifies *Tom*, not *woman*.)

Teacher Notes

Points to remember

1. A participle is a verbal ending in *-ing* (present) or *-ed*, *-en*, *-d*, *-t*, or *-n* (past) that functions as an adjective, modifying a noun or pronoun.
2. A participial phrase consists of a participle plus modifier(s), object(s), and/or complement(s).
3. Participles and participial phrases must be placed as close to the nouns or pronouns they modify as possible, and those nouns or pronouns must be clearly stated.
4. A participial phrase is set off with commas when it:
   (a) comes at the beginning of a sentence
   (b) interrupts a sentence as a nonessential element
   (c) comes at the end of a sentence and is separated from the word it modifies.

Infinitives

An infinitive is a verbal consisting of the word *to* plus a verb (in its simplest "stem" form) and functioning as a noun, adjective, or adverb. The term *verbal* indicates that an infinitive, like the other two kinds of verbals, is based on a verb and therefore expresses action or a state of being. However, the infinitive may function as a subject, direct object, subject complement, adjective, or adverb in a sentence. Although an infinitive is easy to locate because of the *to* + verb form, deciding what function it has in a sentence can sometimes be confusing.

- *To wait* seemed foolish when decisive action was required. (subject)
- Everyone wanted *to go*. (direct object)
- His ambition is *to fly*. (subject complement)
- He lacked the strength *to resist*. (adjective)
- We must study *to learn*. (adverb)

Be sure not to confuse an infinitive—a verbal consisting of *to* plus a verb—with a prepositional phrase beginning with *to*, which consists of *to* plus a noun or pronoun and any modifiers.

- **Infinitives:** to fly, to draw, to become, to enter, to stand, to catch, to belong
- **Prepositional Phrases:** to him, to the committee, to my house, to the mountains, to us, to this address

An Infinitive Phrase is a group of words consisting of an infinitive and the modifier(s) and/or (pro)noun(s) or noun phrase(s) that function as the actor(s), direct object(s), indirect object(s), or complement(s) of the action or state expressed in the infinitive, such as:

We intended **to leave** early.

The infinitive phrase functions as the direct object of the verb *intended*.

to leave (infinitive)
early (adverb)

I have a paper **to write** before class.

The infinitive phrase functions as an adjective modifying *paper*.

to write (infinitive)
before class (prepositional phrase as adverb)

Phil agreed **to give** me *a ride*.

The infinitive phrase functions as the direct object of the verb *agreed*.

to give (infinitive)
me (indirect object of action expressed in infinitive)
a ride (direct object of action expressed in infinitive)

Teacher Notes

They asked **me** to bring *some food*.

The infinitive phrase functions as the direct object of the verb *asked*.

me (actor or "subject" of infinitive phrase)
to bring (infinitive)
some food (direct object of action expressed in infinitive)

Everyone wanted **Carol** to be **the captain** *of the team*.

The infinitive phrase functions as the direct object of the verb *wanted*.

Carol (actor or "subject" of infinitive phrase)
to be (infinitive)
the captain (subject complement for Carol, via state of being expressed in infinitive)
of the team (prepositional phrase as adjective)

Actors: In these last two examples the actor of the infinitive phrase could be roughly characterized as the "subject" of the action or state expressed in the infinitive. It is somewhat misleading to use the word *subject*, however, since an infinitive phrase is not a full clause with a subject and a finite verb. Also notice that when it is a pronoun, the actor appears in the objective case (*me*, not *I*, in the fourth example). Certain verbs, when they take an infinitive direct object, require an actor for the infinitive phrase; others can't have an actor. Still other verbs can go either way, as the charts below illustrate.

Verbs that take infinitive objects without actors:			
agree	begin	continue	decide
fail	hesitate	hope	intend
learn	neglect	offer	plan
prefer	pretend	promise	refuse
remember	start	try	

Examples:

- Most students *plan* to study.
- We *began* to learn.
- They *offered* to pay.
- They *neglected* to pay.
- She *promised* to return.

In all of these examples no actor can come between the italicized main (finite) verb and the infinitive direct-object phrase.

Verbs that take infinitive objects with actors:			
advise	allow	convince	remind
encourage	force	hire	teach
instruct	invite	permit	tell
implore	incite	appoint	order

Teacher Notes

Examples:

- He *reminded* me to buy milk.
- Their fathers *advise* them to study.
- She *forced* the defendant to admit the truth.
- You've *convinced* the director of the program to change her position.
- I *invite* you to consider the evidence.

In all of these examples an actor is required after the italicized main (finite) verb and before the infinitive direct-object phrase.

Verbs that use either pattern:				
ask	expect	(would) like	want	need

Examples:

- I *asked* to see the records.
- I *asked* him to show me the records.
- Trent *expected* his group to win.
- Trent *expected* to win.
- Brenda *likes* to drive fast.
- Brenda *likes* her friend to drive fast.

In all of these examples the italicized main verb can take an infinitive object with or without an actor.

Punctuation: If the infinitive is used as an adverb and is the beginning phrase in a sentence, it should be set off with a comma; otherwise, no punctuation is needed for an infinitive phrase.

- To buy a basket of flowers, John had to spend his last dollar.
- To improve your writing, you must consider your purpose and audience.

Points to remember:

1. An infinitive is a verbal consisting of the word *to* plus a verb; it may be used as a noun, adjective, or adverb.
2. An infinitive phrase consists of an infinitive plus modifier(s), object(s), complement(s), and/or actor(s).
3. An infinitive phrase requires a comma only if it is used as an adverb at the beginning of a sentence.

Split infinitives

Split infinitives occur when additional words are included between *to* and the verb in an infinitive. Many readers find a single adverb splitting the infinitive to be acceptable, but this practice should be avoided in formal writing.

Examples:

- I like *to* on a nice day *walk* in the woods. (unacceptable)
  On a nice day, I like *to walk* in the woods. (revised)
- I needed *to* quickly *gather* my personal possessions. (acceptable in informal contexts)
  I needed *to gather* my personal possessions quickly. (revised for formal contexts)

© 2011 College Board. All rights reserved.

Teacher Notes

Part 5: Prepositions for Time, Place, and Introducing Objects

One point in time

On is used with days:

- I will see you **on** Monday.
- The week begins **on** Sunday.

At is used with noon, night, midnight, and with the time of day:

- My plane leaves **at** noon.
- The movie starts **at** 6 p.m.

In is used with other parts of the day, with months, with years, with seasons:

- He likes to read **in** the afternoon.
- The days are long **in** August.
- The book was published **in** 1999.
- The flowers will bloom **in** spring.

Extended time

To express extended time, English uses the following prepositions: **since, for, by, from–to, from–until, during, (with)in**

- She has been gone **since** yesterday. *(She left yesterday and has not returned.)*
- I'm going to Paris **for** two weeks. *(I will spend two weeks there.)*
- The movie showed **from** August **to** October. *(Beginning in August and ending in October.)*
- The decorations were up **from** spring **until** fall. *(Beginning in spring and ending in fall.)*
- I watch TV **during** the evening. *(For some period of time in the evening.)*
- We must finish the project **within** a year. *(No longer than a year.)*

Place

To express notions of place, English uses the following prepositions: to talk about the point itself: **in**, to express something contained: **inside**, to talk about the surface: **on**, to talk about a general vicinity, **at**.

- There is a wasp **in** the room.
- Put the present **inside** the box.
- I left your keys **on** the table.
- She was waiting **at** the corner.

To introduce objects of verbs

English uses the following prepositions to introduce objects of the following verbs.

At: glance, laugh, look, rejoice, smile, stare

- She took a quick glance **at** her reflection.
  (*exception with **mirror***: She took a quick glance **in** the mirror.)
- You didn't laugh **at** his joke.
- I'm looking **at** the computer monitor.
- We rejoiced **at** his safe rescue.
- That pretty girl smiled **at** you.
- Stop staring **at** me.

Teacher Notes

Of: approve, consist, smell

- I don't approve **of** his speech.
- My contribution to the article consists **of** many pages.
- He came home smelling **of** garlic.

Of (or about): dream, think

- I dream **of** finishing college in four years.
- Can you think **of** a number between one and ten?
- I am thinking **about** this problem.

For: call, hope, look, wait, watch, wish

- Did someone call **for** a taxi?
- He hopes **for** a raise in salary next year.
- I'm looking **for** my keys.
- We'll wait **for** her here.
- You go buy the tickets and I'll watch **for** the train.
- If you wish **for** an "A" in this class, you must work hard.

Part 6: Identifying Independent and Dependent Clauses

When you want to use commas and semicolons in sentences and when you are concerned about whether a sentence is or is not a fragment, a good way to start is to be able to recognize dependent and independent clauses. The definitions offered here will help you with this.

Independent Clause

An independent clause is a group of words that contains a subject and verb and expresses a complete thought. An independent clause is a sentence.

Jim studied in the Sweet Shop for his chemistry quiz.

Dependent Clause

A dependent clause is a group of words that contains a subject and verb but does not express a complete thought. A dependent clause cannot be a sentence. Often a dependent clause is marked by a **dependent marker word**.

When Jim studied in the Sweet Shop for his chemistry quiz . . . (What happened when he studied? The thought is incomplete.)

Dependent Marker Word

A dependent marker word is a word added to the beginning of an independent clause that makes it into a dependent clause.

When Jim studied in the Sweet Shop for his chemistry quiz, it was very noisy.

Some common dependent markers are: **after**, **although**, **as**, **as if**, **because**, **before**, **even if**, **even though**, **if**, **in order to**, **since**, **though**, **unless**, **until**, **whatever**, **when**, **whenever**, **whether**, and **while**.

Connecting Dependent and Independent Clauses

There are two types of words that can be used as connectors at the beginning of an independent clause: coordinating conjunctions and independent marker words.

1. Coordinating Conjunction

The seven coordinating conjunctions used as connecting words at the beginning of an independent clause are **and**, **but**, **for**, **or**, **nor**, **so**, and **yet**. When the second independent clause in a sentence begins with a coordinating conjunction, a comma is needed before the coordinating conjunction:

Teacher Notes

Jim studied in the Sweet Shop for his chemistry quiz, **but** it was hard to concentrate because of the noise.

2. Independent Marker Word

An independent marker word is a connecting word used at the beginning of an independent clause. These words can always begin a sentence that can stand alone. When the second independent clause in a sentence has an independent marker word, a semicolon is needed before the independent marker word.

Jim studied in the Sweet Shop for his chemistry quiz; **however**, it was hard to concentrate because of the noise.

Some common independent markers are: **also**, **consequently**, **furthermore**, **however**, **moreover**, **nevertheless**, and **therefore**.

Some Common Errors to Avoid

Comma Splices

A comma splice is the use of a comma between two independent clauses. You can usually fix the error by changing the comma to a period and therefore making the two clauses into two separate sentences, by changing the comma to a semicolon, or by making one clause dependent by inserting a dependent marker word in front of it.

Incorrect: I like this class, it is very interesting.

Correct: I like this class. It is very interesting.
- (or) I like this class; it is very interesting.
- (or) I like this class, and it is very interesting.
- (or) I like this class because it is very interesting.
- (or) Because it is very interesting, I like this class.

Fused Sentences

Fused sentences happen when there are two independent clauses not separated by any form of punctuation. This error is also known as a run-on sentence. The error can sometimes be corrected by adding a period, semicolon, or colon to separate the two sentences.

Incorrect: My professor is intelligent I've learned a lot from her.

Correct: My professor is intelligent. I've learned a lot from her.
- (or) My professor is intelligent; I've learned a lot from her.
- (or) My professor is intelligent, and I've learned a lot from her.
- (or) My professor is intelligent; moreover, I've learned a lot from her.

Sentence Fragments

Sentence fragments happen by treating a dependent clause or other incomplete thought as a complete sentence. You can usually fix this error by combining it with another sentence to make a complete thought or by removing the dependent marker.

Incorrect: Because I forgot the exam was today.

Correct: Because I forgot the exam was today, I didn't study.
- (or) I forgot the exam was today.

Teacher Notes

Part 7: Parallel Structure

Parallel structure means using the same pattern of words to show that two or more ideas have the same level of importance. This can happen at the word, phrase, or clause level. The usual way to join parallel structures is with the use of coordinating conjunctions such as "and" or "or."

Words and Phrases

With the -ing form (gerund) of words:

Parallel: Mary likes hiking, swimming, and bicycling.

With infinitive phrases:

Parallel: Mary likes to hike, to swim, and to ride a bicycle.
OR
Mary likes to hike, swim, and ride a bicycle.

(Note: You can use "to" before all the verbs in a sentence or only before the first one.)

Do not mix forms.

Example 1

Not Parallel:
Mary likes hiking, swimming, and **to ride** a bicycle.

Parallel:
Mary likes hiking, swimming, and riding a bicycle.

Example 2

Not Parallel:
The production manager was asked to write his report quickly, accurate ly, and **in a detailed manner**.

Parallel:
The production manager was asked to write his report quickly, accurately, and thoroughly.

Example 3

Not Parallel:
The teacher said that he was a poor student because he waited until the last minute to study for the exam, completed his lab problems in a careless manner, and **his motivation was** low.

Parallel:
The teacher said that he was a poor student because he waited until the last minute to study for the exam, completed his lab problems in a careless manner, and lacked motivation.

Clauses

A parallel structure that begins with clauses must keep on with clauses. Changing to another pattern or changing the voice of the verb (from active to passive or vice versa) will break the parallelism.

Example 1

Not Parallel:
The coach told the players that they should get a lot of sleep, that they should not eat too much, and to do some warm-up exercises before the game.

Parallel:
The coach told the players that they should get a lot of sleep, that they should not eat too much, and that they should do some warm-up exercises before the game.

Teacher Notes

OR
Parallel:
The coach told the players that they should **get** a lot of sleep, not **eat** too much, and **do** some warm-up exercises before the game.

Example 2

Not Parallel:
The salesman expected **that he would present** his product at the meeting, **that there would be** time for him to show his slide presentation, and **that questions would be asked** by prospective buyers. **(passive)**

Parallel:
The salesman expected **that he would present** his product at the meeting, **that there would be** time for him to show his slide presentation, and **that prospective buyers would ask** him questions.

Lists After a Colon

Be sure to keep all the elements in a list in the same form.

Example 1

Not Parallel:
The dictionary can be used for these purposes: to find **word meanings, pronunciations, correct spellings,** and **looking up irregular verbs**.

Parallel:
The dictionary can be used for these purposes: to find **word meanings, pronunciations, correct spellings,** and **irregular verbs**.

Proofreading Strategies to Try:

- Skim your paper, pausing at the words "and" and "or." Check on each side of these words to see whether the items joined are parallel. If not, make them parallel.
- If you have several items in a list, put them in a column to see if they are parallel.
- Listen to the sound of the items in a list or the items being compared. Do you hear the same kinds of sounds? For example, is there a series of "-ing" words beginning each item? Or do your hear a rhythm being repeated? If something is breaking that rhythm or repetition of sound, check to see if it needs to be made parallel.

Part 8: Introduction and General Usage in Defining Clauses

Relative pronouns are **that, who, whom, whose, which, where, when,** and **why**. They are used to join clauses to make a complex sentence. Relative pronouns are used at the beginning of the subordinate clause which gives some specific information about the main clause.

This is the house *that* Jack built.
I don't know the day *when* Jane marries him.
The professor, *whom* I respect, was tenured.

In English, the choice of the relative pronoun depends on the type of clause it is used in. There are two types of clauses distinguished: *defining* (*restrictive*) relative clauses and *non-defining* (*non-restrictive*) relative clauses. In both types of clauses the relative pronoun can function as a subject, an object, or a possessive.

Teacher Notes

Relative Pronouns in Defining Clauses

Defining relative clauses (also known as *restrictive relative clauses*) provide some essential information that explains the main clause. The information is crucial for understanding the sentence correctly and cannot be omitted. Defining clauses are opened by a relative pronoun and **ARE NOT** separated by a comma from the main clause.

The table below sums up the use of relative pronouns in defining clauses:

Function in the sentence	Reference to				
	People	Things/concepts	Place	Time	Reason
Subject	who, that	which, that			
Object	(that, who, whom)	(which, that)	where	when	why
Possessive	whose	whose, of which			

Examples

Relative pronoun used as a subject:

This is the house *that* had a great Christmas decoration.
It took me a while to get used to people *who* eat popcorn during the movie.

Relative pronoun used as an object:

1. As can be seen from the table, referring to a person or thing, the relative pronoun **may be omitted** in the object position:

   This is the man (who / that) I wanted to speak to and whose name I'd forgotten.

   The library didn't have the book (which / that) I wanted.

   I didn't like the book (which / that) John gave me.

   This is the house *where* I lived *when* I first came to the US.

2. In American English, *whom* is not used very often. ***Whom*** is more formal than *who* and is very often omitted in **speech**:

   Grammatically Correct: The woman to *whom* you have just spoken is my teacher.

   Common in Speech: The woman (*who*) you have just spoken to is my teacher.

However, *whom* may not be omitted if preceded by a preposition:

I have found you the tutor for *whom* you were looking.

Relative pronoun used as a possessive:

Whose is the only possessive relative pronoun in English. It can be used with both people and things:

The family *whose* house burnt in the fire was immediately given a suite in a hotel.
The book *whose* author is now being shown in the news has become a bestseller.

General remarks: That, Who, Which compared

The relative pronoun *that* can only be used in defining clauses. It can also be substituted for *who* (referring to persons) or *which* (referring to things). *That* is often used in speech; *who* and *which* are more common in written English.

William Kellogg was the man *that* lived in the late 19th century and had some weird ideas about raising children. (spoken, less formal)

Teacher Notes

William Kellogg was the man *who* lived in the late 19th century and had some weird ideas about raising children. (written, more formal)

Although your computer may suggest to correct it, referring to things, *which* may be used in the defining clause to put additional emphasis on the explanation. Again, the sentence with *which* is more formal than the one with *that*: Note that since it is the defining clause, there is NO comma used preceding *which*:

The café *that* sells the best coffee in town has recently been closed. (less formal)
The café *which* sells the best coffee in town has recently been closed. (more formal)

Some special uses of relative pronouns in defining clauses

that / who

Referring to people, both *that* and *who* can be used. *That* may be used to refer to someone in general:

He is the kind of person *that/who* will never let you down.
I am looking for someone *that/who* could give me a ride to Chicago.

However, when a particular person is being spoken about, *who* is preferred:

The old lady *who* lives next door is a teacher.
The girl *who* wore a red dress attracted everybody's attention at the party.

that / which

There are several cases when *that* is more appropriate and is preferred to *which*.

After the pronouns *all, any(thing), every(thing), few, little, many, much, no(thing), none, some(thing)*:

The police usually ask for every detail *that* helps identify the missing person. (*that* used as the subject)
Marrying a congressman is *all* (that) she wants. (*that* used as the object)

After verbs that answer the question **WHAT?** For example, *say, suggest, state, declare, hope, think, write*, etc. In this case, the whole relative clause functions as the object of the main clause:

Some people *say* (that) success is one percent of talent and ninety-nine percent of hard work.
The chairman *stated* at the meeting (that) his company is part of a big-time entertainment industry.

After the noun modified by an adjective *in the superlative degree*:

This is the *funniest* story (that) I have ever read! (*that* used as the object)

After ordinal numbers, e.g., *first, second, etc.*:

The first draft (that) we submitted was really horrible. (*that* used as the object)

If the verb in the main clause is a form of *BE*:

This is a claim that has absolutely no reason in it. (*that* used as the subject)

Relative Pronouns in Non-Defining Clauses

Non-defining relative clauses (also known as non-restrictive, or parenthetical, clauses) provide some additional information which is not essential and may be omitted without affecting the contents of the sentence. All relative pronouns EXCEPT "that" can be used in non-defining clauses; however, the pronouns MAY NOT be omitted. Non-defining clauses ARE separated by commas.

The table below sums up the use of relative pronouns in non-defining clauses:

Function in the sentence	Reference to				
	People	Things/concepts	Place	Time	Reason
Subject	who	which			
Object	who, whom	which	where	when	why
Possessive	whose	whose, of which			

a. **Relative pronoun used as a subject:**

The writer, **who** lives in this luxurious mansion, has just published his second novel.

b. **Relative pronoun used as an object:**

The house at the end of the street, **which** my grandfather built, needs renovating.

c. **Relative pronoun used as a possessive:**

William Kellogg, **whose** name has become a famous breakfast foods brand-name, had some weird ideas about raising children.

Some Special Uses of Relative Pronouns in Non-Defining Clauses

a. **which**
If you are referring to the previous clause as a whole, use ***which***:
My friend eventually decided to get divorced, **which** upset me a lot.

b. **of whom, of which**
Use ***of whom*** for persons and ***of which*** for things or concepts after numbers and words such as *most, many, some, both, none*:
I saw a lot of new people at the party, some **of whom** seemed familiar.
He was always coming up with new ideas, most **of which** were absolutely impracticable.

Part 9: Sentence Types and Punctuation Patterns

To punctuate a sentence, you can use and combine some of these patterns.

Pattern One: Simple Sentence

This pattern is an example of a simple sentence:

Independent clause [.]

Example: Doctors are concerned about the rising death rate from asthma.

Pattern Two: Compound Sentence

This pattern is an example of a compound sentence with a coordinating conjunction:

Independent clause [,] coordinating conjunction independent clause [.]

There are seven coordinating conjunctions: **and**, **but**, **for**, **or**, **nor**, **so**, **yet**.

Example: Doctors are concerned about the rising death rate from asthma, but they don't know the reasons for it.

Grammar Handbook

Teacher Notes

Teacher Notes

Pattern Three: Compound Sentence

This pattern is an example of a compound sentence with a semicolon.

Independent clause [;] independent clause [.]

Example: Doctors are concerned about the rising death rate from asthma; they are unsure of its cause.

Pattern Four: Compound Sentence

This pattern is an example of a compound sentence with an independent marker.

Independent clause [;] independent marker [,] independent clause [.]

Examples of independent markers are the following: **therefore**, **moreover**, **thus**, **consequently**, **however**, **also**.

Example: Doctors are concerned about the rising death rate from asthma; therefore, they have called for more research into its causes.

Pattern Five: Complex Sentence

This pattern is an example of a complex sentence with a dependent marker.

***Dependent marker* dependent clause [,] Independent clause [.]**

Examples of dependent markers are as follows: **because**, **before**, **since**, **while**, **although**, **if**, **until**, **when**, **after**, **as**, **as if**.

Example: *Because* doctors are concerned about the rising death rate from asthma, they have called for more research into its causes.

Pattern Six: Complex Sentence

This pattern is an example of a complex sentence with a dependent marker following the independent clause.

Independent clause dependent marker dependent clause [.]

Example: Doctors are concerned about the rising death rate from asthma because it is a common, treatable illness.

Pattern Seven

This pattern includes an independent clause with an embedded non-essential clause or phrase. A non-essential clause or phrase is one that can be removed without changing the meaning of the sentence or making it ungrammatical. In other words, the non-essential clause or phrase gives additional information, but the sentence can stand alone without it.

First part of an independent clause [,] non-essential clause or phrase, rest of the independent clause [.]

Example: Many doctors, including both pediatricians and family practice physicians, are concerned about the rising death rate from asthma.

Pattern Eight

This pattern includes an independent clause with an embedded essential clause or phrase. An essential clause or phrase is one that cannot be removed without changing the overall meaning of the sentence.

First part of an independent clause essential clause or phrase rest of the independent clause [.]

Example: Many doctors who are concerned about the rising death rate from asthma have called for more research into its causes.

© 2011 College Board. All rights reserved.

Teacher Notes

Part 10: Making Subjects and Verbs Agree

1. When the subject of a sentence is composed of two or more nouns or pronouns connected by *and*, use a plural verb.

   She and her friends **are** at the fair.

2. When two or more singular nouns or pronouns are connected by *or* or *nor*, use a singular verb.

   The book or the pen **is** in the drawer.

3. When a compound subject contains both a singular and a plural noun or pronoun joined by *or* or *nor*, the verb should agree with the part of the subject that is nearer the verb.

   The boy or his friends **run** every day.
   His friends or the boy **runs** every day.

4. *Doesn't* is a contraction of *does not* and should be used only with a singular subject. *Don't* is a contraction of *do not* and should be used only with a plural subject. The exception to this rule appears in the case of the first person and second person pronouns *I* and *you*. With these pronouns, the contraction *don't* should be used. [Note that formal writing generally avoids the use of contractions.]

   He doesn't **like** it.
   They don't **like** it.

5. Do not be misled by a phrase that comes between the subject and the verb. The verb agrees with the subject, not with a noun or pronoun in the phrase.

   One of the boxes **is** open
   The people who listen to that music **are** few.
   The team captain, as well as his players, **is** anxious.
   The book, including all the chapters in the first section, **is** boring.
   The woman with all the dogs **walks** down my street.

6. The words *each*, *each one*, *either*, *neither*, *everyone*, *everybody*, *anybody*, *anyone*, *nobody*, *somebody*, *someone*, and *no one* are singular and require a singular verb.

   Each of these hot dogs **is** juicy.
   Everybody **knows** Mr. Jones.
   Either **is** correct.

7. Nouns such as *civics*, *mathematics*, *dollars*, *measles*, and *news* require singular verbs.

   The news **is** on at six.

   Note: The word **dollars** is a special case. When talking about an amount of money, it requires a singular verb, but when referring to the dollars themselves, a plural verb is required.

   Five dollars **is** a lot of money.
   Dollars **are** often used instead of rubles in Russia.

8. Nouns such as *scissors*, *tweezers*, *trousers*, and *shears* require plural verbs. (There are two parts to these things.)

   These scissors **are** dull.
   Those trousers **are** made of wool.

9. In sentences beginning with *there is* or *there are*, the subject follows the verb. Since *there* is not the subject, the verb agrees with what follows.

© 2011 College Board. All rights reserved.

Grammar Handbook 431

Teacher Notes

There are many questions.
There is a question.

10. Collective nouns are words that imply more than one person but that are considered singular and take a singular verb, such as: *group*, *team*, *committee*, *class*, and *family*.

The team runs during practice.
The committee decides how to proceed.
The family has a long history.
My family has never been able to agree.

In some cases, a sentence may call for the use of a plural verb when using a collective noun.

The crew are preparing to dock the ship.

This sentence is referring to the individual efforts of each crew member.

11. Expressions such as *with*, *together with*, *including*, *accompanied by*, *in addition to*, or *as well* do not change the number of the subject. If the subject is singular, the verb is too.

The President, accompanied by his wife, is traveling to India.
All of the books, including yours, are in that box.

Sequence of Tenses

Simple Present: They walk.

Present Perfect: They have walked.

Simple Past: They walked.

Past Perfect: They had walked.

Future: They will walk.

Future Perfect: They will have walked.

Problems in sequencing tenses usually occur with the perfect tenses, all of which are formed by adding an auxiliary or auxiliaries to the past participle, the third principal part.

ring, rang, rung
walk, walked, walked

The most common auxiliaries are forms of "be," "can," "do," "may," "must," "ought," "shall," "will," "has," "have," "had," and they are the forms we shall use in this most basic discussion.

Present Perfect

The present perfect consists of a past participle (the third principal part) with "has" or "have." It designates action which began in the past but which continues into the present or the effect of which still continues.

1. Betty taught for ten years. (simple past)
2. Betty has taught for ten years. (present perfect)

The implication in (1) is that Betty has retired; in (2), that she is still teaching.

1. John did his homework. He can go to the movies.
2. If John has done his homework, he can go to the movies.

Infinitives, too, have perfect tense forms when combined with "have," and sometimes problems arise when infinitives are used with verbs such as "hope," "plan," "expect," and "intend," all of which usually point to the future (I wanted to go to the movie. Janet meant to see the doctor.) The

Teacher Notes

perfect tense sets up a sequence by marking the action which began and usually was completed before the action in the main verb.

1. I am happy to have participated in this campaign!
2. John had hoped to have won the trophy.

Thus the action of the main verb points back in time; the action of the perfect infinitive has been completed.

The past perfect tense designates action in the past just as simple past does, but the action of the past perfect is action completed in the past before another action.

1. John raised vegetables and later sold them. (past)
2. John sold vegetables that he had raised. (past perfect)

The vegetables were raised before they were sold.

1. Renee washed the car when George arrived. (simple past)
2. Renee had washed the car when George arrived. (past perfect)

In (1), she waited until George arrived and then washed the car. In (2), she had already finished washing the car by the time he arrived.

In sentences expressing condition and result, the past perfect tense is used in the part that states the condition.

1. If I had done my exercises, I would have passed the test.
2. I think George would have been elected if he hadn't sounded so pompous.

Future Perfect Tense
The future perfect tense designates action that will have been completed at a specified time in the future.

1. Saturday I will finish my housework. (simple future)
2. By Saturday noon, I will have finished my housework. (future perfect)

Part 11: Using Active Versus Passive Voice

In a sentence using **active voice**, the subject of the sentence performs the action expressed in the verb.

The dog ***bit*** **the boy**.

The arrow points from the subject performing the action (the dog) to the individual being acted upon (the boy). This is an example of a sentence using the active voice.

Scientists ***have conducted*** **experiments** to test the hypothesis.

Sample active voice sentence with the subject performing the action described by the verb.

Watching a framed, mobile world through a car's windshield ***reminds*** **me** of watching a movie or TV.

The active voice sentence subject (watching a framed, mobile world) performs the action of reminding the speaker of something.

Each example above includes a sentence subject performing the action expressed by the verb.

Teacher Notes

Examples:

	Active	Passive
Simple Present	• The company ships the computers to many foreign countries.	• Computers are shipped to many foreign countries.
Present Progressive	• The chef is preparing the food.	• The food is being prepared.
Simple Past	• The delivery man delivered the package yesterday.	• The package was delivered yesterday.
Past Progressive	• The producer was making an announcement.	• An announcement was being made.
Future	• Our representative will pick up the computer.	• The computer will be picked up.
Present Perfect	• Someone has made the arrangements for us.	• The arrangements have been made for us.
Past Perfect	• They had given us visas for three months.	• They had been given visas for three months.
Future Perfect	• By next month we will have finished this job.	• By next month this job will have been finished.

Part 12: Irregular Verbs: Overview and List

In English, regular verbs consist of three main parts: the root form (present), the (simple) past, and the past participle. Regular verbs have an *-ed* ending added to the root verb for both the simple past and past participle. Irregular verbs do not follow this pattern, and instead take on an alternative pattern.

The following is a partial list of irregular verbs found in English. Each listing consists of the present/root form of the verb, the (simple) past form of the verb, and the past participle form of the verb.

List of Irregular Verbs in English

Present	Past	Past Participle
be	was, were	been
become	became	become
begin	began	begun
blow	blew	blown
break	broke	broken
bring	brought	brought
build	built	built
burst	burst	burst
buy	bought	bought
catch	caught	caught
choose	chose	chosen
come	came	come
cut	cut	cut

Present	Past	Past Participle
deal	dealt	dealt
do	did	done
drink	drank	drunk
drive	drove	driven
eat	ate	eaten
fall	fell	fallen
feed	fed	fed
feel	felt	felt
fight	fought	fought
find	found	found
fly	flew	flown
forbid	forbade	forbidden
forget	forgot	forgotten

434 SpringBoard® English Textual Power™ Level 4

Present	Past	Past Participle
forgive	forgave	forgiven
freeze	froze	frozen
get	got	gotten
give	gave	given
go	went	gone
grow	grew	grown
have	had	had
hear	heard	heard
hide	hid	hidden
hold	held	held
hurt	hurt	hurt
keep	kept	kept
know	knew	known
lay	laid	laid
lead	led	led
leave	left	left
let	let	let
lie	lay	lain
lose	lost	lost
make	made	made
meet	met	met
pay	paid	paid
quit	quit	quit
read	read	read
ride	rode	ridden
run	ran	run
say	said	said

Present	Past	Past Participle
see	saw	seen
seek	sought	sought
sell	sold	sold
send	sent	sent
shake	shook	sent
shine	shone	shone
sing	sang	sung
sit	sat	sat
sleep	slept	slept
speak	spoke	spoken
spend	spent	spent
spring	sprang	sprung
stand	stood	stood
steal	stole	stolen
swim	swam	swum
swing	swung	swung
take	took	taken
teach	taught	taught
tear	tore	torn
tell	told	told
think	thought	thought
throw	threw	thrown
understand	understood	understood
wake	woke (waked)	woken (waked)
wear	wore	worn
win	won	won
write	wrote	written

Commonly Confused Verbs

LIE versus LAY

Lie vs. Lay Usage		
Present	**Past**	**Past Participle**
lie, lying (to tell a falsehood)	I lied to my mother.	I have lied under oath.
lie, lying (to recline)	I lay on the bed because I was tired.	He has lain in the grass.
lay, laying (to put, place)	I laid the baby in her cradle.	We have laid the dishes on the table.

Example sentences:

After **laying** down his weapon, the soldier **lay** down to sleep.
Will you **lay** out my clothes while I **lie** down to rest?

Grammar Handbook

Teacher Notes

Teacher Notes

SIT* versus *SET

Sit vs. Set Usage		
Present	**Past**	**Past Participle**
sit (to be seated or come to resting position)	I sat in my favorite chair.	You have sat there for three hours.
set (to put or place)	I set my glass on the table.	She has set her books on my desk again.

Example sentence:

Let's **set** the table before we **sit** down to rest.

RISE* versus *RAISE

Rise vs. Raise Usage		
Present	**Past**	**Past Participle**
rise (steady or customary upward movement)	The balloon rose into the air.	He has risen to a position of power.
raise (to cause to rise)	They raised their hands because they knew the answer.	I have raised the curtain many times.

Example sentence:

The boy **raised** the flag just before the sun **rose.**

Part 13: Capitalization and Punctuation

A Little Help with Capitals

If you have a question about whether a specific word should be capitalized that doesn't fit under one of these rules, try checking a dictionary to see if the word is capitalized there.

Use capital letters in the following ways:

The first words of a sentence

When he tells a joke, he sometimes forgets the punch line.

The pronoun "I"

The last time I visited Atlanta was several years ago.

Proper nouns (the names of specific people, places, organizations, and sometimes things)

Worrill Fabrication Company
Golden Gate Bridge
Supreme Court
Livingston, Missouri
Atlantic Ocean
Mothers Against Drunk Driving

Teacher Notes

Family relationships (when used as proper names)

I sent a thank-you note to Aunt Abigail, but not to my other aunts.
Here is a present I bought for Mother.
Did you buy a present for your mother?

The names of God, specific deities, religious figures, and holy books

God the Father
the Virgin Mary
the Bible
the Greek gods
Moses
Shiva
Buddha
Zeus

Exception: Do not capitalize the non-specific use of the word "god."

The word "polytheistic" means the worship of more than one god.

Titles preceding names, but not titles that follow names

She worked as the assistant to Mayor Hanolovi.
I was able to interview Miriam Moss, mayor of Littonville.

Directions that are names (North, South, East, and West when used as sections of the country, but not as compass directions)

The Patels have moved to the Southwest.
Jim's house is two miles north of Otterbein.

The days of the week, the months of the year, and holidays (but not the seasons used generally)

Halloween
October
Friday
winter
spring
fall

Exception: Seasons are capitalized when used in a title.

The Fall 1999 Semester

The names of countries, nationalities, and specific languages

Costa Rica
Spanish
French
English

The first word in a sentence that is a direct quote

Emerson once said, "A foolish consistency is the hobgoblin of little minds."

The major words in the titles of books, articles, and songs (but not short prepositions or the articles "the," "a," or "an," if they are not the first word of the title)

One of Jerry's favorite books is *The Catcher in the Rye*.

© 2011 College Board. All rights reserved.

Teacher Notes

Members of national, political, racial, social, civic, and athletic groups

Green Bay Packers
African-Americans
Democrats
Friends of the Wilderness
Chinese

Periods and events (but not century numbers)

Victorian Era
Great Depression
Constitutional Convention
sixteenth century

Trademarks

Pepsi
Honda
IBM
Microsoft Word

Words and abbreviations of specific names (but not names of things that came from specific things but are now general types)

Freudian	UN
NBC	french fries
pasteurize	italics

Comma

Use a comma to join two independent clauses by a comma and a coordinating conjunction (*and, but, or, for, nor, so*).

Road construction can be inconvenient, but it is necessary.

The new house has a large fenced backyard, so I am sure our dog will enjoy it.

Use a comma after an introductory phrase, prepositional phrase, or dependent clause.

To get a good grade, you must complete all your assignments.

Because Dad caught the chicken pox, we canceled our vacation.

After the wedding, the guests attended the reception.

Use a comma to separate elements in a series. Although there is no set rule that requires a comma before the last item in a series, it seems to be a general academic convention to include it. The examples below demonstrate this trend.

On her vacation, Lisa visited Greece, Spain, and Italy.

In their speeches, many of the candidates promised to help protect the environment, bring about world peace, and end world hunger.

Use a comma to separate nonessential elements from a sentence. More specifically, when a sentence includes information that is not crucial to the message or intent of the sentence, enclose it in or separate it by commas.

John's truck, a red Chevrolet, needs new tires.

When he realized he had overslept, Matt rushed to his car and hurried to work.

Teacher Notes

Use a comma between coordinate adjectives (adjectives that are equal and reversible).

The irritable, fidgety crowd waited impatiently for the rally speeches to begin.

The sturdy, compact suitcase made a perfect gift.

Use a comma after a transitional element (*however, therefore, nonetheless, also, otherwise, finally, instead, thus, of course, above all, for example, in other words, as a result, on the other hand, in conclusion, in addition*)

For example, the Red Sox, Yankees, and Indians are popular baseball teams.

If you really want to get a good grade this semester, however, you must complete all assignments, attend class, and study your notes.

Use a comma with quoted words.

"Yes," she promised. Todd replied, saying, "I will be back this afternoon."

Use a comma in a date.

October 25, 1999
Monday, October 25, 1999
25 October 1999

Use a comma in a number.

15,000,000
1614 High Street

Use a comma in a personal title.

Pam Smith, MD
Mike Rose, Chief Financial Officer for Operations, reported the quarter's earnings.

Use a comma to separate a city name from the state.

West Lafayette, Indiana
Dallas, Texas

Avoid comma splices (two independent clauses joined only by a comma). Instead, separate the clauses with a period, with a comma followed by a coordinating conjunction, or with a semicolon.

Semicolon

Use a semicolon to join two independent clauses when the second clause restates the first or when the two clauses are of equal emphasis.

Road construction in Dallas has hindered travel around town; streets have become covered with bulldozers, trucks, and cones.

Use a semicolon to join two independent clauses when the second clause begins with a conjunctive adverb (*however, therefore, moreover, furthermore, thus, meanwhile, nonetheless, otherwise*) or a transition (*in fact, for example, that is, for instance, in addition, in other words, on the other hand, even so*).

Terrorism in the United States has become a recent concern; in fact, the concern for America's safety has led to an awareness of global terrorism.

Use a semicolon to join elements of a series when individual items of the series already include commas.

Recent sites of the Olympic Games include Athens, Greece; Salt Lake City, Utah; Sydney, Australia; Nagano, Japan.

Teacher Notes

Colon

Use a colon to join two independent clauses when you wish to emphasize the second clause.

Road construction in Dallas has hindered travel around town: parts of Main, Fifth, and West Street are closed during the construction.

Use a colon after an independent clause when it is followed by a list, a quotation, an appositive, or other idea directly related to the independent clause.

Julie went to the store for some groceries: milk, bread, coffee, and cheese.

In his Gettysburg Address, Abraham Lincoln urges Americans to rededicate themselves to the unfinished work of the deceased soldiers: "It is for us the living rather to be dedicated here to the unfinished work which they who fought here have thus far so nobly advanced. It is rather for us to be here dedicated to the great task remaining before us — that from these honored dead we take increased devotion to that cause for which they gave the last full measure of devotion — that we here highly resolve that these dead shall not have died in vain, that this nation under God shall have a new birth of freedom, and that government of the people, by the people, for the people shall not perish from the earth."

I know the perfect job for her: a politician.

Use a colon at the end of a business letter greeting.

To Whom It May Concern:

Use a colon to separate the hour and minute(s) in a time notation.

12:00 p.m.

Use a colon to separate the chapter and verse in a Biblical reference.

Matthew 1:6

Parentheses

Parentheses are used to emphasize content. They place more emphasis on the enclosed content than commas. Use parentheses to set off nonessential material, such as dates, clarifying information, or sources, from a sentence.

Muhammed Ali (1942-present), arguably the greatest athlete of all time, claimed he would "float like a butterfly, sting like a bee."

Use parentheses to enclose numbered items in a sentence.

He asked everyone to bring (1) a folding tent, (2) food and water for two days, and (3) a sleeping bag.

Also use parentheses for literary citations embedded in text or to give the explanation of an acronym.

Research by Wegener and Petty (1994) supports...
The AMA (American Medical Association) recommends regular exercise.

Dash

Dashes are used to set off or emphasize the content enclosed within dashes or the content that follows a dash. Dashes place more emphasis on this content than parentheses.

Perhaps one reason why the term has been so problematic—so resistant to definition, and yet so transitory in those definitions—is because of its multitude of applications.

In terms of public legitimacy—that is, in terms of garnering support from state legislators, parents, donors, and university administrators—English departments are primarily places where advanced literacy is taught.

Teacher Notes

The U.S.S. *Constitution* became known as "Old Ironsides" during the War of 1812—during which the cannonballs fired from the British H.M.S. *Guerriere* merely bounced off the sides of the *Constitution*.

To some of you, my proposals may seem radical—even revolutionary.

Use a dash to set off an appositive phrase that already includes commas. An appositive is a word that adds explanatory or clarifying information to the noun that precedes it.

The cousins—Tina, Todd, and Sam—arrived at the party together.

Quotation Marks

Use quotation marks to enclose direct quotations. Note that commas and periods are placed inside the closing quotation mark, and colons and semicolons are placed outside. The placement of question and exclamation marks depends on the situation.

He asked, "When will you be arriving?" I answered, "Sometime after 6:30."

Use quotation marks to indicate the novel, ironic, or reserved use of a word.

History is stained with blood spilled in the name of "justice."

Use quotation marks around the titles of short poems, song titles, short stories, magazine or newspaper articles, essays, speeches, chapter titles, short films, and episodes of television or radio shows.

"Self-Reliance," by Ralph Waldo Emerson
"Just Like a Woman," by Bob Dylan
"The Smelly Car," an episode of Seinfeld

Do not use quotation marks in indirect or block quotations. Indirect quotations are not exact wordings but rather rephrasings or summaries of another person's words. In this case, it is not necessary to use quotation marks. However, indirect quotations still require proper citations, and you will be committing plagiarism if you fail to do so.

Mr. Johnson, a local farmer, reported last night that he saw an alien spaceship on his own property.

Italics

Underlining and Italics are often used interchangeably. Before word-processing programs were widely available, writers would underline certain words to indicate to publishers to italicize whatever was underlined. Although the general trend has been moving toward italicizing instead of underlining, you should remain consistent with your choice throughout your paper. To be safe, you could check with your teacher to find out which he/she prefers. Italicize the titles of magazines, books, newspapers, academic journals, films, television shows, long poems, plays of three or more acts, operas, musical albums, works of art, websites, and individual trains, planes, or ships.

Time
Romeo and Juliet by William Shakespeare
The Metamorphosis of Narcissus by Salvador Dali
Amazon.com
Titanic

Italicize foreign words.

Semper fi, the motto of the U.S. Marine Corps, means "always faithful."

Italicize a word or phrase to add emphasis.

The *truth* is of utmost concern!

Italicize a word when referring to that word.

The word *justice* is often misunderstood and therefore misused.

© 2011 College Board. All rights reserved.

Teacher Notes

Hyphen

Two words brought together as a compound may be written separately, written as one word, or connected by hyphens. For example, three modern dictionaries all have the same listings for the following compounds:

hair stylist
hairsplitter
hair-raiser

Another modern dictionary, however, lists *hairstylist*, not *hair stylist*. Compounding is obviously in a state of flux, and authorities do not always agree in all cases, but the uses of the hyphen offered here are generally agreed upon.

1. Use a hyphen to join two or more words serving as a single adjective before a noun:

   a one-way street
   chocolate-covered peanuts
   well-known author

   However, when compound modifiers come after a noun, they are not hyphenated:

   The peanuts were chocolate covered.
   The author was well known.

2. Use a hyphen with compound numbers:

   forty-six
   sixty-three
   Our much-loved teacher was sixty-three years old.

3. Use a hyphen to avoid confusion or an awkward combination of letters:

   re-sign a petition (vs. resign from a job)
   semi-independent (but semiconscious)
   shell-like (but childlike)

4. Use a hyphen with the prefixes *ex-* (meaning former), *self-*, *all-*; with the suffix *-elect*; between a prefix and a capitalized word; and with figures or letters:

   ex-husband
   self-assured
   mid-September
   all-inclusive
   mayor-elect
   anti-American
   T-shirt
   pre-Civil War
   mid-1980s

5. Use a hyphen to divide words at the end of a line if necessary, and make the break only between syllables:

   pref-er-ence
   sell-ing
   in-di-vid-u-al-ist

6. For line breaks, divide already hyphenated words only at the hyphen:

   mass-
   produced

Teacher Notes

Apostrophe

The apostrophe has three uses:

- to form possessives of nouns
- to show the omission of letters
- to indicate certain plurals of lowercase letters

Forming Possessives of Nouns

To see if you need to make a possessive, turn the phrase around and make it an "of the..." phrase. For example:

the boy's hat = the hat of the boy
three days' journey = journey of three days

If the noun after "of" is a building, an object, or a piece of furniture, then **no** apostrophe is needed!

room of the hotel = hotel room
door of the car = car door
leg of the table = table leg

Once you've determined whether you need to make a possessive, follow these rules to create one.

- **add 's to the singular form of the word (even if it ends in *-s*):**

  the owner's car
  James's hat (James' hat is also acceptable. For plural, proper nouns that are possessive, use an apostrophe after the 's': "The Eggles' presentation was good." The Eggles are a husband and wife consultant team.)

- **add 's to the plural forms that do not end in *-s*:**

  the children's game
  the geese's honking

- **add ' to the end of plural nouns that end in *-s*:**

  houses' roofs
  three friends' letters

- **add 's to the end of compound words:**

  my brother-in-law's money

- **add 's to the last noun to show joint possession of an object:**

  Todd and Anne's apartment

Showing omission of letters

Apostrophes are used in contractions. A contraction is a word (or set of numbers) in which one or more letters (or numbers) have been omitted. The apostrophe shows this omission. Contractions are common in speaking and in informal writing. To use an apostrophe to create a contraction, place an apostrophe where the omitted letter(s) would go. Here are some examples:

don't = do not
I'm = I am
he'll = he will
who's = who is
could've= could have (NOT "could of"!)
'60 = 1960

Don't use apostrophes for possessive pronouns or for noun plurals.

Apostrophes should not be used with possessive pronouns because possessive pronouns already

© 2011 College Board. All rights reserved.

Teacher Notes

show possession — they don't need an apostrophe. *His, her, its, my, yours, ours* are all possessive pronouns. Here are some examples:

wrong: **his'** book
correct: **his** book

wrong: The group made **it's** decision.
correct: The group made **its** decision.

(Note: *Its* and *it's* are not the same thing. *It's* is a contraction for "it is" and *its* is a possessive pronoun meaning "belonging to it." It's raining out= it is raining out. A simple way to remember this rule is the fact that you don't use an apostrophe for the possessive *his* or *hers*, so don't do it with *its*!)

wrong: a friend of **yours'**
correct: a friend of **yours**

Proofreading for apostrophes
A good time to proofread is when you have finished writing the paper. Try the following strategies to proofread for apostrophes:

- If you tend to leave out apostrophes, check every word that ends in *-s* or *-es* to see if it needs an apostrophe.
- If you put in too many apostrophes, check every apostrophe to see if you can justify it with a rule for using apostrophes.

Ellipsis

An ellipsis (a row of three dots: ...) must be used whenever anything is omitted from within a quoted passage—word, phrase, line, or paragraph-- regardless of its source or use. It would, therefore, apply to all usage, including technical, non-technical, medical, journalistic, fiction, etc. The usual form is a "bare" ellipsis (just the three dots, preceded and followed by a space), although the MLA Handbook for Writers of Research Papers recommends that the writer enclose an ellipsis in brackets [...] when omitting part of an original quotation, to differentiate instances of deleted text from ellipses included in the original text. In all cases, the entire quoted passage, including ellipses, is preceded and followed by quotation marks and the source properly cited.

Two things to consider: 1) using ellipses is a form of "editing" the source material, so be certain that the final outcome does not change the original meaning or intent of the quoted passage; and 2) if quoted text ends up with more ellipses than words, consider paraphrasing rather than using direct quotes.

Brackets

Brackets are most often used to clarify the meaning of quoted material. If the context of your quote might be unclear, you may add a few words to provide clarity. Enclose the added material in brackets.

Added Material: The quarterback told the reporter, "It's quite simple. They [the other team] played a better game, scored more points, and that's why we lost."

Resources

SpringBoard Instructional Strategies Index

READING STRATEGIES

S STUDENT/**T** TEACHER

STRATEGY		DEFINITION	PURPOSE
Activating Prior Knowledge	T	Providing an opportunity for students to think about what they already know about a concept, place, person, culture, and so on, and to share their knowledge with a wider audience	To prepare students to encounter new concepts, places, persons, cultures, and so on, prior to reading a text
Anticipation Guide	T	Activating thinking about a particular topic by presenting issues or vocabulary prior to reading the text (e.g., word categorization, agree/disagree, opinionnaire)	To provide a focus for reading and encourage students to be actively involved with the text by anticipating issues or new vocabulary
Chunking the Text	T	Breaking the text into smaller, manageable units of sense (e.g., words, sentences, paragraphs, whole text) by numbering, separating phrases, drawing boxes	To reduce the intimidation factor when encountering long words, sentences, or whole texts; to increase comprehension of difficult or challenging text
Close Reading	S	Accessing small chunks of text to read, reread, mark, and annotate key passages, word-for-word, sentence-by-sentence, and line-by-line	To develop comprehensive understanding by engaging in one or more focused readings of a text
Diffusing	S	Reading a passage, noting unfamiliar words, discovering meaning of unfamiliar words using context clues, dictionaries, and/or thesauruses, and replacing unfamiliar words with familiar ones	To facilitate a close reading of text, the use of resources, an understanding of synonyms, and increased comprehension of text
Double-Entry Journal	S	A two-column journal (also called Dialectical Journal) with a student-selected passage in one column and the student's response in the second column (e.g., asking questions of the text, forming personal responses, interpreting the text, reflecting on the process of making meaning of the text)	To respond to a specific passage with comments, questions, or insights to foster active involvement with a text and to facilitate increased comprehension
Graphic Organizer	S	Using a visual representation for the organization of information	To facilitate increased comprehension and discussion
Guided Reading	T	Identifying strategies to guide students through challenging text (e.g., make predictions, mark the text, skim the text)	To help students learn to use a multiplicity of strategies to make meaning from challenging text
Interactive Word Wall	T	Creating an interactive visual display of vocabulary words that serves as a constant reminder of words and groups of words as they are introduced, used, and mastered over the course of a year	To provide a print-rich environment, reinforcement of learned words, a reference for reading and writing, and an ever-present tool for building word knowledge and awareness
KWHL Chart	S	Setting up discussion with use of a graphic organizer. Allows students to activate prior knowledge by answering "What do I *know*?" sets a purpose by answering "What do I *want* to know?" helps preview a task by answering "*How* will I learn it?" and reflects on new knowledge by answering "What have I *learned*?"	To organize thinking, access prior knowledge, and reflect on learning to increase comprehension and engagement

STRATEGY		DEFINITION	PURPOSE
Manipulatives	T	Using a kinesthetic approach to making meaning in which students are asked to assemble parts of a whole as a way of understanding the text.	To provide a tactile and visual means of examining text in order to encourage multiple ways of understanding text
Marking the Text	S	Selecting text by highlighting, underlining, and/or annotating for specific components, such as main idea, imagery, literary devices, and so on	To focus reading for specific purposes, such as author's craft, and to organize information from selections; to facilitate reexamination of a text
Metacognitive Markers	S	Responding to text with a system of cueing marks where students use a ? for questions about the text; a ! for reactions related to the text; and an * for comments about the text and underline to signal key ideas	To track responses to texts and use those responses as a point of departure for talking or writing about texts
Predicting	S	Making guesses about the text by using the title and pictures and/or thinking ahead about events which may occur based on evidence in the text	To help students become actively involved, interested, and mentally prepared to understand ideas
Previewing	S	Examining a text's structure, features, layout, and so on, prior to reading	To gain familiarity with the text, make connections to the text, and extend prior knowledge to set a purpose for reading
QHT	S	Expanding prior knowledge of vocabulary words by marking words with a Q, H, or T (Q signals words students do not know; H signals words students have heard and might be able to identify; T signals words students know well enough to teach to their peers.)	To allow students to build on their prior knowledge of words, to provide a forum for peer teaching and learning of new words, and to serve as a prereading exercise to aid in comprehension
Questioning the Text* *The AP Vertical Teams Guide for English (109-112)*	S	Developing literal, interpretive, and universal questions about the text while reading a text	To engage more actively with texts, read with greater purpose and focus, and ultimately answer questions to gain greater insight into the text
Quickwrite	S	Responding to a text by writing for a short, specific amount of time about a designated topic or idea related to a text	To activate background knowledge, clarify issues, facilitate making connections, and allow for reflection
RAFT	S	Responding to and analyzing text by brainstorming various roles (e.g., self, characters from other texts), audiences (e.g., a different character, a real person), formats (e.g., letter, brochure, essay, travel guide), and topics; readers may choose one particular role, audience, format, and topic to create a new text	To initiate reader response; to facilitate an analysis of a text to gain focus prior to creating a new text
Rereading	S	Encountering the same text with more than one reading	To identify additional details; to clarify meaning and/or reinforce comprehension of texts
Shared Reading	T	Reading the text aloud (usually by the teacher) while students follow along silently, or reading a text aloud with an invitation to students to read along orally	To provide support for students in a group or for the whole class as they interpret and analyze challenging text

*Delineates AP strategy

READING STRATEGIES (Continued)

STRATEGY		DEFINITION	PURPOSE
SIFT* *The AP Vertical Teams Guide for English (17–20)*	**S**	Analyzing a fictional text by examining stylistic elements, especially symbol, images, and figures of speech, in order to show how all work together to reveal tone and theme.	To focus and facilitate an analysis of a fictional text by examining the title and text for symbolism, identifying images and sensory details, analyzing figurative language and identifying how all these elements reveal tone and theme
Skimming/Scanning	**S**	Skimming by rapid or superficial reading of a text to form an overall impression or to obtain a general understanding of the material; scanning by focusing on key words, phrases, or specific details to provide speedy recognition of information	To quickly form an overall impression prior to an in-depth study of a text; to answer specific questions or quickly locate targeted information or detail in a text
SMELL* *The AP Vertical Teams Guide for English (138–139)*	**S**	Analyzing a persuasive speech or essay by asking five essential questions: • **S**ender-receiver relationship—What is the sender-receiver relationship? Who are the images and language meant to attract? Describe the speaker of the text. • **M**essage—What is the message? Summarize the statement made in the text. • **E**motional Strategies—What is the desired effect? • **L**ogical Strategies—What logic is operating? How does it (or its absence) affect the message? Consider the logic of the images as well as the words. • **L**anguage—What does the language of the text describe? How does it affect the meaning and effectiveness of the writing? Consider the language of the images as well as the words.	To analyze a persuasive speech or essay by focusing on five essential questions *The AP Vertical Teams Guide for English*
SOAPSTone*	**S**	Analyzing text by discussing and identifying *Speaker, Occasion, Audience, Purpose, Subject,* and *Tone*	To use an analytical process to understand the author's craft
Summarizing/ Paraphrasing	**S**	Restating in one's own words the main idea or essential information expressed in a text, whether it be narration, dialogue, or informational text	To facilitate comprehension and recall of a text
Think Aloud	**S**	Talking through a difficult passage or task by using a form of metacognition whereby the reader expresses how he/she has made sense of the text	To reflect on how readers make meaning of challenging texts
TP-CASTT* *The AP Vertical Teams Guide for English (94–99)*	**S**	Analyzing a poetic text by identifying and discussing *Title, Paraphrase, Connotation, Attitude, Shift, Theme,* and *Title* again	To use an analytical process to understand the author's craft
Visualizing	**S**	Forming a picture (mentally and/or literally) while reading a text	To increase reading comprehension and promote active engagement with text
Vocabulary Notebook	**T**	Using a format such as a notebook, journal, or personal list to maintain an ongoing list of vocabulary words, definitions, and connection to academic study	To facilitate and sustain a systematic process of vocabulary development

*Delineates AP strategy

STRATEGY		DEFINITION	PURPOSE
Word Maps	S	Using a clearly defined graphic organizer such as concept circles or word webs to identify and reinforce word meanings	To provide a visual tool for identifying and remembering multiple aspects of words and word meanings
Word Sort	T	Organizing and sorting word card manipulatives into categories designated by the teacher or selected by the student and providing a written or oral justification for the classifications	To solidify understanding of word meanings by considering the multiple uses, meanings, and relationships of word parts, words, and groups of words

WRITING STRATEGIES

S T
STUDENT/TEACHER

STRATEGY		DEFINITION	PURPOSE
Adding	S	Making conscious choices to enhance a text by adding additional words, phrases, sentences, or ideas	To refine and clarify the writer's thoughts during revision and/or drafting
Brainstorming	S	Using a flexible but deliberate process of listing multiple ideas in a short period of time without excluding any idea from the preliminary list	To generate ideas, concepts, or key words that provide a focus and/or establish organization as part of the prewriting or revision process
Deleting	S	Providing clarity and cohesiveness for a text by eliminating words, phrases, sentences, or ideas	To refine and clarify the writer's thoughts during revision and/or drafting
Double-Entry Journal	S	Creating a two-column journal (also called Dialectical Journal) with a student-selected passage in one column and the student's response in the second column (e.g., asking questions of the text, forming personal responses, interpreting the text, reflecting on the process of making meaning of the text)	To assist in organizing key textual elements and responses noted during reading in order to generate textual support that can be incorporated into a piece of writing at a later time
Drafting	S	Composing a text in its initial form	To incorporate brainstormed or initial ideas into a written format
Free writing	S	Using a fluid brainstorming process to write without constraints in order to solidify and convey the writer's purpose	To refine and clarify the writer's thoughts, spark new ideas, and/or generate content during revision and/or drafting
Generating Questions	S	Clarifying and developing ideas by asking questions of the draft. May be part of self-editing or peer editing	To clarify and develop ideas in a draft. Used during drafting and as part of writer response
Graphic Organizer	S	Representing ideas and information visually (e.g., Venn diagrams, flowcharts, cluster maps)	To provide a visual system for organizing multiple ideas, details, and/or textual support to be included in a piece of writing
Guided Writing	T	Teacher modeling of the writing that students are expected to produce by guiding students through the organization, generation of ideas, and revision of texts before students are asked to do it	To demonstrate the process of writing by modeling the construction, revision and/or process of crafting texts
Looping	S	Focusing on one section of a text and generating ideas from that section and then repeating the process with the newly generated segments	To refine and clarify the writer's thoughts, spark new ideas, and/or generate new content during revision and/or drafting

WRITING STRATEGIES (Continued)

STRATEGY		DEFINITION	PURPOSE
Manipulatives	T	Providing tactile and kinesthetic experiences to engage students in the process of writing by physically maneuvering words, phrases, or sentences to reconstruct text in as many different ways as possible and to note how meaning changes with each rearrangement	To appeal to kinesthetic learners and help students visualize the form and function of various parts of speech, stylistic concerns, sentence structure, and so on
Mapping	S	Creating a graphic organizer that serves as a visual representation of the organizational plan for a written text	To generate ideas, concepts, or key words that provide a focus and/or establish organization during the prewriting, drafting, or revision process
Marking the Draft	S	Interacting with the draft version of a piece of writing by highlighting, underlining, color-coding, and annotating to indicate revision ideas.	To encourage focused, reflective thinking about revising drafts
Outlining	S	Using a system of numerals and letters in order to identify topics and supporting details and ensure an appropriate balance of ideas	To generate ideas, concepts, or key words that provide a focus and/or establish organization prior to writing an initial draft and/or during the revision process
Quickwrite	T	Writing for a short, specific amount of time about a designated topic related to a text	To generate multiple ideas in a quick fashion that could be turned into longer pieces of writing at a later time (May be considered as part of the drafting process)
RAFT	S	Generating and/or transforming a text by identifying and/or manipulating its component parts of *Role, Audience, Format,* and *Topic*	To consider the main elements of the writer's own work in order to generate a focus and purpose during the prewriting and drafting stages of the writing process
Rearranging	S	Selecting components of a text and moving them to another place within the text and/or modifying the order in which the author's ideas are presented	To refine and clarify the writer's thoughts during revision and/or drafting
Revisiting Prior Work	S	Looking through a collection of previously completed work to identify successes and challenges that may have been encountered with particular formats, conventions, style, word choice, and so on	To build on prior experience in preparation for a new piece of writing and/or to revise a previous piece of writing
Self-Editing/Peer Editing	S	Working with a partner to examine a text closely in order to identify areas that might need to be corrected for grammar, punctuation, spelling	To provide a systematic process for editing a written text to ensure correctness of identified components such as conventions of standard English
Sharing and Responding	S	Communicating with another person or a small group of peers who respond to a piece of writing as focused readers (not necessarily as evaluators)	To make suggestions for improvement to the work of others and/or to receive appropriate and relevant feedback on the writer's own work, used during the drafting and revision process
Sketching	S	Drawing or sketching ideas or ordering of ideas. Includes storyboarding, visualizing	To generate and/or clarify ideas by visualizing them. May be part of prewriting
Substituting	S	Replacing original words or phrases in a text with new words or phrases that achieve the desired effect	To refine and clarify the writer's thoughts during revision and/or drafting

STRATEGY		DEFINITION	PURPOSE
TWIST* *(The AP Vertical Teams Guide for English 167–174)*	S	Arriving at a thesis statement that incorporates the following literary elements: tone, word choice (diction), imagery, style and theme	To craft an interpretive thesis in response to a prompt about a passage
Visual/Auditory Prompts	T	Providing students with visual stimuli (e.g., a piece of art, film clip, visual media) or auditory stimuli (e.g., a piece of music, sound effects, radio broadcast, other auditory expressions) prior to writing	To encourage response to varied stimuli; to provide an opportunity for students of various learning styles to create a written text
Webbing	S	Developing a graphic organizer that consists of a series of circles connected with lines to indicate relationships among ideas	To generate ideas, concepts, or key words that provide a focus and/or establish organization prior to writing an initial draft and/or during the revision process
Writer's Checklist	T	Using a class-developed checklist (that could be written on a bookmark and/or displayed on the wall) to look for specific features of a text and check for accuracy	To focus the editing stage of the writing process on key areas so that the writer can correct common mistakes and include specific components

*Delineates AP strategy

SPEAKING AND LISTENING STRATEGIES

S T
STUDENT/TEACHER

STRATEGY		DEFINITION	PURPOSE
Choral Reading	T	Reading text lines aloud in student groups and/or individually to present an interpretation	To develop fluency; differentiate between the reading of statements and questions; practice phrasing, pacing, and reading dialogue; show how a character's emotions are captured through vocal stress and intonation
Debate	T	Engaging in an informal or formal argumentation of an issue	To provide students with an opportunity to collect and orally present evidence supporting the affirmative and negative arguments of a proposition or issue
Drama Games	T	Participating in creative dramatics (e.g., pantomime, tableau, role playing)	To engage students in the reading and presenting of text and to create meaning through a kinesthetic approach
Fishbowl (Inner/outer circles)	T	Discussing specific topics within groups; some students will form the inner circle and model appropriate discussion techniques while an outer circle of students listen, respond, and evaluate	To provide students with an opportunity to engage in a formal discussion and to experience roles both as participant and active listener; students also have the responsibility of supporting their opinions and responses using specific textual evidence
Notetaking	S	Creating a record of information while listening to a speaker	To facilitate active listening; to record and organize ideas that assist in processing information
Oral Interpretation	S	Reading a text orally while providing the necessary inflection and emphasis that demonstrate an understanding of the meaning of the text	To share with an audience the reader's personal insight into a text through voice, fluency, tone, and purpose

SPEAKING AND LISTENING STRATEGIES (Continued)

STRATEGY		DEFINITION	PURPOSE
Oral Reading	S	Reading aloud one's own text or the texts of others (e.g., echo reading, choral reading, paired readings)	To share one's own work or the work of others; build fluency and increase confidence in presenting to a group
Read Around	T	Practicing oral reading of a selected text and providing students with an opportunity to choose their favorite sentences and/or chunks of text to read to others	To inspire critical thinking and promote fluent and purposeful reading
Rehearsal	T	Encouraging multiple practices of a piece of text prior to a performance	To provide students with an opportunity to clarify the meaning of a text prior to a performance as they refine the use of dramatic conventions (e.g., gestures, vocal interpretations, facial expressions)
Role Playing	S	Assuming the role or persona of a character	To develop the voice, emotions, and mannerisms of a character to facilitate improved comprehension of a text
Socratic Seminar	T	Tying a focused discussion to an essential question, topic, or selected text in which students ask questions of each other; questions initiate a conversation that continues with a series of responses and additional questions	To help students formulate questions that address issues (in lieu of simply stating their opinions) to facilitate their own discussion and arrive at a new understanding; students also have the responsibility of supporting their opinions and responses using specific textual evidence

COLLABORATIVE STRATEGIES

S T
STUDENT/TEACHER

STRATEGY		DEFINITION	PURPOSE
Discussion Groups	S	Engaging in an interactive, small group discussion, often with an assigned role; to consider a topic, text, question, and so on	To gain new understanding or insight of a text from multiple perspectives
Jigsaw	T	By reading different texts or passages from a single text, students become "experts"; they share information from their reading with a specific group, and then return to their initial groups to share their new knowledge	To summarize and present information to others in a way that facilitates an understanding of a text (or multiple texts) without having each student read the text in its entirety
Literature Circles	T	Groups of students read the same text to participate in a mutual reading experience; based on the objective(s) of the lesson, students take on a variety of roles throughout the reading experience; texts may be selected based on individual preferences or on the demands of the text	To provide opportunities for students to interact with one another as they read, respond to, and interpret a common text
Think-Pair-Share	S T	Considering and thinking about a topic or question and then writing what has been learned; pairing with a peer or a small group to share ideas; sharing ideas and discussion with a larger group	To construct meaning about a topic or question; to test thinking in relation to the ideas of others; to prepare for a discussion with a larger group

SOAPSTone:

SOAPSTone	Analysis	Textual Support
Speaker: What does the reader know about the writer?		
Occasion: What are the circumstances surrounding this text?		
Audience: Who is the target audience?		
Purpose: Why did the author write this text?		
Subject: What is the topic?		
Tone: What is the author's tone, or attitude?		

TP-CASTT Analysis

Poem Title:

Author:

Title: Make a Prediction. What do you think the title means before you read the poem?

Paraphrase: Translate the poem in your own words. What is the poem about? Rephrase difficult sections word for word.

Connotation: Look beyond the literal meaning of key words and images to their associations.

Attitude: What is the speaker's attitude? What is the author's attitude? How does the author feel about the speaker, about other characters, about the subject?

Shifts: Where do the shifts in tone, setting, voice, etc., occur? Look for time and place, keywords, punctuation, stanza divisions, changes in length or rhyme, and sentence structure. What is the purpose of each shift? How do they contribute to effect and meaning?

Title: Reexamine the title. What do you think it means now in the context of the poem?

Theme: Think of the literal and metaphorical layers of the poem. Then determine the overall theme. The theme must be written in a complete sentence.

Glossary
Glosario

A

active-voice verbs: a verb form indicating that the subject performs the action
verbos en voz activa: forma verbal que indica que el sujeto realiza la acción

advertising techniques: specific methods used in print, graphics, or videos to persuade people to buy a product or use a service
técnicas publicitarias: métodos específicos usados en impresos, gráfica o videos para persuadir a las personas a comprar un producto o usar un servicio

alliteration: the repetition of initial consonant sounds in words that are close together
aliteración: repetición de sonidos consonánticos iniciales en palabras cercanas

allusion: a reference to a well-known person, event, or place from history, music, art, or another literary work
alusión: referencia a una persona, evento o lugar muy conocidos de la historia, música, arte u otra obra literaria

anaphora: the repetition of the same word or group of words at the beginnings of two or more clauses or lines
anáfora: repetición de la misma palabra o grupo de palabras al comienzo de una o más cláusulas o versos

anecdotal evidence: evidence based on personal accounts of incidents
evidencia anecdótica: evidencia basada en relatos personales de los hechos

annotated bibliography: a list of sources used in research along with comments about each source
bibliografía anotada: lista de fuentes utilizadas en la investigación, junto con comentarios acerca de cada fuente

antagonist: the character who opposes or struggles again the main character
antagonista: personaje que se opone o lucha contra el personaje principal

aphorism: a succinct statement expressing an opinion or general truth
aforismo: afirmación breve que expresa una opinión o verdad general

archetypes: universal symbols—images, characters, motifs, or patterns—that recur in myths, art and literature through the world
arquetipos: símbolos universales —imágenes, personajes, motivos o patrones— reiterativos en los mitos, el arte y la literatura alrededor del mundo

archival footage: film footage taken from another, previously recorded, source
cortometraje de archivo: fragmento de película tomada de otra fuente grabada previamente

argument: a form of writing that presents a particular opinion or idea and supports it with evidence
argumento: forma de redacción que presenta una opinión o idea particular y la apoya con evidencia

argumentation: the structure of an argument includes the *hook* (quotation, example, or idea that catches readers' attention), *claim* (the opinion or thesis statement), *support* (evidence in the form of facts, statistics, examples, anecdotes, or expert opinions), *concession* (the writer's admission that the other side of the argument has a valid point), *refutation* (a well-reasoned denial of an opponent's point, based on solid evidence), and *call to action* (an inspired request of readers)
argumentación: la estructura de una argumentación incluye el gancho (cita, ejemplo o idea que capta la atención del lector), afirmación (declaración de opinión o tesis), apoyo (evidencia en forma de hechos, estadísticas, ejemplos, anécdotas u opiniones de expertos), concesión (admisión por parte del escritor de que la otra parte del debate tiene un punto válido), refutación (negación bien razonada de una opinión del oponente, basada en evidencia sólida) y llamado a la acción (petición inspirada de lectores)

argument by analogy: a comparison of two similar situations, implying that the outcome of one will resemble the outcome of the other
argumento por analogía: comparación de dos situaciones semejantes, infiriendo que el resultado de será parecido al resultado de la otra

aside: a short speech spoken by an actor directly to the audience and unheard by other actors on stage
aparte: alocución breve dicha por un actor directamente al público y que no escuchan los demás actores que están en el escenario

assonance: the repetition of similar vowel sounds in accented syllables, followed by different consonant sounds, in words that are close together
asonancia: repetición de sonidos vocálicos similares en sílabas acentuadas, seguida de diferentes sonidos consonánticos, en palabras que están cercanas

audience: the intended readers, listeners, or viewers of specific types of written, spoken or visual texts
público: lectores objetivo, oyentes o espectadores de tipos específicos de textos escritos, hablados o visuales

audience analysis: determining the knowledge, beliefs, and needs of a target audience in order to reach them successfully
análisis del público: determinar los conocimientos, creencias y necesidades de una audiencia objetivo de modo de llegar a ella con éxito

author's purpose: the specific reason or reasons for the writing; what the author hopes to accomplish
propósito del autor: razón específica para escribir; lo que el autor espera lograr

B

balanced sentence: a sentence that presents ideas of equal weight in similar grammatical forms to emphasize the similarity or difference between the ideas
oración balanceada: oración que representa ideas de igual peso en formas gramaticales similares para enfatizar la semejanza o diferencia entre las ideas

bias: an inclination or mental leaning for or against something, which prevents impartial judgment
sesgo: inclinación o tendencia mental a favor o en contra de algo, lo que impide una opinión imparcial

blank verse: unrhymed verse
verso libre: verso que no tiene rima

blocking: in drama, how actors position themselves in relation to one another, the audience, and the objects on the stage
bloqueo: en drama, el modo en que los actores se sitúan entre sí, con el público y los objetos en el escenario

C

caricature: a visual or verbal representation in which characteristics or traits are exaggerated or distorted for emphasis
caricatura: representación visual o verbal en la que las características o rasgos se exageran o se distorsionan para dar énfasis

characterization: the methods a writer uses to develop characters
caracterización: métodos que usa un escritor para desarrollar personajes

characters: people, animals, or imaginary creatures that take part in the action of a story. A short story usually centers on a *main character*, but may also contain one or more *minor characters*, who are not as complex, but whose thoughts, words, or actions move the plot along. A character who is *dynamic* changes in response to the events of the narrative; a character who is *static* remains the same throughout the narrative. A *round* character is fully developed—he or she shows a variety of traits; a *flat* character is one-dimensional, usually showing only one trait.
personajes: personas, animales o criaturas imaginarias que participan en la acción de un cuento. Un cuento corto normalmente se centra en un *personaje principal*, pero puede también contener uno o más *personajes secundarios*, que no son tan complejos, pero cuyos pensamientos, palabras o acciones hacen avanzar la trama. Un personaje que es *dinámico* cambia según los eventos del relato; un personaje que es *estático* permanece igual a lo largo del relato. Un personaje *complejo* está completamente desarrollado: muestra una diversidad de rasgos; un personaje *simple* es unidimensional, mostrando normalmente sólo un rasgo.

chorus: in traditional or classic drama, a group of performers who speak as one and comment on the action of the play
coro: en el drama tradicional o clásico, grupo de actores que hablan al unísono y comentan la acción de la obra teatral

cinematic elements: the features of cinema—movies, film, video—that contribute to its form and structure: *angles* (the view from which the image is shot); *framing* (how a scene is structured); *lighting* (the type of lighting used to light a scene); and *mise en scène* (the composition, setting, or staging of an image, or a scene in a film); *sound* (the sound effects and music accompanying each scene)
elementos cinematográficos: las características del cine—películas, filmaciones, video—que contribuyen a darle forma y estructura: *angulación* (vista desde la cual se toma la imagen); *encuadre* (cómo se estructura una escena); *iluminación* (tipo de iluminación que se usa para una escena); y *montaje* (composición, ambiente o escenificación de una imagen o escena en una película); *sonido* (efectos sonoros y música que acompañan cada escena)

claim: a position statement (or thesis) that asserts an idea or makes an argument
afirmación: declaración de opinión (o tesis) que asevera una idea o establece un debate

cliché: an overused expression or idea
cliché: expresión o idea que se usa en exceso

climax: the point at which the action reaches its peak; the point of greatest interest or suspense in a story; the turning point at which the outcome of the conflict is decided
clímax: punto en el que la acción alcanza su punto culminante; punto de mayor interés en un cuento; punto de inflexión en el que se decide el resultado del conflicto

coherence: the quality of unity or logical connection among ideas; the clear and orderly presentation of ideas in a paragraph or essay
coherencia: calidad de unidad o relación lógica entre las ideas; presentación clara y ordenada de las ideas en un párrafo o ensayo

commentary: in an expository essay or paragraph, the explanation of the importance or relevance of supporting detail and the way the details support the larger analysis
comentario: ensayo o párrafo expositivo, explicación de la importancia o relevancia de los detalles de apoyo, y la manera en que los detalles apoyan el análisis principal

complex sentence: a sentence containing one independent clause and one or more subordinate clauses
oración compleja: oración que contiene una cláusula independiente y una o más cláusulas subordinadas

complications: the events in a plot that develop the conflict; the complications move the plot forward in its rising action
complicaciones: sucesos de una trama que desarrollan el conflicto; las complicaciones hacen avanzar la trama en su acción ascendente

compound sentence: a sentence containing two independent clauses
oración compuesta: oración que contiene dos cláusulas independientes

concession: an admission in an argument that the opposing side has valid points
concesión: admitir en un debate que el lado opositor tiene opiniones válidas

conflict: a struggle or problem in a story. An *internal conflict*

occurs when a character struggles between opposing needs or desires or emotions within his or her own mind. An *external conflict* occurs when a character struggles against an outside force. This force may be another character, a societal expectation, or something in the physical world.
conflicto: lucha o problema en un cuento. Un *conflicto interno* ocurre cuando un personaje lucha entre necesidades o deseos o emociones que se contraponen dentro de su mente. Un *conflicto externo* ocurre cuando un personaje lucha contra una fuerza externa. Esta fuerza puede ser otro personaje, una expectativa social o algo del mundo físico.

connotation: the associations and emotional overtones attached to a word beyond its literal definition or denotation. A connotation may be positive, negative, or neutral.
connotación: asociaciones y alusiones emocionales unidas a una palabra más allá de su definición literal o denotación. Una connotación puede ser positiva, negativa o neutra.

consonance: the repetition of final consonant sounds in stressed syllables with different vowel sounds
consonancia: repetición de sonidos consonánticos finales en sílabas acentuadas con diferentes sonidos vocálicos

context: the circumstances or conditions in which something takes place
contexto: circunstancias o condiciones en las que algo ocurre

conventions: standard practices and forms
convenciones: prácticas y formas usuales

couplet: two consecutive lines of verse with end rhyme; a couplet usually expresses a complete unit of thought
copla: dos líneas de versos consecutivos con rima final; una copla normalmente expresa una unidad de pensamiento completa

credibility: the quality of being trusted or believed
credibilidad: calidad de ser confiable o creíble

critical lens: a particular identifiable perspective as in Reader Response Criticism, Cultural Criticism, etc., through which a text can be analyzed and interpreted
ojo crítico: punto de vista particular identificable como por ejemplo Teoría de la recepción, Crítica sociocultural, etc., por medio del que se puede analizar e interpretar un texto

cultural conflict: a struggle that occurs when people with different cultural expectations or attitudes interact
conflicto cultural: lucha que ocurre cuando interactúan personas con diferentes expectativas o actitudes culturales

culture: the shared set of arts, ideas, skills, institutions, customs, attitude, values and achievements that characterize a group of people, and that are passed on or taught to succeeding generations
cultura: conjunto de artes, ideas, destrezas, instituciones, costumbres, actitud, valores y logros compartidos que caracterizan a un grupo de personas, y que se transfieren o enseñan a las generaciones siguientes

cumulative (or loose) sentence: a sentence in which the main clause comes first, followed by subordinate structures or clauses
oración acumulativa (o frases sueltas): oración cuya cláusula principal viene primero, seguida de estructuras o cláusulas subordinadas

D

deductive reasoning: a process of using general information from which to draw a specific conclusion
razonamiento deductivo: proceso en que se usa información general para sacar una conclusión específica

denotation: the exact literal meaning of a word
denotación: significado literal exacto de una palabra

detail: a specific fact, observation, or incident; any of the small pieces or parts that make up something else
detalle: hecho, observación o incidente específico; cualquiera de las pequeñas piezas o partes que constituyen otra cosa

dialect: the distinctive language, including the sounds, spelling, grammar, and diction, of a specific group or class of people
dialecto: lenguaje distintivo, incluyendo sonidos, ortografía, gramática y dicción, de un grupo o clase específico de personas

dialogue: the words spoken by characters in a narrative or film
diálogo: palabras que dicen los personajes en un relato o película

diction: the writer's choice of words; a stylistic element that helps convey voice and tone
dicción: selección de palabras por parte del escritor; elemento estilístico que ayuda a transmitir voz y tono

diegetic sound: actual noises associated with the shooting of a scene, such as voices and background sounds
sonido diegético: sonidos reales asociados con la filmación de una escena, como por ejemplo voces y sonidos de fondo

discourse: the language or speech used in a particular context or subject
discurso: lenguaje o habla usada en un contexto o tema en particular

documentary or nonfiction film: a genre of filmmaking that provides a visual record of factual events, using photographs, video footage, and interviews
documental o película de no-ficción: género cinematográfico que realiza un registro visual de sucesos basados en hechos por medio del uso de fotografías, registro en videos y entrevistas

drama: a play written for stage, radio, film, or television, usually about a serious topic or situation
drama: obra teatral escrita para representar en un escenario, radio, cine o televisión, normalmente sobre un tema o situación seria

E

editorial: an article in a newspaper or magazine expressing the opinion of its editor or publisher
editorial: artículo de periódico o revista, que expresa la opinión de su editor

effect: the result or influence of using a specific literary or cinematic device
efecto: resultado o influencia de usar un recurso literario o cinematográfico específico

empirical evidence: evidence based on experiences and direct observation through research
evidencia empírica: evidencia basada en experiencias y en la observación directa por medio de la investigación

epigram: a short witty saying
epigrama: dicho corto e ingenioso

ethos: (ethical appeal) a rhetorical appeal that focuses on ethics, or the character or qualifications of the speaker
ethos: (recurso ético) recurso retórico centrado en la ética o en el carácter o capacidades del orador

evidence: the information that supports or proves an idea or claim; forms of evidence include facts, statistics (numerical facts), expert opinions, examples, and anecdotes; *see also*, anecdotal, empirical, and logical evidence
evidencia: información que apoya o prueba una idea o afirmación; formas de evidencia incluyen hechos, estadística (datos numéricos), opiniones de expertos, ejemplos y anécdotas; *ver también* evidencia anecdótica, empírica y lógica

exaggeration: representing something as larger, better, or worse than it really is
exageración: representar algo como más grande, mejor o peor que lo que realmente es

explicit theme: a theme that is clearly stated by the writer
tema explícito: tema que está claramente establecido por el escritor

exposition: events that give a reader background information needed to understand a story. During exposition, characters are introduced, the setting is described, and the conflict begins to unfold.
exposición: sucesos que dan al lector los antecedentes necesarios para comprender un cuento. Durante la exposición, se presentan los personajes, se describe el ambiente y se comienza a revelar el conflicto.

extended metaphor: a metaphor extended over several lines or throughout an entire poem
metáfora extendida: metáfora que se extiende por varios versos o a través de un poema completo

F

falling action: the events in a play, story, or novel that follow the climax, or moment of greatest suspense, and lead to the resolution
acción descendente: sucesos de una obra teatral, cuento o novela posteriores al clímax, o momento de mayor suspenso, y que conllevan a la resolución

fallacy: a false or misleading argument
falacia: argumento falso o engañoso

figurative language: imaginative language not meant to be taken literally; figurative language uses figures of speech
lenguaje figurativo: lenguaje imaginativo que no pretende ser tomado literalmente; el lenguaje figurativo usa figuras literarias

flashback: an interruption in the sequence of events to relate events that occurred in the past
flashback: interrupción en la secuencia de los sucesos para relatar sucesos ocurridos en el pasado

fixed form: a form of poetry in which the length and pattern are determined by established usage of tradition, such as a sonnet
forma fija: forma de poesía en la que la longitud y el patrón están determinados por el uso de la tradición, como un soneto

foil: a character whose actions or thoughts are juxtaposed against those of a major character in order to highlight key attributes of the major character
antagonista: personaje cuyas acciones o pensamientos se yuxtaponen a los de un personaje principal con el fin de destacar atributos clave del personaje principal

folk tale: a story without a known author that has been preserved through oral retellings
cuento folclórico: cuento sin autor conocido que se ha conservado por medio de relatos orales

footage: literally, a length of film; the expression is still used to refer to digital video clips
metraje: literalmente, la longitud de una película; la expresión aún se usa para referirse a video clips digitales

foreshadowing: the use of hints or clues in a narrative to suggest future action
presagio: uso de claves o pistas en un relato para sugerir una acción futura

free verse: poetry without a fixed pattern of meter and rhyme
verso libre: poesía que no sigue ningún patrón, ritmo o rima regular

G

genre: a kind or style of literature or art, each with its own specific characteristics. For example, poetry, short story, and novel are literary genres. Painting and sculpture are artistic genres.
género: tipo o estilo de literatura o arte, cada uno con sus propias características específicas. Por ejemplo, la poesía, el cuento corto y la novela son géneros literarios. La pintura y la escultura son géneros artísticos.

genre conventions: the essential features and format that characterize a specific genre
convenciones genéricas: características básicas y el formato que caracterizan un género específico

graphics: images or text used to provide information on screen
gráfica: imágenes o texto que se usa para dar información en pantalla

graphic novel: a book-length narrative, or story, in the form of a comic strip rather than words
novela gráfica: narrativa o cuento del largo de un libro, en forma de tira cómica más que palabras

H

hamartia: a tragic hero's fatal flaw; an ingrained character trait that causes a hero to make decisions that ultimately lead to his or her death or downfall
hamartia: error fatal de un héroe trágico; característica propia de un personaje que causa que un héroe tome decisiones que finalmente llevan a su muerte o caída

hero: the main character or protagonist of a play, with whom audiences become emotionally invested
héroe: personaje principal o protagonista de una obra teatral, con el que el público se involucra emocionalmente

hook: an interesting quotation, anecdote, or example at the beginning of a piece of writing that grabs readers' attention
gancho: cita, anécdota o ejemplo interesante al comienzo de un escrito, que capta la atención del lector

humor: the quality of being amusing
humor: calidad de ser divertido

hyperbole: exaggeration used to suggest strong emotion or create a comic effect
hipérbole: exageración que se usa para sugerir una emoción fuerte o crear un efecto cómico

I

iamb: a metrical foot that consists of an unstressed syllable followed by a stressed syllable
yambo: pie métrico que consta de una sílaba átona seguida de una sílaba acentuada

iambic pentameter: a rhythmic pattern of five feet (or units) of one unstressed syllable followed by a stressed syllable
pentámetro yámbico: patrón rítmico de cinco pies (o unidades) de una sílaba átona seguida de una sílaba acentuada

image: a word or phrase that appeals to one of more of the five senses and creates a picture
imagen: palabra o frase que apela a uno o más de los cinco sentido y crea un cuadro

imagery: the verbal expression of sensory experience; descriptive or figurative language used to create word pictures; imagery is created by details that appeal to one or more of the five senses
imaginería: lenguaje descriptivo o figurativo utilizado para crear imágenes verbales; la imaginería es creada por detalles que apelan a uno o más de los cinco sentidos

implied theme: a theme that is understood through the writer's diction, language construction, and use of literary devices
tema implícito: tema que se entiende a través de la dicción del escritor, construcción lingüística y uso de recursos literarios

inductive reasoning: a process of looking at individual facts to draw a general conclusion
razonamiento inductivo: proceso de observación de hechos individuales para sacar una conclusión general

interior monologue: a literary device in which a character's internal emotions and thoughts are presented
monólogo interior: recurso literario en el que se presentan las emociones internas y pensamientos de un personaje

irony: a literary device that exploits readers' expectations; irony occurs when what is expected turns out to be quite different from what actually happens. *Dramatic irony* is a form of irony in which the reader or audience knows more about the circumstances or future events in a story than the characters within it; *verbal irony* occurs when a speaker or narrator says one thing while meaning the opposite; *situational irony* occurs when an event contradicts the expectations of the characters or the reader.
ironía: recurso literario que explota las expectativas de los lectores; la ironía ocurre cuando lo que se espera resulta ser bastante diferente de lo que realmente ocurre. La *ironía dramática* es una forma de ironía en la que el lector o la audiencia saben más acerca de las circunstancias o sucesos futuros de un cuento que los personajes del mismo; la *ironía verbal* ocurre cuando un orador o narrador dice una cosa queriendo decir lo contrario; la *ironía situacional* ocurre cuando un suceso contradice las expectativas de los personajes o del lector.

J

justice: the quality of being reasonable and fair in the administration of the law; the ideal of rightness or fairness
justicia: calidad de ser razonable e imparcial en la administración de la ley; ideal de rectitud o equidad

juxtaposition: the arrangement of two or more things for the purpose of comparison
yuxtaposición: ordenamiento de dos o más cosas con el objeto de compararlas

L

literary theory: attempts to establish principles for interpreting and evaluating literary texts
teoría literaria: intento de establecer principios para interpretar y evaluar textos literarios

logical evidence: evidence based on facts and a clear rationale
evidencia lógica: evidencia basada en hechos y una clara fundamentación

logos: (logical appeal) a rhetorical appeal that uses logic to appeal to the sense of reason
logos: (apelación lógica) apelación retórica que usa la lógica para apelar al sentido de la razón

M

metacognition: the ability to know and be aware of one's own thought processes; self-reflection
metacognición: capacidad de conocer y estar consciente de los propios procesos del pensamiento; introspección

metaphor: a comparison between two unlike things in which one thing is spoken of as if it were another; for example, the moon was a crisp white cracker
metáfora: comparación entre dos cosas diferentes en la que se habla de una cosa como si fuera otra; por ejemplo, la luna era una galletita blanca crujiente

meter: a pattern of stressed and unstressed syllables in poetry
métrica: patrón de sílabas acentuadas y átonas en poesía

monologue: a dramatic speech delivered by a single character in a play
monólogo: discurso dramático que hace un solo personaje en una obra teatral

montage: a composite picture that is created by bringing together a number of images and arranging them to create a connected whole

montaje: cuadro compuesto que se crea al reunir un número de imágenes y que al organizarlas se crea un todo relacionado

mood: the atmosphere or general feeling in a literary work
carácter: atmósfera o sentimiento general en una obra literaria

motif: a recurrent image, symbol, theme, character type, subject, or narrative detail that becomes a unifying element in an artistic work.
motivo: imagen, símbolo, tema, tipo de personaje, tema o detalle narrativo recurrente que se convierte en un elemento unificador en una obra artística.

myth: a traditional story that explains the actions of gods or heroes or the origins of the elements of nature
mito: cuento tradicional que explica las acciones de dioses o héroes, o los orígenes de los elementos de la naturaleza

N

narration: the act of telling a story
narración: acto de contar un cuento

non-diegetic sound: voice-overs and commentary, sounds that do not come from the action on screen.
sonido no diegético: voces y comentarios superpuestos, sonidos que no provienen de la acción en pantalla.

O

objective: based on factual information
objetivo: basado en información de hechos

objectivity: the representation of facts or ideas without injecting personal feelings or biases
objetividad: representación de los hechos o ideas sin agregar sentimientos o prejuicios personales

ode: a lyric poem expressing feelings or thoughts of a speaker, often celebrating a person, event, or a thing
oda: poema lírico que expresa sentimientos o pensamientos de un orador, que frecuentemente celebra a una persona, suceso o cosa

onomatopoeia: words whose sound suggest their meaning
onomatopeya: palabras cuyo sonido sugiere su significado

oral tradition: the passing down of stories, tales, proverbs, and other culturally important stories and ideas through oral retellings
tradición oral: traspaso de historias, cuentos, proverbios y otras historias de importancia cultural por medio de relatos orales

oxymoron: words that appear to contradict each other; e.g., cold fire
oxímoron: palabras que parecen contradecirse mutuamente; por ejemplo, fuego frío

P

parallel structure (parallelism): refers to a grammatical or structural similarity between sentences or parts of a sentence, so that elements of equal importance are equally developed and similarly phrased for emphasis
estructura paralela (paralelismo): se refiere a una similitud gramatical o estructural entre oraciones o partes de una oración, de modo que los elementos de igual importancia se desarrollen por igual y se expresen de manera similar para dar énfasis

paraphrase: to briefly restate ideas from another source in one's own words
parafrasear: volver a presentar las ideas de otra fuente en nuestras propias palabras

parody: a literary or artistic work that imitates the characteristic style of an author or a work for comic effect or ridicule
parodia: obra literaria o artística que imita el estilo característico de un autor o una obra para dar un efecto cómico o ridículo

passive-voice verbs: verb form in which the subject receives the action; the passive voice consists of a form of the verb be plus a past participle of the verb
verbos en voz pasiva: forma verbal en la que el sujeto recibe la acción; la voz pasiva se forma con el verbo ser más el participio pasado de un verbo

pathos: (emotional appeal) a rhetorical appeal to readers' or listeners' senses or emotions
pathos: (apelación emocional) apelación retórica a los sentidos o emociones de los lectores u oyentes

periodic sentence: a sentence that makes sense only when the end of the sentence is reached; that is, when the main clause comes last
oración periódica: oración que tiene sentido sólo cuando se llega al final de la oración; es decir, cuando la cláusula principal viene al final

persona: the voice assumed by a writer to express ideas or beliefs that may not be his or her own
personaje: voz que asume un escritor para expresar ideas o creencias que pueden no ser las propias

personification: a figure of speech that gives human qualities to an animal, object, or idea
personificación: figura literaria que da características humanas a un animal, objeto o idea

persuasive argument: an argument that convinces readers to accept or believe a writer's perspective on a topic
argumento persuasivo: argumento que convence a los lectores a aceptar o creer en la perspectiva de un escritor acerca de un tema

perspective: a way of looking at the world or a mental concept about things or events, one that judges relationships within or among things or events
perspectiva: manera de visualizar el mundo o concepto mental de las cosas o sucesos, que juzga las relaciones dentro o entre cosas o sucesos

photo essay: a collection of photographic images that reveal the author's perspective on the subject
ensayo fotográfico: recolección de imágenes fotográficas que revelan la perspectiva del autor acerca del tema

plagiarism: the unattributed use of another writer's words or ideas
plagio: usar como propias las palabras o ideas de otro escritor

plot: the sequence of related events that make up a story or novel
trama: secuencia de sucesos relacionados que conforman un cuento o novela

poetic structure: the organization of words, lines, and images as well as ideas
estructura poética: organización de las palabras, versos e imágenes, así como también de las ideas

point of view: the perspective from which a narrative is told; i.e., first person, third person limited, third person omniscient
punto de vista: perspectiva desde la cual se cuenta un relato; es decir, primera persona, tercera persona limitada, tercera persona omnisciente

precept: a rule, instruction, or principle that guides somebody's actions and/or moral behavior
precepto: regla, instrucción o principio que guía las acciones y/o conducta moral de alguien

primary footage: film footage shot by the filmmaker for the text at hand
metraje principal: filmación hecha por el cineasta para el texto que tiene a mano

primary source: an original document containing firsthand information about a subject
fuente primaria: documento original que contiene información de primera mano acerca de un tema

prologue: the introduction or preface to a literary work
prólogo: introducción o prefacio de una obra literaria

prose: ordinary written or spoken language using sentences and paragraphs, without deliberate or regular meter or rhyme; not poetry or song
prosa: forma común del lenguaje escrito o hablado, usando oraciones y párrafos, sin métrica o rima deliberada o regular; ni poesía ni canción

protagonist: the central character in a work of literature, the one who is involved in the main conflict in the plot
protagonista: personaje central de una obra literaria, el que participa en el conflicto principal de la trama

Q

quatrain: a four-line stanza in a poem
cuarteta: en un poema, estrofa de cuatro versos

R

reasoning: the thinking or logic used to make a claim in an argument
razonamiento: pensamiento o lógica que se usa para hacer una afirmación en un argumento

refrain: a regularly repeated line or group of lines in a poem or song, usually at the end of a stanza
estribillo: verso o grupo de versos que se repiten con regularidad en un poema o canción, normalmente al final de una estrofa

refutation: the reasoning used to disprove an opposing point
refutación: razonamiento que se usa para rechazar una opinión contraria

reliability: the extent to which a source provides good quality and trustworthy information
confiabilidad: grado en el que una fuente da información confiable y de buena calidad

repetition: the use of any element of language—a sound, a word, a phrase, a line, or a stanza—more than once
repetición: uso de cualquier elemento del lenguaje—un sonido, una palabra, una frase, un verso o una estrofa—más de una vez

resolution (denouement): the end of a play, story, or novel in which the main conflict is finally resolved
resolución (desenlace): final de una obra teatral, cuento o novela, en el que el conflicto principal finalmente se resuelve

résumé: a document that outlines a person's skills, education, and work history
currículum vitae: documento que resume las destrezas, educación y experiencia laboral de una persona

rhetoric: the art of using words to persuade in writing or speaking
retórica: arte de usar las palabras para persuadir por escrito o de manera hablada

rhetorical appeals: the use of emotional, ethical, and logical arguments to persuade in writing or speaking
recursos retóricos: uso de argumentos emocionales, éticos y lógicos para persuadir por escrito o de manera hablada

rhetorical context: the subject, purpose, audience, occasion, or situation in which writing occurs
contexto retórico: sujeto, propósito, audiencia, ocasión o situación en que ocurre el escrito

rhetorical devices: specific techniques used in writing or speaking to create a literary effect or enhance effectiveness
dispositivos retóricos: técnicas específicas que se usan al escribir o al hablar para crear un efecto literario o mejorar la efectividad

rhetorical question: a question that is asked for effect or one for which the answer is obvious
pregunta retórica: pregunta hecha para producir un efecto o cuya respuesta es obvia

rhyme: the repetition of sounds at the ends of words
rima: repetición de sonidos al final de las palabras

rhyme scheme: a consistent pattern of rhyme throughout a poem
esquema de la rima: patrón consistente de una rima a lo largo de un poema

rhythm: the pattern of stressed and unstressed syllables in spoken or written language, especially in poetry
ritmo: patrón de sílabas acentuadas y no acentuadas en lenguaje hablado o escrito, especialmente en poesía

rising action: the movement of a plot toward a climax or moment of greatest excitement; the rising action is fueled by the characters' responses to the conflict
acción ascendente: movimiento de una trama hacia el clímax o momento de mayor emoción; la acción ascendente es impulsada por las reacciones de los personajes ante el conflicto

S

satire: a manner of writing that mixes a critical attitude with wit and humor in an effort to improve mankind and human institutions
sátira: manera de escribir que mezcla una actitud crítica con ingenio y humor en un esfuerzo por mejorar a la humanidad y las instituciones humanas

scenario: an outline, a brief account, a script, or a synopsis of a proposed series of events
escenario: bosquejo, relato breve, libreto o sinopsis de una serie de sucesos propuestos

secondary source: discussion about or commentary on a primary source; the key feature of a secondary source is that it offers an interpretation of information gathered from primary sources
fuente secundaria: discusión o comentario acerca de una fuente primaria; la característica clave de una fuente secundaria es que ofrece una interpretación de la información recopilada en las fuentes primarias

sensory details: details that appeal to or evoke one or more of the five senses--sight, sound, smell, taste, touch
detalles sensoriales: detalles que apelan o evocan uno o más de los cinco sentidos: vista, oído, gusto, olfato, tacto

sensory images: images that appeal to the reader's senses—sight, sound, smell, taste, touch
imágenes sensoriales: imágenes que apelan a los sentidos del lector: vista, oído, olfato, gusto, tacto

setting: the time and place in which a story happens
ambiente: tiempo y lugar en el que ocurre un relato

simile: a comparison of two or more unlike things using the words *like or as*; for example, the moon was as white as milk
símil: comparación entre dos o más cosas diferentes usando las palabras *como o tan*; por ejemplo, la luna estaba tan blanca como la leche

slanters: rhetorical devices used to present the subject in a biased way.
soslayo: recursos retóricos para presentar el tema de modo sesgado.

slogan: a short, catchy phrase used for advertising by a business, club, or political party
eslogan: frase corta y tendenciosa que usa como publicidad para un negocio, club o partido político

social commentary: an expression of an opinion with the goal of promoting change by appealing to a sense of justice
comentario social: expresión de una opinión con el objeto de promover el cambio al apelar a un sentido de justicia

soliloquy: a long speech delivered by an actor alone on the stage
soliloquio: discurso largo realizado por un actor sobre el escenario

sonnet: a fourteen-line lyric poem, usually written in iambic pentameter and following a strict pattern of rhyme
soneto: poema lírico de catorce versos, normalmente escrito en un pentámetro yámbico y que sigue un patrón de rima estricto

speaker: the imaginary voice or persona of the writer or author
orador: voz o persona imaginaria del escritor o autor

stakeholder: a person motivated or affected by a course of action
participante: persona motivada o afectada por el curso de una acción

stanza: a group of lines, usually similar in length and pattern, that form a unit within a poem
estrofa: grupo de versos, normalmente similares en longitud y patrón, que forman una unidad dentro de un poema

stereotype: an oversimplified, generalized conception, opinion, and/or image about particular groups of people.
estereotipo: concepto generalizado, opinión y/o imagen demasiado simplificada acerca de grupos específicos de personas.

structure: the way a literary work is organized; the arrangement of the parts in a literary work
estructura: manera en que la obra literaria está organizada; disposición de las partes en una obra literaria

style: the distinctive way a writer uses language, characterized by elements of diction, syntax, imagery, etc.
estilo: manera distintiva en que un escritor usa el lenguaje, caracterizada por elementos de dicción, sintaxis, lenguaje figurado, etc.

subculture: a smaller subsection of a culture; for example, within the culture of a high school may be many subcultures
subcultura: subsección más pequeña de una cultura; por ejemplo, dentro de la cultura de una escuela secundaria puede haber muchas subculturas

subjectivity: based on one's personal point of view, opinion, or values
subjetividad: en base en nuestro punto de vista, opinión o valores personales

subtext: the underlying or implicit meaning in dialogue or the implied relationship between characters in a book, movie, play or film. The subtext of a work is not explicitly stated.
subtexto: significado subyacente o implícito en el diálogo o la relación implícita entre los personajes de un libro, película, u obra teatral. El subtexto de una obra no se establece de manera explícita.

survey: a method of collecting data from a group of people; it can be written, such as a print or online questionnaire, or oral, such as an in-person interview
encuesta: método para recolectar datos de un grupo de personas; puede ser escrita, como un impreso o cuestionario en línea, u oral, como en una entrevista personal

symbol: anything (object, animal, event, person, or place) that represents itself but also stands for something else on a figurative level
símbolo: cualquier cosa (objeto, animal, evento, persona o lugar) que se representa a sí misma, pero también representa otra cosa a nivel figurativo

symbolic: serving as a symbol; involving the use of symbols or symbolism

simbólico: que sirve como símbolo; que implica el uso de símbolos o simbolismo

syntax: the arrangement of words and the order of grammatical elements in a sentence; the way in which words are put together to make meaningful elements, such as phrases, clauses, and sentences
sintaxis: disposición de las palabras y orden de los elementos gramaticales en una oración; manera en que las palabras se juntan para formar elementos significativos, como frases, cláusulas y oraciones

synthesis: the act of combining ideas from different sources to create, express, or support a new idea
síntesis: acto de combinar ideas de diferentes fuentes para crear, expresar o apoyar una nueva idea

T

target audience: the intended group for which a work is designed to appeal or reach
público objetivo: grupo al que se pretende apelar o llegar con una obra

thematic statement: an interpretive statement articulating the central meaning or message of a text
oración temática: afirmación interpretativa que articula el significado o mensaje central de un texto

theatrical elements: elements employed by dramatists and directors to tell a story on stage. Elements include *costumes* (the clothing worn by actors to express their characters), *makeup* (cosmetics used to change actors' appearances and express their characters), *props* (objects used to help set the scene, advance a plot and make a story realistic), *set* (the place where the action takes place, as suggested by objects, such as furniture, placed on a stage), *acting choices* (gestures, movements, staging, and vocal techniques actors use to convey their characters and tell a story).
elementos teatrales: elementos que utilizan los dramaturgos y directores para contar una historia en el escenario. Los elementos incluyen *vestuario* (ropa que usan los actores para expresar sus personajes), *maquillaje* (cosméticos que se usan para cambiar la apariencia de los actores y expresar sus personajes), *elementos* (objetos que se usan para ayudar a montar la escena, avanzar la trama y crear una historia realista), *plató* (lugar donde tiene lugar la acción, según lo sugieren los objetos, como muebles, colocados sobre un escenario), *opciones de actuación* (gestos, movimientos, representación y técnicas vocales que se usan para transmitir sus personajes y narrar una historia).

theme: a writer's central idea or main message about life; *see also*, explicit theme, implied theme
tema: idea central o mensaje principal acerca de la vida de un escritor; *véase también*, tema explícito, tema implícito

thesis: the main idea or point of an essay or article; in an argumentative essay the thesis is the writer's position on an issue
tesis: idea o punto principal de un ensayo o artículo; en un ensayo argumentativo, la tesis es la opinión del autor acerca de un tema

topic sentence: a sentence that states the main idea of a paragraph; in an essay, it also makes a point that supports the thesis statement
oración principal: oración que establece la idea principal de un párrafo; en un ensayo, también establece una proposición que apoya el enunciado de la tesis

tone: a writer's or speaker's attitude toward a subject
tono: actitud de un escritor u orador acerca de un tema

tragedy: a dramatic play that tells the story of a character, usually of a noble birth, who meets an untimely and unhappy death or downfall, often because of a specific character flaw or twist of fate
tragedia: obra teatral dramática que cuenta la historia de un personaje, normalmente de origen noble, que encuentra una muerte o caída imprevista o infeliz, con frecuencia debido a un defecto específico del personaje o una vuelta del destino

tragic hero: an archetypal hero based on the Greek concept of tragedy; the tragic hero has a flaw that makes him vulnerable to downfall or death
héroe trágico: héroe arquetípico basado en el concepto griego de la tragedia; el héroe trágico tiene un defecto que lo hace vulnerable a la caída o a la muerte

U

understatement: the representation of something as smaller or less significant than it really is; the opposite of exaggeration or hyperbole
subestimación: representación de algo como más pequeño o menos importante de lo que realmente es; lo opuesto a la exageración o hipérbole

V

valid: believable or truthful
válido: creíble o verídico

validity: the quality of truth or accuracy in a source
validez: calidad de verdad o precisión en una fuente

vignette: a picture or visual or a brief descriptive literary piece
viñeta: ilustración o representación visual o pieza literaria descriptiva breve

vocal delivery: the way words are expressed on stage, through volume, pitch, rate or speed of speech, pauses, pronunciation, and articulation
presentación vocal: manera en que se expresan las palabras en el escenario, por medio del volumen, tono, rapidez o velocidad del discurso, pausas, pronunciación y articulación

voice: the way a writer or speaker uses words and tone to express ideas as well as his or her personas
voz: manera en que el escritor u orador usa las palabras y el tono para expresar ideas, así como también su personaje

Index of Skills

Literary Skills

Reading Skills

Writing Skills

Media Skills

Listening and Speaking Skills

Language Skills

Vocabulary Skills

Index of Authors and Titles

Text Credits:

"My Name" from *The House on Mango Street*. Copyright © 1984 by Sandra Cisneros. Published by Vintage Books, a division of Random House, Inc., and in hardcover by Alfred A. Knopf in 1994. By permission of Susan Bergholz Literary Services, New York, and Lamy, NM. All rights reserved.

"Why Couldn't I Have Been Named Ashley" by Immaculeta Achilike. Used by permission.

"Eleven" from *Woman Hollering Creek*. Copyright © 1991 by Sandra Cisneros. Published by Vintage Books, a division of Random House, Inc., New York and originally in hardcover by Random House, Inc. By permission of Susan Bergholz Literary Services, New York, and Lamy, NM. All rights reserved.

"Oranges" from *New and Selected Poems* by Gary Soto. Copyright © 1995 by Gary Soto. Used with permission of Chronicle Books LLC, San Francisco. Visit ChronicleBooks.com

"Spotlight" from *Speak* by Laurie Halse Anderson. Copyright © 1999 by Laurie Halse Anderson. Reprinted by permission of Farrar, Straus and Giroux, LLC.

"Cut" by Bob Green from *Cheeseburgers: The Best of Bob Greene* by Bob Greene, G. K. Hall, 2005. Copyright by Bob Greene. Reproduced by permission of SLL/Sterling Lord Literistic, Inc.

From *Always Running—La Vida Loca, Gang Days in L.A.* by Luis J. Rodriguez. (Curbstone Press, 1993) Reprinted with permission of Curbstone Press. Distributed by Consortium.

"'Race' Politics" from *Poems Across The Pavement* by Luis J. Rodriguez. Copyright © 1998 by Luis J. Rodriguez. Published by Tia Chucha Press. By permission of Susan Bergholz Literary Services, New York, NY and Lamy, NJ. All rights reserved.

From "The Looking Glass Shame" from *Silent Dancing* by Judith Ortiz Cofer. Copyright © 1990 Arte Público Press - University of Houston. Reprinted with permission from the publisher.

"Bethany only looking ahead" by Jan TenBruggencate from *The Honolulu Advertiser*, November 21, 2003. Copyright 2003 The Honolulu Advertiser. Used by permission.

"As If! Marketing to Older Teens" by Judith Rosen from *Publishers Weekly*, July 18, 2005. Used with permission of Publishers Weekly. Copyright © 2009. All rights reserved.

"The Stolen Party" by Liliana Heker, © 1982, which appeared in *Other Fires: Short Fiction* by Latin American Women, edited and translated by Alberto Manguel, © 1985. Reprinted by permission of Westwood Creative Artists Ltd.

"Marigolds" by Eugenia Collier. Originally published in *Negro Digest*, November 1969. Reappeared in *Breeder and Other Stories* by Eugenia Collier, Black Classic Press, 1994. Used by permission of the author.

"Hollywood Outsider Tim Burton," March 5, 2006, CBS News. Reproduced by permission of CBS News Archives.

From *Charlie and the Chocolate Factory* by Roald Dahl, copyright © 1964, renewed 1992 by Roald Dahl Nominee Limited. Used by permission of Alfred A. Knopf, an imprint of Random House Children's Books, a division of Random House, Inc.

"Poetry" from *Selected Poems by Pablo Neruda*, translated by Alastair Reid, edited by Nathaniel Tarn and published by Jonathan Cape. Reprinted by permission of The Random House Group Ltd.

From *Poemcrazy* by Susan G. Woodridge, copyright © 1996 Susan G. Woodridge. Used by permission of Crown Publishers, a division of Random House, Inc.

"Nikki Rosa" from *Black Feeling, Black Talk, Black Judgment* by Nikki Giovanni. Copyright © 1968, 1970 by Nikki Giovanni. Reproduced by permission of HarperCollins Publishers.

"We Real Cool" by Gwendolyn Brooks. Reprinted by consent of Brooks Permissions.

"Fast Break" from *Wild Gratitude* by Edward Hirsch, copyright © 1985 by Edward Hirsch. Used by permission of Alfred A. Knopf, a division of Random House, Inc.

"Identity" by Julio Noboa Polanco. Used by permission of the author.

"Ego Tripping" from *The Selected Poems of Nikki Giovanni* by Nikki Giovanni. Compilation copyright © 1996 by Nikki Giovanni. Reproduced by permission of HarperCollins Publishers.

"Hanging Fire" from *The Collected Poems of Audre Lorde* by Audre Lorde. Copyright © 1978 by Audre Lorde. Used by permission of W. W. Norton & Company, Inc.

"Ode to My Socks" from *Full Woman, Fleshly Apple, Hot Moon: Selected Poetry of Pablo Neruda* by Pablo Neruda, translated by Stephen Mitchell. Translation copyright © 1997 by Stephen Mitchell. Reproduced by permission of HarperCollins Publishers.

From *My Wicked Wicked Ways*. Copyright © 1987 by Sandra Cisneros. Published by Third Woman Press and in hardcover by Alfred A. Knopf. By permission of Susan Bergholz Literary Services, New York, and Lamy, NM. All rights reserved.

"In Response to Executive Order 9066" by Dwight Okita. Used by permission.

"Young" by Anne Sexton, from *All My Pretty Ones*. Copyright © 1962 by Anne Sexton. Reproduced by permission of SLL/ Sterling Lord Literistic, Inc.

"Combing" by Gladys Cardiff, from *Puget Soundings*, March 1971. Used by permission of Gladys Cardiff.

"Harlem (2) ["What happens to a dream deferred..."]" from *The Collected Poems of Langston Hughes* by Langston Hughes, edited by Arnold Rampersad with David Roessel, Associate Editor, copyright © 1994 by the Estate of Langston Hughes. Used by permission of Alfred A. Knopf, a division of Random House, Inc.

"Scars" from *Selected Poems by Daniel Halpern*, copyright © 1994 by Daniel Halpern. Used by permission of Alfred A. Knopf, a division of Random House, Inc.

"American Hero," copyright © 1992 Essex Hemphill from *Ceremonies*, reprinted by permission of The Frances Goldin Literary Agency.

"The Beep Beep Poem" form *Cotton Candy on a Rainy Day* by Nikki Giovanni. Copyright © 1978 by Nikki Giovanni. Reproduced by permission of HarperCollins Publishers.

"kidnap poem" from *The Selected Poems of Nikki Giovanni* by Nikki Giovanni. Compilation copyright © 1996 by Nikki Giovanni. Reproduced by permission of HarperCollins Publishers.

"Jim Crow: Shorthand for Separation" by Rick Edmonds. Reproduced from Forum, the magazine of the Florida Humanities Council, an affiliate of the National Endowment for the Humanities.

From *To Kill a Mockingbird* by Harper Lee. Copyright © 1960 by Harper Lee. Foreword copyright © 1993 by Harper Lee. Reprinted by permission of HarperCollins Publishers.

From *In Defense of To Kill a Mockingbird* by Nicholas J. Karolides, Lee Burress, and John M. Keam, 1993, Scarecrow Press. Used by permission.

Photo credits:

21 BVT/BigStockPhoto.com; **23** abacusmage/ BigStockPhoto.com; **27** andres/BigStockPhoto.com; **28** Mark Ross/BigStockPhoto.com; **31** llandrea/ BigStockPhoto.com; **35** flippo/BigStockPhoto.com; **36** Truckershutterbug/BigStockPhoto.com; **38** mccale/ BigStockPhoto.com; **42** sgame/BigStockPhoto.com; **53** sgame/BigStockPhoto.com; **54** phred/BigStockPhoto. com; **65** InvisibleViva/ BigStockPhoto.com; **66** Vivid Pixels/ BigStockPhoto.com; **68** phodopus/BigStockPhoto.com. **92** Lightbearer/BigStockPhoto.com; **97** Daneel/ BigStockPhoto.com; **98** sundikva/BigStockPhoto.com; **100** toddtaulman/BigStockPhoto.com; **103** nmonckton/ BigStockPhoto.com; **111** Global Photographers/ BigStockPhoto.com; **113** jgroup/BigStockPhoto.com; **114** DonG/BigStockPhoto.com; **115** Honjune/ BigStockPhoto.com; **123** alle/BigStockPhoto.com; **126** victorburnside/BigStockPhoto.com; **129** Djapeman/ BigStockPhoto.com; **149** rachelreveley/ BigStockPhoto.com; **150** Onestepbeyond/BigStockPhoto. com; **154** Joss/BigStockPhoto.com; **156** argus456/ BigStockPhoto.com; **157** digitalr/BigStockPhoto.com. **191** rhambley/BigStockPhoto.com; **192** llandrea/ BigStockPhoto.com; **195** sil63/BigStockPhoto.com; **196** shh-photos/BigStockPhoto.com; **199** leine/ BigStockPhoto.com; **201** HALIMA AHKDAR/ BigStockPhoto.com; **202** zt/BigStockPhoto.com; **203** Max2/BigStockPhoto.com; **205** teekaygee/ BigStockPhoto.com; **211** shippee/BigStockPhoto.com; **215** Albo/BigStockPhoto.com; **219** rbouwman/ BigStockPhoto.com; **220** nitipong_b/BigStockPhoto.com, maximus/BigStockPhoto.com; **223** Catsmeow/ BigStockPhoto.com; **224** digitalphotonut/BigStockPhoto. com; **230** felinda/BigStockPhoto.com; **232** milosluz/ BigStockPhoto.com; **235** mjp/BigStockPhoto.com; **236** Olga Sweet/BigStockPhoto.com; **238** rainette/ BigStockPhoto.com; **240** kjpargeter/BigStockPhoto.com; **242** marilynv/BigStockPhoto.com. **257** serge75/ BigStockPhoto.com; **261** Sarah Nicholl/BigStockPhoto.com. **301** pzAxe/BigStockPhoto.com; **367** Oddphoto/ BigStockPhoto.com; **411** phodopus/BigStockPhoto.com.